Principles and Applications of MALL

Multimedia-Assisted Language Learning

Second Edition

SECOND EDITION

Principles and Applications of

MALL

Multimedia-Assisted Language Learning

Chung Hyun Lee

Bookorea

Principles and Applications of MALL
Multimedia-Assisted Language Learning
Second Edition

This edition published February 25, 2021
The Writer Chung Hyun Lee
The Publisher Bookorea

First edition published 2015
2019, 2017

Printed in Bookorea Publications Ltd.
Lee, Chankyu
Woorim 2A-1007, 146-8 Sangdaewon-dong, Jungwon-gu, Seongnam-si, Gyeonggi-do, South Korea
ZIP: 462-807
TEL: 02-704-7840
FAX: 02-704-7848
E-mail: sunhaksa@korea.com
Homepage: www.bookorea.kr

ISBN 978-89-6324-761-8 (93740) (paperback)
ISBN 978-89-6324-920-9 (93740) (e-book)

Acknowledgements

Many people have supported and encouraged the publication of the second edition of this book. I would like to thank them all. Especially, I would like to express my gratitude to the following.

Very special thanks to outstanding students and now as my colleagues, Mr. Jihoon Pyo and Prof. Jiun Simon Baek for the publication of the second edition, and Prof. Seo Young Yoon, Dr. Jinyoung Lee, Dr. Lee So, and Dr. Hee Yeon Kang, who have offered invaluable insights and information through the years, without whom the publications would not have been possible. I am happy to work with and proud of them. Also, my heartfelt thanks go to Dr. Hyereem Kim for her endless support and encouragement.

I would like to thank all my students for their questions and discussions in MALL and CALL classes, all of which were very useful and helpful for this book. I am also grateful to my colleagues and friends at Hankuk University of Foreign Studies and the Korea Association of Multimedia-Assisted Language Learning (KAMALL) for their support and encouragement.

Finally, many thanks go to the president of Bookorea, Mr. Chankyu Lee, the staff, Ms. Soojin Kim, and others for their enthusiasm and hard work for the book's publication.

I hope that *Principles and Applications of MALL (Multimedia-Assisted Language Learning)* will serve its purpose in providing invaluable knowledge and helpful insights to all those who are looking into researching, developing, and teaching in the field of MALL and mobile-assisted blended learning.

The book I dedicate to all language teachers, students, and researchers in their effort to teach, learn and research English and other foreign languages using MALL.

Preface

Teachers, students, and researchers in foreign language learning and teaching have dreamed about learner-centered, level-differentiated, and autonomous learning environments for the balanced development of listening, speaking, reading, and writing, and particularly for improving communication skills and learner creativity since education began. Through information and communications technology (ICT), digital technologies, multimedia, and multimedia-assisted language learning (MALL) programs and content, what once was a dream in language teaching and learning has now become a real possibility. Face-to-face classes have been expanded to e-learning, online learning, web-based instruction or web-assisted language learning, m-learning, blended learning, mobile-assisted blended learning, and smart education with social network services. In the high-tech era that we live in, ICT, digital technologies, and multimedia contribute to language teaching and learning to the extent that they become essential in language classes. Artificial intelligence, big data, corpus linguistics, and data analytics have recently become important in English teaching and learning. For example, digital technologies are used so widely that language assessment or corpus linguistics without the technologies has become obsolete. The first edition of *Principles and Application of MALL* was published six years ago. There have been rapid changes and increases in using ICT, digital technologies, and multimedia in language teaching and learning for five or six years. This second edition provides new issues, topics, and updates to reflect rapid changes and developments in the fields, based on teachers' and students' voices in language classes and reviews of many journal articles, books, chapters, and web pages.

The second edition aims to provide teachers, students, and researchers with proper knowledge and experiences of effective use of digital technologies in language classes filled with digital native students in the 21st century, based on over 35 years of my ideas, research publications, and teaching materials. The edition covers theories and practices of MALL, MALL and language skills development, hands-on practice of editing, authoring, and learning tools, integration of MALL into language classes through authentic samples, and research on those fields. The book will provide in-depth and much-needed knowledge for learners interested in various aspects of MALL in both macro and micro levels of language skills. It is said that "multimedia will not replace teachers in language classes. However, teachers who use multimedia effectively will replace teachers who do not" (anonymous). It is hoped to better train teachers and researchers in staying abreast of recent trends in classroom practices and gain insight into the future direction of research and practice in language teaching and learning. Teachers can have the ability and insight into integrating MALL into language classes through this edition.

Organization of the Second Edition

The second edition provides teachers, students, and researchers with principles and practices of MALL, i.e., from the theories of MALL, hands-on practice of various editing, authoring, and learning tools, and integration of MALL into the classroom to trends and current issues in computer-assisted language learning (CALL), MALL, web-assisted language learning (WALL), and mobile-assisted blended learning (MABL). The book consists of **an introduction**, including a self-assessment questionnaire on digital technologies, four parts with 12 chapters and appendices.

The three chapters in **Part 1, Pedagogy of MALL,** cover and partly update: 1) theories and practices of MALL; 2) MALL and language skills development; and 3) MALL content evaluation. Chapter 1 addresses multimedia in language teaching and learning, advantages and limitations of multimedia, the roles of multimedia, teacher, and learner, and interaction patterns of MALL, mobile learning and mobile-assisted language learning, blended learning and MABL in ELT&L, the use of artificial intelligence and big data in language learning, computer-assisted language testing, MALL, and instructional models, and conclusion. Chapter 2 focuses on how computers and personal learning devices (PLDs) can contribute to language skills development, how MALL programs and content can be appropriately used in language teaching and learning, and how teaching and learning activities can be effectively employed. Chapter 3 deals with the evaluation and selection of MALL content, websites, and apps, content evaluation criteria and checklists, and effective procedures for content evaluation.

There are some major changes in the chapters of **Part 2, Hands-on Practice of Editing, Authoring, and Learning Tools**: 1) editing tools I: words & texts, images, and cartoons; 2) editing tools II: sounds, videos, and animations; 3) authoring tools; and 4) other learning tools. Chapter 4 presents word cloud creation tools, image editing tools, and cartoon editing tools such as *Tagxedo*, *WordArt, Classcard, Snagit*, *PhotoScape,* and *Make Beliefs Comix*. Chapter 5 introduces sound, video, and animation editing tools such as *Goldwave, Audacity*, *Smartphone Voice Recorder, 1gram player, GOM Cam, Camtasia,* and *Animaker*.

Chapter 6 deals with authoring tools that allow teachers and learners to create content, such as the *Hot Potatoes* suite, which includes six applications, JQuiz, JMix, JCross, JCloze, JMatch, and the Masher. Chapter 7 presents other useful tools available for language teaching and learning, such as learning management systems, collaborative learning tools, grammar, and plagiarism checking tools, web-based mind mapping tools, and corpus-based learning tools such as *Classting, Socrative, Flipgrid, Microsoft Teams, Padlet, OKMindmap, Grammarly, Compleat Lexical Tutor,* and *Mendeley*.

The three chapters in **Part 3, Integration of MALL into the Classroom**, present including new sample lesson plans, teaching methods and techniques, and activities with updated resources: 1) focus on language skills development: listening, speaking, reading, and writing; 2) focus on subskills development: pronunciation, vocabulary, and grammar; and 3) focus on integrated language skills development. Chapter 8 provides teaching and learning materials with new sample lesson plans and teaching methods and techniques for four language skills. Chapter 9 contains teaching and learning materials with new sample lesson plans and teaching methods and techniques for three subskills, pronunciation, vocabulary, and grammar. Chapter 10 presents teaching methods and techniques with a new sample MALL lesson plan for an integrated EFL class, using various multimedia programs and content.

The two chapters in **Part 4, Trends and Current Issues in CALL and MALL** cover updated research on CALL/MALL/WALL (hereafter MALL) and MABL overseas and in Korea. Chapter 11 provides a historical overview and current issues in MALL and MABL research overseas. Chapter 12 presents trends and current issues in MALL and MABL research in Korea.

Last, there are many useful resources in the appendices, such as updated web resources, microteaching evaluation checklist, app evaluation checklists, homepages of MALL, E-learning journals, etc. These updated resources will help teachers and students carry out some tasks and activities suggested at the end of each chapter in classes.

In sum, **the second edition** of *Principles and Applications of MALL* provides theoretical foundations and pedagogical implications of MALL and MABL and practical application to real language classes. The book also addresses current trends and issues in MALL and MABL research based on prestigious professional journals overseas and in Korea. Teachers, students, and researchers who are interested in MALL can refer to the book for understanding the principles of MALL, implementing multimedia programs and content, and sharing professionals' knowledge and experiences in MALL. I hope that the book will help broaden your insight, knowledge, and experiences of MALL. It will prove to be a valuable resource as a textbook and a guidebook to comprehensive research in MALL and MABL for all those who are interested, including scholars, researchers, teachers, and students.

Contents

List of Acronyms

AI	Artificial Intelligence
APP(s)	Application(s)
AR	Augmented Reality
ARS	Automated Response System
BBS	Bulletin Board System
CAL	Computer-Assisted Learning
CALL	Computer-Assisted Language Learning
CALT	Computer Adaptive Language Tests
CAT	Computer Adaptive Tests
CBL	Computer-Based Learning
CBLT	Computer-Based Language Tests
CBT	Computer-Based Tests
CLT	Communicative Language Teaching
CMC	Computer-Mediated Communication
CML	Computer-Managed Learning
CPH	Critical Period Hypothesis
EFL	English as Foreign Language
ELT&L	English Language Teaching and Learning
FLT&L	Foreign Language Teaching and Learning
FTFC	Face-To-Face Communication
ICT	Information and Communications Technology
IRT	Item Response Theory

- ISDN Integrated Services Digital Network
- IT Informational Technology
- IV Interactive Video
- LMS Learning Management System
- MALL Multimedia-Assisted Language Learning
- MABL Mobile-Assisted Blended Learning
- PLDs Personal Learning Devices
- SBL Strong Blended Learning
- SLA Second Language Acquisition
- SNS Social Network Service
- TBLT Task-Based Language Teaching
- TTS Text-To-Speech
- VR Virtual Reality
- WALL Web-Assisted Language Learning
- WBI Web-Based Instruction
- WBL Weak Blended Learning
- WBT Web-Based Language Testing
- WWW World Wide Web
- XR Extended Reality

Introduction

Information and communications technology (ICT), digital technologies, and multimedia in foreign language teaching and learning (FLT&L) have been popular and received students,' teachers' and researchers' attention in recent years. Now, they use digital technologies every day, such as the computer, PLDs, the Internet, the Web, the app, social network service (SNS), etc., in language classes at all school levels. Such phenomena are the result of developments in technology and language teaching methods and approaches such as the Audiolingual Method in the 1960s, Communicative Language Teaching (CLT) in the 1970s, Task-Based Language Teaching (TBLT) in the 1990s, and Content and Language Integrated Learning (CLIL) and Text-Based Instruction (TBI) in the late 1990s-2000s. Despite the increasing popularity of using ICT and multimedia in language classes, some teachers have been skeptical about using them and reluctant to use new or advanced technologies. Some of them consider using technology as not conducive to a humanistic approach to language learning and teaching and think it is challenging to apply technology to communicative approaches.

However, many research studies have suggested that computer-Assisted Language Learning (CALL) or multimedia-Assisted Language Learning (MALL) can be used for a variety of approaches in humanistic and communicative approaches (Baek & Lee, 2018; Chapelle, 2009; S. Cho, 2005; I. C. Choi, 1991; S. Y. Choi, 1993; Cook, 1988; Garrett, 1991; J. I. Han, 2003; Higgins, 1988; Hubbard, 2009; Kelm, 1996; Kern, Ware, & Warschauer, 2004; D. J. Kim, 2002; I. S. Kim, 1996; C. H. Lee, 1998a, 1999, 2000a, 2006, 2009; C. I. Lee, 2005; Lee & Cho, 2019; Lee, Yoon, & Lee, 2013; Stevens, 1989, 1992; K. Sung, 2004; Windeatt, Hardisty, & Eastment, 2000, etc.). Due to their characteristics, such as information transfer and information processing, ICT and multimedia can provide teachers and learners with a great variety of teaching and learning materials according to the current approaches in FLT&L. The teachers can help their students feel motivated and develop target language skills using the materials. Besides, new MALL content and methodological approaches that can be used to practice all four language skills, listening, speaking, reading, writing, and three subskills, pronunciation, vocabulary, and grammar, are being developed and distributed.

Current Trends and Future Developments in FLT&L and MALL

The current trends in education all over the world have emphasized learning a foreign language, especially English, and particularly on communicative skills and oral proficiency under the banner of 'globalism.' Besides, the current issues in English language teaching and learning (ELT&L) in Korea, such as CLT and TBLT, level-specific instruction, self-directed learning, and fostering learners' creativity have brought on a shift in language instruction. Many English as a foreign language (EFL) teaching materials available in Korea are usually inflexibly structured, based on written texts or worksheets, focusing on acquiring linguistic competence. There is no doubt that there is a need for language learning strategies and more open-ended types of activities, such as role-plays, information gap activities, and simulations in a communicative situation, in language classes. In the 21st century, high technologies such as computers, personal learning devices (PLDs)[1], the Internet, the Web, the app, and SNS are available at all school levels and ages from elementary to higher education. High-tech computer hardware and software are being used so pervasively and contribute to the current trends and issues in language learning and teaching. The traditional classroom, i.e., the conventional learning environment, has been expanded from e-learning to online learning, web-based instruction (WBI), u-learning, m-learning, blended learning, MALL, mobile-assisted blended learning (MABL), and smart education with SNS. The majority of teachers and students have realized the potential and value of ICT and multimedia and have become interested in using them in language classes. They consider them as exciting and useful resources, enjoy and accept them readily in language teaching and learning (Baek & Lee, 2018; Choi & Lee, 2003; Kang & Lee, 2016; Knezek, Miyashita, & Sakamoto, 1993; C. H. Lee, 1999; S. Lee, 2005b; Lee & Cho, 2019; Lee & Han, 2000; Lee & Lee, 2012; Lee, Yoon, & Lee, 2013; So & Lee, 2013, 2014). The use of ICT, digital technologies, and multimedia in language classes is now not difficult or requires highly technical skills; instead, they are user-friendly and easy to use and access. With proper training, even teachers who are not familiar with ICT, digital technologies, and multimedia can easily learn to use them effectively in their language classes. There is a need to make more increased use of ICT, digital technologies, and multimedia such as PLDs, the Web, the app, augmented reality (AR), virtual reality (VR), extended reality (XR), SNS, AI chatbots, etc., in FLT&L. MALL and MABL can

---

[1] Personal Learning Devices (PLDs) mean learners-owned devices like tablet PC, personal digital assistant, portable media player, and cellular phone, to name a few.

be used in flexible, entertaining, and creative ways in language classes. It can also provide learners with more opportunities to practice online and reinforce face-to-face interaction on and offline while creating an optimal educational environment.

In particular, AR, VR, XR, and AI chatbots have received high amounts of attention in numerous industrial and educational fields in recent years. Due to the developments of mobile and wearable devices and AI, the realities will be influencing everyday lives. In language teaching and learning, the realities can provide more specific and realistic environments. Learners can break free from simple simulations and learn foreign languages in more complex and realistic simulations and can be exposed to autonomous learning and various experiences. Future School, for example, an environment under development by Korea Education Research information Service (KERIS), is an individualized, creative virtual space catered for students using ubiquitous, augmented, and virtual reality technologies. The establishment of virtual classrooms is another reality in the near future.

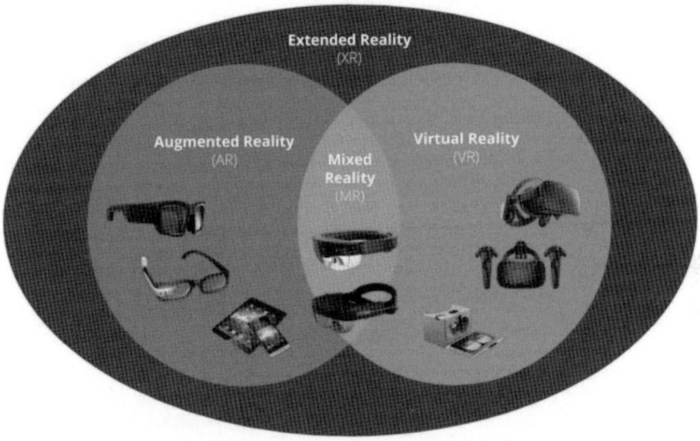

Figure. 2 AR, VR, and XR
(https://www.thoughtworks.com/insights/blog/extending-reality-ar-and-vr-part-i)

Significance of Teacher and Learner Education in MALL

For the successful implementation of ICT, digital technologies, and multimedia in language teaching and learning, hands-on practical teacher and learner education should be prioritized. Furthermore, teachers should seek and contemplate various ways to boost students' self-regulated learning skills and autonomy. Teacher education is now needed to use, evaluate, and modify MALL and MABL programs or content and instructional models in their language classes and design syllabus and content catered to their needs. The role of ICT, digital technologies, and multimedia in FLT&L is that of a tool and now of partnership. It is because their use cannot replace all the teacher's roles in language classes. However, using ICT, digital technologies, and multimedia requires teachers to play other roles besides the instructor's role in the conventional language classroom. The teachers will have to make the most appropriate choice from whatever MALL programs and content are available and use them to achieve the best possible advantage. If students do not understand their learning while using ICT, digital technologies, and multimedia, it is the teacher's responsibility to find the reasons for any misunderstanding and facilitate learning in a more meaningful way. Even most of today's students, called digital natives or screenagers, do not know how to use digital technologies effectively and what their roles and responsibilities are in language learning. Therefore, it is necessary for students to provide practical workshops and hands-on practice to promote digital literacy for language learning. C. H. Lee (1999, 2012) pointed out that a language teacher is an integral part of language classrooms. Teachers who can evolve and meet the needs of the current era can bring about changes in learners. All teachers must evolve into teachers who can use ICT, digital technologies, and multimedia efficiently and effectively. From these points of view, it is said that the availability of hardware and appropriate software and effective teaching methodology is the most significant factors in the successful implementation of ICT, digital technologies, and multimedia in FLT&L.

Figure. 1 Future Classrooms
(https://elearningindustry.com/future-of-education-and-technology)
(https://www.keris.or.kr/eng/cm/cntnts/cntntsView.do?mi=1196&cntntsId=1338)

In sum, in this chapter, I discuss a brief overview of language teaching methods and approaches and MALL, their close relationship with identifying and exploring current trends and future developments in FLT&L and MALL. I also emphasize the importance of teacher and learner education for the successful implementation of ICT, digital technologies, and multimedia in FLT&L.

In the following chapters, we will look at the pedagogy of MALL in-depth in part 1, such as principles and practices of MALL, MALL and language skills development, and MALL content evaluation. Part 2 provides hands-on practice of editing tools (words & texts, images, cartoons, sounds, videos, and animations), authoring tools (*Hot Potatoes*), and learning tools (*Classting, Socrative, Flipgrid, Microsoft Teams, Padlet, OKMindmap, Grammarly, Compleat Lexical Tutor,* and *Mendeley*). Part 3 deals with integrating MALL into the classroom in detail: focus on language skills development: listening, speaking, reading, and writing; focus on subskills development: pronunciation, vocabulary, and grammar; and focus on integrated language skills development. Finally, Part 4 covers a historical overview and current MALL issues based on research conducted from the 1980s to the present and the period and research topics. Research articles in the prestigious international and domestic journals related to MALL and MABL, *Language Learning & Technology (LLT), and Multimedia Assisted Language Learning* (*MALL*) are reviewed in detail.

Tasks for Study and Discussion

The following self-assessment questionnaire explores your knowledge and experience of using digital technologies in language teaching and learning. After completing the questionnaire:

1. Share your experience of using digital technologies with your partner or classmate.

2. Count how many terms that you know in Question 9.

3. Find and write down definitions and concepts of unknown terms via the Internet and the web.

4. Discuss the terms with your partner or classmates.

Self-Assessment Questionnaire on Digital Technology

Please answer the questions.

1. Have you ever read any publications on the use of digital technology:

   in language learning? Yes ___ No ___

   in language teaching? Yes ___ No ___

2. Have you had the experience of using digital technology:

   in language learning? Yes ___ No ___

   in language teaching? Yes ___ No ___

If yes, go to question 3.
If no, go to question 8.

3. Describe what work you have done with digital technology before coming on this course. If possible, write down what sort of digital technologies you have used, what you have used them for, what programs and content you have used, and how much you have used them.

   In language learning

   ____

   ____

   In language teaching

   ____

   ____

4. How often do you use digital technology in language teaching and learning?

   Almost always___ Often___ Sometimes___ Rarely___ Never ___

5. How useful do you think digital technology is:

   in language learning?

   Very useful___ Fairly useful___ Not very useful___ Not useful at all___

   in language teaching?

   Very useful___ Fairly useful___ Not very useful___ Not useful at all___

6. How satisfied are you with using digital technology:

in language learning?

Very satisfied___ Fairly satisfied___ Not very satisfied___ Not satisfied at all___

in language teaching?

Very satisfied___ Fairly satisfied___ Not very satisfied___ Not satisfied at all___

7. What technologies did you use in ELT&L? (Please tick all that apply.)

Audio	____	Video	____	TV (IP TV)	____
Computers	____	Tablet PC	____	CD/DVD-ROM	____
Internet	____	Web	____	Smartphone	____
AR	____	VR	____	XR	____

Other (Please specify.), *e.g., AI chatbot*

8. Please answer only the three of the above technologies that you use the most. Indicate what you think of each item by placing a check (✓) on the line at the point which best represents your view (**For example, if you think that VR is very useful, place a check next to the word very useful on the line**).

	Motivating	___	___	___	___	Demotivating
	Useful	✓	___	___	___	Useless
VR	Helpful	___	___	___	___	Unhelpful
	Easy	___	___	___	___	Complicated
	Satisfying	___	___	___	___	Unsatisfying
	Motivating	___	___	___	___	Demotivating
	Useful	___	___	___	___	Useless
	Helpful	___	___	___	___	Unhelpful
	Easy	___	___	___	___	Complicated
	Satisfying	___	___	___	___	Unsatisfying
	Motivating	___	___	___	___	Demotivating
	Useful	___	___	___	___	Useless
	Helpful	___	___	___	___	Unhelpful
	Easy	___	___	___	___	Complicated
	Satisfying	___	___	___	___	Unsatisfying

9. Do you know what the followings are? (Please check the appropriate column.)

Terms	Yes	Not sure	No	Terms	Yes	Not sure	No
Media technology				WBI			
Digital technology				CALL			
PLD(s)				MALL			
Multimedia				WALL			
Hypertext				MABL			
Web 1.0 – 6.0 (and beyond)				CALT			
UCC				e-learning			
IT				u-learning			
ICT				m-learning			
SNS				Distance learning			
AI				Hybrid learning			
AI chatbot				Blended learning			
Coding				Flipped learning			
Authoring tools				Smart education			
Editing tools				Machine learning			
Learning tools				Deep learning			
LMS				Big data			
CMC				AR			
TTS				VR			
ARS				XR			

Part 1

Pedagogy of MALL

Part 1
Pedagogy of MALL

There has recently been an emphasis on developing communicative skills in FLT&L. However, the ultimate objective of language teaching is to help learners develop all four language skills – listening, speaking, reading, and writing – in a balanced way and three subskills – pronunciation, vocabulary, and grammar. The capabilities and qualities of digital technologies, e.g., computers, PLDs, smartphones, multimedia, the web, social media, and apps, have also continuously developed to suit the needs in teaching and learning of the aforementioned skills. Many distinctive characteristics that ICT and multimedia offer can be applied to any approach from behaviorism to constructivism or connectivism and developing four language skills, the three subskills, and particularly the communicative skills. Teachers and students have recently seen convincing evidence of how CALL or MALL programs and content can be used effectively and clear directions to follow in FLT&L. Although digital technologies and AI can contribute to the development of language skills, it is worth recalling that they cannot replace the teacher. It is the teacher who has the responsibility for creating a meaningful learning environment and facilitating successful language learning, armed with well-organized preparation both technically and pedagogically. Teachers have to apply an appropriate or integrated methodology in MALL and MABL and provide meaningful activities in the right place to achieve their aims and objectives in language classes.

As described in the introduction, three main factors for the successful use of ICT, digital technology, and multimedia in FLT&L are hardware, software, and effective teaching methodology. Due to the Korean government's investment in educational information policy and e-learning in the 21st century, hardware has been distributed to almost all educational institutions from primary and secondary schools to higher education throughout the nation. Considering that the basic hardware is already provided, the availability of software (or courseware or content) and effective teaching methodology will become the keys to successful implementations of MALL and MABL in FLT&L. Well-designed MALL courseware or content that makes the most of the positive attributes of ICT and multimedia can provide maximized motivation, learner retention, interactive learning, and autonomous learning. In short, appropriate evaluation, selection, and implementation of MALL content can positively influence affective factors such as learners' motivation and interest, and in the end, increase learner achievement.

Part 1 focuses on: 1) theories and practices of MALL such as multimedia in language teaching and learning, advantages and limitations of multimedia, the roles of multimedia, teacher, and learner, and interaction patterns of MALL, mobile learning, blended learning, and MABL in ELT&L, the use of artificial intelligence and big data in language learning, computer-assisted language testing, and MALL instructional models and lesson plans; 2) MALL and language skills development including ways of developing the four language skills and three subskills, presentation of various MALL programs and web app content, MALL activities; and 3) MALL and web app content evaluation including evaluation criteria and framework, evaluation checklists, selection, and evaluation process.

Chapter 1

Theories and Practices of MALL

1.1 Introduction

Over the last two decades, the Communicative Approach, the Whole Language Approach, and humanistic (or learner-centered) approaches in FLT&L have assumed greater importance. There is no doubt that there is a growing need for content-based, task-based, and open-ended teaching and learning activities such as role-plays, information gaps, and simulations related to communicative situations. Teachers agree that learners need to be actively involved in the learning process in entertaining and creative ways (Laurillard, 1987).

The most fundamental question to address at this point is whether ICT and multimedia can be conducive to FLT&L and particularly teaching and learning processes. MALL and MABL have been researched concerning the integration of digital technology and multimedia into language teaching and learning theories and practices. As a result, ICT and digital technology, particularly computers, multimedia, PLDs, the Internet, the Web, SNS, and apps, have made substantial contributions to language teaching and learning by accommodating a learning environment that is closer to real-life, boosting motivation, and providing dynamic material, activities, and feedback (Baek & Lee, 2018; Y. Cha, 2007; Chapelle, 2001; Chapelle & Jamieson, 2008; S. Cho, 1998; Choi & Lee, 2020; Hardisty & Windeatt, 1989; Higgins & Johns, 1984; J. B. Hwang, 2007; Jones & Fortescue, 1987; Jung & Chang, 2009; Kang & Lee, 2014, 2020; D. J. Kim, 2000; H. Kim, 2004; S. Y. Kim, 2002; Kim & Lee, 2018; C. H. Lee, 1998a, 1998b, 2000a, 2004, 2006, 2009; S. Lee, 2005a, 2011b; Lee & Lee, 2012; Lee & Cho, 2019; Lee, Yoon, & Lee, 2013; Pyo & Lee, 2019, 2020; So & Lee, 2013, 2014; Warschauer, 1996; Yoon & Lee, 2011b, 2012). Many teachers seem to have realized the value of the technologies in their preparation, management, and organization of lessons and teaching materials. Despite the increased potential, availability, and interest in the use of ICT and multimedia, however, teachers and learners have not actively adopted and used them in actual classrooms (C. H. Lee, 2000a, 2000c; Lee & Han, 2000; Stansbury, 2017) due to the lack of knowledge (knowledge of how they work and how they can be used for FLT&L and experience in MALL. Some teachers, attracted to the glitz of functions and displays, make the mistake of regarding computers as intrinsic goods. The main concern in the context of language teaching and learning is not so much the technology itself but rather the benefits and effectiveness that technology brings to the ultimate goals of improving language competence and enhancing achievement. Therefore, the successful implementation of multimedia in language teaching and learning requires the three core elements of hardware, software, and effective teaching methodology. In recent years, blended learning has become popular in ELT&L due to its positive attributes of blending face-to-face classes and online with ICT and multimedia. Blended learning is an instructional system that opens the door to combining face-to-face classes with online sessions so as to contribute to overcoming the challenges by enriching instruction in multimedia environments (Graham, 2006; Neumeier, 2005).

This chapter covers: first, multimedia in language teaching and learning, including the concept of multimedia and its relationship with second language acquisition (SLA), language learning theories, and language teaching methods; seconds, the advantages and limitations of multimedia; third, the changing roles of teachers and learners in MALL with the interaction patterns of MALL; fourth, the concepts and applications of mobile learning, mobile-assisted language learning, blended learning, and MABL in language classes; fifth, the use of artificial intelligence and big data in language learning; sixth, computer-assisted language testing and its categories such as computer-based language testing, computer-adapted language testing, and web-based language testing; finally, some examples of multimedia-based instructional models and procedures applicable to the actual language classes.

1.2 Multimedia in Language Teaching and Learning

1. What is Multimedia?

It is necessary to clear some confusion on the meaning of 'multimedia,' which is sometimes used synonymously with 'hypermedia' or 'interactive video.' The distinctions are not always clear, and the terms are sometimes used interchangeably (Paine & McAra, 1993; Romiszowski, 1993). Before defining the term, it would be useful to recognize the differences between 'hypertext,' 'multimedia,' and 'hypermedia.'

Hypertext

Hypertext refers to a dynamic and non-linear system for presenting 'active' text, including text, graphics, audio, and video (Megarry, 1989; Preece, 1993). Its key features may be summarized by two terms, 'nodes' and 'links,' which allow learners to determine their routes through materials (Preece, 1993; Romiszowski, 1993). In other words, hypertext is high-level software through which learners search for information and explore knowledge in real-time in non-linear and interactive ways (Megarry, 1989). Hypertext programs can be implemented by incorporating multimedia such as graphics, sounds, videos, and extensive texts. There are many hypertext products. *Authorware*, *Hypercard*, *Toolbook*, and web-editors are examples of hypertext programs.

Multimedia

The term 'multimedia' was widely defined in the 1980s as 'an integrated collection of different media' (Barker & Tucker, 1990; Preece, 1993; Romiszowski, 1988), e.g., the combinations of computer and audio cassette or video cassette recorder. Now, it is necessary to re-define the term due to the emergence of new technologies. The term refers broadly to the application of technology in which various media are used together. Though there are variations of definitions to encompass the enlarged concept, multimedia is defined as "a collation of different media emanating from a single computer system or a network, which can deliver texts, graphics, images, sounds, and moving pictures on the screen" in this book (C. H. Lee, 1998b, p. 28).

Figure 1.1 Multimedia
(https://www.tutorialspoint.com/basics_of_computer_science/basics_of_computer_science_multimedia.htm)

Hypermedia

The term 'hypermedia' is often used to describe a hypertext system or a hypertext application that features a non-linear and real-time branching structure, integrating other media, such as still images, animation, sound, and video (Hall et al. 1989; Paine & McAra, 1993). The definition of hypermedia has grown from a notion synonymous with multimedia in the 1980s to a combination of hypertext and a variety of multimedia (Preece, 1993; Sanne, 1993). The conventional components are videos, images (either pictures or graphics), sounds, and texts, which are put together and implemented in real-time in a non-linear manner. Multimedia is now used synonymously with 'hypermedia' since hypertext is used in all its materials on the computer network.

2. Multimedia, Second Language Learning, and Language Teaching Methods

Historically, multimedia technology, second language acquisition and learning, and language teaching methodology have shared a close relationship in their development. The primary role of media technology is to serve as a substitute agent for teachers and an assistant and learning partner for learners as it facilitates the teaching and learning process and contributes to better achievement in language learning. For instance, the advent of the theoretical tenets of behaviorism and the Audiolingual Method in language learning triggered the use of a radio broadcast, a cassette tape player, an audio lab, and other audio technology. More recently, the influence of the communicative approach has rekindled attention to constructivism. In contrast, the whole language approach has highlighted the importance of learner interest and motivation as well as the interaction between the computer and learner, learner and learner, and learner and teacher through computers, multimedia, the Internet, or the Web.

In this section, the first part will examine the relationship between language acquisition and multimedia, with particular attention to their theoretical connections to neurobiological, cognitive, and affective dimensions. The second section will address computers or multimedia and the theoretical foundations of second language acquisition, structuralism, behaviorism, cognitivism, constructivism, and connectivism. The link between MALL and the language teaching approach, i.e., the Grammar Translation Method (GTM), the Audiolingual Method (ALM), the Communicative Language Teaching (CLT), and Task-Based Language Teaching (TBLT), will also be examined.

Language acquisition and learning, and multimedia

Neurobiological dimension and multimedia

From a neurobiological perspective, multimedia is conducive to language learning in that it tends to stimulate the right hemisphere of the brain more. The Critical Period Hypothesis (CPH), which originates from the first language acquisition theory, has been reported to hold true for second language acquisition (Schumann, 1997; Scovel, 1988). The human brain is broadly divided into two hemispheres and specialized into different functions due to lateralization, with the left hemisphere responsible for linguistic, intellectual, logical, and analytic functions and with the right hemisphere responsible for visual, spatial, and emotional functions. Lateralization and the CPH hold substantial implications for language teaching and learning. It is generally understood that puberty is a critical time for second language learning and that second language learning after this period falls behind in effectiveness. Moreover, given that lateralization is completed during this period, starting second language learning before puberty would seem ideal. The end point of lateralization also indicates that second language can be acquired using both hemispheres of the brain during the period preceding lateralization and that the use of both hemispheres is more effective for language learning than the independent use of one of them (Scovel, 1969). Consequently, infant and young language learners who acquire their second language before the critical period and lateralization seem to stand a better chance than adults.

Given the above hypotheses and findings regarding SLA, the question arises on the role and pedagogical value of multimedia. From a neurobiological perspective, multimedia is said to elicit an active involvement of the right hemisphere that takes control of the visual, spatial, and emotional dimensions. That is, multimedia activates the function of the right brain by expressing and transferring comprehensive data and information in various modalities, including graphics, still images, audio, animation, video, and texts. In light of these facts, it appears that multimedia has the edge over conventional language learning and teaching materials in stimulating the use of the right hemisphere more effectively. The level of the involvement of the right hemisphere reaches its peak during the transition from infancy to the young learner period since the effects of multimedia can optimize the activation of the right hemisphere according to the neurobiological perspectives. Adults whose critical period has passed and whose lateralization is completed may acquire the second language less effectively than do young learners but are still likely to get the function of the right hemisphere optimized through using multimedia.

Cognitive dimension and multimedia

From a cognitive viewpoint, multimedia offers the affordability of learner-centered SLA as part of learners' overall cognitive development. According to Piaget's (1972) stages of intellectual development, between ages 7 and 16, the human brain develops from an operational stage. During this period, the human brain can execute a range of functions from concrete and formal to intellectual and abstract thinking, test hypothesis, and logical analysis. The operational stage corresponds to puberty when lateralization is completed. Unlike the second language learning process of young learners, the process for adults tends to demonstrate the heavy involvement of the left hemisphere, where language learning takes place mainly through the analysis of language forms, memorization, and drills. The mechanical acquisition process stands opposite to the meaningful learning proposed by Ausubel (1964). In order for language learning and teaching to shift from a unidirectional delivery of linguistic knowledge to meaningful learner-centered learning, language teaching methodology, qualifications of teachers, and environmental variables should be considered first.

Based on the cognitive theory, what contributions do multimedia have in second language teaching and learning? In terms of the cognitive perspective of second language acquisition, multimedia serves to optimize the effectiveness of the learner-centered cognitive methodology. Multimedia programs like simulation and task-based activities, in particular, enable self-directed learning that places learners rather than teachers at the center of the learning process. These programs take learners beyond simple responses. For example, problem-solving tasks in a multimedia environment facilitate learners' active participation in the learning process as learners engage in meaningful interaction and collaboration with peers that call for logical and abstract thinking. Moreover, learners become more autonomous in setting and modifying their own goals and plans on a need basis through timely feedback, analysis of the learning process, and provisions of supplementary materials related to the learning objective and content provided by the computer. This active involvement on the part of the learners enables second language learners to monitor their learning ultimately.

Affective dimension and multimedia

Multimedia makes substantial contributions to the affective dimension of language learning. Learners' affective domain has gained more significance in research as a result of level-differentiated instruction. Multimedia can enrich the learning environment by the provision of graphics, audio, and video. The psychological burden or anxiety from pressure in classes can be reduced through multimedia that provides individualized and self-directed learning opportunities. Lowered anxiety and positive attitudes towards learning can lead to higher levels of motivation and interest. Empirical studies by researchers in the field of multimedia have also provided supporting evidence (C. H. Lee, 1999, 2000a; Durndell, Macleod, & Siann, 1987; Khan, 1997; Laurillard, 1995; Perzylo, 1993). Risk-taking and anxiety, among other affective factors, are notable learner factors that can positively or negatively influence second language learning. Learners who are more risk-taking and less anxious stand a better chance of successfully learning a second language than learners who are anxious and risk-avoiding (Dewaele, 2012; Dörnyei, 2009; Smith, Ebert, & Broman-Fulks, 2016). Risk-taking and overcoming anxiety during the language learning process are not simple and easy. This difficulty is obvious in the foreign language learning environment in which learners have few opportunities to overcome anxiety and take risks. It is likely to interfere with effective second language learning. Multimedia provides a solution by creating an authentic or near-authentic learning environment for learners to react to risks and get through their anxiety actively (C. H. Lee, 1999, 2002; Laurillard, 1995). Also, various learner-to-learner, learner-to-teacher, and learner-computer interactions along with individualized and prompt feedback offer learners opportunities to take risks and lower their anxiety. The opportunities that multimedia provides in the affective dimensions will ultimately allow learners to become more independent in their learning. In sum, multimedia contributes to learners' affective and cognitive dimensions where learner-centered language learning is emphasized through task-based activities.

Four language learning theories and multimedia

Behaviorism and multimedia

Historically, structuralism and behaviorism were the most dominant theoretical tenets during the 1940s and 1950s. Structuralism focused on describing and identifying the structural nature of human language, stressing the importance of the structural system in language learning. On the other hand, behaviorism viewed linguistic behavior as a response to stimuli, which can be reinforced and conditioned (Skinner, 1957). The computer was first introduced to language learning in the early 1960s and was influenced by behaviorist theories. Most CALL software or courseware was developed and used to reinforce grammatical structures of language through drills or stimulus-response. The computer's ability to process information and produce quick and accurate output surpassed that of the human brain; subsequently, computers were mainly used for the mechanical and drilled practice of vocabulary and grammar. Later, computers were used for practice in reading and writing at more advanced levels as well. The most well-known example of such a use is PLATO (Programmed Logic for Automatic Teaching Operation), a program developed by the University of Illinois. Warschauer (1996) and Warschauer and Healey (1998) classified the program as behavioristic CALL.

Behavioristic CALL was heavily criticized by some researchers, including Clifford (1987), Hirvela (1988), and Schank (1984). Clifford (1987) argued that the simple feedback of 'correct' or 'wrong' that computer programs provide was formulaic and of little substance. These early CALL programs were criticized for their incompatibility with the humanistic, cognitive, and communicative language teaching and learning approach. However, considering that language learning objectives are a balanced development of the four language skills based on language 'usage' and 'use' as well as communicative competence, criticisms leveled at early CALL programs need to be held back. There is still a need for behavioristic CALL in language teaching methodology that addresses language structure through a behavioristic approach such as the Grammar Translation Method. With the development of technology, behavioristic CALL has progressed, supplemented with the computer's sound system, playing and recording sounds comparable to those heard on an audio system. The Audiolingual Method can be implemented based on structuralistic and behavioristic CALL.

Cognitivism and multimedia

Structuralistic and behavioristic language teaching and learning approaches were criticized heavily during the 1960s. Unlike rote learning, learning from a cognitive perspective is a series of processes in which new information is integrated with what learners already know. Ausubel's meaningful learning theory (1968) explains that newly acquired facts and concepts undergo a process of integration with already existing knowledge. It is referred to as meaningful learning or subsumption. It is the process in which new information interacts with pre-existing knowledge and ultimately becomes a part of the learners' cognitive structure (Brown, 2007a). In this regard, cognitive learning theory bears similarity to information processing theory.

Computers can be applied to the cognitive approach since they enable learners to monitor their performance and learning as needed and adjust learning activities appropriate to their current level. This function carries significance since learners are best aware of what they know and do not know (Higgins & Johns, 1984). On top of effectiveness, computers contribute to boosting intrinsic motivation by accommodating a low-anxiety environment in which individualized and interactive learning can occur as part of problem-solving tasks. Feedback from the computer makes conscious learning possible and prevents learners from repeating the same errors. Learners become aware of various learning strategies applicable to language learning. Warschauer (1996), Warschauer and Healey (1998) defined cognitive CALL as communicative CALL and divided the roles of computers as follows: 1) computer as a tutor; 2) computer as a stimulus; and 3) computer as a tool. Cognitive CALL programs put learners in control of computers while providing various learning materials appropriate to the nature of the activity using effective media such as sounds and videos and feedback. *Fast Food* (British Council, 1986), *Travelling around Korea* (C. H. Lee, 2000d), *Treasure Hunt* (Jacob, 1999) were well-known simulation programs. Chatbots are computer programs that interact with users using natural languages, and well-designed chatbots can be useful for improving communicative skills. In sum, CALL or multimedia programs or chatbots are applicable to the communicative approach or CLT where learners discuss useful strategies to perform a specific task through pair and group activities.

Constructivism and multimedia

Constructivism has captured language learning theorists' and practitioners' imagination as the importance of meaningful social interaction in authentic situations and has gained importance since the 1980s. Constructivists believe that individuals develop their viewpoints (Piaget, 1972; Vygotsky, 1978). Knowledge is individually and socially formed based on previous experiences and is located within learners themselves (Reeves & Reeves, 1997). It is built by one's own experience, and learning is a process in which the experiences are formed. Learners' intent, experience, and cognitive strategies constitute the core elements of constructivism along with social apprenticeship, collaborative groups, or an individual as a member of the global community in the constructivist framework (Spivey, 1997).

The rapid development of ICT and digital technology has pushed multimedia, the Internet, the Web, the app, or CMC technology beyond communicative CALL, contributing to the constructivist learning approach. Warschauer (1996, 2000, 2010) and Warschauer and Healey (1998) classified it as integrative CALL. Integrative CALL makes possible a range of functions from selecting and collecting to storing, distributing quality information and data in high-tech multimedia, including text, visuals, graphics, audio, and video that transcend time and space. Therefore, integrative CALL creates a natural language learning and sociocultural environment in which task-based, content-based, problem-solving, and collaborative language learning become viable. Integrative CALL is also compatible with and applicable to the Whole Language Approach. Recent attention by teachers and learners to asynchronous (e-mail and bulletin board) and synchronous (online chatting and videoconferencing) CMC attests to the advantages that integrative CALL provides. Learners are given control over the interaction in CMC-based classes, and interaction is centered on content, as is the natural environment. This type of interaction and environment promotes intrinsic motivation and interest (Kelm, 1996). An anxiety-free and less threatening environment departs from the conventional classroom environment in that individual learners can communicate in a way that is not confined to patterned dialogues. They can communicate at their own pace, converse naturally, and receive ample feedback from participating learners. In sum, CMC is applicable to a variety of learning environments supported by the constructivist theory.

Connectivism and multimedia

As mentioned so far, there is no doubt that behaviorism, cognitivism, and constructivism are the three major learning theories in language learning over the century from the early 1990s. However, cutting-edge technology has changed human beings' behaviors, thoughts, affections, and lives in the age of digital technology and AI. Language teaching and learning with digital technology and AI can be much more revolutionary than anything teachers and students think and imagine. The students can achieve personalized learning and interact with peers and people worldwide using various digital technologies, e.g., PLDs, multimedia, SNS, apps, etc.

At the beginning of the 21st century, an alternative theory or a pedagogical movement has been proposed to solve the issues, named 'connectivism' by Siemens (2004). Siemens (2005) stated that "connectivism is the integration of principles explored by chaos, network, and complexity and self-organization theories" (p. 7). It refers to connected learning networks or nodes. A node is either a connection point, a redistribution point, or a communication point in a computer network and refers to a point or joint where a connection occurs (https://afteracademy.com/blog/What-is-a-network-and-what-are-the-nodes-present-in-a-network). Siemens (2005) emphasized that "the greater the network of a node, the greater the connection and therefore, the greater the likelihood of learning" (https://en.wikiversity.org/wiki/Connectivism). The principles of connectivism are as follows: 1) Learning and knowledge rests in diversity of opinions; 2) Learning is a process of connecting specialized nodes or information sources; 3) Learning may reside in non-human appliances; 4) Capacity to know more is more critical than what is currently known; 5) Nurturing and maintaining connections is needed to facilitate continual learning; 6) Ability to see connections between fields, ideas, and concepts is a core skill; 7) Currency (accurate, up-to-date knowledge) is the intent of all connectivist learning activities; and 8) Decision-making is itself a learning process. Choosing what to learn and the meaning of incoming information is seen through the lens of a shifting reality. While there is a right answer now, it may be wrong tomorrow due to alterations in the information climate affecting the decision (Siemens, 2004, p.7). Connectivism has also been defined in some ways by some researchers. Corbett and Spinello (2020) defined it as "learning as a networked group effort where learning is a process of connecting people and information sources." Duke et al. (2013, p. 6) described it as "social learning that is networked."

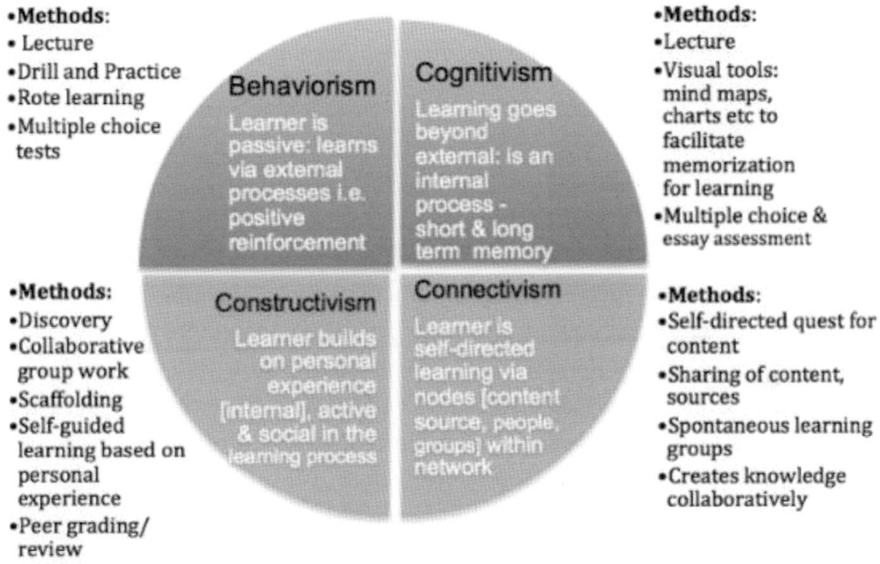

Image shows four perspectives on learning based upon theoretical principles. Instructional methods associated with each, adjacent to respective quadrant. Orange quadrants represent a student-focused learning approach, blue instructor-focused.

Figure 1.2 Four perspectives on learning based upon theoretical principles (https://onlinelearninginsights.wordpress.com/2013/05/15/how-couse-design-puts-the-focus-on-learning-not-teaching/)

However, there are some criticisms against connectivism as a new learning theory. For example, Verhagen (2006) argued that connectivism as a theory is ineffective and "unsubstantiated philosophizing" (p.14). It is influential but will not be perceived as a learning theory without significant empirical studies to inform its development and establish it as a theoretical framework (Bell, 2011; Corbett & Spinello, 2020). Therefore, connectivism is considered a successor to the previous theories such as behaviorism, cognitivism, and constructivism (Bell, 2011; Garcia et al., 2015). For the time being, it may be reasonable that connectivism is the expansion of constructivism in the digital age.

1.3 Advantages and Limitations of Multimedia

Language can best be learned when learners are exposed to the target language and culture. However, in the EFL context in Korea, there are substantial difficulties in accommodating the ideal environment. Multimedia has gained increasing attention as an alternative to the conventional learning environment with PLDs, the Internet, and the Web distributed and used in language teaching and learning in public educational institutions. Because of that, this section addresses the advantages and limitations of multimedia.

1. Advantages of Multimedia

There is a widespread belief that multimedia has considerable potential to contribute to language teaching and learning because of its ability to overcome the limitations of the computer or video. For example, video is an excellent presentational medium, but it is claimed that there is always a danger of 'passive' learning (C. H. Lee, 1998b). Computers have tended to emphasize and refine the didactic element rather than allow interactive learning, i.e., learner-centered learning through interaction between the machine and the learner and between learners (Laurillard, 1987, 1995). However, multimedia can present all media types at a high quality and make language learning more interactive. Such a presentation can result in increased interest, enhanced individualization, higher retention of the material, and improved success rates in FLT&L (Perzylo, 1993). Therefore, the application of multimedia in FLT&L can offer considerable enrichment of the learning environment over that of conventional media or computers, or video (C. H. Lee, 2000a, 2002). This section deals with the main potential of multimedia and the Internet or the Web or the app. The most notable advantages of multimedia include the integration of media, large storage capacity, easy access, the ability to search for information (random access and rapid retrieval information), individualized learning (individualization), interactive learning, increased retention, and motivation (C. H. Lee, 1998b). Each merit will be elaborated in the following sections.

The integration of media

ICT and multimedia can combine all the processing power and control capabilities of the computer with the presentational capacities of audiovisual media (Latchem, Williamson, & Henderson-Lancett, 1993; Rülmann, 1995). This provides learners with many opportunities to keep up with 'real-life language use and culture in real time' in and out of classes. Davey, Jones, and Fox (1995) and Perzylo (1993) claimed that multimedia could enrich the learning experience through exposure to comprehensible language and enhance learners' motivation in the language classroom. For example, while dealing with a specific holiday such as 'Halloween' in Anglophone culture, multimedia can replace text-based language teaching materials used in conventional classrooms, including textbooks or hand-outs. Multimedia provides information and content of the target culture in a more comprehensive manner using related texts, graphics, audio, and video, making the main concept and content more readily understandable.

Large storage capacity

Multimedia can store large amounts of information in digital form. A CD-ROM can store approximately 700-800 MB (Mega Byte: MB). The capacity amounts to over 300,000 pages of text, 150,000 still frames 80-minute long music, and a large amount of text, moving pictures, animations, and audio (Bunzel & Morris, 1992; Latchem, Williamson, & Henderson-Lancett, 1993; Romiszowski, 1993). A DVD can store up to five times as much as a CD-ROM. Recently, portable USB (Universal Serial Bus) flash drives, solid-state drives (SSDs), and external hard disk drives are more popular. They are rewritable and removable so that users can easily store, transport, and erase personal files. A USB flash drive and an external hard drive provide a storage capacity of one terabyte (TB) or even more.

As the terms imply, the Internet or the Web connects computers worldwide, resulting in a scale of astronomical information. Thus, multimedia offers a wider variety of forms of information than any other traditional medium. Teachers in the conventional classroom may have had some difficulties providing learners with various resources and situations. The use of multimedia can allow them to create realistic situations and manage the classroom more easily since it offers various resources and makes the connections between the various resources worldwide (Atkinson, 1992).

Random access and rapid retrieval of information

Besides being easy to use, multimedia allows random access and the rapid retrieval of information. The searching routines in multimedia usually enable users to find information quickly in a straightforward manner, i.e., by clicking or typing words, titles, etc. (Baumbach, 1990). Therefore, learners can save time and concentrate on the subject they are studying (Baumbach, 1990; Fox, Labbett, Matthews, Romano-Hvid, & Schostak, 1992). Hypertext capability allows learners to search for the relevant information through browsing and clicking or typing of words and titles at each phase. In particular, hypertext provides them with an opportunity to navigate through the Web in a non-linear way. These features enable them to develop their information-searching and problem-solving skills by searching for what they want and need from vast amounts of multimedia information. Information searching skills and strategies are required to use materials effectively (Baumbach, 1990; Perzylo, 1993). Multimedia can offer opportunities to simulate a non-formal learning situation for the learners to navigate their own route through the subject matter in a way that is mostly self-directed and personally meaningful (Laurillard, 1987). Some skills, e.g., following directions, identifying problems and solutions, classifying information, editing, refining, and modifying, can lead to successful searches and improve problem-solving skills (Baumbach, 1990). However, the vast amount of information also poses some challenges to the learners in that they have to have information-searching skills and effective strategies. These skills will not be easy for learners to acquire by themselves; therefore, teachers will need to teach them the skills before giving tasks.

Individualization

The hypertext system in multimedia rapidly delivers plentiful audiovisual data and information like sound, text, graphics, and moving pictures in real-time. A variety of materials created and accessed by multimedia can be engaged to cater to different types of learners; learners can control their own pace and level depending on the topic and obtain mastery at each stage in a rich learning environment. Individualized feedback and evaluation at each stage also enhance this mastery. According to Perzylo (1993), a learning process that involves individual monitoring, assessment, and readily available feedback increases learners' control and independence over their learning process. However, individualized learning does not easily take place, and it may take initial trials and errors. For example, multimedia programs differ in the amount and quality of information and the extent of learning objectives and guides for individualized learning. Such differences may pose difficulties for the learners in establishing their own learning goals and objectives. In this case, information-searching skills and strategies become the determinants of self-paced and effective individualized learning that will eventually lead to goal accomplishment. Thus, teachers should guide and train the learners to search for level-appropriate information in a self-directed manner and reconstruct the information to engage in a meaningful learning experience.

Interactive learning

Interactivity commonly refers to the degree of interaction between the computer system and the learner, learner and learner, and interaction between the teacher and the learner. On the other hand, it refers to the degree of interactiveness between the learner(s) and the computer system, learner(s) and learner(s), and learner(s) and the teacher (Barker & Tucker, 1990; Garrett, 1991; Romiszowski, 1993). Thus, interactive learning is a process rather than a technology, implying creating an information-rich learning environment involving interactions between learners and Interactive Video (IV) or multimedia, and between learners through those (Barker & Tucker, 1990). Multimedia can encourage much more interaction between the learner and the system and between learners than the computer alone, due to the distinctive features mentioned above (Gardner & McNally, 1995). These distinctive features enhance various interactions since the exciting and effective learning media provided in MALL minimizes the interaction not directly relevant to the target content and chances for learners to become passive (Dalton, 1990). Moreover, communication between the computer and the learner has become possible due to the development of voice recognition systems that enable learners to enter oral input into the computer. However, teachers' role should not be overlooked despite the remarkable multimedia capacity that enhances the interaction between the multimedia system and the learners.

Figure 1.3 is the modified interaction model of MALL by Gardner and McNally (1995). The potential of multimedia in the teaching and learning of English is not so much in the technology itself but in the increased efficiency in the process of teaching and learning and strengthened interactions between the teachers and learners through the medium of a multimedia system. No matter how much multimedia is accessible in the classroom, it should also be noted that it is still the teachers' and learners' responsibility to apply multimedia to the curriculum as in other learning and teaching approaches. Ultimately, successful interaction in the classroom requires the learners' active participation and a sense of responsibility on the teachers' part.

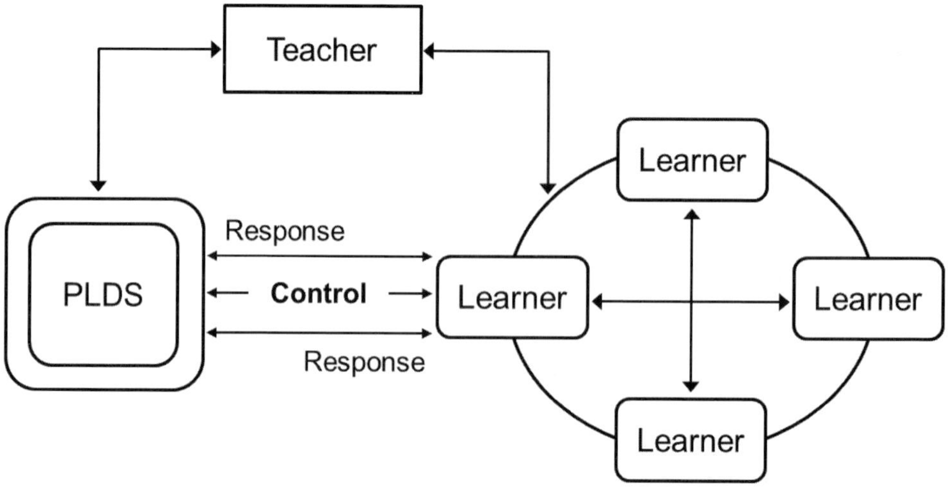

Figure 1.3 Interaction between the learners and between the learners and the machine, using multimedia and PLDs (based on Gardner & McNally, 1995)

Increased retention

Multimedia enables learners to actively engage more of their senses in the learning process (Perzylo, 1993). Adams (1987) and Corston (1993) claimed that people remember 10% of what they read (text), 20% of what they see (still and moving images), 30% of what they see and hear (text, audio, and still and moving images), 70% of what they see, hear and do (text, audio, still and moving images, and interaction). Rülmann (1995) stated that a combination of various materials assures a maximal learning outcome. In this sense, multimedia brings about a maximal understanding of the target language and content and retention of what is learned.

Motivation

Humans innately enjoy seeing, which is why learners enjoy working with visual materials in language learning. Multimedia is a comprehensive audiovisual medium, and for this reason, it is conducive to raising learners' interest and motivation. Findings from related studies indicate that students enjoy working with multimedia-based references (resources) and that they respond to them using positive adjectives such as 'exciting,' 'fascinating,' and 'stimulating' (Baumbach, 1990; Baek & Lee, 2018) and express their willingness to continue to use multimedia in foreign language learning (Laurillard, 1995; C. H. Lee, 1999, 2000a; Lee & Cho, 2019; Norris, Davies, & Beattie, 1990; Perzylo, 1993). In sum, multimedia is generally considered an exciting learning resource that teachers can use to boost students' motivation to learn.

2. The Limitations of Multimedia

As mentioned in the section on the advantages of multimedia, multimedia resources and information can improve the outcomes by facilitating the learning process. However, there are some limitations in using multimedia in the language classroom, despite its powerful digital technology in terms of hardware and software. First of all, the rich and attractive multimedia materials, such as sounds, images, moving pictures, etc. can distract students' attention and hinder the learning process. It is easy for the students to be fascinated by the technology and get distracted. Besides, multimedia programs generally provide learners with a vast amount of help options and feedback. However, some of these strengths make it easier to complete a task and may not necessarily be helpful for interactive learning and individualization. Therefore, both teachers and students need to pay careful attention to the pitfall of systems that produce everything with the simple click of a button or a touch of the screen (Garrett, 1991). This requires that teachers understand the importance of cognitive, problem-solving, interactive learning approaches in language learning, which should be followed by putting the appropriate technological medium in the appropriate place in the overall learning process (Rüschoff, 1993).

1.4 The Roles of Multimedia, Teacher, and Learner, and Interaction Patterns in MALL

The real potential of multimedia lies not so much in the technology but in the courseware that enables learners to access various materials, navigate information, and apply knowledge in meaningful ways (Latchem, Williamson, & Henderson-Lancett, 1993). Using computer-based technology requires teachers and students to change their roles to some extent, compared to the regular classroom. In short, computers can play an essential role as a medium or environment and a partner. The computer has the potential to give students a more profound sense of responsibility and ownership for their learning since they must be continuously active and involved, changing their previous roles as a responder to an initiator according to CALL programs and materials. For example, in instructional CALL programs, the students must answer all the questions, and in collaborative CALL have to initiate and finish activities themselves. The use of multimedia may mean more changes to methodology in teaching and learning styles and teachers' and students' roles than those that any other media technology can produce. In this section, more specific roles of multimedia, the teacher, and learners in MALL will be discussed, followed by discussing the changes in their roles due to the rapidly advancing multimedia technology.

1. The Role of Multimedia

Multimedia can play essential roles as a provider of useful information, a facilitator of pair or group work, and a substitute for teachers in language classes. That is, multimedia creates a learning environment in which learners can be engaged in self-directed and creative learning activities. The role multimedia plays is also compatible with a more traditional pedagogical approach such as rote learning or pattern practice. More specifically, Wright and Dillon (1990) focus on five uses of multimedia: 1) *as a presentation system* - The application here is for conventional lecturing or group teaching; 2) *for independent student learning* - multimedia can be used by students, either individually or in a small group, without the teacher; 3) *as a resource for students in the classroom* - It is the use of multimedia as a resource of enhancing teaching and learning activities; 4) *as an information source* - It is the use of multimedia as a source of information that is of interest, or for reference; and 5) *as a surrogate tutor* - Multimedia can supplement and reinforce teachers' instruction in both main subject and professional studies. The multimedia application can also be designed flexibly for either classroom or self-access use (Perzylo, 1993). However, its more substantial roles seem to be in the categories of the creators of a rich environment. They can demonstrate how best they serve as learning tools and as reference and information sources.

2. The Role of Teacher

According to the role of multimedia as discussed in the preceding section, the teacher's roles develop from one of conventional authorities to those of the consultant and facilitator in order that students can be involved more actively in the learning process. Teachers in multimedia-based instruction should pay extra attention to the importance of providing creative learning activities that multimedia alone cannot provide. They also should make efforts to maximize class efficiency when multimedia comes into play.

For the successful use of multimedia in class, teachers should first and foremost select appropriate multimedia programs. Teachers are required to be aware of learning objectives and content and select appropriate multimedia resources that best represent them. In this regard, before the selection of multimedia resources, teachers require some knowledge that will enable them to make a comprehensive evaluation that takes account of administrative, educational, technical, operational, and ethical aspects (Guidelines for the evaluation of multimedia content will be covered in detail in Chapter 3.).

3. The Role of Learners

The use of computers has enormously increased learners' responsibility in language learning. Despite variations in the extent of the learners' roles, their roles in the multimedia environment starkly contrast with the passive and other-directed roles seen in the conventional classroom. MALL calls for more participation and responsibility on the part of the learners. Classification can be made in accordance with the role of multimedia (courseware). In an instructional program, learners take on an active responder's role rather than that of an initiator. On the other hand, in a collaborative program or in programs where multimedia serves as sources of information, learners take much greater responsibility for their learning by initiating and completing the given task. In sum, learners should not be passive but rather pro-active in their learning. The active attitudes and participation of the learners maximize the outcome of MALL.

4. Multimedia and Patterns of Interaction

There are several kinds of interaction patterns possible with computers in the classroom - individual, in pairs and groups, between (or among) groups, or as a whole class (Hardisty & Windeatt, 1989; Phillips, 1985). In these patterns, the computer can support profitable interaction between the student and the computer and other students, working together at the machine. Thus, the interaction patterns can play a central role in communicative methodology (Hardisty, 1987). The interaction patterns among multimedia, learners, and teachers can be broadly classified into five types, as illustrated in Figure 1.4.

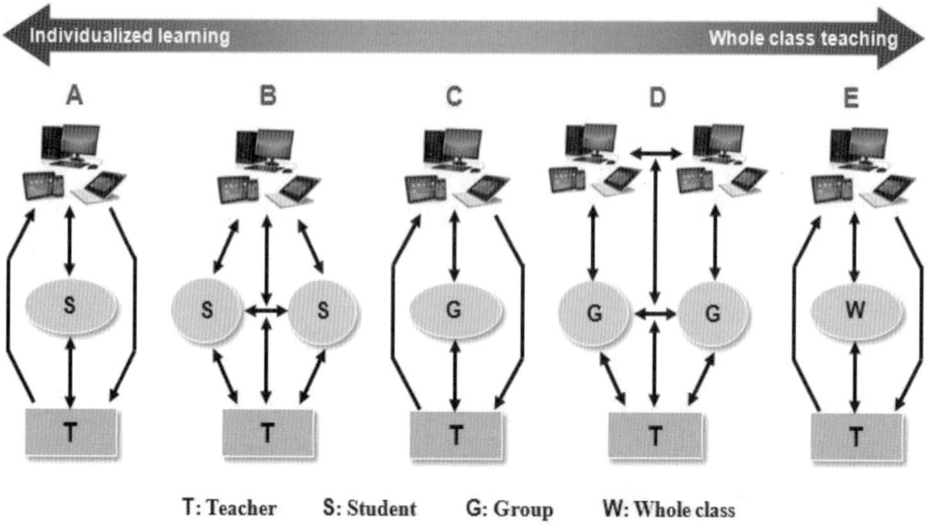

Figure 1.4 Interaction patterns between multimedia, teacher, and learners (C. H. Lee, 1998a)

It should be noted that the number of computers does not necessarily have to be equal to the number of learners. Individual or whole-class instruction is viable even with a small number of computers. First, in one-to-one mode A, the student can work with the computer individually at his/her right level. With network connection, it can also apply to learner-learner interaction. Second, in pair and group work mode (B and C), it aims to generate collaborative activities. The computer can be used to promote interaction between students and among a group of students. Third, in numbers of group mode (D) and expansion of mode (C), it aims to carry out competitive and collaborative activities. The computer can mainly promote interaction among the groups of students in competition with each other, collaborating within each group. Finally, in the whole class mode (E), whole-class activities can be conducted using a computer and projection TV or a projector. The teacher's role will be that of an instructor as in the conventional classroom. However, in modes (A), (B), (C), and (D), the teacher becomes a manager, advisor, facilitator, or partner. In contrast, in mode (E), the teacher's role is identical to that of a conventional classroom. As presented so far, the five interaction patterns in MALL can be conducive to improved learning activities that promote the four language skills and communicative language skills when the identified patterns are appropriately applied to learners' proficiency levels, content flow, and learning and teaching approach. Details on multimedia in the context of communicative and four language skills will be discussed in the next chapter.

1.5 Mobile Learning and Mobile-Assisted Language Learning

Mobile learning using mobile and wearable devices, smartphones, tablet PCs, and apps has been used widely to supplement teaching and learning activities in and out of classes. Even now, most web contents are developed to be synchronized and linked with apps, enabling simultaneous use on both computers and mobile devices. Mobile devices can provide creative and diverse activities conveniently in a classroom without computers. It promotes various interactive forms, teacher to student, student to student, and other interactions that enable learners to benefit from a self-paced, creativity-enhancing education. Learners can also respect individual differences, enabling autonomous learning. Above all, the mobility of mobile learning allows learners to overcome the limits of time and space, enabling them to learn anytime, anywhere.

Figure 1.5 Wearable devices and augmented reality (Schaffhauser, 2017)

The recent appearance and expansion of mobile or wearable devices, e.g., flip phones, smartwatches, smart glasses, etc., is expected to bring about groundbreaking changes in future language education. The devices and similar ones are expected to affect language education immensely. Mobile and wearable devices are combined with augmented reality and commercialized, providing much more realistic learning experiences and engaging activities that offer learners immersive experiences.

In its most straightforward concept, mobile-assisted language learning (MALL) is learning a language through mobile devices. This area has become one of the most popular research fields in recent years and has attracted countless researchers, most likely due to the widespread ownership of mobile devices (Beak & Lee, 2018;

Kukulska-Hulme, 2009; Lee & Cho, 2019; Stockwell, 2008). A great deal of effort has been made to understanding how mobile technologies relate to both traditional and innovative ways of teaching and learning, showing the applicability of mobile learning across a wide spectrum of activities (Beak & Lee, 2018; Cho, 2009; Kukulska-Hulme & Shield, 2008; Stockwell, 2008). It is generally regarded that along with most benefits that are associated with CALL, MALL provides an additional perk of being able to provide learners with the means of studying anytime and anywhere (Beak & Lee, 2018; Cho, 2009; Lee & Cho, 2019; Stockwell, 2008). Other advantages and potential capabilities of MALL include collaborative and individual learning, synchronous and asynchronous learning, motivation, autonomous and socially interactive learning (Kim & Kwon, 2012). Although some take a more rational and tempered attitude towards MALL, arguing that the widespread acceptance of communication technologies in non-learning contexts does not automatically mean that they will be effective in educational contexts, they still hold an optimistic opinion (Levy & Kennedy, 2005). Some hold a more pessimistic attitude, stating many factors that impede their introduction into language learning environments (Dias, 2002; Thornton & Houser, 2002). These views stem from the psychological, pedagogical, and technical barriers that accompany the usage of mobile technologies in the classroom, a probable but valid view of mobile learning being an intrusion of privacy (Dias, 2002), and technical limitations, including the size of the screen and the difficulties of inputting text (Thornton & Houser, 2002). Even one of the many optimists of MALL, Kukulska-Hulme and Shield (2008) stated that activities that capitalize on mobility and portability are not as commonplace as one might hope, and although the "anywhere" may often not be an issue, the "anytime" part is. Therefore, it is exceedingly important to consider careful implementations of MALL in any language learning environment to ensure efficient, effective, and meaningful learning for the students (Kukulska-Hulme & Shield, 2008).

1.6 Blended Learning

Blended learning has begun to gain popularity in education in recent years as technology advanced to a degree where students can access the online environment without difficulty. It is used in many educational fields now, but it has not been long since EFL teachers and students began to consider the possibilities of blending the positive attributes of online and offline learning. The limitations of EFL classrooms are that they are generally overcrowded, and they lack some sessions and interactions to provide ample exposure and meaningful interaction for the students. This commonly results in inadequate exposure and limited opportunities for learners to interact using the target language. Blended learning is considered an alternative due to the positive attributes that it combines them with a face-to-face class. Applicable definitions, concepts, and models of blended learning specifically for the field of EFL are needed to present appropriate and optimal models of blended learning for the development of English skills.

Blended learning is used in education across the discipline as its popularity is increasing in recent years, and there seem to be various ways it has been defined. Some researchers have considered blended learning as the blending of the instructional method (Driscoll, 2002; Rossett, 2002), some as instructional modalities (Bersin, 2003; Singh & Reed, 2001), and others as a combination of online and offline instruction (Rooney, 2003; Young, 2002). In ELT, Yoon and Lee (2010) defined blended learning as "bringing together the positive attributes of online and offline education, including instructional modalities, delivery methods, learning tools, etc., in relation to language teaching and learning approaches and methods in order to reinforce the learning process, bring about the optimal learner achievement, and enhance the quality of teaching and learning" (p. 180). This definition shows the instructional goals and context specific to ELT. In actual practice, there are still disputes over the ways in how EFL courses should be blended. Issues and needs specific to academic disciplines and institution leads to variations and complexity in implementing blended learning in classrooms.

In a general sense, Garrison and Kanuka (2004) categorize blended learning into three categories of online, enhanced, and blended learning, while Graham (2006) distinguishes it as enabling, enhancing, and transforming blended learning. In ELT classrooms, online and offline elements can be blended to supplement each other, but more than that, they can construct an interactive environment that cannot be considered as simple additions or substitutions. C. H. Lee (2004) considered blended learning as the combination of online and offline features for holistic English education. S. Y. Yoon (2011) suggested two levels of blended learning for ELT – weak and strong blended learning (WBL and SBL)[1] – as seen in Table 1.1.

---

1 WBL: The presence or the absence of one environment does not require transforming or reconstructing the teaching methodologies. It aims to provide additional or supplemental activities in one environment to enhance or supplement the other.
SBL: Both online and offline environments are essential, through which transformation and reconstruction of teaching methods and methodologies from the conventional take place. It aims to provide ample exposure and interaction in the online and offline environment.

Table 1.1 Degrees of blended learning (S. Y. Yoon, 2011, p. 239)

	Online only	Online or offline	Online and offline (supplementary)	Online and offline (transformational)	Offline only
C. H. Lee (2004)	-	-	Online and offline holistic English education		-
Garrison & Kanuka (2004)	-	-	-	Blended learning	-
Graham (2006)	-	Enabling blend	Enhancing blend	Transforming blend	-
S. Y. Yoon (2011)	-	-	Weak blended learning	Strong blended learning	-

On developing and implementing blended learning into EFL classrooms, the features of blended learning should be considered as well as the appropriateness of multimedia components. The main features of blended learning to be considered for EFL classrooms are pedagogical instruction and learning experience, individual work, interaction with peers, interaction with the teacher, feedback, discussion and reflection, and multimedia components (Yoon & Lee, 2011b). An example of Yoon and Lee's blended learning model 2011b) for EFL classrooms is presented in Figure 1.6.

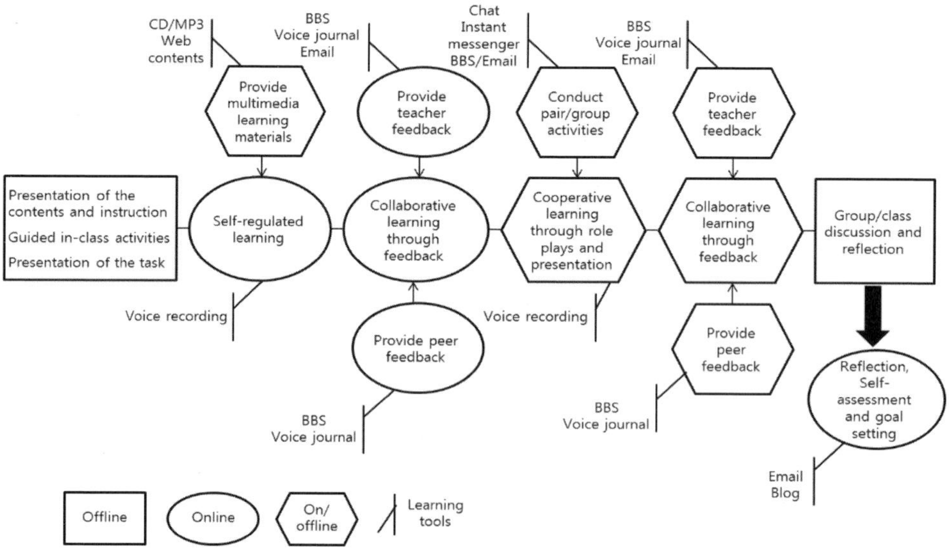

Figure 1.6 The optimal BLS model (Yoon & Lee, 2011b, p. 46)

The optimal BLS (Blended Learning for Spoken Skills) model is developed based on the features of blended learning and multimedia components. It is a comprehensive model for English spoken skill for SBL, which pedagogically transforms online and offline classes to promote the maximized benefits of online and offline classes. The students are given tasks, e.g., pronunciation and listening practices to build on their pronunciation and work on speaking and listening. As the lesson progresses, the students use all three spoken skills of speaking, pronunciation, and listening while carrying out the task. Variation in tasks within the model, such as pair or group work using dialogues, role-plays, presentations, and video production where the students can collaboratively or cooperatively interact, can be considered. Various multimedia components like the bulletin board system (BBS) and voice journal are suggested for use, depending on the types of tasks. The multimedia components that instigated blended learning features in this model were web contents and resources, voice recording, audio samples, BBS, voice journal, and email. They all were found to be useful for the development of English spoken skills.

It can be seen that a bottom-up approach in the development of spoken skills by building up from pronunciation to speaking and listening skills is addressed as a consequence of self-regulated learning. Meanwhile, it also takes on a top-down approach where speaking skill is mainly attended as a recurrent skill. In contrast, pronunciation and listening skills were fostered as nonrecurrent skills from 'cooperated learning through role-plays and presentations.'

The models presented in this section contain the features of blended learning and appropriate multimedia components that promote complex learning and simultaneously maintain students' motivation while being effective and efficient. Likewise, while designing a blended learning course, teachers should keep in mind the appropriateness of teaching and learning tools and their effects on learners. However, there are limitations of blended learning as well. Possible excess in workload for students and the teachers, lack of familiarity in using learning tools, various social issues that may arise due to interacting in a new arena of online environments are some of the limitations (S. Y. Yoon, 2011; Yoon & Lee, 2011b). For efficient and effective integration of media in online and offline classes, teacher training and learner education are essential in initiating a blended learning course. In particular, the teacher needs to be aware of the various learner needs that may arise in a blended learning class and assist the learners who may have difficulties in participating in online and offline environments.

1.7 Mobile-Assisted Blended Learning (MABL)

Language learning using digital technology continues to evolve, in line with emerging technologies. It would be a stretch to label mobile devices as 'new,' but their capabilities and functions continue to improve year by year, and many web contents are being developed and designed to be used simultaneously on almost all multimedia devices (Lee, 2017). Mobile-Assisted Language Learning (MALL) offers the potential to provide creative and various activities conveniently ubiquitously and facilitate innovative interactive forms and enable learners to access a self-paced, autonomous learning environment. It is generally accepted that MALL adds the element of ubiquity to the benefits that are associated with CALL. This ubiquity aspect is particularly beneficial to the blended learning approach, especially in contexts where mobile devices are accepted both inside and outside the classroom. Mobile-assisted blended learning (MABL) is the combination of mobile learning or MALL and blended learning (Baek & Lee, 2018). The framework of MABL classes is shown in Figure 1.7.

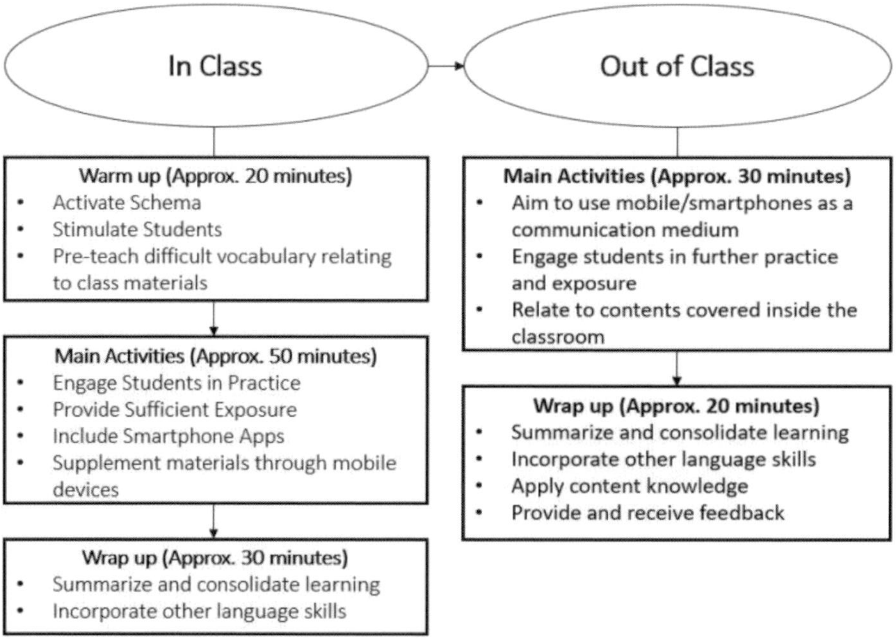

Figure 1.7 The framework of MABL classes (Baek & Lee, 2018, p. 18)

Blended learning combined with mobile devices can offer a substantial increase in the amount of exposure and practice for all four language skills by creating environments that contain seemingly unlimited information, promote interests, motivation and reinforce learning processes (Baek & Lee, 2018; Lee, 2017). MABL can also promote interaction and rapport between teachers and students. As shown in Figure 1.7, for example, using mobile devices as a communication medium means it is another avenue where students can easily reach out to the teachers for help. It can also be a convenient way for a more individualized teacher and peer-feedback be provided in a flexible timeframe.

By incorporating various apps, classrooms can be more easily transformed into an environment where both online and offline aspects are integral to and supplements each other, as illustrated by the procedure of MABL classes in Figure 1.8. The procedure was designed for an English-speaking course at the university level, focusing on enhancing exposure and practice for the students and providing general and in-depth, individualized feedback.

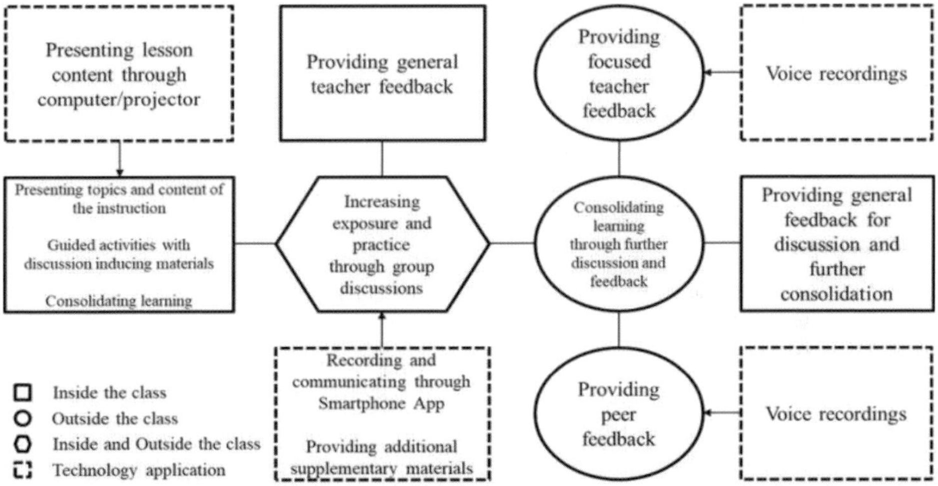

Figure 1.8 The procedure of MABL classes (Baek & Lee, 2018, p.19)

It should be noted that the positive outlook added by the ubiquity of mobile devices is, in fact, a potential. The aspect of 'anywhere, anytime' is indeed possible but not always attainable like the limitations mentioned for blended learning. For example, a student occupied in a part-time job will not be able to participate in 'Out of Class' activities and will have to catch up later. Although this is not detrimental to the students' learning experience, it will require more attention from the teacher and patience from other students. As such, the potential of MABL may be alluring to willing teachers, but it requires careful implementation.

1.8 Artificial Intelligence (AI) and Big Data in Language Learning

With the emerging digital technology and a highly advanced network system in the recent two decades, artificial intelligence (AI) and big data have attracted researchers and teaching practitioners into the language learning disciplines. This recent interest in AI and big data starts with the hypothesis that they are conducive to keeping track of each learner's learning outcomes in language classes while catering to learners' individual needs and goals on developing language skills. AI and big data allow individualized learning in which various learning programs and content can be tailored to each learner in classes. Moreover, it is possible to present learning materials suitable for each learner's current level by analyzing data from reflection logs on LMS (Woolf, Lane, Chaudhri, & Kolodner, 2013). In line with this, this section discusses the possible implications of AI and big data in second and foreign language learning.

1. AI and Language Learning

Artificial intelligence (AI) is not a newly emerged term in this digital era where quick and convenient network services and diverse digital technologies are readily available. The official usage of the term AI was first proposed in a two-month workshop at Dartmouth in 1956. In the workshop, John McCarthy and his colleagues stated that "an attempt will be made to find how to make machines use language, form abstractions and concepts, solve kinds of problems now reserved for humans, and improve themselves" (McCarthy, Minsky, Rochster, & Shannon, 1955, p. 1). This statement also had the primary purpose of distinguishing AI from other fields regarding methodologies and issues that need to be addressed as a separate field, which should try to replicate the capabilities of human beings (e.g., creativity, self-improvement, and natural language use) (Russell & Norvig, 2010). Early research in AI revealed a philosophical distinction between strong AI and weak AI (Kannan & Munday, 2018; Pokrivcakova, 2019). McCarthy et al. (1955) fundamentally insisted on the concept of strong AI, which attempts to develop a human-like cognitive system in machines or computers. It aims to evolve intelligent machines to be equipped with equal intelligence and the self-awareness ability of humankind. In this sense, many researchers concur that developing machines with strong AI will be unlikely actualized soon (Pokrivcakova, 2019). In contrast, weak AI refers to the artificial intelligence that implements a limited part of the human mindset, aiming to solve narrow tasks focusing on a specific problem (Flowers, 2019; Searle, 1980). Google Translator, Papago, Siri, Google Assistant, Grammarly, automated scoring systems are examples of weak AI.

However, recent AI research goes beyond the binary distinction without end goal due to its unpredictable future in the fourth industrial revolution. The research areas become more interdisciplinary than conventional approaches, and its definition has been shifted continuously based on what is required in its interdisciplinarity of research (Dodigovic, 2007; Kannan & Munday, 2018; Pokrivcakova, 2019). Luckin, Holmes, Griffiths, and Forcier (2016) defined the AI in the education field as "computer systems that have been designed to interact with the world through capabilities (for example, visual perception and speech recognition) and intelligent behaviors (for example, assessing the available information and then taking the most sensible action to achieve a state goal) that we would think of as essentially human" (p. 14). Pokrivcakova (2019) maintained that the computer systems in Luckin et al.'s (2016) definition contain various technologies and methods, such as machine learning, adaptive learning, natural language processing, data mining, crowdsourcing, neural networks, or algorithms. Interestingly, there have been efforts to apply AI in language learning with the growing interest in CALL since early 1990. The early studies integrating AI techniques in CALL were called intelligent CALL (ICALL) (Matthews, 1992, 1993). ICALL research areas include intelligent tutoring systems (ITS) and natural language processing (NLP) (Schulze, 2008). ITS are technology-enhanced learning systems developed to facilitate one-to-one individualized learning. These systems are helpful in large-scale classrooms where one-to-one teacher feedback is physically impossible. Also, NLP deals with the specific capabilities of intelligent systems, including natural language understanding and natural language production (Pokrivcakova, 2019). The ICALL research revealed some benefits of using AI in language classes: 1) it is helpful for learners to be engaged in learning activities at their own pace; 2) instant feedback and interaction with technologies are possible for each learner; 3) it is available to predict learners' future outcomes and suggest appropriate learning content and materials; and 4) it is also helpful for teachers to better understand learners' learning strategies and preferences.

ICALL research has been much more sophisticated by encompassing various AI-based tools, programs, and software (Briggs, 2018; Campbell-Howes, 2019; S. M. Lee, 2019). Machine translation, chatbots, and AI writing assistants in language learning have been hot potatoes in the 2010s. Many research studies figured out their pros and cons on developing L2 language skills (Dargan, 2019; Garcia & Pena, 2011; S. M. Lee; 2019; Lotze, 2018; White & Heinrich, 2013). Those AI-based tools are developed based on machine learning, NLP, and deep learning technologies. The recent ITS tools have also been evolved by being integrated with the NLP-based tutoring system and thereby becoming interactive machine learning tutors (Pokrivcakova, 2019). This development expands the opportunities to adapt AI in language learning in providing learners with individualized learning materials, adaptive and intelligent web-based collaborative learning system, more interactive communication with various tools, and increased exposure to the target language. If language teachers want to use chatbots, machine translators, and AI writing assistants in language classes, they do not necessarily become AI experts. Instead, it is essential to understand how to facilitate learners' learning processes with the AI-enhanced programs within a proper pedagogy and learning aims and objectives. In other words, it is undesirable to provide students with needless workloads and repetitive activities through AI-based tools in language classes (Dodigovic, 2009; Pokrivcakova, 2019) with communicative approaches.

Figure 1.9 AI in personalized-learning
https://elearningindustry.com/benefits-of-artifcial-intelligence-in-personalized-learning

2. Big Data and Language Learning

Big data become a very famous term in the recent decade, and its role in society is now noticeably invaluable. According to the *Merriam-Webster Dictionary*, the definition of data is "information in digital form that can be transmitted or processed." It is worth noting that the data has been becoming easy to be gathered, analyzed, and explored with the consistent development of digital technologies. This also indicates what people do on their computers, smartphones, or the Internet can be recorded and analyzed to explore specific patterns and information. These patterns and information from the data are exploited to reveal what people like or dislike. Hurley (2019) mentioned that these data remain useless until analyzed to identify hidden patterns, trends, and associations that generally exist in them.

The concept of big data would ease the process of using data in a much more efficient way. Social media such as Facebook, Instagram, and Twitter use big data to suggest a suitable post, feed, and even advertisements based on each user's interest. Microsoft defined big data as "the term increasingly used to describe the process of applying serious computing power – the latest in machine learning and artificial intelligence – to seriously massive and often highly complex sets of information" (https://news.microsoft.com/2013/02/11/the-big-bang-how-the-big-data-explosion-is-changing-the-world/). As mentioned in the definition, big data and AI are counterparts. In their relationship, AI acts as the brain, and big data present the information and raw data input. To develop artificially intelligent systems, a plethora of data sets are invaluable. This means that AI would become useless without big data. Similarly, big data as the raw data (e.g., text, videos, photographs, and numerical data) is not worth anything. It needs to be connected to AI systems to be analyzed and find patterns and useful information. This process is also known as machine learning and is the sub-field of AI. The machine cannot learn anything without collecting and analyzing the data by AI systems (Hurley, 2019).

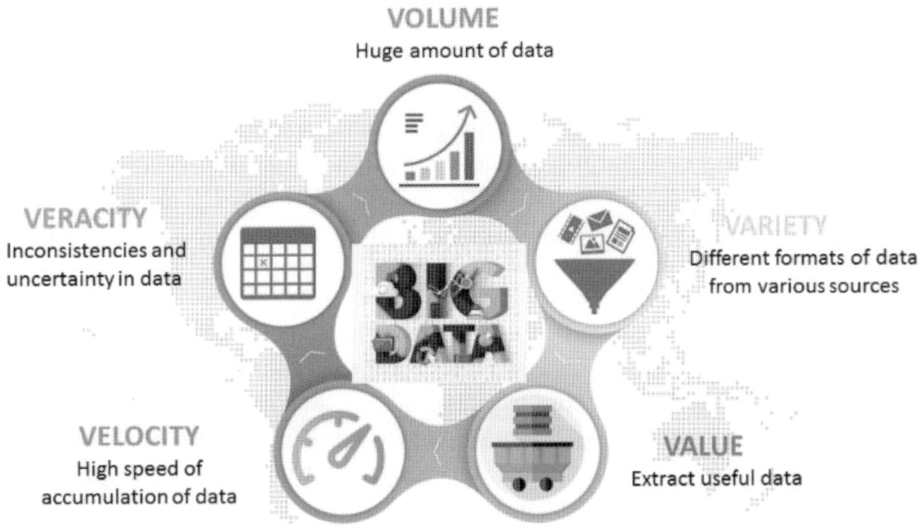

Figure 1.10 Characteristics of Big Data
(https://laptrinhx.com/what-is-big-data-a-beginner-s-guide-to-the-world-of-big-data-1936020691/)

There exist five core characteristics of big data: volume, variety, velocity, value, and veracity (Cope & Kalantzis, 2016; Gartner, 2012; Laney, 2001). The first key to big data is volume, and it is related to the word *big*. To obtain reliable results from the data analytics, it is essential to collect a large amount of data. The more data can be collected and analyzed, the more reliable and valid patterns will be found. Second, variety refers to the diversity of collected data. People left various data after using networked services, allowing the administrators of some websites, programs, or software to collect them. These diverse data can be categorized into three types: structured, unstructured, and semi-structured. They also have varied information that will be useful in some contexts. Third, velocity means the speed of the data processing and movement from flash memory to more extensive memory storage. Nowadays, this data processing and movement can occur almost in real-time. Fourth, value refers to what collected data inherently has. As mentioned already, data itself cannot be understood as it is difficult to discern useful patterns and information without data analytics. After being analyzed, the data can be helpful to those who necessitate them. Thus, the data have the immanent value that must be discovered. Lastly, veracity is related to how accurate and reliable the data sets are. The fifth key characteristic, thus, is related to how large data can be gathered. A large amount of data also guarantees the inherent value of the collected data.

Many researchers in various disciplines have attempted to call big data into their fields, and second and foreign language learning are no exceptions. Mayer-Schönberger and Cukier (2013) insisted that big data anticipates a revolution that will shift the way people live, work, and think. This transformation and change will eventually happen to language learning environments. In the upcoming era of big data, teachers and learners can meet individualized learning needs, responsive and recursive formative evaluations, efficient research for learning strategies, and collaborative learning. Cope and Kalantizis (2016) postulated that analyzing the data in CMC environments is nothing new. Learning management systems (LMS) also provide data-tracking functions and let the language teachers record what students do on the given activities or tasks. This helps the teachers to analyze students' engagement levels and achievement of language skills. With big data in language learning, it will be much easier and faster to collect a large amount of data invaluable to language teachers and learners.

However, the collected data must be explored through some statistical programs. SPSS, R, and SAS are three major statistical programs that can analyze the data from various learning websites, programs, and software. Even though big data in language learning necessitates professional knowledge of collecting and analyzing the data, it helps researchers and teachers employ the data sets in more efficient and effective ways. Big data in language learning helps teachers suggest and develop individualized learning materials through learning analytics, which cannot be done by themselves. Besides, it becomes easy to detect students' weaknesses and strengths in learning a language. The learners can also check their learning outcomes and witness where they are excelling or need more improvements. By reflecting on learning analytics results, learners can make plans for facilitating further gains in their language skills. To do this, consistent teacher education and development will be required.

1.9 Computer-Assisted Language Testing

The recent development in computer hardware and software brought forth advancement in language testing (Bachman, 2000; Brown, 1997). Since the mid-20th century, linguistics and statistics have been integrated and instigated rapid expansion of corpus linguistics, voice recognition technology, automated scoring system, and other related cognitive sciences (I. C. Choi, 2002). These technologies are being vigorously implemented in language testing, resulting in popularity in multimedia-based language testing. It seems that computer-based language tests (CBLT) and computer adaptive language tests (CALT) have attracted attention for a decade or so. In contrast, computer-based tests (CBT) and computer adaptive tests (CAT) have been the focus of much research in the field of psychometrics since the early 1970s because the application of technology to language testing had consistent controversies technology and dimensionality of language ability (Bachman, 1990), the multi-faceted issues on the effects of interactivity of multimedia on language test-takers' performances (Bachman & Palmer, 1996; Choi, Kim, & Boo, 2003). Computer-assisted language testing can be largely categorized into three categories of computer-based language testing (CBLT), computer-adaptive language testing (CALT), and web-based language testing (WBT). The features and characteristics of each are discussed.

1. Computer-Based Language Testing (CBLT)

The attempt to use computers for language testing began as the distribution of computers took on speed. The use of computers in language testing was limited to scoring answers and analyzing, summarizing, and interpreting the results (Bachman, 2000). As personal computers became popular and technology advanced to a higher level, CBLT became a possibility. Language testing took on the more active form where test-takers took the test on computers, and test items were provided on the computer screen as the test progressed.

CBLT has its strengths in comparison to conventional testing methods. The development, administration, scoring, and analysis of the results are quick, accurate, and efficient (Gruba & Corbel, 1997). It allows using color, graphs, images, and audiovisuals in test items (Green, 1988). Computer programs can make it easy to provide variation of test-time types, control time for both test items and the administration of the entire test, to get detailed information such as learner response time, and to administer standardized tests (Bachman, 2000; Gruba & Corbel, 1997). Test items' storage and confidentiality became more efficient than paper tests, and immediate feedback based on learner responses could be provided.

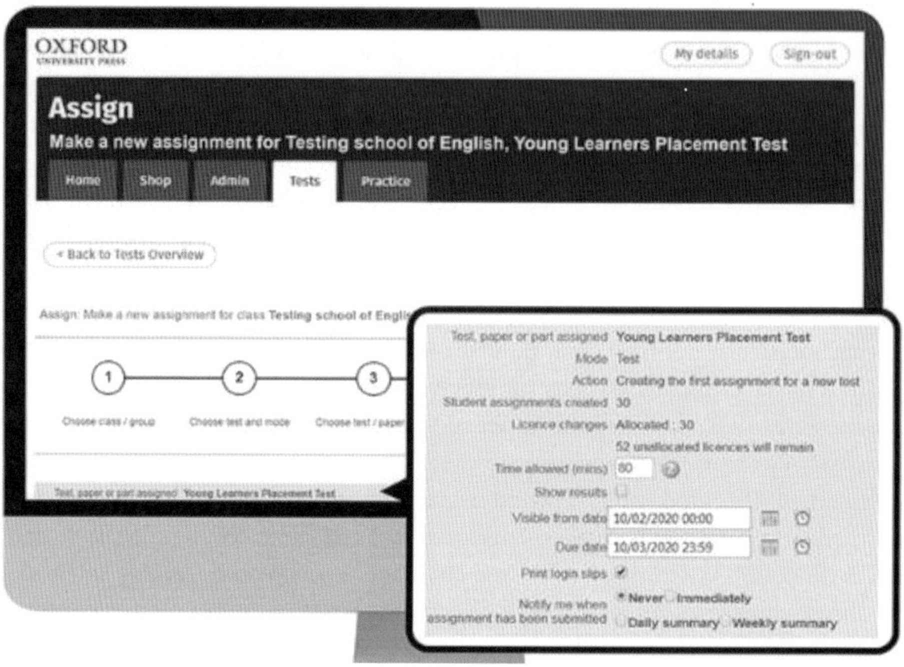

Figure 1.11 Computer-based language testing
(https://elt.oup.com/feature/global/young-learners-placement/)

2. Computer-Adaptive Language Testing (CALT)

With the introduction of item response theory (IRT), CALT has been paid more attention from language test developers and researchers. CALT is a form of testing administered to individuals, and test items that are appropriate for the level of test-takers are chosen and presented to individual test-takers based on IRT and computerized algorithms, control, and multimedia technology (Brown, 1997; Larson, 1998). The difference between CBLT and CALT is that in CBLT, all the test-takers are given the same test items, but in CALT, the test items are chosen from the test bank based on the test-takers' responses to the previous test-items to tailor to the individuals (Chalhoub-Deville & Deville, 1999; Madsen, 1991). That means that in CBLT, it is possible to edit or delete test items before administering the tests, and test-takers can go back to previous test items and make corrections; however, in CALT, changing answers, skipping test items, or editing test items are not possible.

The item difficulty of test items in CALT is pre-calculated and presented based on the test-takers' ability, which is also calculated as they respond to the test-items while the test is being administered. This function provides the test-taker with test items that are level-appropriate, in turn, keeping them motivated to participate in the assessment without giving up due to test items that happened to be too difficult or too easy. It can also reduce predictions and mistakes in the test-takers' responses, increasing the test's reliability (Henning, 1987; Larson, 1998). For administering CALT, test item bank system, test administration system, scoring system, and evaluation and analysis systems are needed (Chalhoub-Deville & Deville, 1999; Dunkel, 1999). These systems, or sub-features, are not run as a whole, but they exist as separate systems in the program and run as needed.

3. Web-Based Language Testing (WBT)

WBT is a form of computerized testing administered on the Web, which is quite useful for distance education or online learning. Since the test is administered online, test-takers can download the test or take the tests directly on the Web regardless of time and location. Roever (2001) pointed out that despite the availability of CBT, WBT is becoming more popular because WBT ensures the freedom of test-takers to choose the time and location of the test, the spread of computers, and the Internet, low-budget online tests, etc. Research and projects on WBT are being conducted in domestic and international academic institutions (Cho, Lee, Kim, Ko, & Jeong, 2008; K. M. O, 2004).

It should be noted that careful and thorough validation of the test must take place in administering WBT with various types of multimedia (Chapelle, Jamieson, & Hegelheimer, 2003; Roever, 2001). Besides, factor analysis and validation of the effects of tests on screen, its design, and the application of technology on tests must be conducted (J. Kim, 2009).

4. Previous studies on CALT

The principles and theories of CALT were introduced by Brown (1997), Larson (1998), and I. C. Choi (2002). Various sub-topics of CALT have been examined, including computational linguistics, development and administration, scoring systems, etc. I. C. Choi (1999) presented how computational linguistics could be applied to language performance testing. Kim and Lim (1998) and J. Kim (2006) focused on the development and administration of testing. Kim and Lim (1998) developed the computer-adaptive English test for elementary school students, and J. Kim (2006) developed a web-based speaking test using Visual Basic 6.0. Computerized testing with conventional testing has been compared. For example, Kenyon and Malabonga (2001) compared examinees' attitudes toward computer-assisted and other proficiency assessments. Sawaki (2001) compared conventional and computerized tests of reading in a second language (L2).

Many studies on testing and assessment have addressed productive skills than receptive skills (Sawaki, 2001; Wagner, 2007). Sawaki (2001) focused on L2 reading, and Wagner (2007) investigated test-takers' viewing behaviors in an L2 video listening test. Studies on testing speaking include measurability of oral fluency through automatic speech recognition for computer-based oral proficiency interview (COPI) (I. C. Choi, 2005), test-takers' anxiety and performance in video conferenced interviews (Craig & Kim, 2010), the effects of tasks on examinee performance in a computer-delivered speaking test (J. Kim, 2011), and the relationship between speaking test administration tools and item types (J. Kim, 2009). Regarding research on writing assessment, H. Lee (2004) examined the reliability of handwritten and computerized ESL writing tests. I. C. Choi (2012) probed the validity of automatic essay scoring-based ratings based on corpus indices and error analysis. The comparison of computer-based ratings and human ratings for L2 writing was a common issue to examine (Choi & Uhm, 2001; H. Lee, 2004). In more recent years, automated scoring systems have been addressed by several researchers. Research on automated scoring systems for writing have dealt with various contexts and test-takers, such as automated scoring of Korean high school students' English composition (Jin & Park, 2012), the effectiveness of automated essay scoring in an EFL classroom at the college level (J. E. Kim, 2014), and the sophistication of an automated scoring system for large-scale essay writing. In terms of automated scoring systems for speaking, Shin, Park, Park, and Yim (2015) have provided implications of utilizing an automated scoring program for English speaking skills.

1.10 MALL and Instructional Models

Multimedia programs or content developed based on distinctive features of multimedia can provide a rich learning environment, individual and collaborative learning, and motivation for English teaching. It, in turn, makes the development of the four language and communicative skills. Teachers and learners get to be more cognizant of the value and importance of MALL, and awareness of MALL will help distribute various multimedia programs in the classroom. However, some studies have reported that the programs are not efficiently used (C. H. Lee, 2002; Lee & Han, 2000). Thus, a growing need for an effective instructional model and procedure is emerging. This section will explore practical instructional models to implement multimedia, the Internet, or the Web in language classes and a blended learning environment. Detailed cases that demonstrate the application of learning and teaching models in MALL will be dealt with in Part 3.

1. Teaching Methodology in MALL

Since the onset of education, teachers have been at the center of it. As CALL or MALL indicates, computers, software, or courseware cannot replace teachers. Thus, teachers should not attempt to use multimedia, including a computer, courseware, or the Web throughout the whole class. It may be more advisable to select them and use them as learning tools. Teachers can flexibly mend and complement the courseware appropriate to the needs and at the same time, apply proper methodology (Hardisty & Windeatt, 1989). It should be noted that CALL or MALL classes require more creative and systematic instruction than conventional classes. Effective instruction can resolve current problems using multimedia, such as lack of software and mismatch between courseware and curriculum or lesson plan. The fundamental methodological solution to the current issues will eventually lead to effective and successful instructions.

Three stages of MALL

A typical listening class is comprised of the three main stages – pre-, while-, and post-listening. Similar stages of pre-, while-, and post-computer work stages were suggested (Hardisty & Windeatt, 1989; Higgins & Johns, 1984; C. H. Lee, 1998a; Windeatt, Hardisty, & Eastment, 2000). Based on the three stages of computer work, C. H. Lee (1998a) came up with detailed procedures and stage-specific activities for MALL or WBI.

First, the pre-computer stage prepares learners for practical computer work with a couple of activities for a warm-up and activating schema. For instance, an overview of the lesson is introduced by discussing related topics and learning vocabulary. In this stage, teachers are advised to inform learners of precise directions on tasks to perform, how to make use of the program, and the role that learners should take on. It is also helpful for the teacher to address the whole class on the learning objective and what it involves by a projector, a projection TV, a visual presenter, and handouts, so that main computer work does not go amiss. Second, the while-computer stage is where learners get engaged in the main learning activities and tasks. As presented in Figure 1.4, it can be carried out with each learner working on individual computer work or work in pair- or group work. In this stage, teachers should take the facilitator role without interfering with computer work unless learners ask for help. Instead, teachers should take on a monitoring role, supervising how activities are performed and how interactions are taking place. Last, the post-computer stage is where the lesson is supplemented and consolidated through extra work or assignments.

In sum, the three stages will serve in making the most effective use of multimedia in the learning and teaching of English. However, computers do not necessarily have to be used all the time in the three stages. It is more advisable to incorporate computers on a need basis as a supplementary tool.

Instructional models of MALL

Based on the procedure suggested by Hardisty and Windeatt (1989), C. H. Lee (1998a), and Windeatt, Hardisty, and Eastment (2000), Figure 1.12 presents an integrated model of a MALL lesson for four language skills development. Specific MALL lessons for four language skills, three subskills, and integrated language skills will be presented in Part 3, 'Integration of MALL into the Classroom' in detail. Given that websites or apps can neither run the whole stretch of class nor replace teachers, it seems reasonable to judge when multimedia should be incorporated into the larger context of the main lesson and content. Thus, the following instructional model is organized in accordance with the three computer work stages. First, during the pre-computer work stage, the teacher presents the main topic of the lesson and uses brainstorming to activate learners' schema. In this stage, learners briefly study the key vocabulary related to the topic and engage in individual or pair- or group-work depending on the needs and flow of the lesson. Teachers should inform learners of the nature of the program to be used or how to use it before using them.

Second, during the while-computer work stage, learners get involved in learning activities available in various forms: texts, sounds, moving pictures to exercise, and do tasks. Different interaction patterns are also necessary to encourage meaningful learning as learners start with listening, after which follows speaking, reading, and writing in the model. As designing the model, it is essential to strike a balance between top-down and bottom-up comprehension practice to develop well-balanced comprehension skills within the program's content or learning flow. Other websites can also be suggested to supplement and consolidate the language skill(s) practiced whenever necessary. The teachers' role at this point is to observe, control, and monitor learners' performance. They are also supposed to respond to questions as they participate as an instructor, facilitator, or partner.

Third, during the post-computer work stage, the content covered is summarized. The skills that the learners had difficulty with are supplemented or intensified with further practice. If the program is designed for four language skills or focused on particular skills such as reading and writing, oral practice (activities) such as role-play, simulation, and discussion can be used to reinforce during this stage. Reading or writing skills can also be practiced by providing learners relevant websites to read and write more. In the case of programs mainly focused on spoken skills (listening and speaking), reading and writing skills can be supplemented by providing relevant topics and websites or apps before the class.

A MALL instructional model for language skills development

The model presented in Figure 1.12 is an integrated example of instruction and procedure that encompasses the four language skills, but it can be modified to focus on specific skills. As explained, during the while-computer work stage, learners first engage in individual work practicing listening or pronunciation with apps or video clips in the websites.

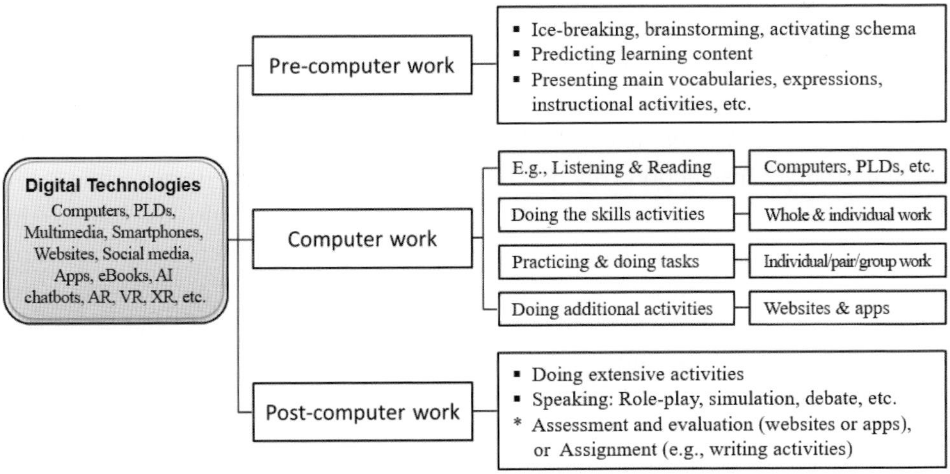

Figure 1.12 A MALL instructional model for four language skills development

The top-down, bottom-up, and interactive approaches are likely to improve well-balanced listening skills. When apps are also used as the primary material, it is crucial to have the learners practice further, using relevant websites that provide listening materials appropriate to their levels. Second, during the post-computer work stage, the content learned should be wrapped up and linked to other skills. Role-play, simulation, and discussion are useful activities that can be supplemented for other oral skills, and reading and writing about the topic based on the information in the relevant websites can also be useful.

A sample model for reading can start with learning the given sentences, related materials, images, and graphics (and moving pictures) during the pre-computer work stage. Individual work during the while-computer work stage can involve reading various sentences and practicing vocabulary and grammar. As was the case with listening, both top-down, bottom-up, and interactive reading skills should be promoted for balanced development. Similar to the previous instructional model, pair- and group work and other practices to reinforce and consolidate the skills covered can also be incorporated using websites that provide level-appropriate materials for the learners. Finally, during the post-computer work stage, the lesson can be wrapped up, and based on the content learned, other oral/aural practices such as role-play, simulation, and discussion can be provided. Writing skills can also be practiced using relevant websites.

A reading strategy instruction model for blended learning

As attention seemingly shifts towards the process rather than the product of L2 reading, research into both learners' reading strategy use and strategy instruction has become one of the dominant areas in L2 reading. Reading strategy instruction can help learners improve their reading comprehension (Abbott, 2006; Macaro & Erler, 2008; Mokhtari & Reichard, 2004). According to Suh and Lee (2014), the reading strategy instruction can be composed of three stages (pre-, while-, and post-reading stages) and the following six phases: 1) teacher's introduction of the reading strategies; 2) student and teacher discussion on the benefits of the reading strategies; 3) teacher's modeling of the strategy use; 4) students' guided practice of the strategy use; 5) students' individual practice of the strategy use; and 6) student and teacher reflections and feedback (see Figure 1.13). The reading strategy instruction consists of three sessions each week. The students have two offline sessions (one hour per session) and one online session, and the instructional procedure in blended learning is designed based on Neumeier's (2005) framework of parameters and Yoon and Lee's blended learning models (2011b) for designing a blended learning environment.

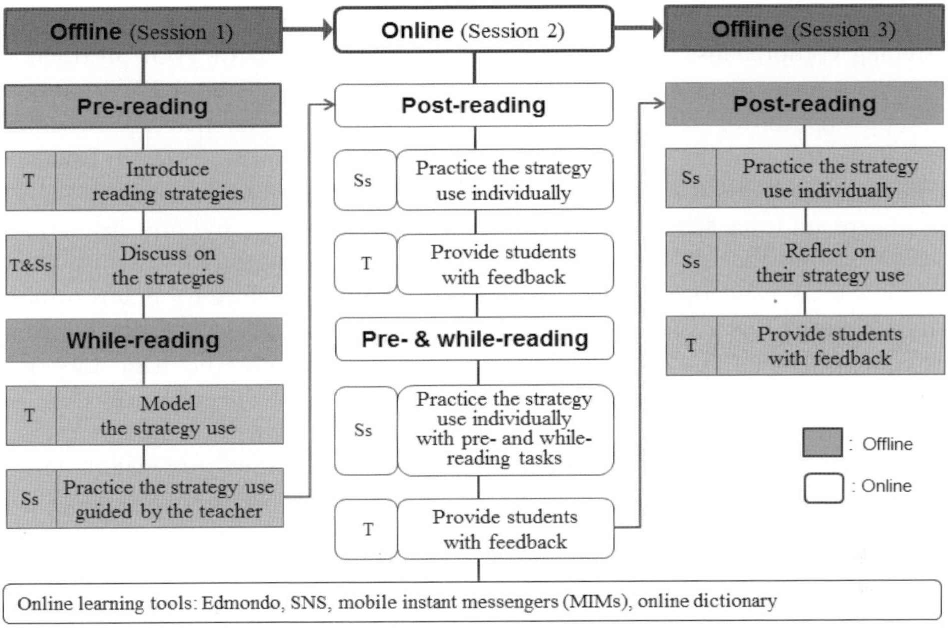

Figure 1.13 A reading strategy instruction model for blended learning (Suh & Lee, 2014, p. 306)

Phases 1, 2, 3, and 4 of the strategy instruction are implemented in the first offline session. The students learn new pre-, while-, and post-reading strategies, discuss the strategies, and observe the teacher's modeling of the strategy use. They also practice the instructed strategies with the guide and help of the teacher. In phase 5, the students have an online session. They practice a post-reading strategy while performing a task. They are also given new reading materials and are asked to read them and perform pre- and while-reading tasks likely to elicit the deployment of the instructed strategies. After the online session, the students have the second offline session (phase 6), practicing the post-reading strategy using the material they read during the online session. Then, the students are given some time to share their reflections, and the teacher provides feedback on the students' use of the strategies in the online session.

An instructional model for focus on form instruction in blended learning

Focus on form (FonF) instruction with communicative activities has received wide attention in grammar teaching and learning for the last decades. The successful implementation of FonF instruction appears to require enough time for ample input and production in appropriate circumstances. Blended learning can be applied to students with FonF instruction for developing their grammar knowledge and listening comprehension. There is an instructional model for FonF instruction through listening activities in blended learning, as shown in Figure 1.14. The model can be utilized for effective teaching and learning of grammar and listening simultaneously and suggested to be flexibly applied and implemented in language classes for FonF instruction in blended learning.

There are three stages of listening activities: pre-, while-, and post-listening in the offline session. At the pre-listening stage, first, background information of listening texts, new vocabularies, and main topics are introduced for brainstorming and preparing the main activities. The while-listening stage consists of three listening activities. The first listening activity is for predicting the main story of a listening text with a visual mode; learners are asked to guess the main story through the visual mode and share ideas with their peers. The second listening activity aims to comprehend the main ideas via comprehension questions that include target forms with textual enhancement. In the last listening activity, learners have communicative activities for production using target forms with peers, and learners are required to use these target forms to complete given activities. Last, the post-listening activities include summarizing the main ideas and sharing reflections using target forms.

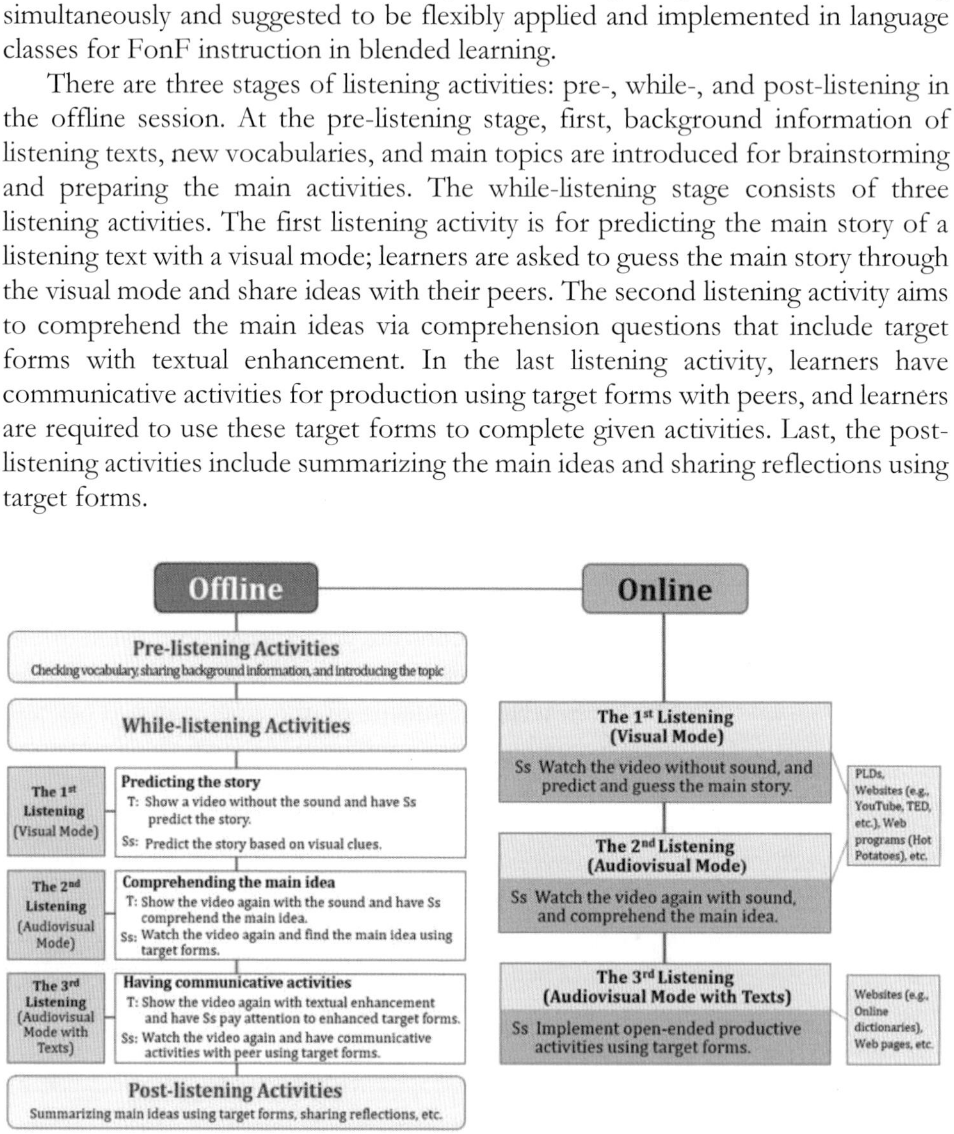

Figure 1.14 An instructional model for FonF instruction in Blended Learning through Listening Activities (Kang & Lee, 2020, p. 685)

In the online tasks, the intention is to promote autonomous learning in an online environment. Learners are required to follow the same procedures as in the three listening stages in the offline session. Like the offline session, first listening aims to predict and guess the main idea with visual mode without sound. In the second listening, learners are asked to re-watch the video with sound and determine the main idea with comprehension questions using target forms. Learners carry out open-ended productive activities using target forms in the final listening activity.

Specific lesson plans based on the instructional models for MALL and blended learning will be presented in chapters 8, 9, and 10.

A framework of MALL lesson plans

Some may think that it is easy to teach English to young learners or students at secondary school because the content is simple and not difficult. However, they are learning English in an EFL situation and need to improve their English proficiency in a limited time. Therefore, teachers must be well aware of their learners' characteristics, the goals and objectives of the curriculum, effective teaching methods, and knowledge of English and have experience. Multimedia and its content can instill motivation and interest in learners while providing various learning materials, allowing learners to choose appropriate learning materials for efficient language learning. For effective ELT&L to use MALL, it is essential to consider the process of teaching and learning.

A typical English class is comprised of three stages, introduction, development, and consolidation. Pre-, while-, and post-computer work in MALL can be fitted in the development stage. Based on the three stages, the detailed procedure and stage-specific activities in MALL are as follows. See Part 3 for various samples of MALL lessons.

Introduction

The introduction includes greeting, review, the introduction of goals, etc. Using realia (possibly multimedia content) in the introduction part of the class to greet students effectively gets students' attention and interest. Teachers can ask about sport or the date using a calendar or the weather using a weather map and pictures. When reviewing the previous lesson, it is helpful to use websites or webpages, or apps previously used to remind students of their things. Teachers need to take time for Q & A and introduce the learning goal of the lesson.

Development

There are three steps of the development stage consisting of pre-computer work, computer work, and post-computer work.

Pre-computer work

It is good to familiarize the students with the topic before presenting the multimedia content by discussing ideas or experiences related to the topic. The following activities, such as brainstorming and semantic mapping, are effective ways to activate schemata.

Computer work

The bottom-up approach looks at details about presented language materials. It can help the students to learn language analytically by beginning with details and expanding to overall ideas. Appropriate activities and tasks are as follows: learning the sounds and letters, then reading vocabulary or sentences; doing sentence completion activities and graph, picture, or map completion activities; finding keywords and main ideas, etc.

The top-down approach checks if the students understand the general topic or details of the language materials presented. It is easier to apply to intermediate and above-level students than beginners since it begins with the overall ideas and narrows down to smaller features. Talking about the topic or detail, exchanging opinions through group activities and teacher models are some examples.

It is ideal to combine the top-down and bottom-up approaches. It provides the students with a fair chance to learn through the approach preferred by students of different levels in a group. Multimedia content useful for this is e-textbook, related websites, and teacher-made PowerPoint presentations, etc.

Post-computer work

In the post-computer work, teachers can give the students a chance to summarize and use the learned content after checking for comprehension. Suggested activities are as follows: expressing opinions about the learning content; role-plays; practice questions or quizzes, etc.

Consolidation

It is essential to give time to review what students learned in consolidation. Teachers can provide the lesson summary and check-up activities. Finally, teachers can give homework and end the class.

Table 1.2 A framework of MALL lesson plans

Procedures	Teacher activities	Student activities	Resources
		INTRODUCTION	
Greeting	• Exchange greetings. • Make small talks on health, sports, the latest news, weather, day/date, etc.	• Exchange greetings. • Repetition	• Health/Sports/News/ Weather chart • Calendar, etc.
Review & introducing goals	• Review the previous lesson. • Introduce learning aims and objectivities.	• Remember previous lesson. • Repeat learning aims and objectivities.	• Websites • Apps • eBooks
		DEVELOPMENT	
Pre-computer work	• Activate schema. • Enhance motivation • Predict learning content using pictures and others. • Present main vocabulary and expressions.	• Describe ideas or experience related to the topic. • Semantic-mapping • Predict learning content using pictures.	• Brainstorming software • Pictures and videos from the Web
Computer work	• Level appropriate language learning activity • Check for understanding of top-down and bottom-up resources presented in class. • Take questions and present resources for areas difficult to understand.	• Level appropriate language learning activity • Looking for topic • Looking for details • Sentence completion • Table, picture, map completion	• Teacher made content • Related websites/ webpages • Apps • PPT presentation • SNS
Post-computer work	• Give a chance for use and usage of the presented learning content. • Integrate the learned skills.	• Present opinions. • Role play • Quiz	• Related websites • Webpages • Apps • SNS
		CONSOLIDATION	
	• Summarize and check for understanding. • Give homework and prepare for the next class. • End class.	• Describe learned content. • End class.	• PPT presentation

1.11 Conclusion

The primary purpose of multimedia-assisted language learning (MALL) is to achieve the prime goal in FLT&L, learners' four language skills development, particularly learners' communicative competence, by reinforcing teaching and learning processes with multimedia advantages. It is time to reconsider and clarify the following issues for the effective use of multimedia in foreign language teaching and learning: First, what is multimedia, and what is the trend of digital multimedia technology?; Second, what kind of contribution can multimedia make to teaching and learning foreign languages?; Third, what is the relationship between MALL and second language acquisition/learning?; Fourth, how can multimedia be used effectively in the language learning process?; Fifth, can multimedia change the way learners think, perform, and learn?; and sixth, can MALL be applied to the theories and practices of FLT&L?

Multimedia has many distinct advantages, such as a high level of interactivity, individualization, increased retention, motivation, etc., and these can make positive contributions to FLT&L. It offers lots of potential in FLT&L. Teachers and students can use various digital, robust, and interactive materials in the language classroom. Therefore, MALL can be used with any approach from behaviorism to constructivism and connectivism. It can also be applied to developing all four language skills, reading, writing, listening, and speaking, including three subskills (pronunciation, vocabulary, and grammar), provided appropriate teaching methodology and techniques are used. The role of computers and PLDs in FLT&L is that of tool and, recently, of partnership. The teacher's role is still central in MALL. It is clear that teachers must be given appropriate time off for technical and pedagogical preparation and that proper teacher training, mainly focused on hands-on practice and methodological solutions, is essential for the effective use of multimedia in FLT&L.

The use of multimedia as a tool and a partner provides them with opportunities to experience and use real-life authentic language and brings various interaction patterns into the classroom due to its distinctive features. Many research studies have reported that multimedia or web app content is easy for learners to use and motivates them in learning foreign languages. However, information searching skills require learners to use a variety of multimedia materials. The teachers will have to focus on tasks and activities teaching enabling skills.

It is worth noticing that multimedia has distinctive characteristics in making positive contributions to FLT&L but some limitations. In addition to the technical problems, there is a danger that multimedia will be misused and overused, as mentioned in the previous sections. However, most limitations could be overcome by teachers through proper preparation and training, particularly workshop-based teacher training focused on providing the teachers with not only technical but methodological knowledge and skills with the help of experts.

Finally, it is entirely up to the teachers to select multimedia or the web app content appropriately to create a variety of learning environments in language classes and attain the prime objectives, teaching and learning a foreign language successfully. Sample instructional models in the last portion of the chapter are presented with the hope that teachers can modify and apply them in teaching contexts.

Tasks for Study and Discussion

1. Teachers and learners are very interested in the use of ICT and digital technology in FLT&L. Why?

2. What are the three crucial factors for the successful implementation of multimedia in FLT&L?

3. Describe the following terms briefly.
   1) AI chatbot
   2) CMC
   3) Interactive learning
   4) Individualization
   5) Behaviorism/Cognitivism/Constructivism/Connectivism and multimedia
   6) Blended learning
   7) MABL
   8) Big data
   9) CALT
   10) Three stages of MALL

4. MALL can be used with any approach from behaviorism to constructivism or connectivism in FLT&L. Why & How? Please describe it briefly concerning language learning theories.

5. What are the advantages and limitations of multimedia?

6. What are the roles of multimedia, teachers, and students in FLT&L? Under what circumstances can they change?

7. What are some of the interaction patterns which are possible with computers/multimedia in the language classroom?

8. Describe the three stages in MALL and the teacher's roles in each stage for the successful implementation of MALL.

9. Some research studies report that ICT and multimedia have not been widely used in the language classes. Why? Give your own opinion on how you as a teacher can cope with the current difficulties and problems in to encourage wider use in the future.

10. What are the issues and prospects of using digital technology in ELT&L?

Chapter 2

MALL and Language Skills Development

2.1 Introduction

It was claimed that CALL was suitable for some reading and writing skills development but may not be appropriate for speaking skills, particularly free-spoken activities in the 1980s. However, there has been enormous progress over the past three decades in CALL or MALL. In terms of the current developments of hardware and software in digital technologies and methodological considerations, CALL or MALL can expand the range of activities available to developing four language skills - listening, speaking, reading, writing, and three subskills - pronunciation, vocabulary, and grammar.

The multimedia computer (hereafter computer) is now a medium or an environment in which various language teaching methods and language skills can be implemented. Computers and PLDs can do far more in CALL/MALL/WALL (hereafter MALL) and MABL than only carry out simple learning tasks, such as stimulus-response type activities in some skills. For example, they can interact with students in various ways and individualize the learning process (Baek & Lee, 2018; C. H. Lee, 1998a, 2000a, 2006; Lee & Cho, 2019; Lee, Yoon, & Lee, 2013; Windeatt, Hardisty, & Eastment, 2000; Wyatt, 1984; Yoon & Lee, 2009). In short, MALL can be designed to integrate into the Grammar Translation Method, cognitive learning, communicative and humanistic approaches, and be used for the development of the four language skills and the three subskills in FLT&L (Cook, 1988; C. H. Lee, 2006; Stevens, 1992). MALL should be re-evaluated since it can be used with any approach from behaviorism to constructivism and with any language skill and the integrated four language skills.

Therefore, this chapter will closely look at MALL and MABL, which are available in language classes and language skills development: 1) to demonstrate to language teachers and learners how computers and PLDs can contribute to developing the four language skills and three subskills; 2) to present appropriate MALL programs and content that can be used in language teaching and learning; and 3) to suggest some teaching and learning activities that can be employed in each language skill.

2.2 Computers and Listening with Pronunciation

The computer can carry out various approaches, skills, and activities in the area of listening. The computer alone, i.e., without other peripherals such as sound cards and speakers, cannot offer as many practical benefits to the area of listening as it can provide for reading or writing. The use of computers in listening depends on the type of hardware, although it can produce synthesized speech if a built-in speaker is available. Using computers and smartphones, MP3, voice recognition technology, the Web, the app, and social media can be the best way of tackling various kinds of listening skills and activities.

Listening involves phonological perceptions of discrete or connected sounds and morphological, lexical, and grammatical processing. The fundamental goal of these perceptions and analytic processing is listening comprehension which requires an integration of bottom-up and top-down processes. The bottom-up processing refers to how listeners understand by starting with the smallest units of the acoustic message (phonemes or individual sounds), which is combined words, constituting phrases, clauses, sentences, and finally, ideas and concepts. The processing is one of the areas where MALL can be used most effectively in subskills-oriented listening activities.

On the other hand, top-down processing emphasizes using previous knowledge in processing a text, either aural or written, rather than focusing on individual sounds and words. The top-down processing is based on the idea that listeners rely on prior contextual knowledge to decode individual sounds. Listeners have pre-established knowledge of texts, context, and subject matters, and discourse structure stored in long-term memory, and this knowledge referred to as 'schema.' This prior knowledge compensates for the problems at micro levels such as sound discrimination, syntax, or semantics (Flowerdew & Miller, 2005). The final processing that combines the two approaches is interactive processing (Rumelhart, 1994). The interactive processing was originally developed in relation to reading. However, as a similar receptive skill, it is applicable equally to listening, where the language is processed simultaneously at various levels: phonological, syntactic, semantic, and pragmatic levels, interacting with one another. This real-time processing of information involves both top-down and bottom-up processing. MALL content, due to its distinctive characteristics, can also facilitate both of the processing approaches.

1. The Use of Computers in Listening

Using synthesized and digitized speech

There are two ways of using computers in improving listening skills: computer-generated speech (i.e., synthesized speech) and digitized speech on a hard disk, CD/DVD-ROM titles, websites, and apps. Examples of computer-produced synthesized speech can be found in many AI chatbots, *NaturalReader* (https://www.naturalreaders.com/), *Voki* (http://www.voki.com), etc.

In using synthesized speech for listening, it should be noted that the speech quality may not high enough for direct use since it may not produce an accurate and clear sound that students need. The benefits it offers can be limited for second language students in developing listening skills, particularly in subskills-oriented listening activities, such as pronunciation, stress, and intonation.

Figure 2.1 The screenshot of *willbot* (https://www.williambot.com/en/)

Although software regarding digitized speech and moving pictures has limitations, it has undergone rapid development, and recent software has demonstrated authentic sound quality. It can store numerical encoding of an actual utterance and regenerate the utterance at playback time. It can store not only a great deal of high-quality visual images but the sound of the original utterance on a hard disk, or a smartphone, or the Web. Digitized speech can be easily stored in the memory of computers and smartphones. For example, the listening passages are recorded on a hard disk, and rapid and exact access can be obtained to any speech segment on the disk. Spoken responses, hints, and instructions can be selectively played back to students, depending on their answers, from the system (Wyatt, 1984). Thus, using digitized speech with the additional peripherals, teachers can find useful ways to offer students much more effective listening skills and activities.

Using information and communications technology (ICT)

The more recent development of ICT and multimedia for listening is reflected in the widespread use of podcasts and CMC, which enabled audio and videoconferencing with advances in mobile and broadband technologies. Podcasts are audio or video files published on the Web, designed to be downloadable to an MP3 player or laptop for future listening (McMinn, 2008). With widespread availability and mobility, podcasts provide creativity and the continuation of L2 listening practice beyond the classroom context. Empirical evidence from previous studies (e.g., O'Bryan & Hegelheimer, 2009; Weinberg, Knoerr, & Vandergrift, 2011) indicates that these podcasts reinforced the listening strategies taught in class by providing learners with opportunities to review and practice strategies through lectures and tasks out of the classroom.

Interactive listening has become possible with more authentic and high-quality real-time media, including Internet voice and video applications such as *Skype* and *Zoom* (Vandergrift & Goh, 2012). There is empirical research that compared the effects of video, audio CMC, and face-to-face communication (FTFC) with the findings that support the effects of video CMC reaching as a high level of understanding as that of FTFC (Yanguas, 2010). Oral CMC seems to offer great potential, particularly for learners in contexts with little exposure to a target language, since oral CMC can offer similar contexts for learning to authentic FTFC.

One of the fundamental features of computers in developing listening skills is the help options. Help options include not only rewind, pause, and repeat functions but also a dictionary, cultural notes, transcripts, subtitles, feedback, and an expert's module to develop learners' metacognitive knowledge for comprehension (Vandergrift & Goh, 2012). Tracking the use of these help options can provide teachers with strategic actions that learners take as they listen and enable them to guide learners to make better use of particular support functions. For instance, a study by Roussel, Rieussec, Nespoulous, and Tricot (2008) tracked and recorded learners' mouse movements and identified four distinct usages: 1) a global listening followed by detailed listening, frequently using pauses and immediate rewinds; 2) a detailed listening with frequent pauses followed by more global listening; 3) global listening only; and 4) detailed listening with frequent pauses.

Empirical evidence for the advantage of adding a visual element for listening comprehension is not conclusive. Moreover, the potential help of the visuals for listening comprehension may pose issues in determining the extent of the construct of listening comprehension, e.g., in assessment (Vandergrift & Goh, 2012). However, Mayer (2002a, 2002b), Paivio (1986), and Heo and Lee (2019) report that L2 listeners can comprehend better when aural and visual information are provided together since the two modes of information can reinforce each other, making it more accessible for retrieval.

The limitations of the traditional audio language lab are being overcome as the computer makes listening and viewing more interactive. There are some listening instructions and activities using digitized speech in computers, PLDs, websites, and apps, e.g., listening strategies, subskills-oriented listening, pronunciation, and listening comprehension. (Baek & Lee, 2018; Cho, 2009; Heo & Lee, 2019; C. H. Lee, 2006; Lee & Lee, 2012; Windeatt, Hardisty, & Eastment, 2000; Yoon & Lee, 2009).

2. Three Types of Listening Activities Using Computers

Subskills-oriented listening activities

It is undoubtedly important for learners to hear English sounds and to make sounds of English correctly. In teaching spoken language, therefore, one of the teacher's roles is to help learners perceive sounds and produce appropriate sounds in the language classroom (Kenworthy, 1987). Learners also need to work hard, particularly in 'listening' to English sounds and take responsibility for their learning.

As mentioned in the previous section, MALL can offer many benefits for learners in listening and practicing pronunciation, sounds, stress rhythm, and intonation based on the subskills-oriented listening activities such as practicing sounds, stress pattern, linkage and simplification, sound/spelling correspondences, and clusters of sounds. In particular, recent listening apps can provide learners with more opportunities to listen to English sounds and practice them in a ubiquitous environment, enabling autonomous learning and interacting with the teacher and other learners.

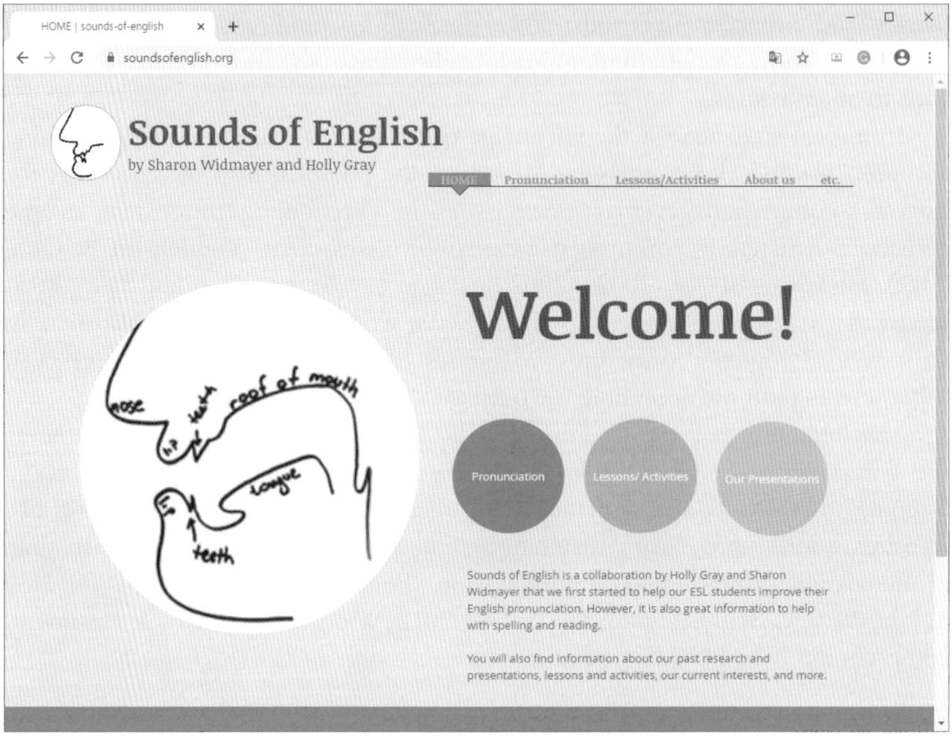

Figure 2.2 The main screen of *Sounds of English*
(https://www. soundsofenglish.org)

Some of useful websites and apps for improving pronunciation are as follows: *American English Pronunciation* (https://pronuncian.com/), *English Pronunciation* (http://play.google.com/store/apps/details?id=com.study.english.pronunciation), *English Listening* (https://play.google.com/store/apps/details?id=com.talkenglish. listening), *Learn English Listening* (https://play.google.com/store/apps/details? Id=com.ocoder.learn.english.free), *Pronunciation and Conversation* (https://www. thoughtco.com/esl-pronunciation-and-conversation-4133093), *Sounds of English* (https://www.soundsofenglish.org), *Sounds: Pronunciation* (https://play.google.com /store/apps/details?id=com. macmillan.app.soundsfree), etc.

Listening comprehension activities

One of the most recent and dominant trends is the strategy-based approach, also known as the process-based approach. The underlying assumption of this approach is that listening involves both conscious control and automatic control of the listener. The conscious aspects of the purposeful thinking process and actions based on it are viewed as 'strategies,' and expert listeners have been observed to employ planning and selection of effective strategies (Ross, 1997). Strategy training in L2 listening has been a popular area of research and pedagogy since O'Malley and Chamot (1990) and Oxford (1990) attempted to identify and categorize the types of strategies at various levels. More recently, Vandergrift (1997) has presented a comprehensive listening strategy taxonomy that refined the previously proposed ones. The listening strategy taxonomy classifies listening strategies into three categories of metacognitive, cognitive, and socio-affective types. Metacognitive listening strategies are referred to as strategies that oversee and control the cognitive process of listening comprehension, while cognitive strategies directly affect comprehension and compensate for missing part of the input. Socioaffective strategies are not direct strategies but those that impact the affective dimension involved in listening comprehension.

A large number of listening strategies and comprehension activities can be carried out efficiently in MALL, which shares some features with listening comprehension in the use of audio technology and PLDs, but in a much more enhanced form (Chapelle & Jamieson, 2008; Fox, 1990, Hardisty & Windeatt, 1989; Heo & Lee, 2019). For example, teachers can give students a story for listening comprehension on the websites and apps and ask them to predict what is likely to be coming next when listening, since a passage can be stopped at appropriate points to check on their comprehension of general points or important details. If they are unclear on such points, they can be routed back to listen to the section containing the information they missed and continue listening to the passage. After listening to the story, students can answer listening comprehension questions by interacting with the computer keyboard and screen, and they can provide them with help, hints, and all branching actions (Heo & Lee, 2019; Vandergrift & Goh, 2012; Wyatt, 1984).

Dictogloss and note-taking activities

Dictogloss and note-taking activities can also be carried out and enhanced with word processors in MALL. First, for example, students listen to a lecture presented for note-taking on the cassette recorder. While and after listening to it, students can take their notes on a word processor file, which can be a 'blank sheet,' allowing each student to type in a personal selection of notes in response to a listening passage (Leonard, 1985), or incomplete notes to help them complete an outline displayed on the screen. The latter would sharpen the students' ability to pick out what is essential to the lecture and what is peripheral to it, although it is not a completely free note-taking exercise, since headings and sentences are provided to steer them in the direction of the required information (Higgins & Johns, 1984). If they have gaps in their notes or misunderstandings during listening, they can return to the appropriate section of the listening passage. Most importantly, a variety of hints and suggestions to meet their students' level can be provided by the teacher, including the complete transcription of the lecture or a guide note.

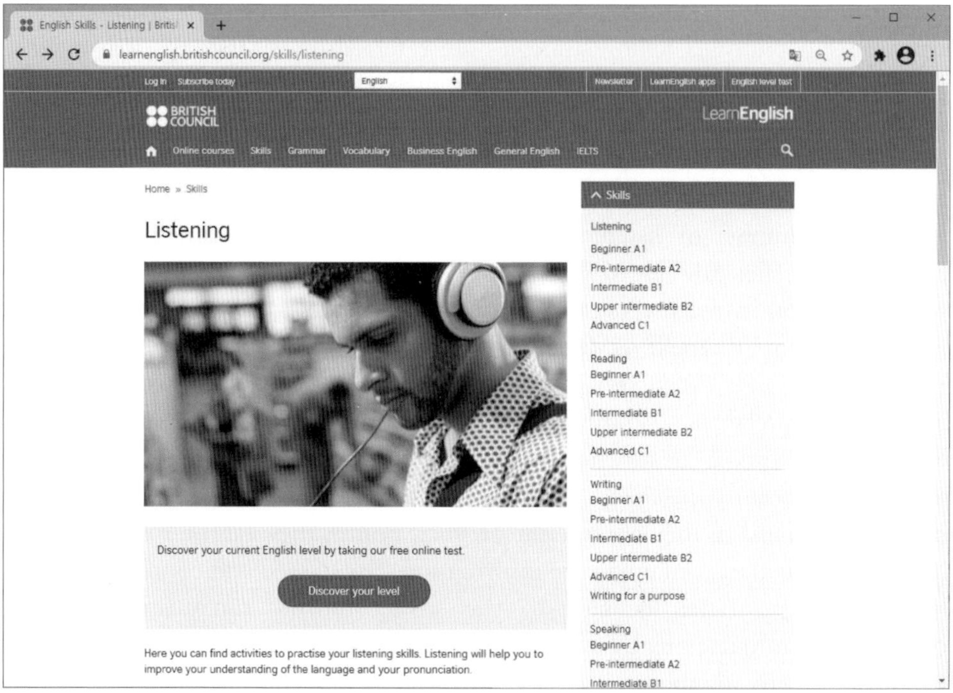

Figure 2.3 The main screen of *Learn English,* Listening (https://learnenglish.britishcouncil.org/skills/listening)

Some useful webpages and apps for improving listening skills are as follows: *Esl-Lounge Student* (https://www.esl-lounge.com/student/listening.php), *Focus on English* (https://www.focusenglish.com), *Learn English* (https://learnenglish.britishcouncil.org/skills/listening), Learning English Podcasts (https://player.fm/

featured/learning-english), *National Public Radio* (https://www.npr. org), *Naturalreader* (https://www.naturalreaders.com/), *PBS News hour* (https://www. pbs.org/newshour/podcasts), *Podcasts in English* (https://www.podcastsinenglish. com/index.shtml), *Randall's Cyber Listening Lab* (https://www.esl-lab.com), *TED* (https://www.ted. com), *VOA Learning English* (https://learningenglish.voanews. com), *Voki* (https://www. voki.com), *YouTube* (https://www.youtube.com), *English Listening Player* (https://play.google.com/store/apps/details?id=com.talk english.player), *English Listening* (https://play.google.com/store/apps/details?id= com.talkenglish.listening), *Learn English Listening* (https://play.google.com/store/ apps/details?id=com.ocoder.learn.english.free), etc.

2.3 Computers and Speaking with Pronunciation

Pessimistic views of CALL have been expressed, claiming that computers cannot be used with communicative approaches. However, programs and methodological considerations applicable to the communicative approach and developing speaking skills have developed away from the often criticized 'drill and practice' of the early years in CALL. Indeed, if the content of MALL programs and smartphone apps meets some of the requirements of communicative methodology, i.e., real communication and language use by learners, communication activities can be promoted by digital technology, AI, and MALL (Baek & Lee, 2018; Cook, 1988; Hardisty, 1987; C. H. Lee, 2000a, 2004, 2017; Lee, Yoon, & Lee, 2013; Stevens, 1992; Yoon & Lee, 2009).

1. The Use of Computers in Speaking

There are two ways that MALL can be adapted to developing speaking skills. First, there can be interactions between language learners and the computer itself, which is natural man-machine interaction. Second, there can be interactions between learners while using computers where they can provide learners with learning environments, i.e., 'something to talk about' in online and offline environments (Baek & Lee, 2018; Jones & Fortescue, 1987; Lee, 2000, 2017; Lee & Pyo, 2003; Stevens, 1992; Yoon & Lee, 2009).

Natural man-machine interaction

The application of AI, e.g., natural language parsing using database management programs and expert systems, allows computers to engage in natural conversation with learners. Some progress in AI-based CALL and AI chatbots has been made, which shows some possibilities in this area. For example, a computer program, *TELL ME MORE* (1998, 2002) shows that it can distinguish among several dozen words or expressions and engage in limited dialogue with learners, responding to some questions about selected subjects. Learners can engage in speaking skills into practice, listening and answering the program's questions and determining the outcome of each conversation. The program evaluates the learner's pronunciation and responds accordingly.

AI chatbots and humanoid AI have recently developed to allow apps and robots to communicate with human beings in Figure 2.4. It is still early to say that the development of AI can solve the current issues, making natural conversation with computers and learners possible in language learning. Beatty (2003) stated that expert systems and natural language processing are likely to be partially addressed by researchers and practitioners in the coming years. Even if the robots can communicate with students as unrestrictedly as human beings by every possible means, teachers and students must not entirely rely on them. It is worth noticing that communication activity essentially remains something human, cultural, personal, and unprogrammed (Hope, Taylor, & Pusack, 1984; C. H. Lee, 1998a, 2000a).

Figure 2.4 Conversing with Sophia, an advanced AI humanoid robot (https://chainbulletin.com/chain-2020-conference-gathers-almost-14000-people/)

Methodological considerations for communicative interaction

So far, as stated in the preceding section, the level of communication in the application of AI and speech recognition is more limited than what teachers and learners have expected in the field of language teaching and learning. Therefore, it seems reasonable to consider how MALL can be integrated into communicative approaches and activities.

Littlewood (1981) grouped the main communicative activities to enhance the functional and structural aspects of language within the classroom situation into two areas, using language to share information and using language to process information. Cook (1988) suggested that integrating CALL into communicative language teaching is to make the most of its ability to interact with students. In short, two main communicative activities applicable to CALL are 'information transfer (information gap)' and 'information processing (simulation).' There is no argument that computers can facilitate information transfer and processing (Hardisty, 1987; Stevens, 1992). In particular, Stevens (1992) pointed out that simulations can provide genuine communicative interaction when students work together in pairs or groups at workstations, stimulating them to lively discussions, disputes, and cooperative decision-making.

2. Three Types of Speaking Activities Using Computers

There are three possible ways of using computers in developing speaking skills. They are generally identified as subskills-oriented, guided, and free-spoken activities in online and offline environments. In particular, graphics, sounds, videos, and web app content in multiple modes are being used to provide learners with authentic activities and tasks that encourage interaction (Grabe & Grabe, 2007; C. H. Lee, 2004, 2006, 2012, 2017).

Subskills-oriented speaking activities

The correct pronunciation is essential for students to speak eligibly, and they must study pronunciation and its features, such as intonation. Computers with digitized speech in addition to the peripheral equipment (e.g., microphone, loudspeaker, sound card, etc.) and smartphones can encourage the students to practice the subskills more effectively than a cassette recorder or audio language lab since they can provide students with immediate and proper feedback (Baek & Lee, 2018; Jones & Fortescue, 1987). For example, there are various websites and apps available for practicing pronunciation and intonation, and look up the websites and apps introduced in the previous 'Subskills-oriented listening activities' section, e.g., *American English Pronunciation* (https://pronuncian.com/), *English Pronunciation* (https://play.google.com/store/apps/details?id=com.study.english.pronunciation), *Sounds of English* (https://www.soundsofenglish.org/), etc.

Voice recordings have been used to provide repeated and individual practices for students in teaching pronunciation and speaking (Baek & Lee, 2018; Neri, Cucchiarini, Strik, & Boves, 2002; Walker, 2005; Yoon & Lee, 2009). The framework of using voice recording was provided by Walker (2005): 1) the text to be recorded should be integrated into the rest of the language practice dealt with in class; 2) the learners must be familiar with the text before recording; 3) the length of the text should be no longer than 2 minutes and appropriate for the target learners; and 4) cooperative learning should be promoted before and during recording. Smartphones, *RhinoSpike* (https://rhinospike.com), and many voice recorder apps provide easy and convenient methods to record voices and sounds.

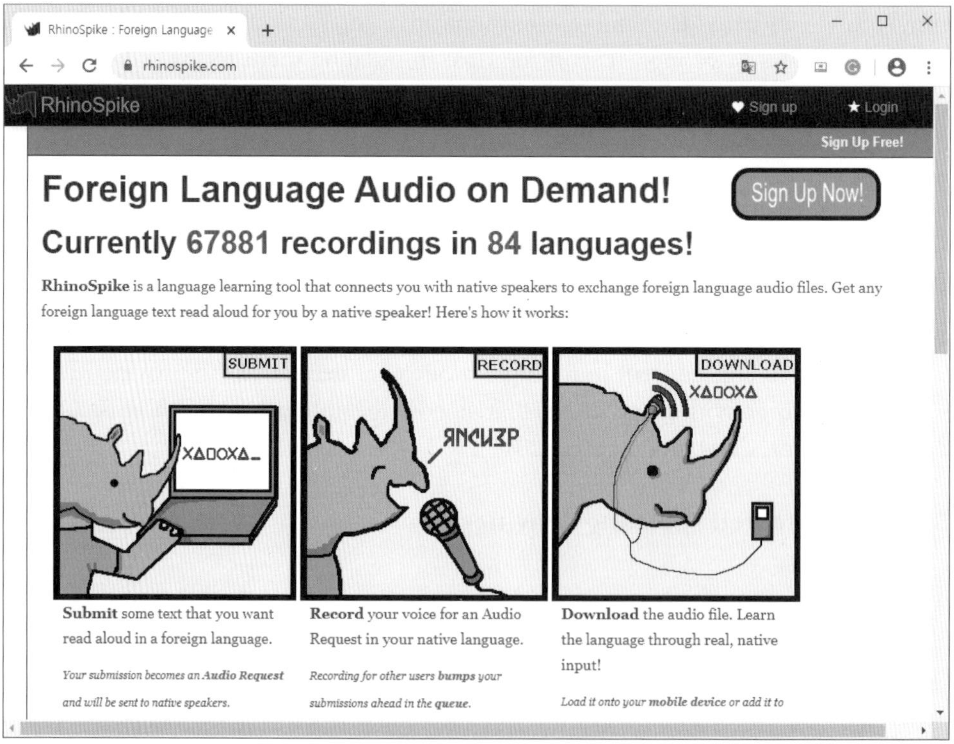

Figure 2.5 The main screen of *RhinoSpike* (https://rhinospike.com)

Guided and free-spoken activities

Students can develop their speaking skills through communicating with their teachers and colleagues. Considerable emphasis should be given to guided and free-spoken activities to encourage interaction between students in the classroom, including information gaps, simulations, role-plays, and discussions. In terms of current and developing hardware and software capabilities, it has been proven that computer programs and apps can offer rich and flexible environments to carry out these activities to help students improve speaking skills. Here, three main communicative activities applicable to MALL, information gaps, simulations, and CMC, are discussed in detail.

Information transfer (Information gap)

'Information gap' refers to a situation where information is known by only one learner (or some) in communication between two learners (or more), and the other learner must elicit that information (Littlewood, 1981; Richards, Platt, & Platt, 1992). It can also be a situation in which learners have different information and exchange their information to get a complete solution to the task (Hardisty, 1987).

Information transfer (information gap) activities can be applied to the medium of computers. Computers can provide various information with textual, auditory, and visual cues, e.g., a short report, pictures, map, diagram, timetable, etc., which are often used for information gap activities in the classroom. CALL activities involving information transfer can be a stimulus for communication between students (Taylor, 1986). For example, a CALL activity using *Storyboard* from *Wida Software* (Higgins & Davies, 1982) can be applied to information gap activities. It is a 'total cloze' activity for students to reconstruct a text that is entirely obliterated on the screen (Jones, 1998). They have to reconstruct it by guessing single or more words with some information. One of the exercises, 'Asking the way' can be used in rebuilding a text with the help of a map in which an information gap between students can be formed if they have two or more computers (see Figure 2.6).

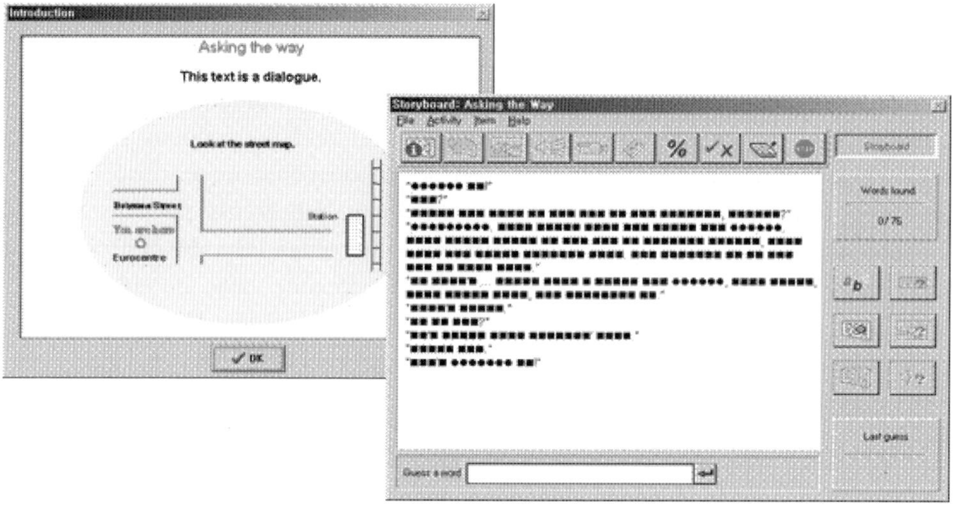

Figure 2.6 The sample of information gap activity using *Storyboard* (Lee, 2000a)

When teachers put two or more students into this activity at two computers (i.e., a student sees the map, and another student does not have any information except for a title, punctuation, and spacing intact, but must reconstruct the text), they can ask for help to solve problems posed by the program (C. H. Lee, 2000a). Active interaction between students takes place in an attempt to reconstruct the text (Hardisty, 1987). Thus, the activities using computers can provide students with the same environment as the traditional media or richer sources in some cases.

Information processing (simulation)

Information processing (simulation) activities can be performed by any simulation, whether on the computer or traditional media (Hardisty 1987; Jones & Fortescue, 1987; Stevens, 1992). Jones (1982) defined that a simulation is the reality of function in a simulated and structured environment. 'Simulation' in language teaching and learning can be defined as any learning activity which reproduces or simulates realistic situations, which involve much interaction between learners and decisions (Higgins & Jones, 1984; Richards, Platt, & Platt, 1992).

Undoubtedly, the computer is a powerful tool in modeling reality within the language classroom due to its distinctive features that allow it to present and process a variety of information immediately and accurately (Stevens, 1992). First, computer simulations such AR and VR are proven to be beneficial in simulating more abstract situations and can overcome the limited availability of physical apparatus, which are often too time-consuming or costly in the conventional language classroom (Cummins et al., 1987; Godwin-Jones, 2016; Hennessy & O'Shea, 1993; Richardson, 2016). Second, they allow learners to manipulate not only realism but reality itself and alternative realities (Hennessy & O'Shea, 1993; Jones, 1986). In other words, they can provide learners with unique and extended sources, particularly in the development of concepts and communication skills in the classroom (Cummins et al., 1987). Computer simulations can provide learners with useful sources and a motivating stimulus for speaking in the classroom so that they can carry out language use activities and practice it (Jones, 1986; Stevens, 1992). However, the success in using simulations depends upon teachers' guidance and students' attitudes. Their value for FLT&L is not found in the program or content itself but the process, and that is why well-designed simulations are useful (Jones, 1982).

There have been several simulation programs and adventures which have a great potential for facilitating communicative tasks, e.g., *Drops AR* (https://languagedrops.com/), *English Pin* (https://play.google. com/store/apps/details?id=com.Archipin.Epin.Tourist&hl=en_US), *Mondly AR* (https://www.mondly.com/ar), *Mondly VR* (https://www.mondly.com), *Fast Food* (British Council, 1986), *Travelling around Korea* (C. H. Lee, 2000d), etc.

Figure 2.7 The screenshot of *Mondly VR* (https://www.mondly.com)

Learner-learner interaction using CMC technology

One of the CMC technologies that enable authentic real-time communication for the development of speaking skills is videoconferencing. Previously, the high cost of hardware caused videoconferencing to be less accessible, but with the fast-growing computer technology and related industry in recent years, it has become more readily available in the FLT&L classrooms. The capabilities and strengths of videoconferencing when compared to man-machine interaction lie in authentic interactivity supported by synchronous visual and oral interaction and opportunities to produce natural language use during meaning negotiation outside the classroom. Empirical evidence supports the effect of videoconferencing on the development of speaking skills in various learning contexts (Chen & Wang, 2008; Levy & Stockwell, 2007; Loranc-Paszylk, 2015; Smyth, 2005; Wang, 2004). Besides, interaction patterns including learners-to-learner and group-to-group are viable (Fabos & Young, 1999; Larreamendy-Joerns & Leinhardt, 2006). CMC-based multimedia technology promotes cultural awareness through international networks (Levy & Stockwell, 2007; Nakano, 2007) since videoconferencing has often been between the native speaker(s) or teachers and non-native learners.

Kakao Talk (http://www.kakao.com), *Microsoft Teams* (https://products.office.com/ko-kr/microsoft-teams/group-chat-software/), *Skype* (http://skype.daesung.com/eng/main.Asp), and *Zoom* (https://zoom.us/) are examples of commercialized videoconferencing tools introduced and evaluated.

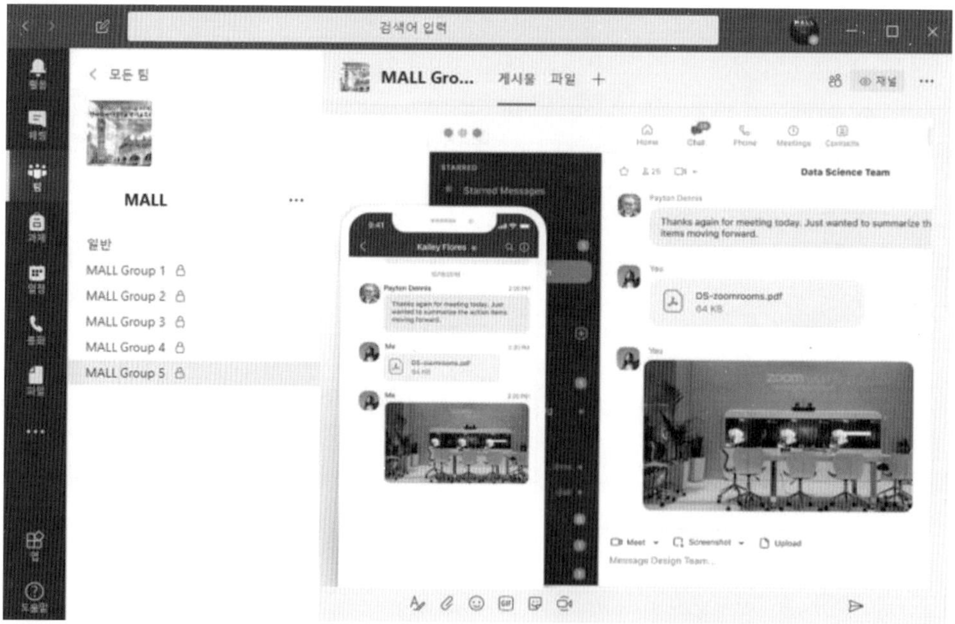

Figure 2.8 The screenshot of *Microsoft Teams*

As stated so far, the methodological use of MALL can be applied to the communicative approach based on the three main activities, information transfer, information processing, and CMC. Computer simulations can be used in developing speaking skills, provided appropriate teaching methodology and techniques are used. They provide learners with enhanced or new forms of activities that can help in developing speaking skills. In short, computer simulations can reproduce or simulate real situations, and they can provide students with a focus for communicative activities and a variety of storylines to talk about in EFL speaking classrooms.

However, information gap activities and simulations need careful preparation and careful management by teachers. If the computer becomes the center of the activities and dictates all the simulation steps, it may interfere with the communicative and simulative processes that should develop between students (Legenhausen & Wolff, 1987). With well-planned, imaginative uses of commercial packages and authoring tools, teachers can help students improve their speaking skills. Teachers have to keep in mind that methodological approaches can solve the problems like misconceptions about the lack of suitability of computers for speaking skills and lack of software. If the computer becomes the focus of the activities without specific technical and pedagogical preparation in using computer simulations, it can have little effect on language teaching and learning. Teachers should always keep in mind that the ultimate aims of using computer simulations are to have students take responsibility for language learning in the student-centered learning environment, control their learning, and promote the creative use of language.

The followings are some of the useful websites and tools for improving speaking skills: *Drops AR* (https://languagedrops.com/), *English Pin* (https://play.google.com/store/apps/details?id=com.Archipin.Epin.Tourist&hl=en_US), *Focus on English* (http://www.focusenglish.com), *Kakao Talk* (http://www.kakao.com), *Listen to English Online* (http://eleaston.com/listen. html), *Mondly AR* (https://www.mondly.com/ar), *Mondly VR* (https://www.mondly.com), *On-Line News Hour* (http://www.pbs.org/newshour/newshour_index. html), *Randall's Cyber Listening Lab* (http://www.esl-lab.com), *RhinoSpike* (https://rhinospike.com), *Skype* (http://skype.daesung.com/eng/main. asp), *The English Listening Lounge* (http://www.englishlistening.com), *Voki* (http://www.voki. com), *Xtranormal* (http://www.xtranormal. com), etc.

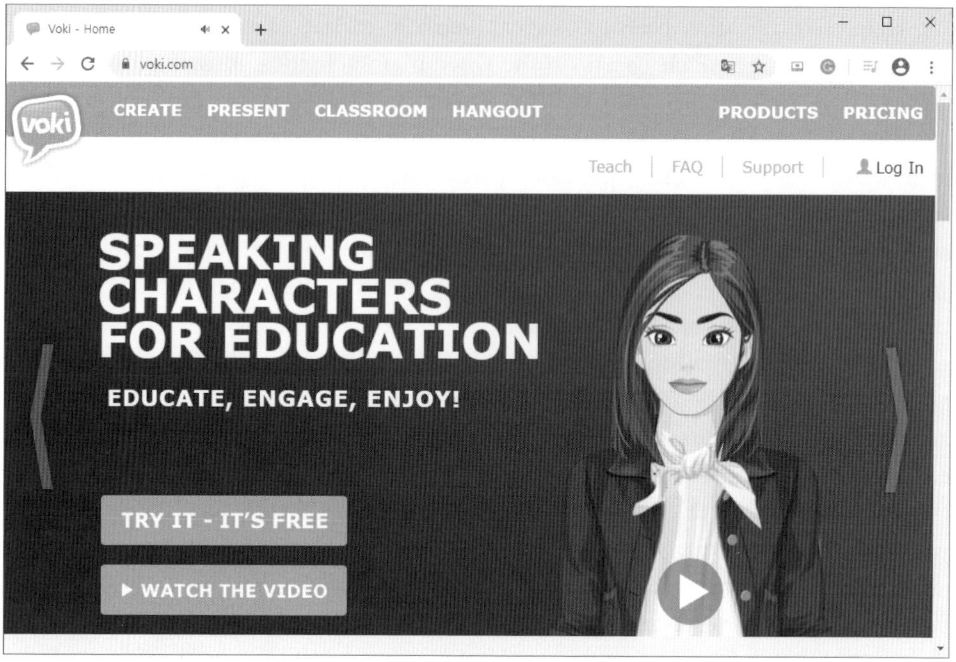

Figure 2.9 The main screen of *Voki* (http://www.voki. com)

2.4 Computers and Reading with Vocabulary

The computer can play an essential and extensive role in improving reading skills and strategies by its attributes. In other words, the computer can be easily applied to the area of teaching and learning reading skills and strategies due to its advantages, e.g., free choice of tasks from a large number of texts and exercises, immediate feedback, visual clues and sound effects, random access, the 'Help' system, record-keeping, self-pacing, interactivity, etc. These make the computer a suitable tool for carrying out specific skill and strategy practice and activities required in reading, although there are some limitations concerning MALL activities, e.g., possible side effects of using PLDs, the use of ready-to-use programs, etc. (Fox, 1986; Hardisty & Windeatt, 1989; C. H. Lee, 2006; Yoon, Lee, & Lee, 2013). The problems can be solved when the computer in reading activities is seen as one component of a lesson, rather than the lesson itself, and when methodological solutions can be applied to software (Windeatt, 1987). For example, other media such as digital presenters and written materials can be used in a MALL lesson as aids to compensate for the limitations of the computer.

Reading skills and strategies instruction in MALL

Teaching and learning reading skills and strategies have received attention in L2 reading research and practice (Fox, 1990; Nuttall, 1996, 2005). Many text-based and reading-oriented websites are useful learning environments in which a variety of reading skills and strategies can be practiced and improved. First, intensive and extensive reading, skimming and scanning, and speed reading are required for effective reading comprehension (Day & Bamford, 2002; Grellet, 1981; Nuttall, 2005; Yamashita, 2004). See 'Activities for improving five reading skills' section in detail.

Second, teaching students how to utilize reading strategies effectively has been an important consideration in reading classes since it can help the students improve in strategy use and reading comprehension (Macaro, 2006). Therefore, reading strategy instruction has become one of the significant issues in L2 reading. Strategy instruction is usually defined as explicit instruction on strategy use practices to improve L2 learners' reading comprehension (Taylor, Stevens, & Asher, 2006). According to Grabe and Stoller (2002), eight main features of strategy instruction of L2 reading are necessary.

First, teachers need to explain what strategies are and why they are important. Second, students need to discuss the types of strategies and reasons for using them. Third, students are encouraged to use and practice strategies. Fourth, teachers need to model expert reading behavior through reading and thinking aloud. Fifth, students read and think aloud, experimenting with different strategies. Sixth, students receive feedback on their strategy use. Seventh, students explain their strategy use and its benefits. Last, the class has a content base to use strategies to learn content information while reading.

Another significant factor that has affected reading strategy instruction is the development of media technology. It helps L2 learners effectively practice reading strategies by taking advantage of various reading resources on the Web. Besides, teachers can utilize diverse materials and teaching and learning tools at their disposal. In particular, with the continuing development of multimedia, strategy use and strategy instruction in online learning environments have been increasingly investigated in L2 reading research, focusing on identifying certain patterns of strategy use and its effects on reading comprehension (Akyel & Erçetin, 2009; Anderson, 2003; Chun, 2001; Coiro & Dobler, 2007). It was found that the patterns of strategy use were affected by students' proficiency levels and contexts (Anderson, 2003; Chun, 2001). For example, Akyel and Erçetin (2009) explored the strategies used by advanced English learners while reading online. They found that the patterns of reading strategy use online were slightly different from those used while reading printed texts. Moreover, some new strategies emerged, including using online resources, utilizing annotations, and navigating through texts.

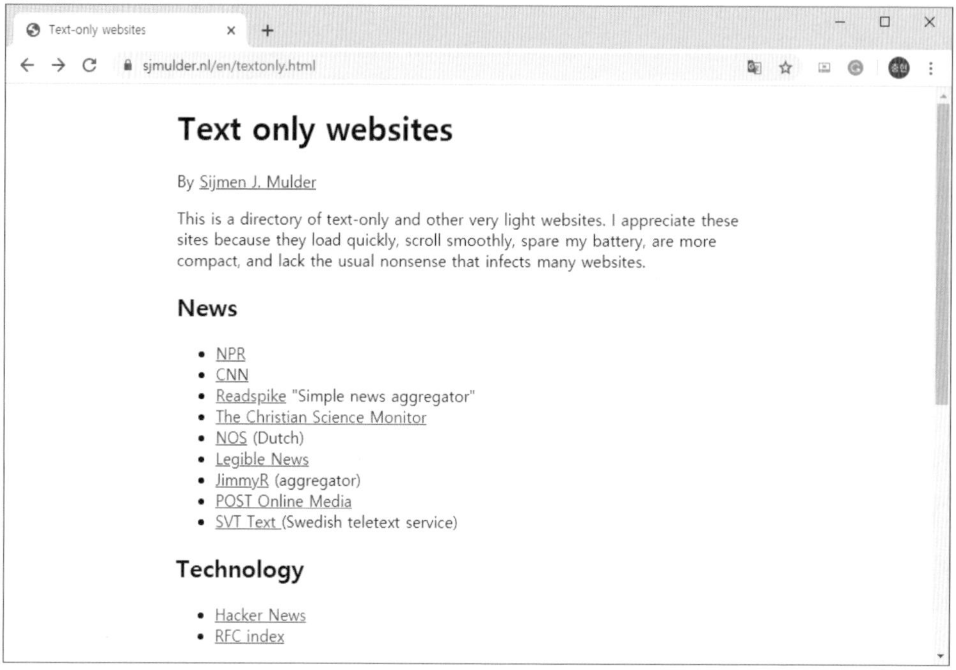

Figure 2.10 The main screen of text only websites

1. The Use of Computers in Reading

Using websites and apps

MALL activities are based on techniques in use in the teaching and learning of reading in the conventional classroom but can significantly improve subskills-oriented reading and five reading skills, intensive and extensive reading, skimming and scanning, and speed reading (Fox, 1986). The reading skills can be practiced much more easily on the computer (i.e., through the MALL reading activities) than in written or other media. For example, using websites and apps for reading can allow students to carry out various exercises and activities for extensive reading like finding information and data related to a theme they are studying with many language texts and high-quality visual materials.

Using digital textbooks and e-textbooks

Digital textbooks and e-textbooks use the same content as the printed textbooks and multimedia content such as texts, video clips, animation, virtual reality, access to search engines, and a variety of interactive tools. The hardware used for digital textbooks is the tablet PC networked to the teacher's computer and an electronic blackboard. Students can use an electronic pen to take notes or highlight contents in the textbooks and save them for later viewing (KERIS, 2008, 2017).

The digital textbook not only expands teaching and learning of L2 reading, but it makes what was impossible with printed textbooks possible. For example, video clips of interviews with authors can show students what the authors had in mind more personally than via paper. AR technology or animation of volcano eruption can visually assist science lessons. In foreign language reading classes, authentic audio and video files can provide much-needed ample exposure to the target languages and a high level of understanding in reading.

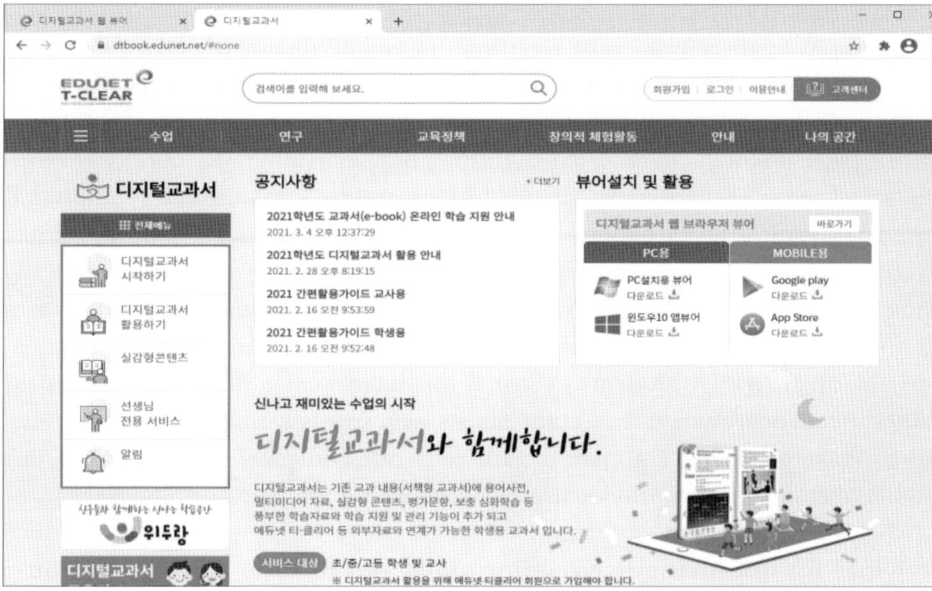

Figure 2.11 English digital textbook (https://dtbook.edunet.net/#none)

2. Three Types of Reading Activities Using Computers

In terms of current MALL reading programs and content, MALL reading activities for improving subskills-oriented and five reading skills can generally be categorized as follows: subskills-oriented reading activities; familiar activities or some extensions of them already in use in printed or other materials; and newer or more innovative activities (C. H. Lee, 1998a, 2006; Wyatt, 1984).

Subskills-oriented reading activities

Subskills-oriented reading activities use the computer's ability for information-processing to produce a flexible reading environment in which students can find the information they need and want (Fox 1986; C. H. Lee, 1998a). For example, the computer dictionary, particularly on websites and apps, is one promising feature that computers can offer. It is usually much more detailed and comprehensive than conventional dictionaries. When reading a text, the dictionary can provide learners with various information on new or difficult words and vocabulary. Such information includes lexical data like definition, example contexts, and collocations, along with information on semantic fields and synonyms, and grammatical information on how to recognize nouns and verbs in a passage (Fox, 1990).

There are many commercial electronic or online dictionaries, e.g., *Cambridge Dictionaries Online* (http://dictionary.cambridge.org), *Collins COBUILD English Dictionary* (http://www.collinsdictionary.com/dictionary/english), *Daum Dictionary* (http://dic.daum.net), *Dictionary.com* (http://dictionary.reference.com), *Merriam-Webster Learner's Dictionary* (http://www.learnersdictionary.com), *NAVER Dictionary* (http://dic.naver.com), and *Oxford English Dictionary* (http://www.oed.com), etc. The dictionaries allow students instant and flexible access to any items, words and vocabulary, grammar, etc., with minimum disruption of a reading task via a keyboard or mouse. During a reading task on the computer, teachers can encourage students to search for the meanings related to the context using the dictionary when they come across new words, vocabulary, and phrases, and to make a list and compare it with each other in pairs or a group. In this manner, dictionaries can provide useful assistance for students' reading tasks.

Activities for improving five reading skills and reading comprehension

Reading involves a variety of skills. What principles and strategies will be necessary for learners to develop reading skills for academic purposes? Greenall and Swan (1986) pointed out that effective reading means reading accurately and efficiently and understanding as much from the passage as learners need to achieve their purposes. A good reader can read better and faster with full comprehension (Nuttall, 1996, 2005). To be an efficient reader, in addition to the process of reading, five reading skills will be necessary: 1) intensive reading; 2) extensive reading; 3) skimming; 4) scanning; and 5) increasing reading speed. In addressing reading processing and reading skills, MALL programs, websites, and apps for L2 reading can be easily utilized, considering that even simple activities, such as using search engines, require students to read in English. There are lots of websites and apps for reading in and out of classes, e.g., *Bookly* (https://play.google.com/store/apps/details?id=com.twodoor.bookly&hl=en_US), *BrianPop* (https://www.brainpop.com/), *Goodreads* (https://www.good reads.com/), *Kids Discover* (https://www.kidsdiscover.com/kids-discover-online/), *LearnZillion* (https://learnzillion.com/p/), *LibraryThing*(https://www.librarything.com/), *New Readers Press* (https://www.newreaderspress.com/news-for-you-online), *Newsela* (https://newsela. com/), *Oceanhouse Media* (http://www.oceanhousemedia.com/), *Skybrary* (https://www.levarburtonkids.com/skybrary), *WOW in the World* (https://www.npr. org/podcasts/510321/wow-in-the-world), etc.

Intensive and extensive reading

Grellet (1981) defined intensive and extensive reading as follows. First, intensive reading involves reading shorter texts to extract specific information. It is an accuracy activity involving reading for detail. Second, extensive reading includes reading longer texts, usually for one's pleasure. It is a fluency activity, mainly involving global understanding. The two skills, despite areas of overlap, involve different objectives and different skills. Intensive reading involves a close examination of the text to get the full meaning (Munby, 1968). It means reading for exact information, reading for implied meaning, summarizing between sentences and paragraphs, and integrating data from the text with the reader's own knowledge and/or experience (Munby, 1968). Intensive reading aims to arrive at an in-depth and detailed understanding of the text: not only of what it means but also of how the meaning is produced (Nuttall, 1996, 2005).

In extensive reading, on the other hand, students can develop the habit of reading for pleasure which involves the ability to read quickly (Munby, 1979). Munby (1979) adds that this reading skill is also essential for assignments that involve reference work, i.e., training in how to look for specific information that is required, where the answer does not lie conveniently in one book with a useful index, and where a person does not have time to read each line carefully as with intensive reading. In short, it involves reading for some especially required information or getting the gist or general picture of the passage, chapter, or book. However, the two skills are not mutually exclusive - each one supports the other.

Skimming and scanning

Skimming and scanning are closely connected to reading speed. In both, readers are not reading a text word by word, but are forcing their eyes over the print at a rate that permits them to take in, maybe, the beginning and ends of paragraphs, chapter headings, subtitles, bold-face type, and so on (Nuttall, 1996, 2005). These terms are sometimes used indiscriminately. However, Nuttall (1996, 2005) pointed out that skimming should probably not be done competitively, as more is involved than only eye movement. Grellet (1981) also defined them as follows: 1) Skimming - Quickly running one's eyes over a text to get the gist of it; and 2) Scanning - Quickly going through a text to find a particular piece of information. For example, one often skims through a passage to see what it is about before deciding whether it is worth scanning a particular paragraph for the information one is looking for (Grellet, 1981; Nuttall, 2005). Thus, skimming and scanning are essential skills for getting main ideas and finding specific information. Grellet (1981) suggested that predicting, previewing, and anticipation are specific reading techniques necessary for skimming and scanning.

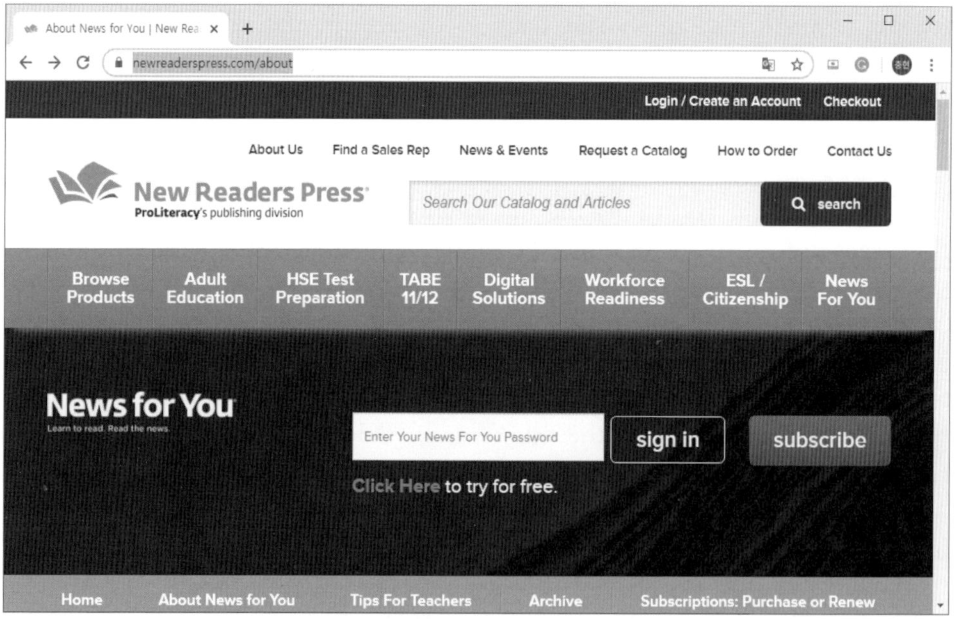

Figure 2.12 The main screen of *News for You*
(https:// www.newreaderspress.com/news-for-you-online)

Increasing reading speed

Reading speed and comprehension are closely linked. Even if someone reads reading materials with full understanding, he is not necessarily a good reader if he reads them slowly. A very slow reader is likely to read with insufficient understanding. To be a good reader, learners should have both reading speed and comprehension (Nuttall, 1996, 2005). Most of the EFL students are generally slow in reading. Their reading speed (in the case of undergraduates) is approximately half as much as that of native speakers (Yun & Lee, 2001). They do not know how to read effectively nor how to increase their reading speed. Eye movements, sense groups, and flexibility are significant factors in improving reading speed (Nuttall, 1996, 2005). Good readers make fewer eye movements than poor ones - their eyes take in several words at a time. One characteristic of efficient readers is their ability to chunk a text into sense units, each consisting of several words and taken in by one fixation of their eyes. Another is their flexibility. According to their purpose, they will vary their speed and their whole manner of reading (Nuttall, 2005).

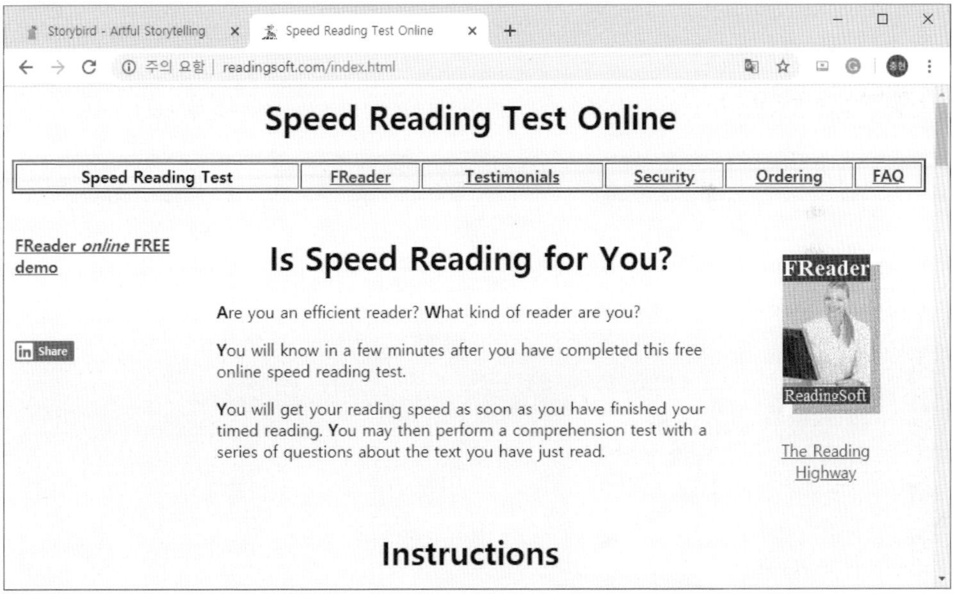

Figure 2.13 The main screen of *Rocket Reader* (https://www. readingsoft.com/)

Some useful websites and apps for increasing reading speed are as follows: *Letter Chase Reader* (https://www.letterchase.com), *Rocket Reader* (http://www.rocket

reader.com), *Speed Reading* (https://play.google.com/store/apps/details?id=com.speedreading.alexander.speedreading), *Speed Reading App: How to Read Faster* (https://play.google.com/store/apps/details?id=com.speedreading.braintrasers), *Speed Reading Test Online* (https://www. readingsoft.com/), *Speed reading: the best!* (https://play.google.com/store/apps/details?id=world.easysolution.speedreading), etc.

Newer or more innovative activities

The Internet, websites, apps, e-mail, BBS, and SNS can provide students with another way of developing reading skills, particularly intensive and extensive reading, skimming and scanning, speed reading, extracting main ideas, inferring, etc., and reading comprehension ultimately, since they have a vast amount of materials to read in the target language, such as letters, information, data, advertisements, even academic writing (e.g., articles and theses), etc. For example, teachers can give students a task (e.g., what is an AI chatbot?). They can search or retrieve and read the materials related to it intensively or extensively. They can also scan and skim them.

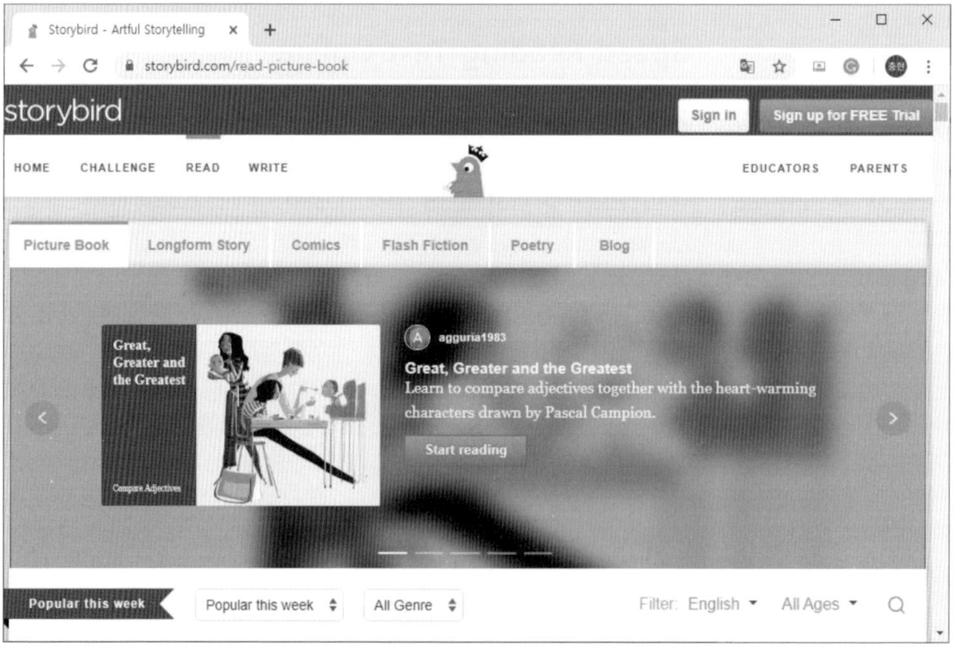

Figure 2.14 The screenshot of *Storybird* (http://storybird.com)

Thus, reading the materials from websites, web pages, and apps must be a new, flexible, and active way to enable students to carry out reading exercises in FLT&L. Some websites and webpages are available for extensive reading, e.g., under the heading of 'Literature,' 'Newspapers,' 'Encyclopaedias,' 'History,' 'Reference,' etc. The students can also create their newspaper or storytelling based on searching, retrieving, and reading the materials.

Some of useful websites are as follows: *BrianPop* (https://www.brainpop.com/), *Crayon* (http://crayon.net), *Interactive Learning Resources* (http://literacynet.org/cnnsf/week.html), *New Readers Press* (https://www.newreaderspress.com/news-for-you-online), *Newsela* (https://newsela.com/), *LibraryThing* (https://www.librarything.com/), *Storybird* (http://storybird.com), etc.

2.5 Computers and Writing with Grammar

The best way for students to learn how to write well is through writing itself, to write and write (Huffman & Goldberg, 1987). However, writing is a complex process. Learners have to create ideas and compose the ideas into the written structure adapted to their goals, which includes content, organization, and the consummation of subskills needed for writing such as vocabulary, spelling, grammar and structure rules, and punctuation, etc., and reading as well (Hamp-Lyons & Heasley, 1987, Jones & Fortescue, 1987; So & Lee, 2013; Tribble, 1996; Williams, 2005a).

The teaching and learning of L2 writing involve several factors, such as the writing process, peer and teacher responses, writing instruction, and writing (Harmer, 2004; Raimes, 1983; Williams, 2005a). Various approaches to teaching writing, such as the controlled-to-free approach, the free-writing approach, the paragraph-pattern approach, the communicative approach, the process approach, and the genre approach, have been suggested (Hyland, 2002; Tribble, 1996; Williams, 2005a). Of these, the process approach has been the mainstay of L2 writing pedagogy. Williams (2005a) suggested four stages of the writing process: getting started, creating the first drafts, revising, and editing. Harmer (2004) suggested four main elements in the writing process: planning, drafting, editing (reflecting and revising), and the final version. Tribble (1996) also suggested the writing process is composed of prewriting, composing (drafting), revising, and editing.

In this respect, computer-assisted writing can make an immediate and extensive contribution to the features of writing mentioned above due to the advantages of computers, e.g., accuracy and speed of processing conventional tasks, immediate feedback, self-pacing, etc. The word processor has powerful facilities, creating, storing, and editing very simply, quickly, and efficiently, and printing texts with a printer, which can lighten the laborious workload and help the writer cope with the drudgery, and play a significant role in developing writing skills, particularly free writing and the process of writing (Phinney, 1989; Piper, 1987; Windeatt, 1987). In short, it can lighten the students' workload and encourage them to produce revised versions and to complete writing tasks in order to motivate them to write more and cause them to have a positive attitude towards writing more so than the traditional medium of pen and paper (Phinney, 1989; Wyatt, 1984). Windeatt (1987) and Windeatt, Hardisty, & Eastment (2000) added that word processors, chatting programs, and e-mail could offer a partial solution not only to the difficulties which students confront in writing but to the problem which teachers face in trying to find suitable language teaching software.

Now, almost all the students write using keyboards or keypads instead of pen or pencil, and they can tap into an immeasurable amount of information on the Internet. Computer-assisted writing can provide various approaches and activities tailored to meet students' needs and wants, not only subskills-oriented writing but to some extent guided and free or creative writing, in which students can practice and improve specific skills. This section will look at how computers can be used for developing a variety of writing skills as follows: 1) the use of computers in writing; 2) subskills-oriented writing; and 3) guided and free writing.

1. The Use of Computers in Writing

In conventional L2 writing classrooms, the teaching and learning of L2 writing have been considered complex and challenging due to the limited number of class sessions and insufficient time in conventional L2 writing classrooms (So & Lee, 2013; Yoon & Lee, 2010). That is why blended learning, which combines the positive attributes of online and face-to-face instruction, has been suggested to provide sufficient writing opportunities and environments for interaction and communication with peers and a teacher regardless of time or place (Bañados, 2013; Grgurović, 2011; Hinkelman & Gruba, 2012; Nicolson, Murphy, & Southgate, 2011; Yoon & Lee, 2010). In blended learning environments, L2 learners can interact with peers and a teacher using computer-mediated communication technology (Lafford & Lafford, 2005; Lee & Pyo, 2003; Yoon & Lee, 2010).

L2 writing instruction in blended learning

Blended learning has been applied to L2 writing classrooms, and it has been found to foster interaction among students and teachers and have a positive impact on the development of L2 writing skills (Behjat, Yamini, & Bagheri, 2011; Ferriman, 2013; Miyazoe & Anderson, 2010; Yoon & Lee, 2010). So and Lee (2013) have proposed an instructional model for L2 writing in blended learning, considering the online and offline characteristics, instructional design and theory, and L2 writing theory and approaches. An instructional model for L2 writing in blended learning comprises five stages: getting ready to write, drafting, revising, producing the final draft, and reviewing. Also, writing activities and instructions are suggested to reinforce the writing process and satisfy the students' academic needs with various learning tools.

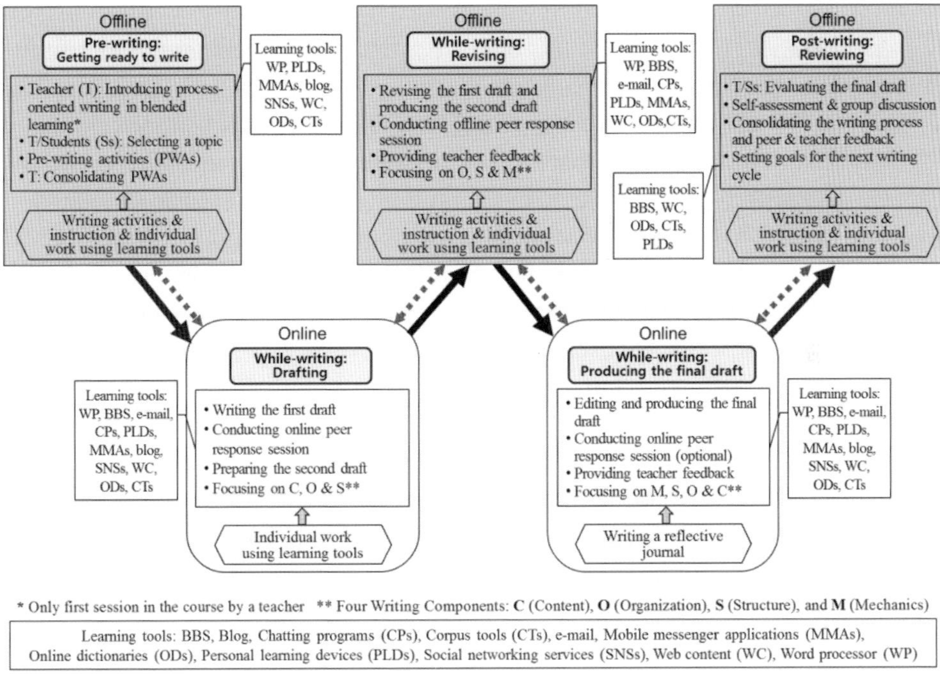

Figure 2.15 The instructional model for L2 writing in blended learning (So & Lee, 2013, p. 8)

Peer and teacher response in L2 writing in blended learning

Theoretical background of peer and teacher response in L2 writing

As the process-oriented writing approach has been widely employed in teaching and learning L2 writing, peer and teacher response has gained greater attention in L2 writing. Liu and Hansen (2002) suggested four theoretical stances: process writing theory, collaborative learning theory, Vygotsky's Zone of Proximal Development, and interactionists' view on second language acquisition (SLA). Advantages of peer response include the fact that it provides L2 learners with a real audience to write for and the fact that they can receive feedback appropriate to their level of development from peers who have diverse levels of language and content (Ferris, 2003; Liu & Hansen, 2002). Peer response has also been found to positively impact revision and writing outcomes (Berg, 1999; Min, 2006).

With the development of ICT and CMC tools, such as BBS, instant messenger, and Wiki, peer response has been implemented in online environments (DiGiovanni & Nagaswami, 2001; Hewett, 2006; Jones, Garralda, Li, & Lock, 2006; Liang, 2010; Liu & Sadler, 2003). Such tools and technology help learners give and receive feedback more effectively and efficiently regardless of time and space, allowing them more time and opportunities for interaction than they would have in the conventional classroom. In addition to these CMC tools, PLDs – such as tablet PCs, smartphones, and portable media players – have been used in language learning and teaching contexts (Yoon, Lee, & Lee, 2013).

In addition to peer response, teacher feedback or response has played one of the important roles in teaching and learning L2 writing. Teachers respond to student writing through written commentary or student-teacher conferences. Teachers were found to provide comments on various composition issues, such as grammar, mechanics, lexical choice, content, organization (Conrad & Goldstein, 1999; Ferris, 1995; Williams, 2005a). Empirical research on teacher response or teacher feedback has looked at three major issues: the focus of teacher comments, the form of feedback, and the effects of the feedback on student writing outcomes (Ferris, 2003). Recent studies shed light on the effects of teacher feedback on revision and writing quality. Many studies show that students in L2 writing classrooms considered teacher feedback valuable and useful to improve their writing (Ferris, 1995; Hedgcock & Lefkowitz, 1996). Some studies also demonstrated that students utilized teacher comments in revision (Conrad & Goldstein, 1999; Ferris, 1997, 2001). Regarding the writing quality, empirical research has shown improved student writings (Fathman & Whalley, 1990; Russikoff & Kogan, 1996).

Procedures of peer and teacher response in blended learning

Taking the peer and teacher responses into account, Figure 2.16 illustrates the procedures of peer and teacher responses in blended learning (So & Lee, 2014). It consists of two compulsory peer response sessions and one optional session in a two-week writing cycle. Peers utilized asynchronous and synchronous CMC tools, such as BBS, e-mail, chat programs, and various PLDs for efficient peer response sessions. Teachers need to monitor the online peer response sessions, not giving feedback as the students tend to rely on more teacher comments than on peer comments if teacher feedback was present alongside peer feedback. Teacher feedback is to be given on the participants' second drafts and final drafts.

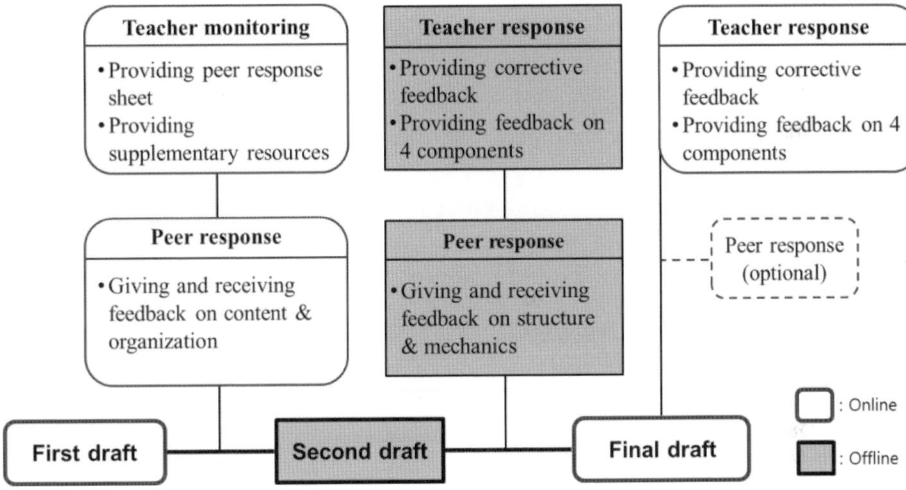

Figure 2.16 Procedures of responses in L2 writing in blended learning (So & Lee, 2014, p. 211)

2. Three Types of Writing Activities Using Computers

Subskills-oriented writing activities

The computer can make a more significant contribution to the area of subskills-oriented writing which mainly deals with accurate form in writing than conventional teaching methods because it functions best in terms of mechanical aspects (Liou, 2013; Yoon & Lee, 2010; So & Lee, 2014; Wyatt, 1984). With the increased interest in the field of subskills-oriented writing in CALL, more software developers have issued specialized packages for use in writing (C. H. Lee, 2006; Phinney, 1989). Many commercial programs available under the heading of 'Word,' 'Vocabulary,' 'Grammar,' 'Spelling,' 'Text,' etc. are related to developing the subskills. However, the quality of the programs varies greatly (Jones & Fortescue 1987), e.g., *English Learner* (http://www.englishlearner.com/index.html), *Guide to Grammar & Writing* (http://www.ccc.commnet.edu/grammar), *Grammarly* (https://www.grammarly.com), *Small Seo Tools* (http://smallseotools.com), *Spellcheck* (http://www.spellcheck.net), *Word and Pictures* (http://www.bbc.co.uk/schools/wordsandpictures), etc. Teachers can also produce more meaningful writing practice exercises suitable for their students' levels than using simple drill exercises in authoring packages and word processing.

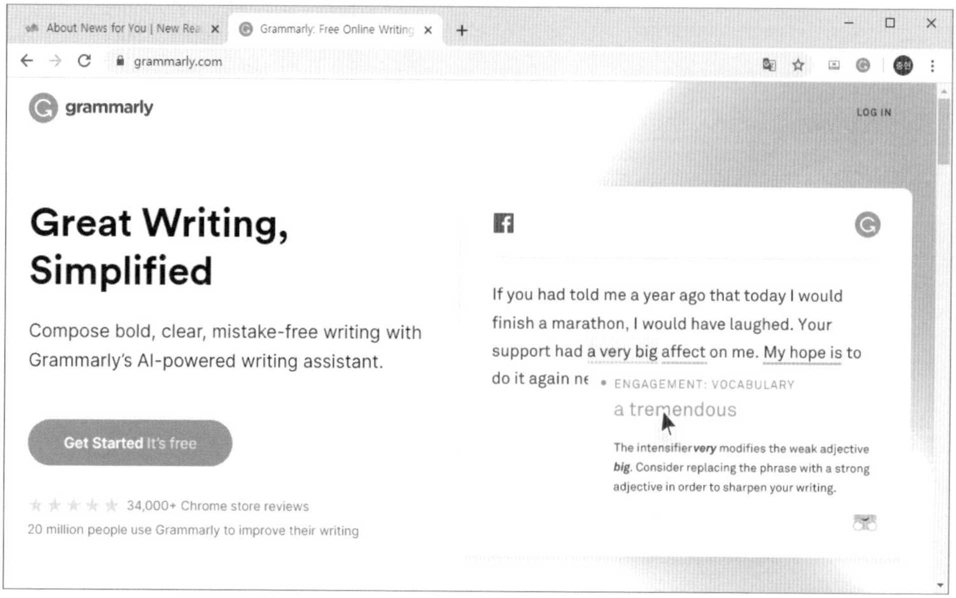

Figure 2.17 The main screen of *Grammarly* (https://www.grammarly.com)

The programs are similar to written materials, but there are generally significant differences. First, they can provide tireless, patient practice, immediate feedback, self-pacing, and individualized attention to students' problems with record-keeping functions. Second, they can be used in process-oriented writing instruction since they can give clear and additional instructions with sound or graphic design at each stage (Hope, Taylor, & Pusack, 1984; Williams, 1991; Wyatt, 1984). Throughout the programs with a mixture of different question types, they can practice and develop the subskills effectively.

Guided writing activities

Another component of many writing curricula is guided writing, in which students are usually given a piece of a model of incomplete passages or paragraphs or text, and they have to rebuild or alter it or create a new version with similar functions and rhetoric (Jones & Fortescue, 1987). For the students, such activities will be useful because the activities can allow them to practice different versions of the same topic, provide checklists for linguistic problems in general, and provide guidelines for free writing (Phinney, 1989).

The computer can also play an extensive role in guided writing since it involves little or no free expression (Wyatt, 1984). Rebuilding, reorganizing (jumbling), revising, editing incomplete texts, exercises, etc. are common aspects of software available in MALL guided writing in more comfortable and more enhanced forms than that of the conventional manner.

Figure 2.18 The main screen of *Guide to Grammar & Writing*
(http://www.ccc.commnet.edu/grammar)

There are some programs *Gapmaster*, *Matchmaster*, and *Storyboard* from Wida Software, and websites for guided or controlled writing, *Guide to Grammar & Writing* (http://www.ccc.commnet.edu/grammar), *LEO* (http://leo.stcloudstate.edu/style /sentencev.html), *Online Writing Lab by D'Youville College* (http://depts.dyc.

edu/learningcenter/owl/index.htm), etc.

In particular, word processors are ideal for guided writing practice and activities. The tasks will be more manageable because it allows students to make changes to texts at any time (Jones & Fortescue, 1987; Windeatt, 1987). All the exercises mentioned above can be carried out on the word processor. Teachers can give students lots of practical instructions and meaningful comments for the exercises, as many as they want. For example, first, teachers can jumble words and sentences or paragraphs within a text. When reorganizing the text, students must extract the meaning from the sentences and texts and be aware of the indications to text cohesion which give a clue to order (Nuttall, 1996, 2005). Second, teachers can delete words or sentences from a passage or dialogue. The students have to rebuild it with the similar strategies above. Third, Jones and Fortescue (1987) suggest another idea for guided writing as follows, "It could be a complete passage which needs changing: a text about the present which the student is asked to change to the past or a description of one person to be changed to a description of another. At a more advanced level, possibilities include a wordy and repetitive text which the student is asked to improve by pruning, an over-informal business letter which needs to be made more business-like" (p. 51).

Free or creative writing activities

The goal of a writing course is ultimate to improve students' free or creative writing. It is claimed that the computer can play essential roles at the word and sentence level but may not offer learners to develop their free or creative writing skills since it cannot monitor the actual content of what they produce (Williams, 1991). However, using word processors, e-mail, BBS, and writing apps can help students develop their free or creative writing skills.

Using the word processors

The word processors can make contributions to free or creative writing. It can help students compose through a series of drafts to a completed version of a paper, in terms of the process and product of writing, encouraging students to brainstorm ideas (Lam & Pennington, 1995). First, free writing will require a warm and supportive, and non-threatening environment considering it is a creative process and is the repetition of the three-writing stages process (Hamp-Lyons & Heasley, 1987).

For EFL students, word processor helps relieve them of the fear of errors at the surface level of writing and concentrate on the process of writing (Piper,

1987). Second, its transitoriness promotes the flow of ideas and encourages more frequent revision (Huffman & Goldberg, 1987). Finally, it offers the students the ability to see the results of proposed changes in context before making a final choice at once (Windeatt, 1987). Therefore, word processors are likely to encourage them to write freely, revise more, and experiment with their ideas on the screen and in a hard copy version of their writing with a printer (Lam & Pennington, 1995). In free or creative writing activities with the word processors, the students can type idea files, headings, lists, pre-writing activities, etc., directly into a word-processed file, which are then available for expansion and further composition. It can allow them to reorganize the parts of the text, insert or delete words, sentences, and paragraphs, and create headings and highlight them as they polish their final products (Hamp-Lyons & Heasley, 1987). For example, students can carry out relevant written work individually, which might be suitable for the writing course as useful free writing activities (Levy & Farrugia, 1988). As the word processors can no longer take part in error correction and free expression beyond the sentence level, the teachers have to take over and help them regarding more advanced features (Hope, Taylor, & Pusack, 1984). The teacher will be a collaborator, consultant, and reader, conferring with students as they write, helping them with decision making, giving on-the-spot instruction (Snyder, 1993).

Using e-mail and BBS

There are also many free or creative writing tasks and activities that teachers can give students in the writing course and help develop the writing skills using e-mail and BBS. Teachers and students have recently realized the potential of using e-mail and BBS in language learning, particularly writing. They can provide exciting and authentic activities for developing and reinforcing writing skills, particularly free or creative writing since they can exchange some written work, everyday information, thoughts, ideas, and opinions on all kinds of subjects in the target language (Goodwin, Hamrick, & Stewart, 1993; Markee, 1994). The students can write and send their message anywhere and any time via a personal computer with the network to anyone who has an e-mail account and receive a reply (Romiszowski, 1988). They have the chance to ask questions about their interests, and if they can get information on different cultural aspects, this can help to ease their adjustment to the new culture, language, and customs (Goodwin et al., 1993). The students can easily have real-time communication and on-line conferences in written form via e-mail. They can also write messages on the word processor and send them to e-mail software, and this provides them with the opportunity to review the structure of written language and contents before sending their sending their messages.

One of the most apparent benefits of using word processors, e-mail, and BBS is to increase interaction between the teacher and the learner(s) in the target language. Goodwin et al. (1993) show an activity available as follows: students, individually, in pairs, and in groups are asked to read an article, write a one-paragraph summary of the content, and respond with their opinions in another paragraph; they focus on reading, summarizing, analyzing, and responding to the texts; and the teacher checks their responses for linguistic and stylistic problems as well as overall organization, and give them feedback. This activity will help students develop specific academic writing, focusing on the content area of writing. E-mail can significantly help them to communicate in written English. That is why the use of e-mail can be called communicative writing.

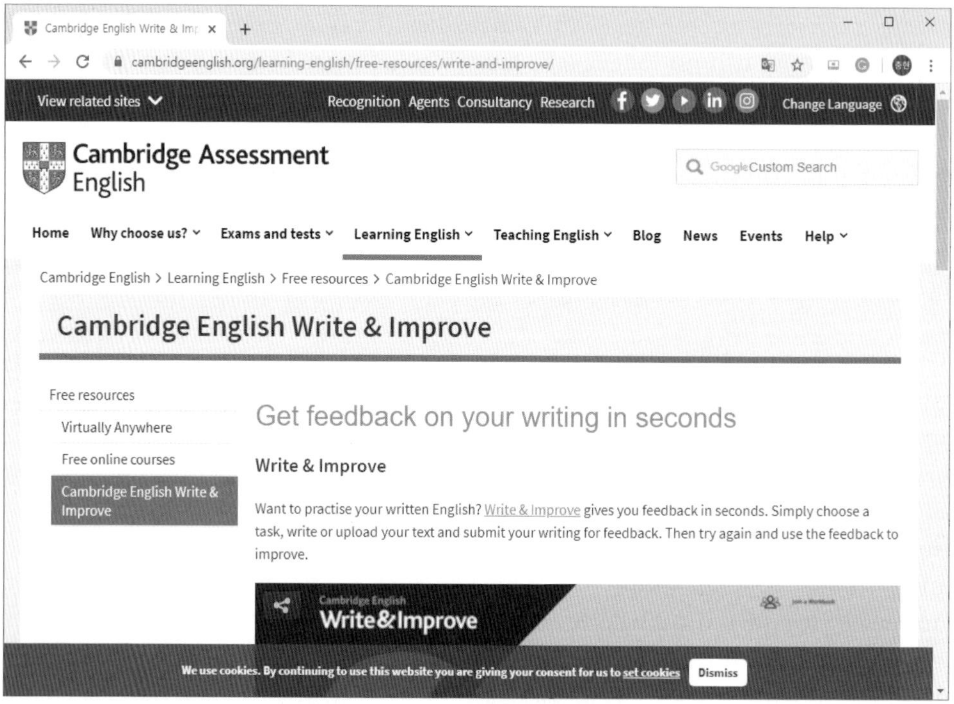

Figure 2.19 The main screen of *Cambridge English Write & Improve* (http:// www.cambridgeenglish.org/learning-english/find-free-resources/write-and-improve)

Some of the useful websites for improving writing skills are as follows: *Cambridge English Write & Improve* (http://www.cambridgeenglish.org/learning-english/find-free-resources/write-and-improve), *Colorado State University's Writing Studio* (http://writing.colostate.edu), *Grammarly* (https://www.grammarly.com), *Purdue's Online Writing Lab* (http://owl.english. purdue.edu), *Small Seo Tools* (http://smallseotools.com), etc.

2.6 Conclusion

Computers, PLDs, websites, apps, and social media can be used in developing not only reading and writing skills but also listening and speaking skills. They help learners carry out conventional tasks and activities with enhanced or new forms of activities that can help develop the four language skills and the three subskills. Moreover, many MALL programs, websites, and apps are used with any approach from behaviorism to constructivism and four language skills and the integrated language skills in language classes.

In using MALL programs, websites, and apps in language classes, the teachers' efforts in using computers and PLDs are more significant than in conventional materials. With well-planned, creative uses of commercial packages, authoring tools, websites, apps, and SNS, teachers can help students improve their language skills. Teachers have to keep in mind that methodological approaches can solve the problems such as misconceptions about the lack of suitability of computers for speaking skills in particular and lack of software. If the computer itself is entirely in the center of the activities without specific technical and pedagogical preparation in using the computer, it can have little effect in FLT&L. With MALL content available, teachers will have to prepare teacher and student support materials such as the program documentation, teachers' notes, students' worksheets, and a lesson plan for the successful use of the content. Besides, using ICT and multimedia in language classes has increased students' responsibility in the learning process. Students need to be aware of why they are using computers and participate actively in the learning process in MALL.

Finally, to effectively use these characteristics, MALL must continue to develop in terms of software or content and methodology. More research, development, training, and evaluation will be required to thoroughly use its potential in language teaching and learning. More empirical research studies in this field will be particularly needed to integrate four language skills development in FLT&L and blended learning.

Tasks for Study and Discussion

1. Which language skill(s) development do you think MALL and MABL can best facilitate?

2. What are the significant features that websites and apps can be applied for teaching and learning each language skill (listening, speaking, reading, writing, grammar, pronunciation, and vocabulary)?

3. How can computers and PLDs play an essential and extensive role in improving listening skills? Please describe two activities available to developing listening.

4. There are two kinds of guided and free spoken activities which can be used to develop speaking skills. What are they?

5. How can computers play an essential and extensive role in improving reading skills? Describe two activities available to developing reading.

6. Describe the advantages of using computers in improving writing skills. Please describe two activities available to developing writing.

7. Select one of the websites or apps for each language skill introduced in the chapter and critically review them in terms of 1) methodology the websites or apps are based on (if any), 2) advantages and limitations, and 3) supplements needed.

Chapter 3

MALL Content Evaluation

3.1 Introduction

There is a close relationship between the availability of software and appropriate teaching methodology. MALL courseware or content that make the most of the positive attributes of multimedia can provide maximized interactive learning, individualized or autonomous learning, learner retention, and motivation in FLT&L (C. H. Lee, 1998a, 2006). It does not mean, however, that using multimedia in FLT&L will ensure effective learning and teaching and bring about improvement in learner's academic achievement. When using MALL courseware or content (MALL content hereafter), teachers and learners must be more proactive and creative than conventional classrooms. Furthermore, they need to be informed and knowledgeable about MALL content and know how to use it. Appropriate content evaluation and the selection and implementation of MALL based on effective teaching methodology can positively influence affective factors such as learners' motivation and interest and increase learner achievement. However, it should be noted that previous literature on CALL or MALL courseware evaluation for FLT&L is mostly from the mid-1980s to mid-1990s. Due to the rapid development and changes in hardware and software technologies, the content evaluation criteria and checklists do not correspond to existing reality. In particular, the domestic literature regarding content evaluation has been limited to introducing and translating studies conducted abroad. There is a dire need to re-evaluate the criteria and checklists and devise suitable for EFL classes based on sound research on continuous revision, modification, and the development of content evaluation. It can provide teachers and developers with useful information for the development of MALL content as well.

This chapter deals with factors that need to be considered in MALL content evaluation, such as evaluation criteria and framework, evaluation checklist, selection, and evaluation process. The following questions are addressed in depth: 1) Are evaluation, selection, and purchase of MALL content carried out properly in ESL and EFL classes?; 2) What kinds of content evaluation criteria and framework are out there, and are they appropriate for the present state of

FLT&L?; 3) What should effective content evaluation criteria and checklists look like and how should they be organized?; and 4) What is the effective and efficient procedure for carrying out a content evaluation based on evaluation criteria? Based on the answers to the questions, this chapter also aims to present evaluation criteria, checklists, and procedures for simple and comprehensive MALL content, websites, or webpages and apps for the appropriate evaluation, selection, and development of MALL content for FLT&L.

3.2 Theoretical Background

There are numerous literature and research studies on theories on CALL and MALL content evaluation. The research studies on theories and practices of software or courseware evaluation are as follows: Alessi and Trollip (1985), Chapelle (2001), Council of Ministers of Education (1985), Eastment (1996), Hawkridge (1990), Hubbard (1987, 1988), Jones and Fortescue (1987), Kim (1999), KMEC (KERIS, 1998), C. H. Lee (2000b, 2002), Lee and Yun (2003, 2005), Levy and Farrugia (1988), Merill (1988), Odell (1986), Robb and Susser (2000), Scarborough (1988), J. B. Son (2005), Windeatt (1995), Windeatt, Hardisty, and Eastment (2000), and others. However, the studies on specific evaluation criteria, standards and checklists, and evaluation procedures for practical use in EFL classrooms by teachers and professionals are few. Because of the advancement in technologies related to hardware and software, there is a need to re-evaluate, revise, and modify the currently existing software evaluation criteria and checklists. This section will first address literature related to MALL content selection, evaluation criteria and checklists, and evaluation procedure.

Selection of MALL Content

Thousands of MALL content, including apps for FLT&L, have been developed and distributed domestically and internationally. It seems that looking into the selection process of content such as how language teachers get information on MALL content, what they take for, and how they choose the content.

Robb and Susser (2000) conducted an online survey for teachers using websites related to FLT&L such as TESLCA-L, NETEACH-L, and JALTCALL. The result showed that 81% used the demo version to choose, and 66% relied on advertisement information. Using evaluation criteria or checklist was 25%, which was lower than those who listened to salespeople or coworkers' recommendations.

Similar results are observed in Korea as well. C. H. Lee (2002) conducted a survey and interviews for junior high school teachers from 1999 to 2001 who participated in in-service teacher training program including MALL courses. 45% relied on the advertisement, 25% used the demo version of the program, 21% relied on recommendations, 8% used evaluation criteria or checklist, and 1% made their selection based on other reasons. The participants responded that even if the demo version was available, they did not use evaluation criteria or checklist due to lack of knowledge and experience.

Can it be assumed that selected MALL content based on advertisements and recommendations is pedagogically effective? Advertisements tend to exaggerate specific features and focus only on some functions of the content. Coworkers' recommendations tend to be subjective, and when course goals and student population changes, selections based on others' recommendations may not prove to hold up to what is expected of the content. Consequently, researchers in MALL suggest using content evaluation criteria and checklists in selecting MALL content to ensure objective and systematic evaluation and selection (Hubbard, 1987; C. H. Lee, 2000b; Lee & Yun, 2003, 2005; Merrill, 1988; Odell, 1986). Hawkridge (1990), for example, criticized the content selection process in British schools and said that content selection should be differentiated from a book or video selection. He said that the qualitative and quantitative evaluations of content should be conducted, including description, analysis, and critique. Odell (1986) also emphasized the importance of objective and systematic evaluation and selection and claimed that the database of evaluation results be made available for researchers and end-users.

Evaluation Criteria and Evaluation Checklist

There have been many research studies on software or content evaluation in both theory and practice, as described earlier. The studies all suggest that CALL or MALL content evaluation criteria should contain a couple of essential elements for evaluation: pedagogical, technical, and/or administrative elements. Hubbard (1988) suggested establishing a content evaluation framework consisting of approach, design, and procedure, and he put a strong emphasis on the approach above all. In other words, he pointed out the necessity to evaluate pedagogical approaches to L2 teaching and learning found in the content, and he also argued that the content evaluation should be flexible so that the teachers can develop their evaluation checklists or modify preexisting ones based on the evaluation framework. In addressing the same issue, C. H. Lee (2000b) made more specific and detailed suggestions and mentioned the followings to be considered before conducting content evaluation: 1) the purposes of evaluation (content purchase, development of MALL content or guidelines, or improvement of existing content); 2) evaluators (MALL specialists, teachers, and students); 3) evaluation methods (evaluation checklists or questionnaire, descriptive analysis, interviews, etc.); and 4) evaluation procedures.

MALL content evaluation criteria and checklists in the past were as follows. Windeatt (1995) stated that the pedagogical goals and objectives of the program, authorability, learner variables, flexibility, general appearance, curriculum compatibility, and adaptability must be included in content evaluation criteria. The evaluation checklists presented by Windeatt, Hardisty, and Eastment (2000, p. 35, 41) are provided in Tables 3.1 and 3.2.

Table 3.1 Evaluation checklist for the webpage appearance and design (Windeatt, Hardisty, & Eastment, 2000, p. 35)

Page	Marks/5	Comment
General appearance Is the page attractive? Why/Why not?		
Clarity Is the page clear? Can you read the information easily?		
Use of color Are the colors attractive? Do they help to make the information easy to read?		
Ease of use Is it easy to move around the page, or to move on to other pages? Is there anything on the page that distracts your attention from the most important information?		
Presentation and accuracy Are there any spelling or grammar mistakes?		
Multimedia Does the page make good use of pictures, sound, animation or video? Does the page take a long time to appear?		
Interest Is the page interesting? Why/Why not?		
Other Criteria		

Table 3.2 Evaluation checklist for the webpage content
(Windeatt, Hardisty, & Eastment, 2000, p. 41)

	Comment
How accurate is the information? How do you know?	
Who provides the information?	
How much do they know about the topic?	
Is more than one side of the argument presented?	
How up-to-date is the information?	
(Add your own questions)	
What is your opinion of this Web document?	

Regarding webpage evaluation, Windeatt, Hardisty, and Eastment (2000) pointed out that reliable and updated information must be presented since anyone can upload information on the Web with varied purposes without any kinds of screening. On that note, they suggested goals and purposes of the web content, author(s) and publishers, updated information, quantity and quality of content, objectivity and accuracy, and overall layout, which are necessary for developing evaluation criteria.

Other checklists have also been developed. Scarborough's (1988) CALL evaluation criteria included screen layout and presentation, technical function, and pedagogical value in L2 teaching and learning. Levy and Farrugia (1988) included content, goals, user's guide, teacher and learner use, feedback, design, authorability, and motivation in evaluation criteria. Eastment's (1996) suggestion included learning goals, ease of installation, ease of use, program design, authorability, and interest. On the other hand, Merrill (1988) focused on two specific areas of instructional criteria and presentation criteria. For instructional criteria, pedagogical goals of content, agreement of pedagogical goals of content and learning objectives, agreement of types of content application and learning objectives. For presentation criteria, presentation of screen layout, movement from screen to screen, ease of use, and interaction were suggested. Council of Ministers of Education's (1985) checklist is more specific in that program goals, pedagogical elements, teaching approaches and methods, technical design, and supportive materials are evaluated in detail.

Research conducted domestically includes I. S. Kim (1999), KMEC (1998), C. H. Lee (2000b, 2002), Lee and Yun (2003, 2005), and J. B. Son (2005). J. B. Son

(2005) suggested pedagogical aspects and technical aspects as evaluation criteria. Pedagogical aspects included the presentation of goals, the accuracy of content, control, feedback, and supportive features, and technical aspects included stability in use, input and output settings, the familiarity of screen layout, the effectiveness of color, image, and sound functions, and hypermedia. I. S. Kim (1999) suggested three major areas of curriculum, L2 pedagogy, and learners, and he focused on evaluating software for L2 learning with guidelines stemming from instructional design and L2 pedagogy. KMEC (1998) took on a more general approach in the evaluation and addressed overall educational software. Its evaluation criteria included: content areas which evaluated validity in the selection, creativity, logical coherence, clarity, ethicality, appropriateness of multimedia; instructional strategies area which included motivation, feedback, and control; and technical and managerial areas which looked into ease of use, stability, functionality, and ease in getting information.

In the research mentioned above on evaluation checklists, it can be seen that essential elements in content such as pedagogical, presentational, and technical elements should be evaluated. However, there seems to be a need to re-evaluate and/or modify the criteria and checklists for the following reasons. First, most of the criteria and checklists are not designed to evaluate MALL content systematically, i.e., websites or apps. Considering that websites and apps are frequently used in L2 classrooms, it is likely that the teachers will find it difficult to use the checklists efficiently and effectively. Second, the criteria and checklists are not consistent with evaluation standards or lack a solid framework on which the evaluation criteria are based. Third, the checklists should allow both quantitative and qualitative evaluation to take place. Each criterion and element of the checklists should have scores and comments based on the evaluation, and total scores and holistic comments should be made available. Fourth, there is a lack in the evaluation of cutting-edge multimedia technologies used in MALL content. For example, voice recognition, web compatibility, authorability, program editing, LMS, etc. need to be evaluated. Fifth, the presence of cultural aspects of the target culture should be evaluated. Sixth, the ethicality of the program is mentioned as a sub-element or not mentioned at all.

Regarding ethicality, C. H. Lee (2000b) stated that ethical problems in the content could have a strong influence on learners. He claimed that it should be considered an independent element in content evaluation so that if the content received 'inappropriateness' in ethicality, it should not be selected. For example, let us take a case of *H* content. *H* content received high scores in pedagogical, technical, and administrative elements but contained much inappropriate content that was unethical and biased so that it received the lowest score possible in ethicality. However, the checklist used at the time of evaluation considered ethicality a sub-element, having a minimal effect on the whole, and the content received an excellent ranking overall. It shows that the checklist used had severe problems, and the evaluation conducted based on that checklist can be misleading.

Evaluation Procedure

MALL content evaluation has been mostly conducted by organizations and institutions that specialize in content development and evaluation rather than by individuals. Consequently, evaluation criteria, procedures, tools, and methods have not been openly introduced to individual teachers. In turn, there are few research studies on the effectiveness and efficiency of the MALL content evaluation process and methods. This lack of guideline, in other words, means potential difficulty in actual use in the teaching field.

Beattie and Preston (1989) claimed that MALL content evaluation needed to begin with defining pedagogical needs and limitations above all. Pedagogical needs refer to teaching and learning goals, learner proficiency level, pedagogical content, etc. Before the content evaluation, hardware should be checked along with other administrative and supportive elements. The demo version of the content that meets the pedagogical needs should be evaluated in its content, pedagogical element, and technical element (Beattie & Preston, 1989). Hubbard (1988), Lee and Yun (2003), and the Council of Ministers of Education (1985) emphasized the importance of proper procedure in CALL courseware evaluation and the necessity of workshops. The Council of Ministers of Education (1985) laid out the procedure for CALL content evaluation: First, accompanying materials and peripheral parts related to the content such as the manual, teacher's guide, and user's guide need to be evaluated. Second, the content as a whole is evaluated for general impression and format. Third, the content is evaluated in detail using a content checklist. Alessi and Trollip (1985) suggested CALL content evaluation should be conducted multiple times for accurate evaluation. Lee and Yun (2003) said that the evaluators should consist of three or five people, and they suggested evaluating three times based on an evaluation checklist to maintain consistency and objectivity.

In the following sections, MALL content evaluation criteria and checklists that are suitable for evaluation specialists and teachers will be introduced. Proper procedures and methods in conducting MALL content evaluation will also be discussed.

3.3 MALL Content Evaluation Criteria and Evaluation Checklists

The Need for MALL Content Evaluation

A tremendous amount of MALL content, including websites and apps, has been developed and distributed with written texts or textbooks. In many educational institutions and classrooms, such MALL content has actively been implemented. However, as mentioned in chapter 1, to make the more extensive and successful use of MALL in FLT&L, proper content evaluation criteria need to be used to select the appropriate content for classroom use.

As C. H. Lee (2000b) and Lee and Yun (2005) said, the purposes of MALL content evaluation are to select appropriate content for purchase and use, to create standards and/or guide in developing MALL content, and to improve existing content. It is assumed that teachers, evaluators, and educational institutions will generally conduct the content evaluation in practical aspects such as price, availability, content, etc. Besides, learner variables like age, proficiency level, interest, etc., are likely to be considered. However, these are the most general aspects of selecting MALL content, and there are many other essential elements to be considered which require professional knowledge and experience. MALL content evaluation criteria and checklists should be used to allow teachers and evaluators to maintain objectivity and consistency in content evaluation while looking into detailed information.

MALL Content Evaluation Criteria and Elements

There is no absolute or perfect set of criteria or checklists for MALL content evaluation. However, to efficiently evaluate the various types of information the content has, evaluation criteria and checklists that look into general and specific aspects should be used. First, the aims and objectives of the content must be presented. Second, administrative elements such as hardware support, program type, publisher information, etc., are looked into. Third, pedagogical elements like learning objectives, learning content, feedback, and assessment need to be evaluated. Fourth, technical elements should be evaluated, including screen displays, ease of use and stability, etc. Fifth, supportive materials should be scrutinized, and finally, yet importantly, ethicality needs to be evaluated. The content evaluation criteria and checklists presented here were developed based on sound theories, previous research, and more than 100 pieces of feedback from teachers and learners from workshops, MALL classes, and teacher training courses. '*' is used to signify the evaluation of websites or webpages.

Aims and objectives

The aims and objectives of each program must be stated on the final copy of MALL content. In other words, learning and teaching goals and objectives need to be presented on the first page, cover, user manual, or the open page of the program or content.

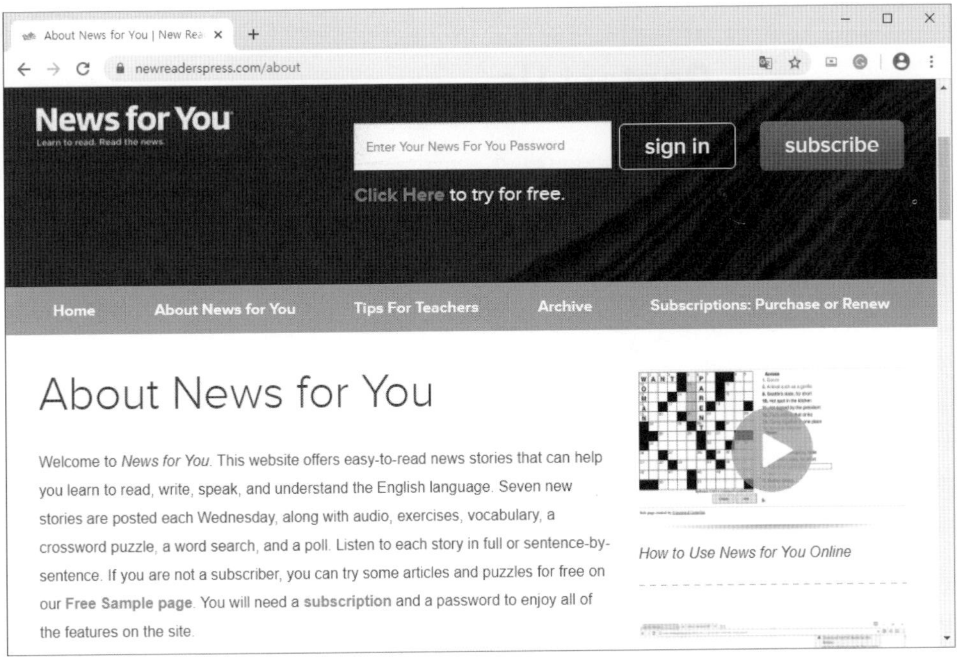

Figure 3.1 Example of aims and objectives

Administrative elements

The end-users such as teachers and students should easily access information such as the title of the program, author(s), publisher(s), the date of publication, price, service environment, program types, and other necessary administrative elements. Information on warranty and support needs to be provided as well. In the case of web content, the date of publication, author(s), or company name should be provided at the bottom of the webpage.

For information on the programming support environment, CPU (Central

Processing Unit), memory, version of OS (Operating System), video card, sound card, etc., should be provided. Moreover, information on program type such as multiple-choice, true-false, total deletion, short answers, gap-filling, sequencing, matching, simulation, etc., should be presented on the program or content. Such information can be presented on the open page of the websites or internally within the content for websites.

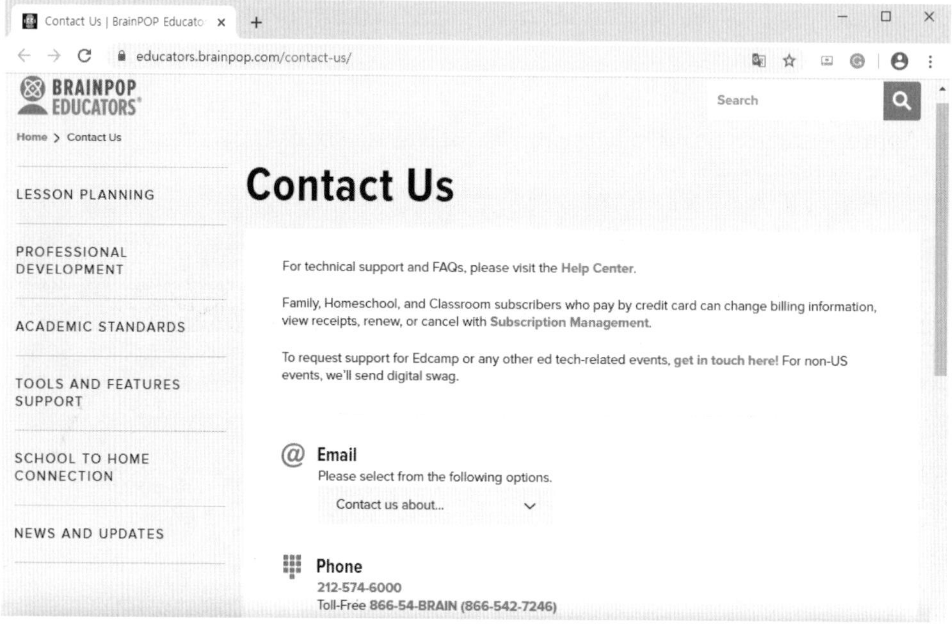

Figure 3.2 Example of administrative elements

Pedagogical elements

Evaluation for pedagogical elements includes learning objectives, learning content, feedback, and assessment. The specific details are provided as follows.

Learning objectives

The learning objectives are evaluated first in MALL content evaluations. In learning objectives, presentation of learning objectives, suitability of learning objectives for learners, suitability of learning content to learning objectives, and appropriateness of learning materials for learning objectives are evaluated.

- Presentation of learning objectives

The learning objectives of each unit of the program/content need to be provided.

- Suitability of learning objectives for learners

The learning objectives of each unit need to suit the cognitive ability and affective aspects of the learners.

- Suitability of learning content to learning objectives

The content of each unit must be appropriate for the learning objectives.

- Appropriateness of learning materials for learning objectives

The learning materials in each unit must be appropriate for the learning objectives.

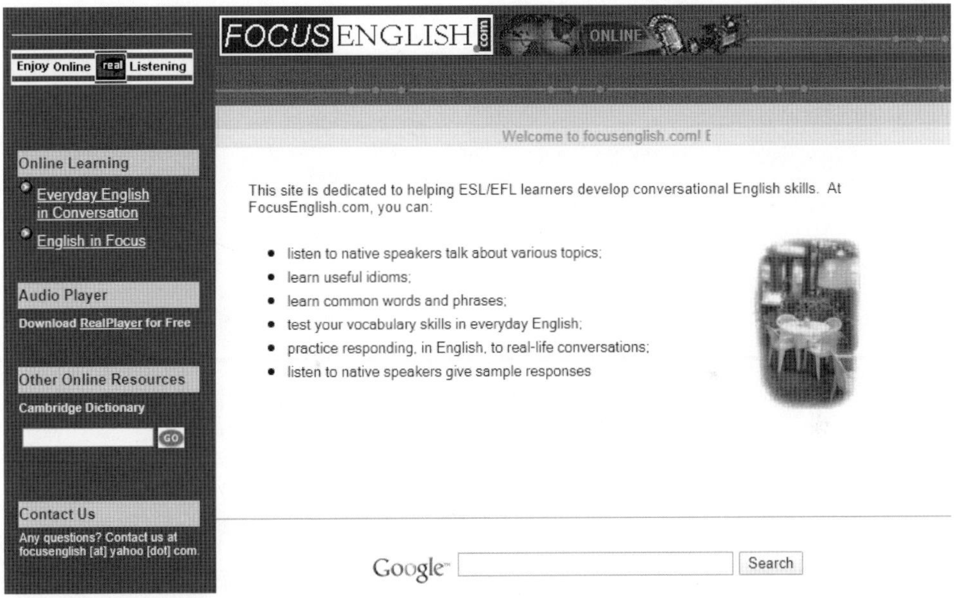

Figure 3.3 Example of learning objectives

Learning content

For evaluating learning content, the suitability of learning content for learners, the suitability of learning materials to learning content, validity in sequencing learning content, appropriateness in quantity, accuracy in learning content, the interaction between learners and learning materials, authenticity in learning content, and up-to-date information* are scrutinized.

- Suitability of learning content for learners

Learning content must be suitable for the learners' needs, age, cognitive ability, and affective domain to provide motivation and interest. It should also be easy to read and understand so that learners can engage in learning independently.

- Appropriateness of learning materials to learning content

In order to deliver learning content to learners effectively, appropriate learning materials or tools need to be selected. Appropriateness of learning materials needs to be evaluated in two folds: appropriateness of learning materials concerning the learning content and appropriateness of multimedia content such as texts, graphics, sounds, videos, etc., to the learning content.

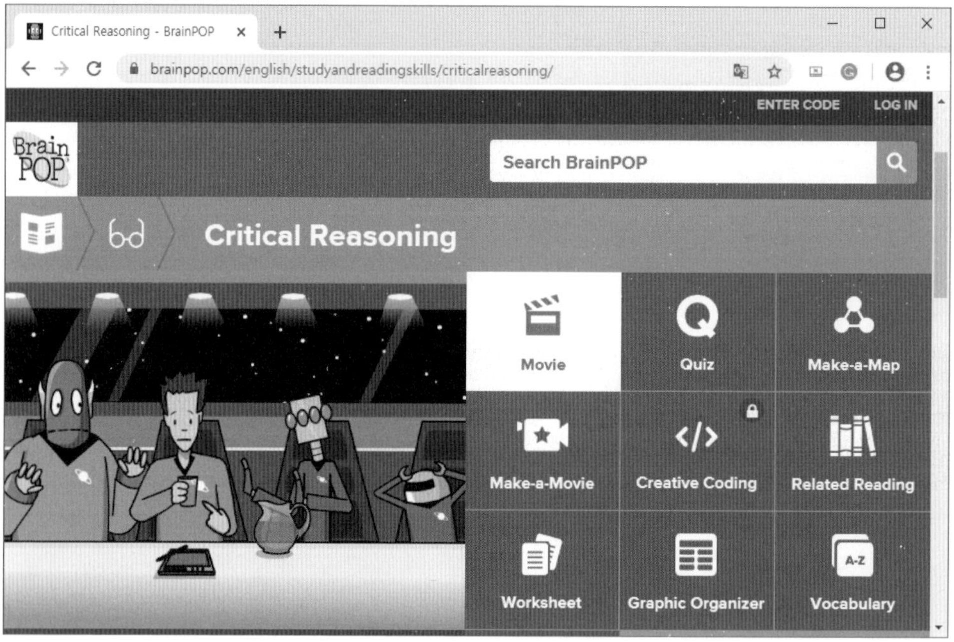

Figure 3.4 Example of learning content

- Validity in sequencing learning content

Learning content needs to be presented so that the whole pictures and details are addressed. For example, repeated practice, cognitive learning, problem solving, constructivism, etc., can be used to provide consistent and reasonable standards for learning based on sound theories of SLA and instructional design. It should be presented gradually in increments that are appropriate for learners' proficiency level to understand learning content. The program should also allow learners to navigate and choose the levels of learning content according to their learning speed and proficiency level.

▪ Appropriateness in the quantity of learning content
The quantity of learning content in each stage needs to be appropriate for learners, and the increase in quantity should be consistent. Learning aids, such as explanations, definitions, examples, images, hints, and help, need to be provided. Level-appropriate practice questions also need to be provided.

▪ Accuracy in learning content
Learning content, answers and explanation for practice questions, and learning aids, such as explanations, definitions, examples, images, hints, and help, must be accurate and be consistent with the learning goals and objectives.

▪ Interaction between learners and learning content
Learning content needs to allow various types of meaningful interaction between learner-to-learner, learner to the computer, group to the computer, group-to-group, etc.

▪ Authenticity in learning content
Learning content must have authenticity. Artificial content should be avoided considering the EFL environment in Korea. In other words, authentic materials and content should be used to promote learners' language skills and communicative competency. Such authentic learning content should also allow learners to be exposed to the target culture.

▪ Up-to-date information*
It is crucial to make sure the information on the Web is updated. The learning content should be updated regularly as well.

Feedback

The presentation of appropriate feedback, a suitable form of feedback for learners, and appropriateness in the content of feedback are evaluated.

▪ Presentation of appropriate feedback
Feedback should be provided in appropriate stages and time based on learners' progress, and the program should allow learners to monitor their progress.

▪ Suitable form of feedback for learners

Feedback needs to be given in a suitable form for the learners' age and level. For example, pictures, buttons, texts, and explanations given as feedback should be appropriate for the learners' ages and levels.

▪ Appropriateness in the content of feedback

Feedback should be given positive and tactful manner to motivate learners. 'Yes or no' type of feedback should be avoided, but feedback should cause learners to reflect and allow them to diagnose their problems and make corrections.

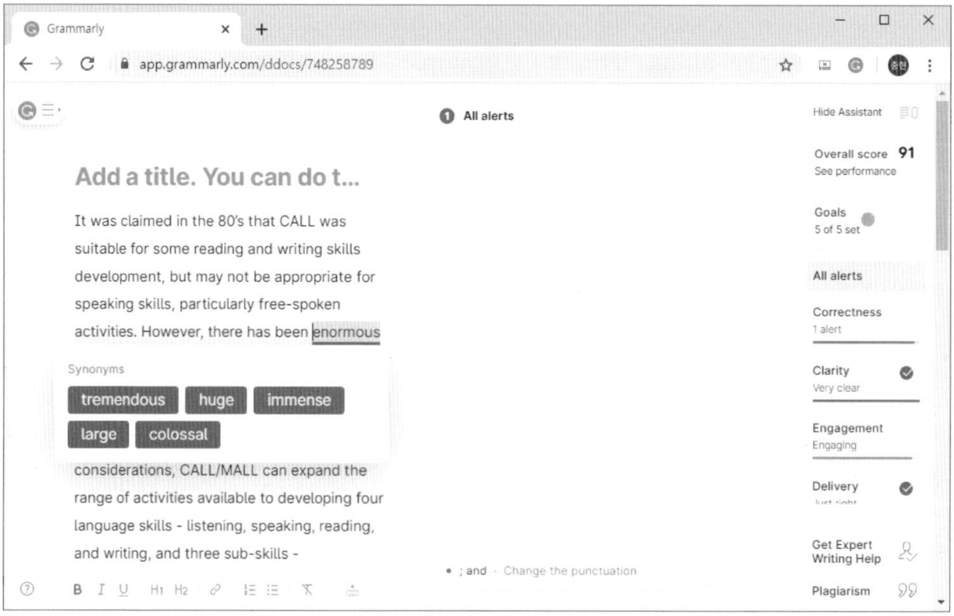

Figure 3.5 Example of presentation of appropriate feedback

▪ Accuracy in the content of feedback

Feedback must be accurate. Feedback and explanation on right answers as well as wrong answers need to be made available and should be accurate.

▪ Appropriate control over feedback

Learners and teachers should be able to control the amount and types of feedback. For example, when feedback is unnecessary, the program should allow learners or teachers to use it without feedback.

Assessment

In the assessment section, presence or absence of tests, appropriateness of test items, diversity and control over test items, and accuracy and systematic test of MALL content are evaluated.

▪ Presence or absence of tests

Pretest or diagnostic assessment should be provided, and appropriate learning content must be presented based on such assessment results. Formative assessment based on the learning content and achievement tests for summative assessment must be provided.

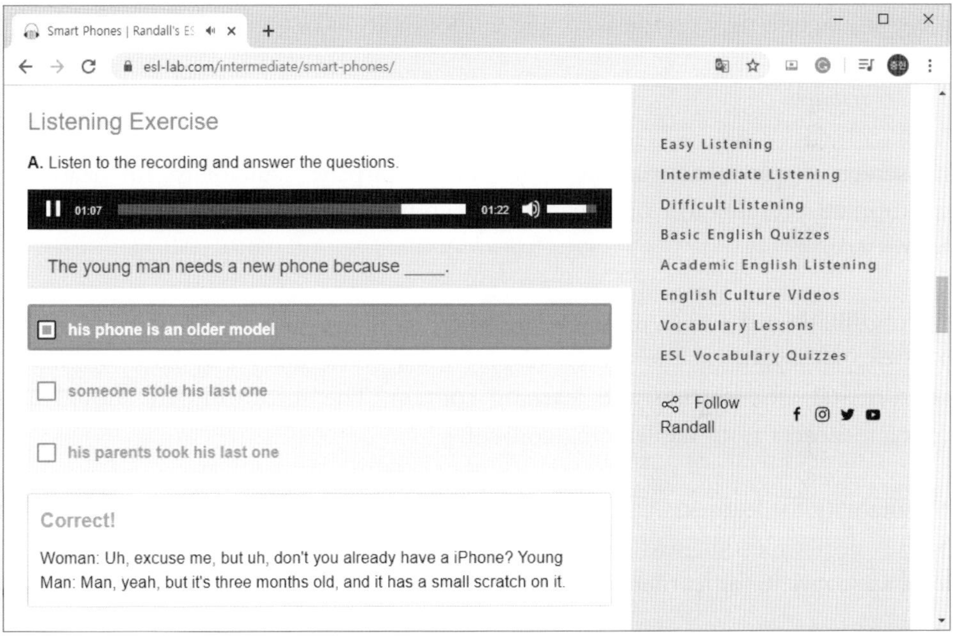

Figure 3.6 Example of tests

▪ Appropriateness of test items

Test items should be level-appropriate and must be based on the learning content of the MALL content.

▪ Diversity and control over test items

Test items should not be fixed but have diversity in types and forms. Besides, teachers or learners should control the difficulties of test items to meet learners' learning progress and levels.

- Accuracy and systematic test results

Test results and statistics must be accurate and systematic. The results should be presented in an easily understandable format using graphs, charts, tables, etc. Analyses of learners' strengths and weaknesses and suggestions for further development have to be provided as well.

Technical elements

Technical elements in MALL content evaluation mainly cover screen displays, color, sound, graphics, moving pictures, ease of use and stability, voice recognition, link-up with the Web, and authorability as main items for evaluation.

Screen displays

In screen displays, coordination of screen displays, suitability for learners, appropriate presentation of the content, and recognition of learning pace are addressed.

- Coordination of screen displays

The overall layout of the screen display must show unity and be coordinated appropriately for learners and learning content. The screen display should not distract learners from the learning content.

- Suitability for learners

Screen display, layout, text size and fonts, icon, button, etc., should be age and level appropriate for learners.

- Appropriate presentation of the content

The presentation of learning content needs to be appropriate in quantity for learners to engage efficiently in learning.

- Recognition of learning pace

Recognition of learning pace is evaluated in two folds. First, learners should be able to recognize where they are in the curriculum or program. Second, information on the learning progress the learners are making within the unit should be provided.

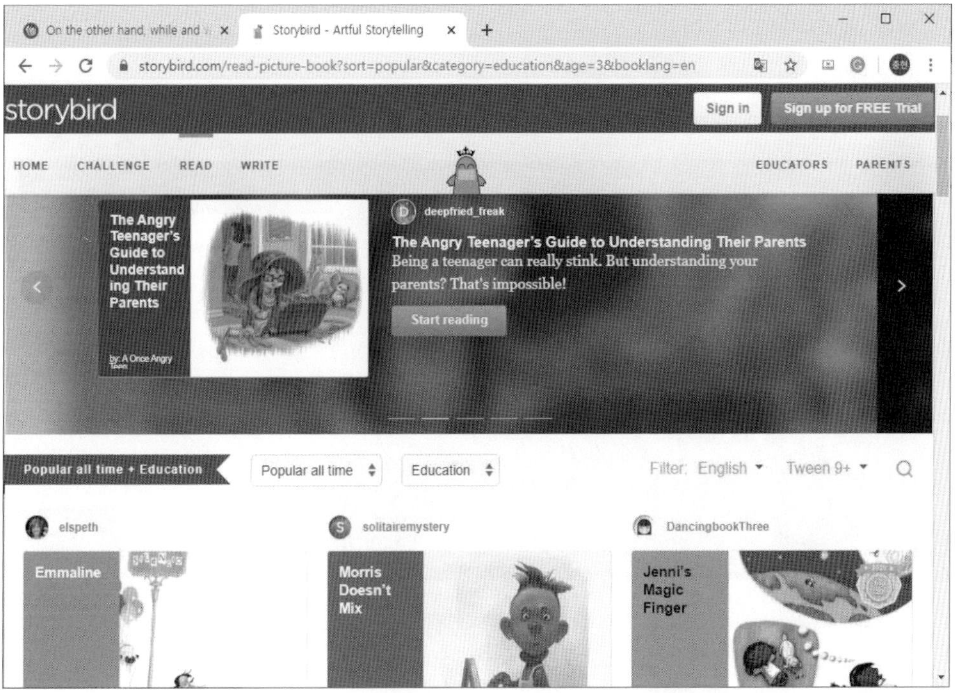

Figure 3.7 Example of screen displays

Colors, sounds, graphics, and moving pictures

▪ Suitability for learners

Colors, sounds, graphics, and moving pictures must be level and age appropriate for learners. They also should engage learners and promote continued interest in learning.

▪ Lucidity of colors, sounds, and graphics

Texts and graphics need to be clear and easy to view. Sounds and moving pictures should not stop, break, pause, etc., and be vividly presented.

▪ Effectiveness of colors, sounds, and graphics

Colors, sounds, and graphics must cause learner interest and motivate learners to engage in learning. They should ultimately be used for educational purposes.

▪ Ease of control

Teachers and learners should be able to control sounds and moving pictures. For example, control of volume, play, stop, fast forward, rewind, screen size, etc., should be made possible.

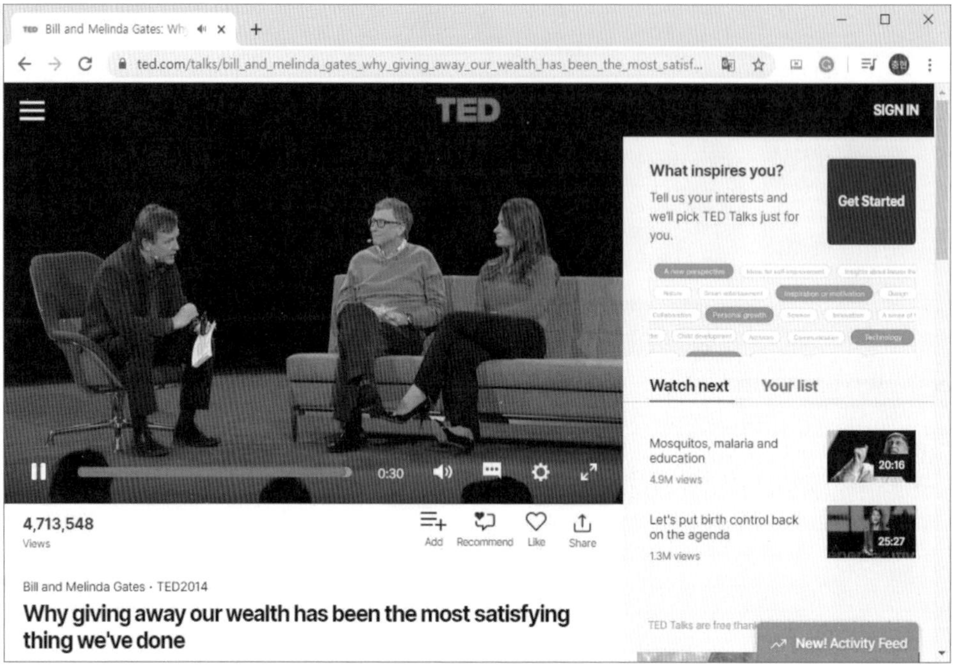

Figure 3.8 Example of colors, sounds, graphics, and moving pictures

Ease of use and stability

Ease of installation, ease of access, self-control of screen movement, closing a program, and functional stability are evaluated.

▪ Ease of installation

The program should be easy to install using a manual or guide for both teachers and learners. If the program has a USB flash drive for installing the program, it should auto-start. If the program has to be downloaded, the installation process should be automatic and straightforward.

▪ Ease of access*

Access to the Web content or starting the program should be quick and easy.

▪ Self-control of screen movement and close

Screen movement from one screen to another should be easy, and the learners should be able to check easily where they are at in the learning process or the program. Exiting and closing of the screen or the program should not be difficult.

▪ Ease of operation
Learners should be able to start the program and use it on their own. Accordingly, icons, buttons, colors, design, and layout in content should be learner appropriate and consistent. Tooltips and help buttons need to be presented on each page.

▪ Functional stability
After installing the program, the program should run without bugs.

Figure 3.9 Example of ease of use and stability

Voice (or text) recognition

The accuracy, educational effectiveness, and stability of voice recognition technology are evaluated. For the written language, the application of text recognition is evaluated.

▪ Accuracy of voice recognition technology
Voice recognition technology needs to recognize the speech accurately produced by learners.

▪ Educational effectiveness of voice recognition technology
Voice recognition technology needs to distinguish learner speech in phoneme, words, and sentence levels and provide feedback. The feedback based on voice recognition technology must be level-appropriate, consistent, and be grounded on sound theories to promote improvement.

▪ Stability of voice recognition technology
Voice recognition technology has to be stable so that it does not interrupt the learners' educational experience.

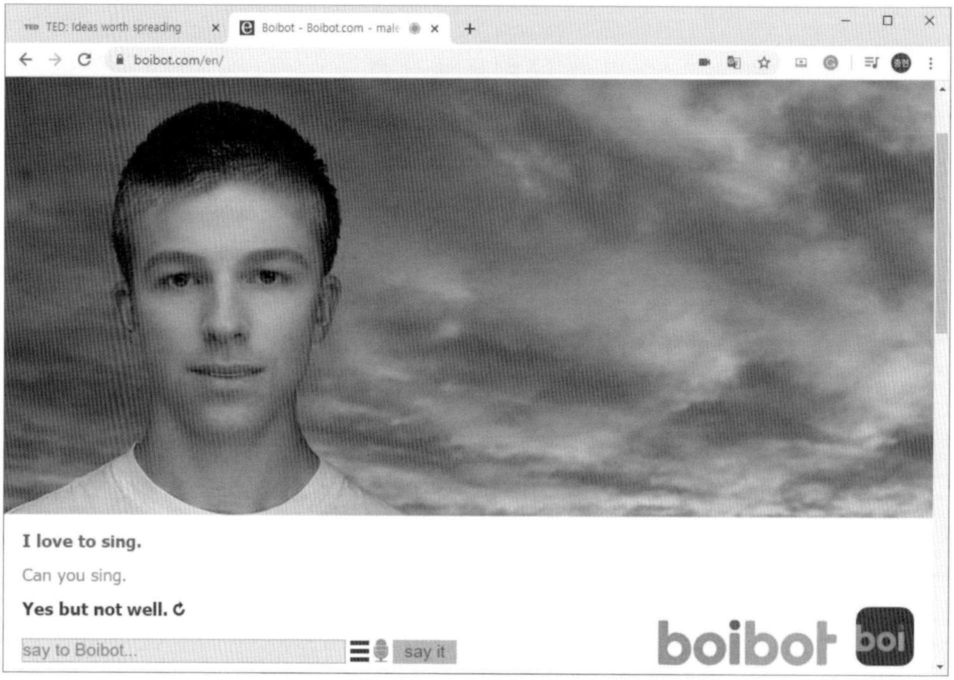

Figure 3.10 Example of voice recognition

Link-up with the Web

Link-up with the Web looks into the stability of the web connection and educational effectiveness of the web-connected materials of MALL content.

▪ Web connection and stability
MALL content should be linked with websites to provide ample learning resources to ensure supplemental and extended learning opportunities. The web connection should not distract learners from learning.

▪ Educational effectiveness of web-connected materials

MALL content should maximize the educational effectiveness of learning goals and objectives. It must be level-appropriate and be linked to useful web resources to provide learners with various resources, information, practice questions, etc. The web-connected materials should encourage learners to engage in autonomous learning.

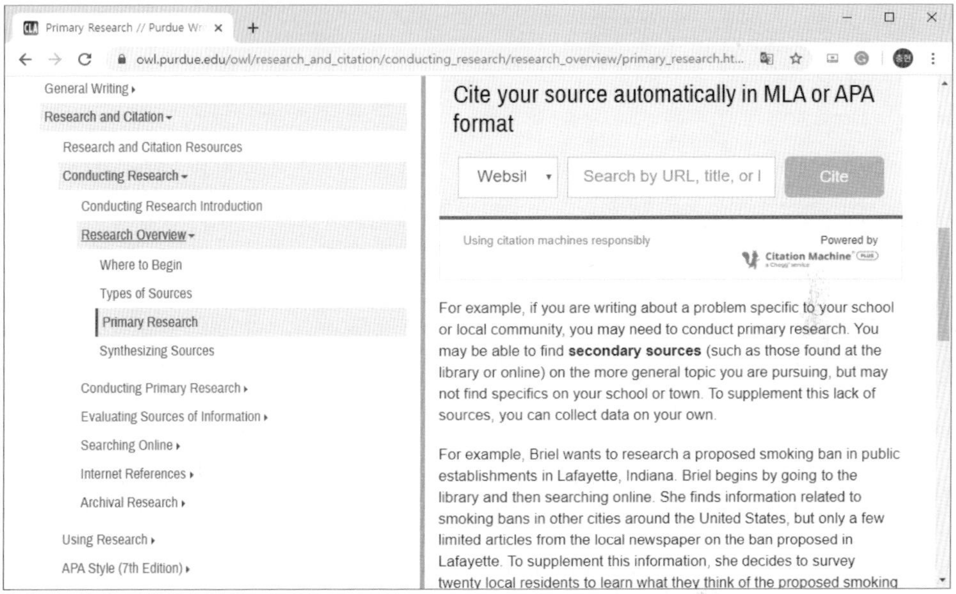

Figure 3.11 Example of the web connection

Authorability

▪ Modification or revision for program

The program should allow room for modification or revision as needed to address the aims and objectives better.

▪ Addition for program

The program should allow possible additions to the content to meet the aims and objectives.

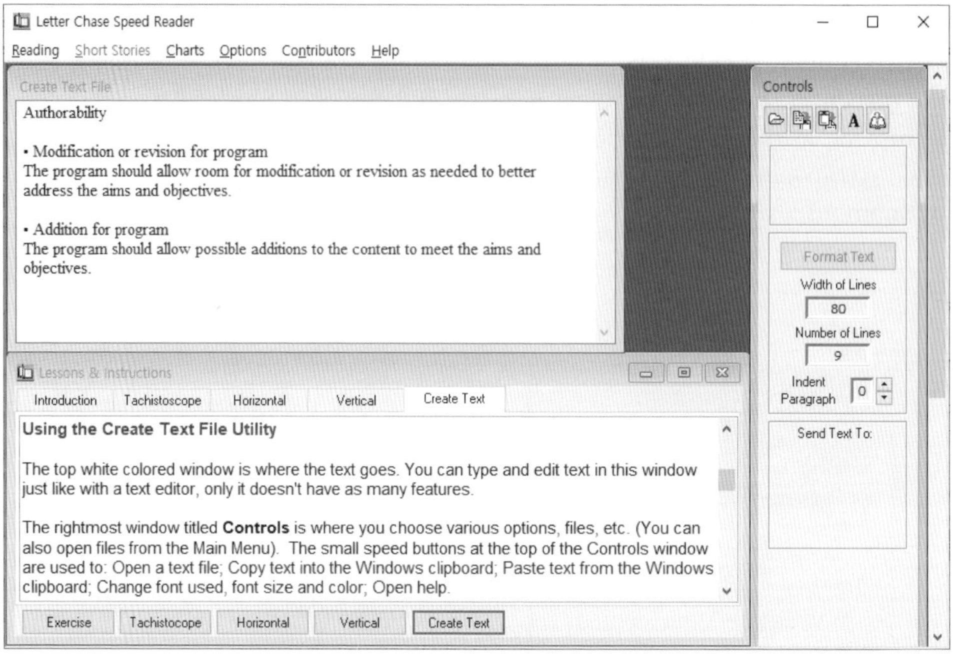

Figure 3.12 Example of authorability

Implementation and supportive elements

The suitability of supportive materials and management systems and ease of implementation are evaluated.

Suitability of supportive materials

The presence or absence of supportive materials and ease of implementation and usefulness are evaluated.

▪ Presence/absence of supportive materials
Appropriate supportive materials need to be provided, such as installation guidelines, FAQ, help, etc., in an appropriate format.

▪ Ease of implementation and usefulness
Supportive materials should be easy to implement and be useful for learning.

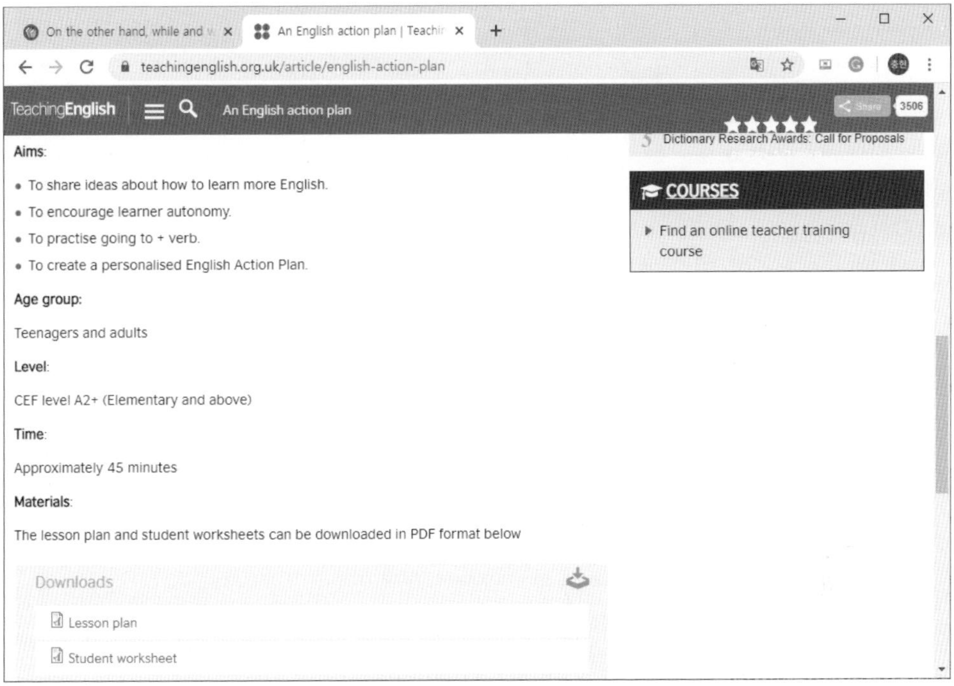

Figure 3.13 Example of suitability of supportive materials

Management system and ease of implementation

In the management system and ease of implementation, items such as a learning management system for recording, managing, and saving learners' progress are evaluated.

- Record and management of accomplishment

The program needs to provide an internal management system for recording and managing learner accomplishment and progress.

- Ease of implementation of the program

The program needs to allow level differentiated content and control of difficulty levels. Besides, the program's content, learner progress, learner accomplishment, etc., need to be printable.

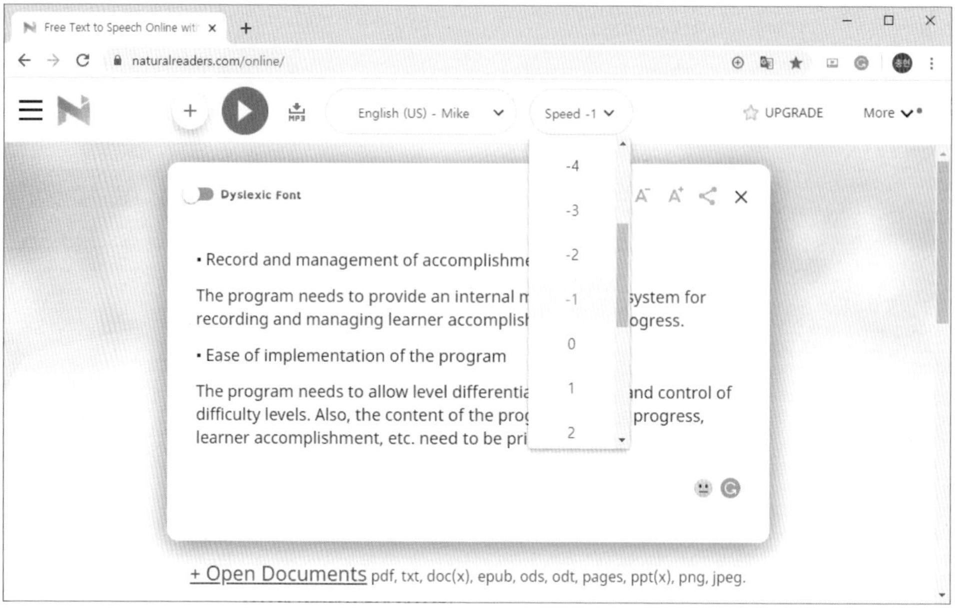

Figure 3.14 Example of suitability of management system and ease of implementation

Ethical elements

Ethical elements are evaluated for discrimination, bias, and violence, and sexually suggestive content.

Discrimination

The program's content should not contain discrimination related to gender, age, race, religion, and culture.

Bias

The program's content should not contain bias for particular notions and theories.

Violence and sexually explicit content

The program's content, including texts, sounds, images, moving pictures, etc., should not contain violence and sexually explicit content.

Access to the harmful sites

The program's content should not be connected to harmful sites.

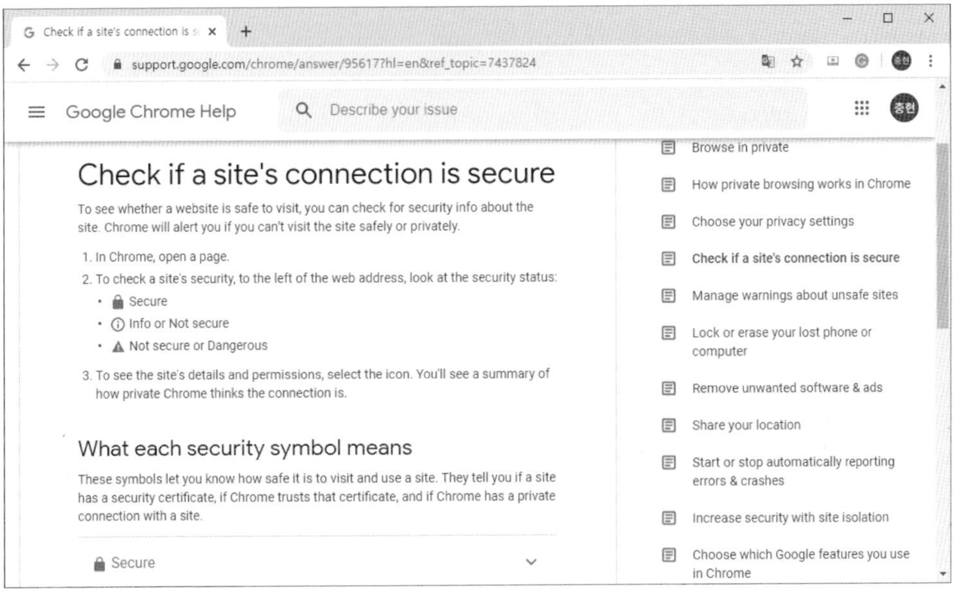

Figure 3.15 Example of ethical elements

Final assessment

In the final assessment, the evaluators describe synthetic judgment based on the quantitative and qualitative evaluation of each sub-element.

MALL Content Evaluation Checklists

Simple and comprehensive MALL content checklists based on the criteria mentioned above and elements are provided in the appendices. As mentioned earlier, there is no such thing as the perfect MALL content criteria and checklists suitable for everyone and every website or app. An evaluator of MALL content should make modifications and revisions according to program goals and objectives, needs, languages, etc. The checklists will contain formative and summative evaluation - first, quantitative evaluation for each element, and based on that, qualitative evaluation should be conducted. At the end of the evaluation process, summative and holistic evaluation should be conducted as well.

3.4 The Implementation of MALL Content Evaluation

How can one conduct MALL content evaluation efficiently using content evaluation criteria and checklists? To conduct the content evaluation using checklists while maintaining objectivity and consistency, evaluators need to be professional in making judgments and putting in time and effort into the process. This section introduces the evaluation procedure and methods that are practical and useful for content evaluators, especially teachers who need to select the appropriate content for language classes.

Evaluation Tools

There are generally three types of MALL content evaluation tools: evaluation checklists (or questionnaires), descriptive questionnaires, and interviews. Evaluation checklists allow summative assessment for each detailed aspect and function of the content as the content runs (see Appendices). It tends to be more objective than descriptive questionnaires and interviews. It should be noted that learner evaluation of content must not be overlooked, so an abridged version of the content evaluation checklist should be given to the learner to investigate their perspectives.

Evaluation Procedure and Methods

The procedure for selecting the most appropriate content for learning objectives, procedure, and syllabus is presented in Figure 3.16. First, look through the list of available MALL content that meets the curriculum standards and learning goals, and select the content to be evaluated. After selecting the content to be evaluated, an evaluation committee should be organized. The committee should consist of three or five members who have the knowledge and experience in content evaluation. If organizing a committee is difficult in the same school or institution, experienced external evaluators should be considered.

The overall procedure of content evaluation is as follows. In step 1 of the evaluation, various accompanying elements and peripheral parts are examined, followed by skimming through the entire content in step 2 for general assessment. If there are items to reconsider or re-evaluate, do so in detail in step 4. Based on quantitative and qualitative assessment gathered, the judgment on the appropriateness of the MALL content is made.

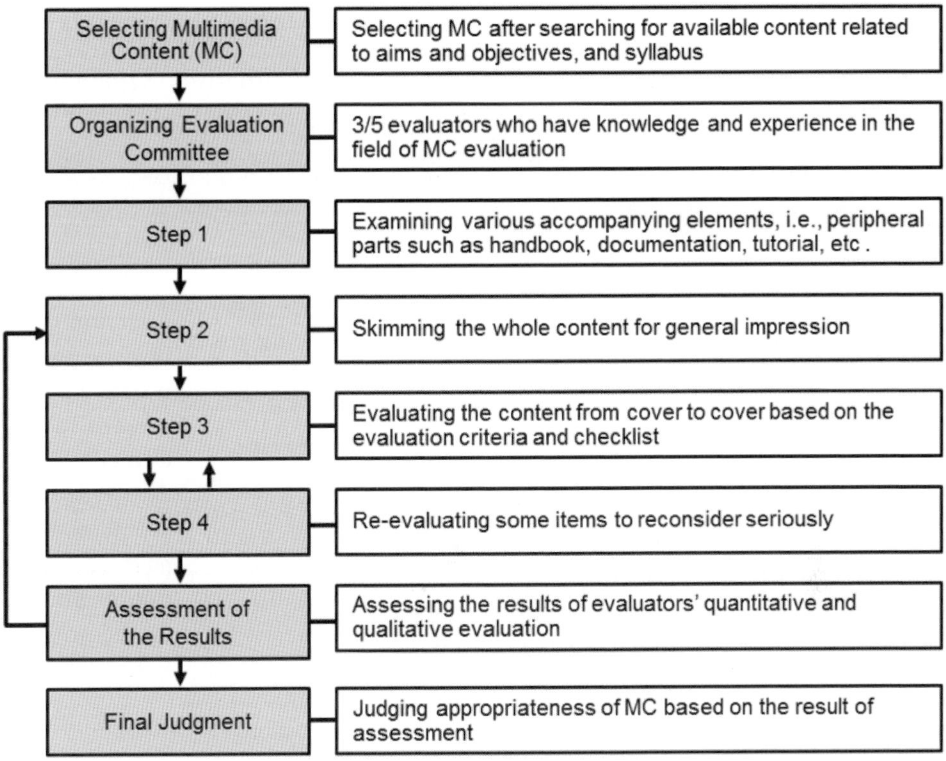

Figure 3.16 MALL content evaluation procedures

In step 3, the evaluation criteria and checklist are used for detailed and systematic assessment of the content in learning objectives, administrative, pedagogical, technical, implementational and supportive, and ethical elements. Step 3 of content evaluation uses the content evaluation checklist, which means both quantitative and qualitative assessments are conducted. With exceptions of ethical elements and the summary, numerical scores are given to each element. The ethical elements are not given a score but are evaluated based on their appropriateness. If the content receives 'inappropriateness' for ethicality, the content must be reconsidered for selection even if other elements have received high scores. The summary of evaluation criteria and elements to be evaluated is found in table 3.3. It should be noted that the scores in Table 3.3 are not absolute and can be readjusted to suit the evaluators' needs.

Table 3.3 MALL content evaluation criteria and elements, and methods

Evaluation criteria	Elements	Quantitative evaluation	Qualitative evaluation
1. Aims & Objectives	Learning and teaching goals (and objectives)	5	Description of positive and negative points of each sub-element Opinions and suggestions for improvement of the program
2. Administrative elements	Author(s), Year Published, E-mail/Homepage, etc.	5	
3. Pedagogical elements	1) Learning objectives 2) Learning content 3) Feedback 4) Assessment	8 20 12 10	
4. Technical elements	1) Screen displays 2) Colors, sounds, graphics, and moving pictures 3) Ease of use and stability 4) Voice (or text) recognition 5) Link-up with the Web 6) Authorability	5 5 6 6 4 4	
5.Implementation and supportive elements	1) Suitability of supportive materials 2) Management system and ease of implementation	4 6 (100)	
6. Ethical elements	1) Discrimination 2) Bias 3) Violence and sexually explicit content 4) Access to the harmful sites	-	Appropriateness or inappropriateness
7. Final assessment	Description of synthetic judgment based on quantitative and qualitative evaluation of each sub-element		

The items that were to be reconsidered or re-evaluated are scrutinized further in step 4. In such cases, steps 3 to 4 complement each other and are conducted to supplement each other. Then the decision for content selection is made using the results of the evaluation up to step 4. If there are differences in the scores (more than 40% in each area) within the committee members, the committee meeting is held, and the content is re-evaluated as a group. If the meeting has the same result, an external evaluator must be consulted for re-evaluation. The evaluation

results are saved and stored in the evaluation database on the school homepage or websites dealing with teaching resources, etc., to serve as valuable resources for teachers, researchers, program developers, and others related to the field.
It is essential that the evaluators must maintain consistency and objectivity. As soon as the decisions are made after the evaluation process, the process should be repeated from step 2. Re-evaluation of the content will be carried on faster than the first time around, and such the process should be repeated at least three times to ensure that consistency and objectivity were maintained. Besides, learner evaluation of the content should be conducted as well.

The MALL content evaluation procedure and methods presented in this chapter were developed for those in charge of forming evaluation committees in educational institutions. Since the procedure is laid out in detail, it seems that program developers and teachers should also use it.

3.5 Conclusion

It is found that regardless of the development and distribution of various types of computers and PLDs, most teachers cannot make the best of what is available in practice. One of the biggest reasons for the problem is identified to be the lack of relevant content that is compatible with the national curriculum as well as the actual classroom activities (C. H. Lee, 1999, 2006; Lee & Han, 2000). It does not mean, however, that the existing content is poorly developed or ineffective for use in conjunction with the textbooks in the language classrooms. It should be noted that the teachers without proper knowledge and experience in MALL content evaluation were unable to make conscious and informed choices in selecting appropriate and effective MALL content for their classrooms. The teachers, however, cannot be responsible for everything. The researchers' and specialists' responsibility is to train teachers on the importance of selecting content, developing proper content evaluation criteria and checklists, and making them available to the teachers (C. H. Lee, 2000b). Besides, domestic organizations specializing in MALL content evaluation have not accumulated and opened data related to content evaluation and evaluation procedures. Therefore, the evaluation, selection, and implementation of appropriate MALL content require all involved - teachers, professionals, and organizations or institutions - to be responsible as a team. Appropriate MALL content must be selected to be compatible with the learning goals and meet EFL classrooms' needs. The systematic and objective evaluation also needs to be conducted based on the content evaluation checklists following a proper procedure. When the appropriate content is selected and implemented based on proper criteria and procedures followed by the effective teaching methodology, teachers can expect learners to develop desired language skills in language classes.

For recognizing the value and importance of MALL content evaluation, this chapter introduces simple and comprehensive content evaluation criteria and checklists appropriate for EFL classes in Korea based on previous research. The evaluation procedures, from selecting content for evaluation to decision-making based on the evaluation result, are provided. It is hoped that MALL content developers, teachers, and MALL specialists can take the content criteria and checklists, and procedures apply them in EFL classes or their specific areas as needed. However, it should be kept in mind that as computer technologies go through rapid changes and development, MALL evaluation criteria and checklists should also be updated from time to time.

In conclusion, the teachers in current EFL classes are more multimedia friendly and aware than before. Many of them are pretty knowledgeable and experienced in using computers and PLDs. It is recommended that for those teachers, conducting MALL content evaluation independently and making independent judgments based on objective results may serve to suit their classrooms instead of solely relying on external information provided. They should be encouraged to make full use of the demo version to evaluate the content before selection. Moreover, to empower the teachers, teacher training and workshop should be conducted to provide knowledge and experience in MALL content evaluation through theory and actual practice. MALL content developers, organizations for the content evaluation, MEST, provincial offices of education, and others should make databases, resources, and facilities available for teachers to evaluate the content and refer to previous evaluations conducted.

Tasks for Study and Discussion

1. What kinds of courseware evaluation criteria and frameworks are out there, and are they appropriate for the present state of FLT&L?

2. What should proper courseware evaluation criteria and checklists cover, and how should they be organized?

3. What is the effective and efficient procedure for carrying out courseware evaluation?

4. Read over the criteria for evaluating MALL content. Do you need to make any modifications? Using the modified criteria, evaluate one of the MALL programs and content such as websites and apps.

5. As the newly appointed MALL expert in an educational institution of your choice (a primary or secondary school, a private institution, etc.), you have been asked to select up to some MALL programs and content to purchase for your institution. Describe the institution briefly, then write down:
   1) What programs do you want to buy?
   2) What would you need to ensure that the programs are used effectively?

6. How can teachers make the best use of the MALL content evaluation form in using web content in their classes?

7. Organize a MALL content evaluation committee and select one of the MALL programs and content to evaluate. Consider the following points.
   1) Are the members well aware of the purposes and the procedures of evaluating the program and content?
   2) Do the members thoroughly understand all the details of the program and content?
   3) What changes should be made to the evaluation category and weight given to each category or sub-category to evaluate the target program and content better?

Appendices: MALL Content Evaluation Checklists

Appendix 1 Simple Evaluation Checklist for MALL

- Evaluator:
- E-mail:
- Date:
- Institution:
- Address/Phone number

Evaluation criteria	Elements	Quantitative evaluation	Qualitative evaluation
1. Aims & Objectives (5)	Learning and teaching goals (objectives)	/5	
2. Administrative elements (5)	Author(s), year published, e-mail/homepage, etc.	/5	
3. Pedagogical elements (50)	1) Learning objectives 2) Learning content 3) Feedback 4) Assessment	/8 /20 /12 /10	
4. Technical elements (30)	1) Screen displays 2) Colors, sounds, graphics, and moving pictures 3) Ease of use and stability 4) Voice (or text) recognition 5) Link-up with the Web 6) Authorability	/5 /5 /6 /6 /4 /4	
5.Implementation and supportive elements (10)	1) Suitability of supportive materials 2) Management system and ease of implementation	/4 /6	
6. Ethical elements	1) Discrimination 2) Bias 3) Violence and sexually explicit content 4) Access to the harmful sites	-	
7. Final assessment	Total: /100		

Ratings:

■ Excellent: Over 90, ■ Good: 80-89, ■ Fair: 60-79, ■ Not Good: Under 59

Appendix 2 Comprehensive Evaluation Checklist for MALL

- Evaluator:
- E-mail:
- Date:
- Institution:
- Address/Phone number

1) Aims and objectives (5 points)				
Presentation of the objectives	**Presence**		**Absence**	
Aims and objectives				
Remarks				
Qualitative evaluation:				
Score				

2) Administrative elements (5)			
Content	Presence	Details	Absence
Title			
Author(s)			
Publisher			
Year published			
Update information			
Address/Tel			
Email/ Homepage			
Hardware support needed			
Program type			
Price			
Remarks			
Qualitative evaluation:			
Score			

3) Pedagogical elements (50)			
Content (Details)		**Score**	**Comments**
Learning objectives (8)	Presentation of learning objectives (2)		
	Suitability of learning objectives for learners (2)		
	Suitability of learning content to learning objectives (2)		
	Appropriateness of learning materials for learning objectives (2)		
Learning content (22)	Suitability of learning content for learners (2)		
	Appropriateness of learning materials to learning content (2)		
	Validity in sequencing learning content (4)		
	Appropriateness in the quantity of learning content (4)		
	Accuracy in learning content (3)		
	Interaction between learners and learning content (3)		
	Authenticity in learning content (4) Up-to-date information* (4)		

Feedback (10)	Presentation of appropriate feedback (2)		
	Suitable form of feedback for learners (2)		
	Appropriateness in the content of feedback (2)		
	Accuracy in the content of feedback (2)		
	Appropriate control over feedback (2)		
Assessment (10)	Presence or absence of tests (2)		
	Appropriateness of test items (3)		
	Diversity and control over test items (2)		
	Accuracy and systematic test result (3)		
Qualitative evaluation:			
Score			

4) Technical elements (30)			
Content (Details)		**Score**	**Comments**
Screen displays (5)	Coordination of screen displays (1)		
	Suitability for learners (1)		
	Appropriate presentation of the content (2)		
	Recognition of learning pace (1)		
Colors, sounds, graphics, and moving pictures (5)	Suitability for learners (1)		
	Lucidity of colors, sounds, and graphics (1)		
	Effectiveness of colors, sounds, and graphics (2)		
	Ease of control (1)		
Ease of use and stability (6)	Ease of installation (USB flash drives) (2) Ease of access (2)*		
	Self-control of screen movement and close (1)		
	Ease of operation (2)		
	Functional stability (1)		

Voice (or text) recognition (6)	Accuracy of voice recognition technology (2)		
	Educational effectiveness of voice recognition technology (2)		
	Stability of voice recognition technology (2)		
Link-up with the Web (4)	Web connection and stability (2)		
	Educational effectiveness of web-connected materials (2)		
Authorability (4)	Modification or revision for program (2)		
	Addition for program (2)		
Qualitative evaluation:			
Score			

5) Implementation and supportive elements (10)			
Content (Details)		**Score**	**Comments**
Suitability of supportive materials (4)	Presence/absence of supportive materials (2)		
	Ease of implementation and usefulness (2)		
Management system and ease of implementation (6)	Record and management of accomplishment (3)		
	Ease of implementation of the program (3)		
Qualitative evaluation:			
Score			

6) Ethical Elements		
Content (Details)	**Appropriateness or inappropriateness**	**Comments**
Discrimination for gender, age, race, region, and culture		
Bias for particular notion and theory		
Violence and sexually explicit content		
Access to the harmful sites		
Qualitative evaluation:		
Appropriateness		

Final assessment	
Final score	

Ratings:
- Excellent: Over 90, ▪ Good: 80-89, ▪ Fair: 60-79, ▪ Not Good: Under 59

'*': For evaluation of websites

Part 2

Hands-on Practice of Editing, Authoring, and Learning Tools

Part 2
Hands-on Practice of Editing, Authoring, and Learning Tools

Cutting-edge technologies such as computers, PLDs, the Web, SNS, CMC technology, speech recognition technology, etc., appear to be available now to some extent at all school levels in Korea. The majority of teachers and students have recently realized the potential and value of the technologies to assist in the preparation, management, and organization of lesson and teaching materials and have used them in language classes for students' spoken and written skills development (C. H. Lee, 1998a, 2006, 2017; Wilson, 1990; Yoon, Lee, & Lee, 2013).

Despite the potential, increased availability, and value of the technologies, teachers' actual use of the technologies in language classes tends to be still low. C. H. Lee (2002) reported that some problems such as lack of knowledge, i.e., knowledge of how they work and how they can be used for FLT&L, lack of experience, and lack of teacher training appear to inhibit the more extensive and successful use of the technologies in language classes.

Technical and pedagogical preparations are the main factors for the successful use of computers in FLT&L. In terms of technical preparation, the teachers should know how the computers work and are familiar with the hardware by either reading the manual or seeking technicians' or experts' help. The teachers have to practice all the necessary properties, functions, and techniques of hardware until they know how the hardware works and feel familiar with using them (Allan, 1985). In short, the teachers do not have to be technical experts or programmers but need to handle the technology and have it under control. In terms of pedagogical preparation, the teachers will always keep in mind whether or not multimedia content is suitable for specific tasks or situations (Windeatt, 1990). The content can be integrated into various syllabi, tasks, and activities in FLT&L. Flexible and imaginative methodological approaches will compensate for any lack of suitable learning content. Therefore, the teachers will need more preparation to integrate new technologies into their existing teaching practices. Although some argued whether it is necessary for teachers to have computer skills for effective teaching or not, computer literacy is necessary for teachers who want to use the technologies effectively in FLT&L (Higgins, 1985; Lian, 1992; Skehan, 1985; Windeatt, Hardisty, & Eastment, 2000). Computer literacy can be defined as knowledge and an understanding of computers (hardware and software) combined with the ability to use them effectively for one's purposes in FLT&L (Ariew & Frommer, 1987; Richards, Platt, & Platt, 1992). This definition of computer literacy may be broad for the teachers since computers require different levels of expertise in the contexts of FLT&L, and questions arise on what kind of computer literacy teachers should have in language classes. Researchers pointed out that the teachers do not need to know everything about programming or the inner workings of a computer, but they need to be familiar with the operation of hardware and software so that they can rely on high-quality software and learn editing and authoring tools (Higgins & Johns, 1984; C. H. Lee, 2002; Skehan, 1985; Windeatt, 1990; Wyatt, 1984; Yoon, Lee, & Lee, 2013). In short, the teachers should have working knowledge and understanding of cutting-edge technologies and content and learn about how the technologies can be used as tools and learning resources for their students in foreign language classes.

Part 2 introduces popular and useful editing and authoring tools, including web content which are available for FLT&L, and presents written tutorials for the main tools to help teachers and students get started quickly and efficiently as follows: 1) words & texts (*Tagxedo* and *Class Card*); 2) images (*Snagit* and *PhotoScape X*); 3) cartoons (*Make Beliefs Comix*); 4) sounds (*Goldwave* and *1gram player*); 5) videos (*Gom Cam, Camtasia,* and *Gom Mix Pro*); 6) animations (*Animaker*); 7) authoring tools (*Hot Potatoes*); and 8) other learning tools such as LMS (*Classting*), a communication and collaboration platform (*Microsoft Teams, Flipgrid,* and *Padlet*), grammar and plagiarism checker (*Grammarly*), mind map (*OKMindmap*), and corpus (*Compleat Lexical Tutor*), a free reference manager (*Mendeley*), etc.

Chapter 4

Editing Tools I: Words & Texts, Images, and Cartoons

4.1 Words and Texts

A large majority of information and data on the Internet are words and texts. It makes the Internet one of the best resources of texts for teaching and learning purposes. Original texts from the Internet or the Web usually require editing to suit the classroom needs, and it takes little effort. First, teachers and students can easily search appropriate texts from websites such as *PBS Newshour* (https://www.pbs.org/newshour), *Reader's Digest* (https://www.rd.com), etc., and select a part of the text or the whole text. Then, they can copy and paste onto other programs such as word processors and presentation programs.

Figure 4.1 The main screen of *Reader's digest*

Text-based learning tools that can be applied to language teaching and learning include word clouds tools. The majority of word cloud tools enable users to enter a text or word bundle, select shapes and colors, and even share through SNS. The following are easily accessible word cloud tools: *TagCrowd* (https://

tagcrowd.com), *Tagxedo* (https://www.tagxedo.com), *Word Art* (https://wordart.com/), *WordItOut* (https://worditout.com), etc. Besides, *Classcard* (https://www.classcard.net) and *Quizlet* (https://quizlet.com) offer genuine platforms for creating word-cards and texts.

Tagxedo

Tagxedo (http://www.tagxedo.com) is a tool that turns words and text into various forms of a word cloud. Words are individually sized and displayed to stand out according to the frequencies of occurrence within the body of texts. How *Tagxedo* can be utilized for language skills development is up to the teachers, but artistic elements can capture learners' imagination and interest. Words being sized according to the frequency of occurrence can facilitate certain activities as part of a class. For example, in a listening activity, a word cloud of vocabulary items to listen can be provided to learners. Learners can use the word cloud to make predictions on the content to listen to can be a proper pre-listening activity to activate learners' schema using words. Figure 4.2 is the main screen of *Tagxedo*. The detailed steps to create your word cloud are as follows.

1) Click 'Create' to get the program started and move to the next window.

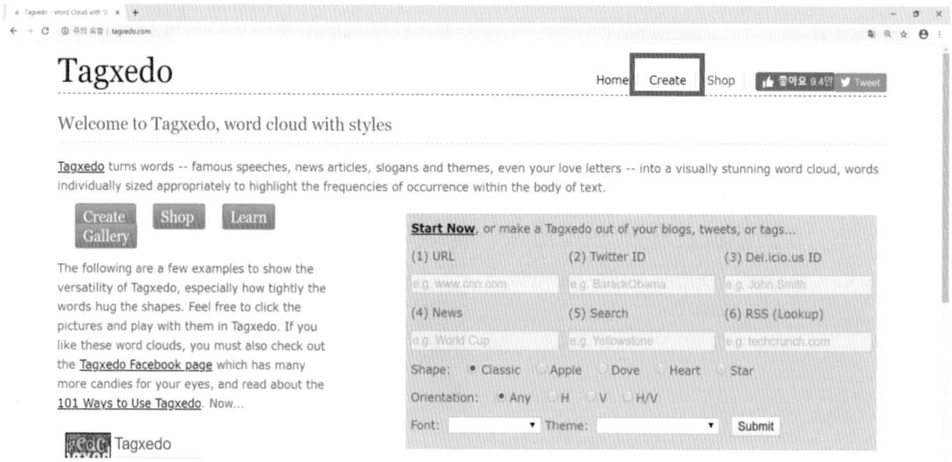

Figure 4.2 The main screen of *Tagxedo*

2) Click 'Load' in the menu to enter a text. Texts can be imported from other sources, XAP, and webpages. Write down words and texts or copy and paste them into the box.

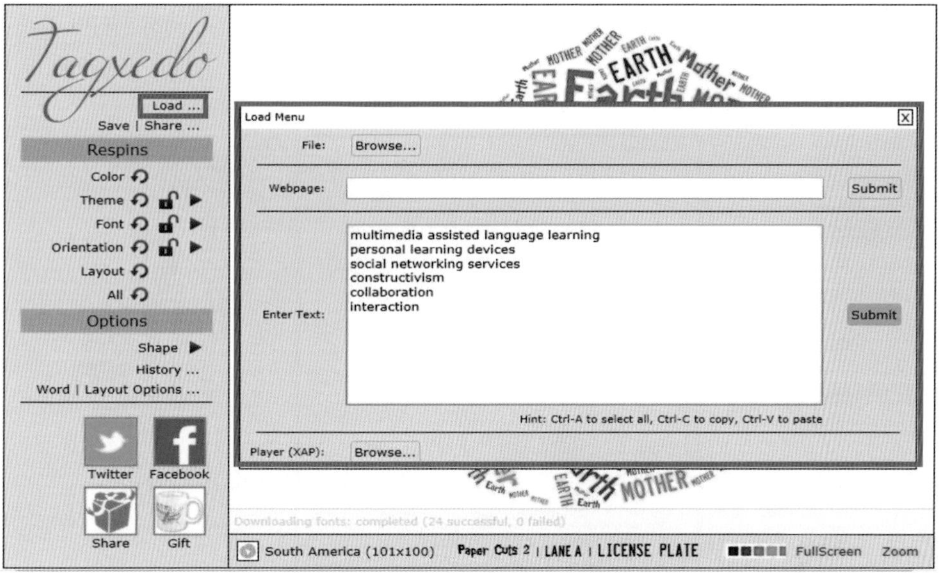

3) Configure the conditions by selecting the options including color, theme, font, orientation (direction), layout, and shape of the cloud to meet your preferences and needs.

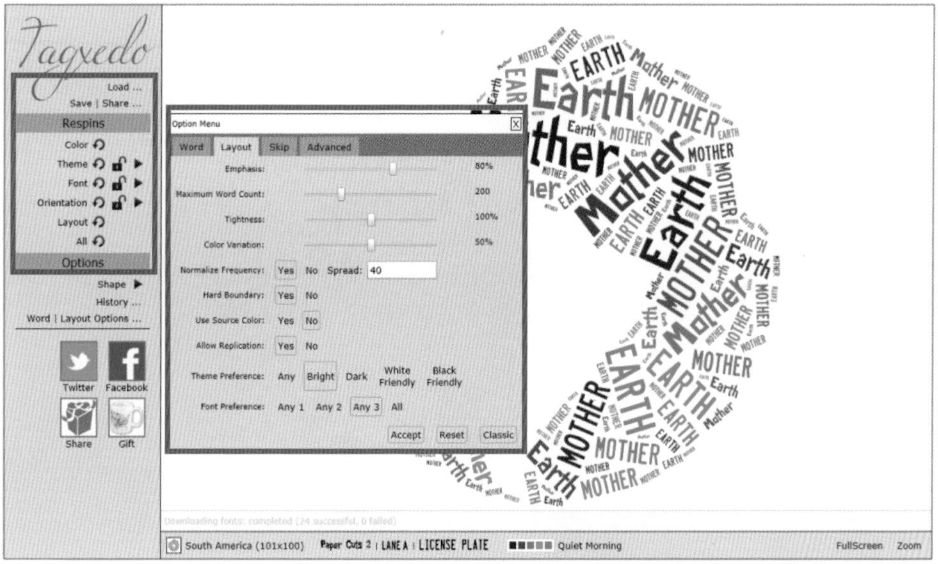

For example, click 'Shape,' and you can choose an image from 'Shape Menu.'

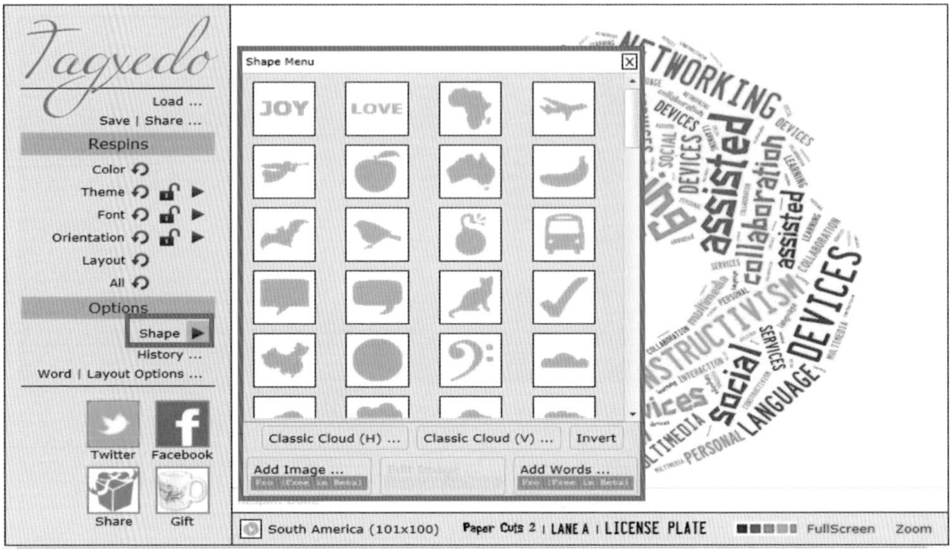

4) Words and general layout can be changed. For example, the 'Skip' function displays word frequency, and words can be deleted if not needed. The same goes for punctuation marks (comma, period, etc.).

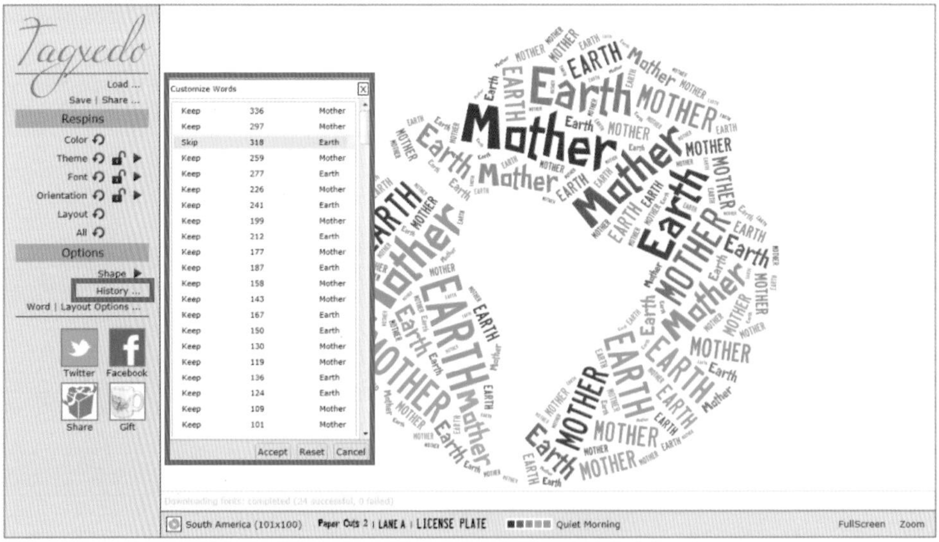

Class Card

Classcard (https://www.classcard.net/) is a website that helps language teachers create various English word-cards for improving learners' word knowledge. *Classcard* is suitable for those teachers teaching elementary and secondary school students as it offers multiple word-cards in English textbooks used in that of levels. This website allows teachers to create their word-cards for students to learn English words through various customizing functions. The customizable word-card functions include Word Set, Sentence Set, Drill Set, and Terminology Set. If word-lists are prepared to create new word-cards, it is easy to produce new word-cards by cut and paste those lists into the website. Moreover, considering the students' level (e.g., elementary, middle, high school level), teachers can extract words from authentic reading materials they want to deal with in their language classes. Based on the content of prepared word-cards, quizzes can also be made to check the students' achievement. The detailed steps for creating your word-cards are as follows.

1) Click [+세트 만들기] (new set) to create Word Set, Sentence Set, Drill Set, and Terminology Set.

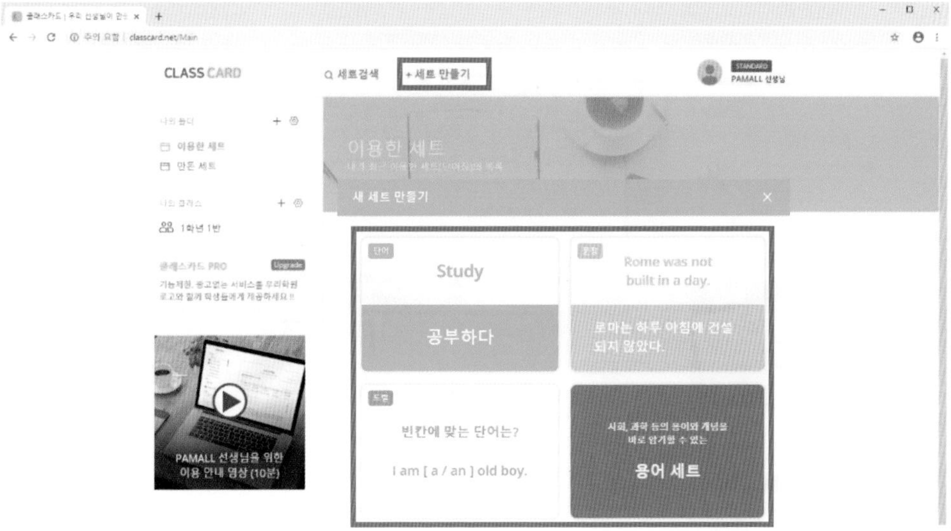

2) Type words and their meanings into boxes or click [엑셀, 한글자료 가져오기] (open Excel files) to create new word cards. If you want to extract words from reading texts, click [본문 단어 추출하기] (the extract words) link to open editing box.

Then, copy and paste the materials you want to extract words and select your students' level.

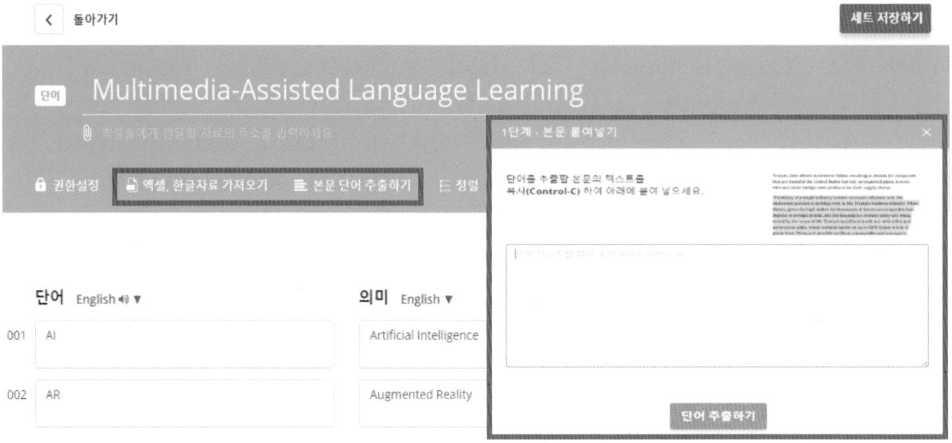

3) After creating the new word-set, you can share it with your students by clicking a 클래스에 추가 (add to class) link in the middle to add the new set in your class on *ClassCard* website.

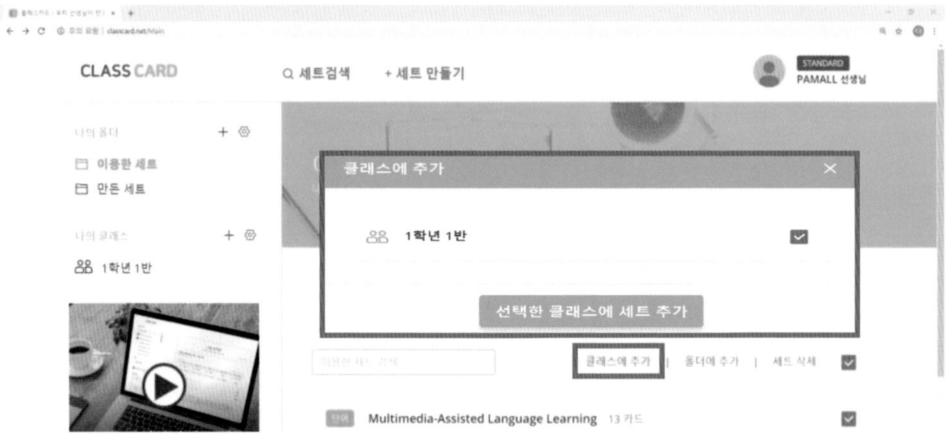

Tasks for Study and Discussion

- Create a vocabulary activity for intermediate level students using *Tagxedo*. Make sure to use various options to customize the word cloud to the goals and objectives of your lesson. Work individually and then share your work with your partners.

*** Sample of vocabulary activity: Vocabulary on Nutrition**

- Objectives: Students will be able to produce word-clouds and images on nutrition for learning vocabulary.

4.2 Images

Images are one of the essential parts of MALL content in FLT&L. They can be easily copied or imported from websites/webpages and apps to the documents of word processors, presentation programs, or SNS. The Internet or the Web provides an enormous amount of images that can be downloaded for FLT&L use.

There are several types of images, such as Bitmap (BMP), Graphics Interface Format (GIF), Joint Picture Experts Group (JPEG), Personal Computer exchange (PCX), and Tag Image File (TIF). First, BMP is "a type of memory organization or image file format used to store digital images. The term *bitmap* comes from the computer programming terminology, meaning just a map of bits, a spatially mapped array of bits" (https://en.wikipedia.org/wiki/Bitmap). Second, GIF is a bitmap image format introduced by CompuServe in 1987 and has gained popularity on the Web due to its wide-ranging support and portability. It is well-suited for more explicit images such as graphics or logos with solid colors (https://en.wikipedia.org/wiki/GIF). Last, JPEG is "a commonly used method of lossy compression for digital images" (https://en.wikipedia.org/wiki/JPEG), particularly for digital photographs. JPEG is one of the most frequently used image formats for digital cameras and other image capture devices. It is one of the most common formats for storing and transmitting photographic images on the Web (https://en.wikipedia.org/wiki/JPEG).

There are various graphic tools which can be downloaded on computers along with manuals and demo versions such as *Adobe Photoshop CC* (http://www.adobe.com), *Illustrator* (https://creative.adobe.com), *Online Image Editor* (http://www.online-image-editor.com), *PIXLR* (https://pixlr.com), *PhotoScape X* (http://x.photoscape.org/), *Snagit* (https://www.techsmith.com/ snagit.html), etc. First of all, saving images or photos from the Web is simple: 1) Place the mouse curser on the image of your choice and click the right button; 2) Save the image as "save image as;" and 3) Select the type of image files and save it.

Figure 4.3 How to save images from the website

Snagit

Snagit (https://www.techsmith.com/snagit.html) is a tool for capturing and editing various multimedia, including texts, images, and moving pictures. *Snagit* allows exporting the edited multimedia content to word processors, presentation programs, or SNS. Its trial version is downloadable from its homepage along with a demo video tutorial with detailed manuals. *Snagit* comprises two parts: the installed camera for capturing an image and recording a video. (See video and written tutorials for *Snagit* and the previous version, https://www.techsmith.com/tutorial-snagit-current.html)

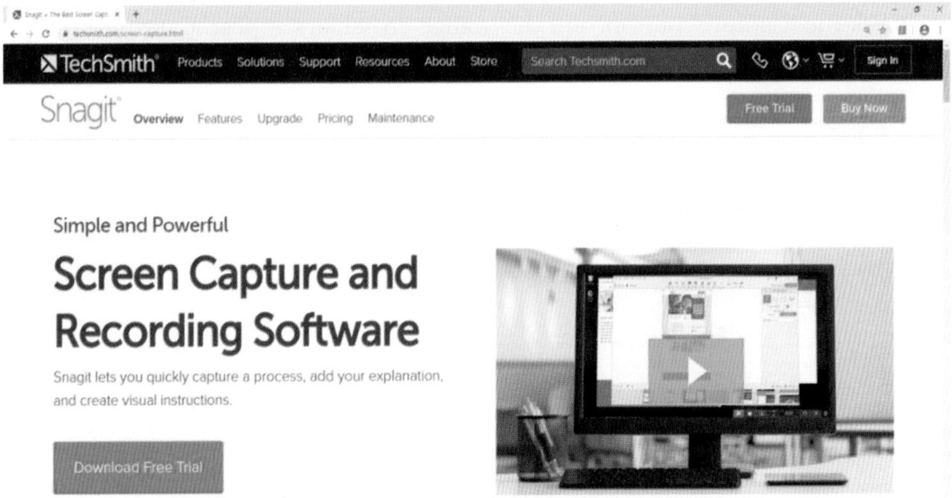

Figure 4.4 The main screen of *Snagit*

1) Place the mouse cursor on the *Snagit* software on the computer screen, and the simplified camera combined with editor shows up as below.
2) Choose a proper function based on your purposes of using a program, which includes All-in-one, Image, and Video.
3) The 'All-in-one' function helps users use either a capture or record tool in a customized area.

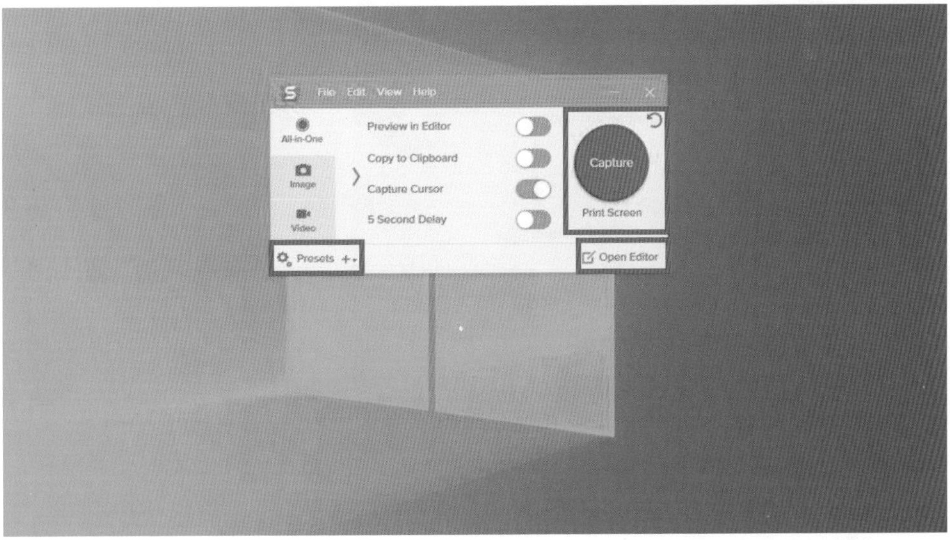

4) Click the 'Capture' button, and the orange crosshairs appear. Capture a region, a window, a full screen, or a scrolling window.

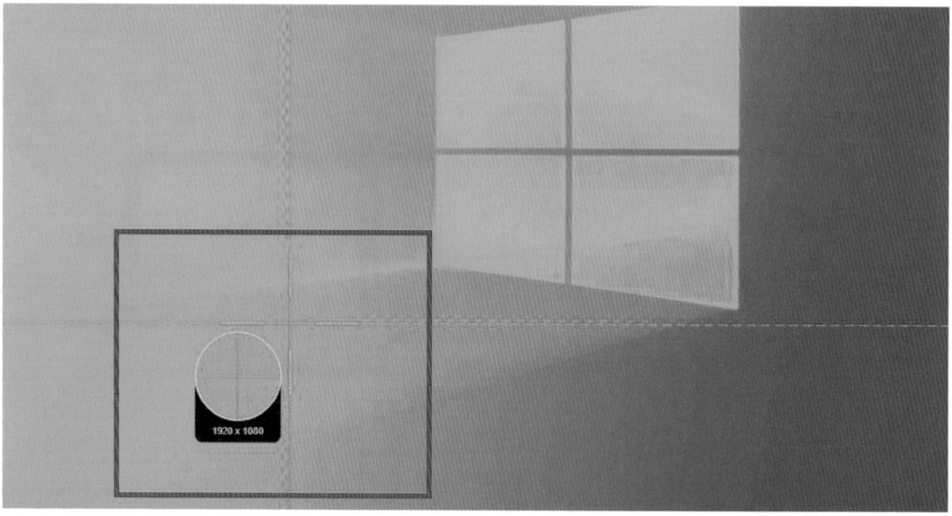

5) To edit, click on the 'Editor' on the left or manually open images from saved files. A captured image will automatically show up.

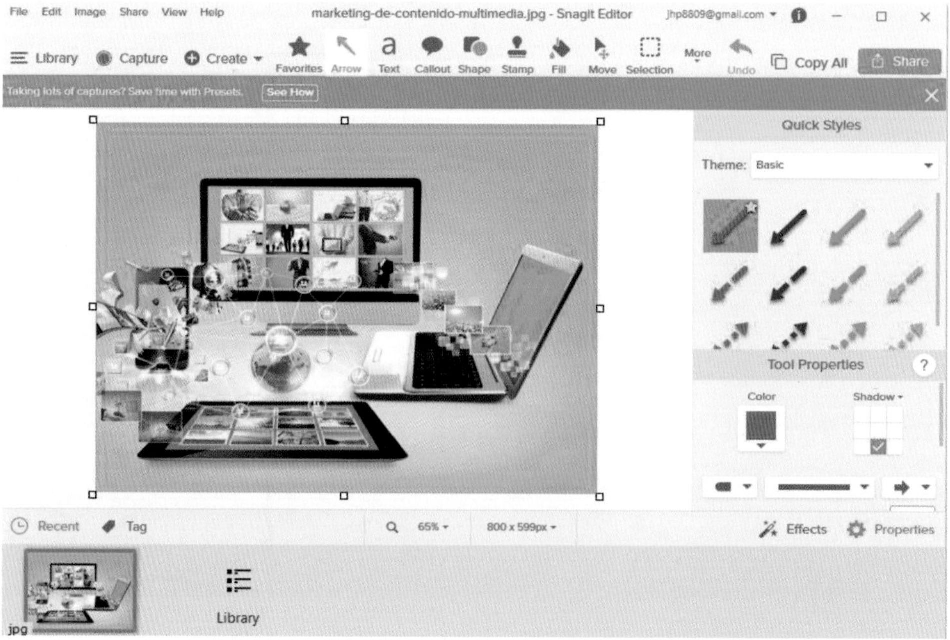

6) Use drawing tools and select styles to edit images.

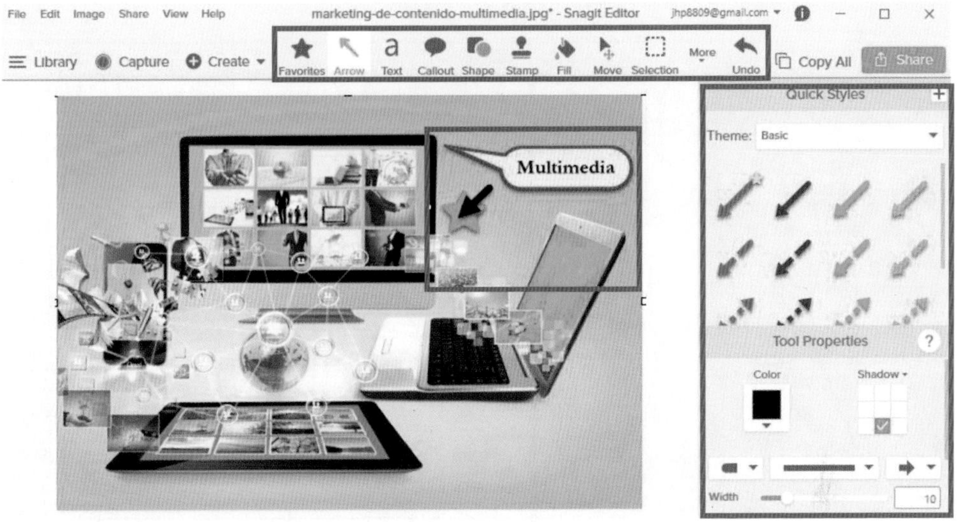

PhotoScape

PhotoScape (http://x.photoscape.org/) is a photo editing software that allows users to fix and enhance pictures in producing a plethora of multimedia content. Teachers can use the software considering the purpose of activities in language classes. The latest version, *PhotoScape X,* is downloadable free of charge. *PhotoScape X* provides diverse modules as follows: viewser, editor, cut out, batch, collage, combine, create GIF, print, screen capture, and color picker. Detailed manuals for each module are offered on its webpage (https://x.photoscape.org/help.php).

1) Refer to the box in the middle for the information on OS compatibility. Click the download button and install the software.

2) Double click the *PhotoScape X* icon to run the program and press the 'Viewer' button.

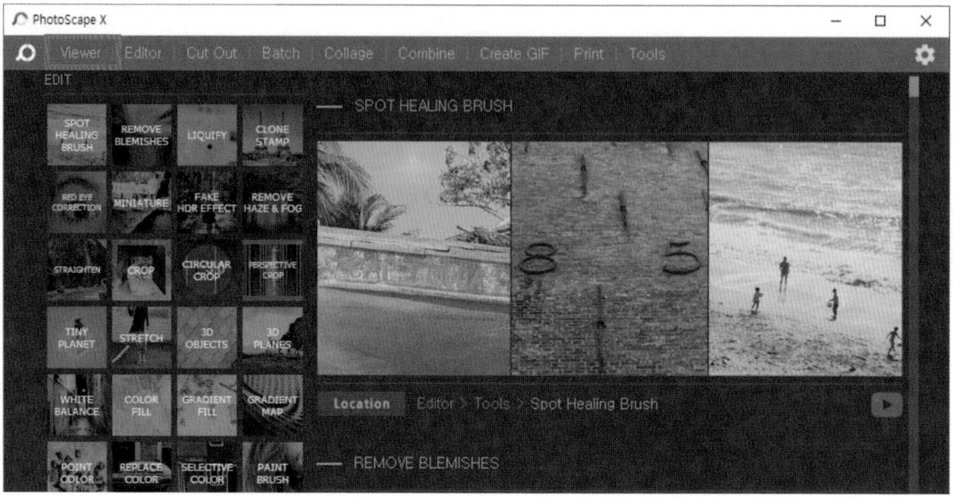

3) In the Viewer module, click a folder on the left side to save pictures from being edited. If you choose an appropriate folder in which various pictures are saved, those pictures are shown on the right side.

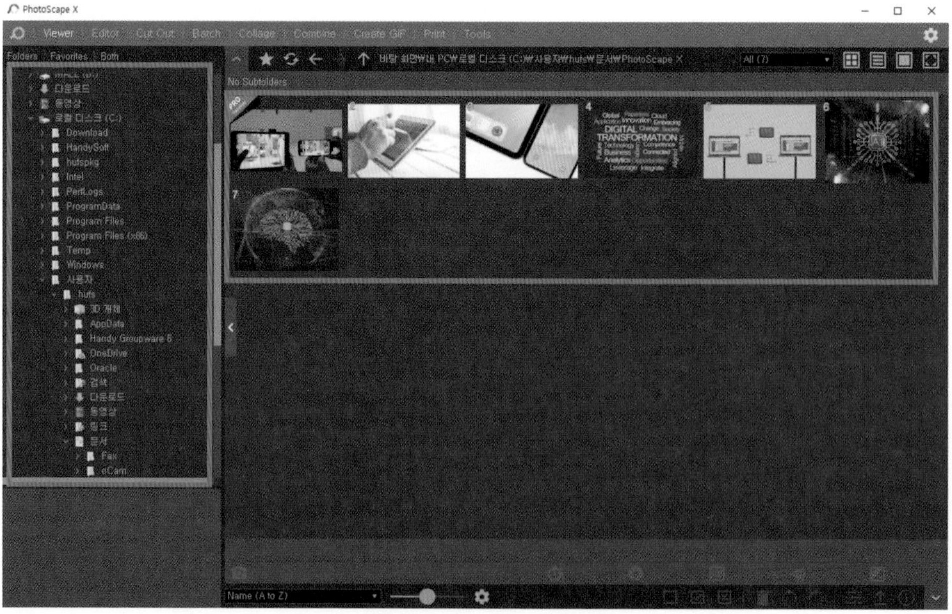

4) Choose a picture that you want to edit and enhance on the right side. Locate the mouse cursor on a picture and press the right button to see editing functions. Click the 'Edit' button to get the 'Editor' module.

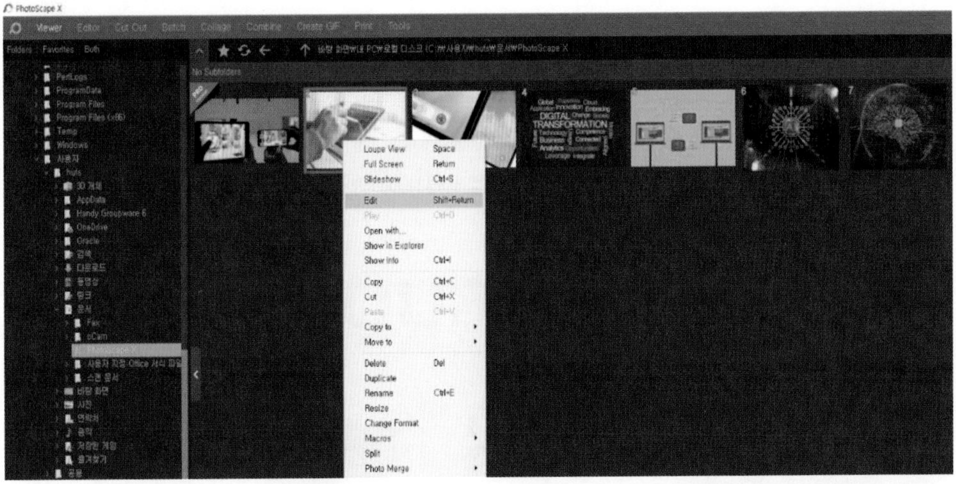

5) If you want to split pictures or drawings into small pieces in making activities for language classes, click the 'split' button on the editing functions. Set a number in each of 'Columns' and 'Rows' based on how many pieces you want to split.

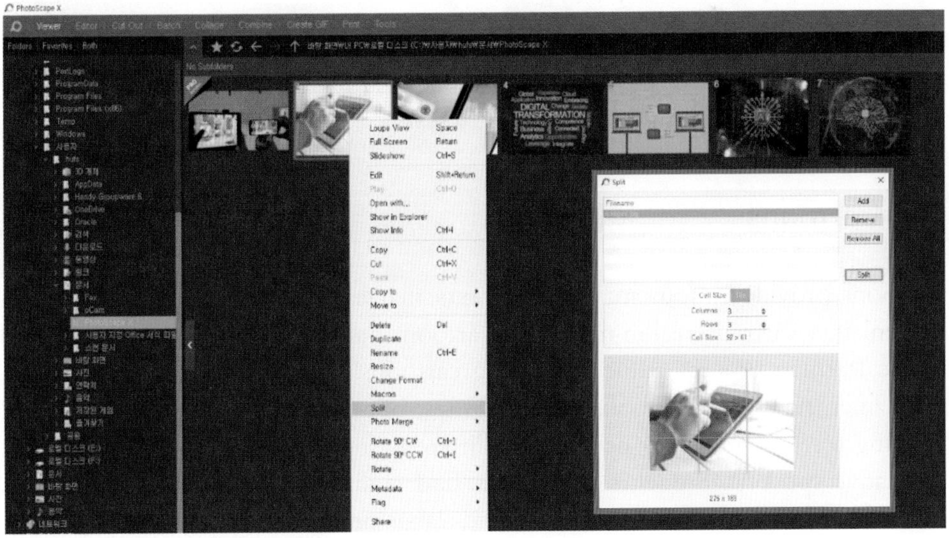

Tasks for Study and Discussion

- Create vocabulary and writing activities on making a budget for shopping with images for beginning and intermediate level students using *Snagit* or *PhotoScape X*. Search for some pictures with your partner. Identify the name of the items in English. Once you identified the names, make a plan for shopping within the $300 budget.

* **Sample of vocabulary and writing activities:** Make a budget for shopping using images.

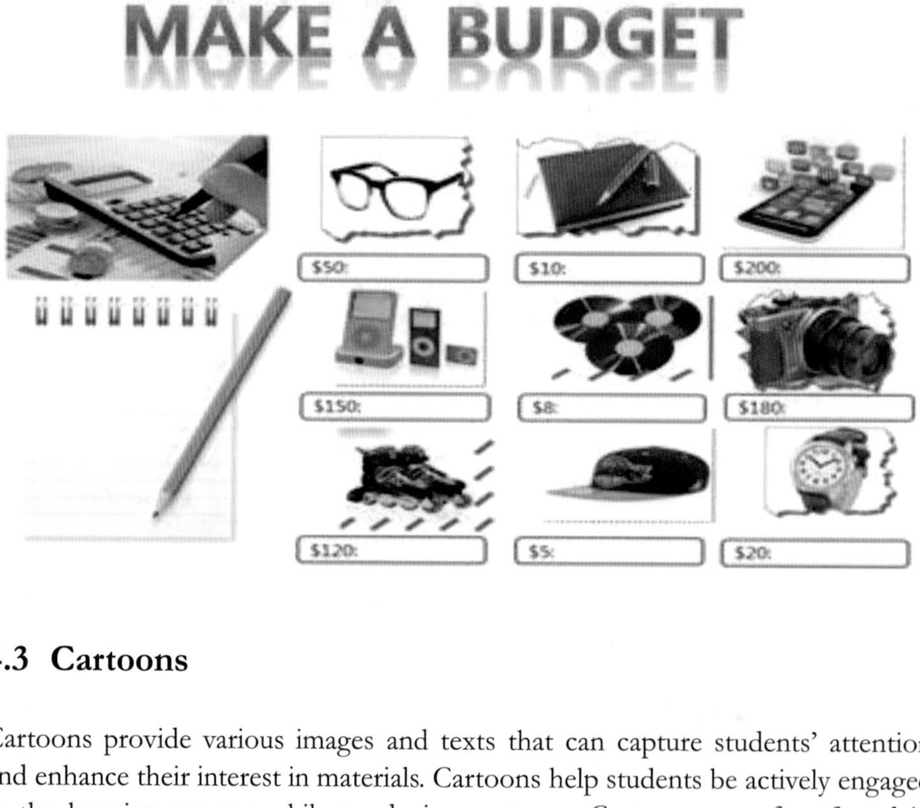

4.3 Cartoons

Cartoons provide various images and texts that can capture students' attention and enhance their interest in materials. Cartoons help students be actively engaged in the learning process while producing cartoons. Cartoons are often found in magazines, newspapers, books, and websites, but the cartoons for teaching and learning foreign languages need to be different from those in such publications for native speakers. Students sometimes find it difficult to understand contexts and expressions like registers, jargons, and slangs presented in cartoons. Thus, it is important to provide cartoons appropriate for students' educational background and language proficiency levels, considering the lesson's objectives. The recent development of technologies allows teachers and students to produce cartoons on the Web.

Several programs and tools are available on the Web, such as *Make Beliefs Comix* (http://www.makebeliefscomix.com/Comix), *Pixton* (http://www.pixton.com), *Comic Creator* (http://www. readwritethink.org/files/resources/interactives /comic), etc. These programs provide layouts, characters, backgrounds so that cartoons can be created very easily. In this section, the ways for creating cartoons through *Make Beliefs Comix* are introduced.

Figure 4.5 The main screen of *Make Beliefs Comix*

Make Beliefs Comix

Make Beliefs Comix (https://www.makebeliefscomix.com/) is one of many websites that provide programs to create cartoons. Users can create their cartoons free of charge without logging in to a website. *Make Beliefs Comix* also offers useful information, including various lesson plans and guidelines for teachers and learners in language classes, utilizing the website as an educational purpose. The following are the detailed steps to create cartoons.

1) Click 'CREATE COMIX' on the left or 'CREATE YOUR COMIX!' in the middle to enter the editor page.

2) Select various of elements of the cartoon, including characters, masks, balloons, background, etc., on the bottom.

3) Choose a character you want to add in your cartoons on the bottom. Scroll below if you would like to see more characters. Click a character that you choose and select appropriate emotions and posture.

4) Choose types of speech balloons. Type words and sentences into the speech balloons.

5) Use various function buttons in the toolbar at the bottom to change image location, size, flip and delete.

Tasks for Study and Discussion

- Create an incomplete cartoon for intermediate to advance level students using *Make Beliefs Comix*. Your students are to fill out the speech balloon(s) and the last box individually. Provide glossary if necessary.

*** Sample of reading, writing, and speaking activities using *Make Beliefs Comix***

Chapter 5

Editing Tools II: Sounds, Videos, and Animations

5.1 Sounds

Sound is one of the most common resources available on the Web and particularly useful for providing authentic materials for teaching and learning listening. Sound files can be used without modification, but in most cases, they need to be customized to meet the target students' needs and the learning environment. Sound files can be produced using *Windows Sound Recorder* or other software developed to record and edit sound files.

Types of sound files include Waveform Audio File Format (WAVE), Musical Instrument Digital Interface (MIDI), MPEG-1 Audio Layer-3 (MP3), RealAudio (RA), Free Lossless Audio Codec (FLAC), etc. *Adobe Audition CC* (https://creative.adobe.com/ko/products/audition), *Audacity* (https://audacityteam.org), *Cool Edit Pro* (https://cool-edit-pro.soft32.com), *Goldwave* (https://www.goldwave.com/goldwave.php), *Gom Audio* (https://audio.gomlab.com), *Sound Forge* (https://sound-forge-audio-studio.en.softonic.com), *1gram player* (https://www.1gram.net/), etc. are some examples of the recommendable shareware that provides recording and editing functions for free. In this section, *Goldwave* is introduced along with its main functions.

Goldwave

Goldwave (https://www.goldwave.com/goldwave.php) is a full-featured digital audio editor that can be easily used by teachers and even learners in creating audio files. Main editing functions include playing, recording, importing, editing, restoring, processing, and converting audio files. Teachers and learners can download the latest version of *Goldwave* from its main webpage.

1) Refer to the red box on the right for information on OS compatibility as shown in Figure 5.1. Press the download button and install the program.

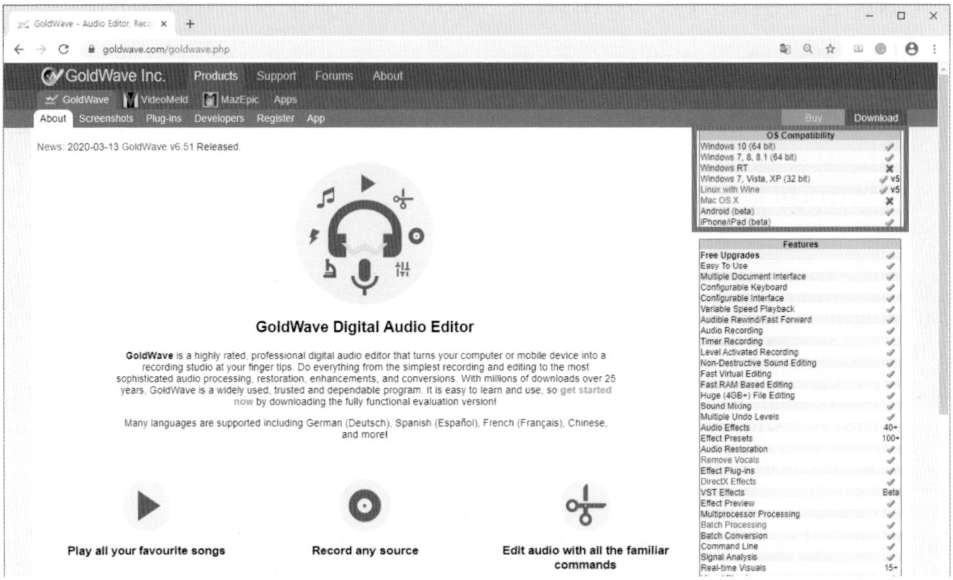

Figure 5.1 The main screen of *Goldwave*

2) Double click on the *Goldwave* icon to run the program and then press the 'New' button.

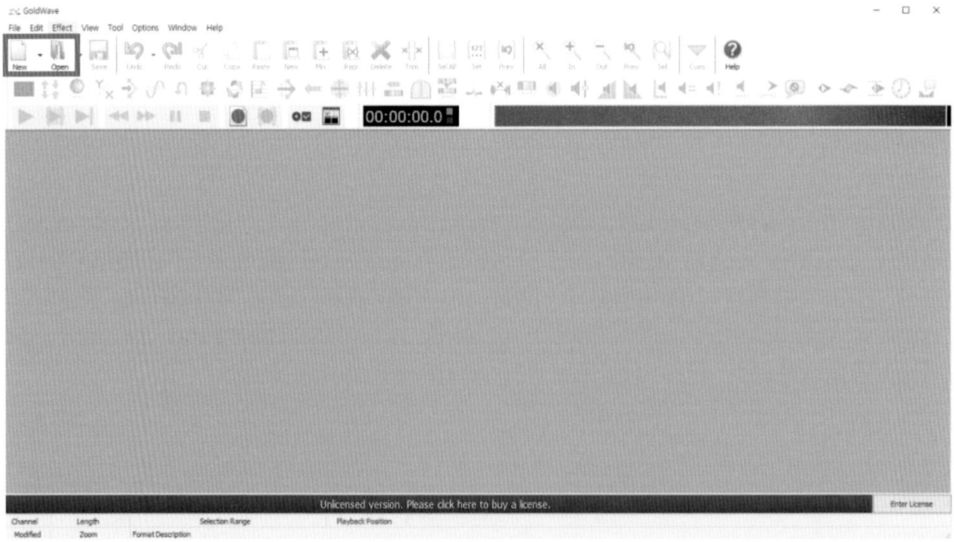

3) Configure the conditions by selecting the options for the recording of a new sound file.

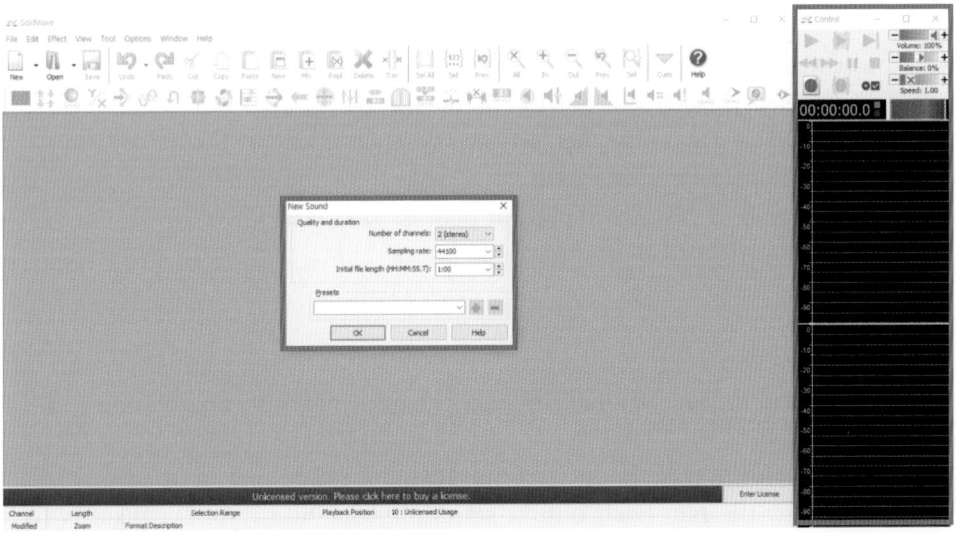

4) The following presents the frequently used editing commands, including main commands and effect toolbar. Click 'Tool' and select 'Control' to make control properties appear.

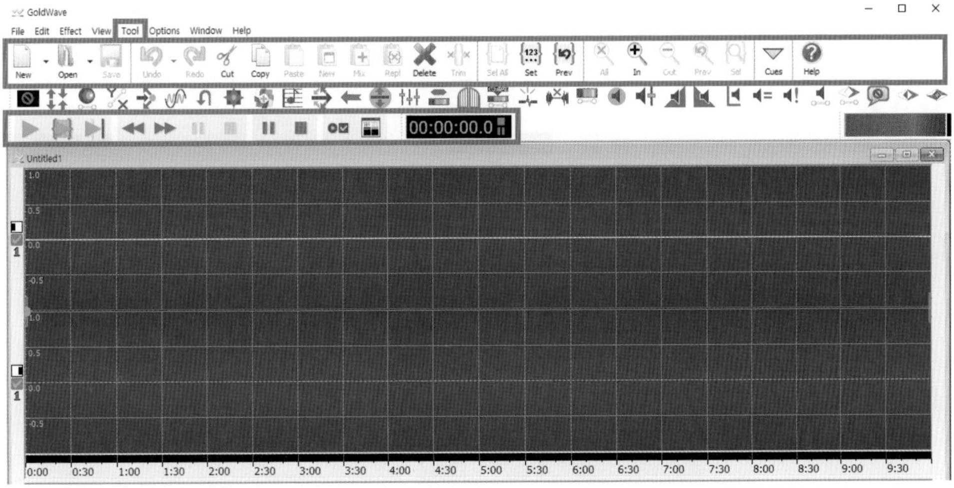

The main commands have the following functions:

- New, Open, and Save: Create a new sound file, open a file and save it.

- Undo/Redo: Undo/redo the previous command.
- Cut, Copy and Paste: Cut, copy, and paste the selected portion of the audio file.
- New: Copy the audio file or create a new audio file using the cut part.
- Mix: Combine two audio files into one.
- Del: Delete the selected portion of the file.
- Trim: Delete the parts other than the designated one by the mouse.
- In and Out: Enlarge or shrink the waveform of the audio file.
- Play: Play all, a designated part, or play up to a certain point.
- Recording: Record all or designated part(s).

Playback

1) Click 'Open' to open an audio file. A progress audio decompression pop-up will show up.
2) Once waveform appears on the sound window, click one of the three 'Play' tabs to play the file. Each button starts playback at a different place, which can be set under the 'Play' tab of the Control Properties window on the main menu. Right-click on one of the play buttons to change the settings quickly.
3) To start playback at a certain point in the sound file, click on the timeline under the waveform in the sound window or right-click on the waveform and choose the 'Play From Here' command from the pop-up menu.

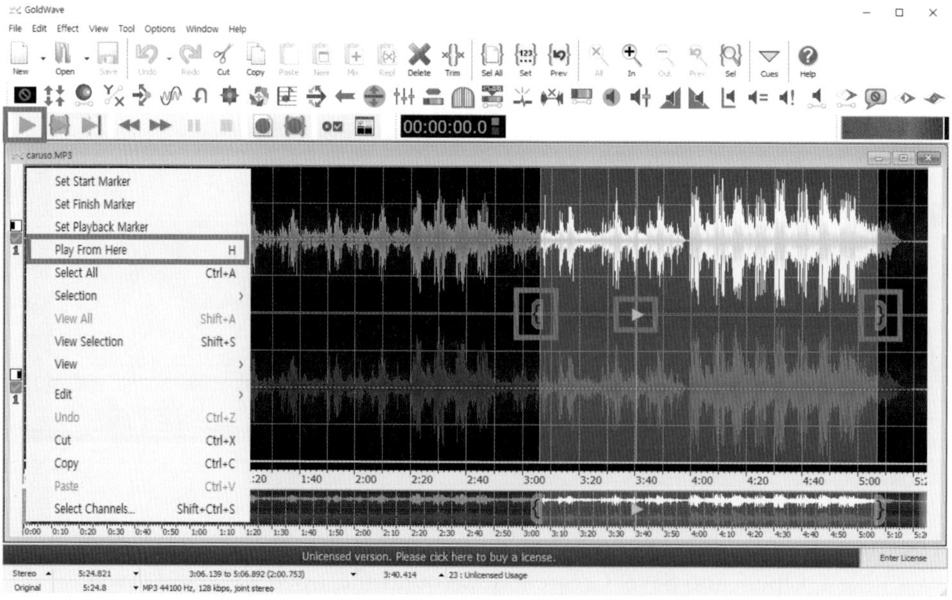

Recording

1) Press the recording button in the control bar, and you can monitor the input. Right-click on the recording key allows you to set the duration.

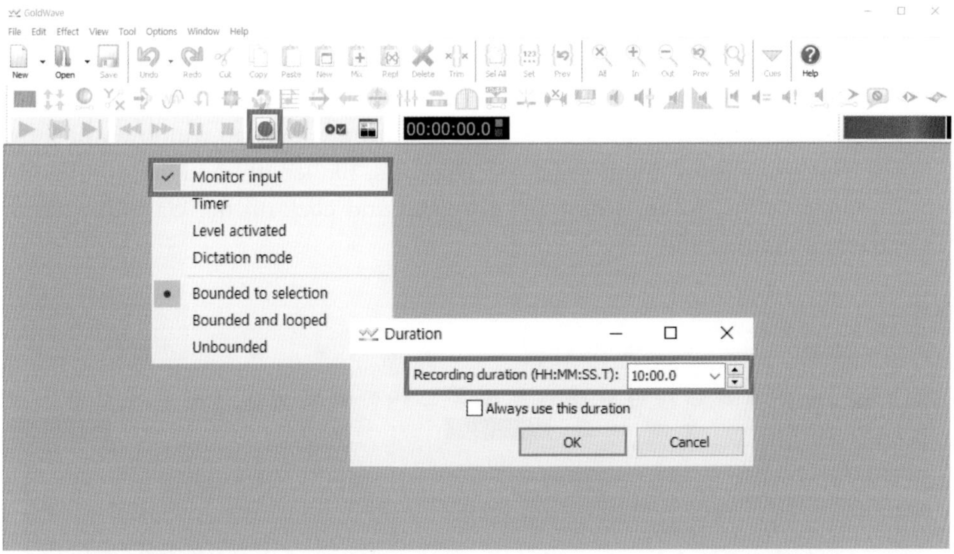

2) Once the recording starts, you will see the waveform on the sound window. Stop or pause key to stop recording before setting the duration or choose the default, and press the stop key when finished.

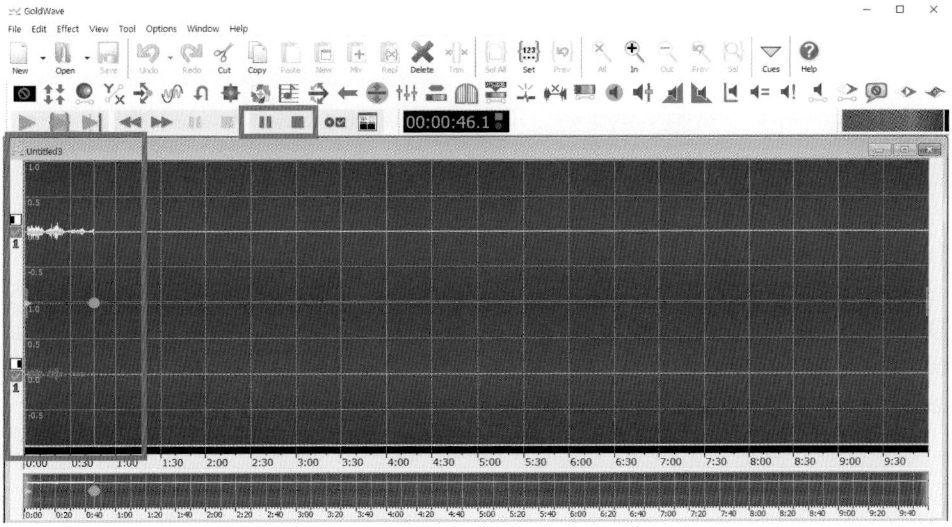

Cutting, pasting, and creating a new file

1) Designate the segment to be cut using brackets. Right-click at the starting point and select 'Set Start Marker.' Locate the cursor at the ending point and right-click to 'Set finish Marker' to set the cutting parameters.
2) Press 'Cut' to cut the designated part.
3) If the cutting from the original file needs to go to a new file, click on the 'New' button to open a new file and click on the 'Paste' button to paste onto the new file. Once you click on the 'New' button, a pop-up window will show up. You can choose the number of channels, file length, and set conditions. Then click 'OK' to get a new file prepared and click on the 'Save' button to save it as another file.

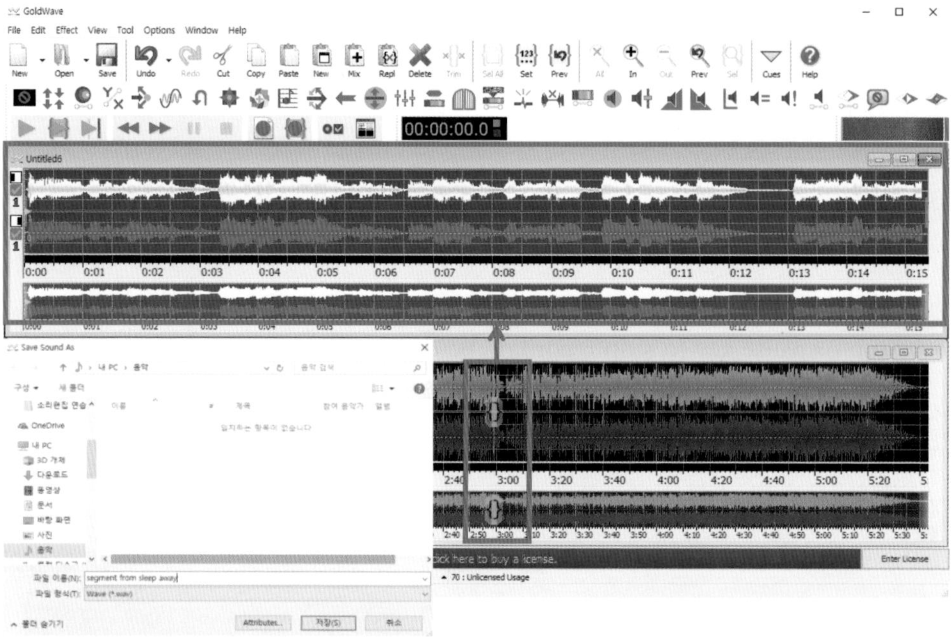

Insert Silence

Designate the segment where you wish to insert silence and click on the 'Edit' button and select 'Insert Silence.' A pop-up will show up for you to choose the length of the silence.

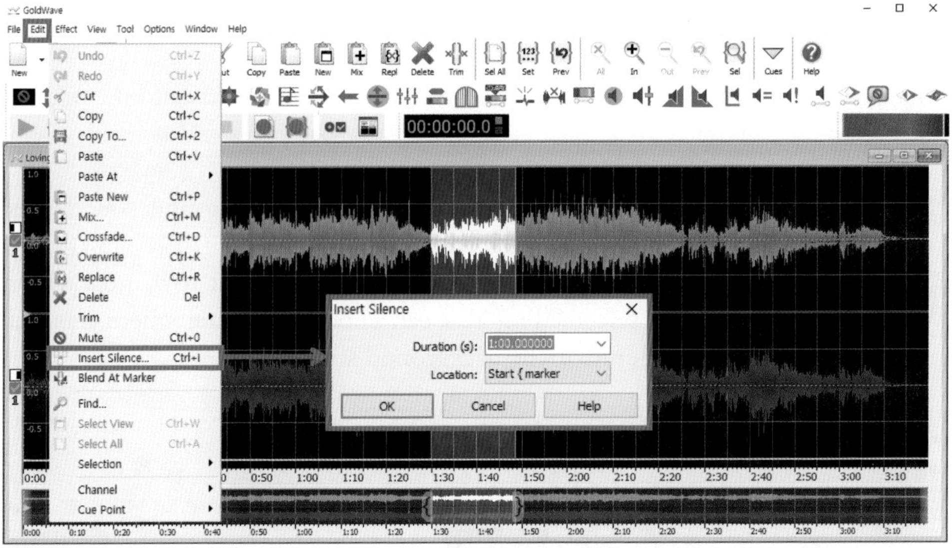

Time Warp

Time warp is a feature that allows the control of the speed of the audio file. To change speed, designate the segment that needs speed change, click on the 'Effect' button on the menu, and select 'Time Warp.'

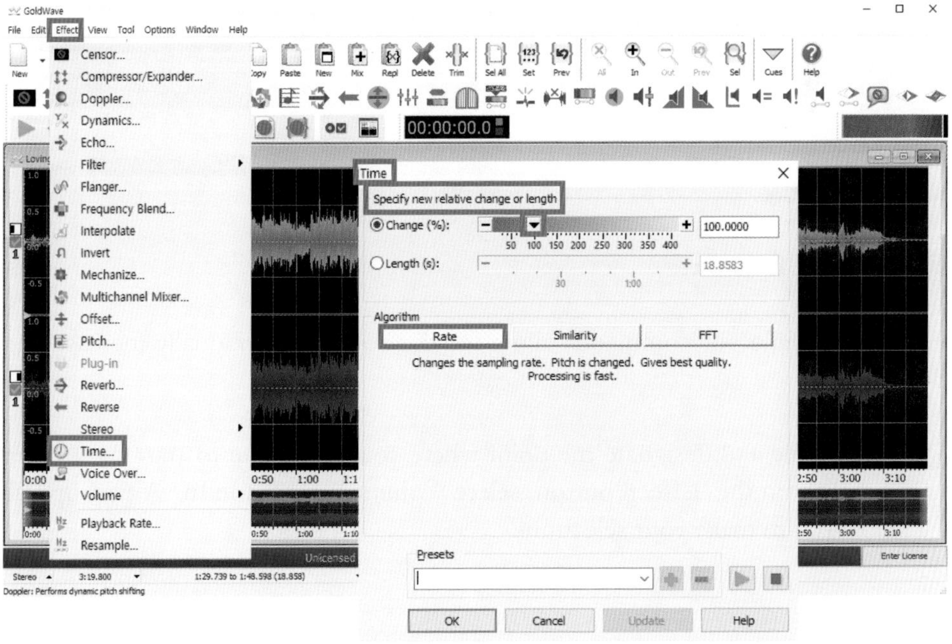

Mix

Mixing is a feature that enables you to set the background sound onto the original file.

1) Press the 'File' button and open the original and background sound files. They come in two sets of the waveform.
2) Designate the segment of the background file in the upper row and click on the 'Edit' button and select 'Mix.' You can choose the time where mix will begin as well as the volume of the background sound.

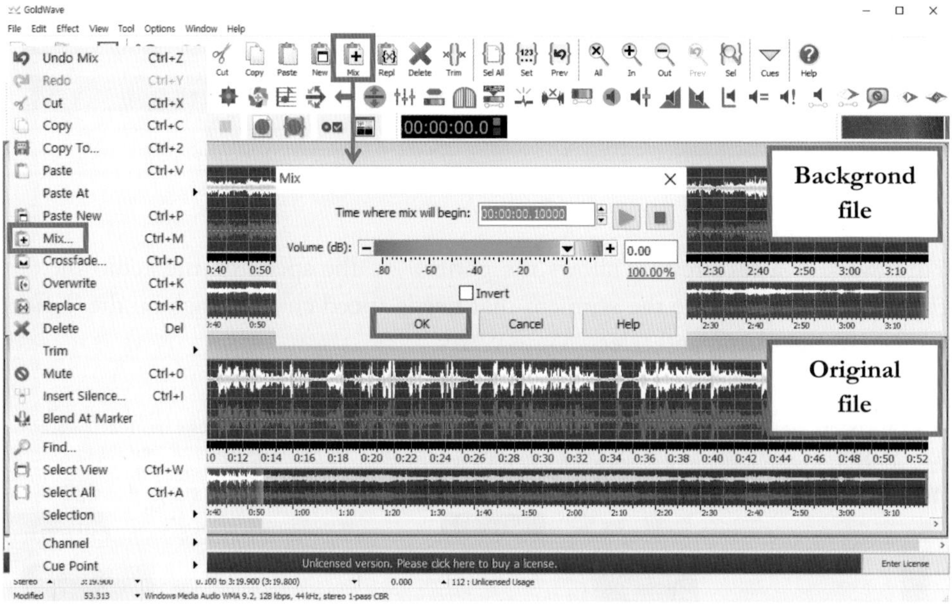

Fade in and fade out

Fade in and fade out commands allow for the volume to gradually increase and decrease.

1) Open a file and designate the point where you would like to start the fade in and click on the 'Effect' button, select 'Volume,' and 'Fade In.' A pop-up will allow you to make your selections.

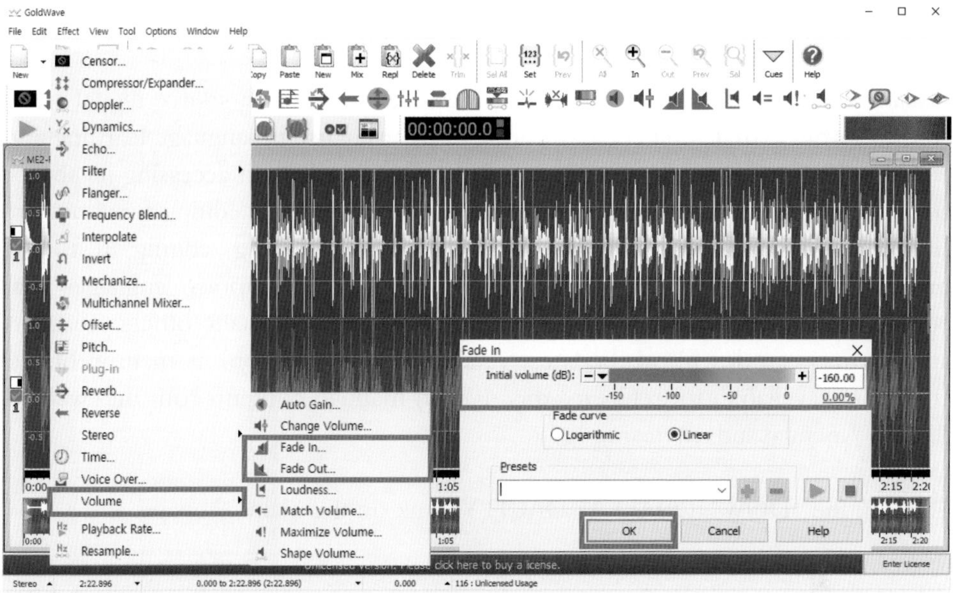

2) The points that are faded in and faded out will show as the fluctuation range of waveform decreases close to a flat line.

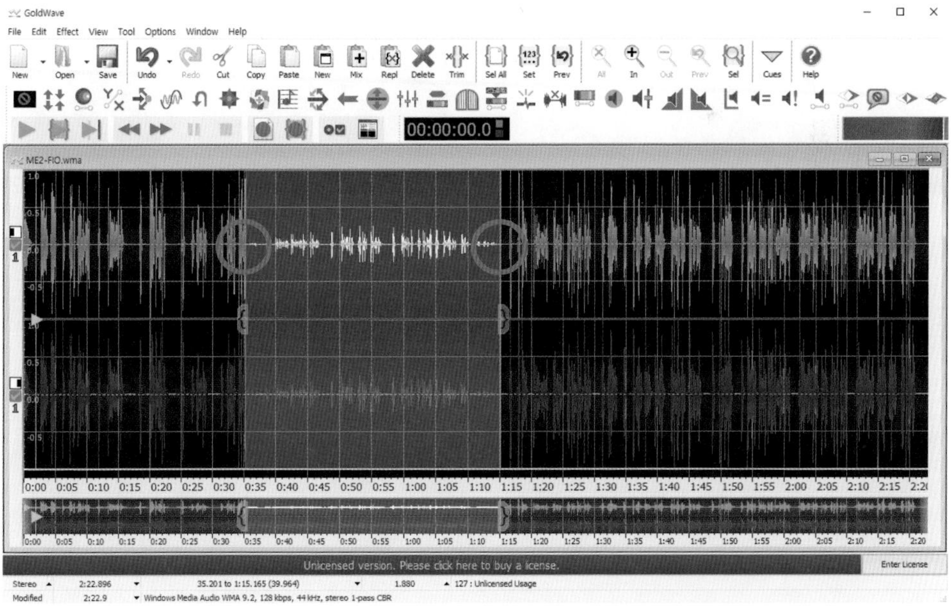

Audacity

Audacity (https://audacityteam.org) provides users with open-source digital audio editing software that teachers and learners can easily use in language learning and teaching. This software is free of cost and offers freedom in accessing its source code; thus, *Audacity* is called the open-source software. Main editing functions are similar to *Goldwave*, including playing, recording, importing, editing, restoring, processing, and converting audio files. *Audacity* offers various languages that contain English, Chinese, Japanese, French, Korean, and many others. Teachers and learners can download the latest version of *Audacity* from its main webpage. It is also available to refer to the *Audacity* manual contents on the website (https://manual.audacityteam.org/).

1) Click the "DOWNLOAD AUDACITY" link on the main webpage.

2) By referring to OS compatibility, download *Audacity* software on your devices.

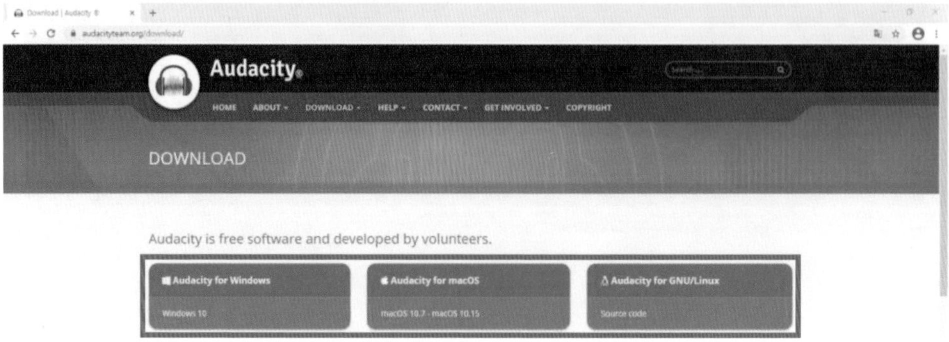

3) Double click the "*Audacity*" icon to run on the software and press the "Open" button in the "File" menu on the menu bar. Select audio files that you want to edit through the software.

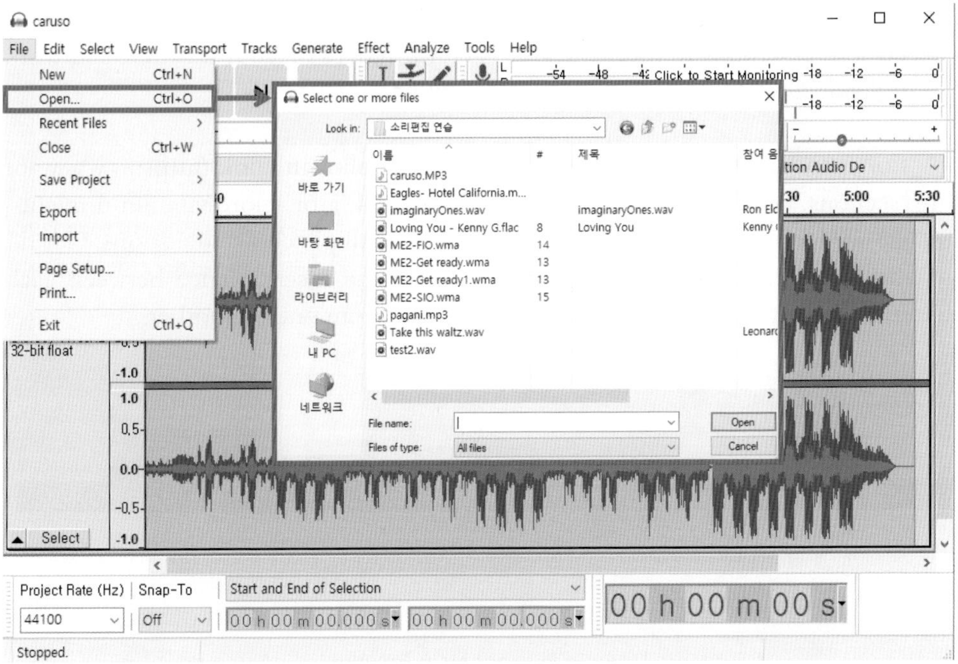

4) Now, it is available to use various editing functions in the *Audacity* software. The functions in the red boxes are some main editing tools of the software.

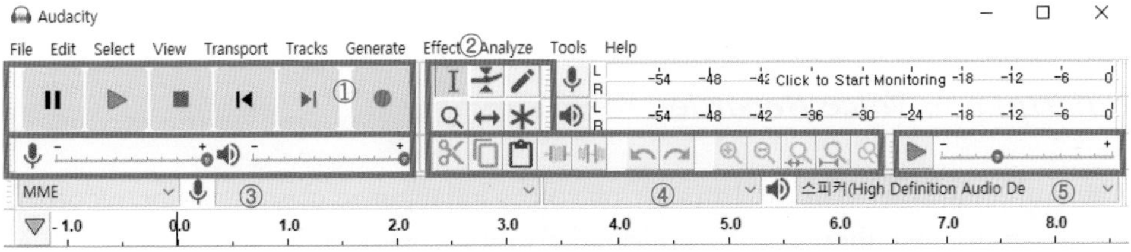

	Names of Toolbars	Functions of Toolbars
①	Transport toolbar	Pause, Play, Stop, Skip to start/end, and Record
②	Tools toolbar	Selection, Envelope, Draw, Zoom, and Time shift
③	Mixer toolbar	Slider recording and Slider playback
④	Edit toolbar	Cut, Copy, Paste, Trim, Silence, Redo, Undo, etc.
⑤	Play-at-speed toolbar	Play-at-speed and Playback speed

Tasks for Study and Discussion

- Create a listening activity for intermediate or advanced level students using *Goldwave* (30 to 60 seconds soundtrack). Make sure to use various functions to customize sounds to meet the goals and objectives of your lesson. First, work individually, and then share your work with your partners.

For example, import the audio file from the following link (https://www.npr.org/sections/health-shots/2017/02/16/515428944/a-bit-more-vitamin-d-might-reduce-winter-colds-and-flu), and make a set of multiple choice questions. Get rid of the parts that are not needed from the file and insert silence between each question so that listeners can shift their attention from one to another.

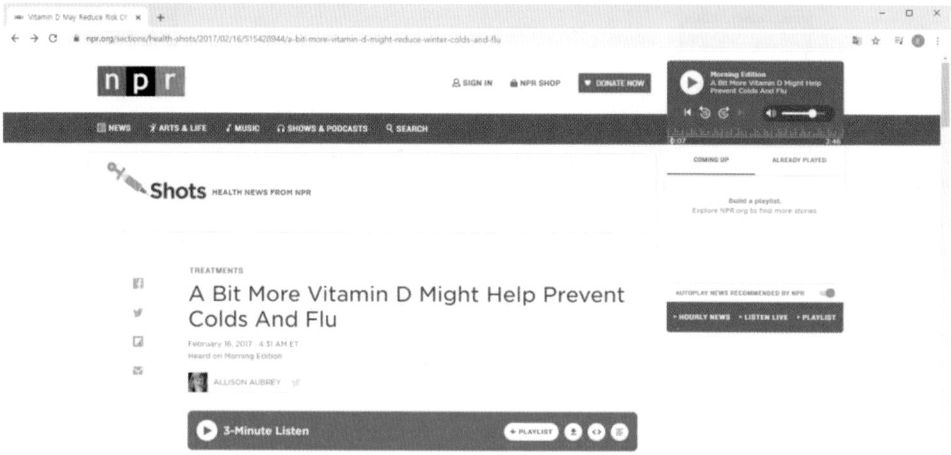

Smartphone Voice Recorder

The authentic voices on the Internet or voices in language classes can be recorded by smartphones rather than complicated software or tools. In speaking classes in FLT&L, learners can record their voices and share those with other learners in practicing the target language. There are two possible options in recording voices through smartphones: downloading apps for recording voices, using a built-in app in smartphones. The built-in app in smartphones also offers simple editing functions for recorded files, which help users delete unnecessary parts in recorded voices.

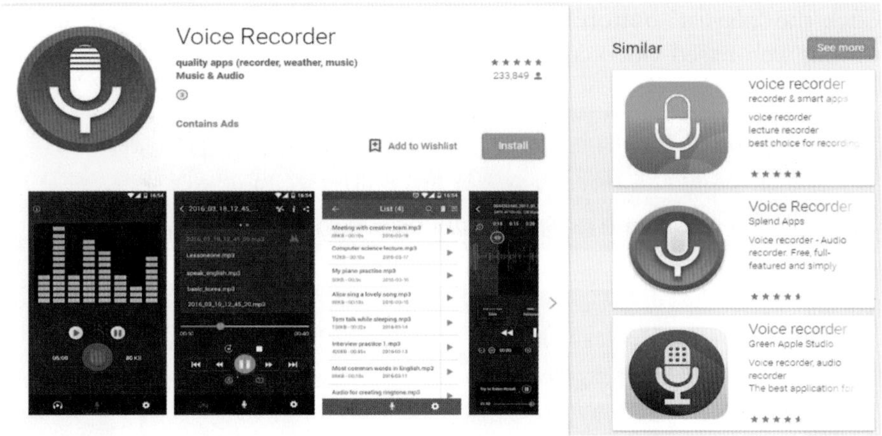

1gram player

1gram player (https://www.1gram.net/) is software whereby users can play sound or video files saved on computers, smartphones, etc. A unique function of *1gram player* is that it allows users to extract and download sound or video files from platforms including YouTube, Naver, and more. The files downloaded through a *1gram player* can be edited and reused while considering copyrights. Downloading sound files is possible for computers and any other devices compatible with *the 1gram player* app. The following demonstrates how to download sound files through the *1gram player* from various web platforms in which a variety of video content is provided.

1) Click 

(PC app download) or 

(Mobile app download) to install an appropriate software to your networked devices.

2) Click the 'playlist' button on the bottom to open the window for accessing various web-based video content platforms through the player.

3) Click the 'download (mp3)' button to open the window for downloading a sound file. The quality of a sound and video file can be adjusted here.

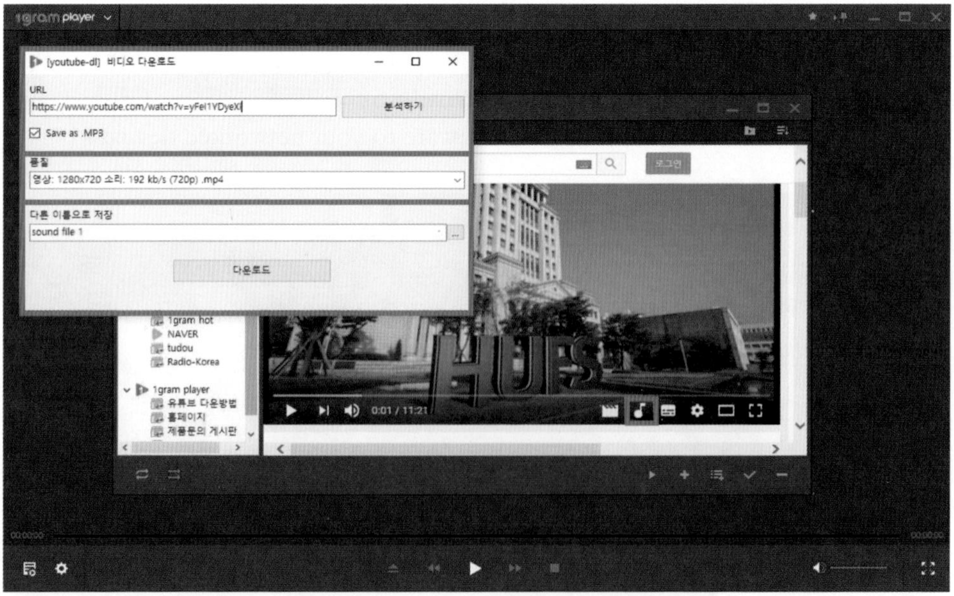

4) Click the 'download (Video)' button next to the 'download (mp3)' button if you want to download a video file itself with the sound and adjust the quality of the video file as described in 3).

5) Select a folder where you want to download voice files through *1gram player* by clicking a button next to 다른 이름으로 저장 (Save the name as). Then, click 다운로드 button to save voice files on your networked devices.

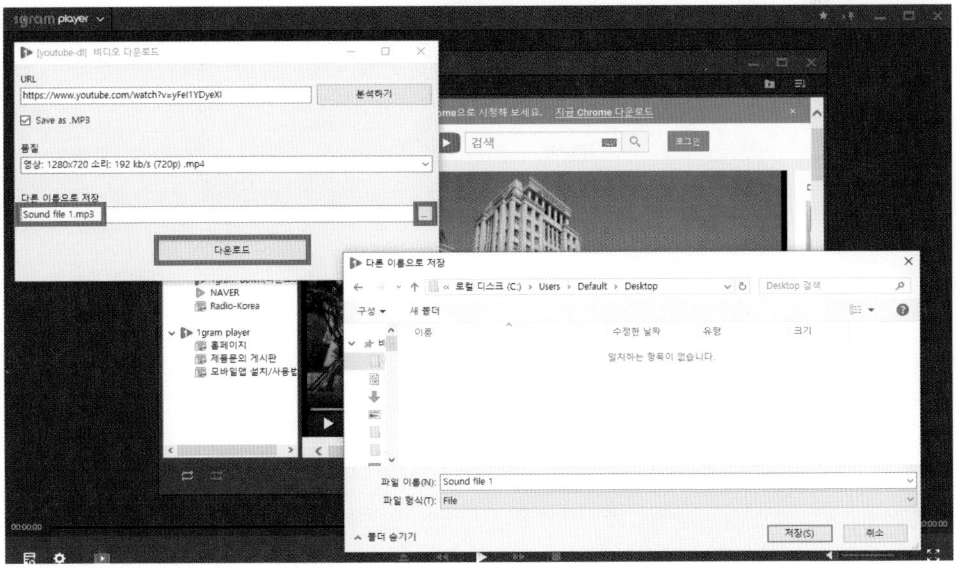

Tasks for Study and Discussion

- Create listening and speaking activities for beginning or intermediate level students by using smartphone recorders or *1gram player*. Make sure to use various sound sources to enhance authentic exposure to the target language. First, work individually, and then share your work with your partners.

For example, listen to the weather reports. What is the weather like in each city? Check (√) the correct weather.

City	Weather			
London	□ rainy	□ warm	□ windy	□ cold
Bangkok	□ humid	□ sunny	□ cloudy	□ wet
Seoul	□ wet	□ snowy	□ warm	□ cold
New York	□ sunny	□ windy	□ wet	□ cold

5.2 Videos

Videos are essential in FLT&L as they provide motivation, authenticity, understanding of a given situation and culture. They are a great help in stimulating and facilitating the learning of a foreign language (C. H. Lee, 2004; Salaberry, 2001; Shumin, 2002; Yoon, Lee, & Lee, 2013). Videos have an advantage in delivering authentic content; therefore, they contribute to enhancing the understanding of the target culture as well as providing indirect contact with speakers of the language (Rivers, 1981). Besides, video is one of the most appreciated classroom teaching and learning materials. In terms of comprehension, it is obvious that non-native speakers of a language rely more heavily on visual clues to support their understanding, and there is no doubt that video is a prominent medium for helping learners interpret the visual clues effectively. Researchers have made various suggestions as to how videos can come into use for language teaching and learning. For instance, Cakir (2006) summarized practical techniques of using videos in language classrooms. The techniques include active viewing, freezing and prediction, silent viewing, sound-on and vision-off activity, repetition and role-play, reproduction activity, and dubbing activity. As Cakir (2006) pointed out, videos are not limited in listening comprehension but can be adapted to foster general spoken skills. In using videos in actual language classes, its purpose should be pedagogical and not for entertainment only. Therefore, C. H. Lee (2004) suggested that 3 minutes is the appropriate length for a video clip to be shown in language classrooms for pedagogical purposes.

However, it is not easy to develop videos and audiovisual materials needed for EFL classrooms due to factors, such as the cost and the amount and time needed. Fortunately, lots of digital videos and audiovisual materials are available on the open web. Therefore, teachers need to search, capture, save, and edit videos appropriate for the objectives and activities in classrooms to suit the needs of the learners. On that note, teachers should keep in mind that copyrights are very important. The captured and edited moving pictures should not be used for profit or any reasons other than educational purposes, and they should be used with permission from the authors.

Video makers and editing tools are available on the Web. Some examples are *1gram player* (https://www.1gram.net/), *Camtasia* (https://www.techsmith.com/camtasia.html), *GOM Cam* (https://www.gomlab.com/gomcam-screen-recording/), *GOM Mix Pro* (https:// www.gomlab.com/gommixpro-video-editing/), *Machete Video Editor Lite* (http://www.machetesoft.com/about-machete-video-editor-lite.html), *MPEG Streamclip* (http://mpeg-streamclip.en.softonic.com/), *WeVideo* (https://www. wevideo.com), *VSDC Video Editor* (http://videosoftdev. com), *Windows Movie Maker* (http://windows.microsoft.com/en-au/windows-live/movie-maker), etc.

GOM Cam

GOM Cam (https://www.gomlab.com/gomcam-screen-recording/) is software for capturing, recording, and creating various multimedia content, including computer screens, images, video content, game screens, and lectures. It allows users to create various multimedia content by recording and extracting sounds and videos on the Internet. While recording computer screens, users can utilize 'Draw' functions on the recorded screens, encompassing text, drawing, highlighting, stamping, and erasing all the draws. These functions can also be employed in a lecture record mode. In the lecture record mode, teachers can import a PowerPoint file prepared in advance for their language classes. It is possible to record the screen of PowerPoint using various support functions. The PowerPoint screen record function for a lecture and webcam or any other video recording devices can be used when preparing a video lecture through *GOM Cam*. Another strength of *GOM Cam* is providing users with various language options (e.g., Korean, English, Chinese, etc.). One of the languages can be selected on the setting menu. The detailed manuals can be found on its website (https://www.gomlab.com/guide/view.gom?product=GOMCAM&language=eng).

- Download a software referring to OS compatibility and double click the *GOM Cam* icon to run the program.

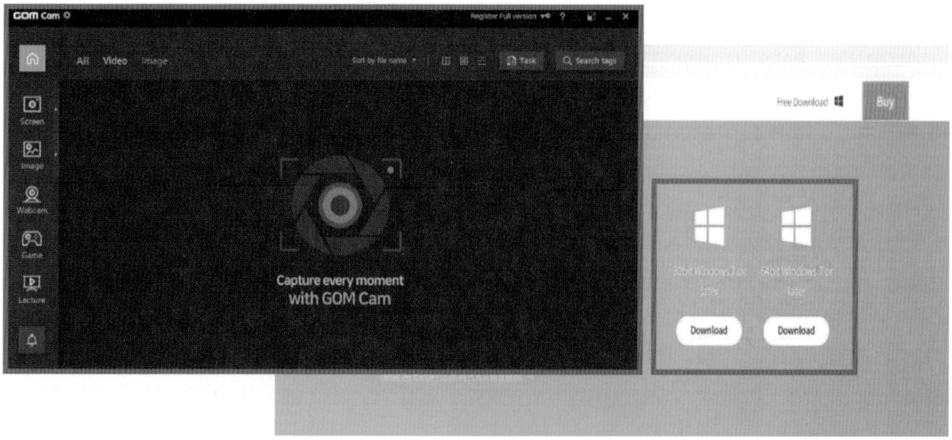

Computer screen record

1) Click the 'Screen' button on the top-left of the *GOM Cam* to select area on the computer screen to be recorded. If you correctly select areas, you can see a toolbox on the top of the selected area. The squared blue line shows which area you chose for recording a computer screen.

2) Click the 'Record' button in the toolbox to start recording a computer screen. You can use the 'Draw' function while recording a video material. If a microphone is connected to your computer, voice or sound can be recorded simultaneously with the computer screen.

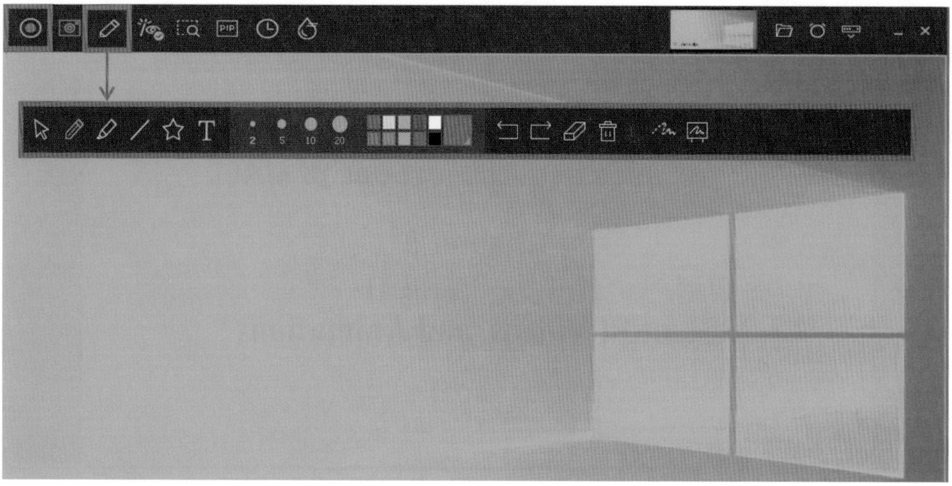

Recording a lecture (PowerPoint)

1) Click the 'Lecture' button on the bottom-left of the *GOM Cam* to open a window for the lecture recording. Open a PowerPoint file by clicking a folder shape in the 'Open PowerPoint file' section.

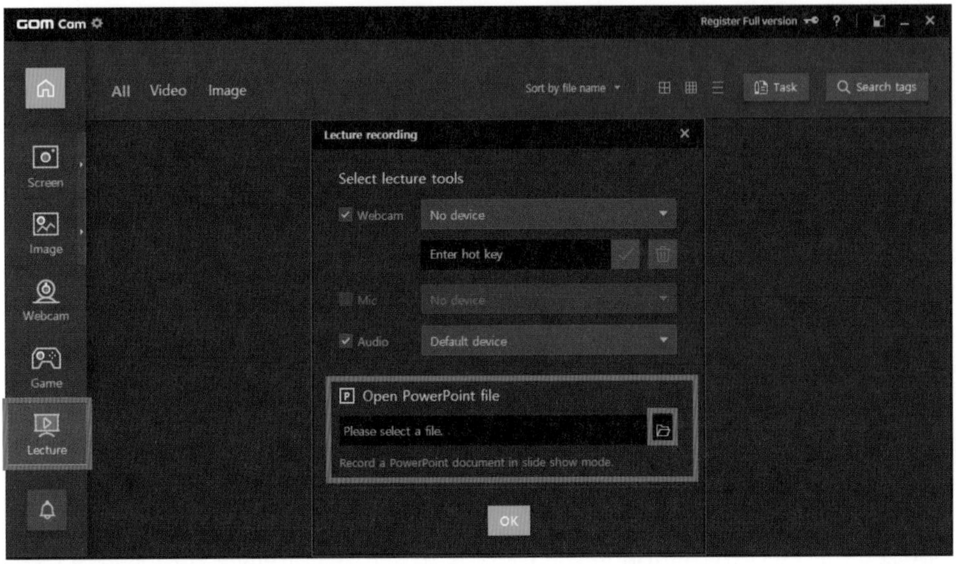

2) If a PowerPoint file is correctly opened through the program, the file shows up in slide mode. Click the 'Record' button on the top to start recording a lecture. You can use other functions on the toolbox at the top.

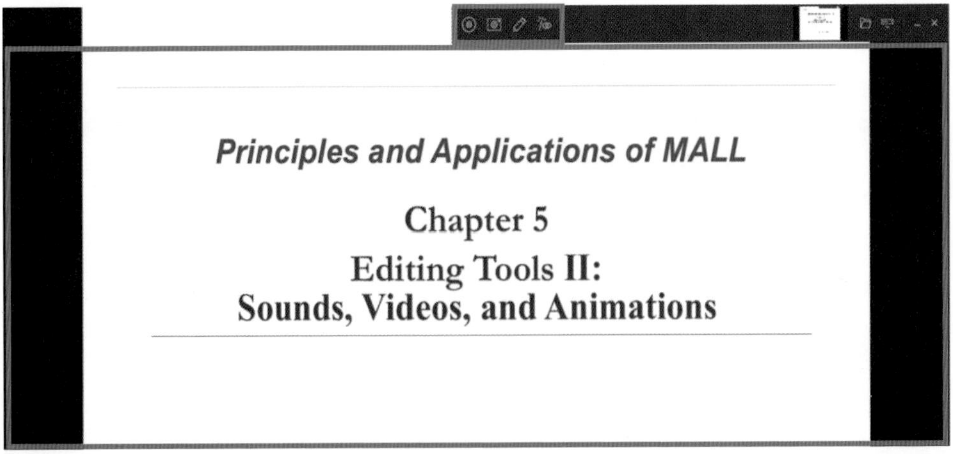

3) For example, click the 'Draw' button to open a box that contains various support functions to draw, highlight, or write text in enhancing the quality of a lecture. Configure detailed settings for each tool (e.g., select, pen, stamp, and font, etc.) by selecting colors and sizes for those.
4) Click the 'Effect setting' button on the top-middle to open the setting window for your lecture. In this setting, you can make use of more sophisticated functions that include connecting with a webcam, importing pictures, and adding a text-marker on the lecture screen.

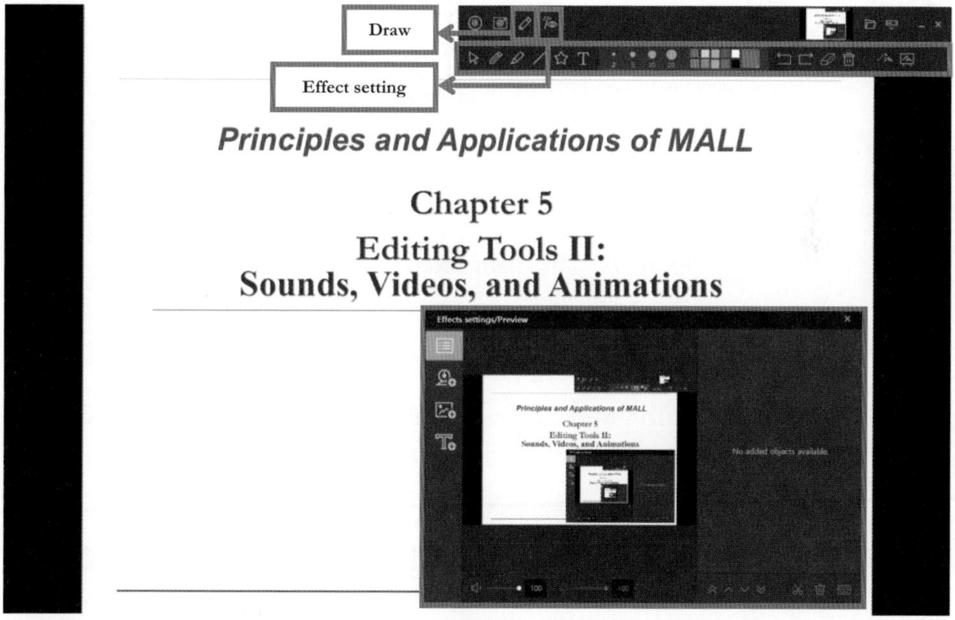

Camtasia

Camtasia (https://www.techsmith.com/video-editor.html) is a video-making and editing tool that allows users to capture and record the computer screen. Users can import and edit video files from a camera or other sources. It is possible to customize videos by adding graphics, animated backgrounds, callouts, and texts and share the end product through SNS. Another strength of *Camtasia* is the step-by-step video tutorials that help users understand the steps for recording, capturing and creating multimedia content (https://www.techsmith.com/tutorial-camtasia.html). A 30 days free trial version is downloadable from the *Camtasia* homepage.

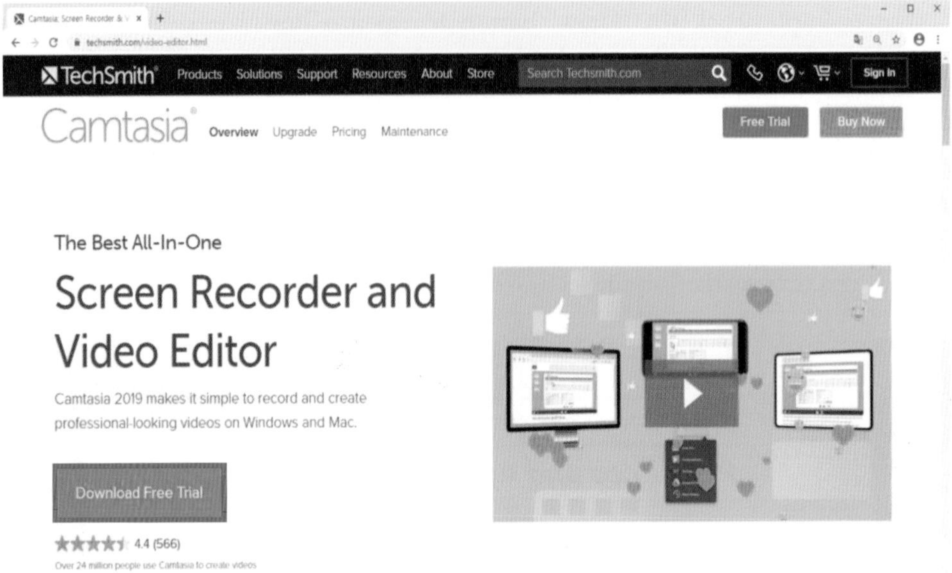

Figure 5.2 The main screen of *Camtasia*

Recording and creating a project file

1) Click the 'Record' button to record or capture the video. You can also click the 'Import Media' button to open a file from another folder. Once the record button is pressed, a task bar shows up to start recording.

2) Prepare the video to be captured. Areas you need to capture can be customized using the options in the 'Select area.' Click the 'rec' button to capture the video. When you finish capturing the video, stop, save, and create a recording file.

3) Once a project file is created and saved, the editor screen comes up with the captured video in the Media Bin section and in the 'Timeline,' and a larger shot in the 'Canvas' section.

GOM Mix Pro

GOM Mix Pro (https://www.gomlab.com/gommixpro-video-editing/) is a similar program to *Camtasia*, which allows users to edit video content. Users can consider two options in downloading the program: *GOM Mix* and *GOM Mix Pro*. These two PC apps share the same functions; However, GOM Mix Pro provides users with more sophisticated functions, various templates, editing filters, and background music. Another different feature between the two apps is that only the *Pro version* furnishes a language setting. One of the languages among English, Korean, Dutch, and Czech languages is choosable in the *Gom Mix Pro* software. The detailed user guide can be found from its website provided in three different languages (https://www.gomlab.com/guide/view.gom?product= GOMMIX).

Download and language setting

1) Download *GOM Mix Pro* free version from the website and double click the icon to run the program.
2) Click the 'Preference' (F5) button on the top-left to open a set box. Select a language you prefer in editing video content from the 'Setting the Language' section in the middle. Click 'OK' to finish the setting the language step.

Add a project file

1) Click the 'Add File' button on the top-right to open a folder to import photos or videos to be edited on the 'project file list' section.

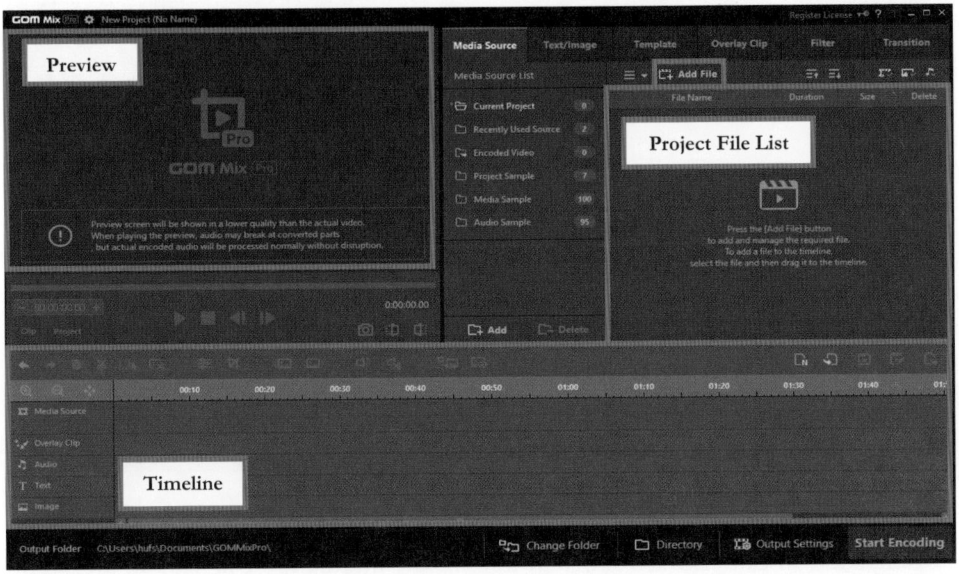

2) Drag and drop or double click project files to add those on the 'Timeline.'

Selecting, deleting, keeping, and splitting the video

1) To cut the video section, click the 'select area' button on the timeline tool. Check a tool description by placing a mouse cursor over the button.

2) Drag two lines in the red part in the timeline considering the portion to be deleted. You can also use shortcut keys in the middle to designate an area. The selected part will be shadowed on the timeline.

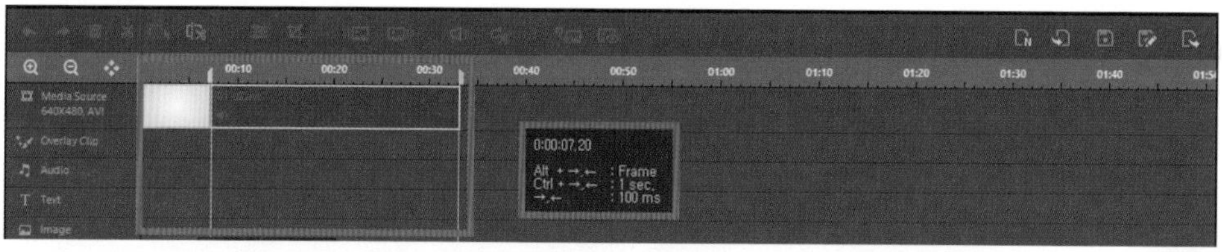

3) After designating an area, click 'Delete/Keep/Split' button on the timeline tool and choose one of the functions to delete, keep, or split selected area.

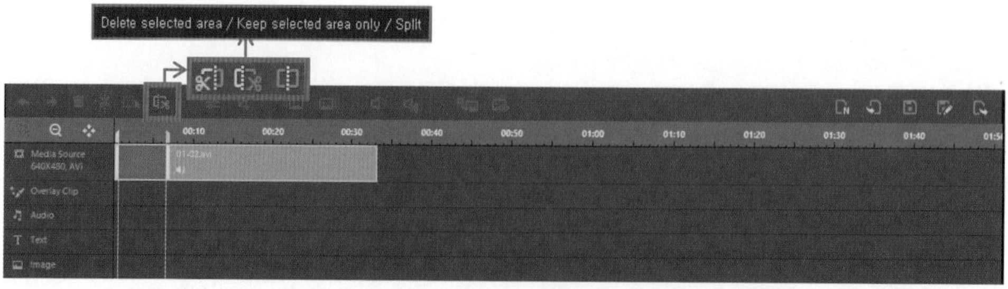

Adding and editing callouts, texts, captions, audio, and other effects

1) Click the 'Text/Image' button to add images, texts, and captions on a video clip and press 'Add New Image' to see various free templates in the program.
2) Select one of the images or callouts and place it in the timeline where necessary. All changes made to the video are shown on the preview screen.

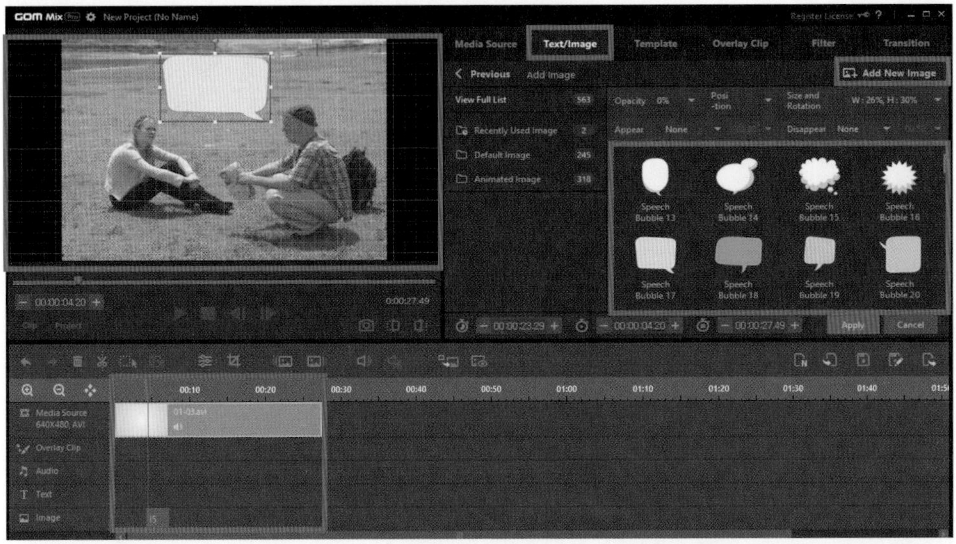

3) If you want to add text on callouts or captions, click the 'Add Text' button on the top-right to open a text box. Type texts in the box and place them in the timeline. Modify the size of the text and caption if necessary.

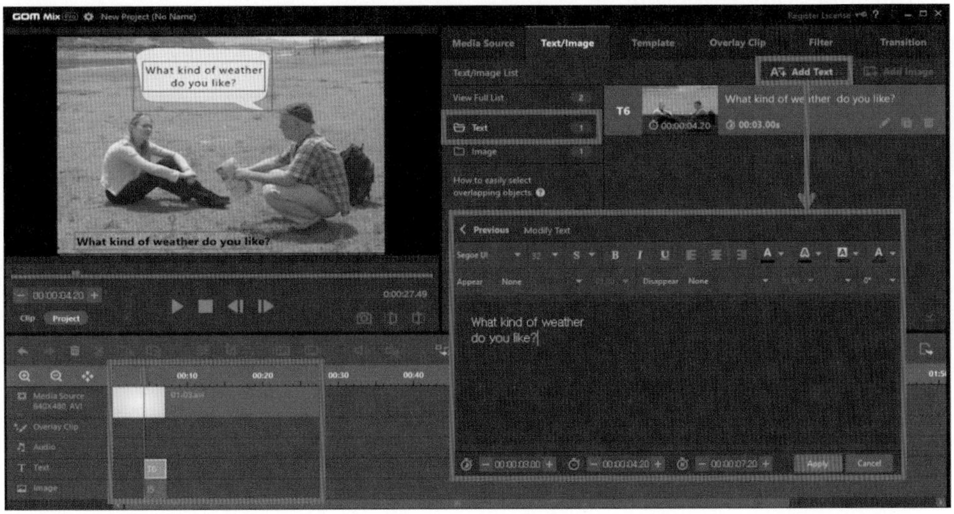

4) Click the 'Audio Sample' button in the 'Media Source' category to add audio files in a video clip. Choose one of the audio samples on the left and double click or drag and drop a file in the timeline. You can add audio files stored on your computer by clicking the 'Add' button in the middle.

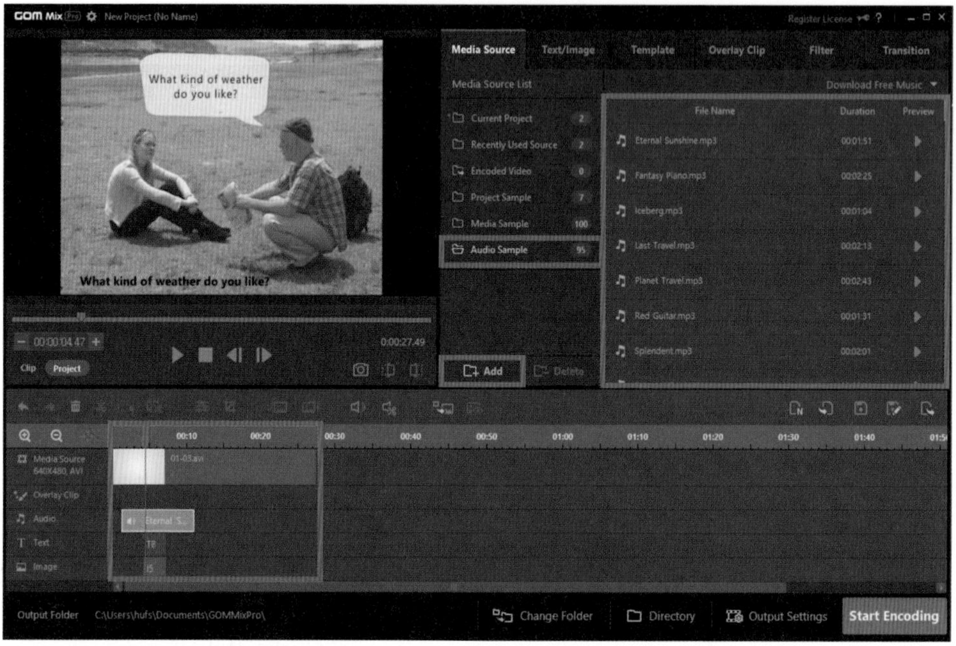

5) *GOM Mix Pro* provides various free effects for editing a video clip. The effects, including Template, Overlay Clip, Filter, and Transition, can be found from categories on the top-right.
6) Click each category and check what effects can be used in your video content.

7) For example, in the 'Transition' category, various free templates are available for editing a video clip. Prepare at least two video projects in the timeline before adding a transition. Double click the transition template on the top-right.

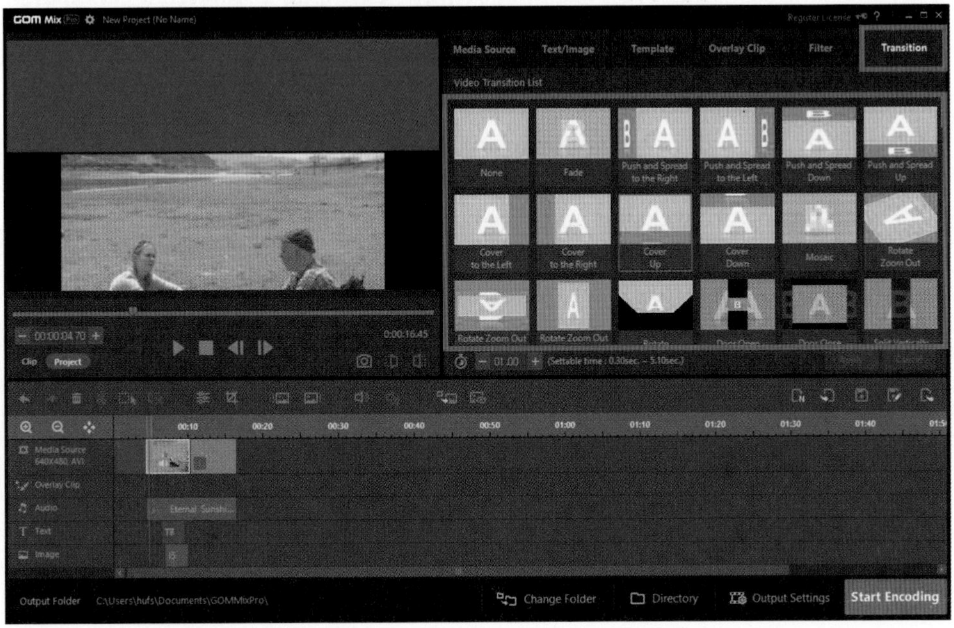

Tasks for Study and Discussion

1. In order to create speaking activities related to speech acts such as requests, apologies, greetings, promises, etc., search for a variety of video content from web resources (Daum, Google, Naver, YouTube, etc.), and then record or download two video clips by using *1 gram plyer,* or *Gom Cam* or *Snagit* or *Camtasia.*

2. Split, cut, and merge the video clips using *Camtasia* or *Gom Mix Pro.* The edited video should include at least a title, caption, callout, and transition.

5.3 Animations

Animations can be interactive instructional materials that facilitate language learning, including open-ended learning environments, simulations, games, drills, tests, and tutorials (Alessi & Trollip, 2001). For example, a storytelling animation is an exciting and lively language learning tool. Animations can be applied to create a storytelling activity where learners can simulate certain situations to fit their stories by manipulating the websites or programs provided (Yang & Chen, 2007). Both 2D and 3D animation-producing webpages and commercialized programs are available, either free or trial versions.

The following are websites and programs for animation tools. First, examples of free programs are *Animaker* (https://www.animaker.com/), *Anim8or* (https://anim8or.com), *Synfig* (https://www.synfig.org), etc. Second, some of the free trial versions are *Animationish* (https://www.animationish.com/), *Lightwave* (https://www.newtek.com/lightwave/2020/), *Motion Studio 4* (http://www.wisdom-soft.com/products/motionstudio.htm), *Pro Motion NG* (https://www.cosmigo.com/), *Toon Boom* (https://www.toonboom.com), etc. *Animaker* is an easy and user-friendly tool that can come in handy for teachers and learners with little experience in producing animations. In this section, *Animaker* is introduced with a detailed user guide and instruction with a sample activity to illustrate how this animation tool can be applied to language teaching and learning.

Animaker

Animaker (https://www.animaker.com/) is one of the tools that can create and share animated videos. Users are provided with many drag-and-drop tools that allow for access to various character models, backgrounds, and other details to create scenario-based videos customizable to the users' needs. *Animaker* provides six different video styles, including 2D, infographics, handcraft, whiteboard, 2.5D, and typography. Users can stick to a single style or mix multiple styles to create the same animation. *Animaker* also holds other assets such as voice recording and text-to-speech function, creating exciting materials for teaching and learning spoken skills. Some features for creating animated videos are easy to find from a customizing toolbox. It is possible to create animations with team members. Figure 5.3 shows the main page of *Animaker.*

1) Click on 'Create' to produce an animated video. Then, click the 'Create a video' button to see various free templates for animations.

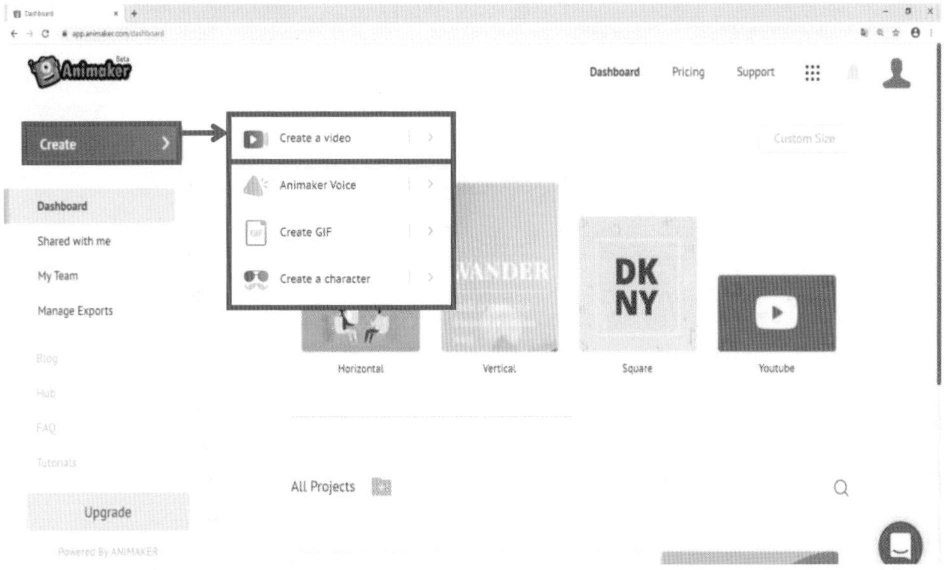

2) You can also customize animations first by clicking links on 'Create a video,' which include Horizontal, Vertical, Square, Youtube, Instagram, and Facebook Cover. To see more options, scroll your mouse to the left or right side.

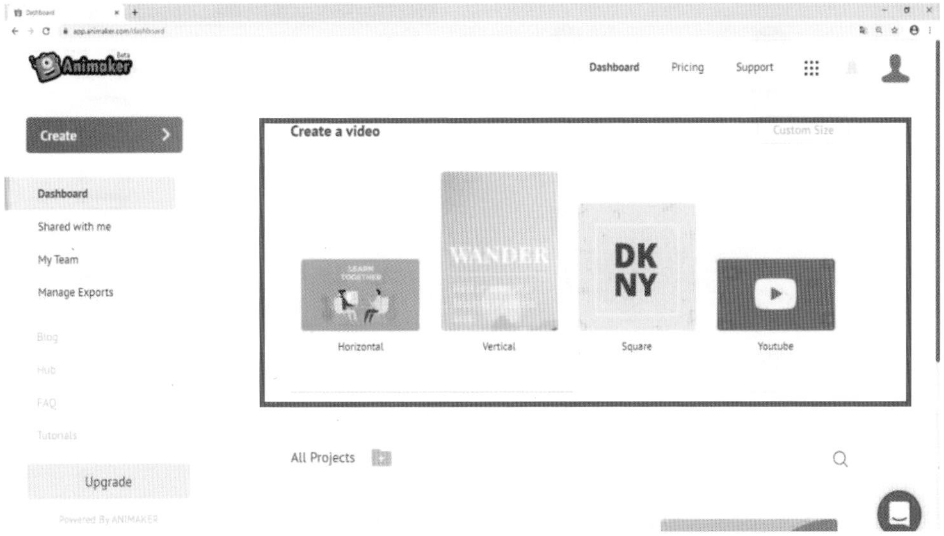

3) Click on 'Backgrounds' and select a proper one from various options on the left for your animations.

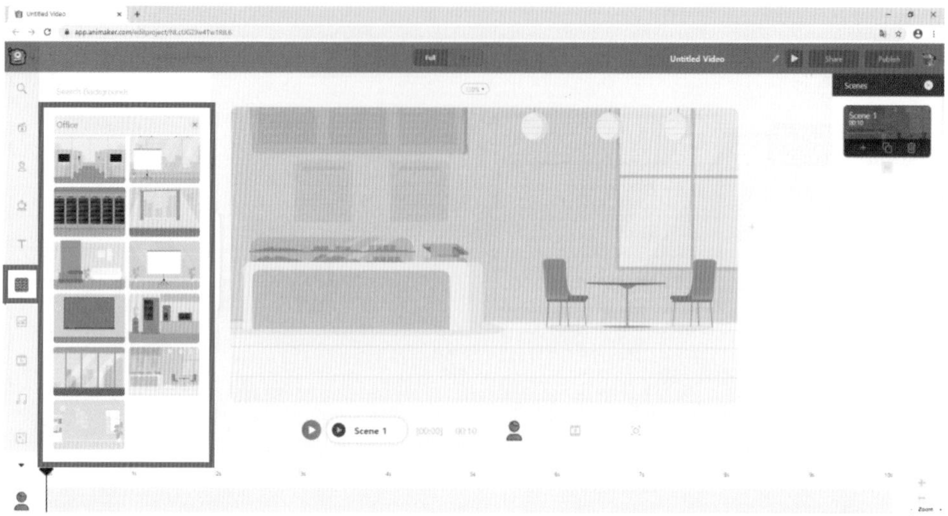

4) When choosing a character, you can set character details such as actions and facial expressions.

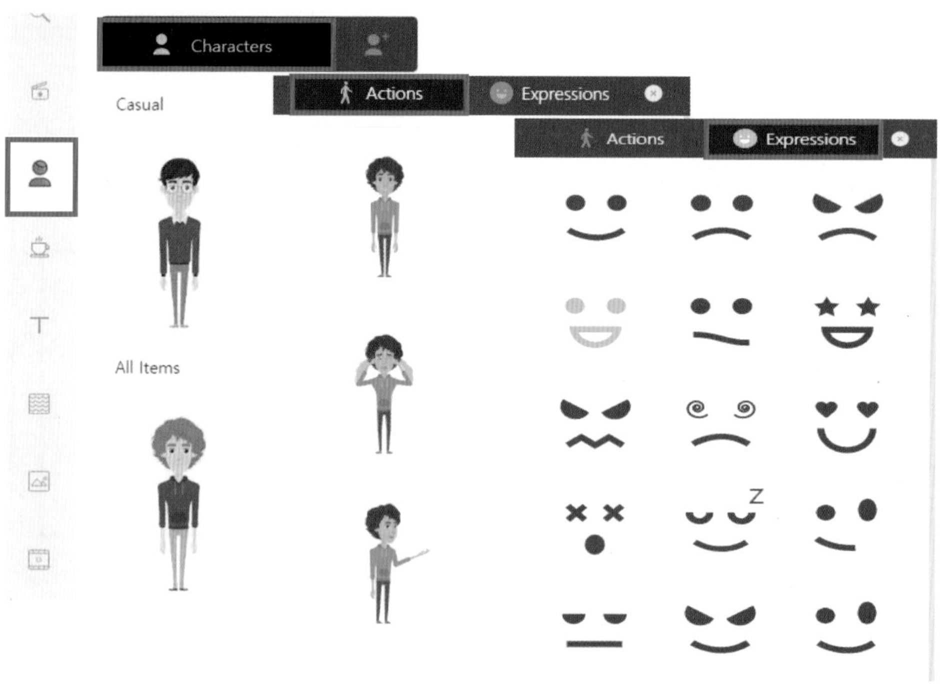

5) Create dialogues adding sounds with the 'Voice-Over' function such as recording voice, text-to-speech, and uploading files.

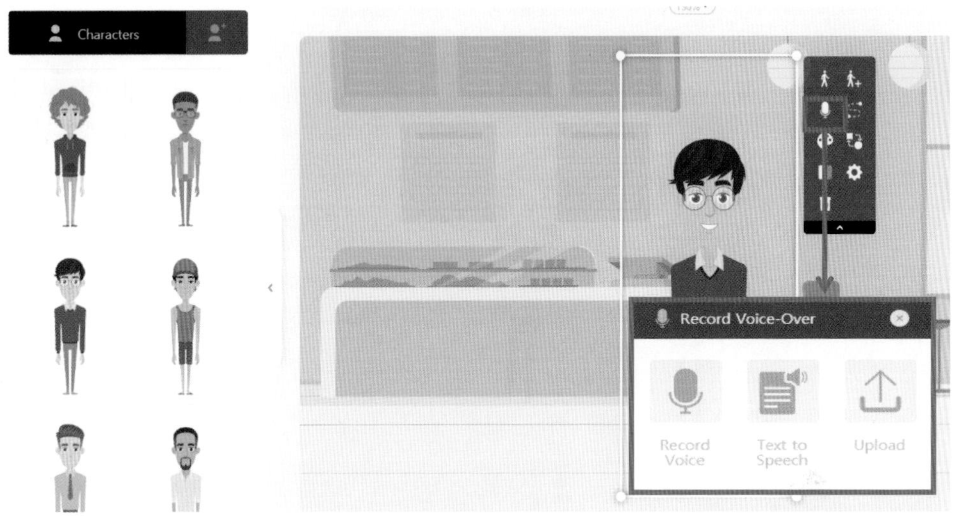

6) Select appropriate Properties, Text, and Music in your scene settings.

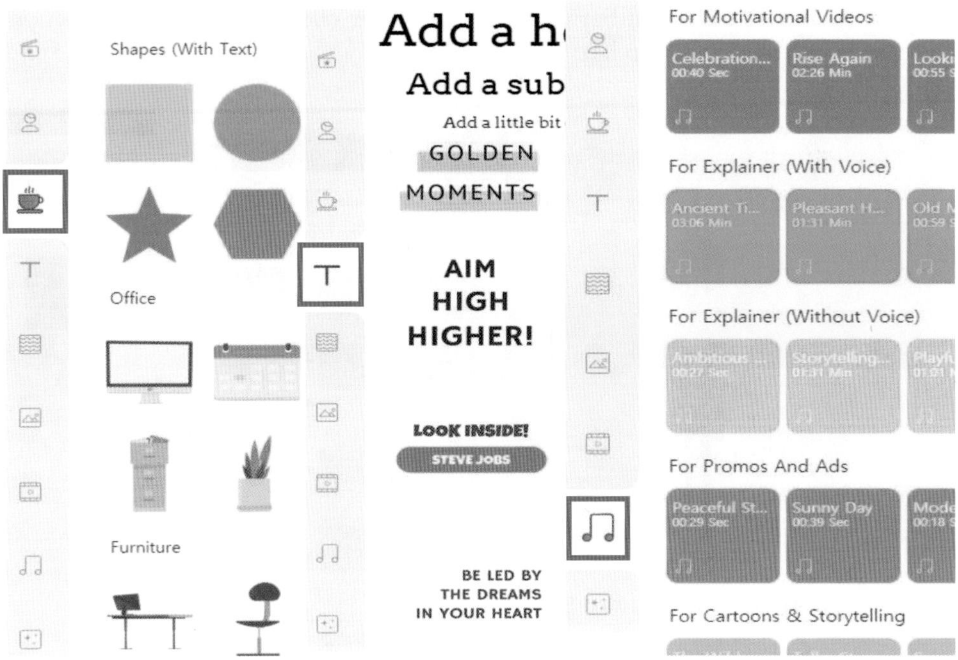

7) Add scenes by clicking the 'Add Scene (+)' button on the top left. The new slot will come up in the timeline. The produced scenes can be duplicated and deleted. The duration of each scene can be adjusted.

8) You can add a transition between two scenes by clicking  (add transition effect) button on the top left.

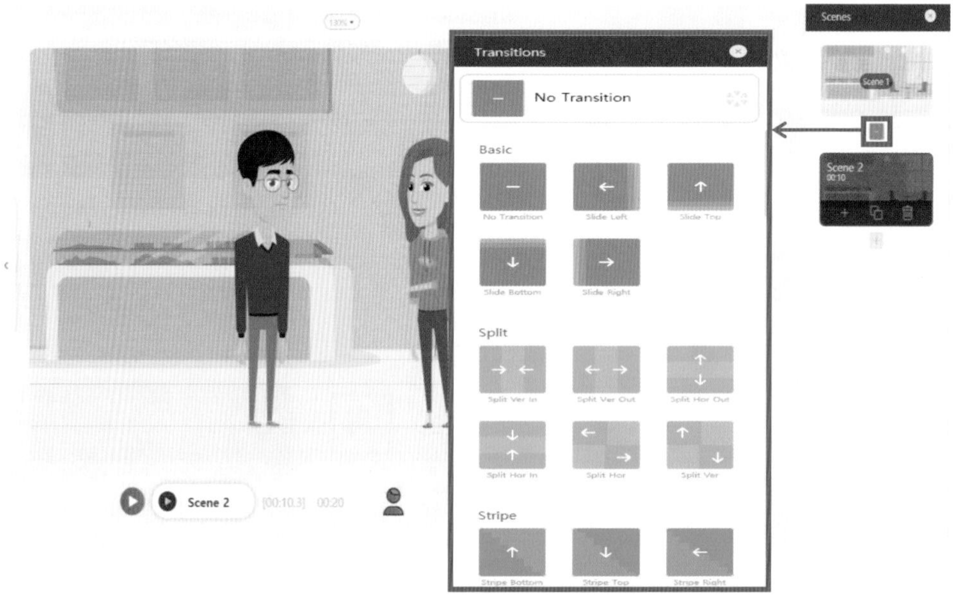

9) Click the 'Share' button to send emails to other people whom you want to give the authority of either view only or edit animations together.

10) Publish the animated video on *Animaker* if desired, or you can embed or share the video on other sites or social media.

Tasks for Study and Discussion

- Create an activity for increasing beginner or intermediate level students' pragmatic competence using *Animaker.* Make use of various characters, backgrounds, and functions to encourage students to participate in the activity. Then publish or share your work on other sites or social media. First, work individually, and then share your work with your partners.

  For example, create an animated video that includes one of the language functions or speech acts such as requests, apologies, compliments, etc.

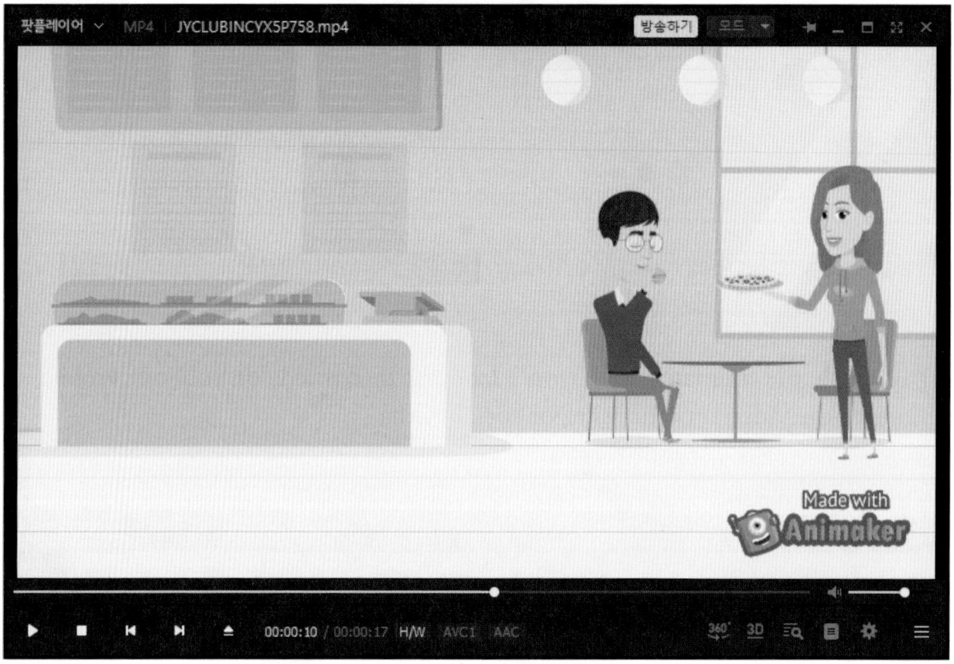

Chapter 6

Authoring Tools

Authoring tools allow users to create content using hypertext and a variety of multimedia applications. They are frequently used to create e-learning modules and link together multimedia objects, such as texts, images, sounds, and videos. The authors (those who use authoring tools) can create useful modules, content, or applications by defining the objects' relationships and sequencing and integrating the objects (Jones, 2003; https://en.wikipedia.org/wiki/Wiki/Authoring _system).

A couple of authoring tools, such as *Hot Potatoes* (https://hotpot.uvic.ca) and *Winwida (WIDA Authoring Suite)* (http://authoring-suite-ii.software.informer.com) are used in FLT&L. In the following section, user-friendly and web-based authoring tools, *Hot Potatoes* and *Socrative* (https://socrative.com/) are introduced.

6.1 *Hot Potatoes*

The *Hot Potatoes* suite is an educational freeware developed by Half-Baked Software for producing web-based exercises for language teachers. It allows teachers to make interactive, web-based exercises that students can access at any Internet-capable computer terminal with a standard Web browser. It uses both HTML and JavaScript. The program's exercise templates allow the users to create exercises on webpages that can be uploaded to a server for easy access.

Teachers can develop unlimited numbers of new exercises to suit the learners' level using texts, sounds, images, moving pictures, and others. They can utilize *Hot Potatoes* to use various types of teaching and learning materials, create new exercises, and edit preexisting exercises. The activities produced using *Hot Potatoes* are easily saved and run on the Web. The program is downloadable from *Hot Potatoes* homepage (https://hotpot.uvic.ca).

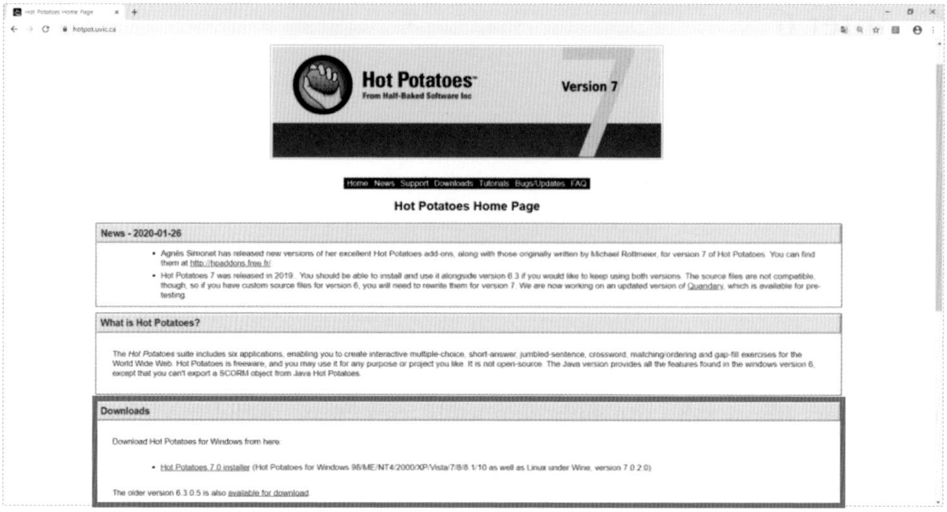

Figure 6.1 The homepage of *Hot Potatoes*

After downloading the *Hot Potatoes 7 installer,* run *Hot Potatoes 7 Setup Wizard* to install the program, as seen in Figure 6.2.

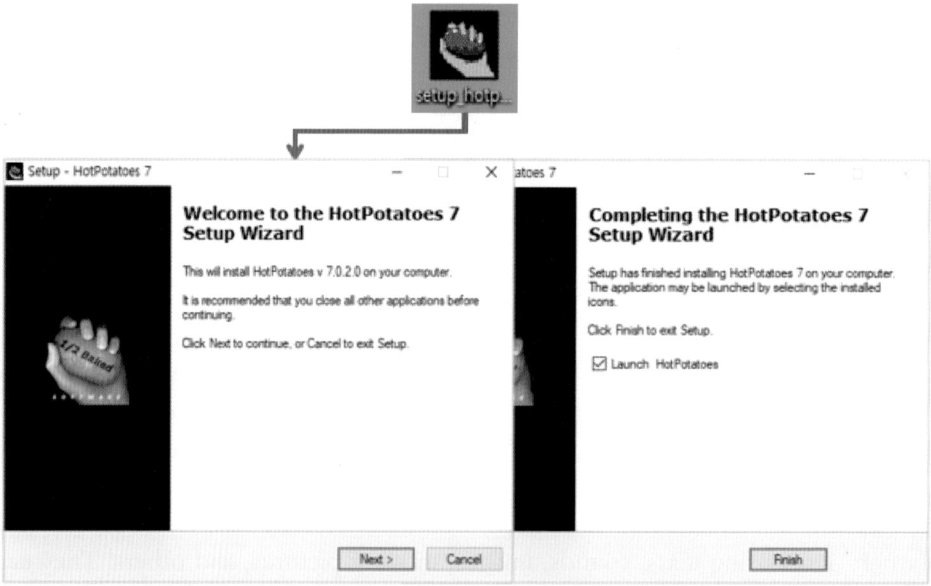

Figure 6.2 The installation process of *Hot Potatoes*

After the completion of the installation, the screen below will appear (Figure 6.3).

Figure 6.3 The main screen of *Hot Potatoes*

Hot Potatoes can create six different types of web-based exercises that can be standalone or be linked to other exercises to form a sequence of tasks: JQuiz, JMix, JCross, JCloze, JMatch, and the Masher. The six programs are referred to as *modules*. Each module can be used to create a different type of interactive, web-based exercise. The exercise types in each module are described in Table 6.1. The Masher is a program that combines all five programs into a bundle.

Table 6.1 The modules of *Hot Potatoes*

Modules	Activity type	What students do
JCloze	Fill-in-the blank exercise	Enter the missing words in a text
JCross	Crossword	Complete a crossword puzzle
JMix	Jumbled-word exercise	Arrange jumbled words into sentences or paragraphs
JMatch	Matching exercise Drag and drop	Match the items in the left column with those in the right column
JQuiz	Multiple-choice quiz Text-entry quiz	Choose the right answer for multiple choice questions or fill in the blank with the right answer
The Masher	Integration of the above activities	

JCloze

Cloze, also known as the cloze test, is a technique used for measuring text difficulty regarding language structure. The text has certain words deleted systematically, and the reader has to supply the information that should go in the blank. In designing a cloze activity, the gapping, or deletion, of words can be based on selecting certain grammar features or being gapped by automatic gapping function, depending on what is being measured. The automatic gap is created by designating the intervals (every 2-5 words) so that the blanks are regularly created at a specific interval.

Creating a new activity with JCloze

1) Click the 'JCloze' icon to get to the screen. Type in the title in the 'Title' area and write the content in the large box.

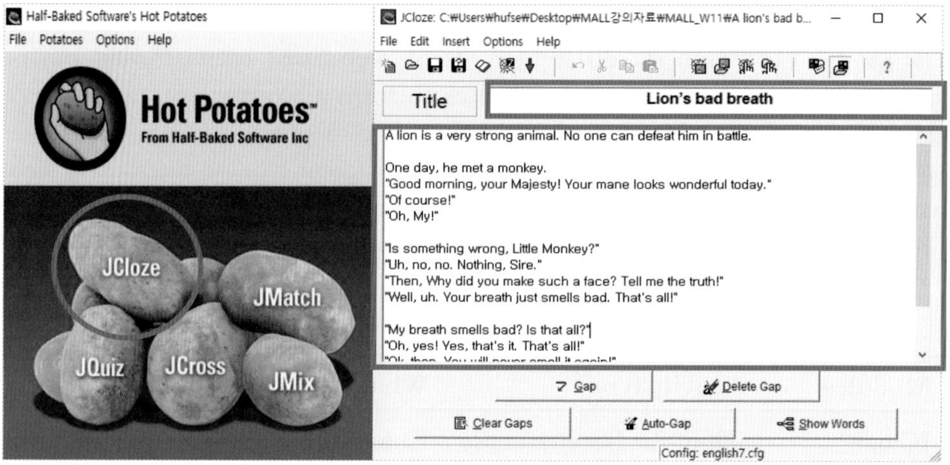

2) Choose and double-click the word you wish to be made blank for gap-filling activity. Then click the 'Gap' button.
3) Add the hint or definition in the 'Clue' box and click 'OK.' You can write other possible answers in the 'Alternative correct answers' box.

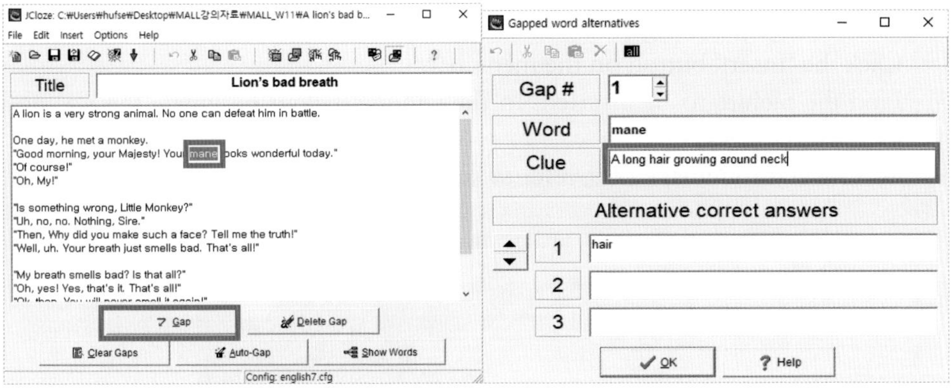

4) Click the 'save' button on the top menu bar to save the exercise. Then click the 'web' button to save it as a web assignment for learners.
5) To verify that the exercise is saved on the Web, click on 'View the exercise in my browser.'

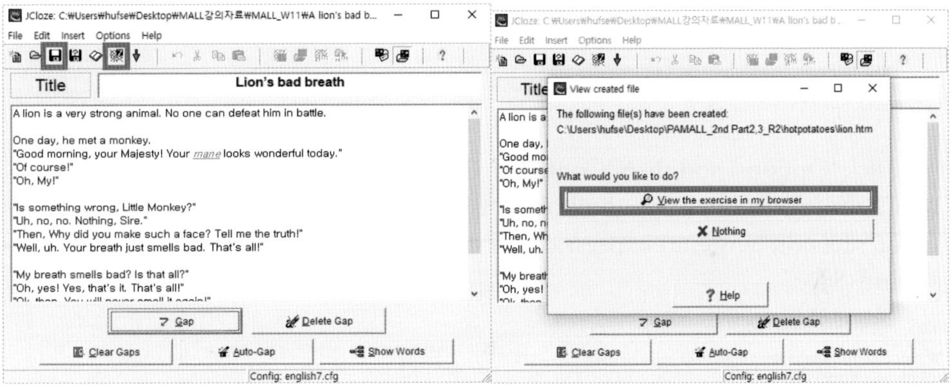

6) The exercise is put on the Web.

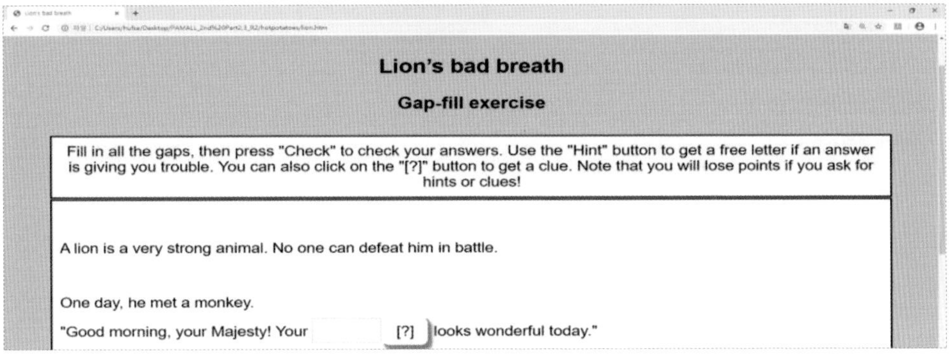

7) Insert images, moving pictures, sounds, or other types of files, if necessary. Click the 'Insert' button on the menu bar.
8) Find the picture to be inserted. In the window below, designate the size and location and click 'OK.'
9) To save and run image files, refer to steps 4), 5), and 6).

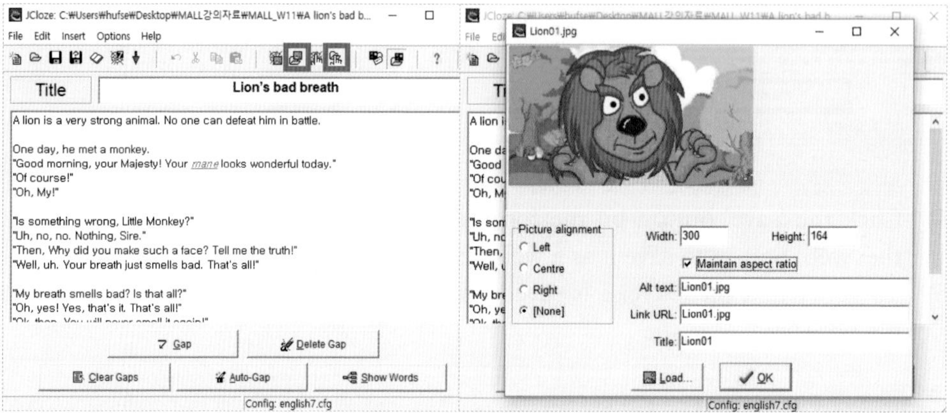

Using options: Setting a time limit

1) Click 'Options' and then 'Configure Output' on the menu bar.
2) Check (√) on 'Set a time limit for this exercise,' and set a time limit in minutes or seconds. Write an expression to indicate that time is up. Then click 'OK' and 'Save.'

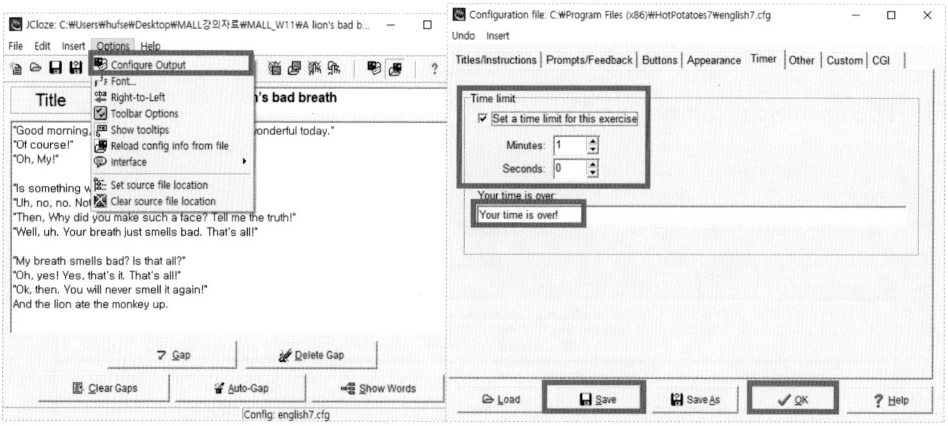

3) The timed exercise is put on the Web.

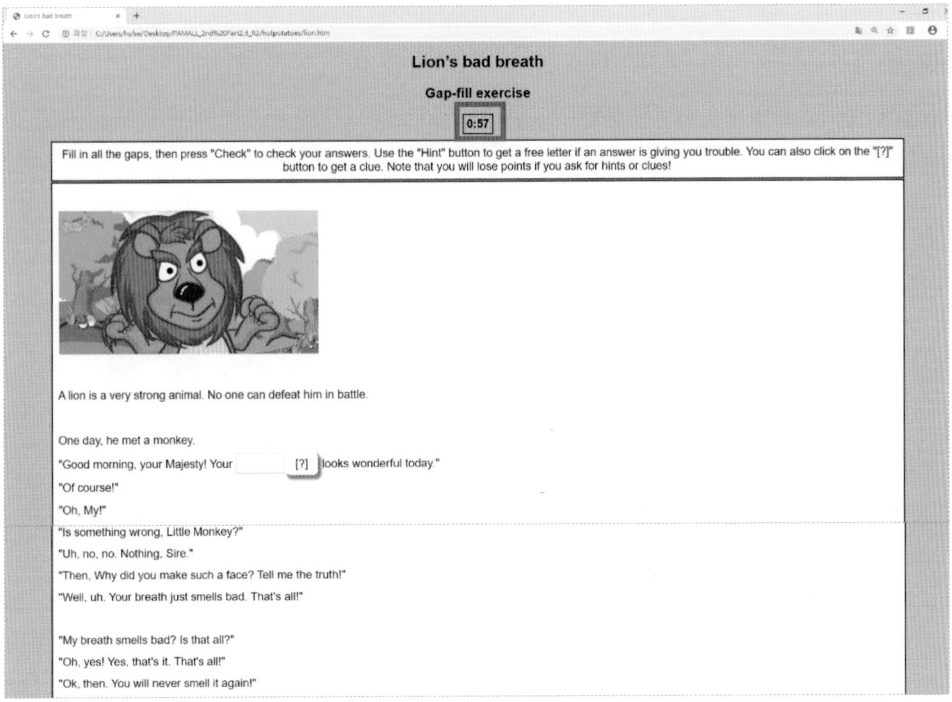

The frequent use of the timer is not recommended, except for testing purposes. Learners may feel anxious and get stressed when they care too much about the time limit. Various options, such as 'Configure Output,' 'Font,' 'Right-to-Left,' etc., are used in the six modules of *Hot Potatoes.*

JMatch

JMatch can be used for general content and various purposes like checking reading comprehension, grammar, and structure. In particular, JMatch is useful for building vocabulary skills. Visuals and audiovisuals can be inserted easily, making it attractive for students to do the activity. In the figure below, images of fruits are on the left column, and the corresponding names for the fruits are presented in multiple-choice answers on the right.

Creating a new activity with JMatch

1) Click 'JMatch' icon to get to the screen. Write in the title in the 'Title' area.

2) Click the 'image' button on the top menu bar to insert images that describe the words on the left. Then write words, phrases, or sentences.

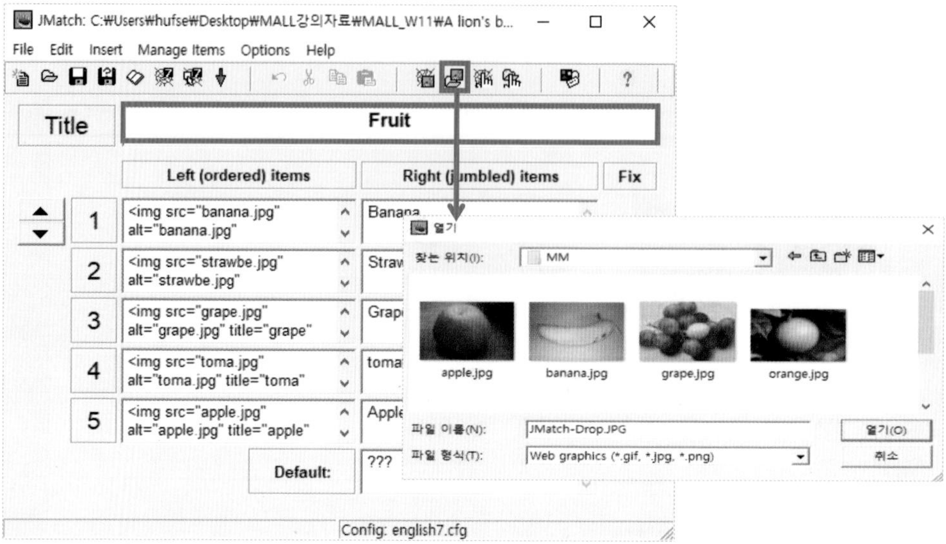

3) Click the 'save' button on the top menu bar to save the added images and descriptions. Then click the 'web' button to save it as a web assignment for learners.
4) The exercise is put on the Web.

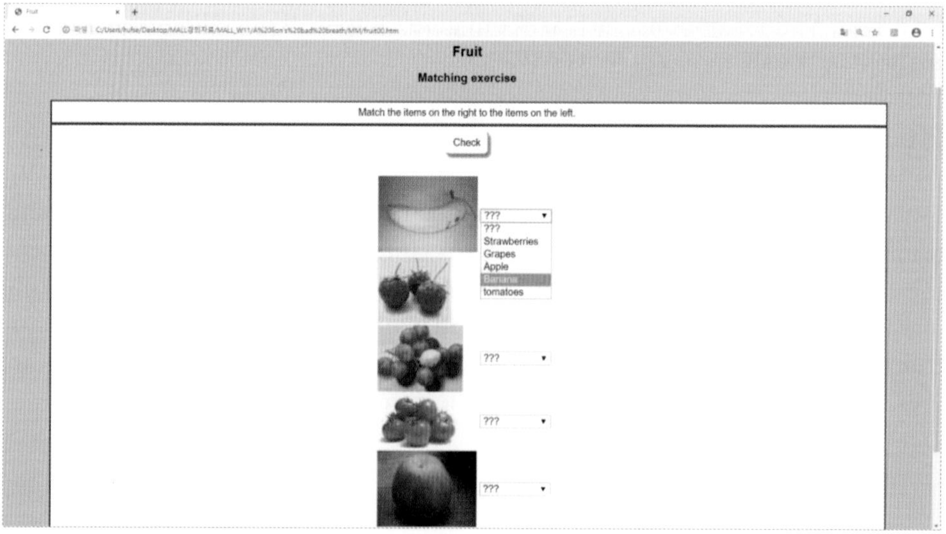

5) JMatch offers two types of matching questions: Drag-and-drop and drop-down forms. Click the 'drag-and-drop Web' button to save it as a Web assignment for learners.

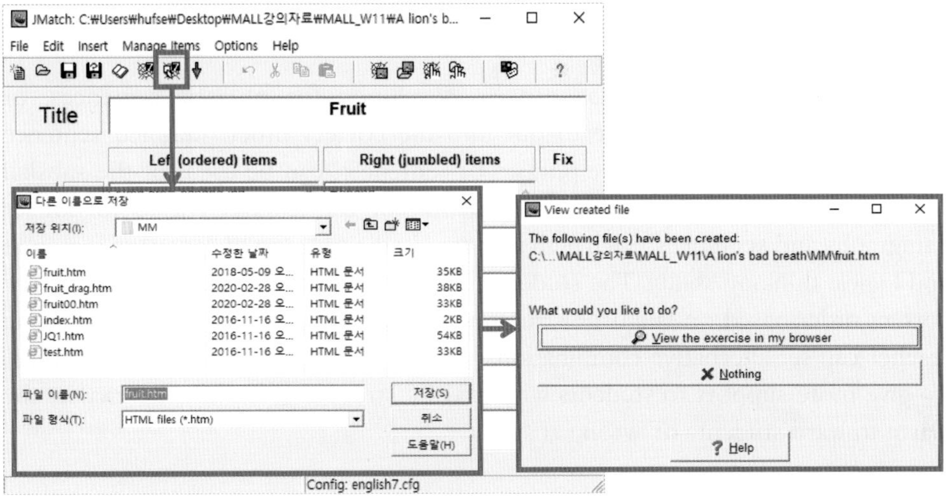

6) The drag-and-drop exercise is put on the Web. You can also set time limits for this activity by manipulating 'Configure output' in the Options menu.

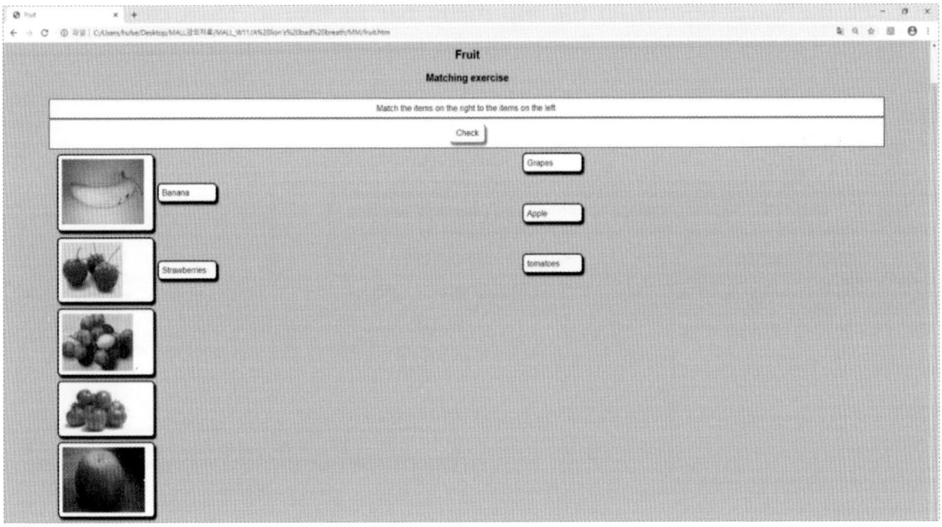

JMix

JMix allows the creation of jumbled sentence activities for writing and grammar skills. Jumbled sentence activities are used for developing students' writing skills in logical thinking and paragraph structure while activating learner strategies like inferring and ordering strategies.

Jumbled sentence activities can be developed for phrases, sentences, or paragraphs that students have to put into the correct order. Jumbled sentence activities for a smaller unit, like phrases or sentences, can be used for the subskill level of grammar structure. The full potential of the JMix activity is for longer paragraphs and sentences. Such activities require knowledge of language structure and logical thinking ability. The students will have to read them and figure out the correct order based on language structure, logical flow, and context. In JMix, the teacher can set alternative combinations so that various answers can be accepted. To give more support to students who may be struggling, the teacher can set the alarm to warn students of wrong answers.

Creating a new activity with JMix

1) Click 'JMix' icon to get to the screen. Write the title in the 'Title' area.
2) Write words, phrases, or sentences in the main sentence box.
3) Click the 'save' button on the top menu bar to save it. Then click the 'web' button to save it as a web assignment for learners.

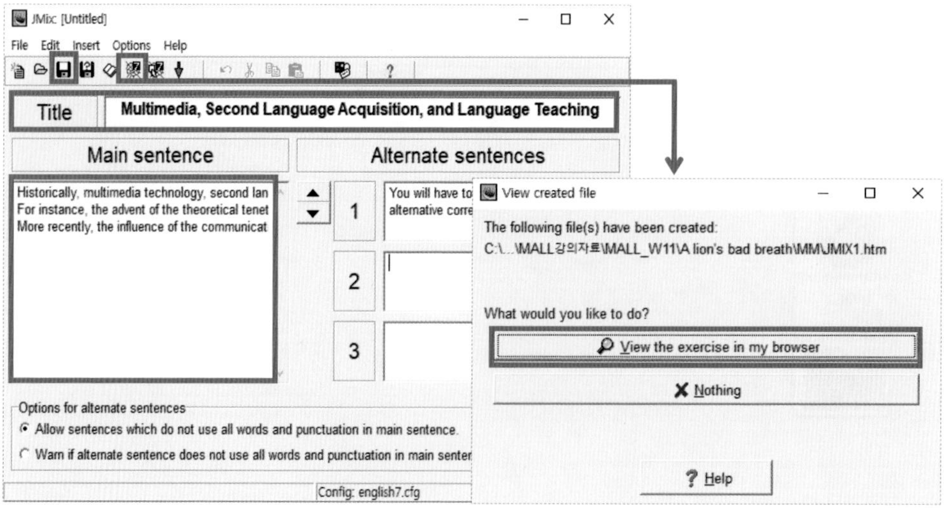

4) The exercise is put on the Web.

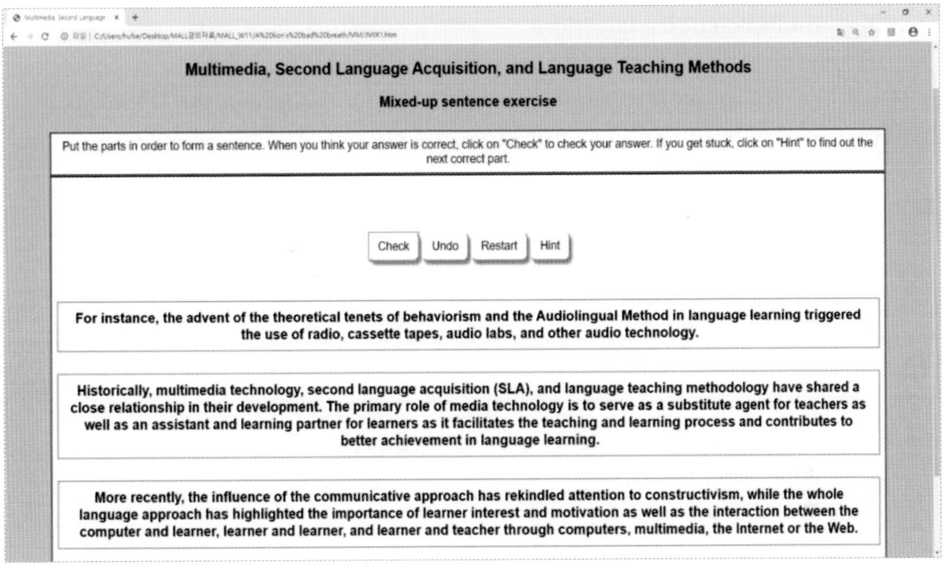

JQuiz

JQuiz can be used mainly to make quizzes, especially in reading. It may be used as a while-reading activity to check the students' reading comprehension, and it may also be used effectively to create a post-reading activity. One of the advantages of JQuiz is that teachers can develop a set of quizzes in various forms, including short answers and multiple-choice questions. In both quizzes, visuals and audiovisuals can be added to provide context and hint for the students.

JQuiz also offers a hybrid type of quiz. The hybrid quiz allows a switch in the versions of quizzes. If a student is unable to answer the short answer question version, the teacher can allow the student to switch to the multiple-choice version. After a set number of attempts specified by the teacher, the quiz converts to a multiple-choice question, giving the students to select the answer from the options. In this way, JQuiz can provide students with the opportunities to engage in problem-solving and high-order reasoning skills through short answers. It also allows scaffolding by providing more clued types of quizzes to support the students.

Creating a new activity with JQuiz

Creating a multiple-choice question

1) Click the 'JQuiz' icon to get to the screen. Write the title in the 'Title' area.
2) Type a question in the 'Question' area and choose 'Multiple-choice.'

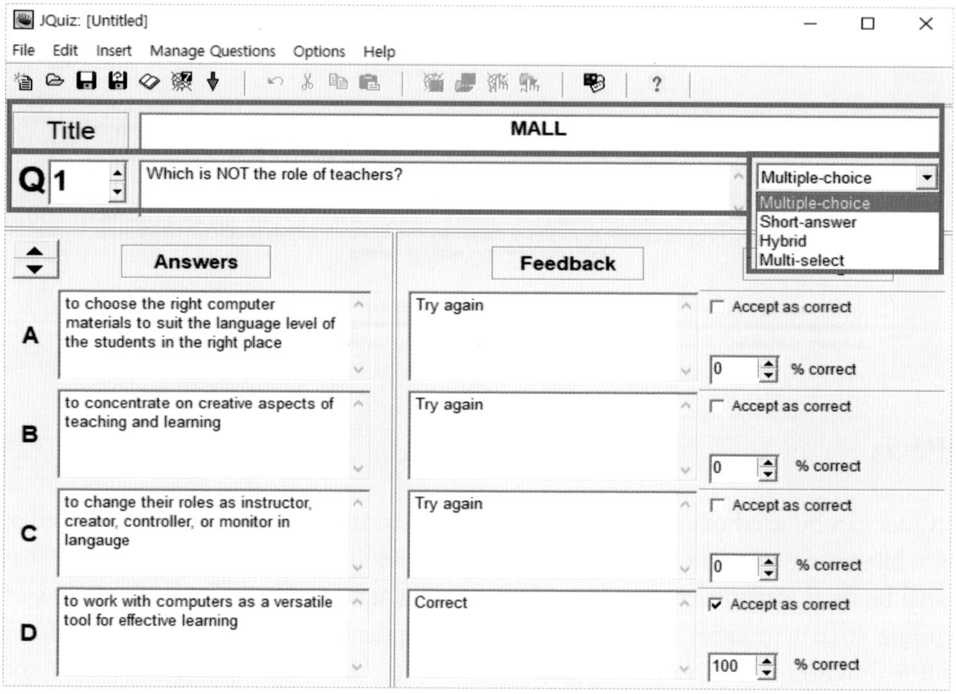

3) Type the answer text in the 'Answers' area and enter feedback next to each answer in the 'Feedback' area. Then check the correct answer in the 'Settings' area.
4) Add questions if necessary (Q1, Q2, Q3, etc.).
5) Click the 'save' button on the top menu bar to save. Then click the 'web' button to save it as a Web assignment for learners.

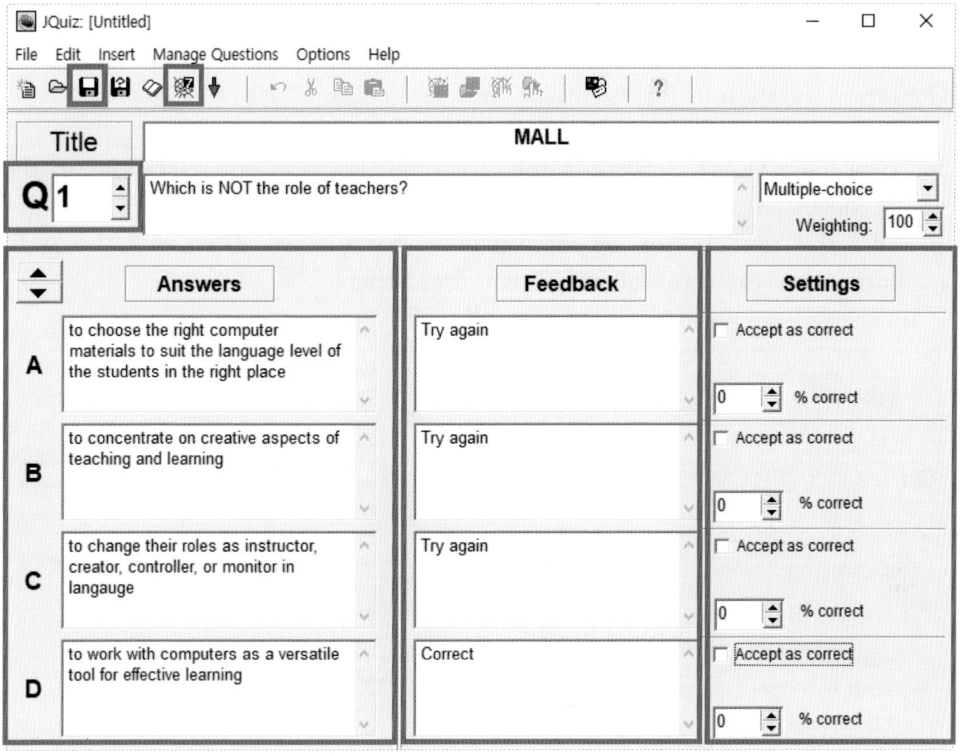

6) The exercise is put on the Web.

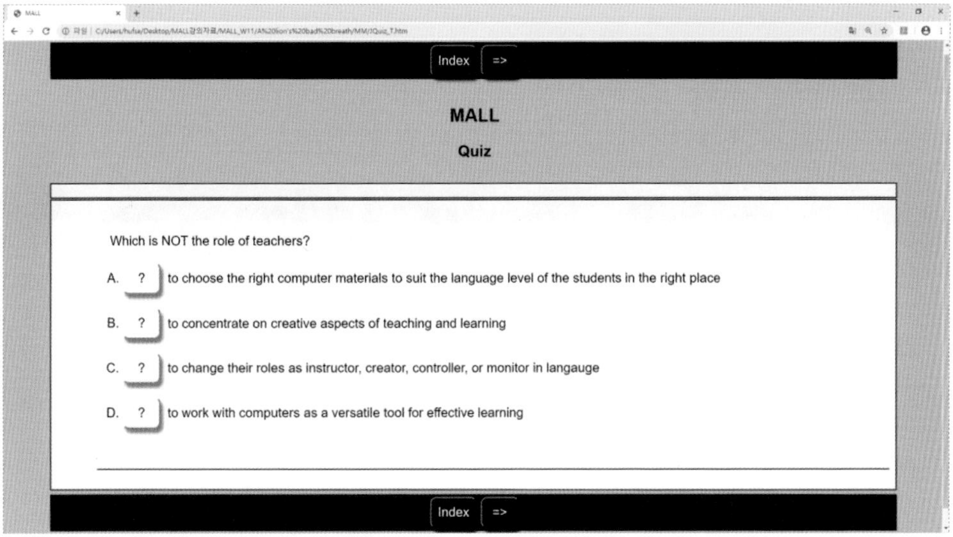

Creating a hybrid question

1) Type a question in the 'Question' area, and choose 'Hybrid' as the quiz type. Then 'include in M/C options' will appear in the 'Settings' area.
2) Type the text for answers in the 'Answers' area, and enter feedback in the 'Feedback' area. Then check the correct answer in the 'Settings' area.
3) Click the 'save' button on the top menu bar to save. Then click the 'web' button to save it as a web assignment for learners.

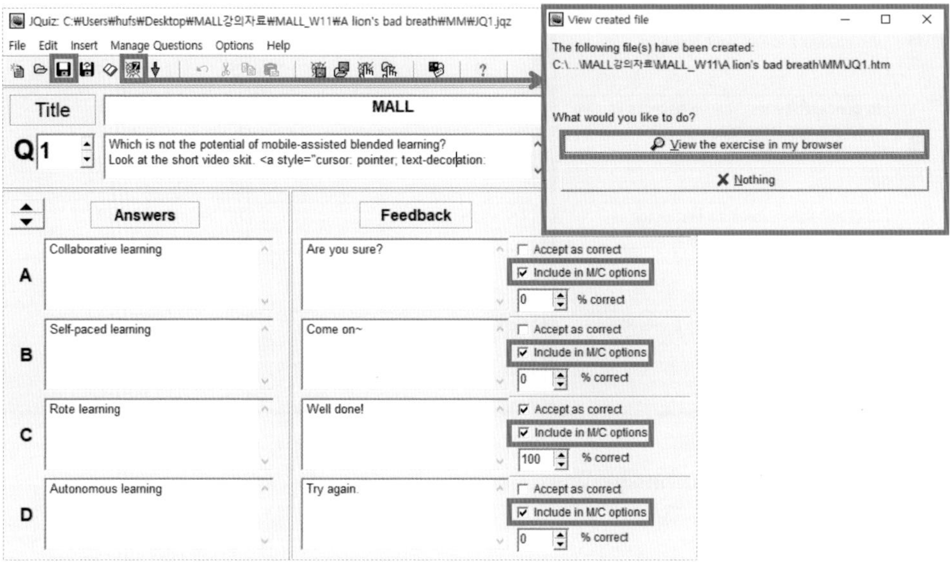

4) The exercise is put on the Web.

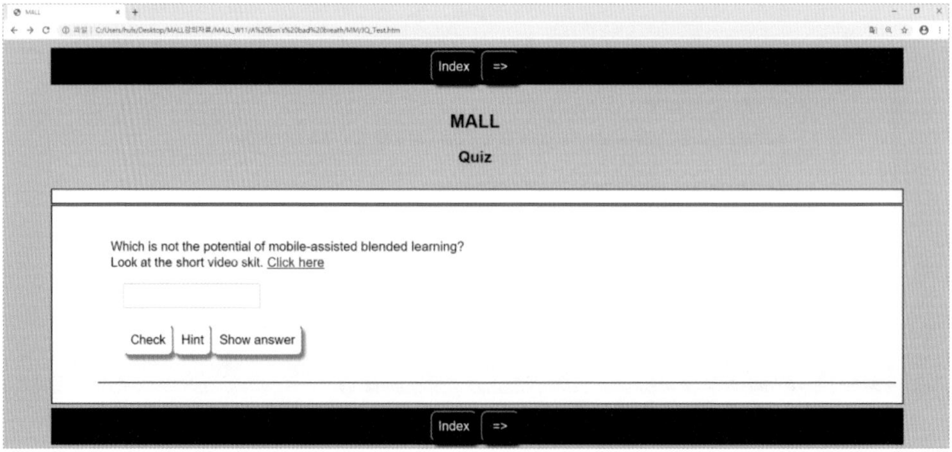

5) When the answer is wrong in the short-answer question, the multiple-choice question will appear with a pop-up.

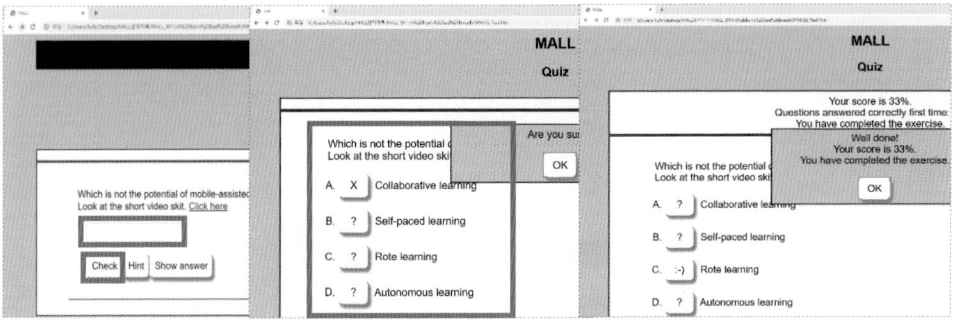

JCross

There are many fun ways to deal with vocabulary in language classes, and a crossword puzzle is one of them. JCross allows teachers to design a crossword puzzle for vocabulary activity. The teacher can provide a list of vocabulary items or enter them one by one. After entering the vocabulary items, JCross automatically produces a crossword puzzle and numbers the words as well. The teacher can provide clues for the vocabulary items to reflect the students' level, needs, and knowledge. There is no separate list of hints, but the students can click on the numbers to see the individual clues.

Creating a new activity with JCross

1) Click the 'JCross' icon to get to the screen. Write the title in the 'Title' area.
2) Write words in the grid to create a crossword.
3) Click 'Add Clues' to write clues for the words entered into the grid and click 'OK.'

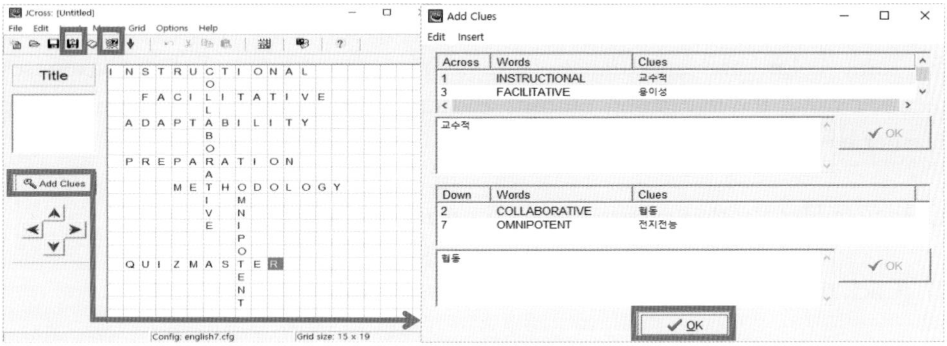

4) Click the 'save' button on the top menu bar to save. Then click the 'web' button to save it as a web assignment for learners.
5) The exercise is put on the Web.

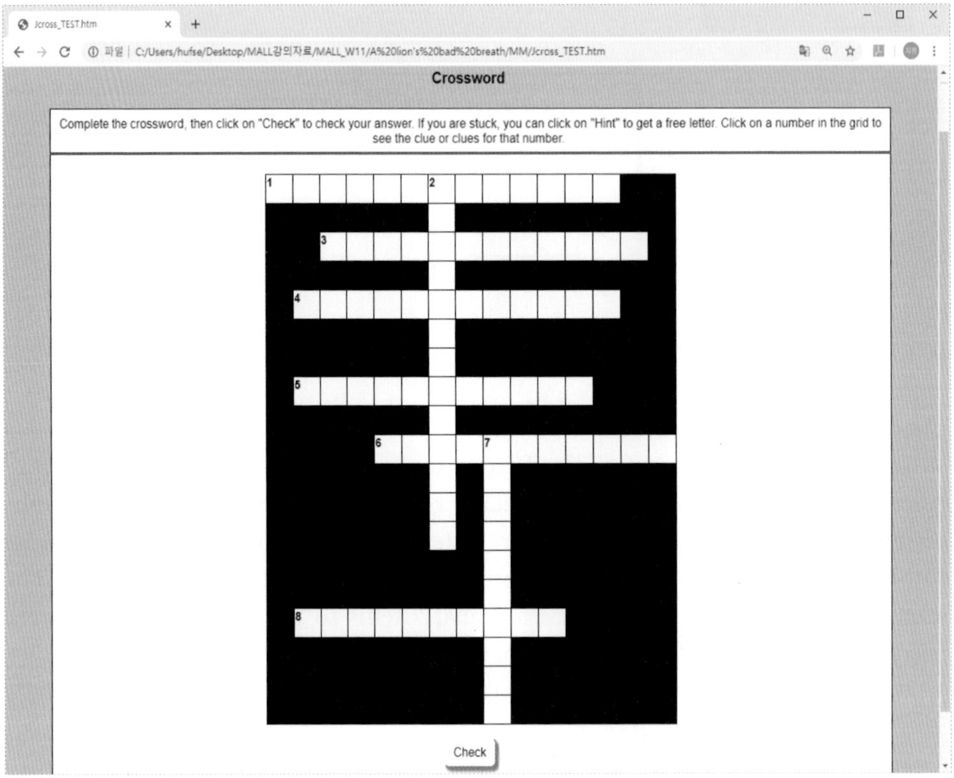

The Masher

The Masher is a tool for automatically compiling batches of Hot Potatoes exercises into units. Imagine that you have five *Hot Potatoes* exercises that form a single unit of materials. You want to build HTML files from all the exercises with the same colors and appearance settings. You also want to link the exercises together using the navigation buttons and create an index file for the unit. The Masher has the function to enable this.

Compiling Hot Potatoes exercises into units with 'The Masher'

1) Click the 'The Masher' icon to get to the screen.

2) Choose files to include in the unit. Then click 'Add files' or drag all the *Hot Potatoes* files you want to include into the 'Files' box.

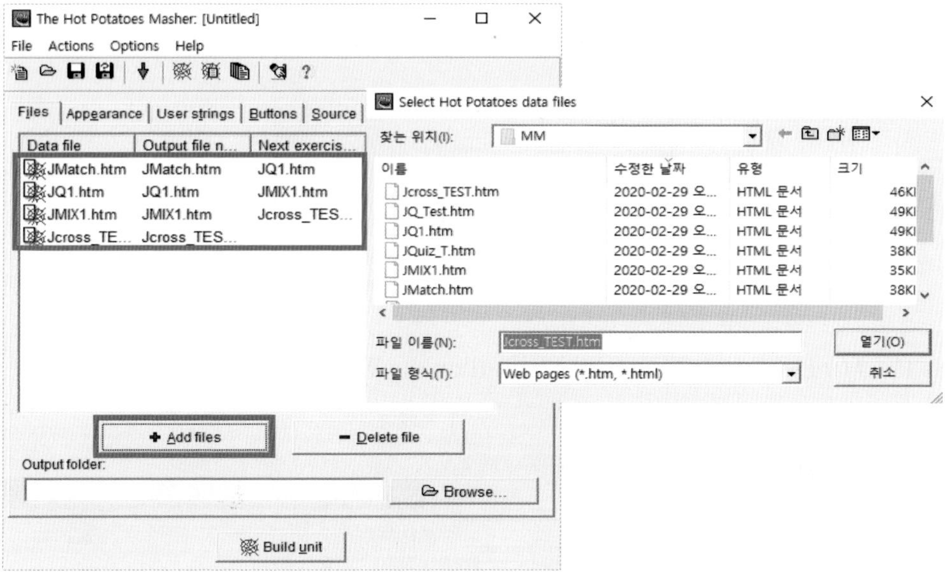

3) Adjust appearance (background graphic URL, font, color, etc.), user strings, buttons, source, and index, if necessary.
4) Click 'Build unit' to compile the *Hot Potatoes* exercises.
5) Click 'Yes' to view the unit on the Web.
6) Click the 'save this project with a new name' button on the top menu bar to save. Then click the 'web' button to save it as a web assignment for learners.

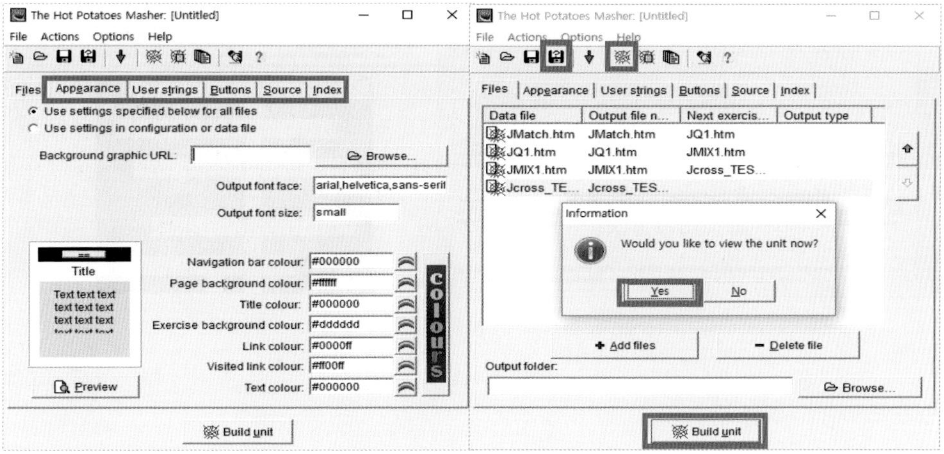

7) The unit is put on the Web with an index page for the entire unit.

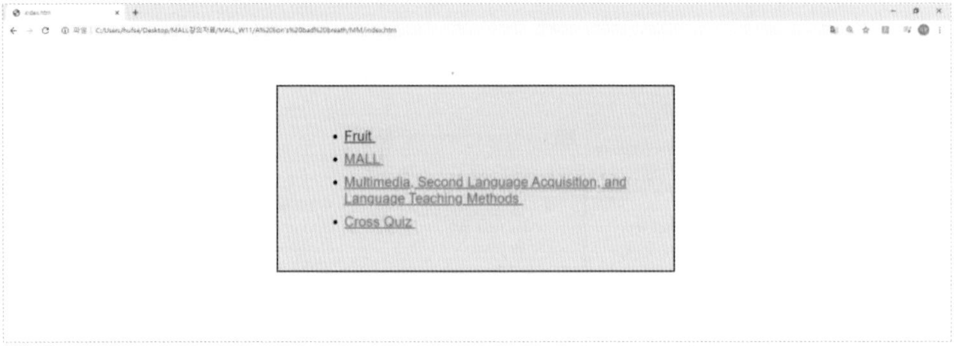

8) The *Hot Potatoes* exercises are compiled on the Web in sequence.

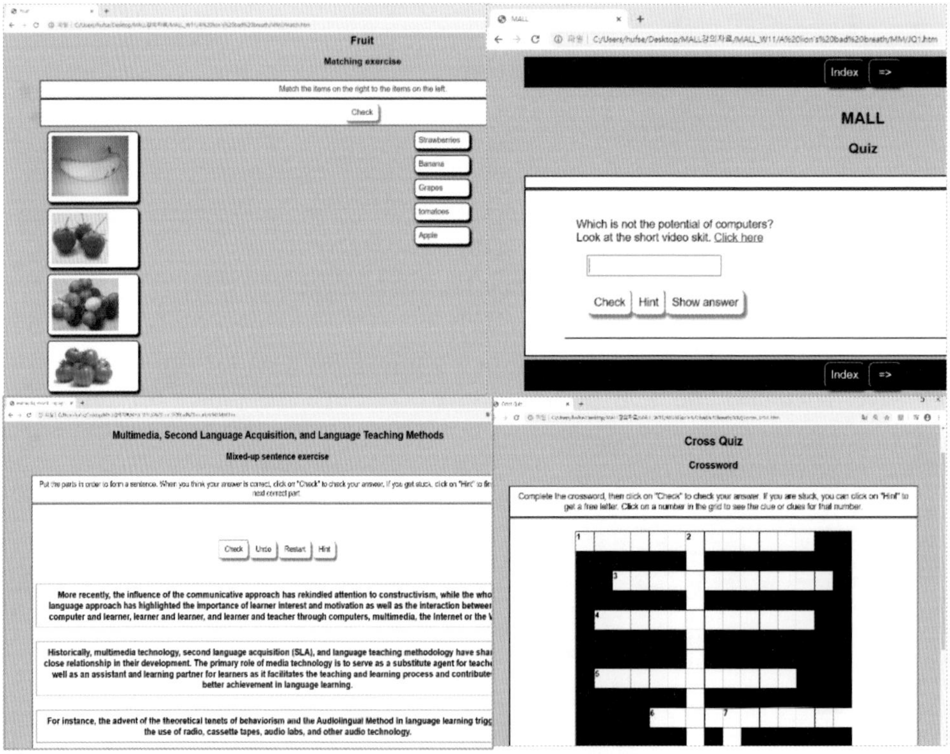

Tasks for Study and Discussion

1. Think about how each module can be used to teach language skills and devise activities appropriate for language skills and modules in the table below. Share your work with partners.

Modules	Language Skills	Activities
JCloze		
JCross		
JMix		
JMatch		
JQuiz		
The Masher		

2. Produce two or three exercises using the six modules of *Hot Potatoes*. Make use of various functions and options. Insert images, sounds, and videos you have produced using *Tagxedo, PhotoScape X, Make Beliefs Comix, Goldwave, Gom Mix Pro,* and *Animaker*. Compile the *Hot Potatoes* exercises into a unit with 'Masher.' First, work individually and then share your work with your partners.

   For example, develop a set of quizzes with JQuiz and a matching exercise with JMatch for beginning and intermediate or mixed-level students in a reading class.

6.2 *Socrative*

Socrative is a formative assessment tool that teachers can create simple quizzes (e.g., multiple-choice, true/false, and short answer questions), space races, and exit tickets for open-ended and reflection questions via Socrative Teacher. Students can take quickly on computers and PLDs and interact with teachers and peers via Socrative Student. The teachers can also gauge student understanding and collect and analyze student data in real-time. It enables teachers to modify their instruction to drive and improve student learning effectively. (https://www.socrative.com/about-us/). Especially through real-time questioning, result aggregation, and visualization, teachers can have instant insight into the levels of understanding and use class time to collaborate and grow as a community of learners.

Socrative on the Web

1) Sign up for using *Socrative* by clicking 

.

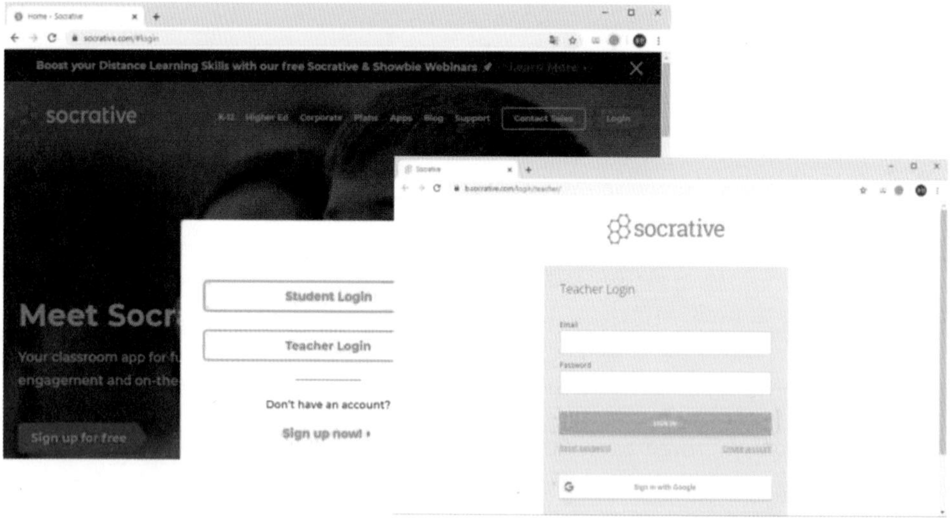

2) Click 'Teacher Login' and input the relevant information to finish registering for Socrative Teacher.
   * After login, you will have your Room Name, e.g., LEE1234.

3) Click 'Quizzes' to create new questions or 'Quick question.'

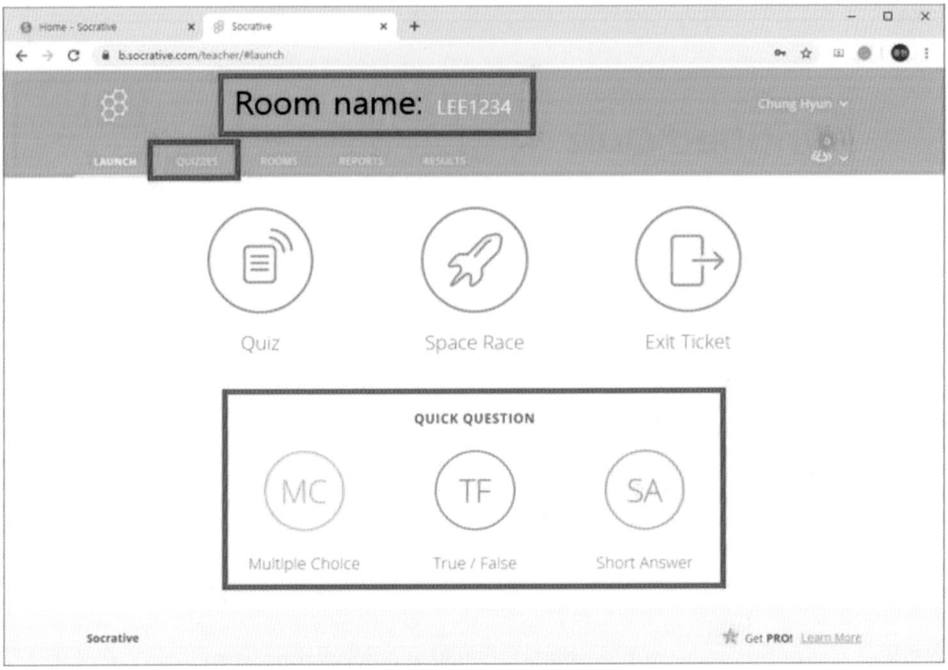

4) Click '+ ADD Quiz' to create new questions or choose the previous questions to edit.

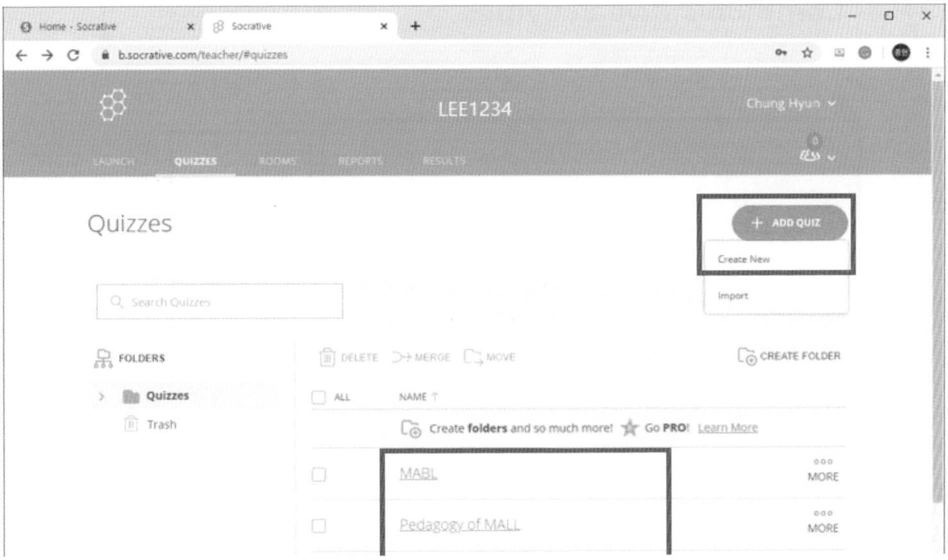

5) Write the title in the Untitled Quiz box and add a question to get started.

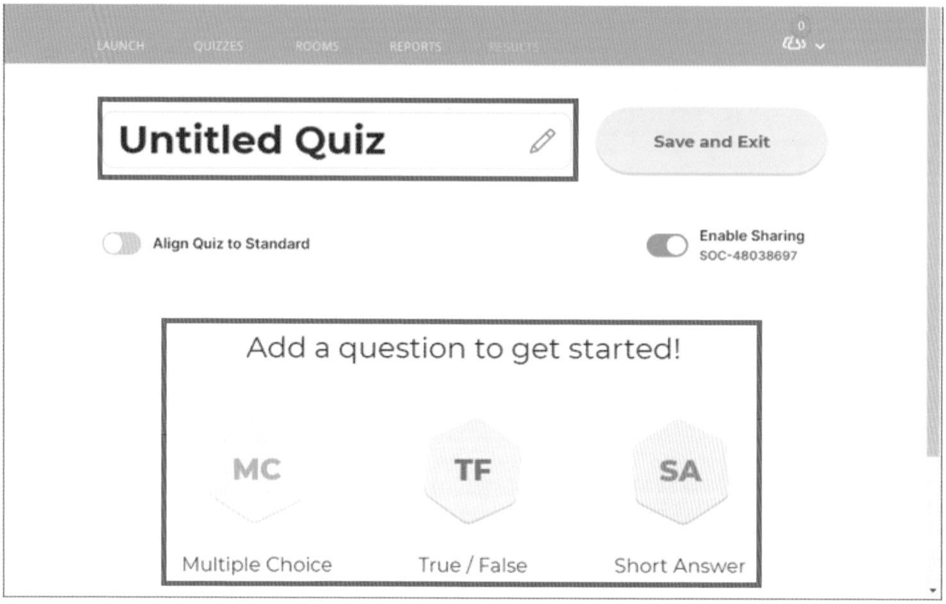

6) Write a new question and answer and click an image button to insert it.
7) Add questions and save and exit.

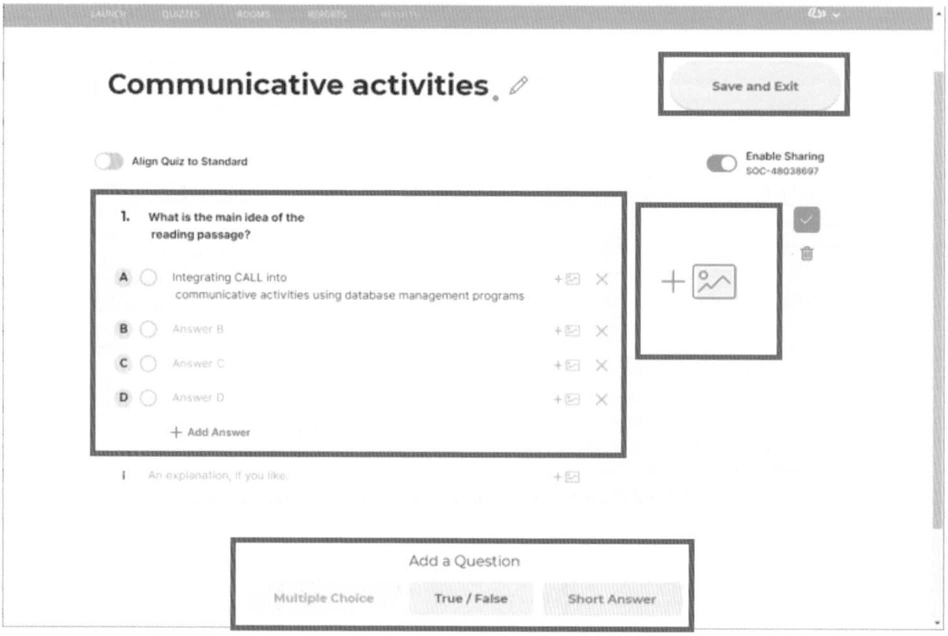

* Edit the previous questions and add more questions.

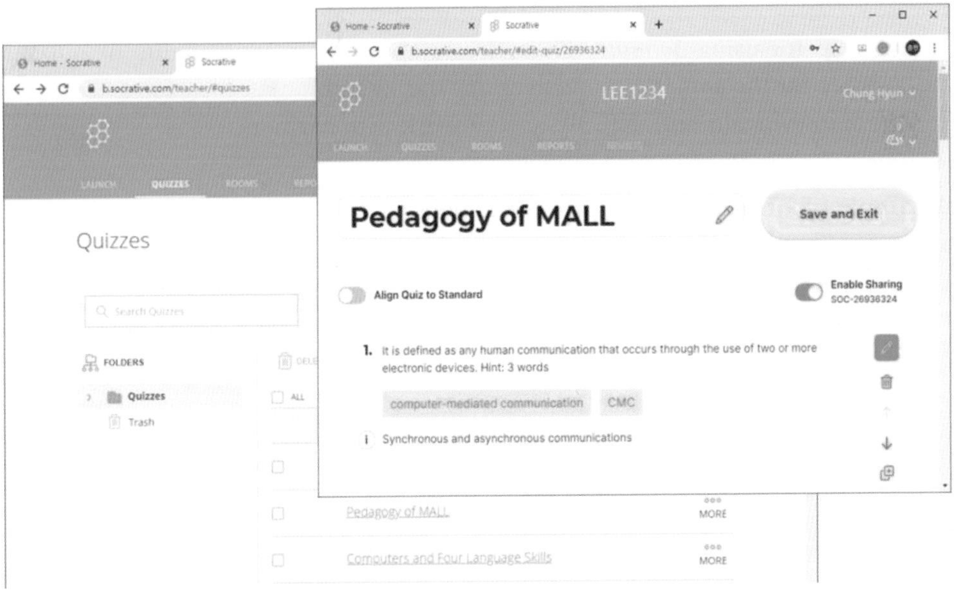

Using *Socrative* Apps

1) Search *Socrative* the 'Google Play Store' or 'AppStore' and download Socrative Teacher and Socrative Student.
2) Write 'Room Name' to sign in to Student Login.

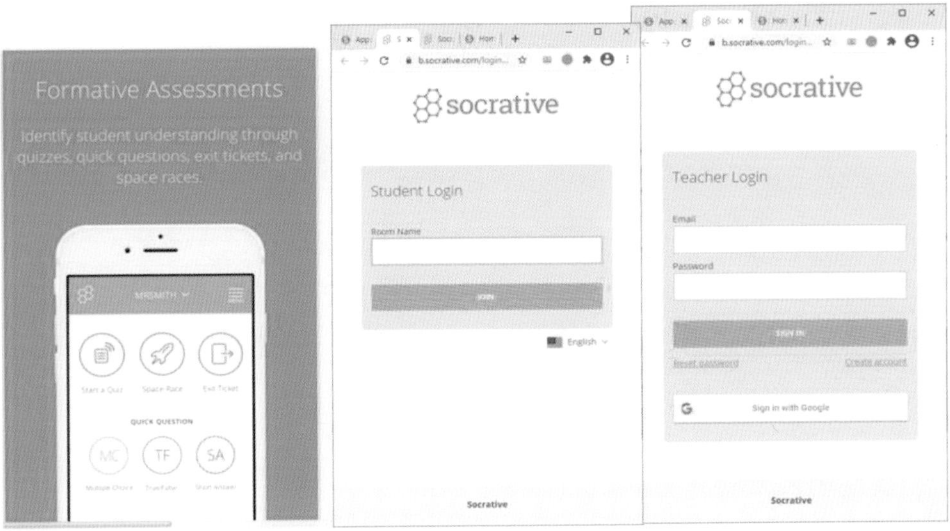

Tasks for Study and Discussion

1. Sign up for using *Socrative.* Then, create appropriate assignments or quizzes suitable for the aims and objectives of your lesson.
2. Work individually and then share your work with partners.

A sample of quiz using Socrative Teacher

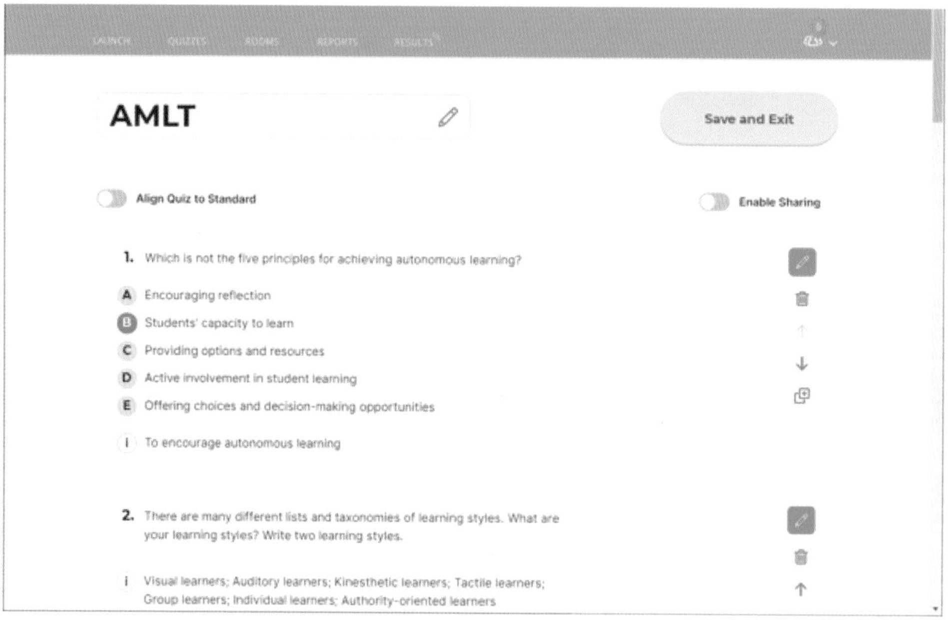

Chapter 7

Other Learning Tools

So far in this book, various editing and authoring tools for FLT&L have been introduced and practiced. This chapter will deal with some other useful tools and websites available for FLT&L, e.g., *Classting* (LMS), *Flipgrid* (a video discussion platform), *Grammarly* (a grammar and plagiarism checking tool), *OKMindmap* (a web-based mind mapping tool), *Compleat Lexical Tutor* (a corpus-based learning tool), etc. They allow teachers and students to facilitate the teaching and learning process, foster interaction and communicate efficiently in FLT&L.

First, LMS is a software system for managing a course, delivering course content, documenting course content, and tracking and reporting students' learning process. For example, *Classting* (https://www.classting.com), *Socrative* (https://socrative.com/), and *Microsoft Teams* (https://www.microsoft.com/ko-kr/microsoft-365/microsoft-teams/download-app) are user-friendly and innovative LMSes. Second, audio/video discussion platforms help learners practice spoken skills through recording and sharing their voices, such as *Flipgrid* (https://www.flipgrid.com) and *Padlet* (https://www.padlet.com). Third, grammar and plagiarism checking tools are available on the Web, such as *Grammarly* (https://www.grammarly.com) and EasyBib (https://writing.easybib.com/). Fourth, web-based mind mapping tools are provided on the Web, such as *OKMindmap* (http://okmindmap.com), *Bubbl.us* (https://bubbl.us/), and *Lucidchart* (https://www.lucidchart.com/pages/). Last, in recent years, due to the development of corpus linguistics, a variety of corpus-based learning tools are available on the Internet, such as *Compleat Lexical Tutor* (http://www.lextutor.ca) and *the Corpus of Contemporary American English* (*COCA*) (http://corpus.byu.edu/coca).

7.1 *Classting*

Classting (https://www.classting.com/) is a web-and mobile-based LMS for educational institutions. It provides cloud hosting services for instructors, students and parents. Once an affiliated account is created, teachers can create classes for students and parents to join, where they access various functions of *Classting*. Teachers can create notices for the whole class, assign and manage homework, while everyone who has been given permission can create posts and albums, and students can submit assignments. *Classting* also has a mobile app to allow teachers to manage their students outside of the classroom and keep track of their classes ubiquitously. The app is available both on iOS and Android devices.

Classting on the Web

Starting *Classting*

1) Sign up for using *Classting* by clicking the green 'Get started in a minute' button.

Figure 7.1 The main screen of *Classting*

2) Choose 'teacher' to start setting up *Classting*.
3) Input the relevant information to finish registering for *Classting*.

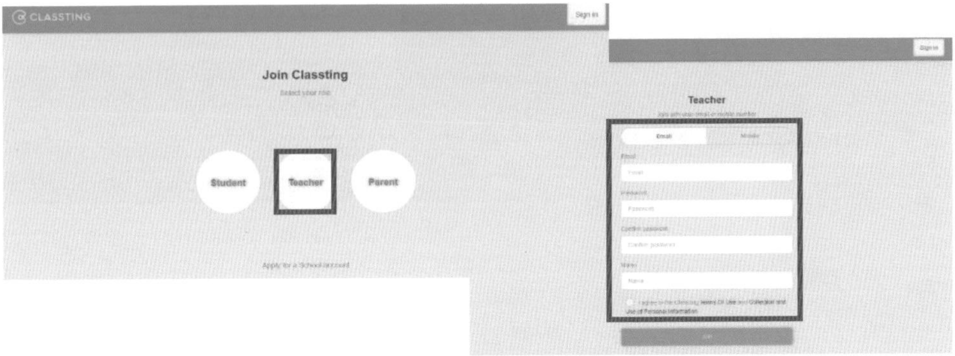

4) Click on the '+' icon to start a new class.
5) Fill in the relevant information. When you start entering the school, choices will appear for the correct institution. For this demonstration, a speaking class was created for the second-year students in a university.

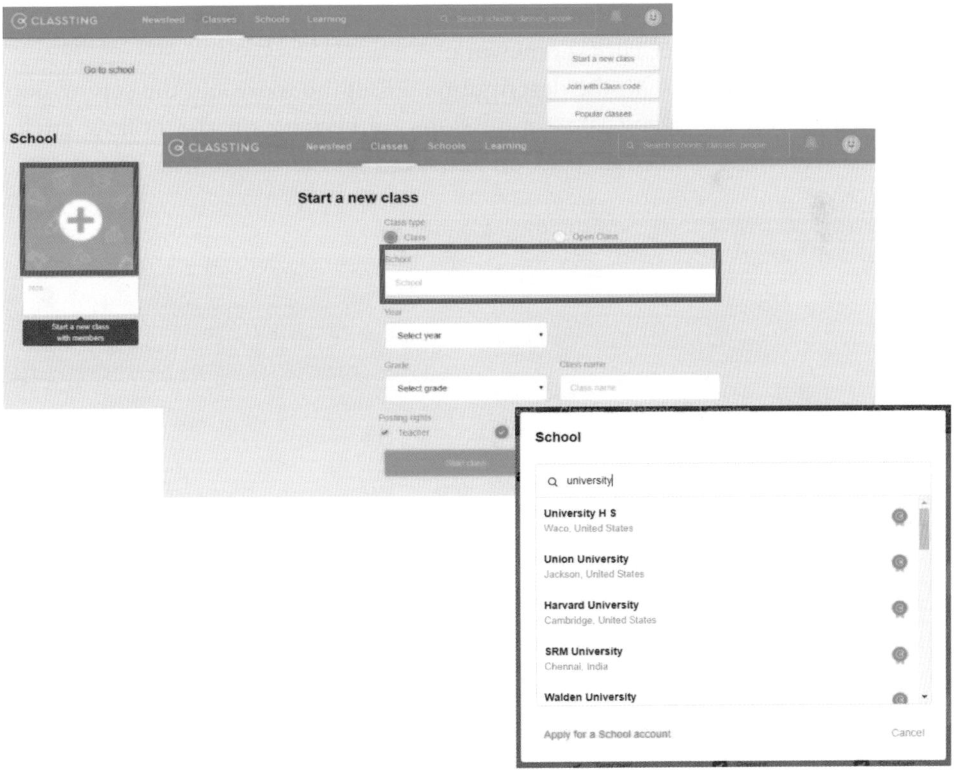

6) Once created, the class landing page will show. Click on 'Invite' to view the code students and parents can use to join the class.

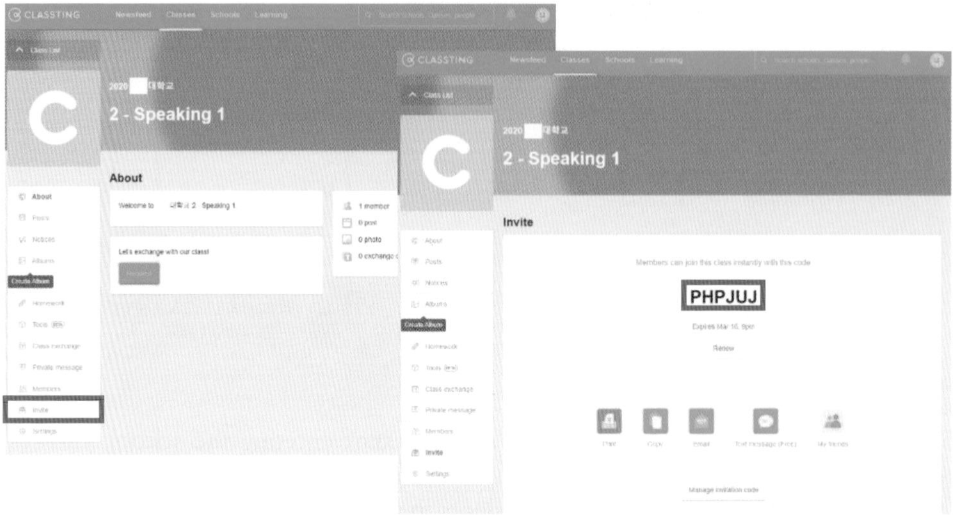

7) To create assignments, click 'homework.'
8) Fill in the title along with the description and set the score and the submission deadline. You can allow late submissions by clicking on the hollow circle. Once everything is filled in, click on "Post" to set the assignment.

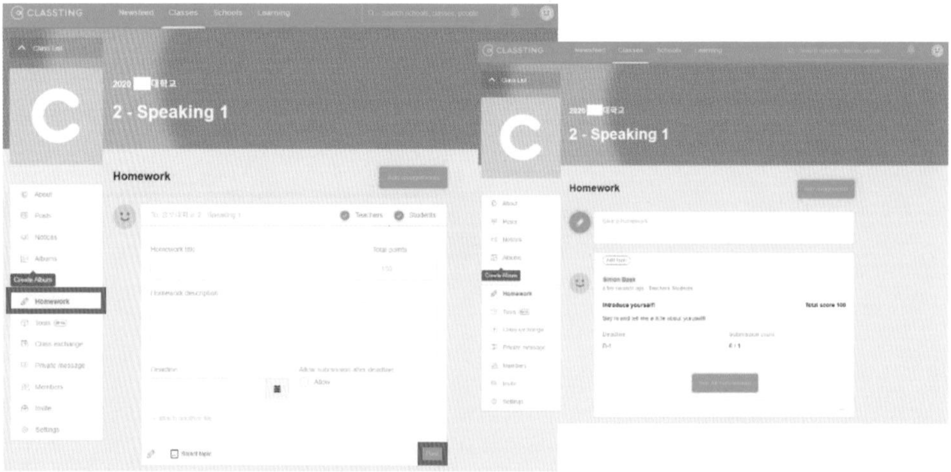

Classting on Smartphones

1) Search *Classting* the 'Google Play Store' or 'AppStore' and download.
2) 'Sign in' will allow using the same teacher credentials from the web version to access the class. Students can choose 'Join' to access the class as students using the code.
3) When joining on a smartphone, there is an additional option to 'Join with mobile number' instead of using an e-mail address.
4) When joining as a student, the app gives an option to choose a name.

5) After choosing the name, the welcome page of the app will be shown. Press the 'Classes' icon at the bottom to begin joining the class using the invite code of the existing class. Students can view notices, post, and submit assignments in the class.

Tasks for Study and Discussion

- Create an online class using *Classting*, invite your group members, and then make a 'homework' activity titled 'What is your favorite learning tool so far?' It is suggested that each person creates a class through the desktop app and then use the smartphone app to do the homework for the group members' classes.

7.2 *Flipgrid*

Flipgrid (https://info.flipgrid.com) is *a video* discussion platform that provides discussion boards where learners can practice speaking skills and interact with pairs and groups. *Flipgrid* aims to bring people together in a more constructive and communicative environment. Video recordings are used with the option of texts as a medium to communicate and interact with others. It offers a talk group of sorts where teachers and students can participate during discussions.

Flipgrid on the Web

1) Sign up for using *Flipgrid.* It is possible to sign up using a Google or a Microsoft account.
2) Click 'START MY GRID' on the landing page after login.

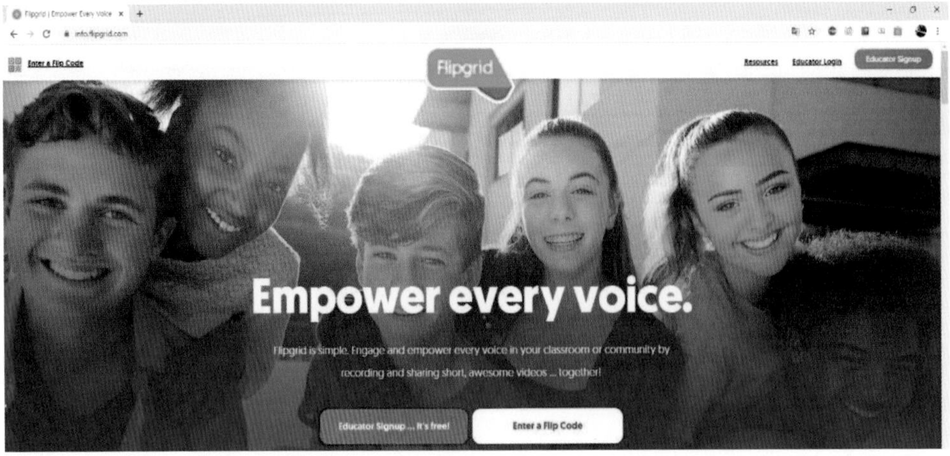

Figure 7.2 The main screen of *Flipgrid*

3) Enter a name for the grid and select the grid-type. The grid type dictates who can join the discussion. At the bottom, a 'Flip Code' is randomly generated for people to join the grid, which can be changed. Once decided, click 'Next'.
4) Enter as many domains as needed to allow students to join the grid. The domains students use must be precise and be included here for them to join.

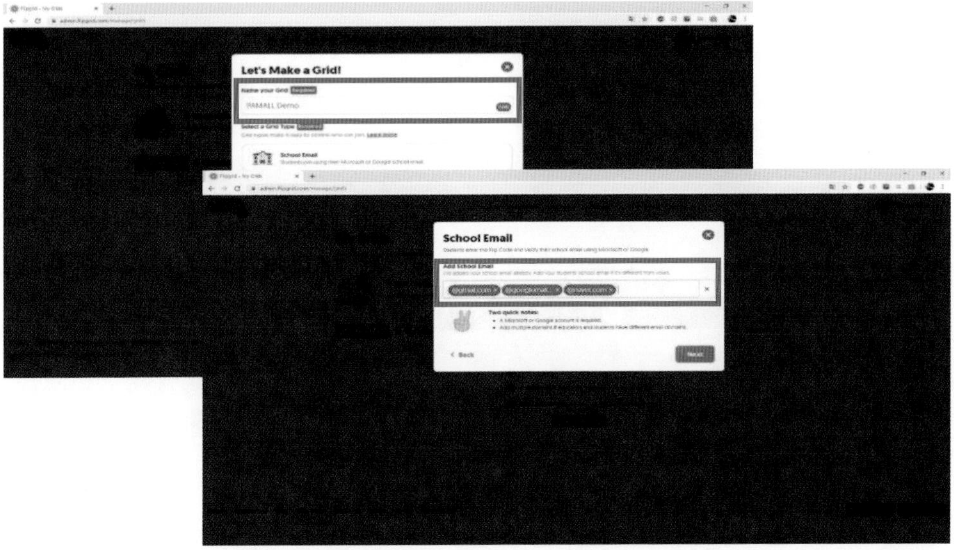

5) Click 'Next' until you can click on 'Go to your Grid' to start the discussion.
6) There should be a topic added automatically on the grid page. The topic can be edited, or other topics can be added. Other options can be used as needed.

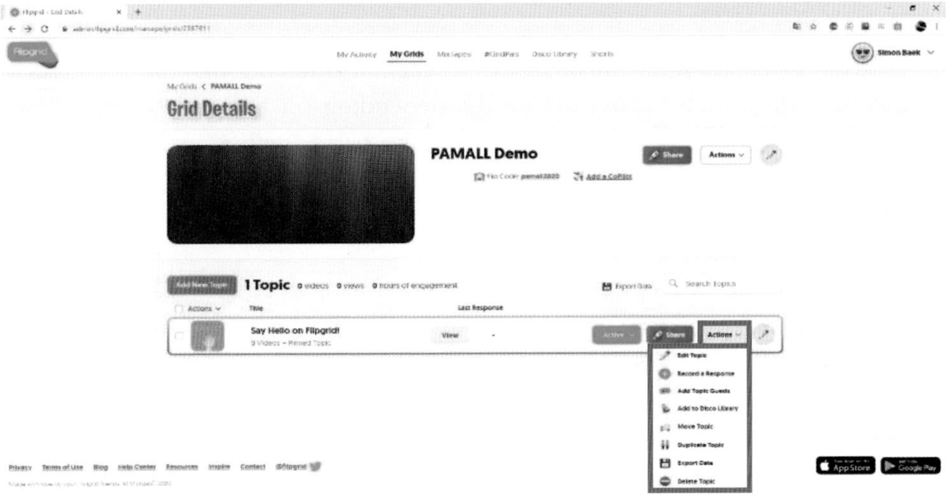

7) Press the 'Record a Response' button to record a new video. From the PC, the video will require a webcam. Alternatively, a custom or a blank background can be chosen.
8) Pressing the 'Next' button will allow you to review the recording before proceeding or add additional content. It is also possible to add yellow sticky notes on the video, as shown below.

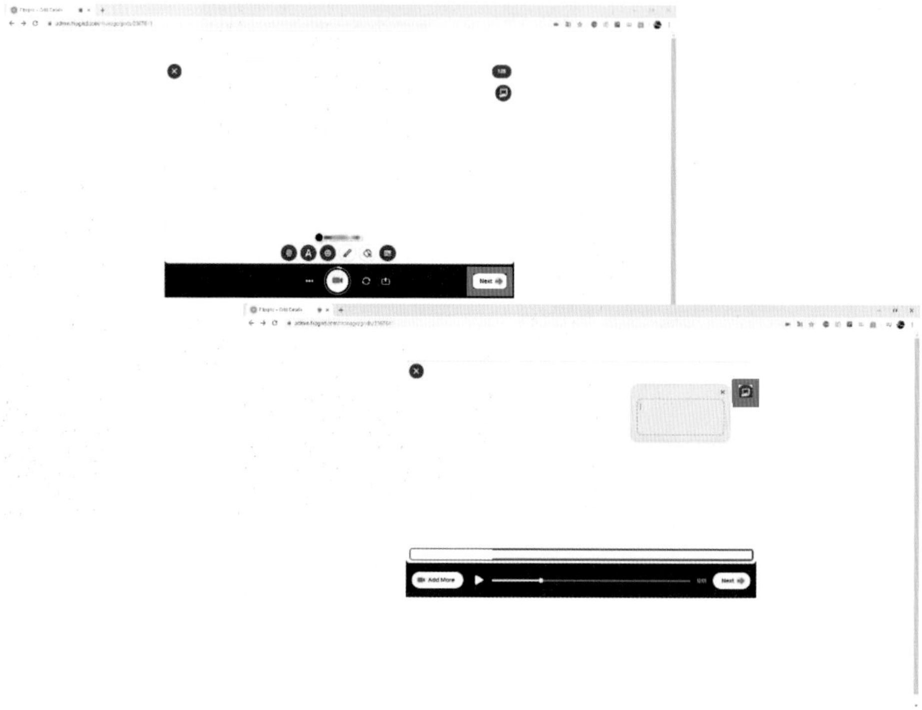

9) After the recording is finished, the teacher or students may be required to take a selfie for the video thumbnail, depending on the grid settings. Once this is done, it is possible to choose a display name (with an optional title and link) and submit the recorded video.
10) Once the video is posted, it should show up on the grid, which can be edited, downloaded, deleted, and more.
11) Clicking on the video created by the 'Teacher' (or any others) will allow students to give a 'reply' (green chat bubble icon), which takes them to another recording page.
12) Once a reply is given, the video will have additional icons at the bottom for adding a reply and for currently existing replies to that video. Click on the second icon to listen to the reply.

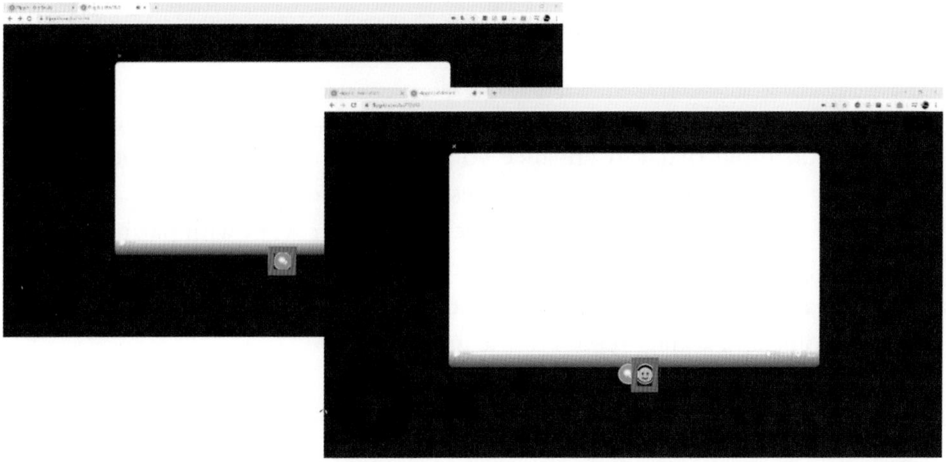

Flipgrid on Smartphones

1) Search *Flipgrid* on the 'Google Play Store' or 'AppStore' and download.
2) Choose the user type ('Student,' 'Educator,' or 'Guest').
3) Either input the code for the Grid or use the QR code.

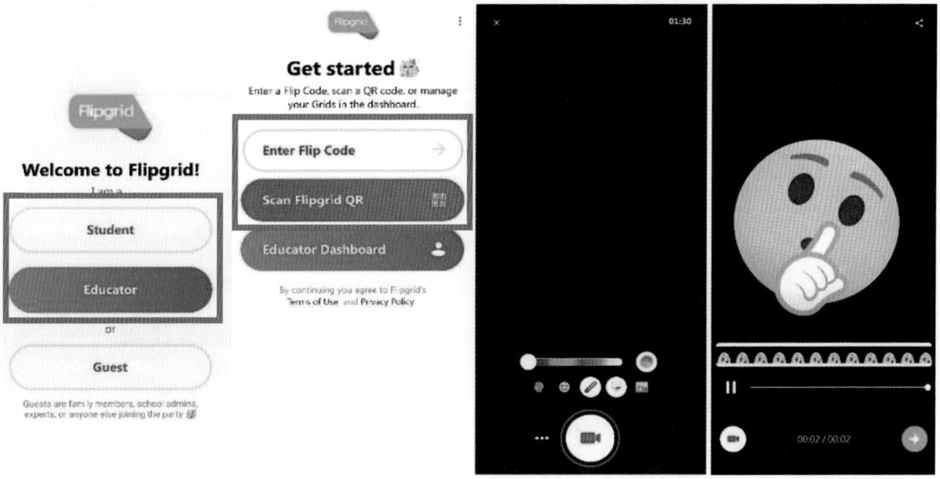

4) Once connected, the grid should show all current responses to the topic. Touch the green circle icon at the bottom right of the screen to add a response. The recording procedure should be very similar to the PC version.

Tasks for Study and Discussion

1. Create a grid for speaking or a pronunciation course. Then, create a discussion topic that can enhance your students' speaking or pronunciation skills by having them create video messages. Invite your friends (partners) to join the grid. Work individually and then share your work with partners.

2. Participate in the discussion and interact with friends (partners) by responding to the topic and adding replies to the grid.

A sample of *Flipgrid* activity: Discussion on Natural Disasters

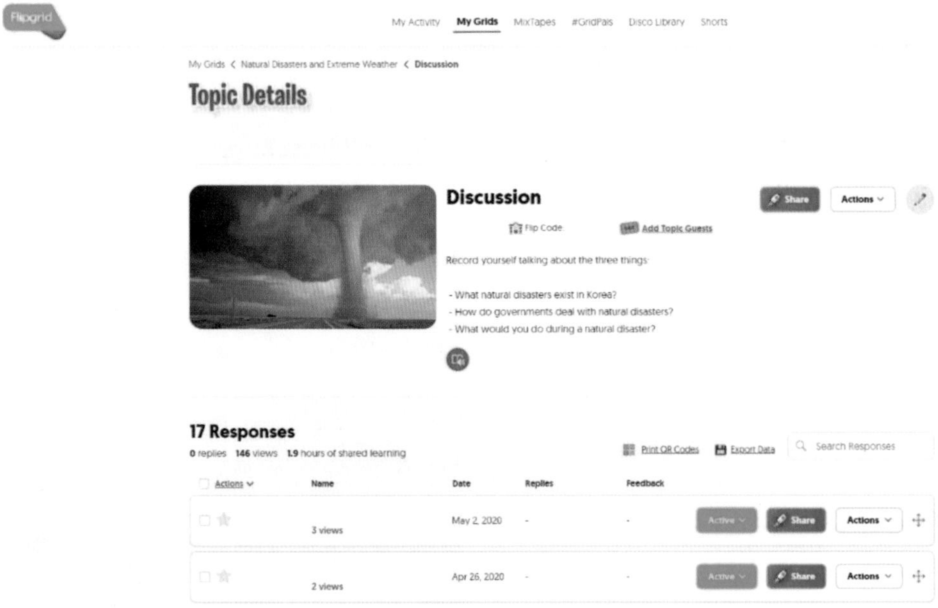

7.3 *Padlet*

Padlet (https://www.padlet.com) is a web-based collaborative workspace where users can create information boards, documents, and webpages that are easy to view. It is like paper for your screen. Its houses various types of presentation type boards,' each displaying information in different formats. These different formats are 'Wall,' 'Canvas,' 'Stream,' 'Grid,' 'Shelf,' 'Backchannel,' 'Map,' and 'Timeline.' All these formats share the same method in adding multimedia information.

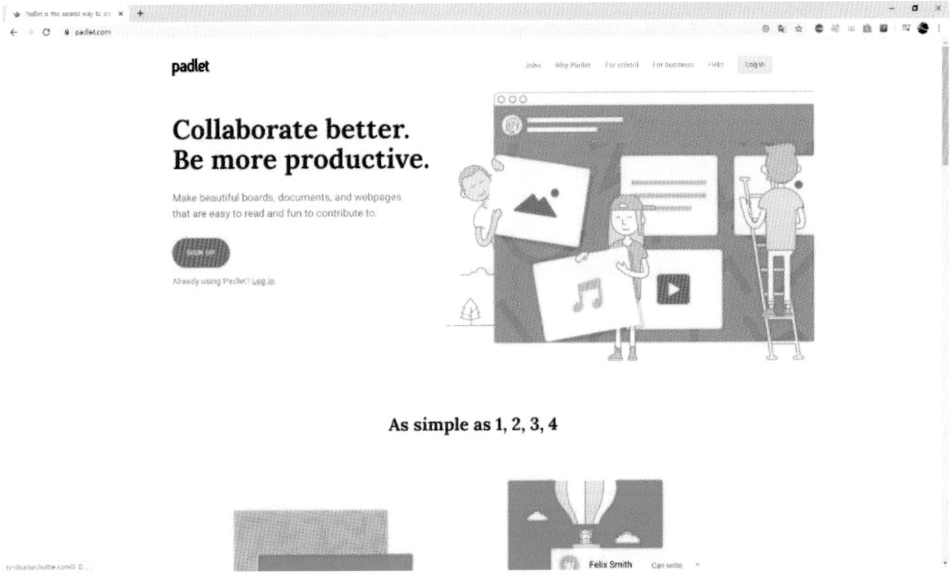

1) Once signed in, it is possible to make, join or browse padlets others created. Click on the 'MAKE A PADLET' button to start using *Padlet*.

2) Any of the following boards can be chosen depending on the teacher, but for this demonstration, we will choose the 'Wall.' Click 'SELECT' below 'Wall.'

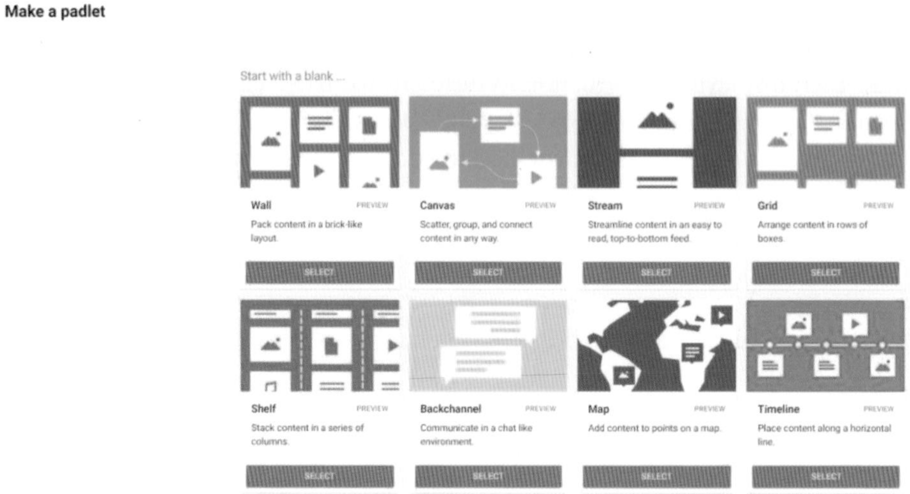

3) The appearance of the 'Wall' can be changed before any posts. Make as many adjustments as needed and click on 'NEXT.'
4) Click 'START POSTING' if satisfied with the appearance of the 'Wall.'

5) Click on the '+' to add a multimedia post to the board. It gives you some options. From left to right, these options are uploading from desktop, posting a link, searching google, taking a picture and more.
6) On the top right of the screen is the 'SHARE' button. Click this to get a variety of options to share the 'Wall' with the students.

7.4 ***OKMindmap***

OKMindmap (http://okmindmap.com) provides a web-based mind mapping tool that allows for clustering ideas on topics more clearly than unstructured brainstorming does. *OKMindmap* provides a user-friendly interface that can be easily edited and expanded. *OKMindmap* does not require the installation of any plug-in services or flash. Users can collaborate synchronously as a group and create a mind map on the Web. Created mind maps can be saved as various types of files and exported and shared via SNSs, such as *Twitter, Facebook,* and *Delicious.*

1) Click 'Start *OKMindmap*' to start the program.

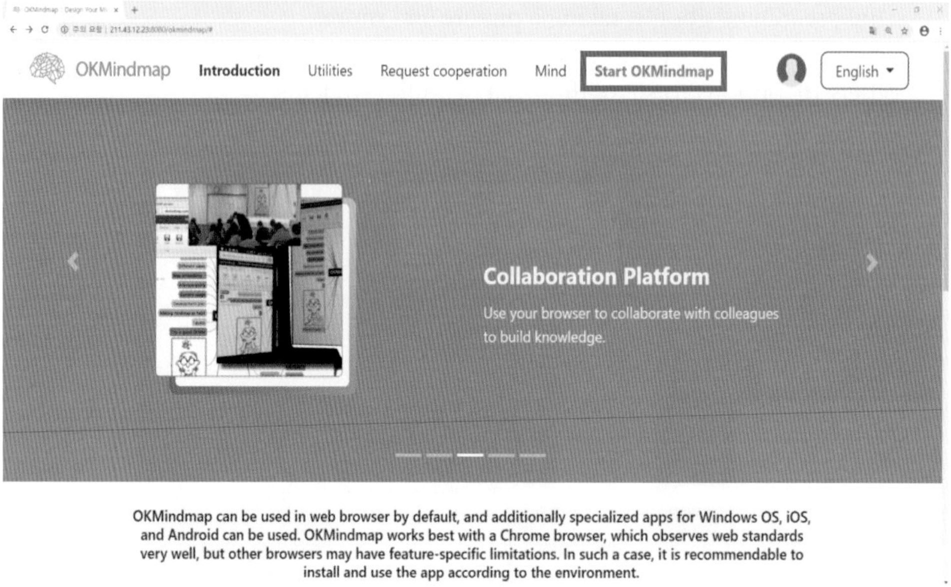

Figure 7.3 The main screen of *OKMindmap*

2) Click 'Create new mindmap' in the middle to create a new mind map. Choose appropriate 'Map Style' among four different types of figures and click the 'Create' button to start editing a new mindmap.

3) The new mind map can be created with the assigned title. Choose appropriate functions in the toolbox to create child or sibling nodes, insert images, video files, hyperlinks, and edit nodes in customizing text colors, background colors, or lines.

4) Click 'Sibling' or 'Chile' in the toolbox on the bottom to create nodes. Type words, phrases, or sentences in each node.

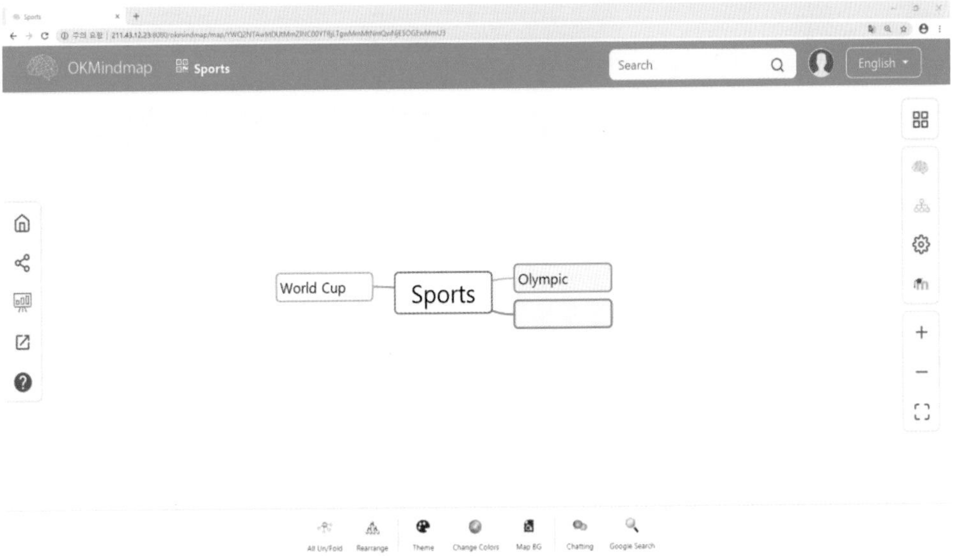

5) Click 'Hyperlink,' 'Image,' and 'Video' on the bottom menu bar to insert images, video files, and hyperlinks in a mindmap.

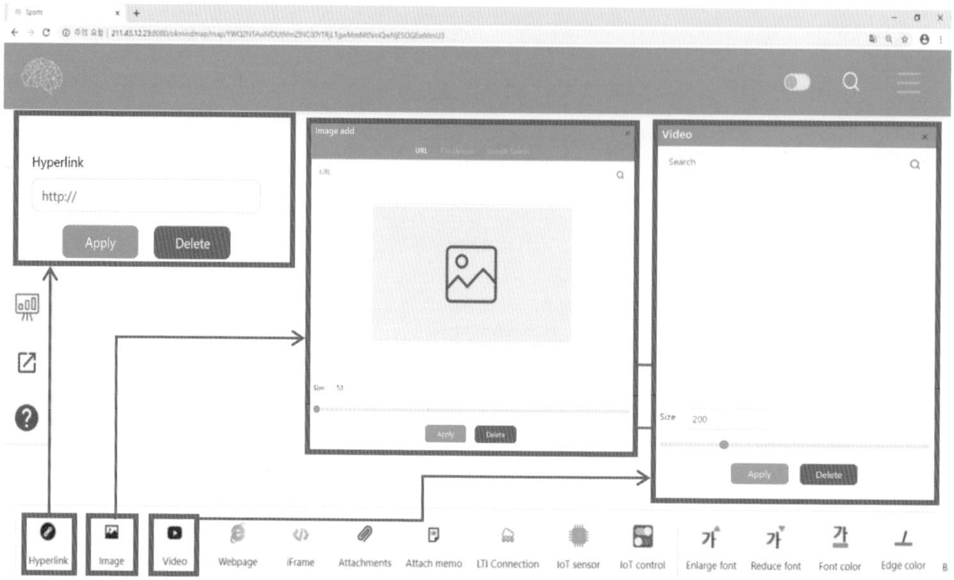

6) Images can be directly uploaded or by *Google Search*. Type words or phrases to search appropriate images and adjust the size. Click 'Apply' to insert the image. Video files and hyperlinks can also be inserted with the same procedure.

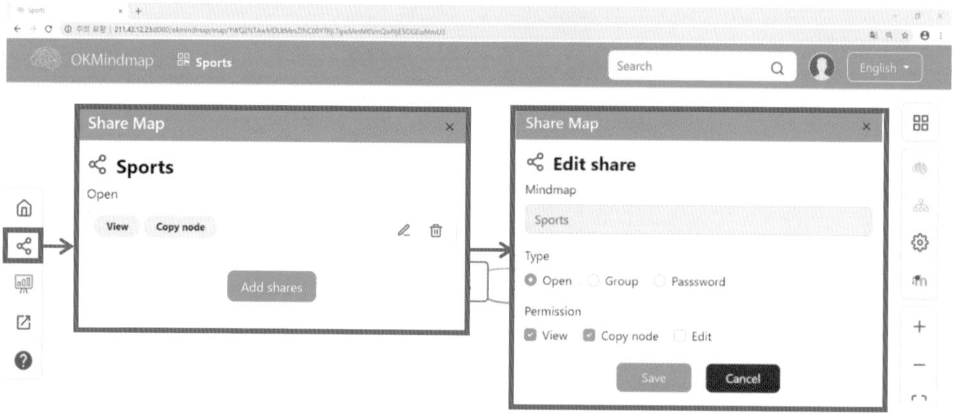

7) Click 'Share' on the right to share the map with groups. Decide on the type (Open, Group, and Password) and permission (View, Copy node, and Edit) and click 'Save.'

Tasks for Study and Discussion

1. Create an activity for teaching one of the four language skills and three subskills using *OKMindmap*. Insert images, videos, and hyperlinks and edit your mind map with diverse colors.

2. Share your mind map via your SNSs and export it as other types of files. Work individually and then share your work with partners.

7.5 *Microsoft Teams*

Microsoft Teams (https://teams.microsoft.com/) provides an authentic place where users can collaboratively work or study together. *Microsoft Teams* apps are compatible and linked across computers, smartphones, and tablets. *Microsoft Teams* is a computer-mediated communication (CMC) tool that makes both synchronous and asynchronous communication possible. After creating a team and inviting members through apps, all members can share various types of documents produced through *Microsoft 365* apps (Word, PowerPoint, Excel, etc.) and chat, meet and even call to collaborate on those shared documents. Teachers can assign various tasks for their learners and use learning management systems (LMS) provided throughout the apps. *Microsoft Teams* offers video tutorials on its website (https://docs.microsoft.com/en-us/MicrosoftTeams/enduser-training).

1) Download *Microsoft Teams* software on your computer by clicking a link in the middle. You can also download a mobile app on your PLDs if necessary.

Figure 7.4 The main page of *Microsoft Teams*

2) Double click the *Microsoft Teams* icon to run the program. You can also use *Microsoft Teams* on the Internet by signing up on its website without the download. Both the Internet and computer apps have similar appearances.

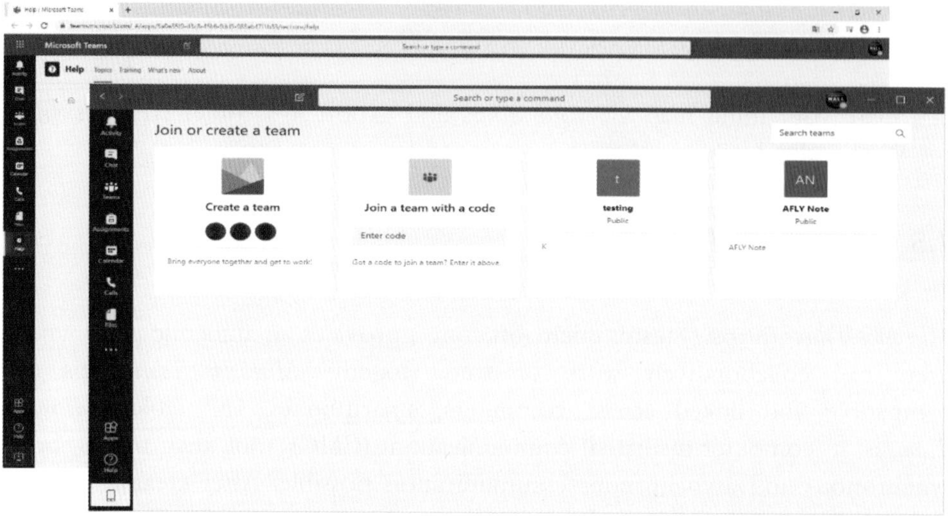

3) Any modifications in *Microsoft Teams* on computers are directly synchronized to the mobile apps downloadable from the Play, Apple, and Microsoft stores.

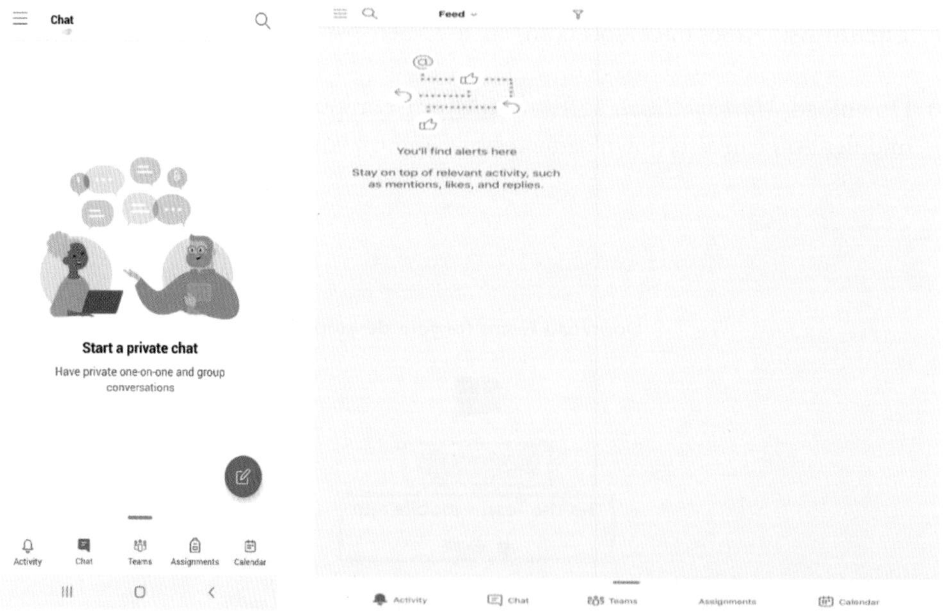

Create a team

1) Users are required to create a team in the *Microsoft Teams* apps to work with other members. Click the 'Create team' button in the squared 'Create a team' box on the top-left.

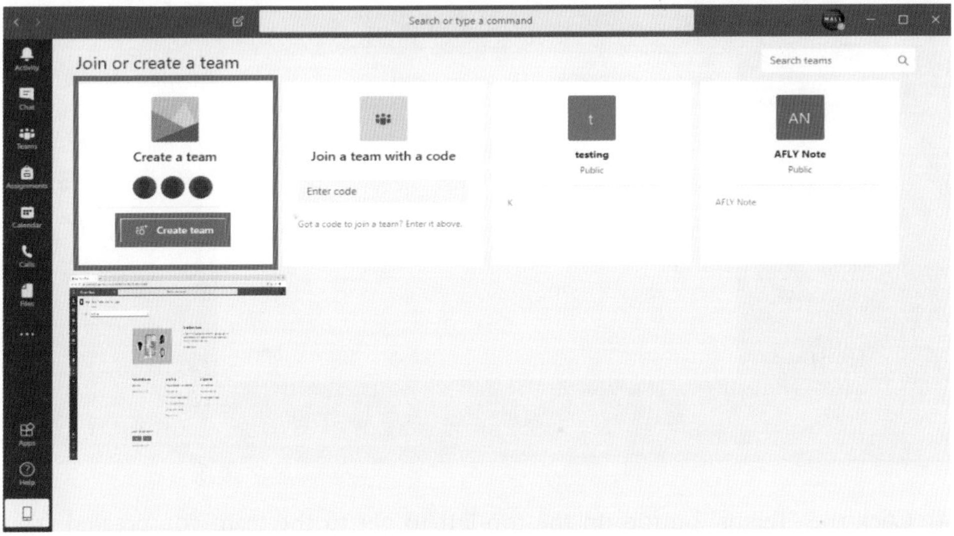

2) Type appropriate 'Team name' and 'Description.' Then, select 'Privacy' options of either private or public for your team.

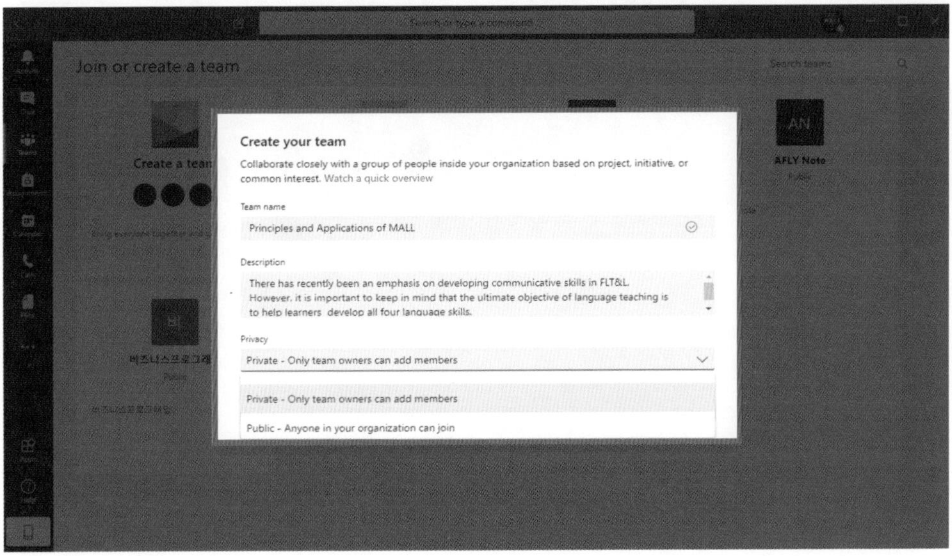

3) Invite members to your team by typing a name or group and check whether you choose an appropriate person to be added to your team. Click on 'Close' to finish the final step of creating a team.

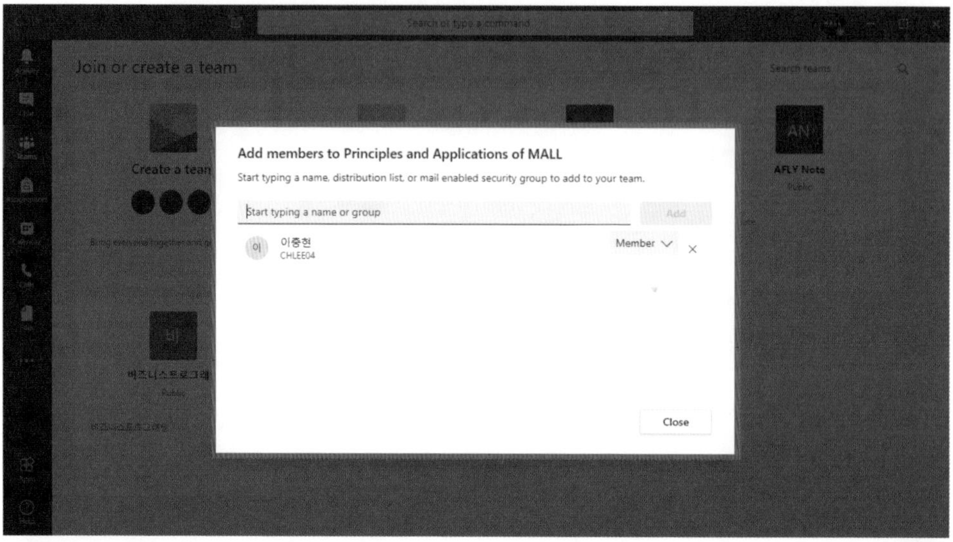

4) Click the 'Teams' button on the top-left to get to the team you created. You can start various activities that include posting, uploading files, and wiki-based tasks.

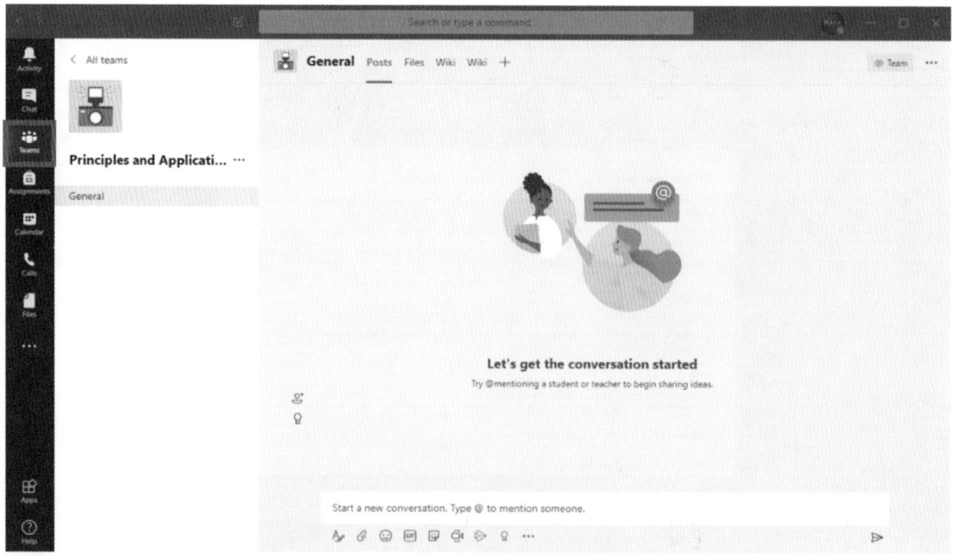

Uploading and co-editing files

1) Click the 'Collapse compose box' on the bottom to post comments with various support functions, including Bold, Italic, Underline, Text highlight, Text color, etc.

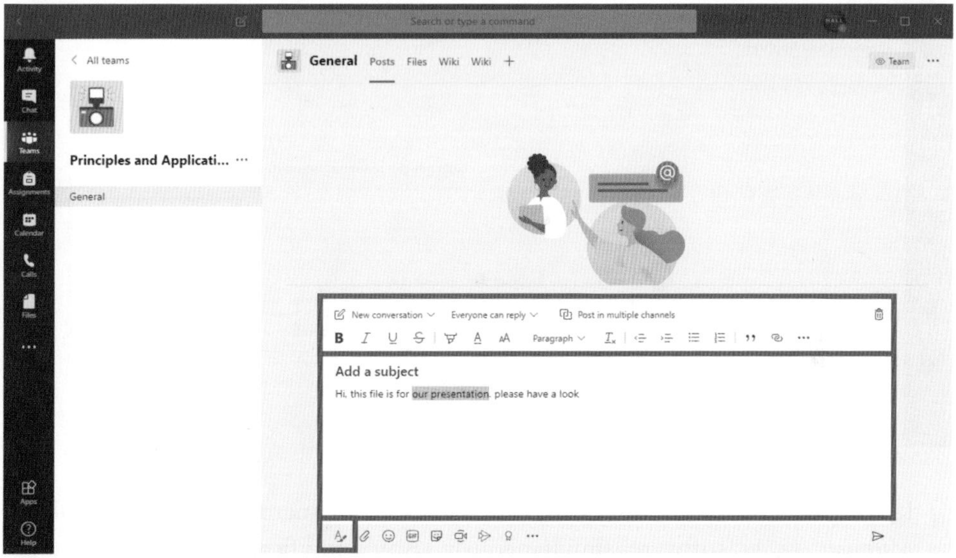

2) Click the 'Attach' button on the bottom to upload files with comments.

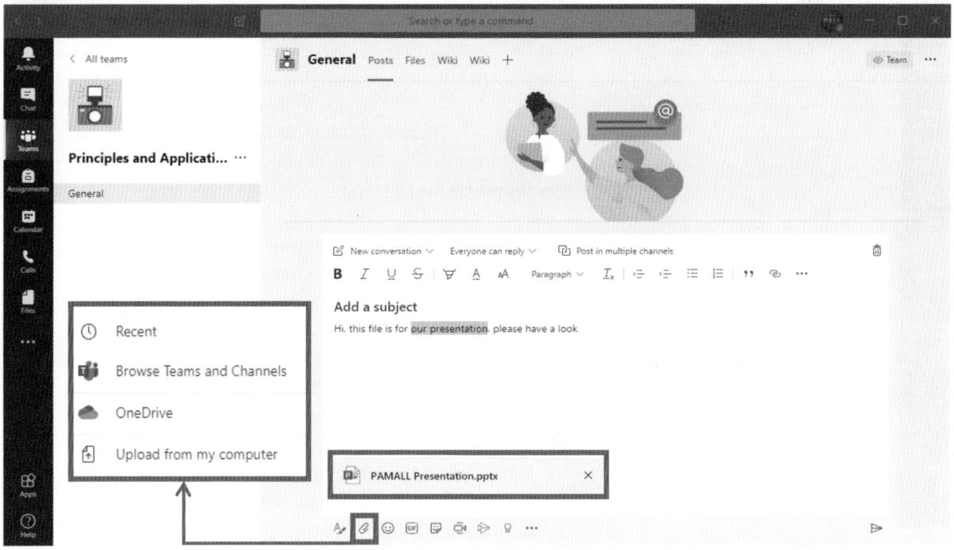

3) Click 'More attachment option' on the uploaded file in a comment box. Choose an appropriate option from the editing place list.

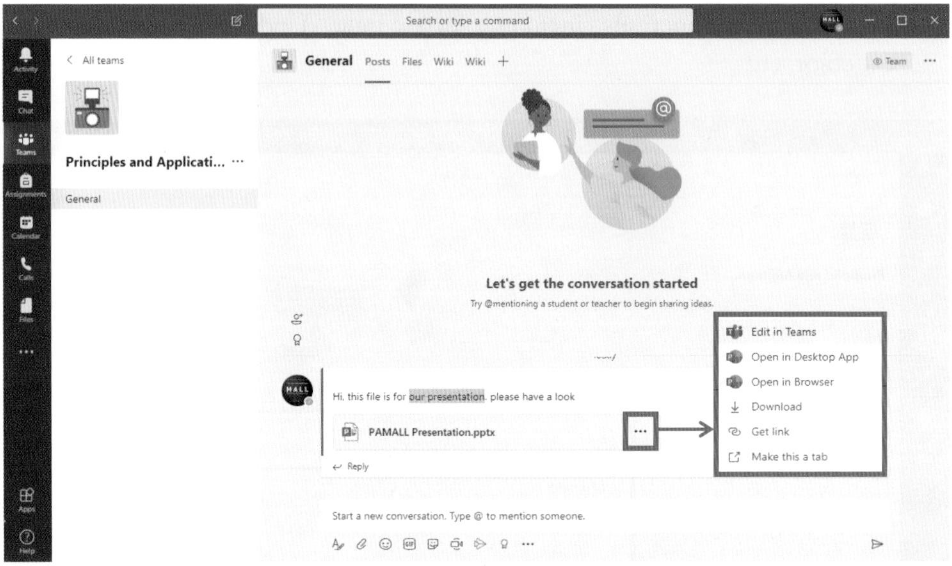

4) If you choose 'Edit in Teams,' it enables team members to edit a file in *Microsoft Teams* software simultaneously. Any modifications on the file are automatically saved to facilitate team collaboration.

5) You can easily access uploaded files by clicking the 'Files' button on the top.

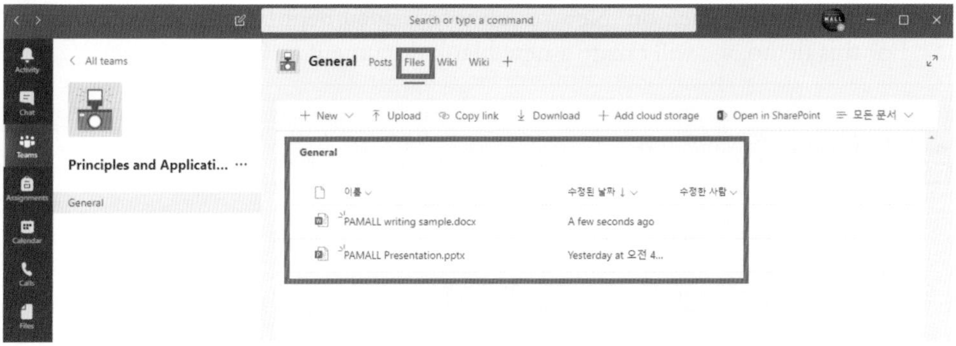

7.6 *Google Drive*

Google Drive (http//:www.drive.google.com) is a free online cloud storage service available for all Google account owners. *Google Drive* can be used as a personal storage space that can be easily accessed anywhere and create documents that are compatible with and offer the essential functions of *Microsoft Office*. The most beneficial aspect of this tool is that everyone who has access to a document can edit and comment on it, making *Google Drive* a handy tool for giving and receiving feedback, as well as collaborative writing.

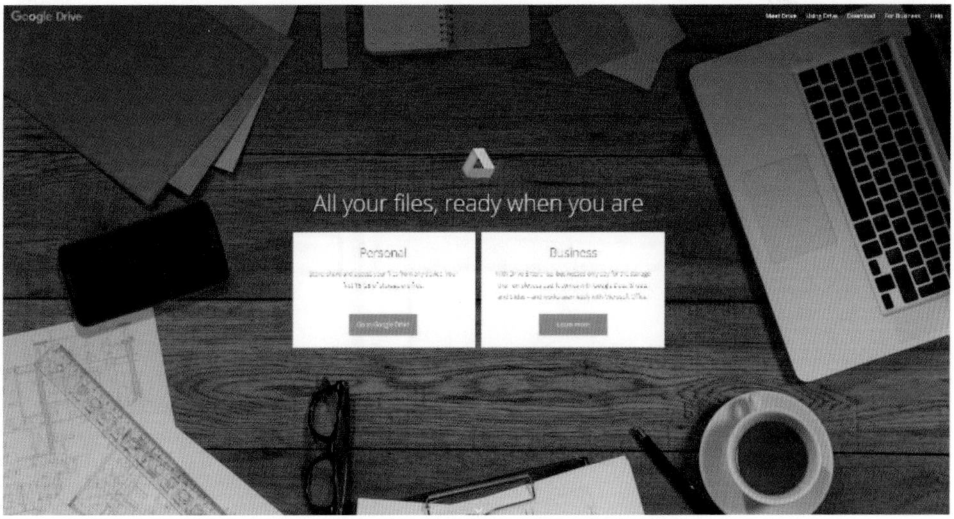

Figure 7.5 The main screen of *Google Drive*

1) Click 'Go to Google Drive' in the box labeled 'Personal' and log in using your Google account.
2) Once logged in, click on 'New' to choose a document type you want to create. For this demo, we will create a new blank document in Google Docs.'

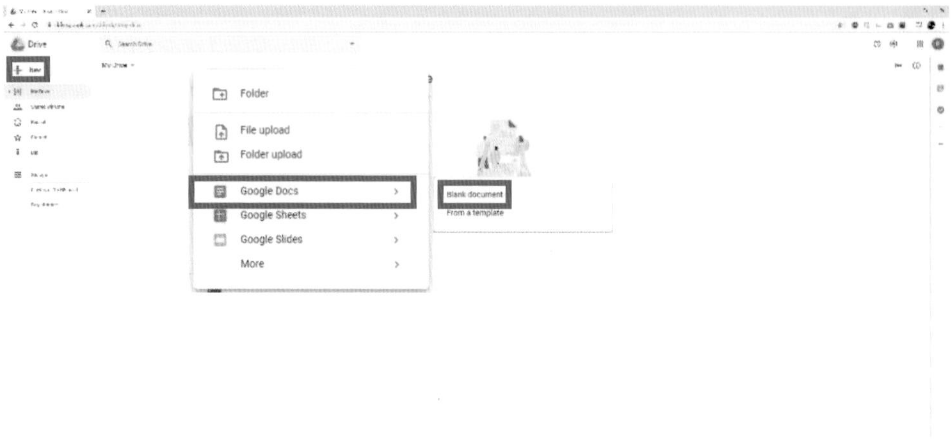

3) To share the document, simply click on the blue "Share" button. If the document is untitled it will prompt you to name the document.
4) Either enter the recipients' email addresses or click on the "Get shareable link" text on the top right of the box.

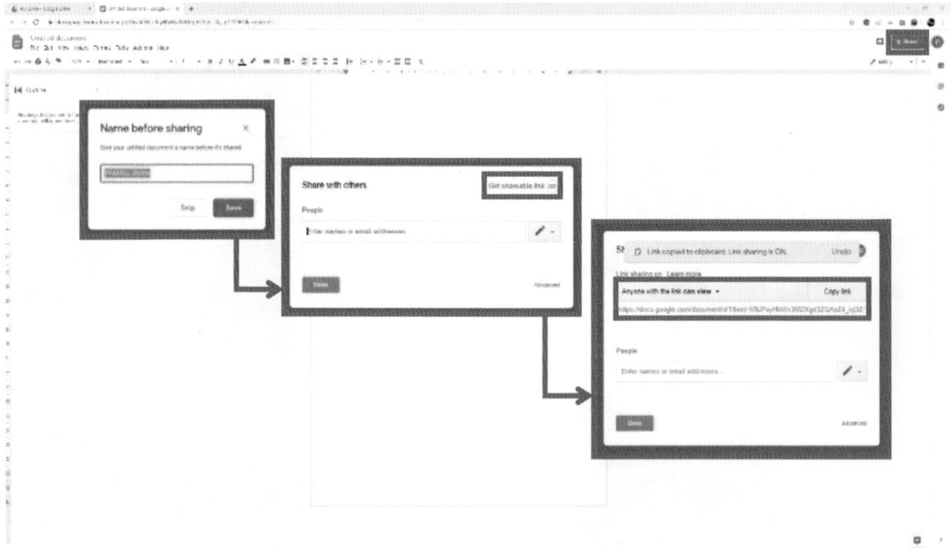

5) The link can be used to access, edit, and comment on the document.

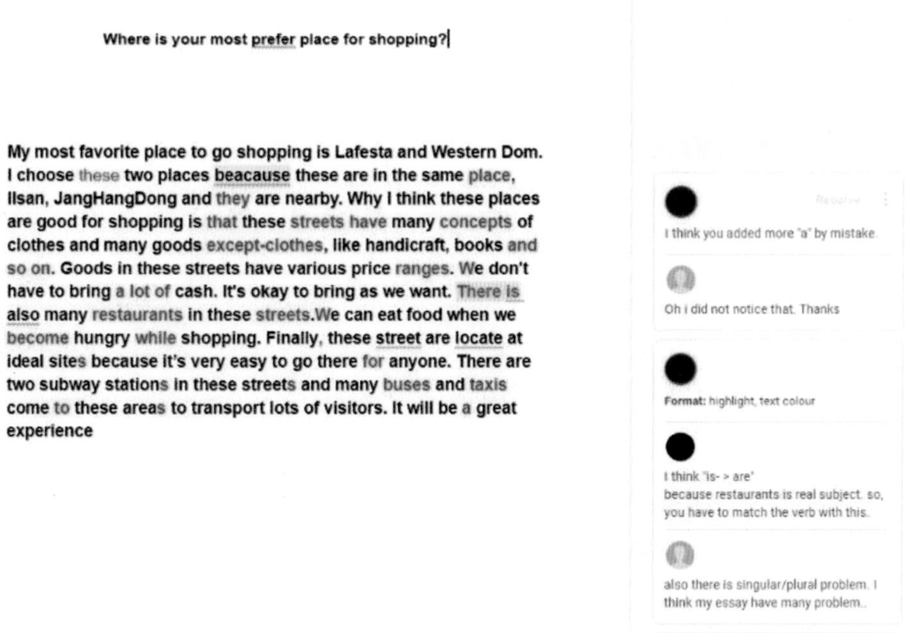
Where is your most prefer place for shopping?

My most favorite place to go shopping is Lafesta and Western Dom. I choose these two places beacause these are in the same place, Ilsan, JangHangDong and they are nearby. Why I think these places are good for shopping is that these streets have many concepts of clothes and many goods except-clothes, like handicraft, books and so on. Goods in these streets have various price ranges. We don't have to bring a lot of cash. It's okay to bring as we want. There is also many restaurants in these streets.We can eat food when we become hungry while shopping. Finally, these street are locate at ideal sites because it's very easy to go there for anyone. There are two subway stations in these streets and many buses and taxis come to these areas to transport lots of visitors. It will be a great experience

I think you added more "a" by mistake

Oh i did not notice that. Thanks

Format: highlight, text colour

I think "is- > are"
because restaurants is real subject. so, you have to match the verb with this.

also there is singular/plural problem. I think my essay have many problem..

Tasks for Study and Discussion

1. Write a short essay using either *Microsoft Teams* or *Google Drive* with the topic of 'blockbuster movies,' and share with your group members.

2. Proofread, correct, and comment on your group members' essays, giving feedback where possible.

7.7 *Grammarly*

Grammarly (http://www.grammarly.com) is a grammar checking tool that scans a text for grammatical errors and plagiarism. *Grammarly* corrects over 250 grammatical mistakes and catches spelling errors and inappropriate vocabulary usage considering contextual meanings. Grammarly can analyze various writing genres, such as general, academic, business, technical, creative, and practical writing.

1) Click 'Login' to start using *Grammarly*.

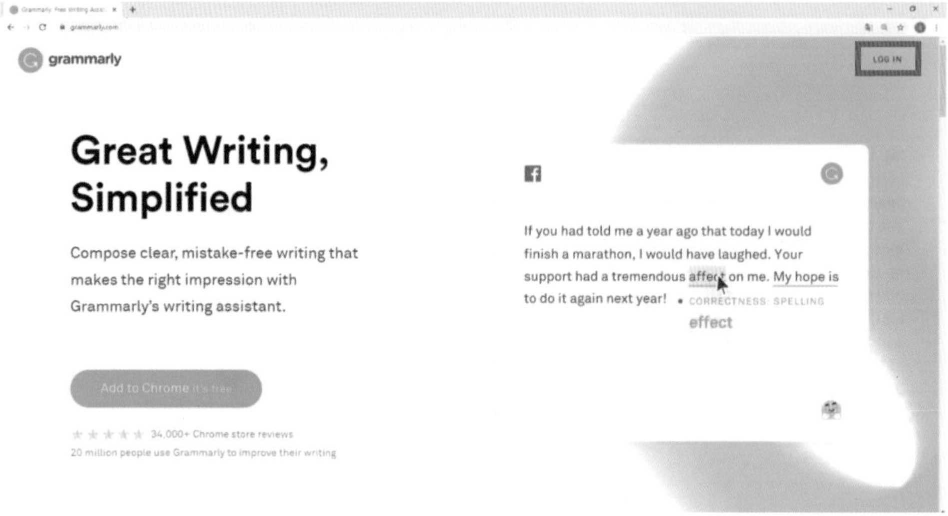

Figure 7.6 The main screen of *Grammarly*

2) Set goals first to get tailored suggestions for your writing. It is possible to set the levels of Audience, Formality, Domain, Tone, and Intent.

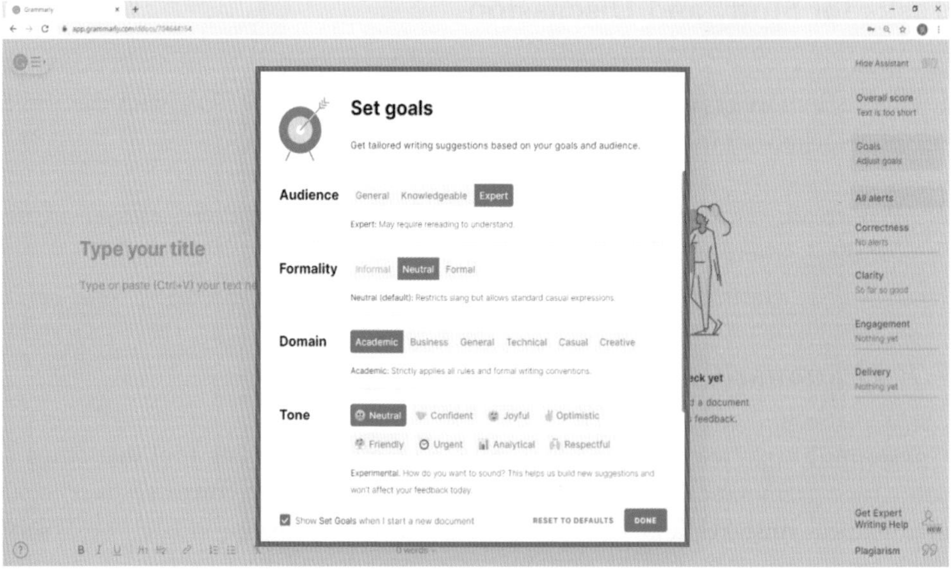

3) Type a title in the title area and type or paste the text in the content area. You can adjust goals again by clicking a 'Goals' button on the top-right.

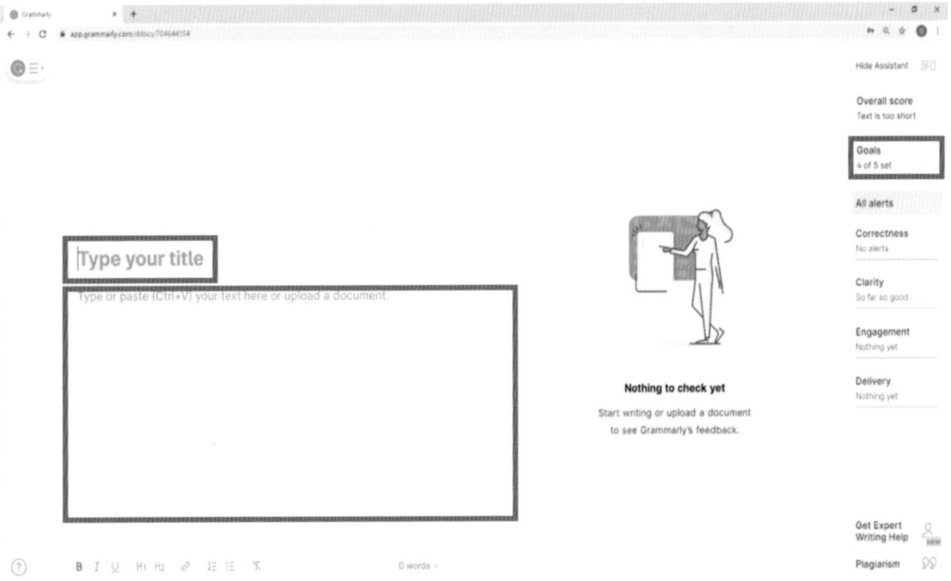

4) *Grammarly* will automatically fix errors on the content if users click suggestions in all alerts section on the right. All the suggestions for errors or mistakes appear in the green box.

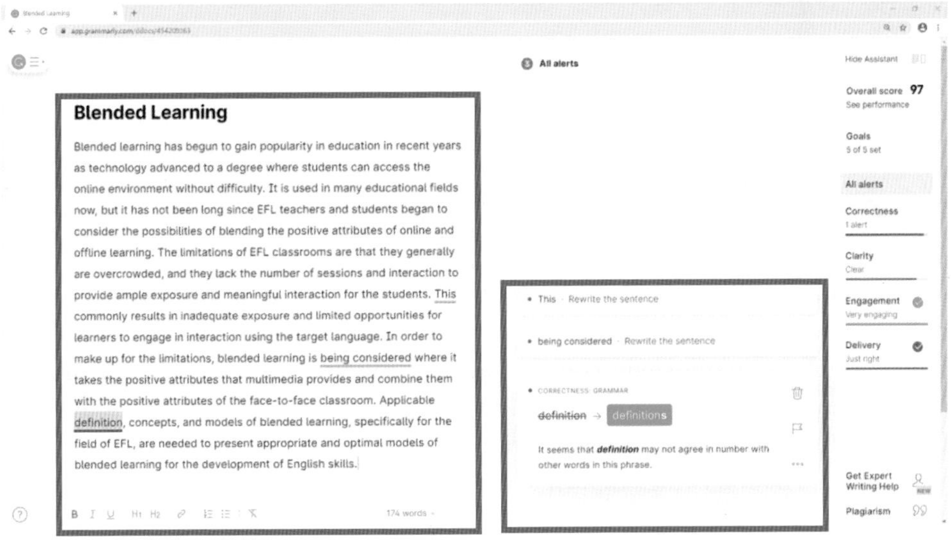

5) If you want to check the part that errors or mistakes occur, click buttons below the 'All alerts' encompassing Correctness, Clarity, Engagement, and Delivery.

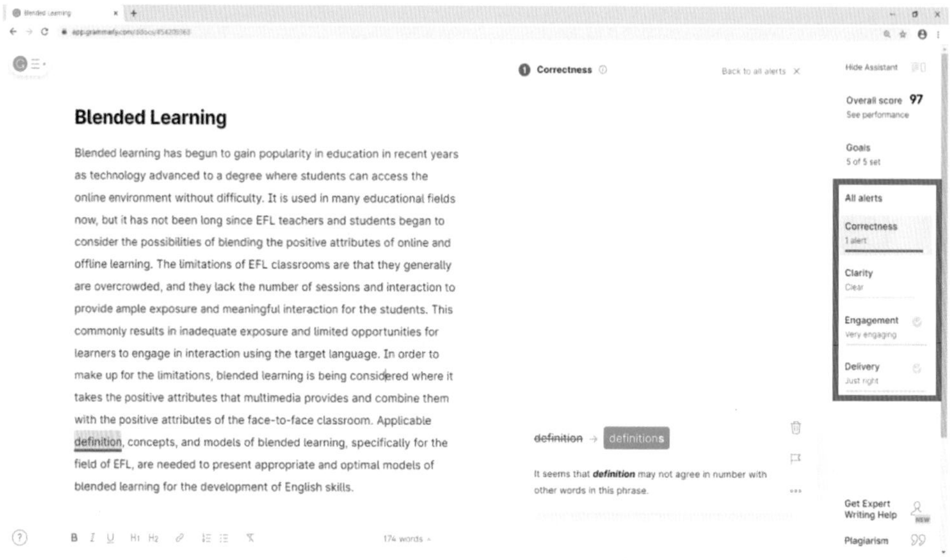

Tasks for Study and Discussion

1. Check your text using *Grammarly*. Share the results with partners.

2. Create a writing activity for intermediate or advanced students to enhance their writing skills using *Grammarly*.

7.8 *Compleat Lexical Tutor (Lextutor)*

Compleat Lexical Tutor (henceforth, *Lextutor*) (http://www.lextutor.ca) is a free online tool for language learning and corpus-based research analysis. The main functions of *Lextutor* include concordancer, vocabulary profiler, exercise maker, interactive exercises, etc. *Lextutor* is comprised of four sections, as shown in Figure 7.7. The functions marked with red colored 'M' can also be used in a mobile app. The followings explain some major functions in *Lextutor*.

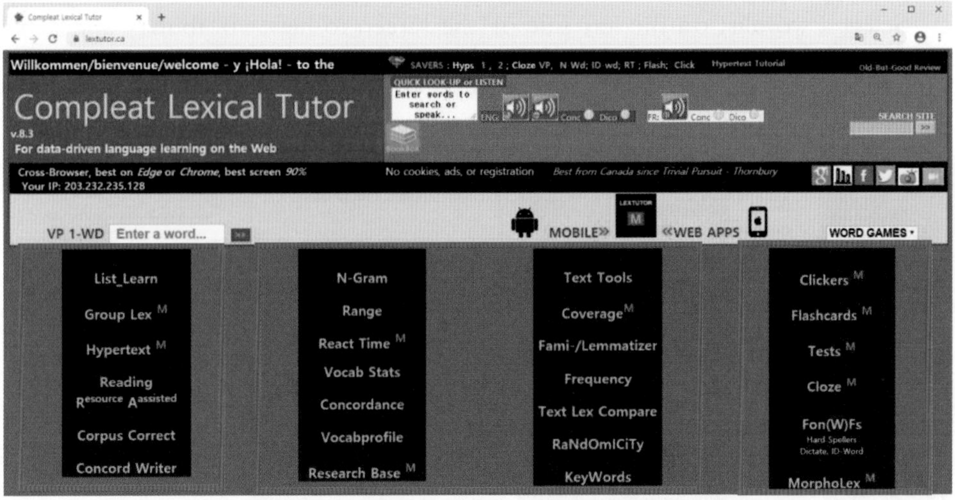

Figure 7.7 The main screen of *Compleat Lexical Tutor*

List_Learn Home

Lextutor provides word lists for vocabulary learning. The database for the target vocabulary comes from Classic, BNC, and COCA word lists.

1) Select one of the word lists among English Classic, BNC (1k-20k), and BNC-COCA (1k-25k) by clicking each of the links.

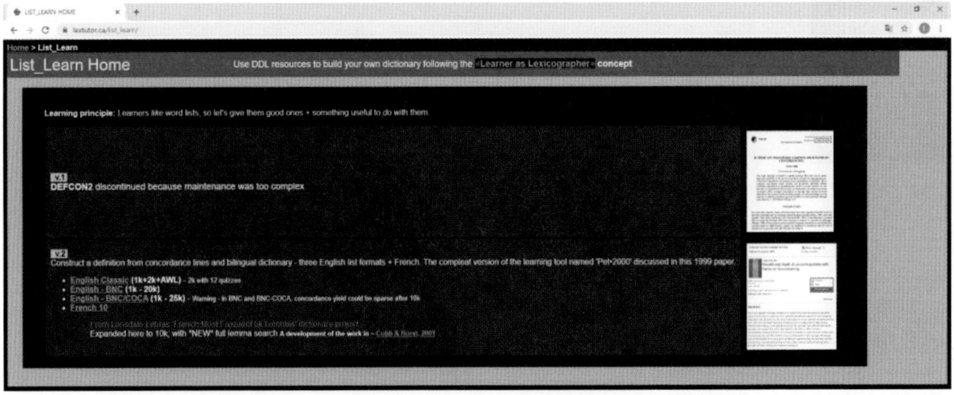

2) Select a wordlist on the left side of the screen to have vocabulary appear in the section below.

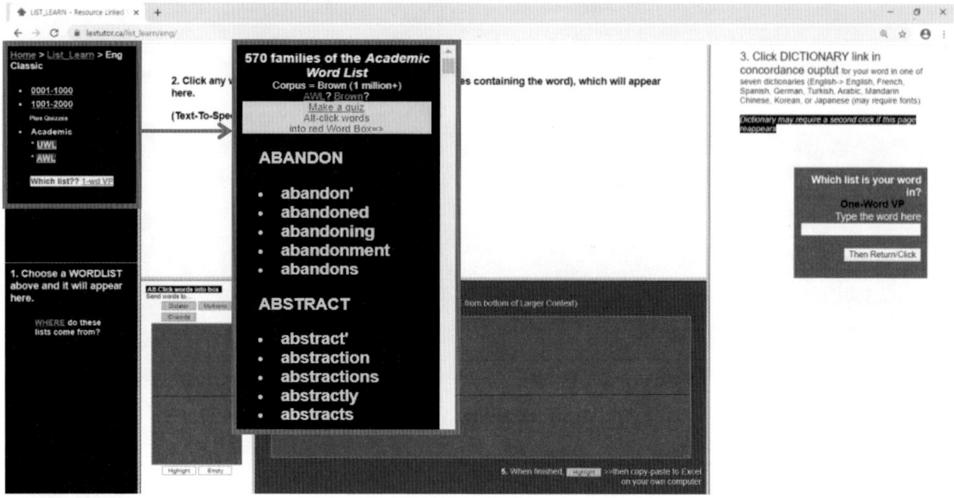

3) Double click the word in order to access concordance lines.

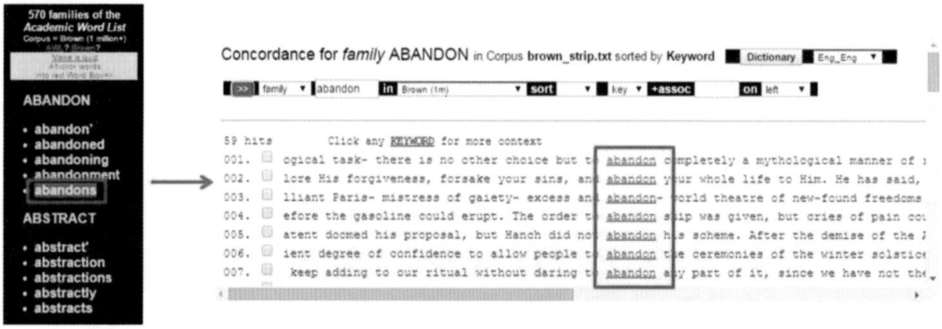

4) Click the word to see the usage of the word in context.

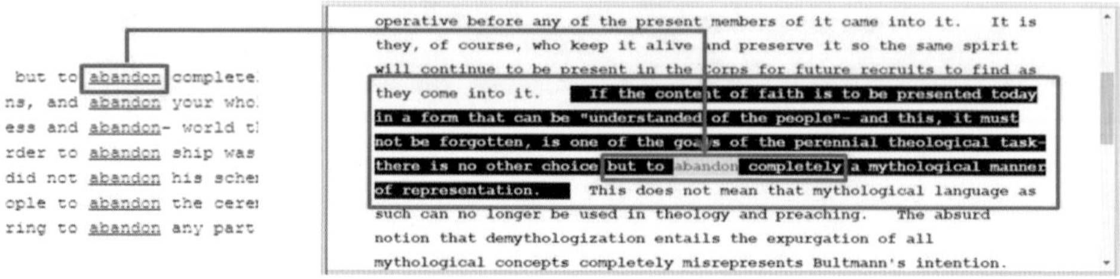

5) Click 'Save' at the bottom of the text to save the data on specific words, examples, and meanings.

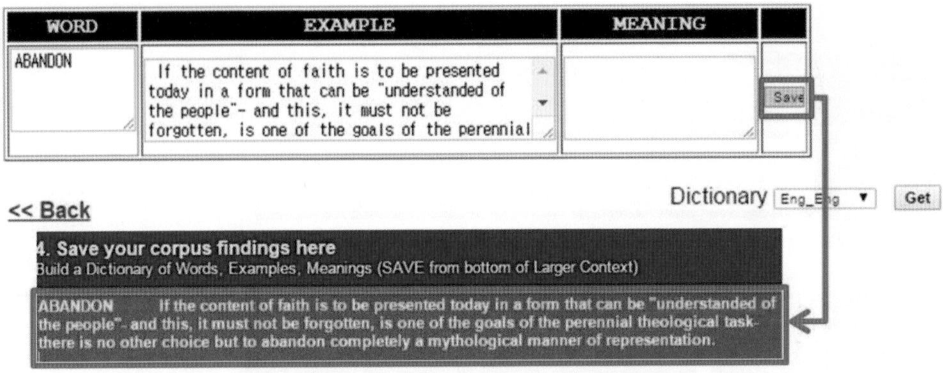

6) Select the dictionary type such as Eng-Eng or Eng-Kor (your native language). Then, click 'dictionary' to search the meaning of words.

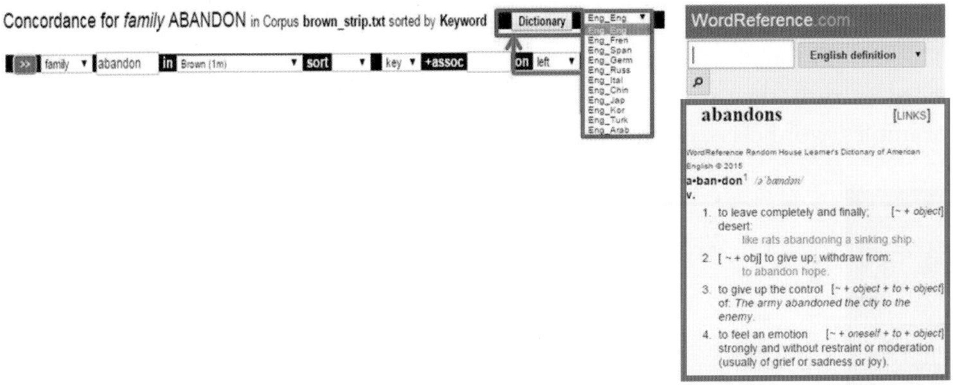

7) When finished, click 'highlight' to copy the text, then paste on your document to the word processor, excel, etc., depending on the needs.

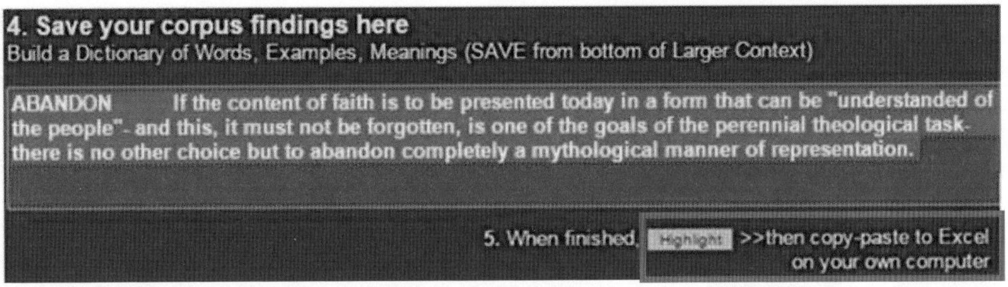

8) The last page of the list-learn function is presented in the image below.

Group Lex

The second function for users is 'Group Lex' that can help create a quiz and add word entry if they want. As seen in the figure below, words are presented with examples, word class, definition, and groups they belong to.

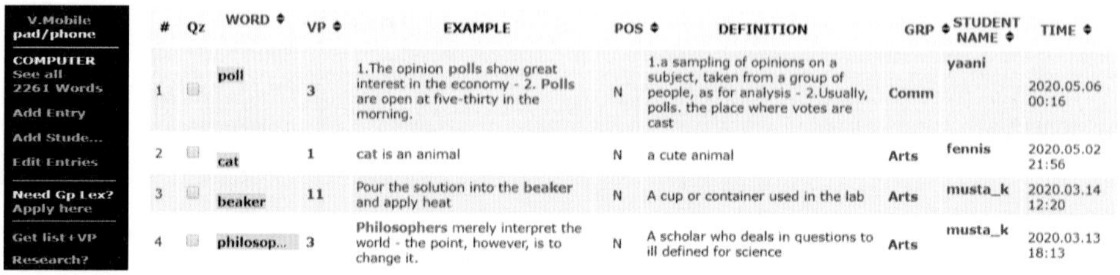

1) To add entry, enter a word in 'NEW WORD' with its example and definitions, and select the word class and group.

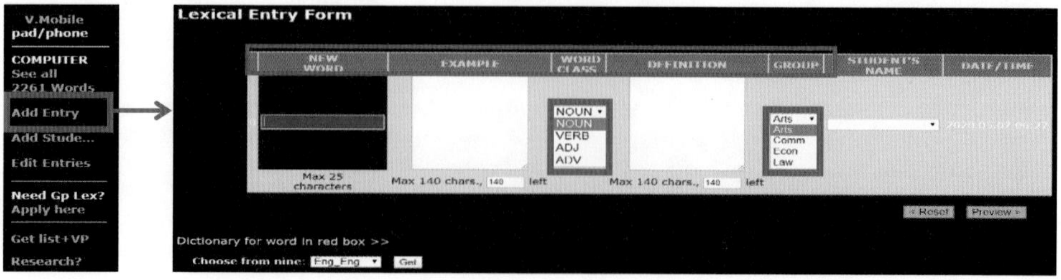

2) In order to make a quiz, select the 'Print' or 'Interactive' options. Click one of the buttons ranging from 'Check1st 10,' to 'Check10th 10' or 'Any 20' or 'None.' Then, click 'Quiz checked.'

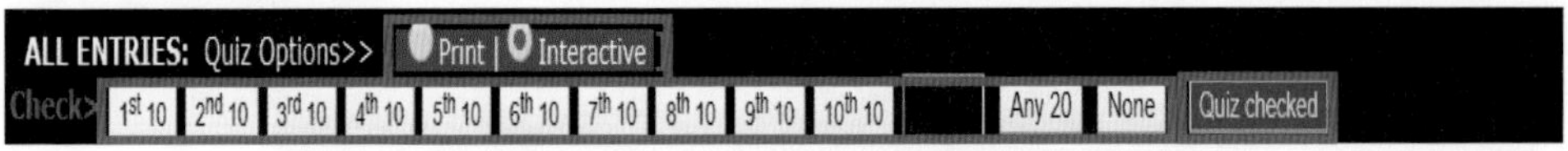

3) 'Print' option provides the quiz in the print format without any feedback. On the other hand, the 'Interactive option' makes a web-based vocabulary test. 'Check' provides the test results of the solved quizzes.

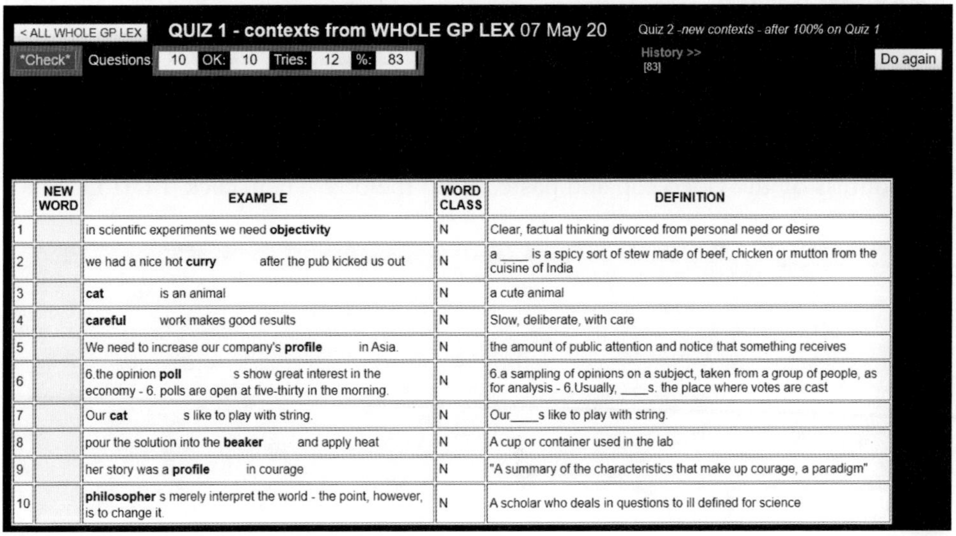

	NEW WORD	EXAMPLE	WORD CLASS	DEFINITION
1		in scientific experiments we need **objectivity**	N	Clear, factual thinking divorced from personal need or desire
2		we had a nice hot **curry** after the pub kicked us out	N	a ____ is a spicy sort of stew made of beef, chicken or mutton from the cuisine of India
3		**cat** is an animal	N	a cute animal
4		**careful** work makes good results	N	Slow, deliberate, with care
5		We need to increase our company's **profile** in Asia.	N	the amount of public attention and notice that something receives
6		6.the opinion **poll** s show great interest in the economy - 6. polls are open at five-thirty in the morning.	N	6.a sampling of opinions on a subject, taken from a group of people, as for analysis - 6.Usually, ____s. the place where votes are cast
7		Our **cat** s like to play with string.	N	Our____s like to play with string.
8		pour the solution into the **beaker** and apply heat	N	A cup or container used in the lab
9		her story was a **profile** in courage	N	"A summary of the characteristics that make up courage, a paradigm"
10		**philosopher** s merely interpret the world - the point, however, is to change it.	N	A scholar who deals in questions to ill defined for science

Hypertext

Hypertext allows users to create their text with multiple resources, including speech, concordance, dictionary, audio or video clip, and other Internet resources. There are two options: text+speech+concorcance+dictionary and text+speech+media+dictionary. This section of the book will explain how a video clip and Internet resource can be added to a text.

1) Before creating the hypertext material, select the text available on the Internet, such as Internet news, web-based novel, *TED*, *Youtube*, and etc. If you want to use a clip from *Youtube*, go to 'http://www.youtube.com' and select the video. Then, move on to the 'Hypertext Builder Home' option as below.

2) Click 'HYPERTEXT II.'

3) Type the title of the text and enter the main text in the box. Copy the URL address of the video clip and paste it into the box. Then, click 'BUILD.'

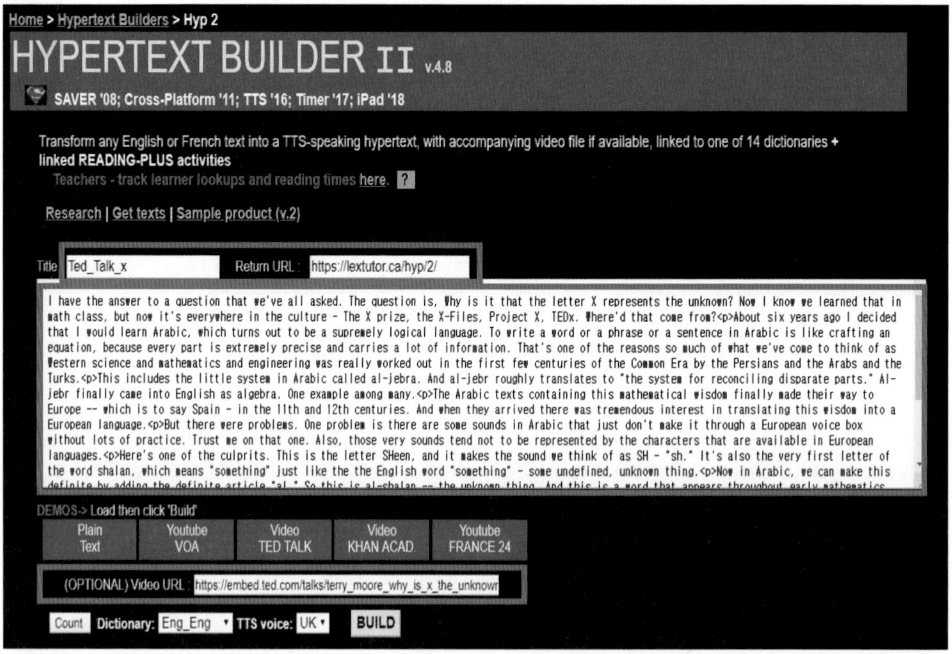

4) Double click an unknown word in the text and click a 'DEFINE' button so that the meaning of the word in the dictionary shows up on the right corner of the window.

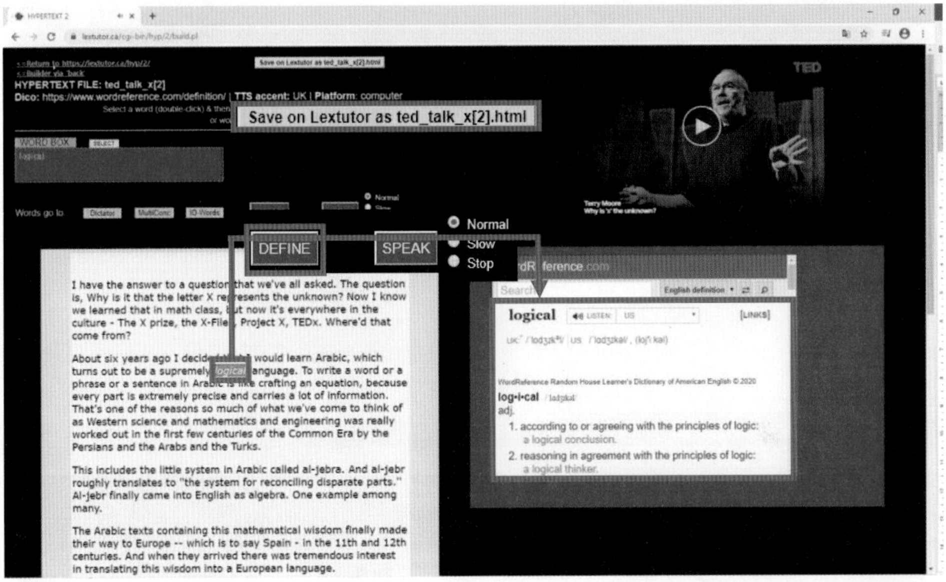

5) Click on 'Save on *Lextutor* as ted_talk_x[2]' on the top to create the URL address of the hypertext material just created.

Your hypertext file has been saved at this address on Lextutor's server:

https://lextutor.ca/hyp/2/users2/ted_talk_x[2].html

Corpus Correct

Corpus correct provides users with opportunities to correct erroneous sentences, utilizing concordance lines provided. It promotes data-driven and inductive grammar learning.

1) Select one of the grammar points categorized into preposition, singular-plural, word order, gerund-infinitive, simple past-present perfect, conditionals, and formulaics.

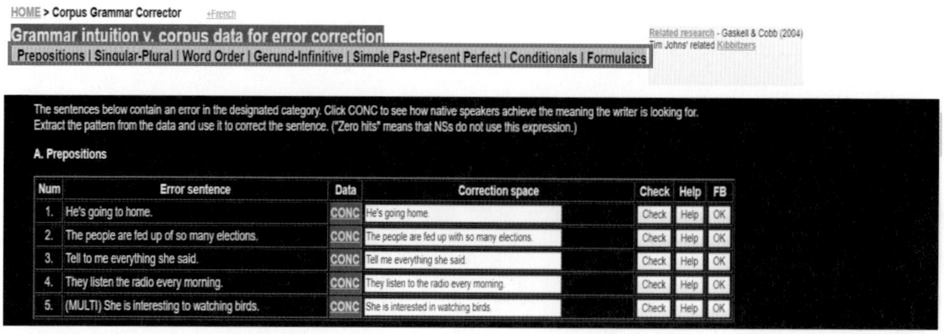

2) Click the 'CONC' button in order to bring the concordance lines related to the error.

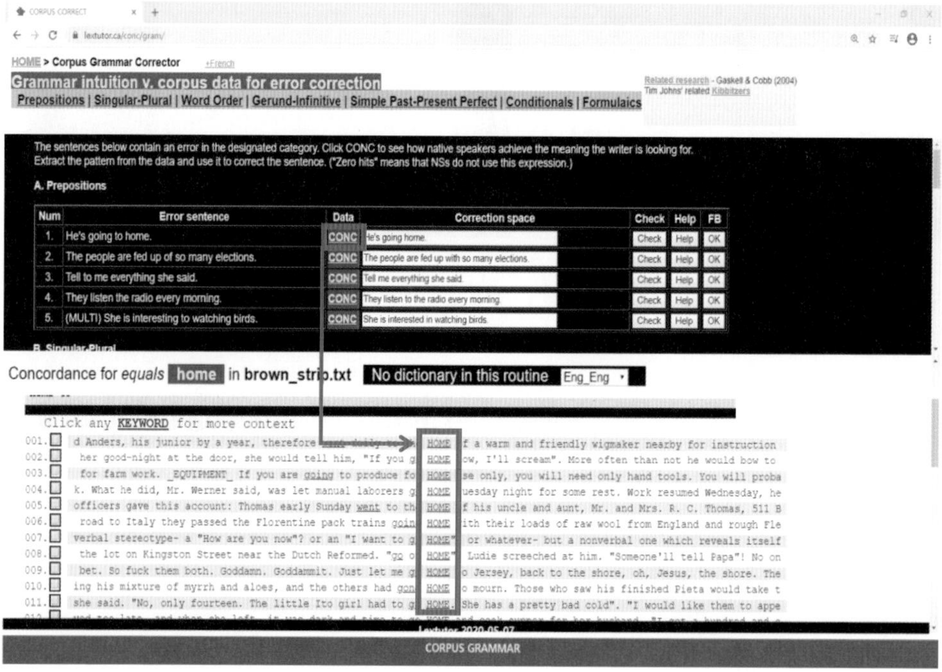

3) Examine the sentence error based on the data in concordance lines and correct them in the correction space.
4) As seen in the next page's image, click the button 'Check' to check the answer. The 'Help' button provides the correct answer.

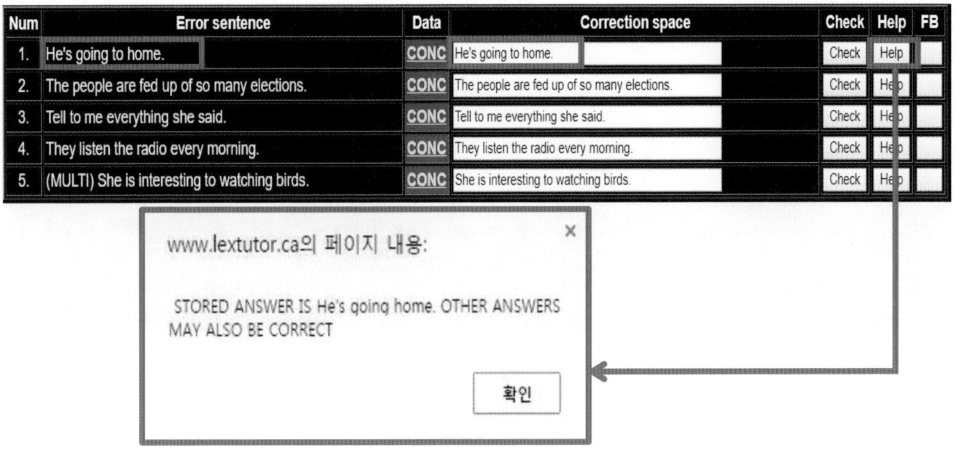

Concordancers

Lextutor provides two types of concordancers: corpus and text concordances. The former lists words, phrases, or distributed structures from various corpora such as Brown corpus, BNC (British National Corpus), and other specified corpora. On the other hand, the latter provides concordance lines from your texts.

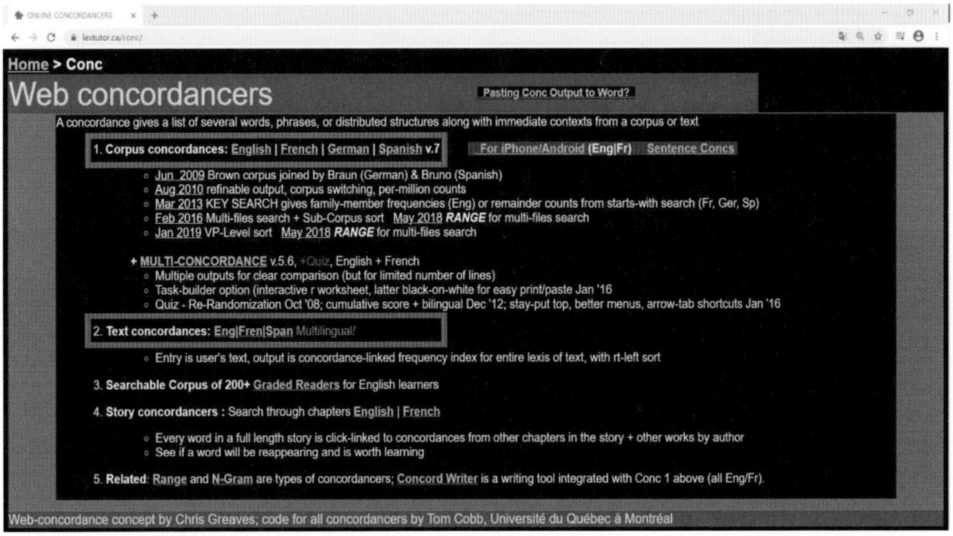

Corpus concordances

1) In order to start corpus concordances, click the language to build concordance lines.

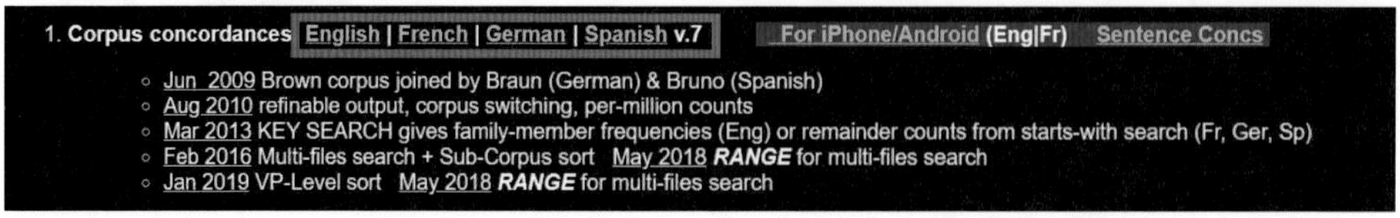

2) Set the options to build concordance lines with a keyword in the context.

3) Type a keyword in the box and select the corpus.

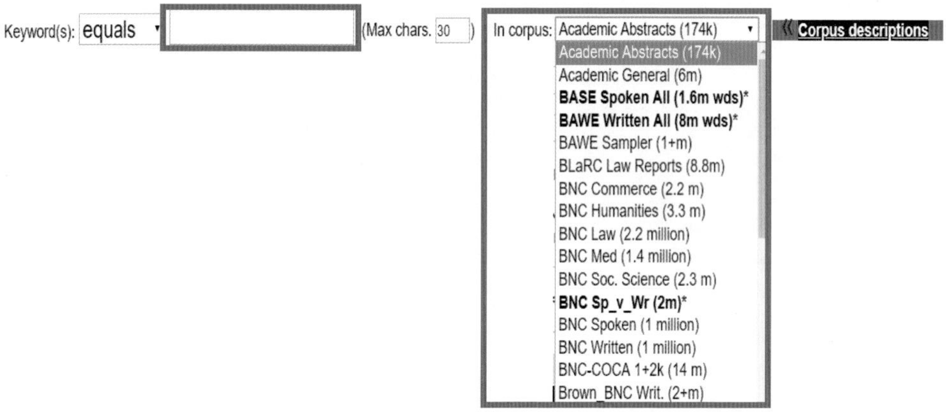

4) Set the conditions in the 'CONTROLS' section.

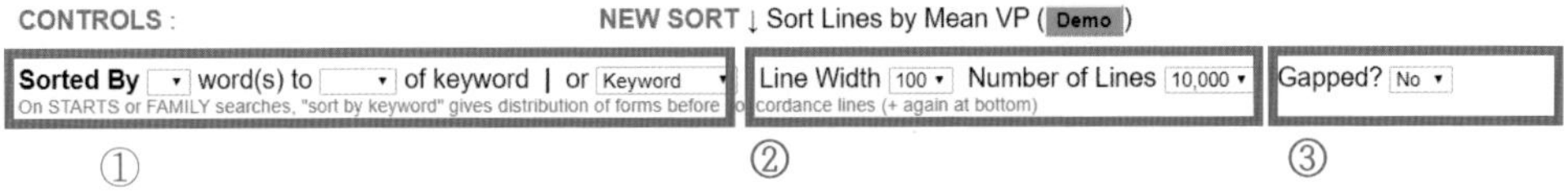

② Choose the range of collocation with keywords. For example, if you choose 'Sort By 1 word to Left of the keyword,' the result shows the frequent word on the left side of the keyword and its concordance lines.
③ Select the width of concordance lines and the number of lines.
④ Choose 'yes' in the 'Gapped' option if you want to place a gap or space where the keyword is supposed to be.

5) Type the word if you want to see the usage of the keyword with the associated word. Specify the location of the word by designating the number of words. The word will come with to the left and the right.

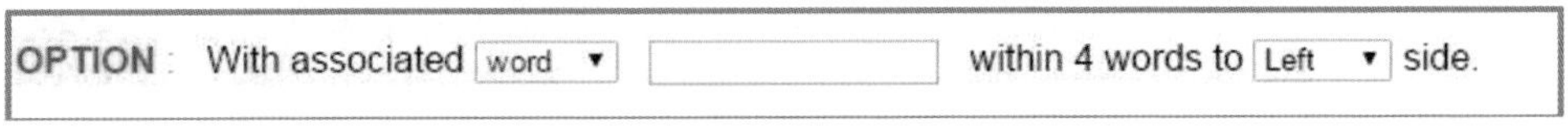

6) When finished, click 'Get concordance.' The image below is the result page of the corpus-based concordance function when typing the word 'money' as a keyword. The result displays concordance lines, associated word collocation placed on the left side, and potential collocation based on Brown corpus. If you want to see the usage of the keyword in the text, click on any keyword.

Multi concordance

'Multi concordance' is another function of corpus-based concordances. It allows users to build a concordance with two and more keywords and to create teaching materials and quizzes for language classes.

1) Click 'Multi Concordance.'

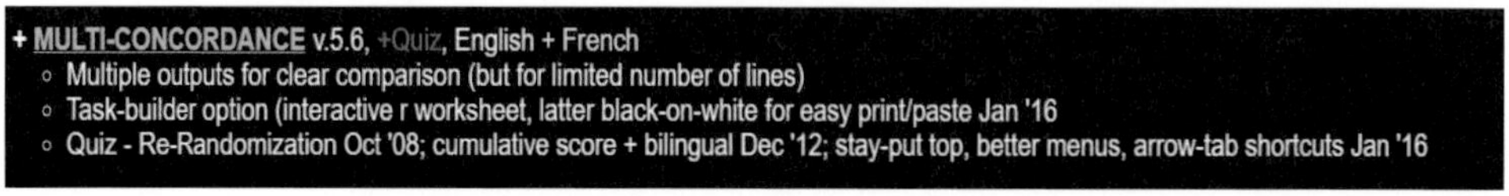

2) Enter the words in the red box and select the corpus in the drop-down.
3) Choose the number of and width of concordance lines and select the output modes. Then, click 'Build.'

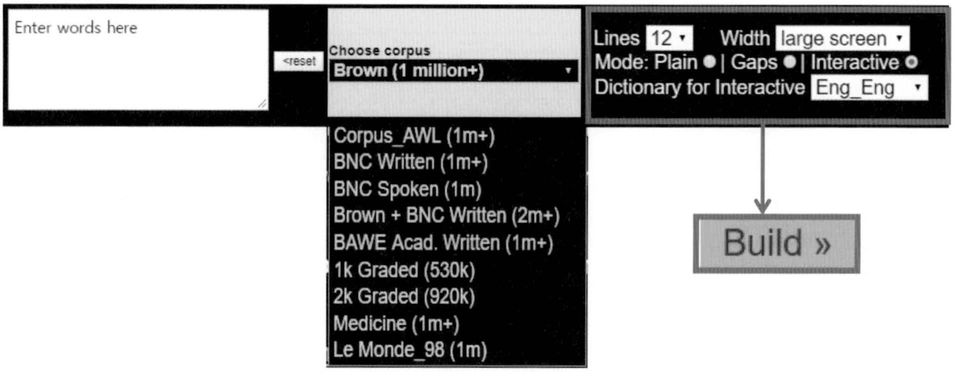

4) There are three output mode options, 'Plain,' 'Gaps,' and 'Quiz.' 'Plain' mode provides Keyword in Context (KWIC) without gaps. In the 'Gaps' mode, keywords are indicated in the blanks. It allows users to create language related exercises. Last, the 'Quiz' option offers an online quiz. Learners are supposed to replace the gaps with an item from the drop-down distracters with feedback. All three options can be saved with a URL address. The following three figures are the result pages of 'Plain,' 'Gaps,' and 'Quiz' modes when the words 'in addition, furthermore, for example, however, therefore, and in other words' are entered.

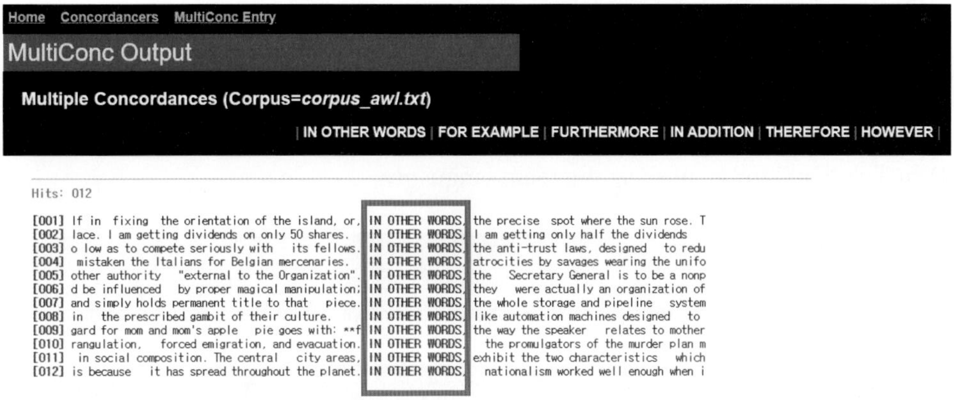

Figure 7.8 The result of plain output mode

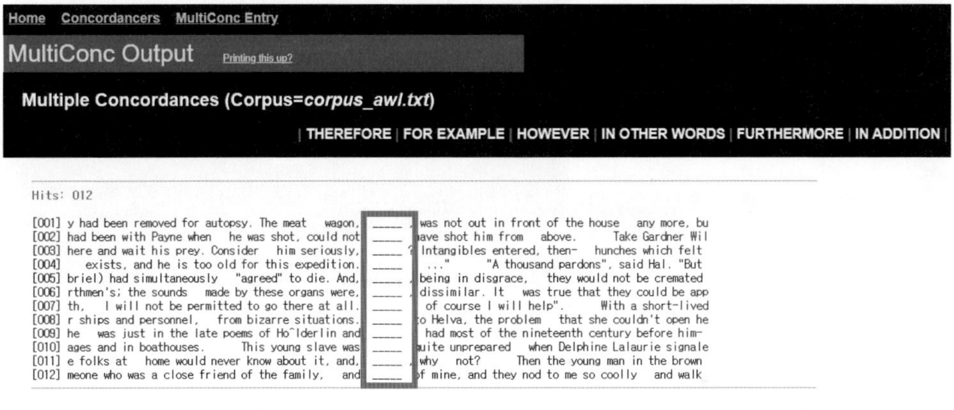

Figure 7.9 The result of gaps output mode

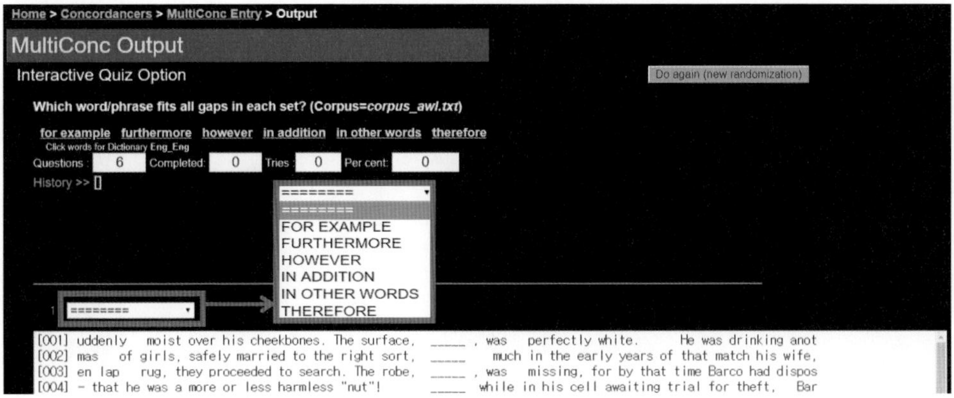

Figure 7.10 The result of quiz output mode

Text concordances

Text concordances enable users to get concordance lines from their texts.

1) Click 'Eng' for English as the main language.

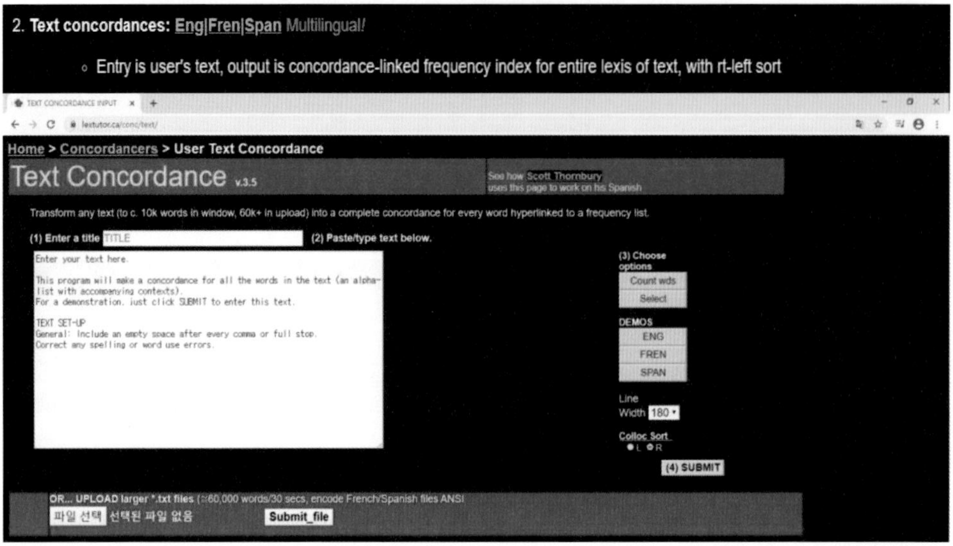

2) Enter the title of the text and type a text in the box. A file and text can also be uploaded.

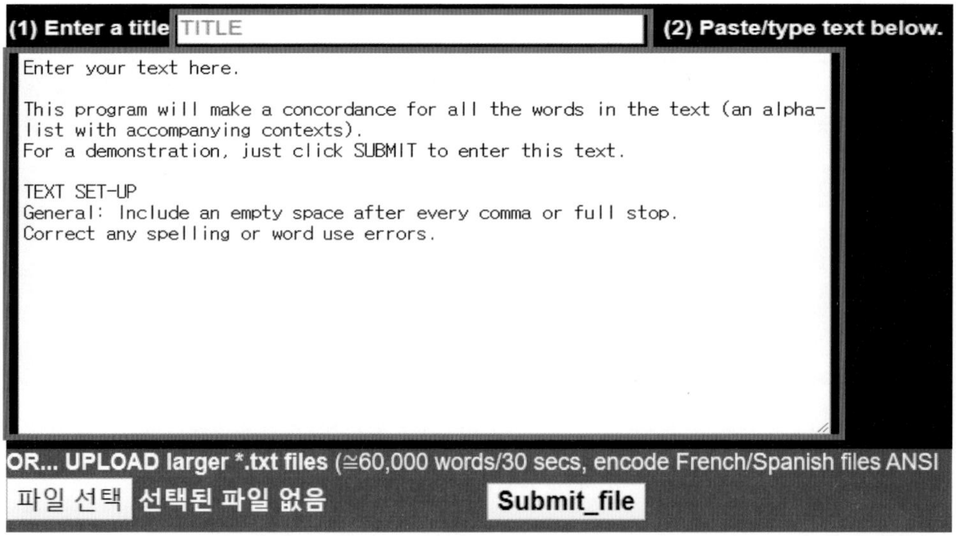

3) Choose the options, and then click 'Submit_file.'

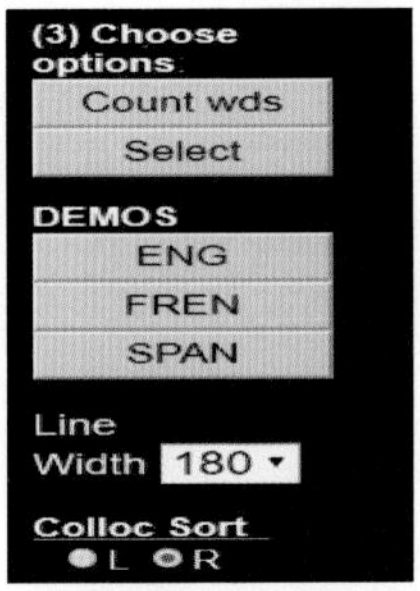

- Count Wds: count the number of tokens and types.

- Demos ENG/FREN/SPAN: provide demonstration.

- Line Width: select the width of the concordance line.

- Colloc Sort: interactive left-right collocate sort options.

4) The result page of the text-based concordance function is presented in the image below. Users can print or save the result.

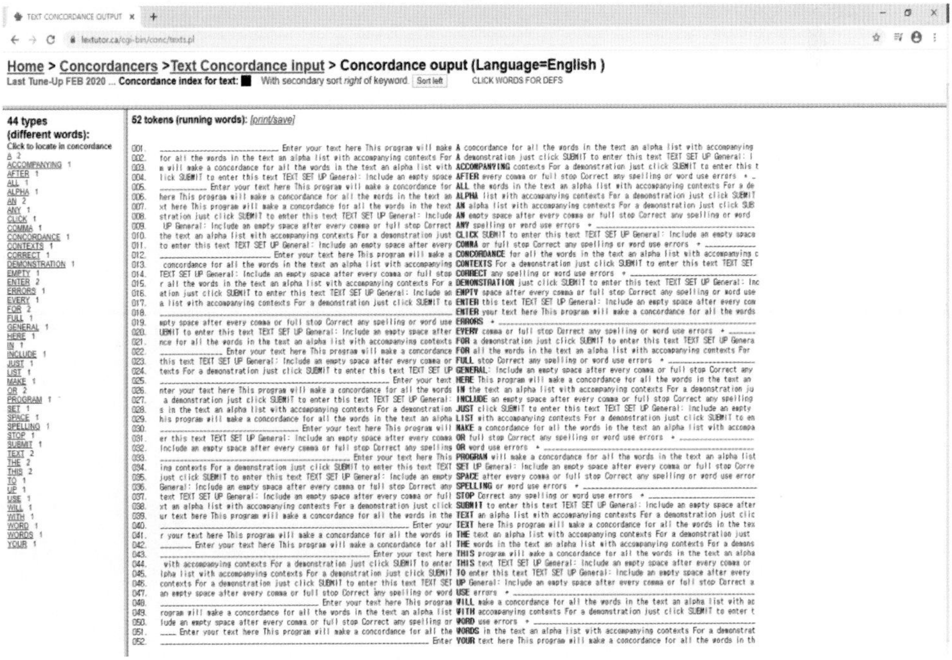

Frequency

Frequency provides a word frequency list, number of tokens and types, and type-token ratio of texts or corpora. The following figure is the home screen of Frequency.

1) Click 'English' in the Menu option.

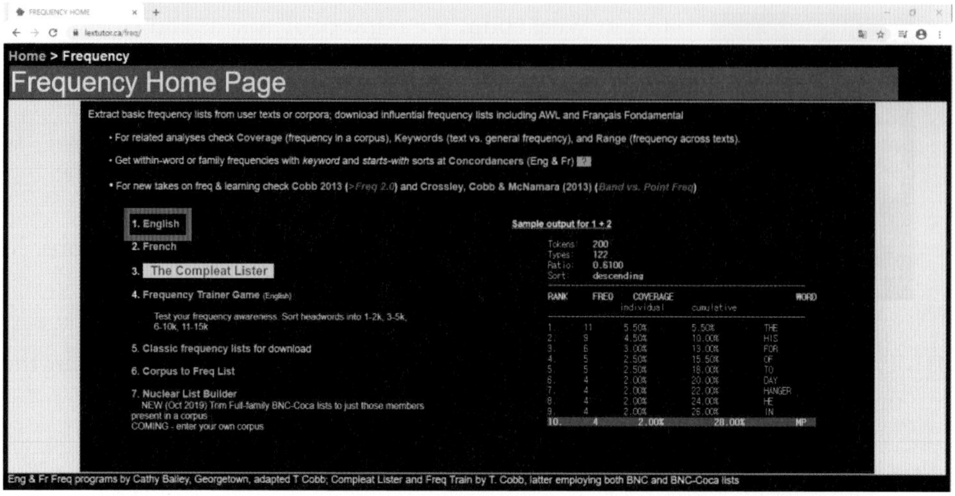

2) Type the title and type or paste a text in the box or upload a text file. Click 'Submit_window' to move to the result page.

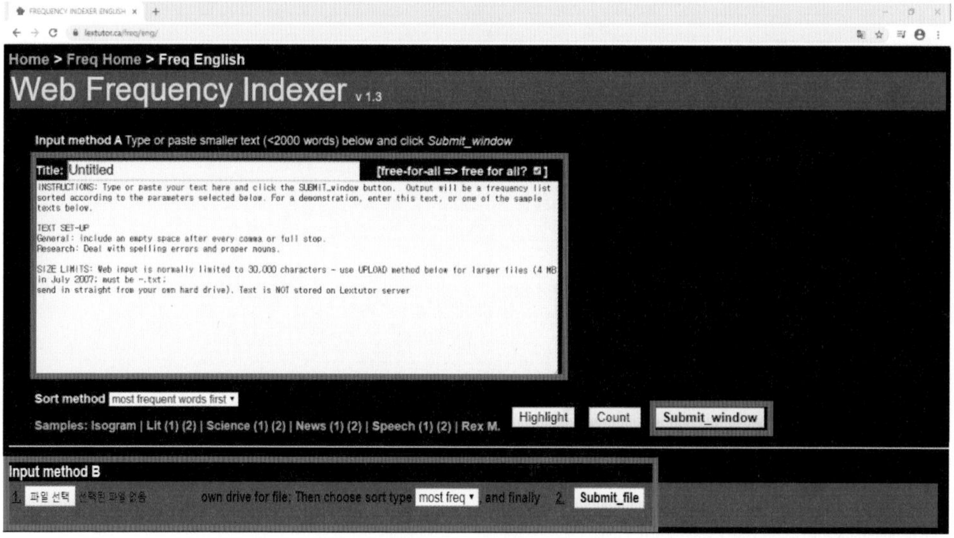

3) The following is the result page of 'frequency.'

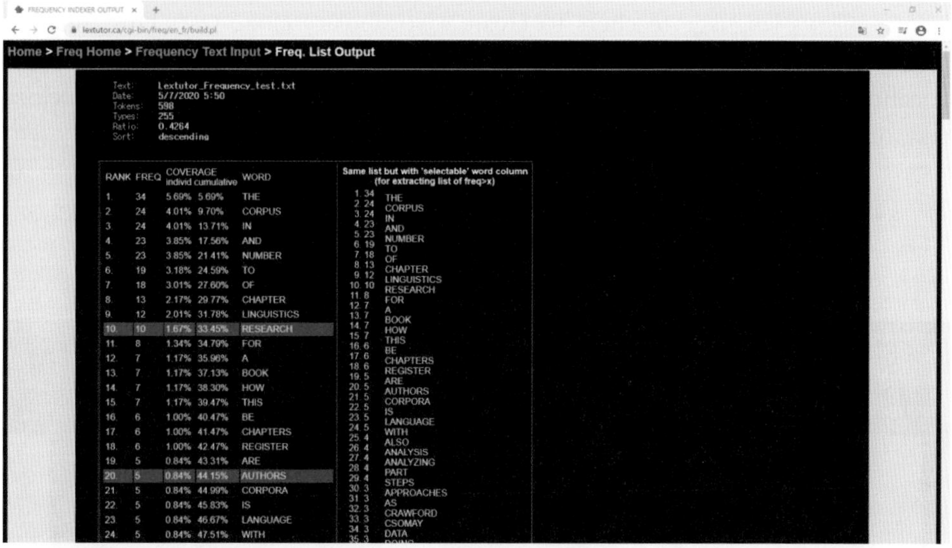

Famous frequency lists for download

Famous frequency word lists can be downloaded, printed, and saved from the *Lextutor* website.

1) Click 'Classic frequency lists' on the Frequency homepage.
2) Select the frequency list to be downloaded, printed, and saved.

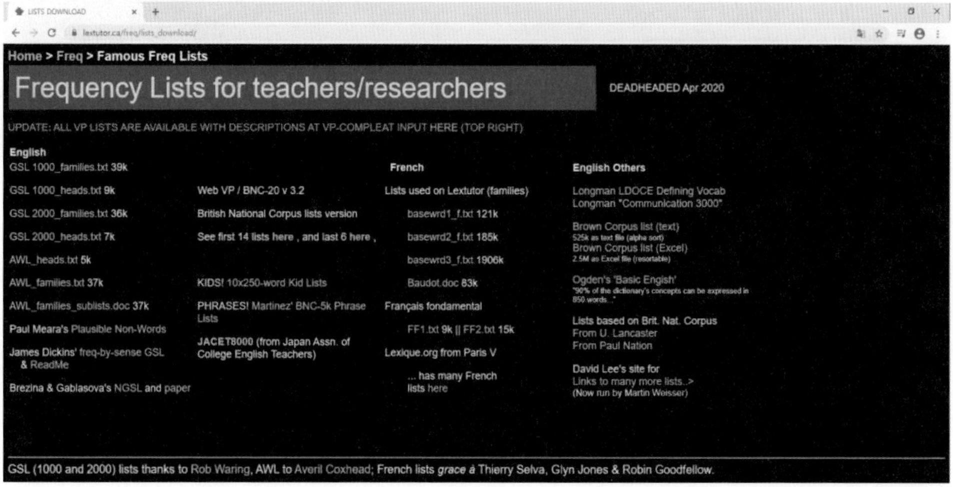

Cloze

'Cloze' allows language teachers to create a vocabulary cloze test. This function provides two main types of cloze tests: deletion cloze (random and rational) and vocabulary profile clozes (frequency-based). In this section, rational deletion cloze text, one of the most frequently used forms, will be introduced.

1) Click on the 'English + French.'

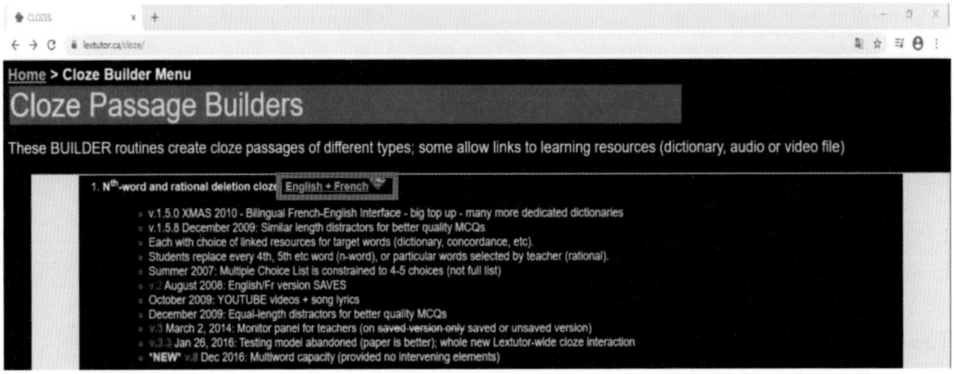

2) The following is the first page for making the 'N-word' or 'Rational Cloze test.'

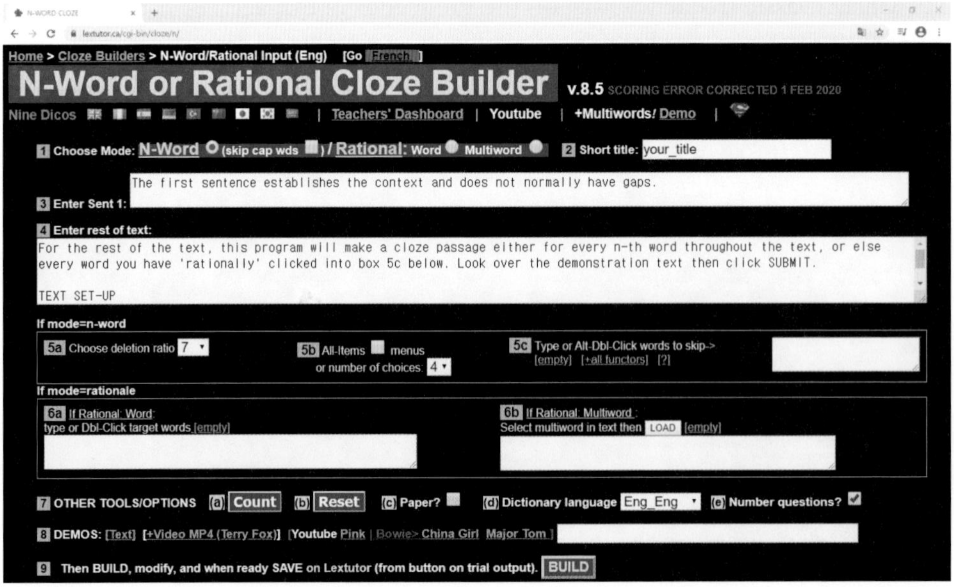

3) Check 'Multiword' in 'Rational' and enter the title.

4) Type the first sentence of the text in 'Enter 1st sentence,' and the rest of the text goes in the box.

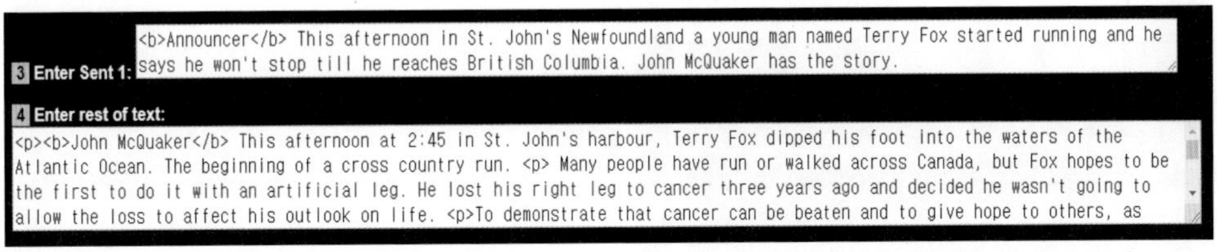

5) Double click the words in which you want to make an item. The selected words will show up on a squared box in the '6a' menu.

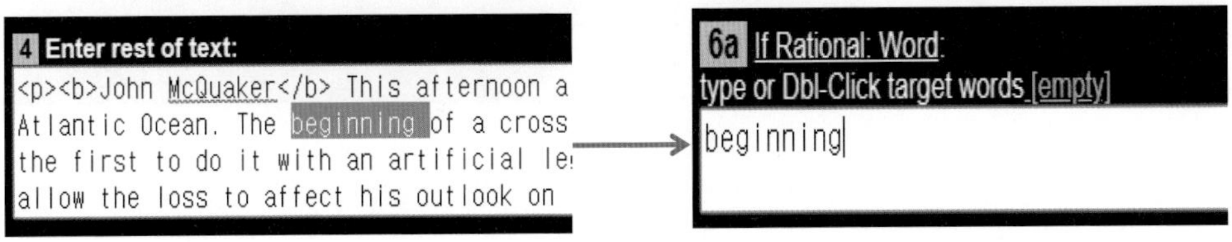

6) Select multi-words from the entered text and click the 'LOAD' button on the '6b' menu.

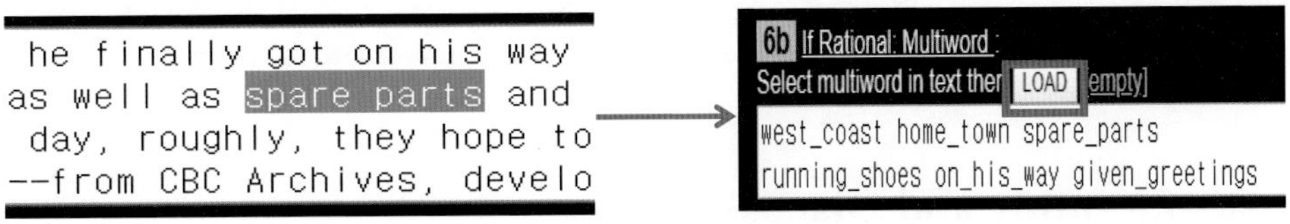

7) Choose the test modes: paper or computer-based. If you want to add a video or a clip from *Youtube*, copy the URL address and paste it into 'Media URL.'

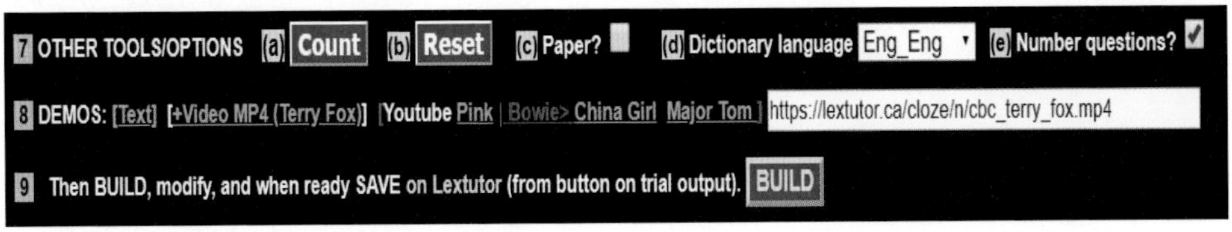

The image below is an example of a cloze test where a clip from *Youtube* is embedded.

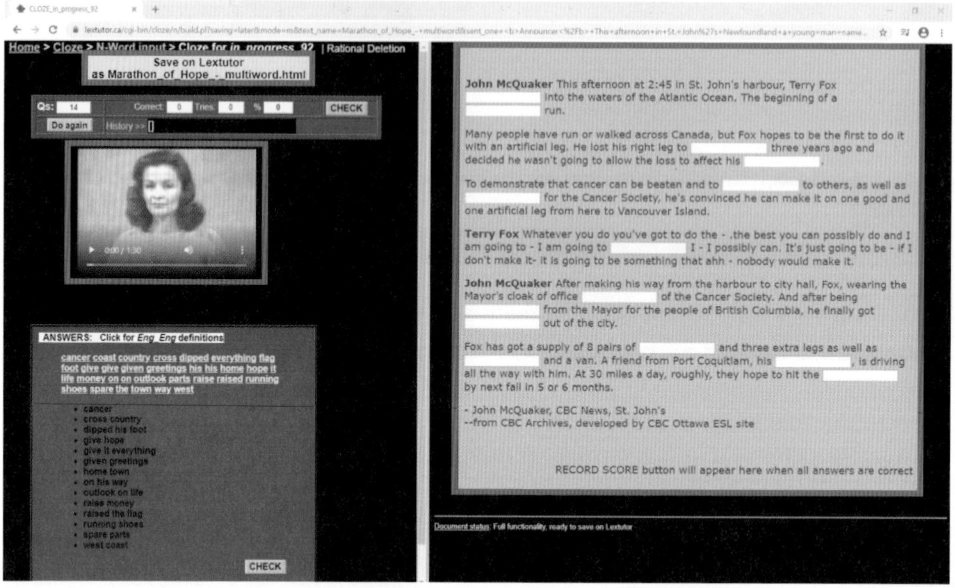

8) Click the button 'Save on *Lextutor* as title.html' to save the test and create the URL for the test (e.g., http://www.lextutor.ca/cloze/n/users/Let_it_Be.html)

Your cloze passage has been saved at this address on the Lextutor server:

https://www.lextutor.ca/cloze/n/users/Marathon_of_Hope_-_multiword.html

If your file has the default name of "in_progress" it will be deleted after one day unvisited.

The file will remain on lextutor server for ~~one year~~ 100 DAYS unvisited, indefinitely if visited even just once per 100 days.

Tasks for Study and Discussion

1. Create a hypertext file for a reading activity using a video file or a sound file.

    1) Search for movies, news, songs, and video clips on the Internet.
    2) Work individually. Then share your work with partners.

2. Create a vocabulary test using the 'Cloze test' type with resources from the video clip, MP3 file, concordance, dictionary, etc.

7.9 *Mendeley*

Mendeley (http://www.mendeley.com) is a free program and ubiquitous web tool for research purposes. The main functions of *Mendeley* boast convenient access to any documents, articles, and journals anywhere. It is also a useful program to organize document files that have been accessed and/or downloaded.

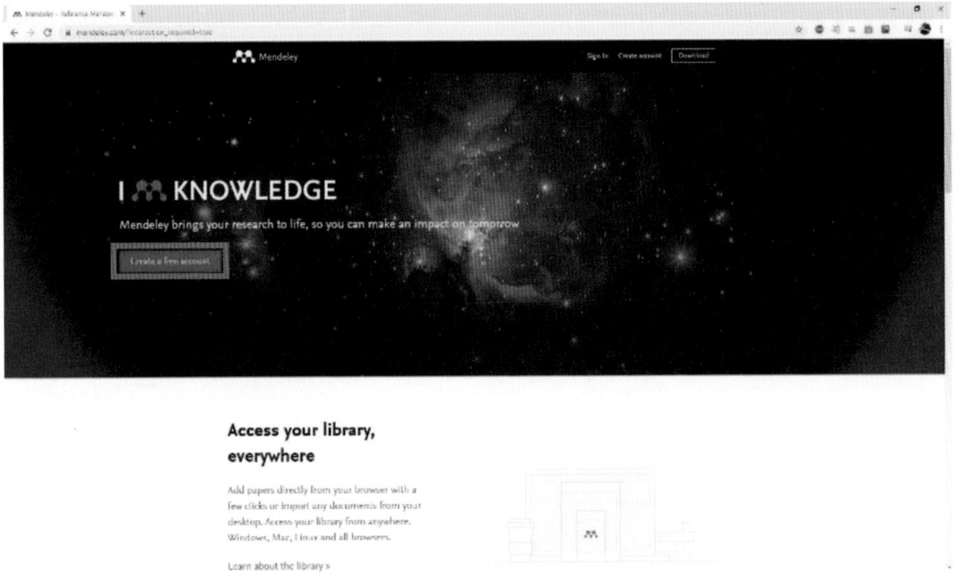

Figure 7.11 Main screen of *Mendeley*

1) Click on the red 'Create a free account,' enter your email address and other required information to complete registration.
2) Once on the account page, click on the red 'Get reference manager' to download the *Mendeley* program.

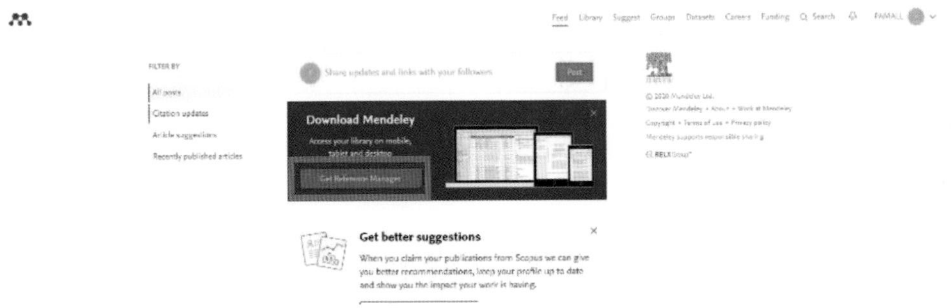

3) Either click on 'Import documents or library' or the button above 'Add' to have *Mendeley* register the document(s) into its system. The added file should appear on the program, with additional info (if available) showing up on the right panel.
4) Click the 'Sync' button to synchronize the document(s) in the program with your account. This should make the file available on the website and other mobile devices that have *Mendeley* installed.

Tasks for Study and Discussion

1. Download research articles of your interest, save them to your *Mendeley* desktop app, then sync your files to the *Mendeley* library.

2. Search for the articles using the *Mendeley* desktop app or website using keywords related to the articles.

Part 3

Integration of MALL into the Classroom

Part 3
Integration of MALL into the Classroom

Some teachers are accustomed to using ICT and multimedia, but other teachers are nervous about using them and show skepticism toward them. It is true that using ICT and multimedia requires technical and pedagogical preparation, including some knowledge and experiences of hardware and software. In particular, digital technologies such as PLDs, multimedia, and social media require working knowledge of ICT and result in changes in teachers' and learners' roles. Therefore, teachers will need to integrate their existing teaching practices with technology, which may differ from the conventional teaching tools that the teachers are familiar with.

Research on improper use of ICT and multimedia in language classes shows that if a MALL lesson is not adequately planned and organized, the valuable teaching and learning time will be wasted (Baek & Lee, 2018; Cho & lee, 2019; C. H. Lee, 2006; Schmid, 1989; Windeatt, Hardisty, & Eastment, 2000). Inappropriate use of ICT and multimedia causes negative attitudes towards MALL for both teachers and students. For that reason, many researchers have emphasized the importance of hands-on practice and actual use of the computer and social media in the language classroom. Indeed, the main factors in the successful use of computers in FLT&L will be technical and pedagogical preparation and their actual use in language classes.

In terms of pedagogical preparation, teachers need to keep in mind that whether or not MALL content is suitable for specific tasks or situations depends on how it is used (Windeatt, 1990; Windeatt, Hardisty, & Eastment, 2000). The content can be integrated into various syllabi, tasks, and activities in FLT&L through flexible and imaginative methodological approaches, which will compensate for the lack of suitable content that the teachers often claim. Windeatt (1990) suggested that teachers should consider the following questions before using the content: 1) What is the content intended to teach or practice?; 2) What does the content teach or practice?; 3) How can it be used with your students? Think of three ways to use it with your students; and 4) What are possible shortcomings of the content? Think of three improvements that can be made to the content.

For the effective and successful use of multimedia and MALL content, teachers and students need to be familiar with their basic properties and functions. Second, they need to know what MALL content can do in FLT&L. Last, they need to find out how MALL content can develop specific language skills. This chapter aims to understand how to integrate MALL into various contexts in the language classroom and produce MALL lesson plans, including tasks and activities for actual language classes.

Chapter 8

Focus on Language Skills Development: Listening, Speaking, Reading, and Writing

8.1 Listening

A wide array of pseudo-authentic audio and audiovisual materials comes into use as valuable resources for developing L2 listening skills. Sounds and videos from websites and apps have been the most widely used. Popular websites such as *CNN student news* (http://www.edition.cnn.com/cnn10), *English Listening* (https://play.google.com/store/apps/details?id=com.talkenglish.listening), *NPR (National Public Radio)* (https://www.npr.org), *Podcasts in English* (https://www.podcastsinenglish.com/), *TED Ed* (https://ed.ted.com), *Voice of America* (https://www.voanews.com), etc. provide downloadable transcripts and listening materials. Researchers have identified and suggested taxonomies of listening activities that can come in handy for teachers in diversifying and selecting the most effective activities for the material (Brown, 2007b; Byrne, 1986; Heo & Lee, 2019; Ur, 1984). Matching the activity and the content is highly significant and can make teaching and learning listening more motivating and effective. Recent trends in the teaching practice of L2 listening comprehension also encourage interaction between/among learners to have learners co-construct the content (Goh & Taib, 2006; Vandergrift & Tafaghodtari, 2010). In this section, the teaching methods and techniques for listening are presented with a sample MALL lesson plan, using an authentic audio clip and authoring tools for improving listening comprehension and strategies.

1. The Audio Material for Teaching Listening

The audio clip selected and used for the lesson plan is from the program entitled *'All tech considered,'* a special series provided by the *NPR* (https://www.npr.org). *NPR* runs multiple programs ranging from up-to-date news to in-depth discussion of certain social and international issues to culture. The clip is concerned with how technology divides generations (https://www.npr.org/

templates/story/story.php?storyId=105751918). The original clip is 3 minutes 24 second-long, but the excerpt for the sample lesson lasts 2 minutes and 25 seconds. It is a clip that includes an interview with experts and the host presenting the coverage. The clip was edited to control the length and pauses inserted when a paragraph switch roughly corresponds to the content changes, using *Goldwave* version 6.51 (https://www.goldwave.com). Aso, *Tagxedo* (https://www.tagxedo. com) and *Hot Potatoes* (https://hotpot.uvic.ca) were used in the pre- and while-listening stages.

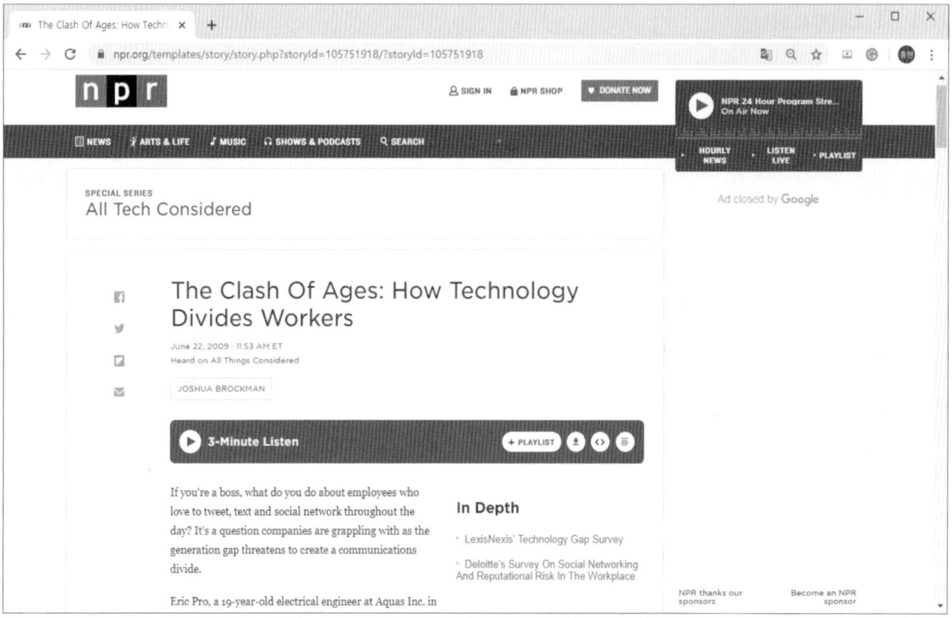

Figure 8.1 The screenshot of *NPR* (*National Public Radio*)

2. A Sample Lesson Plan for Listening Using an Audio Clip

The sample lesson plan presented gives a brief introduction to how the learning tools and content can be adapted and blended in intermediate to advanced listening classes. The lesson plan starts with an introduction on how to prepare the setting and the students, how the main listening activities are instructed, and finally wraps up with a short post-listening activity. Teaching methods and techniques with a sample MALL lesson plan are presented as a separate section with concrete examples and specifications of each activity in each stage of the class.

Title The clashes of ages: How technology divides workers

Theme Listening to an authentic audio clip

Aims To practice listening for the gist and detail in an audio clip on the Web and to employ appropriate listening strategies

Level Intermediate and above

Time 50 minutes

Preparation *Hardware*

- One computer per student (or group of three to four students) with an Internet connection
- A beam projector and a whiteboard
- PLDs in case networked computers are not available.

Software

- Audio clip, 'The clashes of ages: How technology divides workers' from *National Public Radio* (https://www.npr.org)
- Other websites providing authentic audios or videos
- *Goldwave*, *Tagxedo,* and *Hot Potatoes*
- *Gom player* and *Windows Media Player*
- *MS Teams*, *KaKao Talk*, etc.

Procedures *Pre-computer work:* Pre-listening (10 minutes)

- Give an overview of the class and a concise introduction to how to download the main audio file, open the main listening activity, and operate control functions.
- Divide the students into groups of three or four.
- Lead the students into the topic by giving a general question on the topic using the available advance organizers (e.g., title, questions, images) to activate any prior knowledge
- Have the students make predictions of words using a word cloud and provide a matching activity to check vocabulary.

Computer work: While-listening (30 minutes)

- Have the students listen to the first segment of the audio clip as a whole class and ask a question on the main idea or what

Procedures

is expected. Ask them how making predictions using clues helps them get prepared.

- From the second segment, have the students listen to it individually and give them time to interact with peers to collaborate on what they understood.
- As the students collaborate, encourage them to confirm by re-listening to the clip and resolve differences.
- Upon completing one or two segments, play them back to the whole class and provide feedback.
- Repeat this cycle as target segments are covered.

Post-computer work: Post-listening (10 minutes)

- Get the students into groups of three or four.
- Have the students discuss the segments that they had difficulty with and how they resolved those problem areas (using online collaboration tools, if needed).
- Have the students complete the questionnaire for listening strategies and compare the results of other members.
- Have them share the effective ways to resolve problems they experienced as a whole class.

3. Teaching Methods and Techniques for Listening

Listening classes generally follow three stages: pre-computer work (pre-listening), computer work (while-listening), followed by post-computer work (post-listening). Each stage works towards the students' better comprehension with the help of multimedia.

Pre-computer work: Pre-listening

The pre-listening stage and the activities play an important role, as corroborated from many research studies (e.g., Berne, 1995; Elkhafaifi, 2005; Lee & Lee, 2012; Schmidt-Rinehart, 1994). The primary goals of pre-listening are first to activate the students' prior knowledge using advance organizers or related texts, images, and even videos, and second, to inform background knowledge and vocabulary to make predictions on what is to come. In this lesson plan, a general question is given to the students to think about, and a visual word cloud with concrete words used in the clip is presented.

Lead-in

- Prepare the title and related images and show them to the students.
- Pose a general question regarding the title (e.g., what do you think it means by "The clashes of ages: How technology divides workers) to the whole class.

Activity: Making predictions

- Present a word cloud prepared (e.g., using *Tagxedo*) through the projector to the whole class and give them time to browse the words and think briefly about how they relate to the title.

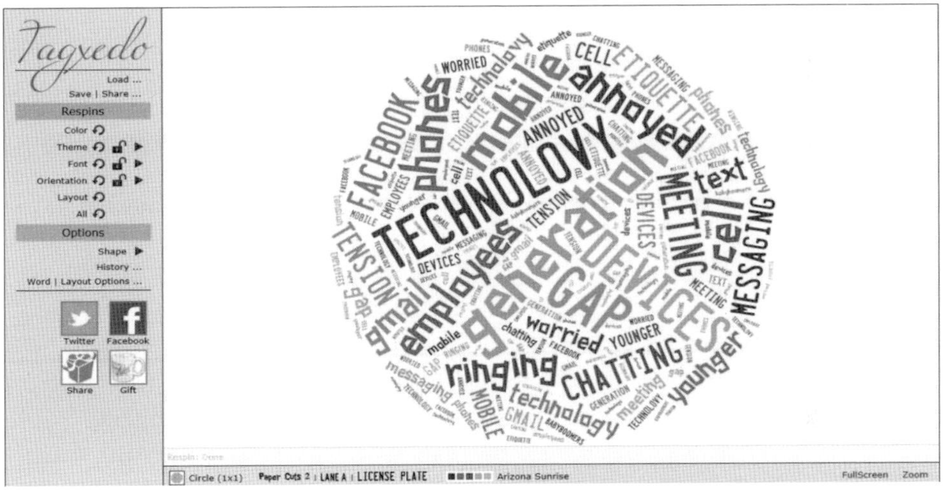

Figure 8.2 A sample word cloud using *Tagxedo*

- Have the students break into groups of three or four and make predictions of the content using the sample word cloud.
- Once the students share ideas and come up with some predictions, have them present to the whole class.
- Have them explain how their prediction relates to the specific words in the word cloud.

Activity: Vocabulary check

- Present the J-match activity on the words and definitions and have the students do the matching.

- Read each word for them with accurate pronunciation and have them select the definition. For instance, ask "What does it mean by a baby boomer?" and have the students read the definition aloud.
- As the students answer, refer to the matching activity and have the students confirm on the screen.

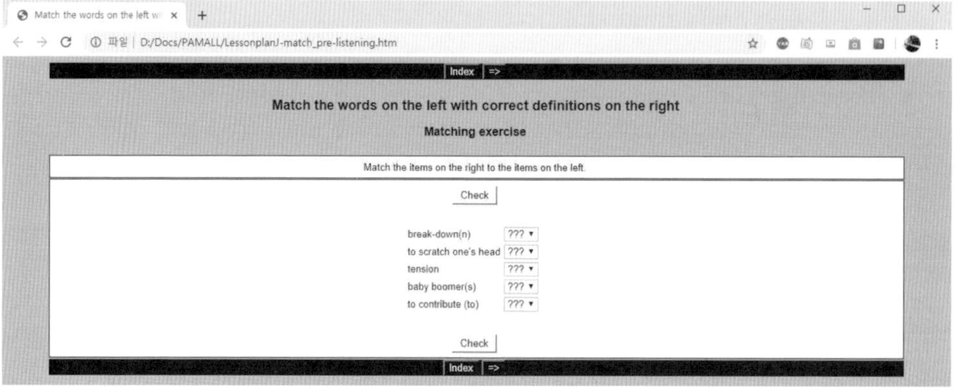

Figure 8.3 A pre-listening activity (JMatch) for checking vocabulary

Optional activity 1

A URL to the prepared activity can be distributed to individual students (e.g., matching or multiple-choice questions in *Hot Potatoes*). Have the students work on the meaning of the new words in context individually on their computers.

Optional activity 2

Lists of words can be given with concrete contexts (e.g., with a sentence or a short paragraph), and have learners guess the meanings of words using the context clues.

Computer work: While-listening

The while-listening stage is where the main listening and comprehension activity is performed. The students can work individually, and then they are encouraged to collaborate on the meaning by confirming and resolving differences. Various types of concrete activities are available (e.g., multiple-choice question, true/false question, short answer question, cloze test, and dictogloss or reconstruction of the text), and a few of them can be combined depending on the extent of clues the students might need. The student-led listening activity is followed by the teachers' feedback and additional instruction on useful listening strategies or techniques regarding the particular problems the students might have had.

Listening comprehension

Listening comprehension activities start with looking for the main idea and then the details. JQuiz from *Hot Potatoes* is used to create multiple-choice questions that address both the main idea and details. Another thing to pay attention to is the strategic scaffolding that may help the students make another attempt based on the clue. Scaffolding is provided upon clicking the question mark.

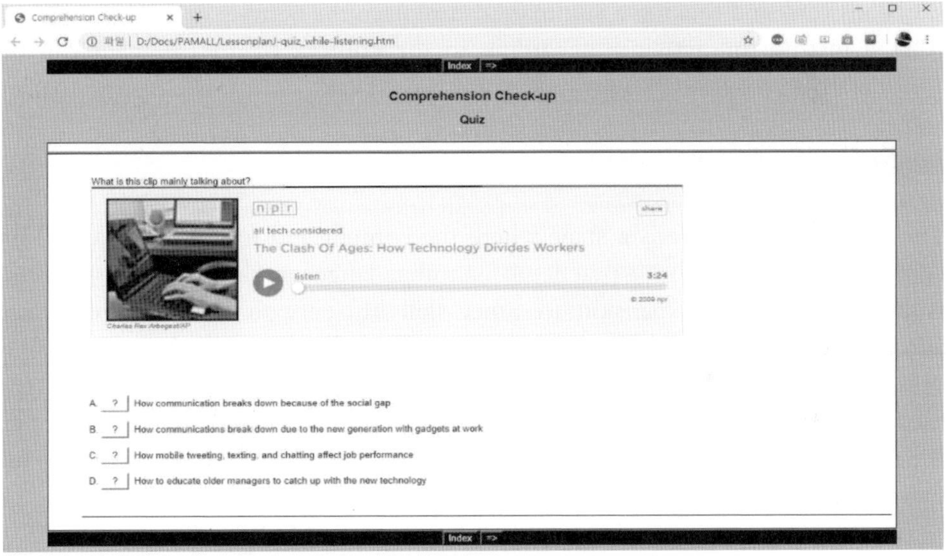

Figure 8.4 A comprehension activity (JQuiz)

Activity: Getting the main idea and details

- Get the students to listen to the first segment and choose the right answer to the question. The first question regards the main idea of the whole clip that requires a top-down approach.
- After the first round of listening, get the students to confirm and compare what they understood about the segment with others.
- When the students answer the question and express uncertainty over their

choices and comprehension, guide them to the scaffolds provided and let them re-listen to the segment. Scaffolds are accessible at the click on the question mark at the beginning of each statement.

- After having the students check the scaffolds, allow them to listen to the segment individually using the embedded audio clip above the questions.
- When the cycle is over, provide feedback and move on to the next segment.
- When all segments are covered, re-play all the segments, stop and then give further clarifications as needed.
- Provide the transcript for further clarification.

Optional activity

Different types of comprehension activities such as filling out information grids, short answers, and making a summary can replace the activity in the lesson plan. Also, a mixture of activities according to the content of the segment can be considered as an option.

Post-computer work: Post-listening

The post-listening stage is a stage where the content and topic are expanded by engaging the students in a practice of another language skill such as speaking, reading, or writing. Expansion to other skills, if enough time and focus are allocated, can allow developing integrated-skills. For example, a short discussion or a debate can promote students' speaking skills with the same topic. As for reading skills, the students can be encouraged to read a passage on a related topic. A writing activity based on reading or summarizing the content can be a useful example of an expansion activity for the main listening.

In the post-listening stage, the students discuss and share the segments that they had difficulty with and how they resolved those problem areas. Completing the metacognitive awareness listening questionnaire (MALQ) (Vandergrift, Goh, Mareschal, & Tafaghodtari, 2010), a validated questionnaire made up of 21 statements on L2 listeners' metacognitive strategies, leads the students to reflect and reinforce general and specific listening strategies.

Activity: Consolidation of listening strategies

The students are supposed to go over the questionnaires and compare them with those of other members. They can keep track of the changes by doing the questionnaire at a specific interval (e.g., once in three or four weeks).

Table 8.1 Metacognitive awareness listening questionnaire
(Vandergrift, Goh, Mareschal, & Tafaghodtari, 2010)

Planning-evaluation	1. Before I start to listen, I have a plan in my head for how I am going to listen.	1	2	3	4	5	6
Directed attention	2. I focus harder on the text when I have trouble understanding it.	1	2	3	4	5	6
Person knowledge	3. I find that listening in English is more difficult than reading, speaking, or writing in English.	1	2	3	4	5	6
Mental translation	4. I translate in my head as I listen.	1	2	3	4	5	6
Problem-solving	5. I use the words I understand to guess the meaning of the words I don't understand.	1	2	3	4	5	6
Directed attention	6. When my mind wanders, I recover my concentration right away.	1	2	3	4	5	6
Problem-solving	7. As I listen, I compare what I understand with what I know about the topic.	1	2	3	4	5	6
Person knowledge	8. I feel that listening comprehension in English is a challenge for me.	1	2	3	4	5	6
Problem-solving	9. I use my experience and knowledge to help me understand.	1	2	3	4	5	6
Planning-evaluation	10. Before listening, I think of similar texts that I may have listened to.	1	2	3	4	5	6
Mental translation	11. I translate keywords as I listen.	1	2	3	4	5	6
Directed attention	12. I try to get back on track when I lose concentration.	1	2	3	4	5	6
Problem-solving	13. As I listen, I quickly adjust my interpretation if I realize that it is not correct.	1	2	3	4	5	6
Planning-evaluation	14. After listening, I think back to how I listened and about what I might do differently next time.	1	2	3	4	5	6
Person knowledge	15. I don't feel nervous when I listen to English.	1	2	3	4	5	6
Directed attention	16. When I have difficulty understanding what I hear, I give up and stop listening.	1	2	3	4	5	6
Problem-solving	17. I use the general idea of the text to help me guess the meaning of the words that I don't understand.	1	2	3	4	5	6
Mental translation	18. I translate word by word as I listen.	1	2	3	4	5	6
Problem-solving	19. When I guess the meaning of a word, I think back to everything else that I heard to see if my guess makes sense.	1	2	3	4	5	6
Planning-evaluation	20. As I listen, I periodically ask myself if I am satisfied with my comprehension level.	1	2	3	4	5	6
Planning-evaluation	21. I have a goal in mind as I listen.	1	2	3	4	5	6

- Get the students to go over the questionnaire and mark it.
- Have the students compare the results of other group members.
- Have the students compare and report if they find any changes over the period.

8.2 Speaking

As mentioned in the previous chapters, if a variety of websites and apps are well-developed and effectively used, they can enrich video resources. Some distinctive characteristics that videos offer can be applied to improving the four language skills and three subskills, mainly speaking or the communicative skills in FLT&L (C. H. Lee, 2006). In short, multimedia content with sounds and moving pictures presents authentic language and situations. It shows individuals interacting with each other in a full context. These can provide learners with a wide range of stimuli and sources of motivation which can provoke active spoken work (Hill, 1989). Teachers should keep in mind that they have to give learners a chance to talk about through various tasks and activities in language classes as much as they can. How can teachers integrate video materials into the communicative activities, and what techniques and activities can teachers use? This section will present teaching methods and techniques with a sample MALL lesson plan for applying a video clip to speaking or communicative activities.

1. The Video Material for Teaching Speaking

The title of the video clip used in the lesson plan is '*Nice to Meet You Too,*' which is excerpted from *ALL in ONE Student Book 1* (Lee, Kwak, & Lynch, 2004). Its materials contain eight video clips intended for both classroom use and self-study to learn English speaking and listening skills. The conversation introduces the third-party introduction. The language is informal even though two of the people do not know each other. Language teachers and students can enjoy the target language conversation in either small-size or full-screen video mode and actively participate in the conversations based on real-life situations and everyday expressions. A part of the video material (see Figure 8.5), which was edited using *Gom Mix Pro*, and the video script are as follows.

Sue: Hey, Fred! How have you been?
Fred: Hi, Sue. Long time no see. I've been just fine.

Sue: Fred. I'd like you to meet my best friend, Eunju.
Fred: Hi, Eunju. Nice to meet you.
Eunju: Nice to meet you too.
Fred: I've heard a lot about you.
Eunju: All good I hope.

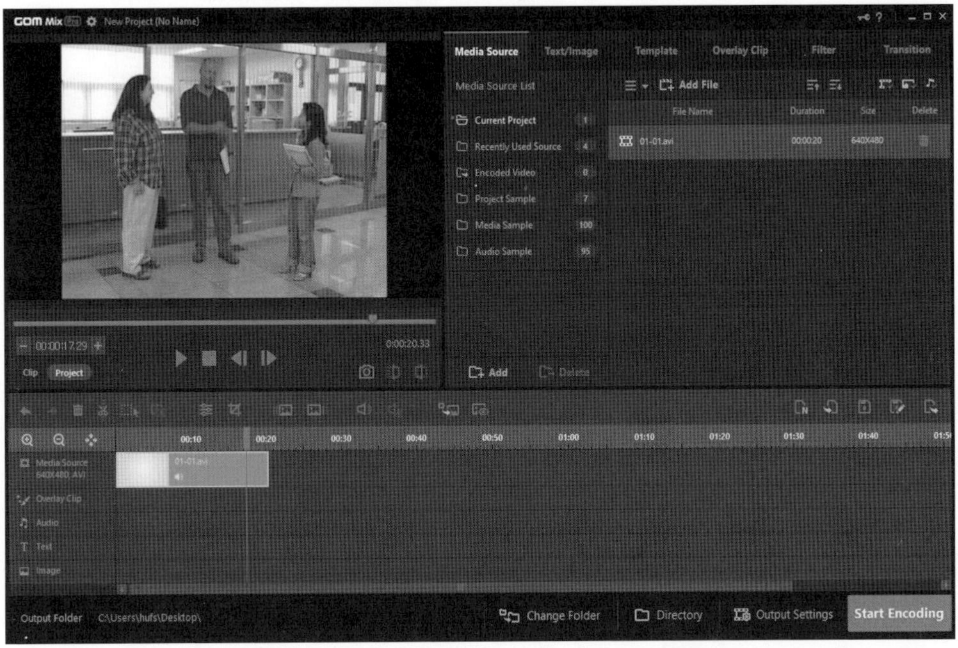

Figure 8.5 A video clip using *Gom Mix Pro*

2. A Sample Lesson Plan for Speaking Using a Video Clip

This sample lesson plan is intended for language teachers who have less experience working with videos on the computer or the Web. More experienced teachers, of course, will have their own techniques and procedures for conducting some tasks and activities in the use of videos and similar animations. It covers preparing, setting up, conducting the tasks and activities for the class, and, finally, a follow-up based on the students' responses. Detailed procedures are presented in the next section.

Title Nice to meet you too.

Theme Greetings and introducing yourself and others

Aims To practice greetings and the language of introduction, especially commonly-used language function in a real-life situation

Level Elementary and above

Time 50 minutes

Preparation *Hardware*

- One computer per student (or group of three students) with an Internet connection or PLDs
- A beam projector and a whiteboard

Software

- A video clip, 'Nice to meet you too.' Alternatively, choose one of the videos dealing with greetings and introducing yourself and others from *YouTube* (https://www.youtube.com).
- Find some other VOD (Video On Demand) sites and websites dealing with them. Check the sites for suitability of content.
- *GOM Mix Pro*
- *Tagxedo, Flipgrid, Animaker*, etc.

Procedures *Pre-computer work:* Pre-speaking (10 minutes)

- Explain the general principles of using video in FLT&L and how to use the video materials on the Web.
- Divide the students into groups of three or four.
- Have students think about the topic and activate any prior knowledge they may have about it.
- Pre-teach some vocabulary in the material unknown to students using *Tagxedo* or JMatch like the pre-listening activity in the previous section. Include useful expressions.

<u>Procedures</u> *Computer work:* While-speaking (25 minutes)

- Have the students watch the video clip individually or in groups of three.
- First of all, tell the students to watch the short video clip without sound.
- After watching it, ask the students some questions or write down the questions on the board to guess or predict what is going on.
- Tell the students to listen to the sound without viewing and ask them to match the scene they saw.
- Have the students watch the video clip with the sound at this time and ask them whether their predictions are right or not.
- Have the students watch the video clip again, pausing for repetition, and ask the students to repeat it in their groups.

Post-computer work: Post-speaking (15 minutes)

- Have the students practice in their groups. Switch roles.
- Get the students to work in pairs.
- Have one of them introduce the other members of the group in front of the class.
- Make a short animation using *Animaker* and their voices in group work. (Give this activity to the students as homework if there is not enough time.)

3. Teaching Methods and Techniques for Speaking

In general, the teachers can divide video materials into three stages for classroom activities, pre-computer work (pre-viewing), computer work (viewing), and post-computer work (post-viewing). Through each stage and its related classroom activities, teachers can integrate them into the communicative activities.

Pre-computer work: Pre-speaking

This stage introduces the topic to deal with and the vocabulary, using illustrations as clues from the particular sections of the sequence. This increases students' active involvement, i.e., a discussion which involves guessing or predicting what is going on (Allan, 1985; Tomalin, 1986). In this stage, teachers can teach students vocabulary in the context of the situations and encourage them to make predictions on the topic. Teachers can use the following procedures (Tomalin, 1986).

- Freeze the picture on the screen at an appropriate point, using the pause button.
- Point to the thing to be taught and, if possible, elicit what it is from students. If not, give the word.
- Get students to repeat it.
- Go on to the next item.

Vocabulary check

- Write the following words or phrases and/or expressions on the board or tell them to speak loudly. Alternatively, present a word cloud prepared (e.g., using *Tagxedo*) through the projector to the whole class and give them time to browse the words.
- Ask the students if they can explain what they mean, and then explain them.
- Make the students repeat after you.

"Long time no see." This term is used among friends who have not seen each other for some time.

"I've heard a lot about you." This term lets a person know that their friend thinks a lot of them, building somewhat of a personal bond.

Activity: Prediction

- Have the students look at the picture.
- Ask them if they know who they are, where they are, and what they are doing. (They are friends. They are saying hello, and one of them introduces his/her best friend to another in front of their department or office.)

Computer work: While-speaking (Viewing and practicing speaking)

In this stage, the students watch the video and listen to the sound. The stage can be divided into three steps - silent viewing, sound without viewing, and viewing with sound. Each step can promote learners' speaking and listening skills using video, audio, and textual aid (C. H. Lee, 2004; Yoon, Lee, & Lee, 2013).

Silent viewing (Sound off and vision on) and sound only (Sound on and vision off)

It often separates the aural and visual clues. First, in viewing without sound, the students can concentrate on the environment, gestures, facial expressions, posture, and action. It consists of a range of activities in which they get training in interpreting visual clues to meaning and a chance to predict certain kinds of language that they will hear later (Lonergan, 1984; Tomalin, 1986).

Second, in sound without viewing (sound only), the students cannot see the screen, but the sound can be heard. This activity can also focus on a useful communicative activity in which they visualize a scene or an object from what is said (Tomalin, 1986).

Activity

- First of all, tell students to watch the short video skit without sound. Ask students the following questions or write down the questions on the board.
  - "Who are they?"
  - "Where are they?"
  - "What are they doing?"
- Play the video sequence without the sound. After watching it, have the students guess or predict what is going on.
- Tell the students to listen to the sound without viewing, and ask them to match the scene they saw.

Viewing with sound and practicing speaking

The students now have both aural and visual clues. Silent viewing and sound only can be used to complete this stage. They have a range of tasks, which involve intensive study of meaning. The teachers can give more viewing comprehension questions and tasks. This activity allows them to practice their language use.

Activity

- When students have made their predictions in the previous stage, play the video sequence with the sound at this time to check their predictions.
- Ask the students whether their predictions were right or not.
- Ask students the following questions.
  - "What are the names of the people in the conversation?"
  - "Who is Sue's best friend?"

- Do a quick check to make sure that they all got the answers correct.
- Watch again, pausing for choral repetition, and make the students repeat after watching the video.
- Watch the video a third time, reading along as they watch, if necessary.
- Ask the students to play a role in group work of three in the same situation.

Post-computer work: Post-speaking

Through this stage, teachers can check whether the students were following the sequence or not. The teachers can give them various activities to review and extend their learning in the previous two stages, e.g., retelling the story, role-play, and discussion. These activities can also be integrated into communicative activities well. First, retelling the story allows them to improve the skill of gist listening and grammatical competence. For example, narrative recall can be used to provide controlled practice for verb tenses (Lonergan, 1984). Second, role-play is an activity that takes place at the middle or end of the sequence. It can also be a suitable type of communicative activity since it allows the students to transfer the language they have learned in the video materials to their use (Tomalin, 1986). Finally, video is often a richer stimulus to the discussion because of its motivating effect than other media. Teachers can let students have pair and group discussions based on the live audiovisual presentation. This activity encourages them to develop their general language fluency and find out what personal difficulties they have in expressing themselves in a target language.

Post-speaking activities

Activity 1

Work in groups of four. Practice the conversation with partners. In this conversation, two people are introducing his/her friend to other peoples. "I'd like you to meet." is that structure that is introduced and is perfect for the situation.

- Get the students into groups of four.
- Have the students practice with their partners.

Activity 2

Work in pairs. Introduce yourself by taking turns asking and answering the questions with the following examples. Then introduce your partner to the class.

Questions

Q1: How do you do?/ Hello?/ HI!
Q2: What's your name?
Q3: How do you spell that?
Q4: Where are you from?

Answers

A1: How do you do?/ Hello?/ HI!
A2: My name is … /I'm…
A3: It's E-U-N-J-U.
A4: I'm from… / I come from...

This activity will help students to practice the vocabulary and forms that they have been introduced to.

- Write the question structures upon the board.
- Ask a couple of students around the class one question at a time. (In this way, your class will have a sample of how the question may be answered before doing the exercise.)
- Now drill each question several times.
- Have students repeat each question after you.
- Then have the students practice the dialogues.
- One student should ask the questions while the other answers them.

Optional activity

- Make a short animation using *Animaker* and their voices in a group work of three.

8.3 Reading

Reading is an area that has benefitted the most in terms of the quality and number of resources available with the development of ICT and multimedia for FLT&L. A large influx of resources ranging from e-books, mobile apps, and reading-oriented websites in various genres are easily accessible. Websites and apps can serve as reading materials since texts and images are the fundamental elements of various types of hypertext. The issue, therefore, is not so much the matter of locating resources as that of locating and selecting reading materials that are conducive to the improvement of reading skills. What also distinguishes teaching methods of reading from other productive skills, including speaking and writing, is the existence of a universal approach applicable to reading the majority of genres. The interactive approach to L2 reading has been the dominant approach suggested by many studies (e.g., Alptekin, 2006; Carrell, Devine, & Eskey, 1988; Chun & Plass, 1996). Multimedia content has enriched the resources and presented help options, most notably, multimedia annotation, with which readers can get assistance (Abraham, 2008; Lin & Chen, 2007; Sakar & Ercetin, 2005). A sample lesson plan incorporates activities that encourage collecting background knowledge, reading interactively using scaffoldings, and representing the topic or the theme into a cartoon.

1. E-Text for Teaching Reading

The e-text used for the sample lesson plan is an article from the website titled *News for You* (https://www.newreaderspress.com/news-for-you-online). This website offers news articles updated regularly and audios of the full texts, exercises, and vocabulary help. The hypertext immediately offers definitions to words that the students may find difficult.

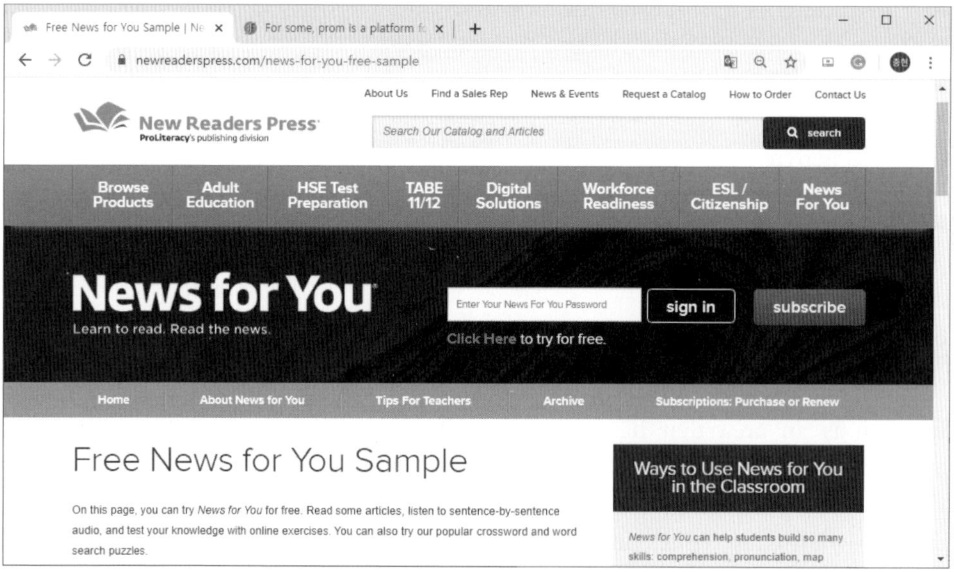

Figure 8.6 The main screen of *News for You*

The website provides various reading activities to choose from (e.g., crossword, making an acrostic, fact-finding, headline matching, etc.). The suggested activities may encourage the students to interact with one another while they are engaged in reading.

2. A Sample Lesson Plan for Reading Using a News Article

The lesson plan below provides a brief overview of the main features and procedures of a multimedia-based reading class. The news article is from *News for You*, and it is divided into three stages of pre-reading, while-reading, and post-reading. *PhotoScape X, Snagit, Make Beliefs Comix, Hot Potatoes,* and *Padlet* are used for developing materials and activities.

Title	Changing trend of prom
Theme	Reading a news article on changing trend of prom
Aims	To practice reading skills using a news article and to create a cartoon related to the topic of the news
Level	Intermediate and above
Time	50 minutes
Preparation	*Hardware*

- One computer per student (or group of three students) with an Internet connection or PLDs
- A beam projector and a whiteboard

Software

- E-text 'Some students make prom about good deeds, social change' from the website (*News for You*)
- Three or more hypertext links to reading websites
- *Padlet* (https://www.padlet.com), *OKMindmap* (http://okmindmap. com)
- JQuiz in *Hot Potatoes* (https://hotpot.uvic.ca)
- *Make Beliefs Comix* (https://www.makebeliefscomix.com)
- *PhotoScape X* (http://x.photoscape.org/), *Snagit* (https://www.techsmith.com/ snagit.html), etc.

Procedures *Pre-computer work:* Pre-reading (10 minutes)

- Explain the general principles of reading approaches and useful strategies.
- Divide the students into groups of three or four.
- Have the students get to the website and get them pre-registered.
- Have the students collect ideas and create a mind map using the words and concepts suggested to activate their schema.

Computer work: While-reading (25 minutes)

- Have the students listen to the edited audio version of the text as a whole class.
- Have the students think of the main idea and compare it with group members.
- After getting the students to share the main ideas, provide the reading text with comprehension questions appropriate to the content.
- Encourage the students not to refer to the definitions straight but instead try to apply inferring strategies.
- Provide answers to the questions and take questions.

Post-computer work: Post-reading (15 minutes)

- Get the students into groups of three.
- Have the students create a cartoon that can effectively suggest the topic of the news using *Make Beliefs Comix*.
- Have groups vote on the cartoon that best represents the main idea.

3. Teaching Methods and Techniques for Reading

The lesson is divided into three stages: pre-computer work (pre-reading), computer work (while-reading), and post-computer work (post-reading). It incorporates related activities to each stage: mind mapping to activate the students' background knowledge at the pre-reading stage, multiple-choice comprehension questions using strategic at while-stage, and making a cartoon that elicits a visual representation of the written text at the post-reading stage.

Pre-computer work: Pre-reading

Pre-reading is a stage where the main goal is to prepare the students to be better tuned for the general topic and possibly the content. Collecting ideas using visual mind mapping, verbal discussion, or making predictions using advance organizers (e.g., title, questions, related images, etc.) are the typical activities used at this stage. In the lesson plan, *OKMindmap* was used to engage the students in a mind-mapping activity.

Mind mapping

Mind mapping as part of brainstorming ideas is one of the most effective activities used for activating the students' schema and is applicable across language skills, particularly to listening and reading (Hammadou, 2000). Visual elements such as images and videos on the mind map can make the brainstorming process more motivating.

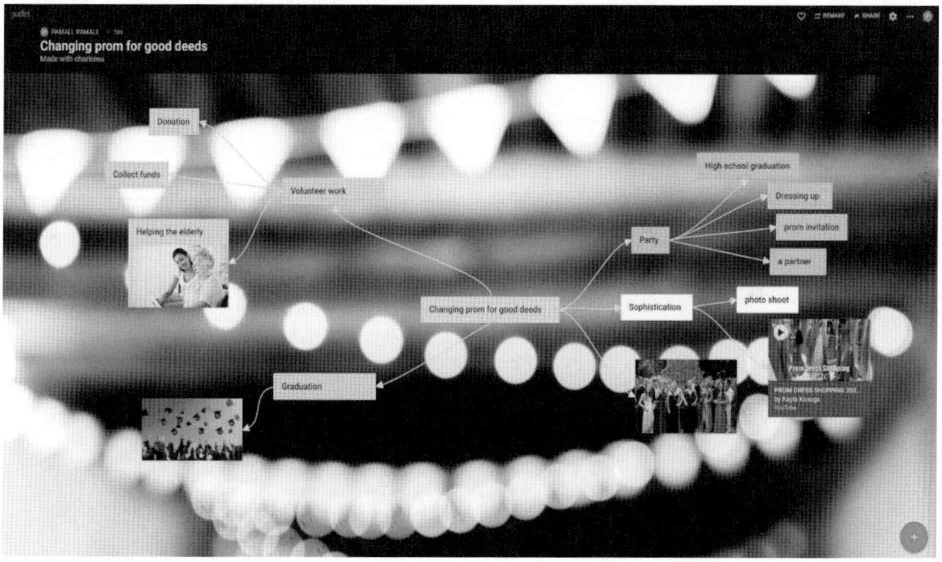

Figure 8.7 A sample mind map using *Padlet*

Activity: Making predictions via mind mapping

- Log in to the *Padlet* and get ready to start the mind map as a whole class activity.

- Have the students come up with words, phrases, concepts, and ideas and present them.
- In case the students are short of ideas, give more examples to the students.
- Ensure that the students give attention to all the key concepts in the given topic phrase (i.e., changing prom for social goods).

Computer work: While-reading

During the while-reading stage, the main reading text is introduced with comprehension activities. Skimming and scanning skills, and top-down and bottom-up approaches are used as the students read along. Strategic scaffoldings can be timely provided prior to providing the meanings. Also, frequently required strategies such as inferring unknown words using context clues or linking the meaning of a particular portion to the overall topic should be practiced. In this lesson plan, a set of multiple-choice questions added with strategic scaffoldings is used. The activity was created using JQuiz, as in Figure 8.8.

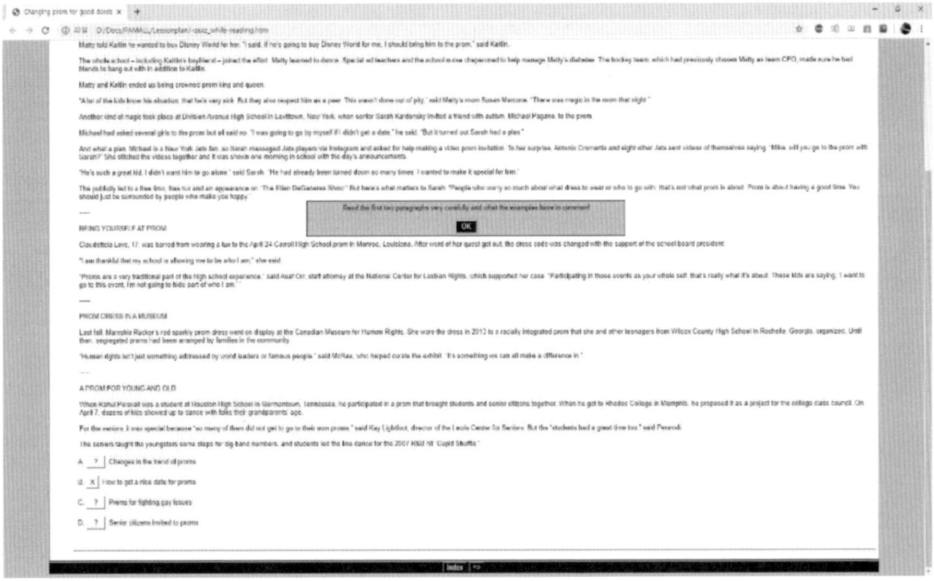

Figure 8.8 A sample multiple choice question (JQuiz) with strategic scaffolding

Activity: Reading comprehension

- Provide the students with a set of comprehension questions embedded with scaffolds.

- Have the students individually go over multiple-choice questions with strategic scaffoldings as feedback for wrong answer choices.
- Once the comprehension activity is completed, present the students with a useful strategic approach to specific areas that the teacher pre-determined to be challenging.

Optional activity: Reconstructing the content

- To ensure that the students have a full understanding of the text, mixed statements can be provided to be re-ordered by the flow of the text using JMix. This activity is more applicable to text that contains time factors.

Post-computer work: Post-reading

A variety of activities can follow up on the while-reading stage. First, further reading on a similar topic can be provided to intensify the skill and consolidate reading approaches. Second, ask the students to search at least a relevant topic on the web for autonomous learning, extensive reading, and improving skimming and scanning skills. Third, reading can be expanded into other language skills such as speaking or writing.

In this lesson plan, a speaking and writing activity of making a cartoon that best represents the topic as a post-expanding activity is used as the post-reading activity.

Activity: Making a cartoon

- Get the students to work in groups of three and create a cartoon with 5-6 panels, using *Make Beliefs Comix* (http://www.makebeliefscomix.com).
  * Get the students to work individually to encourage them to think independently, if there is enough time left, and create a cartoon with 2-3 panels. (Give this activity to the students as homework if there is not enough time.)
- First, get them to think back on the topic and what images should be included.
- Second, have the students choose the characters and the scenes and then write a short text and add callouts.
- Share the cartoons and get the students to vote for the best one.

Figure 8.9 A sample cartoon on the topic using *Make Beliefs Comix*

8.4 Writing

The development of computer programs, word processors, and social media has highly influenced teaching and learning L2 writing. In particular, word processors, spelling and grammar checkers, online dictionaries, corpus-based tools, e-mail, discussion boards, and websites allow students to compose, revise, correct, store, and share texts (Pennington, 2004; Williams, 2005a). Writing on the computer has had a positive effect on student writing quality (Goldberg, Russell, & Cook, 2003; C. H. Lee, 2006). The various computer programs and social media need to be effectively integrated into teaching L2 writing. This section will present teaching methods and techniques with a sample MALL lesson plan for L2 writing using the process-oriented approach.

1. Computer-Assisted Writing with Learning Tools

The computers have enabled the implementation of the process-oriented approach in L2 writing classes more effectively and efficiently than pen and paper-based writing. In particular, word processors significantly impact how L2 writers compose and revise the drafts (See Figure 8.10). Most students can now use word processors without difficulties, such as typing or operating the system, so they can save time for composing and revising instead of using pen and paper.
Time and feedback are considered crucial factors in the process-oriented writing approach (Raimes, 1983). The students need to have time for getting ideas, drafting, and revising. Feedback plays a vital role in the process-oriented writing approach since the students can figure out the discrepancy between what the writers intend to express and what the readers understand while receiving feedback. A variety of computer programs and CMC technology provide the

students with sufficient time and opportunities to give and receive feedback. They share their drafts with peers and the teacher through CMC technology, such as BBS and e-mail, and give feedback using BBS, e-mail, or SNSs.

The process-oriented approach to teaching writing emphasizes the process that writers go through. The process includes planning, drafting, revising, and editing (Harmer, 2004; Williams, 2005a). In more recent years, reviewing is added in the process-oriented approach in blended learning (So & Lee, 2013), aiming to reinforce learning and writing experiences. Each stage can be intensified using computer programs and different types of learning tools available on the Web. For example, a pre-writing activity can be conducted using *Tagxedo* or *OKMindmap* to brainstorm ideas for the topic. BBS can be used as a platform for sharing the drafts and interacting with each other (See Figure 8.10). The following sample lesson plan shows how computer programs and learning tools are integrated into an L2 writing class based on the process-oriented writing approach.

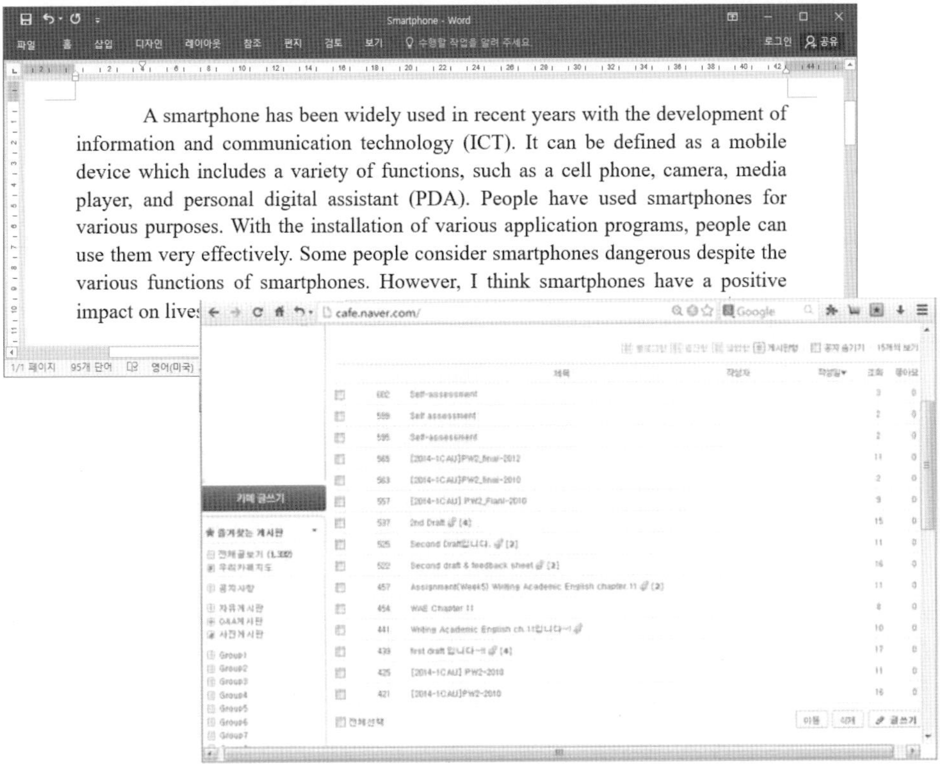

Figure 8.10 Word processor and BBS

2. A Sample Lesson Plan for Computer-Assisted Writing

The sample lesson plan is intended for language teachers who adopt the process-oriented approach in their L2 writing classes. It covers three writing stages, the pre-writing stage, the while-writing stage, and the post-writing stage. It also provides the specification of the computer programs and learning tools. The students work with computers to compose with word processors and share their drafts through BBS in class. The lesson plan can be used in the blended learning environment, applying the instructional model for L2 writing in blended learning (So & Lee, 2013). Detailed techniques and procedures are presented in the next section.

Title Do you agree or disagree with this idea?

Theme Writing an argumentative essay

Aims To write an argumentative essay and to provide quality peer feedback for revision

Level Intermediate to advanced

Time 150 minutes

Preparation *Hardware*

- One computer per student with an Internet connection or PLDs
- A beam projector and a whiteboard

Software

- *Tagxedo* (http://www.tagxedo.com/)
- *Okmindmap* (http://www.okmindmap.com)
- *Grammarly* ((http://www.grammarly.com)
- Bulletin Board System (BBS)

Procedures *Pre-computer work*: Introducing an argumentative essay (20 minutes)

- Introduce and explain an argumentative essay and its organization. Use the resources on *Purdue's Online Writing Lab* (https://owl.english.purdue.edu/owl/resource/685/05/)

<u>Procedures</u>

- Divide the students into groups of three for the writing activities.

Activity: What is an argumentative essay? (10 minutes)

- Have the students visit *Tagxedo*.
- Have the students create a word cloud of an argumentative essay.
- Have the students share the word clouds with group members.

Computer work: Pre-writing stage and while-writing stage (110 minutes)

Pre-writing stage: Mind mapping using *OKMindmap* (15 minutes)

- Introduce a topic (Do smartphones make us feel lonelier?).
- Introduce mind mapping to the students.
- Have the students visit *OKMindmap* website.
- Have the students create a mind map.
- Have the students share the mind maps with group members.
- Ask the students to present the mind map to whole class

While-writing stage: Drafting, revising, and producing the final draft (95 minutes)

<u>Producing the first draft</u> (30 minutes)

- Have the students compose the first draft.
- Monitor the students and help the students, if necessary.
- Have the students upload the first draft to the group BBS.

<u>Conducting peer response</u> (30 minutes)

- Have the students read group members' first drafts.
- Have the students give peer feedback face-to-face using the memo function in word processors for recording.

<u>Revising the first draft and producing the second draft</u> (15 minutes)

- Have the students reflect on peer feedback using the feedback-revision table.
- Have the students revise the first draft and produce the

Procedures

second draft using a word processor.

Grammar checking and producing the final draft (20 minutes)

- Have the students check the grammar and mechanics of the second draft using *Grammarly*.
- Have the students visit *Grammarly* website.
- Have the students revise the second draft and produce the final draft.
- Monitor students and give feedback.

Post-computer work: Post-writing stage (20 minutes)

Reviewing

- Have the students evaluate their final drafts.
- Have the students write down the improvements, problems, the short-term and long-term goals in BBS.
- Have the students share the evaluation and goals with group members and give each other final comments.
- Have the students present the evaluation and goals to the whole class.
- Consolidate the class with the final comments.

3. Teaching Methods and Techniques for Writing

Students produce three to four drafts based on feedback from peers and the teacher in the process-oriented approach. The class consists of three stages of pre-computer work, computer work, and post-computer work. In the pre-computer work, the main features and organization of the argumentative essay are introduced and explained. The computer work is composed of drafting, revising, and producing the final draft. In the post-computer work, the students review their final drafts as well as the writing process.

Pre-computer work: Introducing an argumentative essay

In this stage, the features and organization of the argumentative essay are explained. Resources on the Web can be utilized, e.g., *Purdue's Online Writing Lab* (https://owl.english.purdue.edu/owl/resource/685/05). The following activity is conducted to raise students' awareness of the features of the argumentative essay. The students can review the argumentative essay and its organization by making a word cloud using *Tagxedo*.

Activity: What is an argumentative essay?

- Introduce and explain the features and organization of the argumentative essay. Information on the Web can be provided for the students.
- Have the students visit the *Tagxedo* website (http://www.tagxedo.com).
- Have the students create a word cloud of the argumentative essay.
- Have the students save the word cloud as an image file and upload it to BBS.
- Have the students share their word clouds and talk about the features of the argumentative essay in groups.

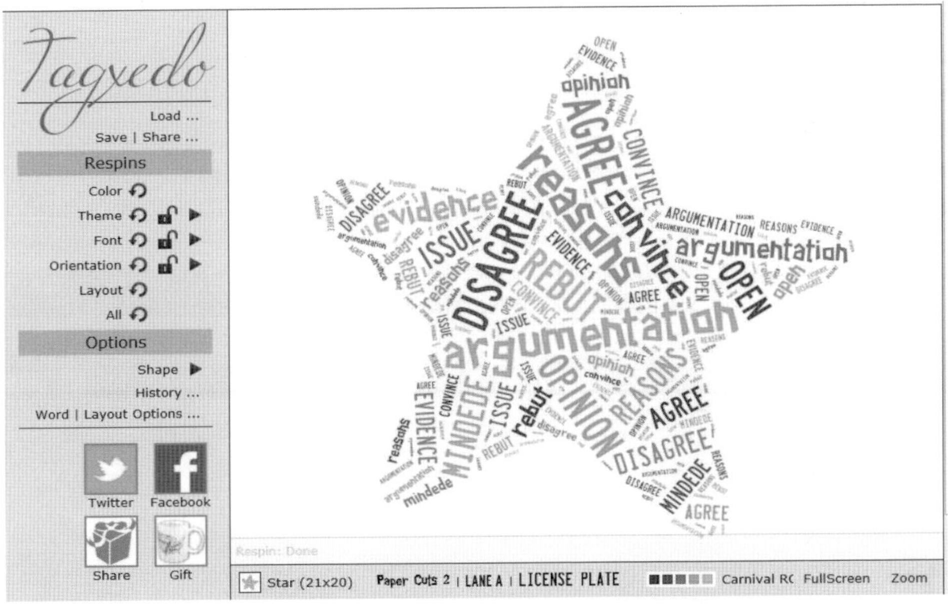

Figure 8.11 A sample word cloud using *Tagxedo*

Computer work: Pre-writing stage and while-writing stage

The students conduct a variety of tasks in the two stages: pre-writing stage and while-writing stage. They conduct a pre-writing activity for gathering ideas and organizing the essay. Then, they produce the first draft, conduct a peer response activity, revise the first draft, produce the second draft, check grammar of the second draft, and produce the final draft. The teacher monitors students' tasks and gives feedback when necessary.

Pre-writing stage: Mind mapping using OKMindmap

Mind mapping is an attractive pre-writing activity since it does not require students to develop and organize ideas fully. It also allows students to make a clear relationship between subtopics (Williams, 2005a). *OKMindmap* is a web-based mind mapping service that does not require any installation of plug-ins for web browsers. The students and teachers can use this service conveniently and efficiently. The procedures of the pre-writing activity using *OKMindmap* are as follows.

- Introduce mind maps to the students, including the main functions and features.
- Have the students visit *OKMindmap* website.
- Have the students create a mind map on the topic.
- Have the students save the mind map as an image and upload it to BBS.
- Have the students share and compare their maps.
- Ask the students to present their mind maps to the whole class.
- Have the students make an additional outline if they find it necessary.

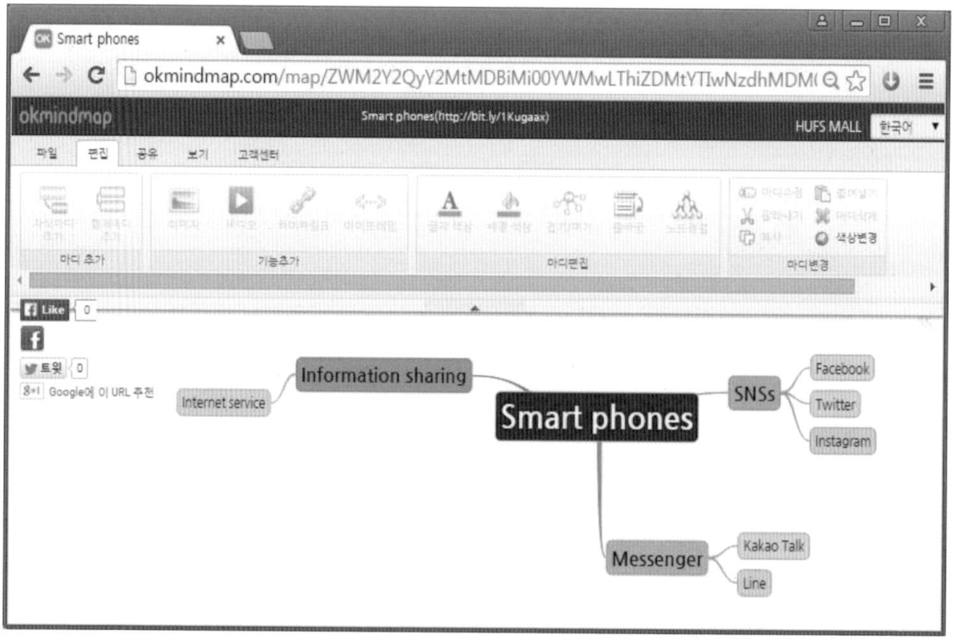

Figure 8.12 A sample mind map using *Okmindmap*

While-writing stage: Drafting, revising, and producing the final draft

Producing the first draft

- Have the students write the first draft based on the mind map and outline using word processors.

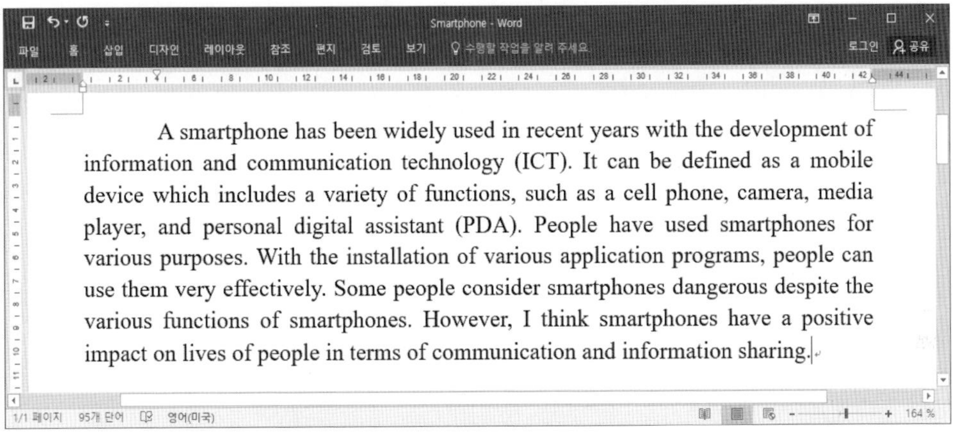

- After producing the first draft, have the students upload their first draft to group BBS.

Conducting peer response

- Have the students download group members' first drafts and read them for a peer response activity.
- Have the students conduct the peer response activity face-to-face. The students are recommended to use the memo function provided in word processors to write down peer comments.

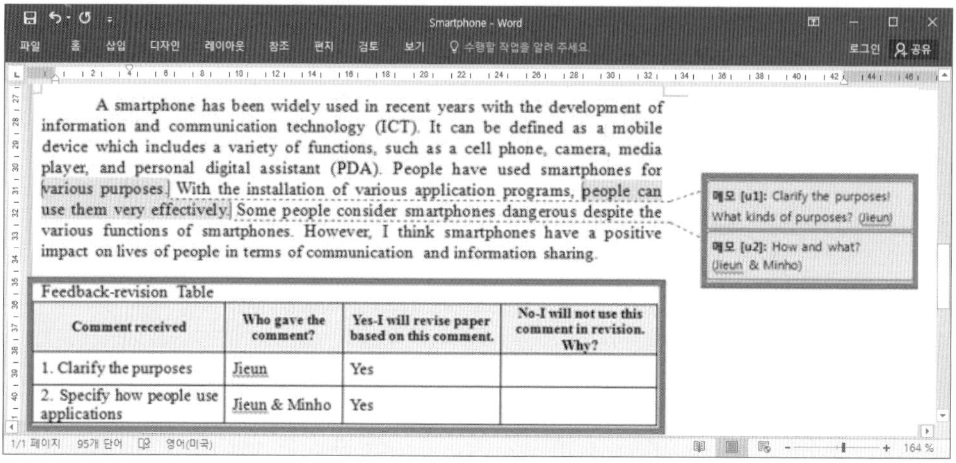

A smartphone has been widely used in recent years with the development of information and communication technology (ICT). It can be defined as a mobile device which includes a variety of functions, such as a cell phone, camera, media player, and personal digital assistant (PDA). People have used smartphones for various purposes. With the installation of various application programs, people can use them very effectively. Some people consider smartphones dangerous despite the various functions of smartphones. However, I think smartphones have a positive impact on lives of people in terms of communication and information sharing.

Feedback-revision Table

Comment received	Who gave the comment?	Yes-I will revise paper based on this comment.	No-I will not use this comment in revision. Why?
1. Clarify the purposes	Jieun	Yes	
2. Specify how people use applications	Jieun & Minho	Yes	

Revising the first draft and producing the second draft

- Have the students draw a feedback-revision table to reflect on the feedback that they received.
- Have the students revise the first draft and produce the second draft based on the feedback-revision table using word processors.

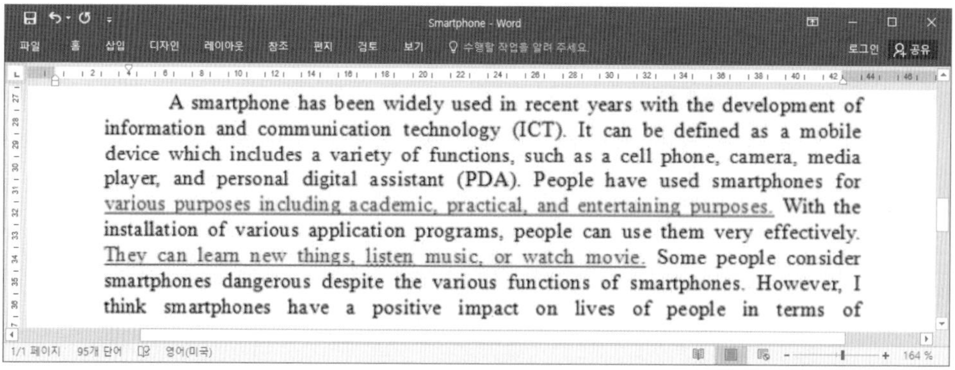

A smartphone has been widely used in recent years with the development of information and communication technology (ICT). It can be defined as a mobile device which includes a variety of functions, such as a cell phone, camera, media player, and personal digital assistant (PDA). People have used smartphones for various purposes including academic, practical, and entertaining purposes. With the installation of various application programs, people can use them very effectively. They can learn new things, listen music, or watch movie. Some people consider smartphones dangerous despite the various functions of smartphones. However, I think smartphones have a positive impact on lives of people in terms of

Grammar checking and producing the final draft

- Have the students check the grammar of the second drafts using *Grammarly*.

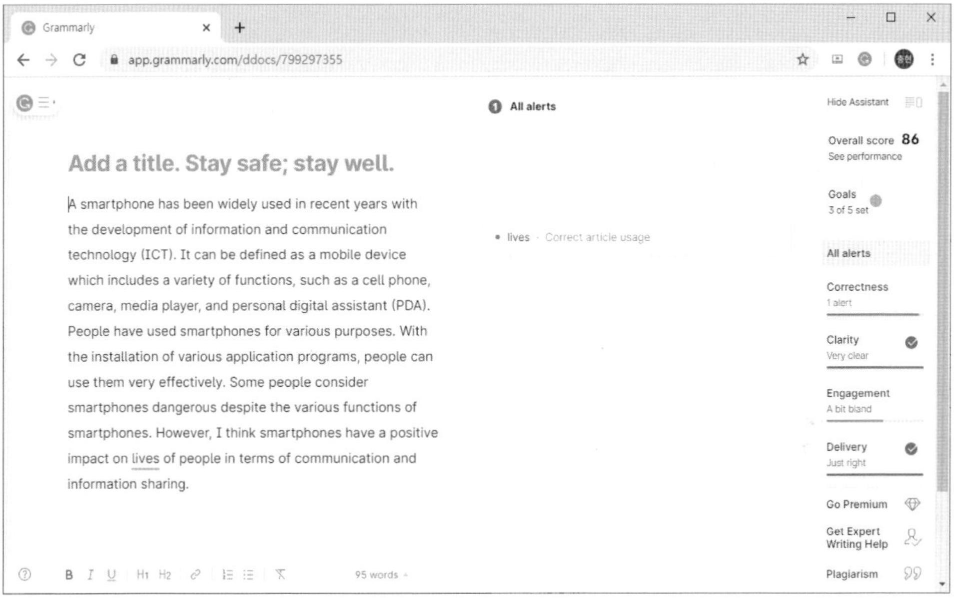

- Have the students revise the second draft and produce the final draft based on Grammarly's feedback..
- Have the students upload their final draft to group BBS.
- Have the students give each other final comments on the final draft.

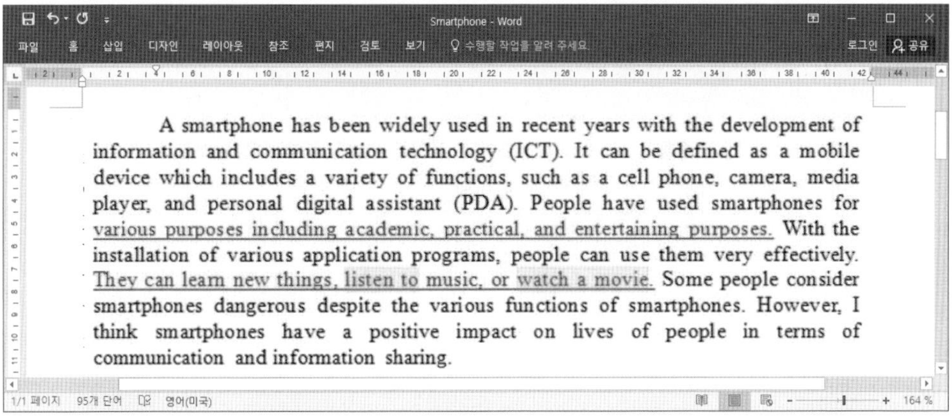

Post-computer work: Post-writing stage

In the post-writing stage, the students review and evaluate the writing process as well as the final drafts. They set short-term and long-term goals for further writing.

- Have the students evaluate their final drafts and write down improvements, problems, and short-term and long-term goals for self-assessment in BBS.

- Have the students share the self-assessment results with group members and set group goals for further writing.
- Ask the students to present individual and group self-assessment results to the whole class.
- Consolidate the class with the final comments.

Tasks for Study and Discussion

- Create a teaching plan for your target students for the language skill of your choice. Make sure to use various websites and apps to meet the goals and objectives of your lesson based on the sample lesson plans.

  - Remember to provide theoretical background and materials, lesson plan, and teaching methods and techniques. Work individually, and then share your work with partner.

Chapter 9

Focus on Subskills Development: Pronunciation, Vocabulary, and Grammar

9.1 Pronunciation

The rise of CLT has shifted the goals of teaching and learning pronunciation (Tarone, 2005). As meaning and communicative fluency have been emphasized in CLT, English teachers have paid more attention to clear, comprehensive, and intelligible pronunciation (Brown, 2007b; Celce-Murcia, Brinton, & Goodwin, 1996). For teaching and learning pronunciation, two major approaches, the bottom-up and the top-down approaches have been suggested. The bottom-up approach focuses on mastering individual sounds from phonemes to allophones, while the top-down approach addresses the sound system as a natural stream of speech, focusing on stress, rhythm, and intonation. The current approach to teaching pronunciation takes on both approaches, acknowledging that both segmental (consonants and vowels) and suprasegmental (stress, rhythm, and intonation) features need to be taught in balance.

Multimedia can provide students with an interactive environment where the students can utilize various resources, such as images, videos, quizzes, and they can share and give feedback through BBS or voice e-learning tools. This section will present teaching methods and techniques with a sample MALL lesson plan for teaching pronunciation using voice recordings and resources on the Web.

1. Voice Recordings for Teaching Pronunciation

Voice recordings have been used for teaching and learning pronunciation with the development of digital technology and PLDs (Baek & Lee, 2018; Neri, Cucchiarini, Strik, & Boves, 2002; Walker, 2005; Yoon & Lee, 2009). Yoon and Lee (2009) presented the three significant benefits of using voice recordings. First, it provides learners with opportunities for individual and repeated practice in a non-threatening environment. Second, the students can have a chance for output that peers and the teacher can assess. Last, the students can raise their awareness for pronunciation through giving and receiving corrective feedback.

Smartphones and tablets provide a built-in recording function. It enables students to directly record their voices and upload their recordings in SNS or BBS. Then they listen to peers' recordings and give feedback (Baek & Lee, 2018). Besides, various resources on the Web provide the students with meaningful materials such as images, video clips, exercises, and quizzes. The following sample lesson plan shows how learning tools and resources on the Web are utilized in an English pronunciation class.

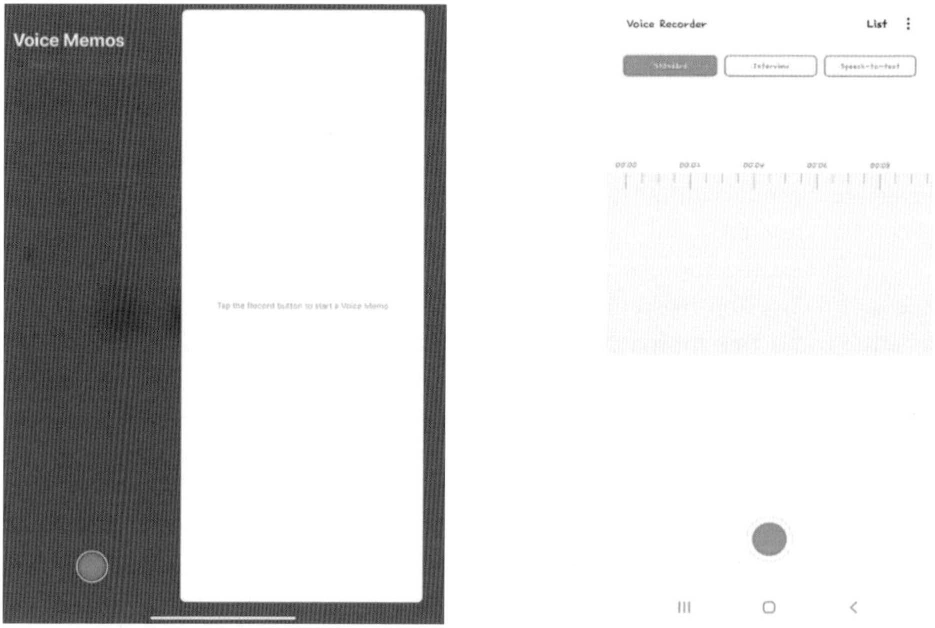

Figure 9.1 Voice recorders in mobile devices

2. A Sample Lesson Plan for Teaching Pronunciation

This sample lesson plan is for language teachers who use voice recordings and web resources for teaching pronunciation. It addresses two consonants, L and R, with resources on the Web and voice recording. The content of the lesson plan is based on Units 8 (Consonant L) and 9 (Consonant R) from *Principles & Practices in English Pronunciation* (Yoon & Lee, 2011a). This sample lesson plan can be integrated into a speaking lesson, particularly the post-computer work stage. Detailed techniques and procedures are presented in the next section.

Title Little Red Riding Hood

Theme Consonants L and R

Aims To pronounce consonants L and R intelligibly

Level Beginner to Intermediate

Time 20 minutes

Preparation *Hardware*

- One computer per student with an Internet connection or PLDs
- A beam projector and a whiteboard
- One headset and microphone per student

Software

- YouTube, *American English Pronunciation Practice* (http://www.manythings.org/pp)
- *Sounds of English* (https://www.soundsofenglish.org)
- Voice recording apps in smartphone or tablet
- *MS Teams* or *Flipgrid*

Procedures *Post-Computer work:* Pronunciation (20 minutes)

- Explain how the sounds of consonants L and R are made and show the students the images of the two positions of vocal organs.
- Show the students the video clips of the articulation of two words. Use the resources on *Sounds of English.*
- Have the students practice minimal pairs of L and R consonants.
- Use the resources on *American English Pronunciation Practice.*
- Have the students record *Little Red Riding Hood* by using their PLDs and upload files on BBS
- Have the students give peer feedback to partners.
- Ask the students to read *Little Red Riding Hood* to the whole class.
- Give the students feedback.
- Give the students homework (Tongue Twisters) for practicing consonants L and R.

3. Teaching Methods and Techniques for Pronunciation

Teachers can teach students two consonants, L and R, using resources on the Web and voice recording programs in the post-computer work of teaching. The teachers can divide the resources into the three stages of class activities, presentation, activity I (minimal pair), and activity II (voice recording). First, students watch the videos and listen to /l/ and /r/ sounds on *Sounds of English*, and second, practice minimal pairs of /l/ and /r/ sounds and answer quizzes on *American English Pronunciation Practice*. Last, the students record their pronunciation using recording programs and receive feedback from one another using *MS Teams* or *Flipgrid*.

Presentation (Explanation)

- Explain how sounds of the two consonants are made with the place and manner of articulation.
- Show the students the images and video clips of sounds of two consonants. Use the resources on *Sounds of English* (https://www.soundsofenglish.org).

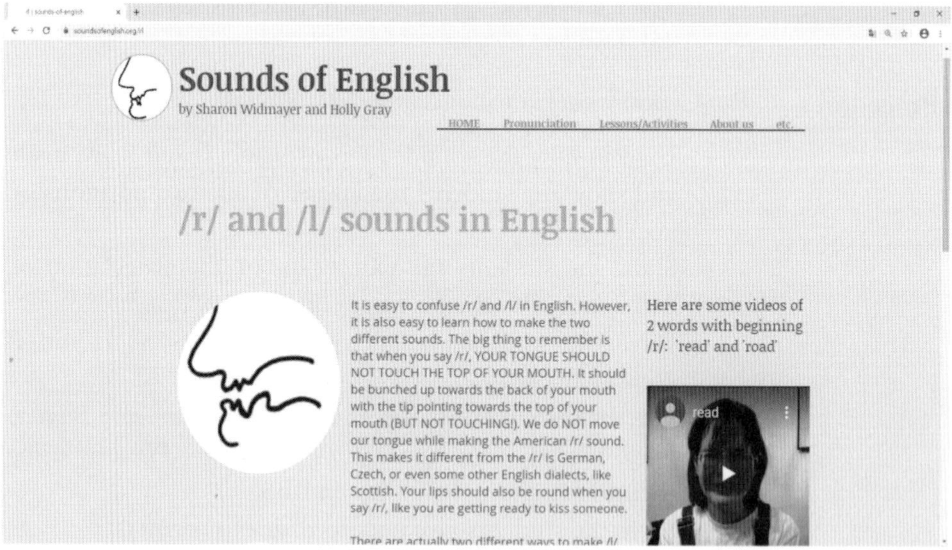

Figure 9.2 Explanation of consonants L and R from S*ounds of English*

Activity I (Minimal pair)

- Have the students practice minimal pairs of /l/ and /r/ sounds and conduct quizzes on *American English Pronunciation Practice* (http://www.manythings.org/mp/m11.html).

- Have the students share the results of quizzes with partners.

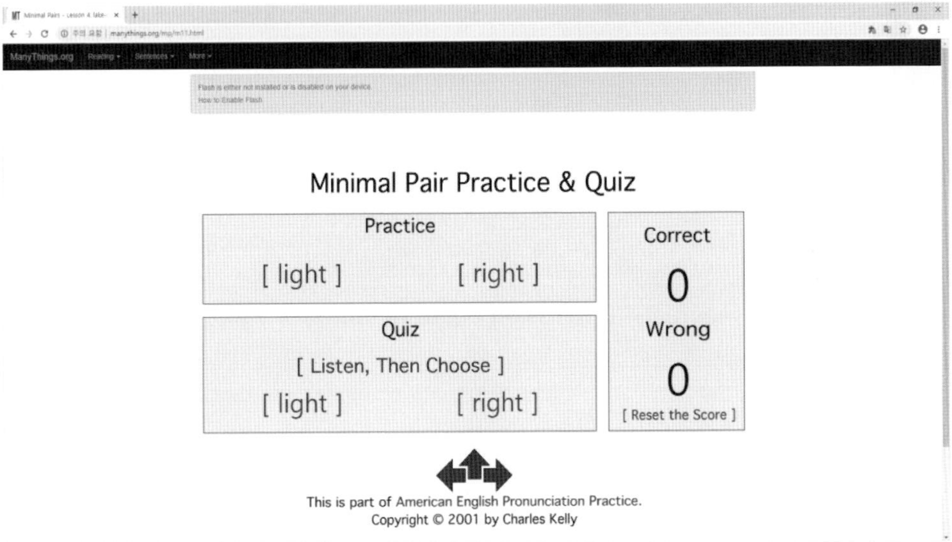

Figure 9.3 Minimal pair practice and quiz (http:/www.manythings.org)

Activity II (Voice recording)

- Have the students focus on /l/ and /r/ sounds in the passage "*Little Red Riding Hood*" (Yoon & Lee, 2011a, p. 62).
- Have the students read aloud the passage for practice, using recording programs (e.g., *Sound Recorder* or *Goldwave*) or smartphones and headsets with microphones.
- Have the students record the passage through voice recorders in their PLDs and upload files on *Microsoft Teams* or SNS or BBS.
- Have the students listen to partners' recordings and give feedback to the partners.

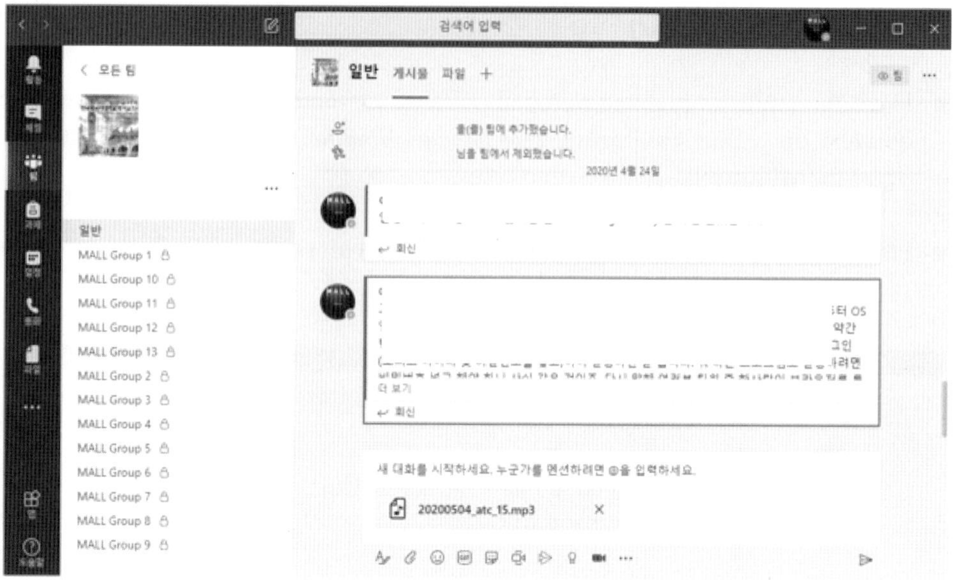

Figure 9.4 Discussion board of *Microsoft Teams*

Consolidation

- Ask the students to read the passage aloud to the whole class.
- Give feedback to the student.
- Give homework: Practicing Tongue Twisters and recording them using voice recorders in PLDs for additional practice of /l/ and /r/ sounds. Try to say the following tongue twisters as fast as possible, but correctly.

Tongue Twisters (Yoon & Lee, 2011a, p. 62)

1. Roberta ran rings around the Roman ruins.
2. Literary literature literally lasts a really long time.
3. It's the right light with the glimmer in the mirror.
4. Laura and Larry rarely lull their rural roosters to sleep.

9.2 Vocabulary

Vocabulary plays an important role in language learning. Wilkins (1972) highlighted the importance of vocabulary for communication, asserting that "without grammar very little can be conveyed, without vocabulary nothing can be conveyed" (p. 111). Researchers believe that learning vocabulary from context helps learners retain vocabulary because the context requires learners' ability to infer or guess the meaning of vocabulary (McCarthy, 1990; Nation, 2013; Oxford & Scarcella, 1994). Learning from context includes learning from the conversation, extensive reading, listening to stories or films (Nation, 2013). It is suggested that authentic materials need to be integrated into a curriculum for learners' vocabulary development (Rott, 1999).

This section introduces a sample vocabulary activity (lesson) as a part of a reading lesson. The vocabulary activity (lesson) includes diverse materials and learning tools such as E-text, *English Online* (http://www.english-online.at), *COCA* (http:// corpus.byu.edu/coca), *Hot Potatoes* (https://hotpot.uvic.ca), and *OKMmindmap* (www.okmindmap.com),

1. E-Text for Teaching Vocabulary

E-text used for the lesson plan is an article from *English Online* (https://www.english-online.at/). English Online provides hundreds of articles in a variety of topics, such as art and architecture, biology, culture and traditions, etc., as seen in Figure 9.5. The articles are modified for learners of English. At the end of the articles, a vocabulary list is presented.

Figure 9.5 The main screen of *English Online*

2. A Sample Lesson Plan for Teaching Vocabulary Using *Tagxedo* and Jcross

This sample activity can be used as a pre-reading activity to check the vocabulary presented in a reading passage.

Title Vaccines – Antibodies that protect us from diseases

Theme The vocabulary related to vaccines

Aims To familiarize the vocabulary to promote reading comprehension and to know the meaning of vocabulary

Level Intermediate and above

Time 10 minutes

Preparation *Hardware*

- One computer per student (or group of three students) with an Internet connection or PLDs
- A beam projector and a whiteboard

Software

- E-text 'Vaccines – Antibodies that protect us from diseases' from *English Online* (http://www.english-online.at)
- *OKMindmap* (http://www.okmindmap.com)
- *COCA* (https://corpus.byu.edu/coca)
- JCross in *Hot Potatoes* (https://hotpot.uvic.ca)

Procedures *Computer work:* Pre-reading (10 minutes)

- Introduce the article from *English Online* to the students. (http://www.english-online.at/health_medicine/health_medicine-index.htm)
- Have the students skim and scan the passage.
- Have the students look for the main idea and keywords.
- Have the students create an outline of the passage based on the main idea and keywords using *OKMindmap*.
- Have the students share their mind maps with partners.

- Have the students get concordance lines of unknown words from *COCA* (https://corpus.byu.edu/coca)
- Have students do a crossword puzzle of the vocabulary in the reading passage.

3. Teaching Methods and Techniques for Vocabulary

The students carry out the following vocabulary activities as a part of the pre-reading stage. The activities include creating an outline using a mind map and doing a crossword puzzle of the vocabulary presented in the reading passage.

Creating an outline of the passage using a mind map

- Introduce the website of *English Online* to the students.
- Have the students skim and scan the reading passage (Vaccines – Antibodies that protect us from diseases) on the computer.
- Have the students look for the main idea and keywords of the passage.
- Introduce the website of *OKMindmap* to the students.
- Have the students create an outline of the passage using *OKMindmap* based on the main idea and keywords.
- Ask the students to share the mind maps with partners.

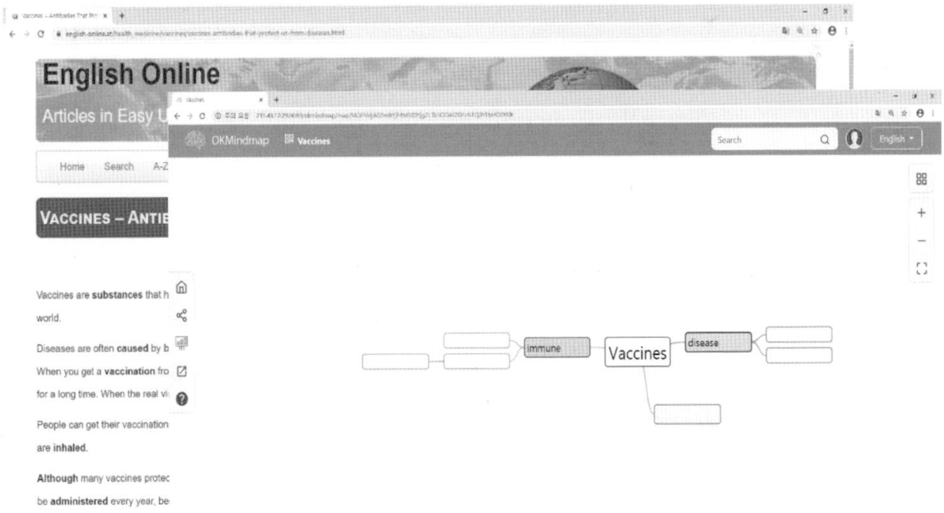

Figure 9.6 E-text and mind map

Getting concordance lines from corpus

- Have the students visit the webpage of *COCA* (https://corpus.byu.edu/coca).
- Have the students get concordance lines of unknown words in the reading passage.
- Have the students observe and write down examples of a word and regularities in use from the concordance lines.
- Have the students share the notes with partners.

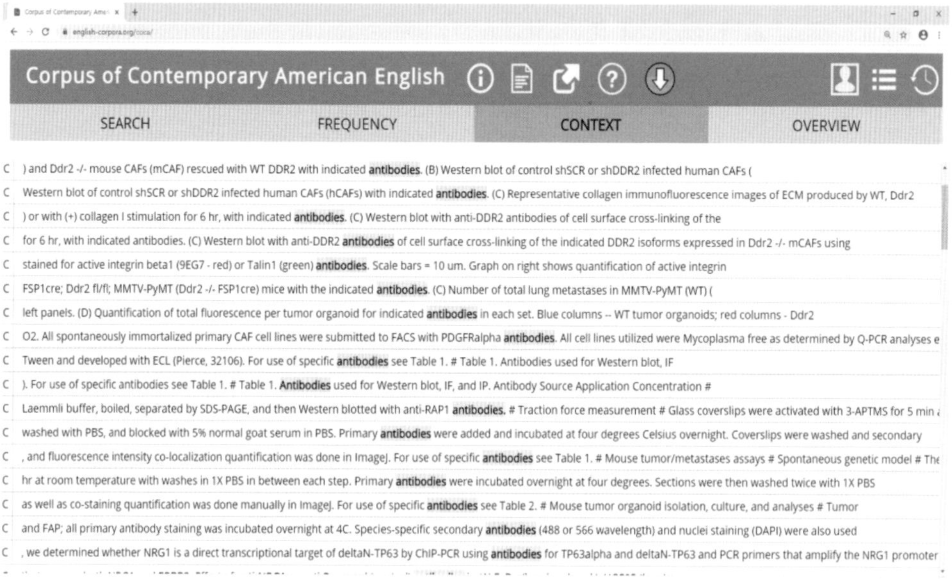

Figure 9.7 Concordance lines from *COCA*

Doing a crossword puzzle

- Provide the students with a crossword puzzle of the vocabulary in the reading passage.
- Have the students individually do the crossword puzzle.
- When finished, ask the students to compare the answer.
- Ask the students to present the answer to the whole class.

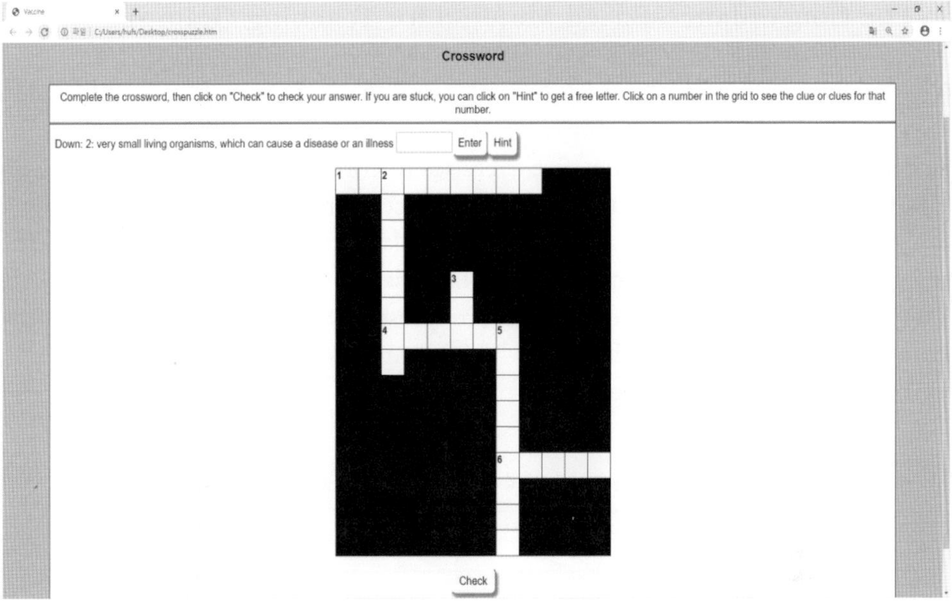

Figure 9.8 JCross puzzle of vaccines

9.3 Grammar

The development of communication skills has recently been central to the teaching and learning of languages, but students also have to learn grammar, especially in an EFL situation (Ellis, 2006; Nassaji & Fotos, 2010; Rutherford, 1987; Thornbury, 1999). Students need to learn grammar in terms of the importance of not only fluency but also accuracy. Grammar instruction helps students pay attention to language form and enhance their awareness of specific grammar rules (Schmidt, 1990). In more recent years, form-focused instruction within the communicative framework has been widespread for teaching and learning grammar (Brown, 2007b; Ellis, 2006; Williams, 2005b). Form-focused instruction ranges from explicit metalinguistic explanations of rules to noticing and consciousness-raising (Ellis, 2006; Schmidt, 1990; Williams, 2005b).

This section will introduce the activity based on data-driven learning. Students learn grammar rules inductively through examples of concordance lines provided by *Lextutor* (http://www.lextutor.ca).

1. The Concordance-Based Material for Teaching Grammar

The concordance-based material is made using the online concordance program '*Lextutor*.' *Lextutor* offers making and editing tools for teaching and learning materials. This material includes five exercises to correct the wrong sentences with concordance lines. The example sentences of concordance lines are from Brown corpus. *Lextutor* provides two types of materials, a computer-based concordance material, and a paper-based concordance material, as seen in Figures 9.9 and 9.10. The examples of concordance lines are presented by clicking 'Click' in the computer-based material. The paper-based material can be provided with both exercises and concordance lines.

Correct the sentences below.
The sentences below contain an error. 'Click' to see how native speakers use prepositions in the sentences.

Error Sentence	**Correct Sentence**	**Data**
I'll visit you in Monday.		Click
Korea hosts the 17th World Cup with Japan, at 2002.		Click
Exercise can help you sleep better in night.		Click
The train leaves Seoul on six o'clock.		Click
The fun festival was held in March 8.		Click
The weather is hot on August.		Click

The sentences below contain errors. Correct the sentences based on the data.

Error Sentence	Correct Sentence
I'll visit you in Monday.	

Hits: 012

[001] ms the Vietnamese withdrawal was not genuine, and on **MONDAY** a Foreign Ministry spokesman, Prachyadavi Tavedikul,
[002] or consideration at a meeting of finance ministers on **MONDAY**. �oreign News Page 9 891006 Soviet threat "eased
[003] The coup leader, Major Moises Giraldi, was buried on **MONDAY** beside three other rebel graves. Only close family
[004] , Marie-Elisabeth Cons- Boutboul, who was charged on **MONDAY** with being an accessory to the murder of her son-in
[005] was broadcast on the city tannoy system in Leipzig on **MONDAY** afternoon. It is thought to have helped calm tension
[006] thodox organ of the Free German Youth (FDJ), which on **MONDAY** attacked "pervasive bossiness" by the President of t
[007] leaders, for instance, issued "Four Urgent Pleas" on **MONDAY** night - the first being an appeal to East Germans "f
[008] r AS 70,000 East Germans streamed through Leipzig on **MONDAY** night in the largest demonstration the German Democ
[009] ainstream Conservative Party, takes over formally on **MONDAY**. �oreign News Page 10 891012 Old guard rebels By
[010] loch for helping to quell crowd problems at Hanley on **MONDAY** night. Bulloch was knocked out after 53 seconds of
[011] condition in hospital after collapsing at his home on **MONDAY**. Graziano, 68, won the world title in 1947 with a si
[012] a fourth-quarter rally by the Philadelphia Eagles on **MONDAY** night to win 27-13. The Bears, with four wins this

Hits: 012

[001] most breaking as he warned over Western television on **WEDNESDAY** night that East Germany's ferment could end like
[002] us would-be refugees. Film of the riots in Dresden on **WEDNESDAY** have reached the West, with evidence that they we
[003] da government. In two sessions, one with Mr Mobutu on **WEDNESDAY**, and another with Mr Savimbi on Thursday, Mr Bus
[004] churchmen - including Archbishop Desmond Tutu - next **WEDNESDAY**, the first sign that he will live up to election

Figure 9.9 Computer and paper-based concordance materials

2. A Sample Lesson Plan for Teaching Grammar Using Concordance-Based Material

This sample activity is intended for one of the activities in communicative writing with time-related prepositions. This activity aims to promote data-driven learning of grammar rules.

Title When is your birthday?

Theme The preposition related to time

Aims To use correct preposition related to time from given data

Level Intermediate and above

Time 10 minutes

Preparation *Hardware*

- One computer per student (or group of three students) with an Internet connection or PLDs
- A beam projector and a whiteboard

Software

- *Lextutor* (http://www.lextutor.ca)
- *Guide to Grammar and Writing* (http://www.ccc.commnet.edu/GRAMMAR)

Procedures *Computer work:* Pre-writing stage (10 minutes)

- Introduce *Lextutor* to the students and have them visit the website of *Lextutor.*
- Explain the general principles of concordance programs and their use.
- Explain how the data are interpreted in the concordance line.
- Provide the computer-based concordance material for the students.
- Have the students do the exercise in the computer-based concordance material.
- Have the students compare the results with the partners.

Procedures
- Ask the students to present the results to the whole class.
- Provide the answer and feedback for the students.
- Present the students with a quiz on *Guide to Grammar and Writing.*
- Have the students take the quiz and check the answer.
- Have the students report the results to the teacher through LMS.
- Provide feedback on the quiz for the students.

3. Teaching Methods and Techniques for Grammar

In this lesson, students will understand prepositions related to time through exercises to correct sentences as a part of the pre-writing stage. First of all, upload exercises file on LMS or send the file by e-mail to open the file on their computer. If it is not available to use computers, prepare a paper version of the material.

Doing exercises in a computer-based concordance material

- Explain how to read concordance data in detail (e.g., click with 'Ctrl' key, etc.)
- Have students find the incorrect part in the sentence.

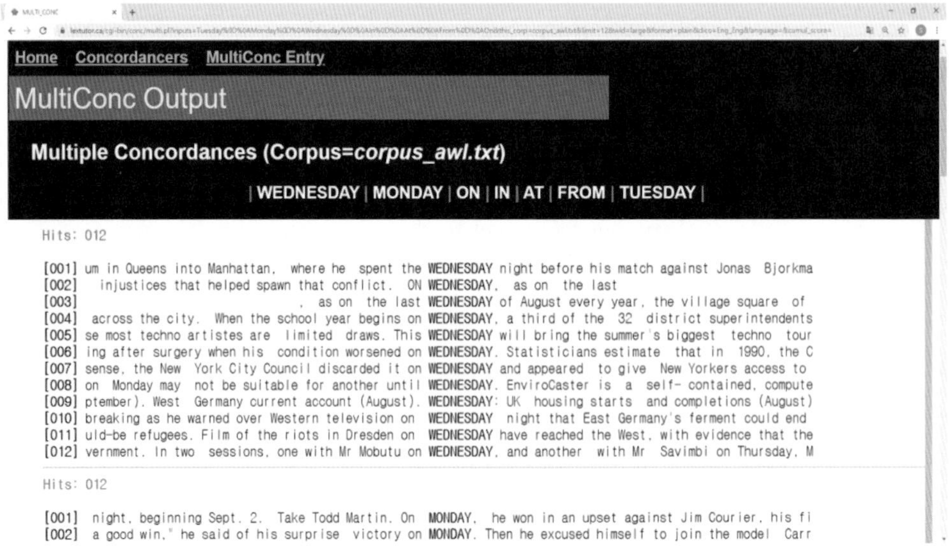

Figure 9.10 Concordance lines from *Lextutor*

- Ask students to examine the concordance lines to see how the native speakers use prepositions.
- Have the students write the correct sentence based on the data.
- Have the students share and compare the results with the partners.
- Ask the students to present the results to the whole class.
- Provide the answer and feedback for the students.

Taking a quiz on the Web

- Introduce the webpage of *Guide to Grammar and Writing* (http://www.ccc.commnet.edu/GRAMMAR)
- Present the students a quiz with *Guide to Grammar and Writing.*
- Have the students take the quiz and check the answer.
- Have the students compare the results of the quiz.
- Have the students report the results to the teacher through LMS.
- Provide feedback on the quiz for the students.

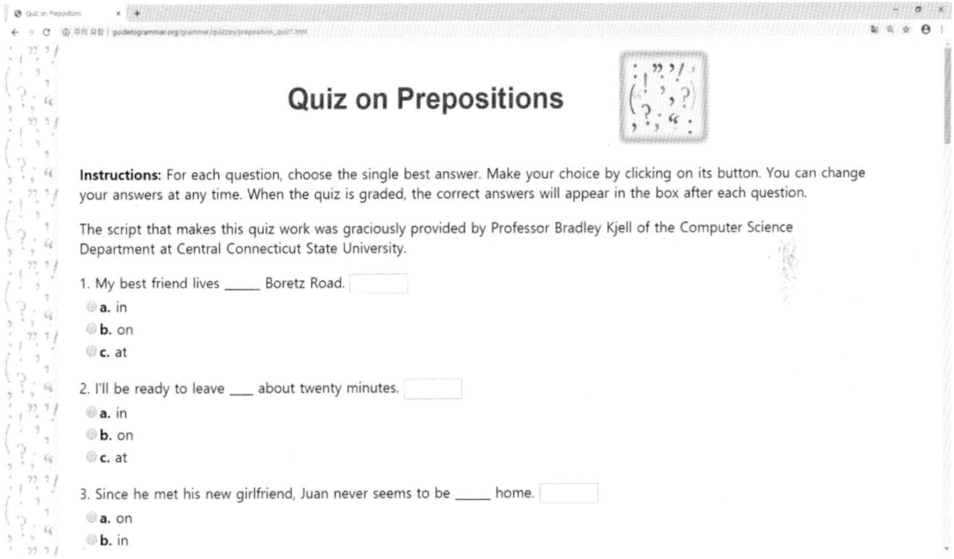

Figure 9.11 A quiz sample of *Guide to Grammar and Writing*

Tasks for Study and Discussion

■ Create a teaching plan for your target students for the language subskill of your choice. Make sure to use various websites and apps to meet the goals and objectives of your lesson based on the sample lesson plans.

- Remember to provide theoretical background and materials, lesson plan, and teaching methods and techniques. Work individually, and then share your work with your partners.

Chapter 10

Focus on Integrated Language Skills Development

Teaching and learning integrated language skills promote more than multiple language skills, such as listening, speaking, reading, writing, pronunciation, vocabulary, and grammar. More recently, it necessitates teaching the combination of the skills in a contextualized manner. For instance, teaching reading can be naturally related to writing and vocabulary, while speaking can be easily combined with pronunciation, listening, and pragmatics (Hinkel, 2006). Integrated instruction to language teaching and learning is based on the assumption that people develop language skills "not in isolation, but tandem" (Hinkel, 2006, p. 113), and language teaching should reflect this process. Focusing on the context and authentic purposes, the integrated approach bears similarity to the communicative approach. Content-based, task-based, and topic-based instructions are typical examples where integrated language skills are required and can be incorporated into the pedagogy. A body of related research in content-based instruction examined the effectiveness of such instruction directly and indirectly and provided empirical support for the view (McCarthy & O'Keeffee, 2004; Murphy, 1991; Snow, Met, & Genesee, 1989), while others take on a skeptical view towards its effectiveness (e.g., Dupuy, 2000). Despite such skepticism and the lack of empirical evidence, teaching multi-skills in context has become one of the most frequent approaches the ESL and EFL textbooks are comprised of. Similar types of content-based and contextualized learning have emerged in MALL as well.

Web-based language learning is one example where learners interact with native speakers through e-mail, audio- and video-conferencing, text-based chatting, etc. (Chung, Graves, Wesche, & Barfurth, 2005; O'Rourke, 2005; Schwienhorst, 2003). ICT and multimedia in integrated skills learning contribute to creating an environment where learners exchange information, discuss content, and develop their language skills. Integrated skills learning, however, poses a lot of practical challenges in accommodating the exchange, and many topics or theme-based courseware that encompasses multi-language skills have become available. Although the courseware may be considered less authentic and meaningful, technological advantages such as voice recognition, immediate feedback, and individualized and self-paced learning system certainly compensate for its innate limitations. This section presents teaching methods and techniques with a sample MALL lesson plan for integrated language skills.

10.1 Multimedia Content for Teaching Integrated Language Skills

This section presents various multimedia programs and content, such as e-text from *USA TODAY* (http://traveltips.usatoday.com/make-reservations-hotel-business-54718.html), *Hot Potatoes*, Socrative, *Tagxedo*, *Flipgrid*, *ZigZag On Earth* (http://www.zigzagonearth.com/10-steps-to-choose-your-ideal-next-travel-destination), etc. It is noteworthy that *Flipgrid* uses voice recording technology that enables interaction with the multimedia devices, teachers, and learners, as learners practice speaking. *USA TODAY* is a website that provides up-to-date news in the USA and provides resourceful archives easily accessible using topic words. The web content provides authentic language input for the learners.

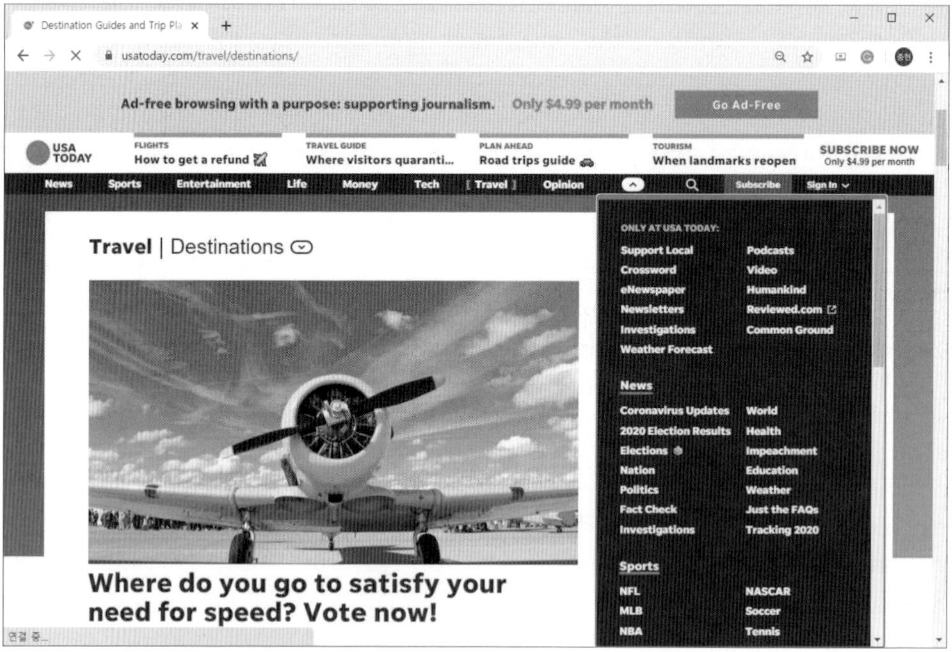

Figure 10.1 The main screen of *USA TODAY*

First, pre-computer work focuses on introducing the topic of travel, clarifying skill-specific objectives. For the primary skills of the lesson, listening, speaking, and reading, *YouTube, Hotpotatoes* (JQuiz), *Socrative*, *ZigZag On Earth*, and *USA*

Today were used. Listening aims to enhance the students' ability to understand typical dialogue and expressions used in traveling contexts, specifically in making a reservation. Speaking also deals with a similar context where typical sentences are presented for controlled speaking practice. Reading involves an e-text on making a reservation and following comprehension activity created by *Hot Potatoes*. The lesson is wrapped up by practicing three subskills (pronunciation, vocabulary, and grammar) and extra short writing activity of making an itinerary.

The website called *ZigZag On Earth*, which provides useful tips and information on well-known tourist attractions worldwide, is used. Figure 10.2 presents the website *ZigZag On Earth* for speaking practice.

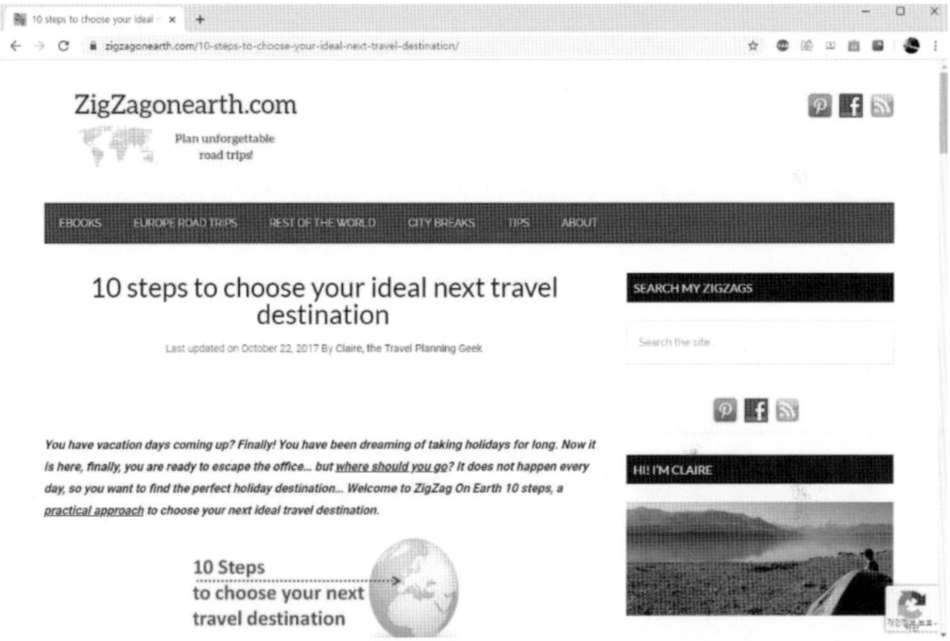

Figure 10.2 The main screen of *ZigZag On Earth*

As for the subskills of the lesson, pronunciation and vocabulary practices were provided to the students using *Flipgrid* and *Socrative*. *Flipgrid* offers an environment where teachers and students can record video recordings or voices on a blank screen, which can be posted, similar to that of a BBS. *Socrative* enables teachers to create "rooms" where premade quizzes can be "launched" to the students and be tracked in real-time. With the above tools, learners can always come back to remind themselves what they have learned and keep track of their learning process and outcomes.

10.2 A Sample Lesson Plan for Teaching Integrated Language Skills

The following lesson plan is designed to cover one of the five segments of the whole topic, organizing and carrying out travel plans. It can be flexibly adjusted to do individual and self-directed learning with the content appropriate to their level, interacting with the computer. It can also be applied to classes designed for learner-learner interaction when the network connection is in place. Before implementing these tools, learners should be aware of the basic concepts of MALL and the organization, content, and manuals of all of the included programs. This will help facilitate effective class management. The lesson to be introduced is on travel, and specifically on making a reservation.

Title Travel plans

Theme Organizing and carrying out travel plans

Aims To reserve a room in a telephone conversation, to use vocabulary and expressions about travel, and to plan an itinerary

Level Intermediate to Advanced

Time 100 minutes

Preparation *Hardware*

- One computer per student with an Internet connection or PLDs
- A beam projector and a whiteboard
- One headset and microphone per student

Software

- *Flipgrid* (https://www.flipgrid.com)
- *Socrative* (https://www.socrative.com)
- *Tagxedo* (http://www.tagxedo.com)
- *Hot Potatoes* (https://hotpot.uvic.ca)
- E-text 'How to make reservations in a hotel for business' from the website *USA TODAY* (https://traveltips.usatoday.com/make-hotel-reservation-14354)
- *ZigZag On Earth*
- *YouTube* (http://www.youtube.com)

Procedures *Pre-computer work:* (10 minutes)

- Introduce the unit and present the main objectives of the lesson.
- Introduce websites and the programs used in the lesson (E-texts, *USA TODAY, ZigZag On Earth*, *Flipgrid, Socrative, Tagxedo*, *Hot Potatoes,* etc.)

Activating schema

- Show the students a video clip (50 places to see before you die).
- Ask them to think about their travel experiences.
- Ask them to share their experiences in groups.
- Ask them to present their experiences to the whole class.

Vocabulary

- Ask the students to come up with the vocabulary related to travel and enter the vocabulary in *Tagxedo* to create a word cloud.
- Present the word cloud to the students.
- Have the students create a word cloud of travel.
- Have them share the word cloud in groups.

Computer work: (60 minutes)

Listening

- Introduce a dialogue on hotel reservations to the students.
- Have the students listen to the dialogue and identify key phrases.
- Have them do listening comprehension exercises and check the answers.

Speaking

- Have the students watch the video and do the expression dialogue exercises and check the answers.
- Have the students record the answers.
- Have them do a role-play with partners.
- Have them log on to the website *ZigZag On Earth* (http://www.zigzagonearth.com/10-steps-to-choose-your-ideal-next-travel-destination) and go over the 10 tips to

<u>Procedures</u>

choose a destination and make sure that the students fully understand the direction.

- Have them work with their partners and follow the direction.
- Have a few pairs present their destinations to the class.

Reading

- Provide the students with the URL of a reading passage. (http://traveltips.usatoday.com/make-hotel-reservation-14354.html)
- Have them predict the content of the reading passage based on the title.
- Have them read the passage on individual computers.
- Have them write down the unknown words in each mind map and predict the words.
- Have them look up the online dictionaries for the words.
- Have them share their mind maps and discuss the content of the reading passage with the discussion questions
- Have them do exercises on *Hot Potatoes* for comprehension check-up.

Post-computer work: (30 minutes)

Language in use

Pronunciation

- Have the students listen to the words related to the situation.
- Have them listen to the keywords.
- Have them practice pronunciation by recording words into the program and compare their own sound wave with that of a native speaker.

Vocabulary

- Have the students go over 'picture-word association' practice and check the answers.

Writing: Planning an itinerary

- Provide websites about the trip (e.g., www.booking.com, www.agoda.com).
- Have the students decide the destination and the hotel.

- Show sample itineraries to students and have them search them on the Web.
- Have them write an itinerary.
- Have them complete an itinerary as homework.

10.3 Teaching Methods and Techniques for Integrated Language Skills

The sample lesson for developing integrated skills is divided into three stages: pre-computer work, while-computer work, and post-computer work. During the pre-computer work, lesson objectives and detail of each target skill and subskills are introduced, and learners' schema is activated through e-texts and web-based programs, *Tagxedo, OKMindmap,* and *YouTube.* During the while-computer work, the main activities for the target skills, including listening, speaking, and reading, are presented. Along with a *YouTube* video, a reading passage from *USA Today*, and some websites for related images were used for activities. The post-computer work includes a unit completion report, pronunciation, vocabulary, grammar, speaking, and a short writing activity.

1. Pre-computer Work

During the pre-computer work, the overall theme of travel is introduced, and learners' schema on travel is activated. A video clip is presented to help activate schema on travel, and *Tagxedo* is used to familiarize the students with related vocabulary. At this stage, the teacher is supposed to make sure that the students understand what specific language skills, functions, and vocabulary will be covered and ideas about travel.

Activating schema

- Have the students watch a video clip and tell the teacher if there are any ideas and words that they can relate to ("It looks like a part of an old palace," "It looks ancient," etc.).
- Ask back the reasons for the ideas and write them on the board.

Figure 10.3 A video clip from *YouTube*

Vocabulary

- Present the word cloud that includes related vocabulary so that learners can detail their ideas and prior knowledge. See Figure 10.4.
- Have the students to read the words aloud that stand out and have them elaborate on those words using their experiences.

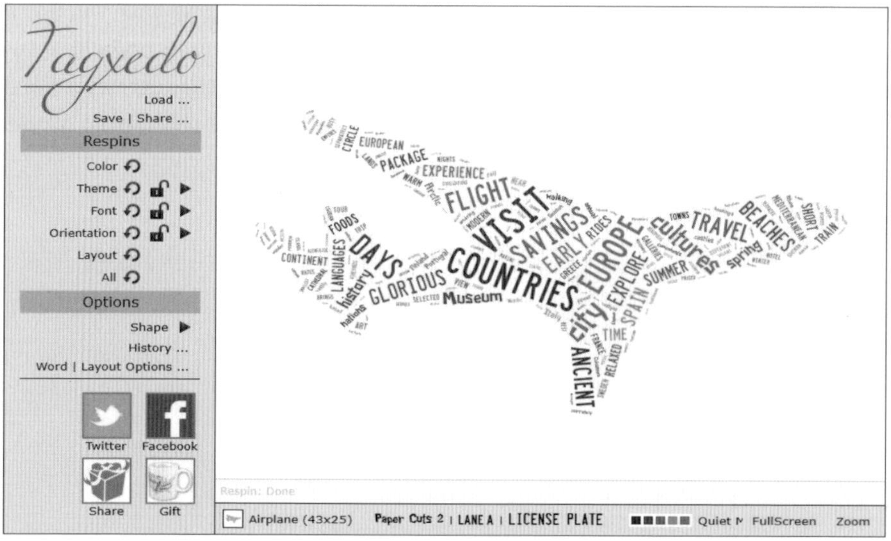

Figure 10.4 A word cloud on travel created by *Tagxedo*

2. While-computer Work

While-computer work focuses on listening, speaking, and reading skills using the same topic of travel.

Listening

Activity: Listening to a dialogue

While it starts with a dialogue in a *YouTube* video, the video shows a hotel reservation dialogue between two people with stock images slideshow.

- Have the students listen to a part of the dialogue and identify key phrases used to make the reservation. See Figure 10.5.
- Have them compare the key phrases with their neighbors.
- Have them discuss any other details mentioned in the video.

Figure 10.5 Hotel reservation dialogue

Activity: Listening comprehension check-up

This section of the lesson provides a listening comprehension practice based on the short dialogue above. Once an answer is selected, immediate feedback is provided so that the students can make another attempt.

- Have the students open the JQuiz html file that includes the hotel reservation dialogue.
- Have them complete the comprehension activity (JQuiz).
- If the students chose the wrong answer, have them make another attempt before skipping or checking the answer.

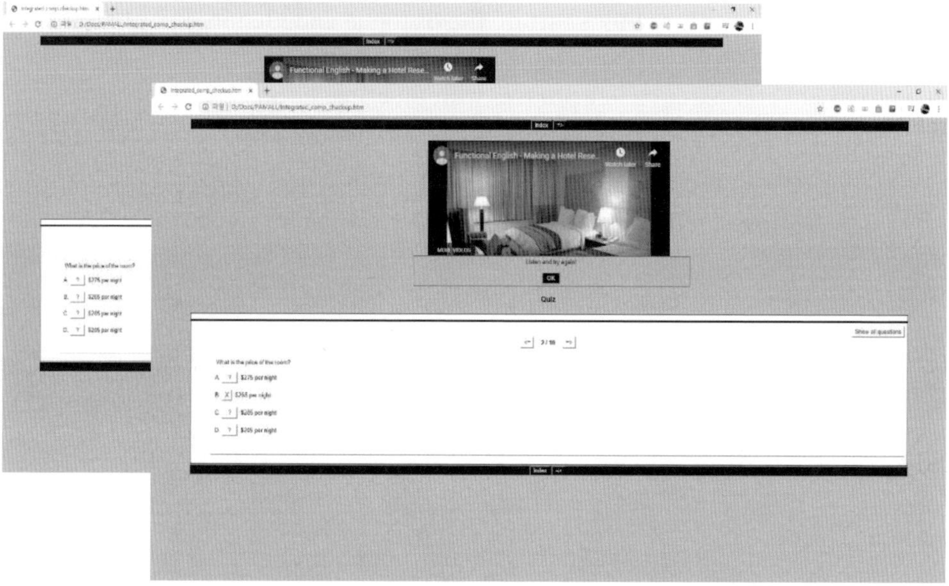

Figure 10.6 Comprehension with text support

Speaking

The speaking activity in the lesson plan breaks down to two parts. First, it begins with controlled speaking activity based on the expressions they already practiced in listening section. The first speaking activity is to practice dialogue on making a reservation. The students will begin with a role play in pairs. The second one is the development where the students are supposed to extend the given dialogues for two more turns each.

The second part of the speaking activity is a guided speaking activity using a website called *ZigZag On Earth,* following steps to choose a destination. The material to be used for the guided speaking practice is '10 steps to choose your ideal next travel destination' form *ZigZag On Earth* (http://www.zigzagonearth.com/10-steps-to-choose-your-ideal-next-travel-destination).

Activity: Controlled speaking

Sample Dialogue

A: *Good Morning.*
B: *I would like to reserve a room, please.*
A: *When will you arrive?*
B: *I will land at LA International Airport on July the 20th.*

A: *Good afternoon, Hilton LA Airport. How can I help you?*
B: *I would like to reserve a room, please.*
I would like to reserve some rooms at your hotel.
I will be with three colleges and my wife. My wife and I will need a double room.

- Have the students pair up and take a role (either A or B).
- Have them do a short role-play using the three dialogues until they get familiar with the expressions.
- Have them do the role-play without looking at the dialogues.
- Once the students are ready with the dialogues, have them extend each dialogue with two more turns for each speaker.

Activity: Guided speaking

- Have the students pair up, go over the first five steps, and ask the teacher any words they do not understand. Figure 10.7 shows the detailed steps to decide on a destination.
- Make sure all the students understand the first five steps.
- Have the students work with their partners and follow the direction.
- As the students complete the task, have them share their ideas with their partners.
- After the students complete the first five steps, have them move on to the next five steps.

- Upon completion of the ten steps, have the students share their details about how they decided on a destination with the whole class.

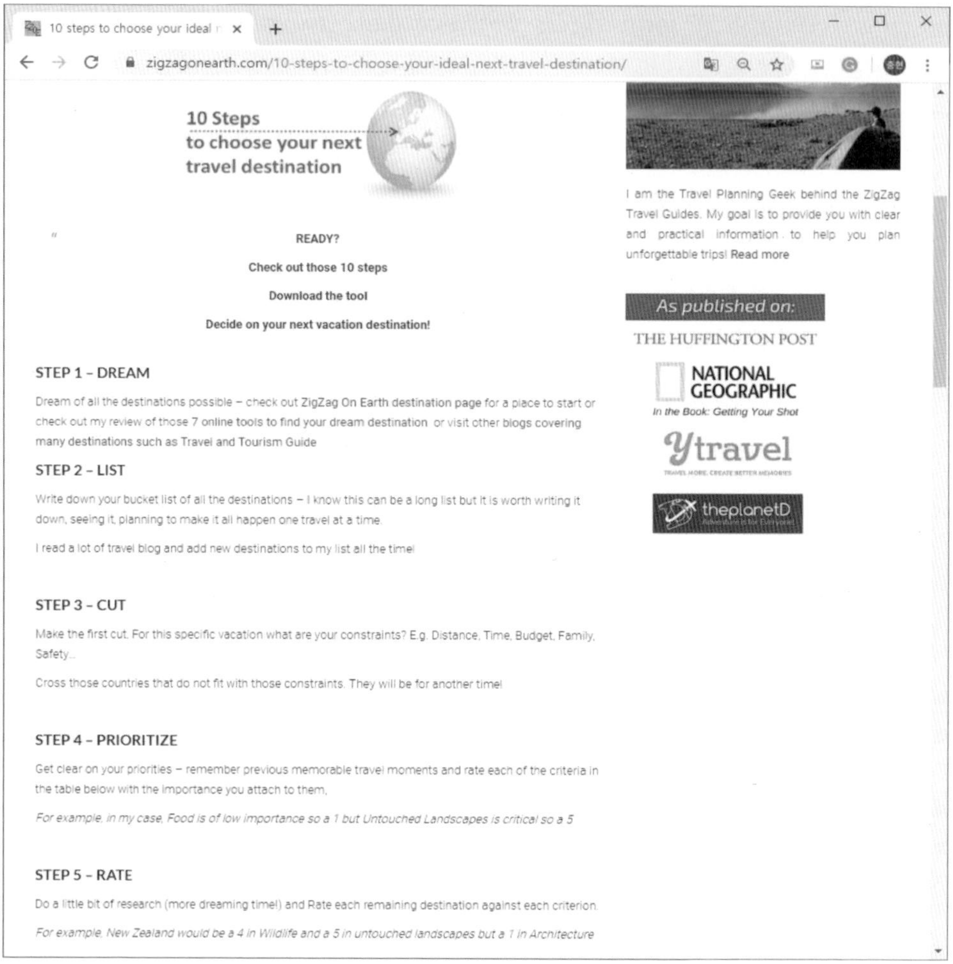

Figure 10.7 Ten steps to choosing a destination

Reading

For teaching reading skills, e-text on the Web (*USA TODAY*) is provided for the students. The e-text is entitled 'How to Make a Hotel Reservation.' The reading part starts with skimming, followed by scanning. The main activity type is multiple-choice questions that are aimed to have the students practice both skills. The e-text on making reservations for a business event is from *USA TODAY*.

- Have the students read the text focusing on what the main content is about. See Figure 10.8 for the e-text.
- Have the students write down the unknown words in mind maps and predict the meaning of words. Then have them look up the online dictionaries for the unknown words.
- Remind them that the purpose of the reading for the first time is not to translate each word into Korean but use the multiple-choice question as presented in Figure 10.9 to grasp the main idea.
- After having the students find the main idea, give instructions on how news articles are organized.
- Once the main idea is explained along with instruction on text organization, have the students do exercises using JQuiz for comprehension check-up.

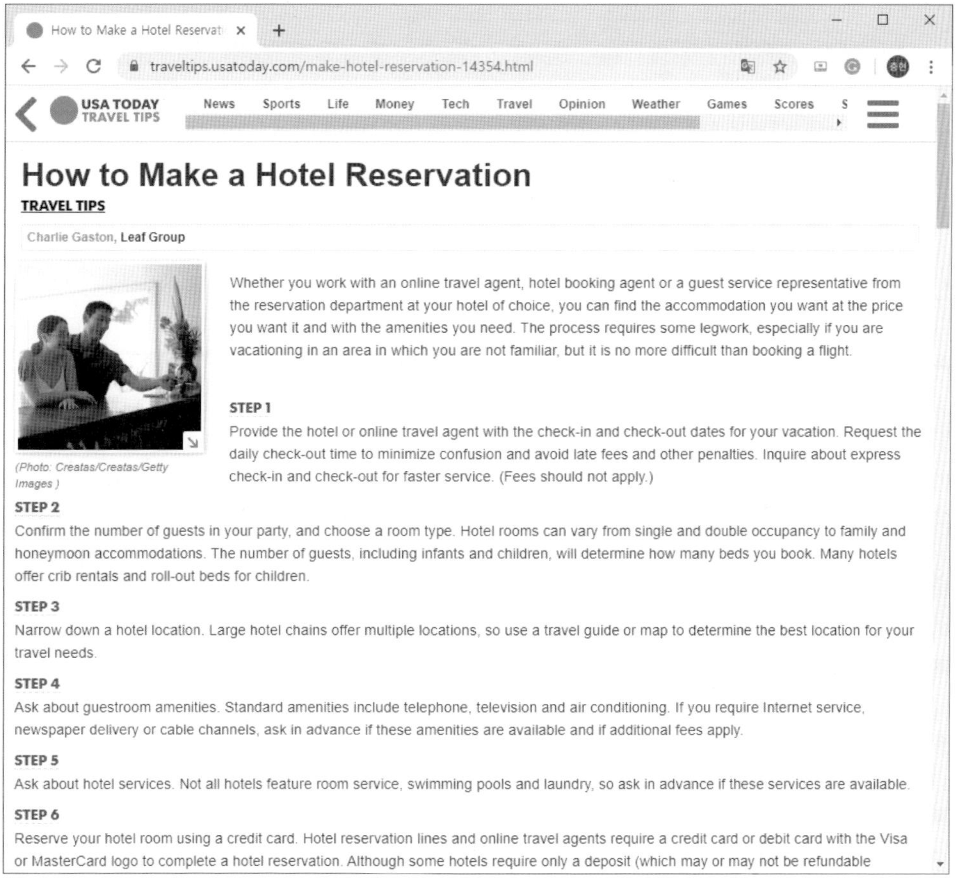

Figure 10.8 The e-text from *USA TODAY*

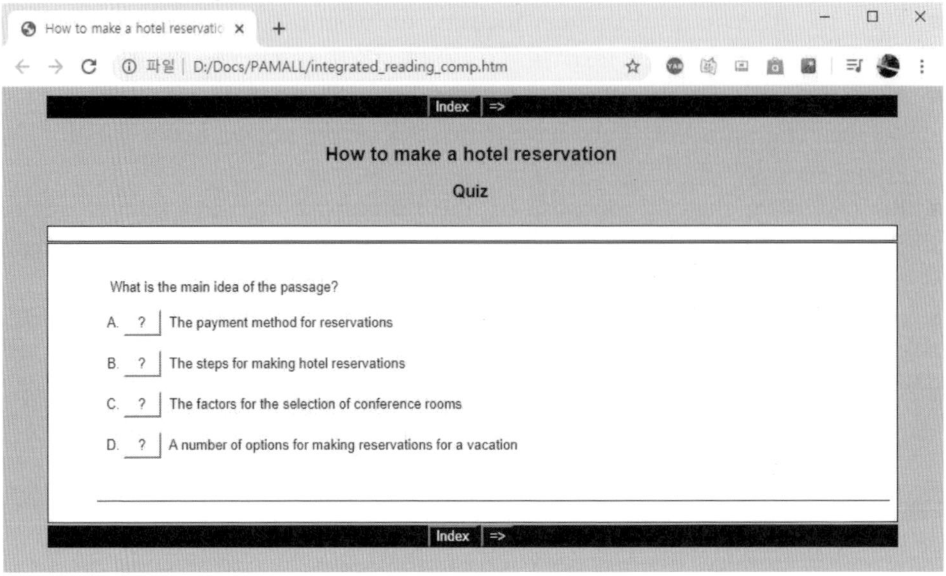

Figure 10.9 A sample multiple-choice question on comprehension

3. Post-computer Work

Language in use

Pronunciation

The exercises for pronunciation practice on target phrases are conducted in *Flipgrid*. By having the teacher and the students record, the students can check their pronunciation and compare it with that of the teacher. The students can listen to the subtle differences in their pronunciation and of a native speaker. Figure 10.10 illustrates the practice.

- Have the students listen to the provided example and record their own pronunciation.
- Have them compare their sound with that of the teacher. Figure 10.11 shows the sample pronouncing practice activity screen on *Flipgrid*.
- Following pronunciation practice with the target phrase, have the students move onto the next practice where they are to practice using a video dialogue.

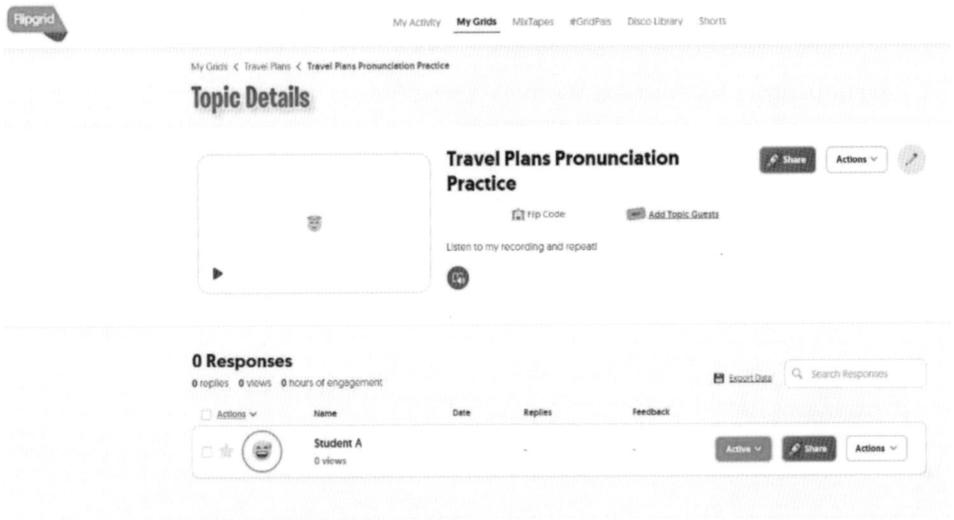

Figure 10.10 *Flipgrid* pronunciation practice activity

- Have them listen to the video, choose three sentences to practice, and record their pronunciation, taking care of the suprasegmental features in the sentence. Figure 10.11 illustrates the practice activity.

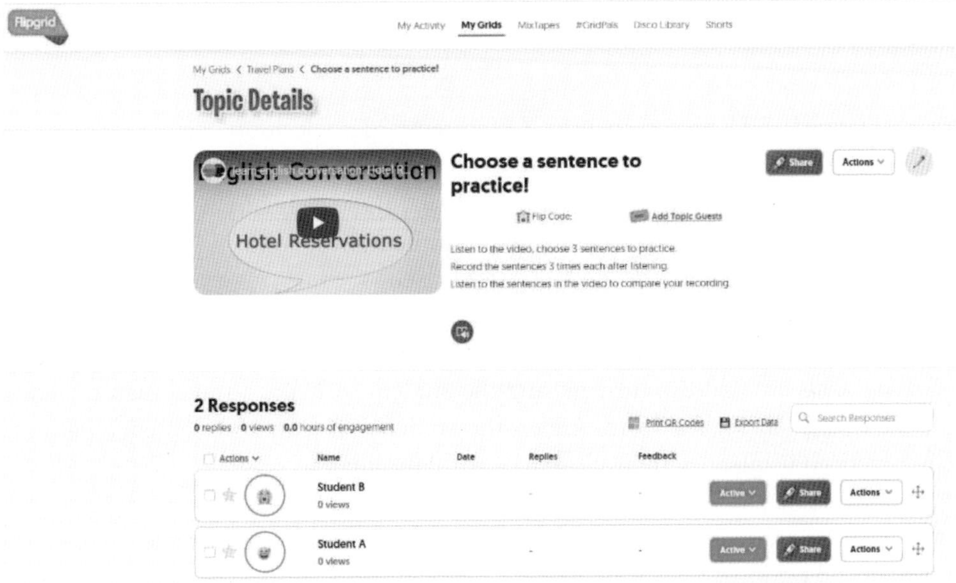

Figure 10.11 The screenshot of sentence pronunciation

Vocabulary

The section provides 'Picture-Word Association' to match the picture with the right caption (word). Figure 10.12 is the screenshot of the vocabulary practice section.

Figure 10.12 The screenshot of picture-word association using *Socrative*

- Have the students join the *Socrative* room for the vocabulary activity.
- Have the students match the images with the right words.

Writing

Writing skills are addressed by getting the student to make a travel plan referring to the images in Figure 10.13. Given the students' level, short sentence patterns are practiced using an activity close to a real-life situation.

- Have the students work in a group of three or four and complete the travel plan to London.
- The teacher provides a list of words that the students may need.

- Have the students share information about the places they have selected to visit and share with the members.

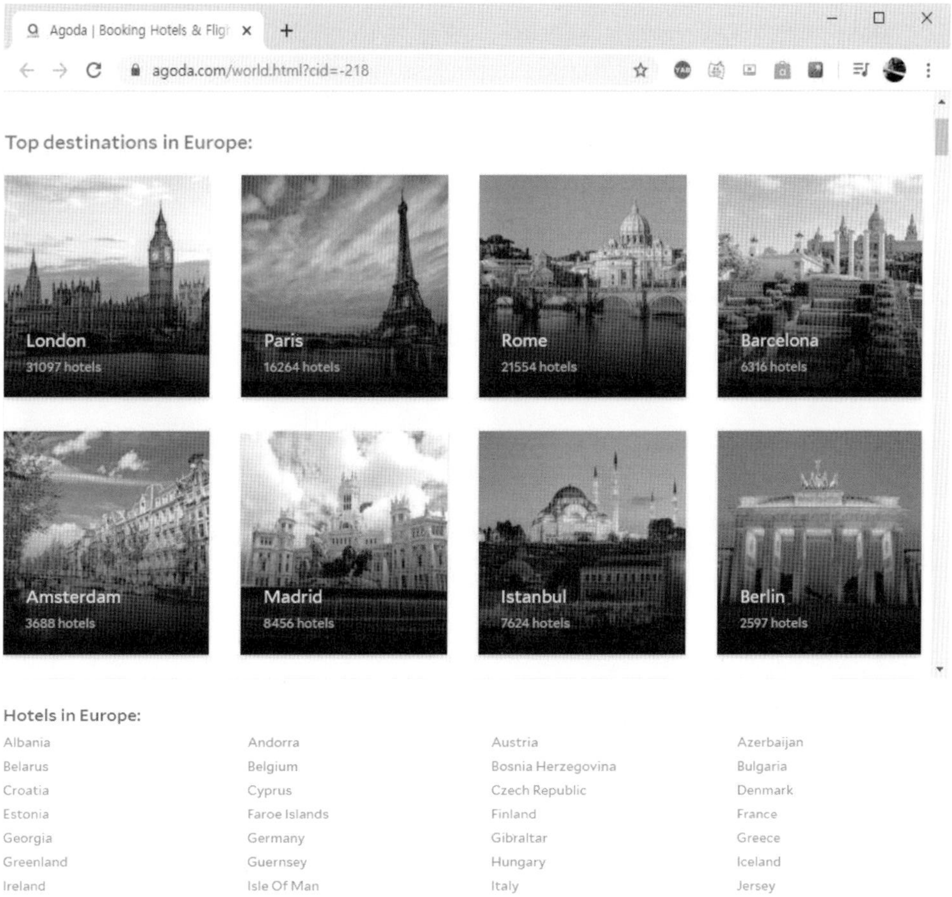

Figure 10.13 Sample images of top destinations in Europe

- Along with the destinations, have the students find what each attraction is famous for and write extra sentences about the information they found from the Web.
- Once the itinerary is completed, have the groups post their itinerary in the class BBS and share itinerary and information.

Tasks for Study and Discussion

- Create a teaching plan for your target students for integrated language skills. Make sure to use various websites and apps to meet the goals and objectives of your lesson, referring to the sample lesson plan.

  - Remember to provide theoretical background and materials, lesson plan, and teaching methods and techniques. Work individually, and then share your work with partners.

Part 4

Trends and Current Issues in CALL and MALL

Part 4
Trends and Current Issues in CALL and MALL

The use of media technology and digital technology in FLT&L is closely related to changes in language teaching methods and their development in both hardware and software (Phillips 1985; van Els, Bongaerts, Extra, van Os, & Janssen-van Dieten, 1984). The history of modern media technology began in the late 1950s and early 1960s. Audio technology and language laboratories, along with the Audiolingual Method and the development of the tape recorder, had permeated all levels of foreign language teaching and learning (Zettersten, 1986). They had certain advantages – presenting communication in action and providing learners with the opportunity to practice with spoken materials (Edelhoff, 1978; Tomalin, 1986). However, the results seem to have generally been unsuccessful, since the tape recorder or the language laboratory was integrated into a 'total' teaching system, which often replaced the teacher without considering what the most appropriate role of audio technology and language laboratories was and what methodology was most appropriate (Sherrington, 1973; Tomalin, 1986; van Els et al., 1984).

The boom of the 1960s did not continue despite the potential of audio technology and language laboratories. Many teachers and students seemed to grow tired of language laboratories and leave them unused or little used in many schools (Zettersten, 1986). It was caused by a lack of awareness, ignorance, and slow and insufficient research studies into the technologies' use (Fox, Matthews, Matthew, & Rope, 1990; Garrett, 1991). However, audio technologies are still used to deliver controlled pattern practice, drills, and testing in schools and higher education (Pusack & Otto, 1990).

The decline of audio technology and language laboratories in the 1970s was affected not only by their problems, as stated above, but also by the arrival of video and computers (van Els et al., 1984). The use of computers was largely restricted to mainframe computers that were not well suited to teachers' and students' needs and were often inaccessible (Hainline, 1987; Pusack & Otto, 1990). More importantly, the development of suitable software in the educational fields lagged behind that of hardware (O'Shea & Self, 1983; Zettersten, 1986).

The decade of the 1980s put microcomputers into the hands of language teachers due to the rapid development of new technologies based on computers and microelectronics in industry and commerce. There was a massive spread of cheaper but better quality microcomputers after the mid-1980s (Pusack & Otto, 1990; Zettersten, 1986). A combination of audio, video, and computing media, i.e., interactive video in a single learning station, was also demonstrated, though insufficient materials and software were an obstacle to the broader application of this technology. Meanwhile, an emphasis on communicative and student-centered approaches in FLT encouraged new efforts to exploit media technologies effectively (Fox et al., 1990; Pusack & Otto, 1990).

Since the 1990s, ICT and computers have gone under revolutionary development. Many language teachers and learners adopt computers and new technologies, and social media in their learning and teaching. CALL and MALL have been an important research field that reflects on these drastic changes in technologies and the trends and issues of ELT&L. There are many research studies in CALL and MALL. This part presents a historical overview, the trends and issues in CALL and MALL research overseas and in Korea from the 1980s to the present.

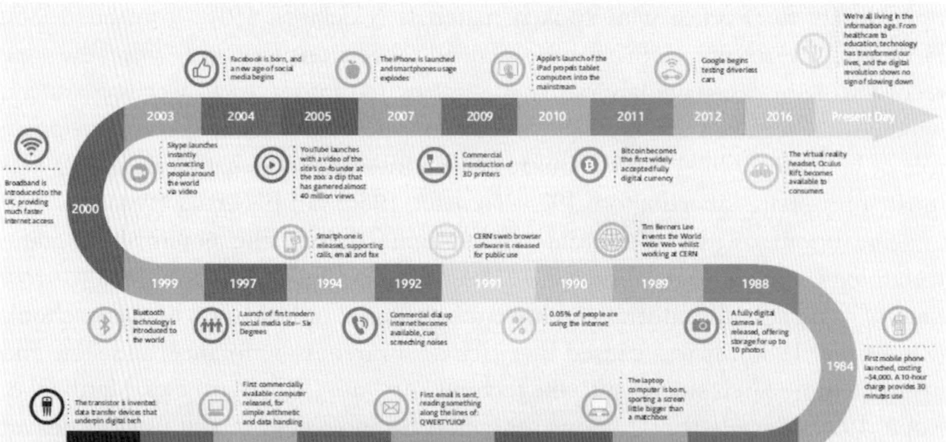

Figure 11.1 A brief history of the digital revolution (https://stfc.ukri.org/files/digital-revolution-infographic/)

Chapter 11

Research on CALL and MALL Overseas

11.1 Introduction

This chapter covers CALL and MALL research conducted from the 1980s to the present, along with the period and research topics. From the 1980s to the beginning of the 1990s, computers and advanced technologies were not frequently implemented in language teaching and learning practices, so little empirical research was carried out. Instead, researchers introduced computer hardware and software appropriate for language teaching and learning. They also suggested the general principles and application methods for CALL and MALL and the ways of teacher training. From the mid of 1990s to the present day, empirical research has been conducted on language skills and specific sub-areas, such as testing, courseware design and evaluation, teacher education, etc.

In this chapter, research trends are addressed based on periodical time and research topics. Research articles in *Language Learning & Technology,* one of the prestigious international journals related to CALL and MALL, are reviewed in detail. *Language Learning & Technology* (*LLT*) is an internationally renowned journal indexed in the Social Sciences Citation Index (SSCI). The articles in *LLT* were collected from the first issues to the latest issue (2015 spring). The collected articles were divided into five periods, media technology period (1980s-mid-1990s) and the four periods suggested by Kang and Lee (2014): 1) 1997-2002 (the software period); 2) 2003-2007 (the Internet period); 3) 2008-2012 (the mobile period); and 4) 2013-2020 (the social media period). Finally, the list of publications in the 1980s – Mid-1990s and the chronological table of *LLT* are provided.

11.2 1980s – Mid-1990s: The Media Technology Period

1. The Advent of Computers for FLT&L

First, the educational uses of computers gathered momentum after the mid-1960s (Ahmad, Corbett, Rogers, & Sussex, 1985; Higgins & Jones, 1984; O'Shea & Self,

1983). Pennington (1991) stated that the application of computers in linguistics and language learning was tied in with highly specialized work on modeling language according to mathematical and logical properties.

Figure 11.2 Simon, the first personal computer (1950)
(http://www.vintagecomputer.net/simon.cfm)

These are some of the fields of research and practice that today can be applied to the field of computers in language teaching and learning (Pennington, 1991). The use of computers in language teaching and learning took a concrete shape at the University of Illinois (the PLATO project) and Stanford University (the computer-based foreign language teaching project) in North America, and the University of Essex (the Scientific Language Project) in Britain from the end of 1960s (Ahmad et al., 1985; Higgins & Jones, 1984; O'Shea & Self, 1983). CALL research in the mid-1960s began to examine its cost and educational effectiveness (Hainline, 1987). At that time (1965-1975), CALL was almost entirely geared towards tutorials and teaching the written language, i.e., drill and practice – grammar explanation and exercises – for beginners on terminals tied to a mainframe computer (Ahmad et al., 1985; Hainline, 1987).

Teachers could not access computers at work and home until the late 1970s with the advent of the relatively cheap microcomputer (Zettersten, 1986). Some writers, such as Ahmad et al. (1985), Cameron (1989), Chapelle and Jamieson (1989), Hardisty and Windeatt (1989), Higgins and Johns (1984), Hope, Taylor, and Pusack (1984), Jones and Fortescue (1987), Kenning and Kenning (1983), Last (1984), O'Shea and Self (1983), Pennington (1989), Wyatt (1984), etc. described the possibilities of CALL using microcomputers or mainframe computers. Some of them have discussed applying computers in the four language skills, listening, speaking, reading, and writing. The potential of CALL has been demonstrated in hundreds of programs or software created from the 1980s (Hope, Taylor, & Pusack, 1984; Stevens, 1989).

Teacher training for media technology has also been considered an important and serious issue. The calls for more familiarity with the hardware and software, teacher training to achieve it, and encouragement to develop new approaches to instruction in general or language teaching have been consistently found in the international literature (Rich, 1991). The examples are found in Alberta Education (1987), C. H. Lee (1998a), OECD (1987), UNESCO (1988), etc.

2. The Convergence of Technologies

There has been continuous development in the capabilities of existing media technologies based on computers and microelectronics. Previous generations of devices were being replaced by new storage media, such as laser discs, which offered much greater storage capabilities, speed, and accuracy. Computers can now carry out many tasks simultaneously through parallel processing (Dever & Pennington, 1989; Phillips, 1985). On the other hand, in contrast to the past decades, the development of software has tended to gain upon that of hardware. Many advanced programming languages and authoring languages – languages designed specifically for producing educational software – e.g., C++, *Guide*, *Toolbook*, etc., have been developed, which help teachers to write appropriate programs generating various kinds of language learning exercises (Dever & Pennington, 1989; Pennington, 1991).

Figure 11.3 CD-ROM titles and a DVD/CD drive

There has also been a convergence of technologies as audio and video technologies have been combined with computers. For instance, CD-ROM multimedia and interactive video (i.e., computer-controlled videotape or videodisc) can play video sequences with much greater speed and accuracy under computer control than videotape (Fox et al., 1990; Laurillard, 1987).

3. The Application of Artificial Intelligence

The application of artificial intelligence (AI) to computers has shown new possibilities in man-machine interaction. Dever and Pennington (1989), Phillips (1985), and Winston (1987) claimed that programs must have the capability of interacting with users in a way that simulates natural language use. Thus, many AI studies sought to develop a greater knowledge of natural language processing (Barchan, 1986). Computer speech recognition has become a reality in CALL. Some programs have adopted speech recognition technology, such as *TriplePlay Plus*! from Syracuse Language Systems, *Think and Talk* from the Language Company, etc.

4. New Information Technology

The arrival of new information technology (NIT) in the 1980s and at the beginning of the 1990s played a leading role in using media technology in education and FLT&L (Rich, 1991). The lower cost and more remarkable power of microcomputers combined with their spread in the rest of society have made them an irresistible force in FLT&L (Jones, 1991). Educational authorities at all levels have put great effort into equipping schools with computers and CD-ROM titles, training teachers and students in their use, and experimenting with various aspects of media technology (Rich, 1991). Many researchers and educational planners have been absorbed in research on how NIT can help teachers and learners in language teaching and learning (Feurzeig, 1988; Garrett, 1991; Rich, 1991).

5. The Development of Existing Media Technologies

The new generation teachers and education planners' increased media technology literacy helped reduce the reluctance to use it, particularly advanced technologies (Knezek, Miyashita, & Sakamoto, 1993). As a result, there was reasonably massive distribution of media technology to the language classroom, which was applied both efficiently and effectively (Licklider, 1987; Rich, 1991). Teachers and students could use computers and CD-ROM multimedia for enhancing the language teaching and learning process at school and home. Significantly, each learner or a small group of learners was equipped with the computer as an exciting medium for individualization and problem-solving.

A convergence of hardware and software developments was found in the 1990s. Software became both more intelligent and more powerful due to the application of hypertext. The increased power of software facilitated the creation of dynamic and non-linear learning environments so that media technology became more interactive and user-friendly. Computers that use expert systems and parallel processors became widely available for FLT&L (Pennington, 1991). It made room for more natural man-machine interaction. Their development had a significant impact in the field of FLT&L. Therefore, the combination of increased processing power and the ability to address directly much larger amounts of memory, together with intelligent software, means that computer-based learning (CBL) and computer-managed learning (CML) systems which assign a more fundamental, active and controlling role to computers than in computer-assisted learning (CAL) would be adopted more effectively and efficiently than has been the case in education so far (Ahmad et al., 1985; Nickerson, 1988; Phillips, 1985).

6. The Integration of Media Technologies

Media technology was integrated with communications technologies, particularly satellite-delivered and cable-delivered signals (video and text), overcoming some of the limitations inherent in each. They helped bring the outside world, i.e., authentic materials, into the teaching and learning situation (Fox et al., 1990; Hill, 1991).

Satellites can provide a rich layer of language resources that can be exploited for FLT&L since the satellite signal can cover a large portion of the earth, depending on the location (Fox et al., 1990; Hill, 1991). It was also reported that electronic mail and computer and video conferencing would be affected by the enhanced facilities of Integrated Services Digital Network (ISDN), which offered simultaneous transmission of voice, data, and images through the modification to the telephone network (Fox et al., 1990). The Internet, which was developed primarily in academic and corporate research institutions, caught teachers' and students' imagination in the classroom and the general public. The Internet was considered to offer more powerful functions for use as an upgrade to e-mail and as a tool in distance learning and searching for various kinds of information in language teaching and learning (Fox et al., 1990).

11.3 1997 – 2002: The Software Period

1. MALL Theory, Conceptualization, and Pedagogy

The development of information and communication technology (ICT) has facilitated MALL research and pedagogy. Several initial studies published in *LLT* have introduced CALL and MALL theory and principles. Chapelle (1997) reviewed CALL literature and asserted the need for empirical research methods for CALL. Ortega (1997), in the same issue, presented processes and outcomes in networked classroom interaction. Students' perceptions and behaviors in technological environments have been examined (Stepp-Greany, 2002; Weasenforth, Biesenbach-Lucas, & Meloni, 2002). Some scholars have addressed the methodological issues of research (Ayoun, 2000; DuFon, 2002; Hegelheimer & Chapelle, 2000; Hulstijn, 2000). They included web-based elicitation tasks (Ayoun, 2000), ways of eliciting L2 production data by using computers (Hulstijn, 2000), methodological issues in learner-computer interaction research (Hegelheimer & Chapelle, 2000), and video recording for ethnographic SLA research (DuFon, 2002).

Figure 11.4 Various kinds of software
(https://www.coderus.com/software-101-a-complete-guide-to-the-different-types-of-software/)

2. E-Learning, Online Learning, and WBI

Research on various learning environments has been conducted. Osuna and Meskill (1998) implemented the World Wide Web to integrate the Spanish language and culture, and Lamy and Goodfellow (1999) examined the reflective conversation in the virtual language classroom. Also, social dimensions in a telecollaborative foreign language study were examined (Belz, 2002).

3. Listening and Speaking

A few studies have been conducted on listening and speaking in this period. One study addressed a model for listening and viewing comprehension in multimedia environments (Hoven, 1999). In this study, Hoven (1999) proposed an instructional design model grounded in sociocultural theory for a self-access language learning environment through listening and viewing comprehension.

4. Reading and Writing

Work on reading and writing relates to literacies. As new technologies have emerged, perspectives on literacy have been changed. *LLT* published a special issue on literacies and technologies in 2000. This issue contained a variety of topics of literacies essential in the new millennium. Murray (2000) reported that changes in the technologies of literacy influenced literacy practices and communities. Richards (2000) attempted to redefine literacy in the electronic age, considering hypermedia and internet communication. Kramsch (2000) focused on authenticity and authorship in the computer-mediated acquisition of L2 literacy, and Kasper (2000) examined ESL students' engagement in the development of multiliteracies. In addition to literacies, two studies are concerned with reading (Chun & Plass, 1997; Lomicka, 1998). Chun and Plass (1997) investigated text comprehension in multimedia environments, and Lomicka (1998) examined the effects of multimedia annotations on reading comprehension.

5. Pronunciation, Vocabulary, and Grammar

Research on pronunciation was not conducted so much in this period. One study addressed automatic speech processing for foreign language pronunciation tutoring (Eskenazi, 1999). Studies on vocabulary have dealt with diverse multimedia and technologies (Al-Seghayer, 2001; De Ridder, 2002; Ghadirian, 2002; Groot, 2000; Laufer & Hill, 2000; Nikolova, 2002; Wood, 2001). The implemented multimedia and technologies are CALL dictionary (Laufer & Hill, 2000), multimedia annotation modes (Al-Seghayer, 2001), authoring of multimedia materials on student acquisition of vocabulary (Nikolova, 2002), the highlighting of hyperlinks (De Ridder, 2002), and the screening and arranging of texts for controlled exposure to vocabulary (Ghadirian, 2002).

Regarding grammar, input and output practice in educational software for L2 acquisition was examined by Nagata (1998), and the construction of grammatical knowledge was revealed through the use of user-behavior tracking technologies (Collentine, 2000).

6. Computer-Mediated Communication (CMC)

The development of technologies has facilitated interaction and communication among students and teachers. A network-based classroom was adopted to promote interaction between students (Sengupta, 2001). Computer-mediated communication (CMC) has begun to be implemented for teaching and learning language in this period (Biesenbach-Lucas & Weasenforth, 2001; Blake, 2000; González-Bueno 1998; Sotillo, 2000; Toyoda & Harrison, 2002). Several researchers have addressed E-mails (Biesenbach-Lucas & Weasenforth, 2001; González-Bueno, 1998). Asynchronous and synchronous CMC was dealt with by Blake (2000), Sotillo (2000), and Toyoda and Harrison (2002). Among those, text-based chats were examined in detail by Blake (2000) and Toyoda and Harrison (2002).

7. Courseware Design and Evaluation

Technological development has a positive impact on the design and development of courseware and software. As the user interface of foreign language multimedia software has been significant, Plass (1998) suggested a cognitive approach as one of the solutions. Speech technology (Ehsani & Knodt, 1998) and signal analysis software for teaching discourse (Chun, 1998) were suggested.

8. Assessment and Testing

Assessment and testing are the main areas that computers and the web can be applied to the development and administration of tests and assessments (Brown,

1997; Dunkel, 1999; Kenyon & Malabonga, 2001; Roever, 2001; Sawaki, 2001). Research studies introduced the use of computers for language testing (Brown, 1997), development and use of computer-adaptive tests (Dunkel, 1999), and web-based language testing (Roever, 2001). Some studies were carried out to compare the conventional and computer-assisted tests (Kenyon & Malabonga, 2001; Sawaki, 2001).

9. Teacher Education

Teacher education for using technology in language teaching and learning is addressed by some researchers (Doering & Beach, 2002; Egbert, Paulus, & Nakamichi, 2002; Meskill, Mossop, DiAngelo, & Pasquale, 2002). It includes expert and novice teachers' perceptions of technology (Meskill et al., 2002), the role of technology in teacher education for CALL instruction (Egbert, Paulus, & Nakamichi, 2002), and pre-service teachers' literacy practice through technology tools (Doering & Beach, 2002).

10. Corpus

It is noteworthy that corpus linguistics has been integrated into teaching and learning languages. In 2001, *LLT* published a special issue that addressed corpus linguistics. The issue had diverse topics for the use of corpus in language teaching and learning as follows: 1) students' approaches to corpus investigation (Kennedy & Miceli, 2001); 2) using corpora for academic purposes (Thompson & Tribble, 2001); 3) lexical behavior in academic and technical corpora for the implications of ESP development (Fuentes, 2001); and 4) the use of a parallel corpus and concordance for language learners (John, 2001; Lixun, 2001).

11.4 2003 – 2007: The Internet Period

1. MALL Theory, Conceptualization, and Pedagogy

MALL theory and pedagogy have expanded in scope, focusing on diverse teaching and learning contexts. For example, Parks, Huot, Hamers, and H.-Lemonnier (2003) focused on an innovative program in a Quebec high school, which involved project-based teaching in networked classrooms. They provided pedagogical implications for language learning. Levy and Kennedy (2004) suggested a task-cycling pedagogy through stimulated reflection and audio-conferencing in foreign language learning. Morris (2005) examined the provision of corrective feedback and learner repair in child-to-child conversations using a software program, *Blackboard,* in an elementary Spanish immersion class.

2. E-Learning, Online Learning, and WBI

Many studies on e-learning, online learning, WBI, and distance learning were conducted. In particular, *LLT* published a special issue on distance learning (Doughty & Long, 2003; Pawan, Paulus, Yalcin, & Chang, 2003; Sampson, 2003; Strambi & Bouvet, 2003; Tudini, 2003). These studies addressed a variety of topics of distance learning, such as optimal psycholinguistic environments (Doughty & Long, 2003), flexibility and interaction (Strambi & Bouvet, 2003), learners' needs (Sampson, 2003), patterns of engagement and interaction of in-service teachers (Pawan, Paulus, Yalcin, & Chang, 2003), and the roles of native speakers in chat (Tudini, 2003). Hampel and Hauck (2004) and Wang (2004) also examined supporting tools for distance learning, audio conferencing, and desktop video conferencing, respectively. The other studies dealt with foreign language students' interaction and behaviors in the electronic discussion (Hanna & De Nooy, 2003), the impact of a web-based course on EAP students' acquisition (Chen, Belkada, & Okamoto, 2004), and the negotiation of cultures in cyberspace (Reeder, Macfadyen, Roche, & Chase, 2004).

Figure 11.5 Online learning at HUFS

3. Listening and Speaking

Inquiry on technology and L2 oral proficiency development has flourished. In 2005, *LLT* published a special issue on technology and oral language development. The studies in this issue dealt with the relationship between synchronous CMC, working memory, and L2 oral proficiency development (Payne & Ross 2005), an integration of collaborative and individual learning through a combination of CALL programs and online activities with face-to-face conversation class (Barr, Leakey, & Ranchoux, 2005), students' conversations and negotiated interaction in text and voice chat rooms (Jepson, 2005), a methodological consideration of speech synthesis for CALL (Handley & Hamel, 2005), French learners' oral interaction in computer in the project-oriented CALL classroom, and the analysis of oral skills in voice e-mail and online interviews (Volle, 2005). Regarding listening, the research topics have been more sophisticated. Grgurović and Hegelheimer (2007) examined students' use of subtitles and the transcripts during listening, and Verdugo and Belmonte (2007) adopted digital stories for teaching young Spanish learners of English to improve listening comprehension.

4. Reading and writing

Research on reading has continued as multimedia or online learning environment provides learners with supporting tools. Lin and Chen (2007) used visualization and advance organizers to reading authentic EFL text in a multimedia environment. Murphy (2007) explored Japanese students' English reading comprehension exercises online, focusing on the effects of feedback, proficiency, and interaction. It is noteworthy that a mobile device was used to support a peer-assisted learning system for collaborative EFL reading (Lan, Sung, & Chang, 2007). In terms of writing, Chen (2006) explored a Taiwanese graduate student's literacy development in e-mail writing. Bloch (2007) focused on the benefits of the blog and described one immigrant student's use of blogs in an L2 writing course.

5. Pronunciation, Vocabulary and Grammar

Research on vocabulary has expanded in scope compared to the other skills, pronunciation, and grammar. The research included L2 vocabulary recognition and recall using pictorial and written test items (Jones, 2004), the expansion of academic vocabulary with an interactive online database (Horst, Cobb, & Nicolae, 2005), the effects of L1 and L2 glosses on incidental vocabulary learning (Yoshii, 2006), and

L2 learners' online dictionary use and its effect on L2 word retention (Peters, 2007). Huang and Liou (2007) incorporated vocabulary learning into an automated graded reading program. One study on pronunciation was found (Hardison, 2004). This study explored the effectiveness of computer-assisted prosody training with visual feedback.

6. Computer-Mediated Communication (CMC)

The development of technologies has accelerated the research on CMC in foreign language teaching and learning. A handful of publications addressed multiple aspects of the implementation of CMC technologies (Biesenbach-Lucas, 2005, 2007; Fitze, 2006; Jiang & Ramsay, 2005; Lai & Zhao, 2006; D. S. Shin, 2006; Vandergriff, 2006; Warner, 2004). They deal with various playful uses of language in synchronous network-based medium, the MOO (Warner, 2004), students' e-mail writing topics and patterns (Biesenbach-Lucas, 2005, 2007), the rapport-building process through CMC in Chinese as a foreign language class (Jiang & Ramsay, 2005), ESL students' context configuration in their learning practices through CMC (D. S. Shin, 2006), and ESL students' noticing in text-based chat (Lai & Zhao, 2006). Besides, conventional classrooms and CMC use have been compared (Fitze, 2006; Vandergriff, 2006). Fitze (2006) compared ESL students' discourse and participation in face-to-face and written electronic discussion, and Vandergriff (2006) compared the L2 students' use of reception strategies, such as reprises and hypothesis testing in traditional face-to-face and SCMC discussions.

7. Collaborative Learning

In this category, telecollaboration was a central concern. In 2003, *LLT* published a special issue on telecollaboration. The topic of this issue was intercultural communication in telecollaboration, including intercultural communication through Internet communication tools (Thorne, 2003), the development of intercultural competence in a German-American e-mail partnership based on linguistic approaches (Belz, 2003), intercultural learning in a Spanish-English e-mail exchange (O'Dowd, 2003), and language students' negotiation of meaning and code-switching in the MOO at a German and a North American university (Kötter, 2003). Besides, Arnold and Ducate (2006) viewed discussion boards as an interactive venue for language teachers and examined prospective foreign language teachers' social and cognitive collaboration in the asynchronous discussion boards.

8. Courseware Design and Evaluation

A couple of designs for materials and activities have been suggested with different purposes. González-Lloret (2003) developed a task-based CALL activity delivered via the Internet to foster communication and interaction. Richards (2005) examined the changing requirements and new possibilities of integrating ICT into formal education and suggested that teachers need to be designers rather than transmitters when implementing ICT-supported learning activities.

11.5 2008 – 2012: The Mobile Period

1. MALL Theory, Conceptualization, and Pedagogy

MALL was considered to be capable of fostering learner autonomy. *LLT* viewed learner autonomy as one of the crucial concepts in language learning and teaching and published a special issue on learner autonomy and new learning environments in 2011. This issue contained a variety of topics related to learner autonomy, such as learner autonomy in a task-based 3D world (Collentine, 2011), a collaborative digital video project for fostering learner autonomy in English for science (Hafner & Miller, 2011), the role of blogging for promoting learner autonomy as well as intercultural competence (L. Lee, 2011), and self-study with language learning software (Nielson, 2011).

Figure 11.6 Mobile learning
(https://elearningindustry.com/mobile-learning-strategy-tips-creating)

2. E-Learning, Online Learning, and WBI

As mobile learning is considered the next generation of e-learning, researchers have focused on mobile learning. In this period, Chen, Hsieh, and Kinshuk (2008) addressed the issues of content adaptation in mobile language learning. They examined the effects of short-term memory and content representation type on learning performance.

3. Blended Learning

Research on blended learning has begun in this period. Blake, Wilson, Cetto, and Pardo-Ballester (2008) measured oral proficiency in distance, face-to-face, and blended classrooms, and Hinkelman and Gruba (2012) described power in blended language learning programs in Japan.

4. Listening and Speaking

Interest in the use of videos in teaching and learning L2 listening has increased. Winke, Gass, and Sydorenko (2010) examined the effects of captioning during video-based listening activities, and Cross (2011) explored the role of the visual content for L2 listeners comprehending news video texts.

5. Reading and Writing

Compared to the two previous periods, research on writing has flourished in this period. Various topics of L2 writing research were addressed. Corpus has been integrated into teaching and learning L2 writing (Chen & Baker, 2010; Kennedy & Miceli, 2010; H. Yoon, 2008). H. Yoon (2008) explored the influence of corpus technology on L2 academic writing, and Kennedy and Miceli (2010) introduced learners to a corpus and reported its effectiveness on creative writing. Collaboration and peer response have also been significant in L2 writing research. The research dealt with students' attention to form in Wiki-based collaborative writing (Kessler, 2009), synchronous online peer response groups in EFL writing (Liang, 2010), and L2 learners' writing conventions in collaborative writing (Elola & Oskoz, 2010). The automated writing evaluation program was implemented in the EFL writing classes (Chen & Cheng, 2008). Chen and Baker (2010) identified frequently-used word combinations in writing by using an automated frequently-driven approach.

6. Pronunciation, Vocabulary, and Grammar

Research in pronunciation has expanded in scope, showing a variety of topics on teaching and learning pronunciation. The topics were the effects of transient visual feedback on increasing pitch variation in oral presentations (Hincks & Edlund, 2009), the effects of computer-assisted pronunciation readings on ESL learners' suprasegmental factors and overall comprehensibility (Tanner & Landon, 2009), and the role of podcasting in developing students' pronunciation (Ducate & Lomicka, 2009), and the software development for pronunciation practice and feedback (Warren, Elgort, & Crabbe, 2009). Work on vocabulary has continued as well. It examined the effects of different types of treatments and interventions, including the effects of multimedia glosses on L2 text comprehension and vocabulary learning (Yanguas, 2009), the effect of input modality (audio, video, and captions) on vocabulary acquisition (Sydorenko, 2010), and the effect of video game interactivity on L2 vocabulary recall (deHaan, Reed, & Kuwada, 2010). Stockwell's (2010) study is noteworthy due to integrating mobile phones for vocabulary activities. In terms of grammar, Sauro (2009) investigated the impact of two types of computer-mediated corrective feedback (reformulation and metalinguistic information) on developing L2 adult learners' grammar knowledge.

7. Computer-Mediated Communication (CMC)

Research on CMC has been varied and sophisticated. Asynchronous CMC has been utilized in different teaching and learning contexts. The researcher addressed diverse issues, such as the role of offline metalanguage talk in ACMC (Kitade, 2008), the assessment issues in asynchronous forums in EAP (Kol & Schcolnik, 2008), and the use of blogs (Sun, 2009; Sun & Chang, 2012; Yang, 2011). Regarding synchronous CMC, Collentine (2009) revealed learners' use of holistic language units in multimodal and task-based synchronous CMC, and Smith (2012) employed eye-tracking technology as a measure of noticing of explicit recast during task-based synchronous CMC. L2 learners' interaction in oral task-based synchronous CMC was examined by Yanguas (2010). Tandem language learning was also explored by several scholars (Bower & Kawaguchi, 2011; Kabata & Edasawa, 2011).

8. Collaborative Learning

In this category, attention has been given to telecollaboration, including a variety of issues. Ware and O'Dowd (2008) examined L2 learners' corrective feedback on their partners' use of the target language in telecollaboration. Vinagre and Muñoz (2011) illustrated the impact of computer-mediated corrective feedback on L2 accuracy development in telecollaborative exchanges. Helm, Guth, and Farrah (2012) qualitatively explored the impact of linguistic, technical, and educational hegemonies on the development of English learners in Hebron, Palestine, Padova, and Italy in a telecollaboration project. Fuchs, Hauck, and Müller-Hartmann (2012) explored learner autonomy through multiliteracy skills development in a task-based telecollaboration format. L. Lee's (2008) study dealt with a focus on form through collaborative scaffolding in export-to-novice interaction.

11.6 2013 – 2020: The Social Media Period

1. MALL Theory, Conceptualization, and Pedagogy

Lai (2013) focused on L2 learners' self-directed use of technology for learning purposes in Hong Kong. Based on survey results, Lai (2013) suggested that greater attention be given to attitudinal factors (e.g., language learning motivation, perceived usefulness of technology for learning, etc.) for promoting language learners' self-directed use of technology. Cerezo (2016) investigated computer-generated corrective feedback in Spanish language development with 52 learners at a university in the United States. The type and amount of computerized input-based practices were implemented for the L2 language improvement.

2. Social Network Services (SNS) and Smart Education

Interest in the use of social network services has increased with developing mobile technologies and social media tools. Kim, Rueckert, Kim, and Seo (2013) reported M.A. students' perceptions on the use of mobile devices and their experiences. Wang and Smith (2013) examined students' learning experiences in reading and grammar learning through mobile phones and suggested six criteria for successful mobile learning. Identity is one of the main issues in SNSs (Chen, 2013; Klimanova & Dembovskaya, 2013). Chen (2013) examined two multilingual writers' literacy practices in social networking communities, and Klimanova and Dembovskaya (2013) explored L2 identity and discourse in the social networking space in Russian. Some new cutting-edge technologies and tools have been implemented for L2 teaching and learning. Language learners' views on podcasting through iTunes U were explored by Rosell-Aguilar (2013). Lys (2013) utilized iPads for the oral proficiency development of advanced learners. Benson (2015) reported qualitative findings on commenting behaviors on the YouTube platform regarding how translanguaging interaction in comments triggers language and intercultural learning. Similarly, Kulavuz-Onal and Vásquez (2018) conducted research on translingual practice in a Facebook group. Isbell (2018) explored Korean online informal language learning (OILL) in the online community. Learner attitudes, usage, and progress in language learning social network sites were explored by Lin, Warschauer, and Blake (2016) through the survey and individual case study. Mompean and Fouz- González (2016) figured out whether utilizing Twitter could increase learner participation and had effects on the pronunciation of EFL students.

Figure 11.7 Social networking in schools
(https://www.teacherboards.co.uk/community/the-effects-of-social-media-in-student-teens/)

3. E-learning, Online Learning, and WBI

Effective and efficient language learning through various online environments has been an issue in L2 research for recent decades. The research conducted by Arndt and Woore (2018), for instance, compared two different online materials, including written blog posts and video blogs, in vocabulary learning. The findings reported that EFL learners could gain distinctive types of vocabulary knowledge through the two different media. Lee (2016) researched learner autonomy for four-skill-integrated tasks in online language courses at a beginning level. Lee (2019) showed the relationship between quantity and diversity of informal digital learning of English (IDLE) practices and language performances. Some studies examined online learning for young learners (Dooly, 2018; Hannibal Jensen, 2019). Dooly (2018) explored how young learners were engaged in language tasks through technology-enhanced learning environments. Hannibal Jensen (2019) examined young learners' motivation and their engagement in web-based L2 language learning.

4. Corpus

Corpus studies have specified with the sophisticated web search engines and the emergence of various corpus linguistics tools. Studies on corpus linguistics were mostly related as follows: 1) improving learners' L2 reading skills (Hadley & Chales, 2017); 2) developing L2 writing skills (Cotos, Link, & Huffman, 2017; Elgort, 2017; Yoon, 2016); 3) enhancing capabilities of communication in the target language (Bardovi-Harlig, Mossman, & Su, 2017; Furniss, 2016); 4) the benefits of corpus linguistics on building up vocabulary and grammar knowledge (Ackerley, 2017; Lee, Warshauer, & Lee, 2017; Li, 2017; Vyatkina, 2016); and lastly 5) teacher training (Guichon, 2017; Leńko-Szymańska, 2017). Corpus studies in L2 writing dealt with developing academic writing skills while indicating the need to help L2 learners be aware of a specific genre (Cotos, Link, & Huffman, 2017; Elgort, 2017; Yoon, 2016). Bardovi-Harlig, Mossman, and Su (2017) and Furniss (2016) reported how corpus linguistics affects the learners' awareness of pragmatics in the target language. Corpus studies on improving vocabulary and grammar knowledge were likely to using data-driven learning (Hadley & Charles, 2017; Leńko-Szymańska, 2017; Vyathkina, 2016), utilizing direct corpus on collocation competence in academic writing (Li, 2017), and employing concordance-based electronic glosses (Lee, Warschauer, & Lee, 2017).

5. Reading and Writing

A few studies on reading have been conducted in recent years. Of these, Park, Yang, and Hsieh (2014) examined L2 readers' information-seeking strategies and decision-making processes when they read online. Park and Warschauer (2016) showed how technology-enhanced syntactic enhancement affected L2 reading and writing development. On the other hand, research on writing has continued and flourished. Peer interaction has been highlighted in L2 writing; hence, research has looked at the details of online peer feedback and collaborative writing (AbuSeileek

& Abualsha'r, 2014; King, 2015; Saeed & Chazali, 2017; Yang & Meng, 2013; Yim & Warschauer, 2017). For example, Yang and Meng (2013) investigated the impact of online peer feedback training on students' text revision, and AbuSeileek and Abualsha'r (2014) did the effect of using computer-mediated corrective feedback on EFL learners' writing outcomes. Aydin and Yildiz (2014) adopted Wikis to promote collaborative writing in an EFL writing course in Istanbul, Turkey. Some other issues have been examined in L2 writing research. Li and Hegelheimer (2013) developed a web-based mobile application for grammar exercises and examined its effects on self-editing in L2 writing. Yoon and Jo (2014) compared the effectiveness and learning strategy use in corpus-based writing revision. Xu and Ding (2014) explored Chinese EFL writers' pausing patterns in an argumentative writing task with the help of software programs (Inputlog 4.0 and Camtasia 6.0). Dzekoe (2017) depicted how multimodal composing activities influenced ESL students' self-revision in academic writing. Gao and Ma (2019) investigated the effects of automated metalinguistic corrective feedback on L2 writing development (See Appendix 1 for more research about reading and writing in LLT journal).

6. Listening and Speaking

Studies on L2 listening and speaking skills development have been conducted by using video sources. For example, Koyama, Sun, and Ockey (2016) investigated the effects of a preview (question stem and answer option) on video-based multiple-choice formats in assessing listening comprehension with English learners in Japan. Gass, Winke, Isbell, and Ahn (2019) explored how video captions assisted language learners' comprehension based on *multimedia theory*, focusing on working memory and eye-tracking study. Tseng and Yeh (2019) focused on the impact of video and written feedback in speaking practices.

7. Pronunciation, Vocabulary, and Grammar

Research on three subskills has continued. First, in terms of pronunciation, Olson (2014) showed a systematic analysis of the effectiveness of a visual feedback paradigm for segmental production. Qian, Chukharev-Hudilainen, and Levis (2018) suggested a system for segmental perceptual training for phonological perception with positive evidence from Russian-speaking English learners. Second, vocabulary research has been varied, including the relationships among anonymity, motivation, participation in discussion, and L2 vocabulary learning in synchronous and asynchronous online environments (Li & Cummins, 2019; Polat, Mancilla, &

Mahalingappa, 2013), online strategy instruction for the integration of dictionary skills into language awareness (Ranalli, 2013), the effects of captioning on video comprehension and incidental vocabulary learning (Perez, Peters, Clarebout, & Desmet, 2014), form-focused approaches through podcasts in L2 vocabulary classes (Marefat & Hassanzadeh, 2016), the effects of different types of gloss presentation (i.e., L2 definition, aural, and video animation) in vocabulary learning (Ramezanali & Faez, 2019), the relationship between playing commercial-off-the-shelf games and L2 vocabulary learning (Sundqvist, 2019). Lastly, in terms of grammar, Cornillie, Van Den Noortgate, Van Den Branden, and Desmet (2017) examined English grammar automaticity by exploiting mini-games and tracking L2 learners' behaviors.

8. Computer-Mediated Communication (CMC)

CMC continues to be a significant concern in MALL research. McNeil (2014) explored sources of foreign language anxiety in an oral asynchronous CMC environment. Monteiro (2014) investigated the effects of corrective feedback (metalinguistic feedback and recast) and focused tasks on developing L2 knowledge during video conferencing. Tare, Golonka, Vatz, Bonilla, Crooks, and Strong (2014) analyzed the outcomes from two types of out-of-class activities (interactive chat and independent writing). Interlanguage errors in synchronous and asynchronous communications with computer-aided analysis were identified by McDonald, García-Carbonel, and Carot-Sierra (2013). Chinese EFL teachers' interaction and socio-cognitive presence in synchronous CMC were explored by Wu and Zhang (2014). Fong, Lin, and Engle (2016) examined the uptake of positioning statements through online conversations. Golonka, Tare, and Bonilla (2017) explored peer-to-peer interactions through text chat to scrutinize what types of interaction occurred in text chat, presenting the more significant language gains. Yanguas and Bergin (2018) compared language-related episodes (LREs) in two different tasks (jigsaw and dictogloss) and two different modes (video SCMC and audio SCMC) in terms of the results in a number, focus, and outcome, respectively. Moreover, there have been CMC studies related to task-based language teaching (TBLT) (Balaman, 2018; Granena, 2016; Ziegler, 2018). Balaman (2018), for example, explored L2 learners' task engagement processes through online environments by observing context-specific learner interaction. Ziegler (2018) investigated what and how learners make plans and use those in pre-task planning through SCMC (see Appendix 1 for more research concerning CMC).

9. Collaborative Learning

Studies in LLT regarding collaborative learning have focused on collaborative writing in online environments. Bikowski and Vithanage (2016) researched the effects of collaborative writing in a web-based context on developing individual L2 writing skills at a university in the United States. Li and Zhu (2017) showed L2 learners' dynamic interaction when performing two writing tasks (a research proposal and an annotated bibliography) in a wiki site with the 12 students enrolled in an EAP writing course. Hsu and Lo (2018) also revealed collaborative writing in the wiki-based context with the 52 learners of English at a Taiwanese university.

10. Teacher Education

The roles of language teachers have been changed as new technologies have been implemented in language classes. *LLT* published a special issue on teacher education and CALL in 2015. This issue included various topics of teacher education and CALL, such as in-service language teachers' training to telecollaboration (O'Dowd, 2015), ESL teacher training in the 3D virtual world (Kozlova & Priven, 2015), teachers' perspectives on their learning from a CALL teacher education program (Chao, 2015), EFL teachers' knowledge and competencies of CALL (Liu & Kleinsasser, 2015), the impact of a CALL teacher education workshop (Tai, 2015), foreign language teachers' perceptions of the affordances of two CMC tools (Haines, 2015), pre-service English teachers' awareness on digital literacy and fair and safe use of digital materials (Shin, 2015), and how regular digital literacy practices influenced teachers' professional development on teaching with technologies. (Tour, 2015).

11. Telecollaboration

In this section, telecollaboration, which emphasizes developing intercultural competence and language abilities through web-based interaction, is a primary concern. Cunningham (2017) researched request production in web conferences between L1 and L2 speakers of German. In 2019, the LLT journal published a special issue on telecollaboration. Cunningham (2019) explored L2 learners' performances concerning content knowledge on the genre-specific 'oral interview' through SCMC. Lee and Song (2019) compared three different learning conditions (i.e., a study abroad, telecollaboration, and on-campus language study) on developing intercultural communicative competence (ICC) regarding cognitive, affective, and behavioral aspects. Oskoz and Gimno-Sanz (2019) researched the telecollaboration between Spanish and US students concerning expressing their ideological positions in online discussions during one semester. Some studies on telecollaboration cover teacher education (Fuchs, 2019; Grau & Turula, 2019). Fuchs (2019) examined critical incidents of backdrops in telecollaboration on social media between English learners in Hong Kong and student teachers in Germany. Grau and Turula (2019) revealed how pre-service teachers could be successful telecollaboraters, investigating Polish and German students' perceptions of intercultural competences, attitudes, and beliefs as follow-up research of O'Dowd (2015).

Figure 11.8 Telecollaboration
(https://www.anandtech.com/show/12766/microsoft-announces-the-surface-hub-2)

12. Assessment and Testing

Long, Shin, Geeslin, and Willis (2018) testified Bachman's (2005) assessment use argument (AUA) to explore evidence regarding interpretations and utilization of the scores on a new Spanish language placement test. Matthews and Wijeyewardene (2018) revealed the relationship between automated computational evaluation and experienced human accessors in scoring L2 writing. Roussel and Galan (2018) investigated the impact of clicker-use in a legal German lecture, which had a dual focus on developing both language and content with French students of Law.

13. Courseware Design and Evaluation

The development of digital technology enables L2 researchers to examine digital textbooks in language classes. Bikowski and Casal (2018) explored the learning processes of L2 students and engagement by using customized digital textbooks on mobile devices with 13 students enrolled in a business English class at a university in the United States. It revealed how interaction with digital textbooks and mobile devices influenced students' learning processes analyzed by Throne's (2003) framework.

11.7 Conclusion

Language Learning & Technology (LLT) is one of the prestigious international journals, and its content varies from CALL and MALL theory and principles to language skill development and teacher education with the latest technology. It can provide the teachers, learners, and researchers with wide-ranging perspectives in second language learning and CALL and MALL. The journal articles introduce the world-wide trends and issues of CALL and MALL, such as software, culture, Internet, WBI, CAT, CMC, and blended learning. For example, there were many studies on the introduction of technology and software as new tools of teaching and learning in the first period (1997-2002), so called the software period. In the last period (2013-2020), called the social media period, research was conducted examining the perspectives and effects of applying new technologies to language classes such as smartphones, SNS, apps, and mobile networking.

The overview of such journal articles can guide teachers and researchers and allow them to make field-specific applications in domestic arenas. Teachers, learners, and researchers should keep track of the trends and issues of CALL and MALL in *LLT* and other prestigious international journals overseas and apply them to their practices in FLT&L.

Tasks for Study and Discussion

- Find out about 10 articles (5 quantitative and 5 qualitative research articles) related to your research topic from *LLT* journal articles. Work individually, and then share your work with your partners.

  1) Describe the purposes, research questions, main methods, and conclusion of the articles briefly.
  2) Describe how they relate to your study.

Appendices

Appendix 1 List of Publications in the 1980s – Mid-1990s

The 1980s – Mid-1990s	
The advent of computers for FLT&L	• Ahmad, K., Corbett, G., Rogers, M., & Sussex, R. (1985). *Computers, language learning and language teaching*. Cambridge: Cambridge University Press. • Higgins, J., & Johns, T. (1984). *Computers in language learning*. London: Collins ELT. • O'Shea, T., & Self, J. (1983). *Learning and teaching with computers*. Brighton, Sussex: Harvester Press. • Pennington, M. C. (1991). The Road Ahead: A forward-looking view of computers in language learning. *Computer Assisted Language Learning*, *4*, 3-19. • Hainline, D. (1987). Computers in language instruction - trends and possibilities. In D. Hainline (Ed.), *New developments in computer-assisted language learning* (pp. 1-8). London: Croom Helm. • Hope, G. R., Taylor, H. F., & Pusack, J. P. (1984). *Using computers in teaching foreign languages*. Englewood Cliffs, New Jersey: Prentice-Hall. • Zettersten, A. (1986). *New technologies in language learning*. Oxford: Pergamon. • Chapelle, C. A., & Jamieson, J. (1989). Research trends in computer-assisted language learning. In M. C. Pennington (Ed.), *Teaching languages with computers* (pp. 47-60). La Jolla: Athelstan. • Hardisty, D., & Windeatt, S. (1989). *CALL*. Oxford: Oxford University Press. • Jones, C., & Fortescue, S. (1987). *Using computers in the language classroom*. Harlow, Essex: Longman. • Kenning, M. J., & Kenning, M. M. (1983). *Introduction to computer assisted language teaching*. Oxford: Oxford University Press. • Last, R. (1984). *Language teaching and the microcomputer*. Oxford: Basil Blackwell.

The advent of computers for FLT&L	• Stevens, V. (1989). A direction for CALL: from behavioristic to humanistic courseware. In M. C. Pennington (Ed.), *Teaching languages with computers*, (pp. 31-44). La Jolla: Athelstan. • Rich, T. (1991). Computer technology and education: past performance and future promise. *Educational & Training Technology International, 28*, 147-53.
The convergence of technologies	• Phillips, M. (1985). Educational technology in the next decade: an ELT perspective. In C. Brumfit, M. Phillips, & P. Skehan (Eds.), *Computers in English language teaching. ELT Documents 122* (pp. 99-120). Oxford: Pergamon. • Pennington, M. C. (1989). Applications of computers in the development of speaking and listening proficiency. In M. C. Pennington (Ed.), *Teaching Languages With Computers* (pp. 99-122). La Jolla: Athelstan. • Pennington, M. C. (1991). The Road ahead: A forward-looking view of computers in language learning. *Computer Assisted Language Learning, 4,* 3-19. • Fox, J. (1990). A microcomputer-based approach to training in second language reading skills. *Computer-Assisted Language Learning, 1*, 29-40. • Laurillard, D. (1987). The problems and possibilities of interactive video. In A. Jones, E. Scanlon, & T. O'Shea (Eds.), *The computer revolution in education: New technologies for distance* (pp. 129-142). Brighton, Sussex: Harvest Press.
The application of artificial intelligence (AI)	• Phillips, M. (1985). Educational technology in the next decade: an ELT perspective. In C. Brumfit, M. Phillips, & P. Skehan (Eds.), *Computers in English language teaching. ELT Documents 122* (pp. 99-120). Oxford: Pergamon. • Winston, P. H. (1987). An introduction to artificial intelligence. In E. Scanlon & T. O'Shea (Eds.), *Educational computing* (pp. 181-192). Chichester: John Wiley and Sons. • Dever, S. Y., & Pennington, M. C. (1989). Computer capabilities underlying computer-learner interaction. In M. C. Pennington (Ed.), *Teaching languages with computers* (pp. 11-28). La Jolla: Athelstan. • Barchan, J. (1986). New approaches to computer aided language learning. In K. C. Cameron, W. S. Dodd, & S. P. Q. Rahtz (Eds.), *Computers and modern language studies* (pp. 93-99). Chichester: Ellis Horwood Ltd.

New information technology	• Rich, T. (1991). Computer technology and education: past performance and future promise. *Educational & Training Technology International, 28*, 147-53. • Garrett, N. (1991). Technology in the service of language learning: trends and issues. *The Modern Language Journal, 75*, 74-98. • Feurzeig, W. (1988). Apprentice tools: students as practitioners. In R. S. Nickerson & P. P. Zodhiates (Eds.), *Technology in education: Looking toward 2020* (pp. 97-120). Hillsdale, New Jersey: REA.
The development of existing media technologies	• Knezek, G., Miyashita, K., & Sakamoto, T. (1993). Cross-cultural similarities in attitudes toward computers and the implications for teacher education. *Journal of Information Technology for Teacher Education, 2*, 193-204. • Licklider, J. C. R. (1987). Information technology, education and the American future. In E. Scanlon & T. O'Shea (Eds.), *Educational computing* (pp. 253-270). Chichester: John Wiley and Sons.
The integration of media technologies	• Hill, B. (1991). *Making the most of satellites and interactive video.* London: CILT. • Fox, J., Matthews, A., Matthews, C., & Rope, A. (1990). *Educational technology in modern language learning.* Sheffield: Training Agency.

Appendix 2 The Chronological Table of *LLT*

The Software Period (1998-2002)	
MALL Theory, Conceptualization, and Pedagogy	• Ayoun, D. (2000). Web-based elicitation tasks in SLA research. *Language Learning & Technology, 3*(2), 77-98. • Chapelle, C. A. (1997). Call in the year 2000: Still in search of research paradigms? *Language Learning & Technology, 1*(1), 19-43. • DuFon, M. A. (2002). Video recording in ethnographic SLA research: Some issues of validity in data collection. *Language Learning & Technology, 6*(1), 40-59. • Hegelheimer, V., & Chapelle, C. A. (2000). Methodological issues in research on learner-computer interactions in CALL. *Language Learning & Technology*, *4*(1), 41-59. • Hulstign, J. H. (2000). The use of computer technology in experimental studies of second language acquisition: A survey of some techniques and some ongoing studies. *Language Learning & Technology*, *3*(2), 32-43. • Ortega, L. (1997). Processes and outcomes in networked classroom interaction: Defining the research agenda for L2 computer-assisted classroom discussion. *Language Learning & Technology*, *1*(1), 82-93. • Pass, J. L. (1998). Design and evaluation of the user interface of foreign language multimedia software: A cognitive approach. *Language Learning & Technology*, 2(1)35-45. • Stepp-Greany, J. (2002). Student perceptions on language learning in a technological environment: Implications for the new millennium. *Language Learning & Technology*, *6*(1), 165-180. • Weasenforth, D., Biesenbach-Lucas, S., & Meloni, C. (2002). Realizing constructivist objectives through collaborative technologies: Threaded discussions. *Language Learning & Technology*, *6*(3), 58-86.
E-Learning, Online Learning and WBI	• Belz, J. A. (2002). Social dimensions of telecollaborative foreign language study. *Language Learning & Technology*, *6*(1), 60-81. • Lamy, M. N., & Goodfellow, R. (1999). "Reflective Conversation" in the virtual language classroom. *Language Learning & Technology*, *2*(2), 43-61. • Osuna, M. M., & Meskill, C. (1998). Using the World Wide Web to integrate Spanish language and culture: A pilot study. *Language Learning & Technology*, *1*(2), 71-92.

Listening and Speaking	• Hoven, D. (1999). A model for listening and viewing comprehension in multimedia environments. *Language Learning & Technology, 3*(1), 88-103.
Reading and Writing	• Chun, D. M., & Plass, J. L. (1997). Research on text comprehension in multimedia environments. *Language Learning & Technology, 1*(1), 60-81. • Lomicka, L. (1998). "To gloss or not to gloss": An investigation of reading comprehension online. *Language Learning & Technology, 1*(2), 41-50.
Pronunciation, Vocabulary and Grammar	• Al-Seghayer, K. (2001). The effect of multimedia annotation modes on L2 vocabulary acquisition: A comparative study. *Language Learning & Technology, 5*(1), 202-232. • Collentine, J. (2000). Insights into the construction of grammatical knowledge provided by user-behavior tracking technologies. *Language Learning & Technology, 3*(2), 44-57. • De Ridder, I. (2002). Visible or invisible links: Does the highlighting of hyperlinks affect incidental vocabulary learning, text comprehension, and the reading process. *Language Learning & Technology, 6*(1), 123-146. • Eskenazi, M. (1999). Using automatic speech processing for foreign language pronunciation tutoring: Some issues and a prototype. *Language Learning & Technology, 2*(2), 62-76. • Ghadirian, S. (2002). Providing controlled exposure to target vocabulary through the screening and arranging of texts. *Language Learning & Technology, 6*(1), 147-164. • Groot, P. J. (2000). Computer assisted second language vocabulary acquisition. *Language Learning & Technology, 4*(1), 60-81. • Laufer, B. & Hill, M. (2000). What lexical information do l2 learners select in a call dictionary and how does it affect word retention? *Language Learning & Technology, 3*(2), 58-76. • Nagata, N. (1998). Input vs. output practice in educational software for second language acquisition. *Language Learning & Technology, 1*(2), 23-40. • Nikolova, O. R. (2002). Effects of students' participation in authoring of multimedia materials on student acquisition of vocabulary. *Language Learning & Technology, 6*(1), 100-122. • Wood, J. (2001). Can software support children's vocabulary development? *Language Learning & Technology, 5*(1), 166-201.

Literacy	• Kasper, L. F. (2000). New technologies, new literacies: Focus discipline research and ESL learning communities. *Language Learning & Technology*, *4*(2), 105-128. • Kramsch, C. (2000). Authenticity and authorship in the computer-mediated acquisition of L2 literacy. *Language Learning & Technology*, *4*(2), 78-104. • Murray, D. E. (2000). Changing technologies, changing literacy communities? *Language Learning & Technology*, *4*(2), 43-58. • Richards, C. (2000). Hypermedia, internet communication, and the challenge of redefining literacy in the electronic age. *Language Learning & Technology*, *4*(2), 59-77.
Computer-Mediated Communication (CMC)	• Biesenbach-Lucas, S., & Weasenforth, D. (2001). E-mail and word processing in the ESL classroom: How the medium affects the message. *Language Learning & Technology*, *5*(1), 135-165. • Blake, R. (2000). Computer mediated communication: A window on L2 Spanish interlanguage. *Language Learning & Technology*, *4*(1), 120-136. • González-Bueno, M. (1998). The effects of electronic mail on Spanish L2 discourse. *Language Learning & Technology*, *1*(2), 55-70. • Sengupta, S. (2001). Exchanging ideas with peers in network-based classrooms: An aid or a pain. *Language Learning & Technology*, *5*(1), 103-134. • Sotillo, S. M. (2000). Discourse functions and syntactic complexity in synchronous and asynchronous communication. *Language Learning & Technology*, *4*(1), 82-119. • Toyoda, E., & Harrison, R. (2002). Categorization of text chat communication between learners and native speakers of Japanese. *Language Learning & Technology*, *6*(1), 82-99.
Courseware Design and Evaluation	• Chun, D. M. (1998). Signal analysis software for teaching discourse intonation. *Language Learning & Technology*, *2*(1), 61-77. • Ehsani, F., & Knodt, E. (1998). Speech technology in computer-aided language learning: Strengths and limitations of a new CALL paradigm. *Language Learning & Technology*, *2*(1), 45-60.

Assessment and Testing	• Brown, J. D. (1997). Computers in language testing: Present research and some future directions. *Language Learning & Technology*, *1*(1), 44-59. • Dunkel, P. (1999). Considerations in developing or using second/foreign language proficiency computer-adaptive tests. *Language Learning & Technology*, *2*(2), 77-93. • Kenyon, D. M., & Malabonga, V. (2001). Comparing examinee attitudes toward computer-assisted and other oral proficiency assessments. *Language Learning & Technology*, *5*(2), 60-83. • Roever, C. (2001). Web-based language testing. *Language Learning & Technology*, *5*(2), 84-94. • Sawaki, Y. (2001). Comparability of conventional and computerized tests of reading in a second language. *Language Learning & Technology*, *5*(2), 38-59.
Teacher Education	• Doering, A., & Beach, R. (2002). Preservice English teachers acquiring literacy practices through technology tools. *Language Learning & Technology, 6*(3), 127-146. • Egbert, J., Paulus, T. M., & Nakamichi, Y. (2002). The impact of CALL instruction on classroom computer use: A foundation for rethinking technology in teacher education. *Language Learning & Technology*, *6*(3), 108-126. • Meskill, C., Mossop, J., DiAngelo, S., & Pasquale, R. K. (2002). Expert and novice teachers talking technology: Precepts, concepts, and misconcepts. *Language Learning & Technology*, *6*(3), 46-57.
Corpus	• Fuentes, A. C. (2001). Lexical behaviour in academic and technical corpora: implications for ESP development. *Language Learning & Technology, 5*(3), 106-129. • John, E. S. (2001). A case for using a parallel corpus and concordancer for beginners of a foreign language. *Language Learning & Technology, 5*(3), 185-203. • Kennedy, C., & Miceli, T. (2001). An evaluation of intermediate students' approaches to corpus investigation. *Language Learning & Technology, 5*(3), 77-90. • Lixun, W. (2001). Exploring parallel concordancing in English and Chinese. *Language Learning & Technology*, *5*(3), 174-184. • Thompson, P., & Tribble, C. (2001). Looking at citations: Using corpora in English for academic purposes. *Language Learning & Technology, 5*(3), 91-105.

The Internet Period (2003-2007)	
MALL Theory, Conceptualization and Pedagogy	• Levy, M., & Kennedy, C. (2004). A task-cycling pedagogy using stimulated reflection and audio-conferencing in foreign language learning. *Language Learning & Technology*, *8*(2), 50-68. • Morris, F. (2005). Child-to-child interaction and corrective feedback in a computer mediated L2 class. *Language Learning & Technology*, *9*(1), 29-45. • Parks, S., Huot, D., Hamers, J., & Lemonnier, F. H. (2003). Crossing boundaries: Multimedia technology and pedagogical innovation in a high school class. *Language Learning & Technology*, *7*(1), 28-45.
E-Learning, Online Learning and WBI	• Chen, J., Belkada, S., & Okamoto, T. (2004). How a web-based course facilitates acquisition of English for academic purposes. *Language Learning & Technology, 8*(2), 33-49. • Doughty, C., & Long, M. (2003). Optimal psycholinguistic environments for distance foreign language learning. *Language Learning & Technology, 7*(3), 50-80. • Pawan, F., Paulus, T. M., Yalcin, S., & Chang, C. F. (2003). Online learning: Patterns of engagement and interaction among in-service teachers. *Language Learning & Technology*, *7*(3), 119-140. • Reeder, K., Macfadyen, L. P., Roche, J., & Chase, M. (2004). Negotiating cultures in cyberspace: Participation patterns and problematics. *Language Learning & Technology, 8*(2), 88-105. • Strambi, A., & Bouvet, E. J. (2003). Flexibility and interaction at a distance: A mixed-model environment for language learning. *Language Learning & Technology, 7*(3), 81-101. • Tudini, V. (2003). Using native speakers in chat. *Language Learning & Technology*, *7*(3), 141-159. • Wang, Y. (2004). Supporting synchronous distance language learning with desktop videoconferencing. *Language Learning & Technology*, *8*(3), 90-121.
Listening and Speaking	• Barr, D., Leakey, J., & Ranchoux, A. (2005). Told like it is! An evaluation of an integrated oral development project. *Language Learning & Technology*, *9*(3), 55-78.

Listening and Speaking	• Grgurović, M., & Hegelheimer, V. (2007). Help options and multimedia listening: Students' use of subtitles and the transcript. *Language Learning & Technology, 11*(1), 45-66. • Handley, Z., & Hamel, M. J. (2005). Establishing a methodology for benchmarking speech synthesis for computer-assisted language learning (CALL). *Language Learning & Technology*, *9*(3), 99-120. • Jepson, K. (2005). Conversations and negotiated interaction in text and voice chat rooms. *Language Learning & Technology*, *9*(3), 79-98. • Payne, J. S., & Ross, B. M. (2005). Synchronous CMC, working memory, and L2 oral proficiency development. *Language Learning & Technology*, *9*(3), 35-54. • Verdugo, D. R., & Belmonte, I. A. (2007). Using digital stories to improve listening comprehension with Spanish young learners of English. *Language Learning & Technology*, *11*(1), 87-101. • Volle, L. M. (2005). Analyzing oral skills in voice e-mail and online interviews. *Language Learning & Technology*, *9*(3), 146-163.
Reading and Writing	• Bloch, J. (2007). Abdullah's blogging: A generation 1.5 student enters the blogosphere. *Language Learning & Technology*, *11*(2), 128-141. • Chen, C. F. E. (2006). The development of e-mail literacy: From writing to peers to writing to authority figures. *Language Learning & Technology*, *10*(2), 35-55. • Lan, Y. J., Sung, Y. T., & Chang, K. E. (2007). A mobile-device-supported peer-assisted learning system for collaborative early EFL reading. *Language Learning & Technology*, *11*(3), 130-151. • Lin, H., & Chen, T. (2007). Reading authentic EFL text using visualization and advance organizers in a multimedia learning environment. *Language Learning & Technology*, *11*(3), 83-106. • Murphy, P. (2007). Reading comprehension exercises online: The effects of feedback, proficiency and interaction. *Language Learning & Technology*, *11*(3), 107-129.

Pronunciation, Vocabulary and Grammar	• Bloch, J. (2007). Abdullah's blogging: A generation 1.5 student enters the blogosphere. *Language Learning & Technology, 11*(2), 128-141. • Chen, C. F. E. (2006). The development of e-mail literacy: From writing to peers to writing to authority figures. *Language Learning & Technology, 10*(2), 35-55. • Horst, M., Cobb, T., & Nicolae, I. (2005). Expanding academic vocabulary with an interactive on-line database. *Language Learning & Technology, 9*(2), 90-110. • Huang, H. T., & Liou, H. C. (2007). Vocabulary learning in an automated graded reading program. *Language Learning & Technology, 11*(3), 64-82. • Jones, L. (2004). Testing L2 vocabulary recognition and recall using pictorial and written test items. *Language Learning & Technology, 8*(3), 122-143. • Peters, E. (2007). Manipulating L2 learners' online dictionary use and its effect on L2 word retention. *Language Learning & Technology, 11*(2), 36-58. • Yoshii, M. (2006). L1 and L2 glosses: Their effects on incidental vocabulary learning. *Language Learning & Technology, 10*(3), 85-101.
Computer-Mediated Communication (CMC)	• Biesenbach-Lucas, S. (2005). Communication topics and strategies in e-mail consultation: Comparison between American and international university students. *Language Learning & Technology, 9*(2), 24-46. • Biesenbach-Lucas, S. (2007). Students writing emails to faculty: An examination of e-politeness among native and non-native speakers of English. *Language Learning & Technology, 11*(2), 59-81. • Fitze, M. (2006). Discourse and participation in ESL face-to-face and written electronic conferences. *Language Learning & Technology, 10*(1), 67-86. • Jiang, W., & Ramsay, G. (2005). Rapport-building through CALL in teaching Chinese as a foreign language: An exploratory study. *Language Learning & Technology, 9*(2), 47-63. • Vandergriff, I. (2006). Negotiating common ground in computer-mediated versus face-to-face discussions. *Language Learning & Technology, 10*(1), 110-138. • Warner, C. N. (2004). It's just a game, right? Types of play in foreign language CMC. *Language Learning & Technology, 8*(2), 69-87.

Collaborative Learning	• Arnold, N., & Ducate, L. (2006). Future foreign language teachers' social and cognitive collaboration in an online environment. *Language Learning & Technology, 10*(1), 42. • Belz, J. A. (2003). Linguistic perspectives on the development of intercultural competence in telecollaboration. *Language Learning & Technology*, *7*(2), 68-117. • Kötter, M. (2003). Negotiation of meaning and codeswitching in online tandems. *Language Learning & Technology*, *7*(2), 145-172. • O'Dowd, R. (2003). Understanding the "other side": Intercultural learning in a Spanish-English e-mail exchange. *Language Learning & Technology, 7*(2), 118-144. • Thorne, S. L. (2003). Artifacts and cultures-of-use in intercultural communication. *Language Learning & Technology*, *7*(2), 38-67.
Courseware Design and Evaluation	• González-Lloret, M. (2003). Designing task-based CALL to promote interaction: En busca de esmeraldas. *Language Learning & Technology*, *7*(1), 86-104. • Richards, C. (2005). The design of effective ICT-supported learning activities: Exemplary models, changing requirements, and new possibilities. *Language Learning & Technology*, *9*(1), 60-79.

The Mobile Period (2008-2012)	
MALL Theory, Conceptualization, and Pedagogy	• Collentine, K. (2011). Learner autonomy in a task-based 3D world and production. *Language Learning & Technology, 15*(3), 50-67. • Hafner, C. A., & Miller, L. (2011). Fostering learner autonomy in English for science: A collaborative digital video project in a technological learning environment. *Language Learning & Technology, 15*(3), 68-86. • Lee, L. (2011). Blogging: Promoting learner autonomy and intercultural competence through study abroad. *Language Learning & Technology, 15*(3), 87-109. • Nielson, K. B. (2011). Self-study with language learning software in the workplace: What happens. *Language Learning & Technology, 15*(3), 110-129.
E-learning, Online Learning and WBI	• Chen, N. S., Hsieh, S. W., & Kinshuk, A. (2008). Effects of short-term memory and content representation type on mobile language learning. *Language Learning & Technology, 12*(3), 93-113.

Blended Learning	•	Blake, R., Wilson, N. L., Cetto, M., & Pardo-Ballester, C. (2008). Measuring oral proficiency in distance, face-to-face, and blended classrooms. *Language Learning & Technology, 12*(3), 114-127. • Hinkelman, D., & Gruba, P. (2012). Power within blended language learning programs in Japan. *Language Learning & Technology, 16*(2), 46-64.
Computer-Mediated Communication (CMC)	•	Bower, J., & Kawaguchi, S. (2011). Negotiation of meaning and corrective feedback in Japanese/English eTandem. *Language Learning & Technology, 15*(1), 41-71. • Collentine, K. (2009). Learner use of holistic language units in multimodal, task-based synchronous computer-mediated communication. *Language Learning & Technology, 13*(2), 68-87. • Kabata, K., & Edasawa, Y. (2011). Tandem language learning through a cross-cultural keypal project. *Language Learning & Technology, 15*(1), 104-121. • Kitade, K. (2008). The role of offline metalanguage talk in asynchronous computer-mediated communication. *Language Learning & Technology, 12*(1), 64-84. • Kol, S., & Schcolnik, M. (2008). Asynchronous forums in EAP: Assessment issues. *Language Learning & Technology, 12*(2), 49-70. • Smith, B. (2012). Eye tracking as a measure of noticing: A study of explicit recasts in SCMC. *Language Learning & Technology, 16*(3), 53-81. • Sun, Y. C. (2009). Voice blog: An exploratory study of language learning. *Language Learning & Technology, 13*(2), 88-103. • Sun, Y. C., & Chang, Y. J. (2012). Blogging to learn: Becoming EFL academic writers through collaborative dialogues. *Language Learning & Technology, 16*(1), 43-61. • Yang, Y. F. (2011). Learner interpretations of shared space in multilateral English blogging. *Language Learning & Technology, 15*(1), 122-146. • Yanguas, Í. (2010). Oral computer-mediated interaction between L2 learners: It's about time. *Language Learning & Technology, 14*(3), 72-93.

Computer-Mediated Communication (CMC)	• Fuchs, C., Hauck, M., & Müller-Hartmann, A. (2012). Promoting learner autonomy through multiliteracy skills development in cross-institutional exchanges. *Language Learning & Technology*, *16*(3), 82-102.
Collaborative Learning	• Lee, L. (2008). Focus-on-form through collaborative scaffolding in expert-to-novice online interaction. *Language Learning & Technology*, *12*(3), 53-72. • Vinagre, M., & Muñoz, B. (2011). Computer-mediated corrective feedback and language accuracy in telecollaborative exchanges. *Language Learning & Technology*, *15*(1), 72-103. • Ware, P. D., & O'Dowd, R. (2008). Peer feedback on language form in telecollaboration. *Language Learning & Technology*, *12*(1), 43-63.
Listening and Speaking	• Cross, J. (2011). Comprehending news videotexts: The influence of the visual content. *Language Learning & Technology*, *15*(2), 44-68. • Winke, P., Gass, S., & Sydorenko, T. (2010). The effects of captioning videos used for foreign language listening activities. *Language Learning & Technology*, *14*(1), 65-86.
Reading and Writing	• Chen, C. F. E., & Cheng, W. Y. E. (2008). Beyond the design of automated writing evaluation: Pedagogical practices and perceived learning effectiveness in EFL writing classes. *Language Learning & Technology*, *12*(2), 94-112. • Chen, Y. H., & Baker, P. (2010). Lexical bundles in L1 and L2 academic writing. *Language Learning & Technology*, *14*(2), 30-49. • Elola, I., & Oskoz, A. (2010). Collaborative writing: Fostering foreign language and writing conventions development. *Language Learning & Technology*, *14*(3), 51-71. • Kennedy, C., & Miceli, T. (2010). Corpus-assisted creative writing: Introducing intermediate Italian learners to a corpus as a reference resource. *Language Learning & Technology*, *14*(1), 28-44. • Kessler, G. (2009). Student-initiated attention to form in wiki-based collaborative writing. *Language Learning & Technology*, *13*(1), 79-95.

Reading and Writing	• Liang, M. Y. (2010). Using synchronous online peer response groups in EFL writing: Revision-related discourse. *Language Learning & Technology*, *14*(1), 45-64. • Yoon, H. (2008). More than a linguistic reference: The influence of corpus technology on L2 academic writing. *Language Learning & Technology*, *12*(2), 31-48.
Pronunciation, Vocabulary and Grammar	• deHaan, J., Reed, W. M., & Kuwada, K. (2010). The effect of interactivity with a music video game on second language vocabulary recall. *Language Learning & Technology*, *14*(2), 74-94. • Ducate, L., & Lomicka, L. (2009). Podcasting: An effective tool for honing language students' pronunciation? *Language Learning & Technology*, *13*(3), 66. • Hincks, R., & Edlund, J. (2009). Promoting increased pitch variation in oral presentations with transient visual feedback. *Language Learning & Technology*, *13*(3), 32-50. • Sauro, S. (2009). Computer-mediated corrective feedback and the development of L2 grammar. *Language Learning & Technology*, *13*(1), 96-120. • Stockwell, G. (2010). Using mobile phones for vocabulary activities: Examining the effect of platform. *Language Learning & Technology*, *14*(2), 95-110. • Sydorenko, T. (2010). Modality of input and vocabulary acquisition. *Language Learning & Technology*, *14*(2), 50-73. • Tanner, M. W., & Landon, M. M. (2009). The effects of computer-assisted pronunciation readings on ESL learners' use of pausing, stress, intonation, and overall comprehensibility. *Language Learning & Technology*, *13*(3), 51-65. • Warren, P., Elgort, I., & Crabbe, D. (2009). Comprehensibility and prosody ratings for pronunciation software development. *Language Learning & Technology*, *13*(3), 87-102. • Yanguas, I. (2009). Multimedia glosses and their effect on L2 text comprehension and vocabulary learning. *Language Learning & Technology*, *13*(2), 48-67.

The Social Media Period (2013-2020)	
MALL theory, Conceptualization, and Pedagogy	• Cerezo, L. (2016). Type and amount of input-based practice in CALI: The revelations of a triangulated research design. *Language Learning & Technology*, *20*(1), 100–123. • Lai, C. (2013). A framework for developing self-directed technology use for language learning. *Language Learning & Technology*, *17*(2), 100-122.
Social Network Service (SNS) and Smart Education	• Benson, P. (2015). Commenting to learn: Evidence of language and intercultural learning in comments on YouTube videos. *Language Learning & Technology* *19*(3), 88–105. • Chen, H. I. (2013). Identity practices of multilingual writers in social networking spaces. *Language Learning & Technology*, *17*(2), 143-170. • Isbell, D. R. (2018). Online informal language learning: Insights from a Korean learning community. *Language Learning & Technology*, *22*(3), 82–102. • Klimanova, L., & Dembovskaya, S. (2013). L2 identity, discourse, and social networking in Russian. *Language Learning & Technology*, *17*(1), 69-88. • Kulavuz-Onal, D., & Vásquez, C. (2018). "Thanks, shokran, gracias": Translingual practices in a Facebook group. *Language Learning & Technology*, *22*(1), 240–255. • Klimanova, L., & Dembovskaya, S. (2013). L2 identity, discourse, and social networking in Russian. *Language Learning & Technology*, *17*(1), 69-88. • Lin, C.-H., Warschauer, M., & Blake, R. (2016). Language learning through social networks: Perceptions and reality. *Language Learning & Technology*, *20*(1), 124–147. • Lys, F. (2013). The development of advanced learner oral proficiency using iPads. *Language Learning & Technology*, *17*(3), 94-116. • Mompean, J. A., & Fouz-González, J. (2016). Twitter-based EFL Pronunciation Instruction. *Language Learning & Technology*, *20*(1), 166–190. • Rosell-Aguilar, F. (2013). Podcasting for language learning through iTunes U: The learner's view. *Language Learning & Technology*, *17*(3), 74-93. • Wang, S., & Smith, S. (2013). Reading and grammar learning through mobile phones. *Language Learning & Technology*, *17*(3), 117-134.

E-learning, Online Learning and WBI	• Arndt, H. L., & Woore. R. (2018). Vocabulary learning from watching YouTube videos and reading blog posts. *Language Learning & Technology*, *22*(1), 124–142. • Dooly, M. (2018). "I do which the question": Students' innovative use of technology resources in the language classroom. *Language Learning & Technology*, *22*(1), 184–217. • Hannibal Jensen, S. (2019). Language learning in the wild: A young user perspective. *Language Learning & Technology*, *23*(1), 72–86. • Lee, J. S. (2019). Quantity and diversity of informal digital learning of English. *Language Learning & Technology*, *23*(1), 114–126. • Lee, L. (2016). Autonomous learning through task-based instruction in fully online language courses. *Language Learning & Technology*, *20*(2), 81–97.
Corpus	• Ackerley, K. (2017). Effects of corpus-based instruction on phraseology in learner English. *Language Learning & Technology*, *21*(3), 195–216. • Bardovi-Harlig, K., Mossman, S., & Su, Y. (2017). The effect of corpus-based instruction on pragmatic routines. *Language Learning & Technology*, *21*(3), 76–103. • Cotos, E., Link, S., & Huffman, S. (2017). Effects of technology on genre learning. *Language Learning & Technology*, *21*(3), 104–130. • Elgort, I. (2017). Blog posts and traditional assignments by first- and second-language writers. *Language Learning & Technology*, *21*(2), 52–72. • Furniss, E. A. (2016). Teaching the pragmatics of Russian conversation using a corpus-referred website. *Language Learning & Technology*, *20*(2), 38–60. • Guichon, N. (2017). Sharing a multimodal corpus to study webcam-mediated language teaching. *Language Learning & Technology*, *21*(1), 55–74. • Hadley, G., & Charles, M. (2017). Enhancing extensive reading with data-driven learning. *Language Learning & Technology*, *21*(3), 131–152 • Han, S., & Shin, J.-A. (2017). Teaching Google search techniques in an L2 academic writing context. *Language Learning & Technology*, *21*(3), 172–194. • Lee, H., Warschauer, M., & Lee, J. H. (2017). The effects of concordance-based electronic glosses on L2 vocabulary learning. *Language Learning & Technology*, *21*(2), 32–51.

Corpus	• Leńko-Szymańska, A. (2017). Training teachers in data-driven learning: Tackling the challenge. *Language Learning & Technology*, *21*(3), 217–241. • Li, S. (2017). Using corpora to develop learners' collocational competence. *Language Learning & Technology*, *21*(3), 153–171. • Vyatkina, N. (2016). Data-driven learning of collocations: Learner performance, proficiency, and perceptions. *Language Learning & Technology*, *20*(3), 159–179. • Yoon, C. (2016). Concordancers and dictionaries as problem-solving tools for ESL academic writing. *Language Learning & Technology*, *20*(1), 209–229.
Reading and Writing	• Abrams, Zs. I. (2019). Collaborative writing and text quality in Google Docs. *Language Learning & Technology*, 23(2), 22–42. • AbuSeileek, A., & Abualsha'r, A. (2014). Using peer computer-mediated corrective feedback to support EFL learners' writing. *Language Learning & Technology*, *18*(1), 76-95. • Dzekoe, R. (2017). Computer-based multimodal composing activities, self-revision, and L2 acquisition through writing. *Language Learning & Technology*, *21*(2), 73–95. • Gao, J., & Ma, S. (2019). The effect of two forms of computer-automated metalinguistic corrective feedback. *Language Learning & Technology*, *23*(2), 65–83. • King, B. W. (2015). Wikipedia writing as praxis: Computer-mediated socialization of second-language writers. *Language Learning & Technology, 19*(3), 106–123. • Li, Z., & Hegelheimer, V. (2013). Mobile-assisted grammar exercises: Effects on self-editing in L2 writing. *Language Learning & Technology*, *17*(3), 135-156. • Park, J., Yang, J. S., & Hsieh, Y. C. (2014). University level second language readers' online reading and comprehension strategies. *Language Learning & Technology*, *18*(3), 148-172. • Park, Y., & Warschauer, M. (2016). Syntactic enhancement and second language literacy: An experimental study. *Language Learning & Technology*, *20*(3), 180–199. • Xu, C., & Ding, Y. (2014). An exploratory study of pauses in computer-assisted EFL writing. *Language Learning & Technology*, *18*(3), 80-96.

Reading and Writing	• Saeed, M. A., & Ghazali, K. (2017). Asynchronous group review of EFL writing: Interactions and text revisions. *Language Learning & Technology, 21*(2), 200–226. • Yang, Y. F., & Meng, W. T. (2013). The effects of online feedback training on students' text revision. *Language Learning & Technology, 17*(2), 220-238. • Yim, S., & Warschauer, M. (2017). Web-based collaborative writing in L2 contexts: Methodological insights from text mining. *Language Learning & Technology, 21*(1), 146–165. • Yoon, H., & Jo, J. W. (2014). Direct and indirect access to corpora: An exploratory case study comparing students' error correction and learning strategy use in L2 writing. *Language Learning & Technology, 18*(1), 96-117.
Listening and Speaking	• Gass, S., Winke, P., Isbell, D. R., & Ahn, J. (2019). How captions help people learn languages: A working-memory, eye-tracking study. *Language Learning & Technology, 23*(2), 84–104. • Koyama, D., Sun, A., & Ockey, G. J. (2016). The effects of item preview on video-based multiple-choice listening assessments. *Language Learning & Technology, 20*(1), 148–165. • Tseng, S.-S., & Yeh, H.-C. (2019). The impact of video and written feedback on student preferences of English speaking practice. *Language Learning & Technology, 23*(2), 145–158.
Pronunciation, Vocabulary and Grammar	• Cornillie, F., Van Den Noortgate, W., Van den Branden, K., & Desmet, P. (2017). Examining focused L2 practice: From in vitro to in vivo. *Language Learning & Technology, 21*(1), 121–145. • Li, J., & Cummins, J. (2019). Effect of using texting on vocabulary instruction for English learners. *Language Learning & Technology, 23*(2), 43–64. • Marefat, F. & Hassanzadeh, M. (2016). Applying form-focused approaches to L2 vocabulary instruction through podcasts. *Language Learning & Technology, 20*(3), 107–127. • Okuno, T., & Hardison, D. M. (2016). Perception-production link in L2 Japanese vowel duration: Training with technology. *Language Learning & Technology, 20*(2), 61–80. • Olson, D. J. (2014). Benefits of visual feedback on segmental production in the L2 classroom. *Language Learning & Technology, 18*(3), 173-192.

Pronunciation, Vocabulary and Grammar	• Perez, M. M., Peters, E., Clarebout, G., & Desment, P. (2014). Effects of captioning on video comprehension and incidental vocabulary learning. *Language Learning & Technology*, *18*(1), 118-141. • Polat, N., Mancilla, R., & Mahalingappa, L. (2013). Anonymity and motivation in asynchronous discussions and L2 vocabulary learning. *Language Learning & Technology*, *17*(2), 57-74. • Qian, M., Chukharev-Hudilainen, E., & Levis, J. (2018). A system for adaptive high-variability segmental perceptual training: Implementation, effectiveness, transfer. *Language Learning & Technology*, *22*(1), 69–96. • Ramezanali, N., & Faez, F. (2019). Vocabulary learning and retention through multimedia glossing. *Language Learning & Technology*, *23*(2), 105–124. • Ranalli, J. (2013). Online strategy instruction for integrating dictionary skills and language awareness. *Language Learning & Technology*, *17*(2), 75-99. • Sundqvist, P. (2019). Commercial-off-the-shelf games in the digital wild and L2 learner vocabulary. *Language Learning & Technology*, *23*(1), 87–113.
Computer-Mediated Communication (CMC)	• Balaman, U. (2018). Task-induced development of hinting behaviors in online task-oriented L2 interaction. *Language Learning & Technology*, *22*(2), 95–115. • Coyle, Y., & Reverte, M. J. (2017). Children's interaction and lexical acquisition in text-based online chat. *Language Learning & Technology*, *21*(2), 179–199. • Dooly, M., & Sadler, R. (2016). Becoming little scientists: technology-enhanced project-based language learning. *Language Learning & Technology*, *20*(1), 54–78. • Fong, C. J., Lin, S., & Engle, A. R. (2016). Positioning identity in computer-mediated discourse among ESOL learners. *Language Learning & Technology*, *20*(3), 142–158. • Giguère, C., & Parks, S. (2018). Child-to-child interaction during eTandem ESL–FSL chat exchanges. *Language Learning & Technology*, *22*(3), 176–192. • Golonka, E. M., Tare, M., & Bonilla, C. (2017). Peer interaction in text chat: Qualitative analysis of chat transcripts. *Language Learning & Technology*, *21*(2), 157–178. • Granena, G. (2016). Individual versus interactive task-based performance through voice-based computer-mediated communication. *Language Learning & Technology*, *20*(3), 40–59.

Computer-Mediated Communication (CMC)	• Hsu, H.-C., & Lo, Y.-F. (2018). Using wiki-mediated collaboration to foster L2 writing performance. *Language Learning & Technology*, *22*(3), 103–123. • Lan, Y. J., Kan, Y. H., Sung, Y. T., & Chung, K. E. (2016). Oral-performance language tasks for CSL beginners in Second Life. *Language Learning & Technology*, *20*(3), 60–79. • McDonald, P., García-Carbonell, A., & Carot-Sierra, J. M. (2013). Computer learner corpora: Analysing interlanguage errors in synchronous and asynchronous communication. *Language Learning & Technology*, *17*(2), 36-56. • Messina Dahlberg, G., & Bagga-Gupta, S. (2016). Mapping languaging in digital spaces: Literacy practices at borderlands. *Language Learning & Technology*, *20*(3), 80–106. • McNeil, L. (2014). Ecological affordance and anxiety in an oral asynchronous computer-mediated environment. *Language Learning & Technology*, *18*(1), 142-159. • Tare, M., Golonka, E. M., Vatz, K., Bonilla, C. L., Crooks, C., & Strong, R. (2014). Effects of interactive chat versus independent writing on L2 learning. *Language Learning & Technology*, *18*(3), 208-227. • Wu, H., & Zhang, W. (2014). Chinese EFL teachers' social interaction, socio-cognitive presence in synchronous computer-mediated communication. *Language Learning & Technology, 18*(3), 228-254. • Wu, Z. (2018). Positioning (mis)aligned: The (un)making of intercultural asynchronous computer-mediated communication. *Language Learning & Technology*, *22*(2), 75–94. • Schreiber, B. R. (2015). "I am what I am": Multilingual identity and digital translanguaging. *Language Learning & Technology*, *19*(3), 69–87. • Yanguas, I., & Bergin, T. (2018). Focus on form in task-based L2 oral computer-mediated communication. *Language Learning & Technology*, *22*(3), 65–81. • Ziegler, N. (2018). Pre-task planning in L2 text-chat: Examining learners' process and performance. *Language Learning & Technology*, *22*(3), 193–213.
Collaborative Learning	• Bikowski, D., & Vithanage, R. (2016). Effects of web-based Collaborative writing on individual L2 writing development. *Language Learning & Technology*, *20*(1), 79–99. • Li, M., & Zhu, W. (2017). Explaining dynamic interactions in wiki-based collaborative writing. *Language Learning & Technology*, *21*(2), 96–120.

Teacher Education	• Chao, C. C. (2015). Rethinking transfer: Learning from call teacher education as consequential transition. *Language Learning & Technology, 19*(1), 102-118. • Haines, K. J. (2015). Learning to identify and actualize affordances in a new tool. *Language Learning & Technology, 19*(1), 165-180. • Kozlova, I., & Priven, D. (2015). ESL teacher training in 3D virtual worlds. *Language Learning & Technology, 19*(1), 83-101. • Kurek, M., & Müller-Hartmann, A. (2019). The formative role of teaching presence in blended Virtual Exchange. *Language Learning & Technology, 23*(3), 52–73. • O'Dowd, R. (2015). Supporting in-service language educators in learning to telecollaborate. *Language Learning & Technology, 19*(1), 63-82. • Shin, S. K. (2015). Teaching critical, ethical, and safe use of ICT to teachers. *Language Learning & Technology, 19*(1), 181-197. • Tai, S. J. D. (2015). From TPACK-in-action workshops to classrooms: CALL competency developed and integrated. *Language Learning & Technology, 19*(1), 139-164. • Tour, E. (2015). Digital mindsets: Teachers' technology use in personal life and teaching. *Language Learning & Technology, 19*(3), 124–139.
Telecollaboration	• Cunningham, D. J. (2017). Methodological innovation for the study of request production in telecollaboration. *Language Learning & Technology, 21*(1), 75–98. • Cunningham, D. J. (2019). Telecollaboration for content and language learning: A Genre-based approach. *Language Learning & Technology, 23*(3), 161–177. • Fuchs, C. (2019). Critical incidents and cultures-of-use in a Hong Kong–Germany telecollaboration. *Language Learning & Technology, 23*(3), 74–97. • Grau, M. K., & Turula, A. (2019). Experiential learning of telecollaborative competences in pre-service teacher education. *Language Learning & Technology, 23*(3), 98–115. • Lee, J. & Song, J. (2019). Developing intercultural competence through study abroad, telecollaboration, and on-campus language study. *Language Learning & Technology,* 23(3), 178–198. • Oskoz, A., & Gimeno-Sanz, A. (2019). Engagement and Attitude in Telecollaboration: Topic and cultural background effects. *Language Learning & Technology, 23*(3), 136–160.

Assessment and Testing	• Long, A. Y., Shin, S.-Y., Geeslin, K., & Willis, E. W. (2018). Does the test work? Evaluating a web-based language placement test. *Language Learning & Technology*, *22*(1), 137–156. • Matthews, J., & Wijeyewardene, I. (2018). Exploring relationships between automated and human evaluations of L2 texts. *Language Learning & Technology*, *22*(3), 143–158. • Roussel, S., & Galan, J.-P. (2018). Can clicker use support learning in a dual-focused second language German course? *Language Learning & Technology*, *22*(3), 45–64.
Courseware Design and Evaluation	• Bikowski, D., & Casal, J. E. (2018). Interactive digital textbooks and engagement: A learning strategies framework. *Language Learning & Technology*, *22*(1), 119–136.
Mobile-Assisted Language Learning (MALL)	• Grimshaw, J., & Cardoso, W. (2018). Activate space rats! Fluency development in a mobile game-assisted environment. *Language Learning & Technology*, *22*(3), 159–175. • Kim, D., Rueckert, D., Kim, D. J., & Seo, D. (2013). Students' perceptions and experiences of mobile learning. *Language Learning & Technology*, *17*(3), 52-73. • Li, Z., & Hegelheimer, V. (2013). Mobile-assisted grammar exercises: Effects on self-editing in L2 writing. *Language Learning & Technology*, *17*(3), 135-156. • Lys, F. (2013). The development of advanced learner oral proficiency using iPads. *Language Learning & Technology*, *17*(3), 94-116. • Rosell-Aguilar, F. (2013). Podcasting for language learning through iTunes U: The learner's view. *Language Learning & Technology*, *17*(3), 74-93. • Wang, S., & Smith, S. (2013). Reading and grammar learning through mobile phones. *Language Learning & Technology, 17*(3), 117-134. • Liu, P. L. (2016). Mobile English vocabulary learning based on concept-mapping strategy. *Language Learning & Technology*, *20*(1), 128–140.
Learner Autonomy and New Learning Environment	• Collentine, K. (2011). Learner autonomy in a task-based 3D world and production. *Language Learning & Technology*, *15*(3), 50-67. • Hafner, C. A., & Miller, L. (2011). Fostering learner autonomy in English for science: A collaborative digital video project in a technological learning environment. *Language Learning & Technology*, *15*(3), 68-86.

Learner Autonomy and New Learning Environment	• Lee, L. (2011). Blogging: Promoting learner autonomy and intercultural competence through study abroad. *Language Learning & Technology, 15*(3), 87-109. • Nielson, K. B. (2011). Self-study with language learning software in the workplace: What happens. *Language Learning & Technology, 15*(3), 110-129.
Less Commonly Taught Language	• Klimanova, L., & Dembovskaya, S. (2013). L2 identity, discourse, and social networking in Russian. *Language Learning & Technology, 17*(1), 69-88. • Ward, M. (2018). Qualitative research in less commonly taught and endangered language CALL. *Language Learning & Technology, 22*(2), 116–132.

Chapter 12

Research on CALL and MALL in Korea

12.1 Introduction

The history of CALL research has not been long in Korea. CALL was introduced at the beginning of the 1990s in Korea. Some researchers presented CALL research findings overseas, including characteristics, potentials and limitations, roles, etc. (I. C. Choi, 1991; S. Y. Choi, 1993, 1994; I. S. Kim, 1996; D. J. Park, 1994; Patterson, 1988).

However, a few empirical studies were conducted in CALL (S. Y. Choi, 1996; S. B. Kim, 1996). S. Y. Choi (1996) and S. B. Kim (1996) examined the effects of CD-ROM titles on the English language development of high school students and college students, respectively. In 1997, fervent research on CALL and MALL began with the establishment of KAMALL (*The Korea Association of Multimedia Assisted Language Learning*) in Korea. The first CALL and MALL professional journal in Korea, *Multimedia Assisted Language Learning* (*MALL*), was first published in 1998. *MALL* is a domestic refereed journal that is enlisted on the National Research Foundation of Korea (NRF). *MALL* has provided many research articles that address a variety of issues of CALL and MALL in Korea.

In this chapter, most research articles in *MALL* are reviewed to provide research trends and issues from 1998 to the present. The collected articles were divided into four periods suggested by Kang and Lee (2014): 1) 1998-2002 (the software period); 2) 2003-2007 (the Internet period); 3) 2008-2012 (the mobile period); and 4) 2013-2020 (the social media and AI period). Finally, the chronological table of *MALL* is provided.

12.2 1998 – 2002: The Software Period

1. MALL Theory, Conceptualization, and Pedagogy

Work on MALL theory and pedagogy has been intensified in this period in Korea. It includes the general principle of the use of multimedia (C. H. Lee, 1998b), the application of e-mail for teaching a foreign language (S. Cho, 1998), teachers' attitudes on the use of computers (C. H. Lee, 1999), the relationship between technology and pedagogy (Myers & Sung, 2002), and knowledge domains for the successful CALL (Levy, 2002).

2. Listening and Speaking

Research on listening and speaking relates to the improvement of students' communicative competence (S. U. Keem, 2000; C. H. Lee, 2000a). Two studies addressed MALL instruction for the cultivation of communicative competence (S. U. Keem, 2000) and the communicative activities that can be applied to CALL (C. H. Lee, 2000a).

Figure 12.1 A CD-ROM title: Arthur's Teacher Trouble

3. Reading and Writing

The development of the web affected the practice of teaching and learning of reading and writing. A large part of the studies is about web-based reading and writing (H. J. Ihm, 2000; D. J. Kim, 2000; H. Kim, 2002). H. Kim (2002) conducted web-integrated reading instruction and provided implications for reading strategy practice. Yun and Lee (2001) implemented CALL software to improve university students' reading speed in English. In terms of writing, D. J. Kim's (2000) study revealed the role of e-mail in teaching English writing in the perspective of constructivism. H. J. Ihm (2000) also examined collaborative learning in a web-based writing program.

4. Pronunciation, Vocabulary, and Grammar

A few studies on three subskills were carried out in this period. Two studies have provided implications and suggestions for teaching grammar and vocabulary (I. S. Kim, 2002; Lee & Yoon, 2000). Lee and Yoon (2000) used a homepage for grammar practice, and I. S. Kim (2002) suggested a computer-assisted vocabulary learning program for university students.

5. Computer-Mediated Communication (CMC)

Inquiries on CMC have identified its use in various contexts (D. J. Kim, 2002; S. Y. Kim, 2002; Min & Choi, 2002). S. Y. Kim (2002) compared college students' reflection on English learning via CMC and face-to-face communication. Min and Choi (2002) used CMC to improve elementary school students' English proficiency. D. J. Kim (2002) presented the pedagogical models for the optical CMC instructions.

6. Collaborative Learning

MALL facilitates collaborative or cooperative learning among the students. Two studies have taken on greater depth in MALL research in collaborative or cooperative learning (Y. S. Jung, 2000; Son & O'Neill, 1999). The major interests of two studies are collaborative e-mail exchange for peer editing (Son & O'Neill, 1999) and the cooperative use of multimedia courseware (Y. S. Jung, 2000).

7. Courseware Design and Evaluation

The development of courseware or program has been important due to its practical aspects. The studies that deal with courseware development and implementation were involved with web-based multimedia content for a listening course (I. S. Kim, 2000), elementary English course design with multimedia technology (J. R. Kim, 1999), and the multimedia CD-ROM courseware for secondary school students (Choi, Kim, Lee, & Sol, 1999).

8. Assessment and Testing

Assessment and testing were one of the central concerns when MALL or CALL came to the fore. Several studies have identified principles of computer adaptive tests (I. C. Choi, 2002; Kim & Lim, 1998; Larson, 1998). The application of computational linguistics to performance tests (I. C. Choi, 1999) and the comparison between computer-based ratings and human ratings (Choi & Uhm, 2001) were addressed as well.

9. Teacher Education

Teacher education is one of the crucial factors in the implementation of CALL and MALL. Several studies have provided implications and suggestions for teacher training (Davies, 2002; J. I. Han, 2001; C. H. Lee, 2002). J. I Han (2001) developed a model of multimedia English education for pre-service teachers. Davies (2002) and C. H. Lee (2002) emphasized the importance of teacher training for the implementation of computers in FLT&L.

10. Other Foreign Languages Education

Computers, multimedia, and the Web were used in teaching and learning other foreign languages, such as Korean, Spanish, and French. H. Y. Lee (2000) applied the Internet to the design for individualized teaching of Korean. J. C. Choi (1999), Choi and Kim (2001), and Kim and Choi (2002) conducted studies on teaching and learning of Spanish. J. C. Choi (1999) developed Internet-based Spanish learning activities through the digital newspaper. Choi and Kim (2001) and Kim and Choi (2002) dealt with web-based Spanish courseware. M. G. Kim (2002) developed a web-based platform for teaching French as a foreign language.

12.3 2003 – 2007: The Internet Period

1. MALL Theory, Conceptualization, and Pedagogy

Research on MALL theory, conceptualization, and pedagogy has become more sophisticated in this period. A variety of issues closely related to English education theory and approaches have been included. K. Sung (2004) incorporated multimedia and inquiry-based approach into teaching English, and S. Lee (2005a) did constructivism into EFL classrooms through technology. Students' self-efficacy beliefs (K. Han, 2004) and learning strategies (Lee & Kwon, 2007) were identified in different contexts. Lee and Lee (2005) revealed teachers' perceptions of cyber homework for primary and secondary school students. J. B. Hwang (2007) examined the effects of focus on form and the use of multimedia on reading comprehension and the acquisition of English grammar.

2. E-Learning, Online Learning, and WBI

Work on e-learning, online learning, and WBI has expanded in scope in this period. The rapid development of technologies has promoted new types of learning environments. It includes Internet-based English assignments in secondary school (Choi & Lee, 2003), web-based L2 tasks (H. Kim, 2004), synchronous online discussion (S. Lee, 2005b), podcasting for English learning (S. Cho, 2006) and web-based English songs for teaching elementary school students (Chung & Choi, 2006).

Figure 12.2 Online Learning at primary school
(https://www.irvinestandard.com/2020/expert-tips-for-online-learning/)

3. Blended Learning

It is a noteworthy fact that blended learning began to be applied to language teaching and learning in this period. Lee and Pyo (2003) conducted a seminal study that revealed the effects of online/offline English language learning at the university level.

4. Listening and Speaking

Listening is one of the language skills that frequently incorporated MALL by researchers (Cha & Rodriguez, 2004; Kim & Kim, 2004; I. S. Kim, 2005; Nam & Jeon, 2006). Several techniques and activities for enhancing listening skills were suggested, including Internet news clips as assignments (Cha & Rodriguez, 2004), Internet assisted instruction (Kim & Kim, 2004; I. S. Kim, 2005), and an English TV program for beginning young learners (Nam & Jeon, 2006). In contrast, research on speaking is rarely found. One study conducted by Choi and Jung (2006) investigated the effects of using a voice bulletin board to improve elementary school students' speaking skills.

5. Reading and Writing

Teaching and learning writing has been positively affected by the development of technologies. A couple of studies deal with different types of writing techniques (Y. V. Chun, 2004; Kim & Shim, 2003). Chun (2004) compared the EFL learners' use of print and online dictionaries in the writing process and Kim and Shim (2003) adopted English writing CD-ROM title for teaching young learners' English writing. S. Lee. (2004) suggested electronic spaces as a new writing and sharing space.

6. Pronunciation, Vocabulary, and Grammar

Research in vocabulary has described the construction of an English word list and the development of its web-based level tests (Kim, O, & Nation, 2005) and an authoring package for English vocabulary learning (C. I. Lee, 2005).

7. Computer-Mediated Communication (CMC)

The application of CMC to foreign language teaching and learning has continued and flourished in this period. Some studies have been conducted on the use of CMC for improving language skills (Ahn & Na, 2005; Y. Cha, 2007; J. T. Chang, 2003; S. Cho, 2005; H. Choi, 2004; Ha & Han, 2006; J. I. Han, 2003, 2005; K. Huh, 2007; S. W. Lee, 2004; E. Y. Park, 2003). Studies deal with the ways of using CMC to improve communicative competence (J. T. Chang, 2003) and language skills (J. I. Han, 2003), strategies for meaning negotiation and self-correction in CMC interaction (E. Y. Park, 2003), the egalitarian features of synchronous CMC (S. W.

Lee, 2004), EFL students' perceptions on text chatting (H. Choi, 2004), the implementation of an intercultural CMC project (Ahn & Na, 2005), the development of CMC activities (S. Cho, 2005), Korean college students' accuracy and form-focused negotiation during text-based chatting the role of meta-awareness and task type on the use of determiners during chatting (Ha & Han, 2006), peer feedback patterns in asynchronous and synchronous CMC modes (Y. Cha, 2007), and the incorporation creativity tasks into CMC environments (K. Huh, 2007).

8. Courseware Design and Evaluation

CALL courseware design and application have become more diversified due to the development of technologies. I. S. Ohm (2003) and H. Kim (2003) presented the design of CALL systems and a homepage respectively. The various programs and content were applied to different teaching and learning contexts (H. Kim, 2007; Kim & Chang, 2005; Kim & Hwang, 2007; K. M. O, 2004). The programs and content involved web-based English achievement testing program (K. M. O, 2004), online college CALL English curriculum (Kim & Chang, 2005), on-class English learning with on-line differentiated content for elementary school students (Kim & Hwang, 2007), and ICT-integrated English curriculum for elementary school (H. Kim, 2007).

9. Assessment and Testing

A small cluster of work on assessment and testing has continued in greater depth. H. Lee (2004) examined the reliability of a repeated testing design, and Choi (2005) explored the applicability of automatic speech recognition technology for computer-based oral proficiency interviews. J. Kim (2006) presented the development of a web-based speaking test using Visual Basic 6.0.

10. Other Foreign Languages Education

A couple of studies were found in this category. S. Cheon (2006) constructed an English loanwords contents (ELC) database for the Korean language. H. Choi (2007) adopted digital mind map software for Russian vocabulary and sentences and suggested more effective methods for the use of a mind map.

12.4 2008 – 2012: The Mobile Period

1. E-Learning, Online Learning, and WBI

The recent development of technologies was reflected in e-learning, online learning, and WBI. More sophisticated studies were conducted to show students' interaction through peer review in the online English class (Jung & Chang, 2009) and elementary English teachers' perceptions and using websites (Park & Lim, 2009). Some new technologies and concepts for FLT&L included a role-playing game (Kim & Jang, 2008), IPTV (S. Lee, 2011a), and video conferencing (S. Lee, 2011b).

2. Blended Learning

During this period, the inquiry on blended learning has been more expanded. Blended learning is applied to different language skills in various teaching and learning contexts. For example, L2 writing was taught in the blended learning environment (S. Y. Yoon, 2011; Yoon & Lee, 2010). The two studies above showed university students' perspectives and effectiveness of blended learning in L2 writing (Yoon & Lee, 2010) and university students' reflection on feedback (S. Y. Yoon, 2011). Blended learning was adopted for teaching and learning L2 listening (Lee & Lee, 2012; Yoon & Lee, 2012). These two initial studies showed university students' perspectives and the effectiveness of blended learning in L2 listening (Lee & Lee, 2012) and the impact of explicit listening instruction on pre-service teachers' practice (Yoon & Lee, 2012). Instructional methods and models were developed and implemented for business English classes (Cha & Kim, 2011) and English teaching at offline universities (Kim & Kim, 2012). Y. Cha (2012) also examined university students' perspectives and learning methods on blended learning in general English classes.

3. Social Network Services (SNS) and Smart Education

SNS and smart education have started to break free from the constraints of time and space in FLT&L due to the development of recent technologies. The suggestions for using smartphones and SNSs in FLT&L have been provided (S. Cho, 2009, 2011; Kim & Kwon, 2012). Twitter is one of the most frequently used SNSs for teaching and learning a foreign language (H. Kim, 2010; Kim, Park, & Baek, 2011; Park & Kim, 2011). Studies examined teachers' efforts to use Twitter

(H. Kim, 2010), the implications for using Twitter in language learning (Kim, Park, & Baek, 2011), and the effects of the English writing activities using Twitter on college students' writing abilities (Park & Kim, 2011).

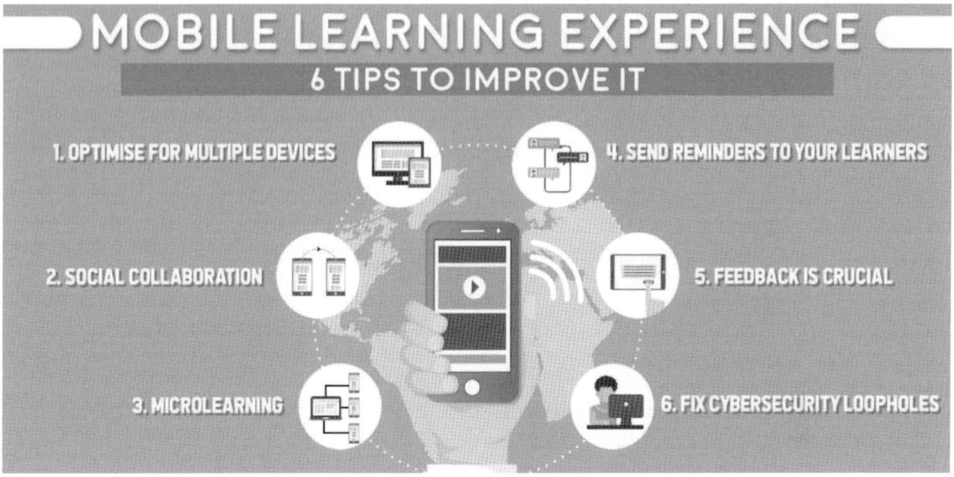

Figure 12.3 M-learning, e-learning, and SNS
(https://playxlpro.com/mobile-learning-experience-5-tips-to-improve-it/)

4. Reading and Writing

Research on reading and writing has rapidly expanded in MALL because the use of computers and technologies has positively influenced the teaching and learning environments, especially for reading and writing. In terms of reading, the development of reading speed is one of the issues (Oh & Choi, 2010; Ryu & Lee, 2011). Oh and Choi (2010) explored the ways of developing speed reading skills using multimedia, and Ryu and Lee (2011) examined the impact of using a web-based speed reading program on the improvement of elementary school students' English reading speed. Internet English storybooks were also adopted for extensive reading (Park & Choi, 2012). The integrated instruction of reading and writing through using multimedia was conducted by K. Huh (2012). Research on writing has been conducted on a web-based writing program and automated essay scoring system (S. Lee, 2008), collaborative writing in weblogs (J. K. Kim, 2009), the comparison between collaborative writing and individual writing (J. K. Pae, 2011), the use of technologies and hypertext to foster collaborative writing (S. Lee, 2012b), electronic teacher feedback and self-evaluation in writing (Jang & Lee, 2012), the effects of e-portfolio on college students' writing ability (J. K. Kim, 2012), and the efficacy of corpus-based pedagogical techniques for academic writing (Schenck & Cho, 2012). One study explored Korean college students' vocabulary profile to predict English reading and writing proficiency (Kim & Ryoo, 2009).

5. Pronunciation, Vocabulary, and Grammar

Research on three subskills has been more sophisticated by using various methods and approaches. First, voice recordings and feedback through BBS have been implemented in teaching and learning pronunciation (Yoon & Lee, 2009). A. Y. Kim (2012) investigated the effects of software (the technology-enhanced accent modification: TEAM) on the improvement of adult ESL students' pronunciation. Second, studies on vocabulary have become more diverse with the development of vocabulary lists (Shin & Jeong, 2009; Shin & Joo, 2008), the implementation of corpora (Y. M. Kim, 2010; Min, Kim, & Kim, 2010), networked computer-supported intentional vocabulary learning (S. Lee, 2012a), and receptive vocabulary size of English and American novels (S. W. Lee, 2012) Last, research on grammar took on the use of web-based English grammar program (Youk & Lee, 2008).

6. Focus on Form

Studies on focus on form encompass the use of CMC technologies such as text-based chat (Y. W. Cho, 2011; Cho & Kim, 2010; Cho, Lee, & Kim, 2012; Hong & Lee, 2008). Hong and Lee (2008) examined Korean adult learners' performance during text-based chat and effects of focus on form on the improvement of language ability. Cho and Kim (2010) explored the feasibility of using text-based chat for communicative focus on form, and Y. W. Cho (2011) measured students' fluency, accuracy, and complexity in chatting after focus on form lessons. Cho, Lee, and Kim (2012) focused on teacher's SLA knowledge during text-based SCMC in their research.

7. Computer-Mediated Communication (CMC)

The implementation of CMC in language teaching and learning has continued, and correspondingly, research in this area has increased (Cha & Park, 2010; Y. S. Jung, 2008; Kim & Lee, 2012; Kwon & Lee, 2011; K. Lim, 2012; Y. S. Shim, 2008). The research topics are diverse, such as the stimulation of meaning negotiation in CMC interaction (Y. S. Shim, 2008), the influence of synchronous interaction on EFL writers' revisions (Cha & Park, 2010), learners' uptake of feedback in text-based synchronous CMC (Kwon & Lee, 2011), and the development of CMC-based English intensive course model for high school students (K. Lim, 2012). Kim and Lee (2012) compared elementary school students' peer feedback patterns for English writing in CMC and face-to-face contexts.

Figure 12.4 Computer-mediated communication (CMC)
(https://study.com/academy/lesson/computer-mediated-communication-definition-types-advantages.html)

8. Collaborative Learning

Collaboration has been highlighted in L2 writing pedagogy, and computers have facilitated collaborative writing and peer response. Research on collaborative learning is, therefore, conducted on writing skills (B. G. Kim, 2010; J. K. Pae, 2012). The studies addressed collaborative discussion and peer review activity in computer-mediated writing (B. G. Kim, 2010) and students' interaction in computer-supported collaborative writing (J. K. Pae, 2012).

9. Courseware Design and Evaluation

A handful of publications have addressed courseware design and evaluation (T. E. Kim, 2010; S. Lee, 2009; Thorne, 2008). Thorne (2008) described a research program examining online communication and gaming as the environment for L2 use and development. Various systems and content have been developed with different foci (Cho, Lee, Kim, Ko, & Jeong, 2008; Jun & Choi, 2008; Kim & Kim, 2010; Moon & Kim, 2012; I. S. Ohm, 2008). These foci include curriculum-based progress monitoring systems (I. S. Ohm, 2008), PDA vocabulary content using cartoon (Jun & Choi, 2008), the model development of web-based language learning programs (Cho, Lee, Kim, Ko, & Jeong, 2008), online-integrated college curriculum for enhancing speaking skills (Kim & Kim, 2010), and web-based English readability index software for Korean elementary school students (Moon & Kim, 2012).

Regarding the evaluation of courseware and programs, S. Lee (2009) evaluated the English learning programs of EBSe, a cable channel that provides English language learning programs. T. E. Kim (2010) also provided the reflection on the use of criterion online writing evaluation service.

10. Assessment and Testing

Much research on testing and assessment published in this period focused on productive skills, speaking, and writing. Some studies have revealed students' anxiety and performance in video conference interviews (Craig & Kim, 2010) and the effects of tasks on examinee performance in a computer-delivered speaking test (H. J. Kim, 2011). Others focused on the development and administration of the tests (J. Kim, 2009, 2011). The studies have dealt with the relationship between speaking test administration tools and item types (J. Kim, 2009) and the validation process for developing a web-based English speaking and writing test (J. Kim, 2011). Regarding writing, Jin and Park (2012) investigated automated scoring of Korean high school students' English composition and I. C. Choi (2012) showed a validation of EFL essay assessment based on corpus indices and error analysis.

11. Teacher Education

Attention has continuously been given to teacher education for the effective implementation of MALL. Several studies addressed a variety of topics, such as the use of the learning management system for academic support (Gye, Chang, & Jung, 2008), the online teacher training program for in-service elementary and secondary school teachers (Lee & Lee, 2009), and the blended TESOL intensive program for teacher trainees (H. D. Kim, 2010). Teachers' perspectives and use of technologies have been revealed with the suggestions and implications (K. Ahn, 2009; H. O. Kim, 2011). Digital portfolios for pre-service teachers (S. Kim, 2012) and a web-based online training program for in-service teachers (Jeon & Kang, 2012) were implemented to improve teaching skills.

12.5 2013 – 2020: The Social Media and AI Period

1. E-Learning, Online Learning, and WBI

Different types of technologies and techniques have been implemented in online learning environments. They include multiplayer online gaming (Lee & Gerber, 2013), mobile technologies and PC (Obari, 2013), writing reflective journal in a blog (J. Kim, 2014), storybook mind mapping (Seo & Lee, 2014), impacting factors for e-learning in the EFL context (Jung, 2016), comparing learning vocabulary versus watching YouTube videos on reading comprehension (Kim & Cha, 2017), a web-portfolio project in a writing course at the college level (S. E. Lee, 2018), the relationship between presences of an online community for inquiry and learners' perceptions on online learning (Mo & Lee, 2017), learners' perceptions of using teachers' websites in Korean language learning (Ahn & Shim, 2015), and technology-enhanced creativity-based English language learning in Korean middle school level (Han, 2017).

2. Blended Learning

Research on blended learning has flourished with a variety of topics in recent years. This research trend indicates the attempts to combine online and offline learning environments. Blended learning is applied to teaching four language skills (Y. Cha, 2014; Kim & Lee, 2018; J. Lee, 2015; Lee & Cho, 2017; Park & Cha, 2013; L. So, 2015; So & Lee, 2016; Yee & Lee, 2017; S. Y. Yoon, 2015) and subskills, in particular, vocabulary (Jung & Lee, 2013; Kim & Moon, 2013; E. Oh, 2017; Yang & Lee, 2017) and language learning strategies (S. Y. Yoon, 2014). Also, mobile devices and smartphones with mobile apps have been integrated into blended learning (S. Jin, 2014; H. S. Kim, 2014; Kim & Yoon, 2014). For example, S. Jin (2014) implemented smartphones for teaching grammar in blended learning and H. S. Kim (2014) examined the effects of using mobile devices for enhancing English reading comprehension in blended learning. Baek and Lee (2018) explored university students' engagement and perceptions of mobile-assisted blended learning (MABL) in English speaking courses.

3. Social Network Services (SNS) and Smart Education

The development of SNS and mobile apps has a significant effect on teaching and learning a foreign language. Different types of SNSs and mobile apps have been implemented, and accordingly, research on this issue has increased. SNSs have been mainly used in teaching and learning L2 writing (Y. S. Cho, 2015; J. I. Han, 2015; S. Jin, 2013; Kim & Park, 2015) and vocabulary learning (S. Jin, 2018). The impact of mobile apps on the improvement of language skills has been investigated (H. Cho, 2018; Choi & Kim, 2013; Ji & Shin, 2019; H. J. Jung, 2017, 2019; H. S. Kim, 2013; S. Y. Kim, 2017; Y. Kwon, 2013; Seo & Choi, 2014; S. Y. Yoon, 2017). The studies addressed mobile apps for the improvement of English listening skills (Kim, 2013) and writing skills (N. S. Jeong, 2017), learner satisfaction and the L2 language development through smart learning (H. J. Jung, 2017, 2019), learner perspectives and experience on using learner response system in the L2 language classrooms (S. Y. Yoon, 2017), influencing factors in smart education at a university level (G. Kim, 2019), problem-based learning with smart learning (S. Y. Kim, 2017), the effects of mobile apps on language learning (Y. Kwon, 2013), CAT app for reading evaluation (Choi & Kim, 2013), Google Forms on the university TOEIC courses (H. Cho, 2018), the use of a mobile speaking app for middle school students (Seo & Choi, 2014), augmented reality-based vocabulary learning for young learners (Ji & Shin, 2019), smart devices on vocabulary learning for L2 students at a beginning level (Park & Lee, 2017), mobile-based game acitivities for vocabulary learning for Korean middle school students (S. Y. Son, 2018), learner interaction in smart English education was also examined (Y. S. Cho, 2015; Jeong, Lee, & Kim, 2013), and effective mobile-assisted blended leaning (MABL) in English classes at the university level (Lee & Cho, 2019) .

4. Listening and Speaking

Research on listening in MALL has continued with varied topics. G. Kim (2018) examined the web-based dictation on developing university students' listening skills. Jung and Cha (2015) investigated the effects of TED shadowing activities on students' listening skills. Although research on speaking has rarely been carried out compared to other language skills, the recent development of technologies has allowed learners to practice speaking skills in online environments. The research includes the effects of speaking tasks and learners' English proficiency on online speaking performance (Y. Choe, 2014), adult learners' participation in web-talking for improving proficiency (Lee & Park, 2014), the effects of self-directed English speaking practice using multimedia (Kim, Cho, & Lee, 2014), and the effects of voice chat on improving EFL students' speaking abilities (N. Y. Kim, 2016).

5. Reading and Writing

Research on reading and writing has become more sophisticated with the use of different programs. Studies on reading have included a learner response system in teaching and learning English reading (Lee & Oh, 2014), self-directed reading in the online environments (Kim & Cha, 2015), mobile-based reading aloud tasks on EFL students' vocabulary learning and reading comprehension skills (N. Y. Kim, 2018), and task complexity on learners' reading fluency, comprehension, and vocabulary learning (Wang, 2018). In terms of writing, different computer writing tools (Wiki and Daedalus) (Kim & Pae, 2013), types of medium (technology-based and paper-based) in corrective feedback (Lee & Astle, 2014), L2 writers' text-borrowing behaviors in summary writing practices (K. S. Kim, 2017), exemplar-based written corrective feedback in EFL multimedia-based writing instruction (Kim & Cho, 2016), digital storytelling on EFL college students' writing skills (P. Kim, 2018), students' perceptions on flipped writing class and influencing factors for satisfaction (M. R. Ahn, 2019), and learner perceptions on the effectiveness of machine translation on their L2 revision (S. Lee, 2019) were examined.

6. Pronunciation, Vocabulary, and Grammar

Research has continued among three subskills in this period. Different types of techniques and tools have been utilized for facilitating vocabulary learning (H. C. Jeon, 2013; Ko & Goranson, 2014; Oh & Park, 2013). For example, H. C. Jeon (2013) made use of e-book content and Oh and Park (2013) smart devices for underachievers' vocabulary learning. N. Kang (2015) compared an offline class with a flipped class for vocabulary and grammar learning. M. H. Ko (2017) investigated the effects of output-based vocabulary feedback by comparing three types of vocabulary learning methods. Regarding English pronunciation, S. Y. Yoon (2013) investigated university students' perspectives on the online English pronunciation class and its effectiveness. Kim and Lee (2015) conducted a case study regarding how peer feedback affected the improvement of pronunciation. Lastly, research on grammar has also been continued. S. Kim (2015) examined how CALL meet learners' individual needs for grammar instruction. H. S. Kim (2019) researched the use of Socrative and Kahoot for EFL learners' grammar learning. Kim and Choi (2019) investigated the incidental development of grammar knowledge through written discourse while focusing on the aspectual distinction.

7. Courseware Design and Evaluation

A variety of programs and models have been developed for language learning and teaching with new technologies (S. Chun, 2016; J. I. Han, 2014; Jeon & Kang, 2013; J. Kang, 2013; Kim & Kim, 2015; Kim & Park, 2016; Lee & Kim, 2014; Yun, Kwon, & Kim, 2015). They include smart English teaching models using QR codes (Jeon & Kang, 2013), online teaching English in English training programs (Lee & Kim, 2014), and the development of mobile apps for speaking instruction for middle school students (Yun, Kwon, & Kim, 2015). Digital English textbooks have been implemented in elementary and secondary schools, and some models have been developed for effective instruction using digital textbooks and courseware evaluation (J. I. Han, 2014; J. Kang, 2013; Kim & Kim, 2015; Kim, Lee, & Lee, 2018; J. Ryu, 2017). J. Kang (2013) applied Technology Acceptance Model to elementary English classrooms and examined the students' acceptance of English textbooks. J. I. Han (2014) implemented learning models of English digital textbooks in middle school, Kim and Kim (2015) explored low achieving high school students' learning needs and provided pedagogical implications, in particular, scaffolding, and Kim, Lee, and Kim (2018) showed design, implementation, and evaluation principles for open learning platforms (OLP) for teacher training.

Figure 12.5 The process of instructional design (https://educationaltechnology.net/wp-content/uploads/2016/12/instructional-design.png)

8. Assessment and Testing

There have been many studies on assessment and testing in the KAMALL journal (Choi & Jang, 2017; Choi & Park, 2016; W. Hong, 2016; J. Kim, 2017; J. E. Kim,

2014; Kim & Park, 2019; Lee & Joo, 2017; Lee & Kim, 2018; Lim, Park, & Si, 2014; Moon & Choi, 2019; Shin, Chon, Lee, & Park, 2017; Shin, Park, Park, & Yim, 2015).

J. E. Kim (2014) and Lim, Park and Si (2014) examined the automated scoring systems for writing, and Shin, Park, Park, and Yim (2015) explored an automatic scoring program for English speaking skills. W. Hong (2016) investigated the effects of presentation modes in CALT on cultural content in EFL classrooms. Choi and Park (2016) examined the efficacy of corpus-driven scoring for computer-based text-to-speech dictation tests at a college level. Choi and Jang (2017) explored the efficacy of a computerized text-to-speech dictation test through automatized error analysis. Lee and Joo (2017) delineated the development of an internet-based English speaking performance assessment support system and investigated its usefulness for teachers and students. Lee and Kim (2018) revealed the effects of task difficulties on university learners' speaking performances and their perceptions of CBT task difficulties. Kim and Park (2019) investigated how task types and scoring constructs affected EFL university students' speaking performance. (See Appendix for more research on assessment and testing in the MALL journal.)

9. Teacher Education

The recent drastic development of digital technologies has laid out continuous research on teachers' professional development. S. H. Lee (2017) explored how non-native English teachers could be empowered by one another through an online community for learning to teach their flipped classroom. H. J. Jung (2018) identified some constructs that caused English teachers' reluctance to use technological innovation in their language classrooms. Kim and Kim (2017) investigated Korean English teachers' future-preparedness about knowledge, attitudes, and perceptions for the fourth industrial revolution.

10. Artificial Intelligence (AI)

The emergence of artificial intelligence (AI) and its sophisticated development in the language field enables L2 researchers and teaching practitioners to conduct studies on developing language skills through AI-based approaches. J. Park (2019) compared AI-based grammar checker with professional human raters. S. Y. Yoon (2019) revealed EFL university students' readiness to use AI for language learning. Some studies have focused on AI-chatbot in language learning and teaching (Kim, Cha, & Kim, 2019; Lee, Kim, Shin, & Yang, 2019; Yang, Kim, Shin, & Lee, 2019). Kim, Cha, and Kim (2019) showed different types of AI-chatbot for language learning. Lee, Kim, Shin, and Yang (2019) explored conversational interaction with AI-chatbot and student users. Yang, Kim, Shin, and Lee (2019) researched the potential and tendencies of using AI-chatbot for young Korean learners of English.

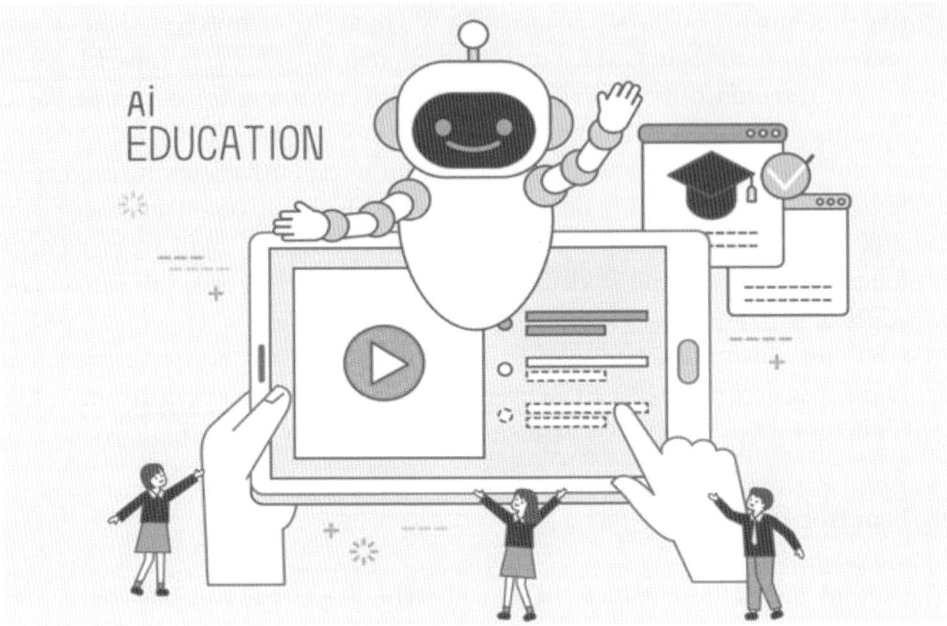

Figure 12.6 AI and Education
(https://www.korea.kr/news/policyNewsView.do?newsId=148875696)

11. Corpus

Corpus has been used in various L2 research fields. Chon and Shin (2013) analyzed spoken and written academic collocations through a corpus-driven approach. Kang and Lee (2014) analyzed topic changes and moves in abstracts of MALL-related articles using corpus data and tools. Kim and Choi (2015) compared the linguistic difficulty among three types of materials for high school students (high school English textbooks, EBS-CSAT prep books, and college scholastic ability tests). Nam and Park (2015) conducted a corpus-based analysis of thematic structures in L2 writing. H. Cho (2016) investigated using corpus in L2 writing to enhance learners' awareness of selected formulaic language. Kang and Lee (2016) compared move structures and lexico-grammatical patterns in CALL research papers with M.A. theses written by Korean graduates. J. Y. Hong (2018) carried out a corpus analysis study concerning the Korean EAP learners' acquisition of rhetorical structure and linguistic features. D. Nam (2018) examined how using the lexical bundle affected prospective science and engineering students' academic L2 writing. Le and Kim (2018) employed corpus analysis to explore the collocational behaviors of two near-synonyms adjectives (*wide* and *broad*) in the Corpus of Contemporary American English (COCA) search engine.

12.6 Conclusion

Based on the review of *MALL* journal articles, it can be summarized that there has been continuous development in ICT and multimedia in hardware and software and their application to practice along with the trends and issues of FLT&L during the last two decades. It is worth noticing that many research articles in MALL have reflected the latest technology available from the end of the 1990s up to the present time. The results of empirical research on the use of various ICT and multimedia are generally positive. ICT and multimedia are more than the sum of the hardware components which constitute them. Due to their distinctive characteristics, ICT and multimedia represent a force for change through their effect on the curriculum, teacher training, and methodology in FLT&L. In recent, blended learning and smart education provide great potential to improve language teaching and learning and opportunities for new teaching methods to enhance learning.

ICT and multimedia must continue to develop in terms of methodology and software or content to realize their characteristics and trends. More research, development, training, and evaluation will be required to make full use of the potential in FLT&L. In particular, more empirical research studies in this field are needed, focused on online learning, blended learning, autonomous learning, and learning strategies in language classes.

Tasks for Study and Discussion

■ Find out about 10 articles (5 quantitative and 5 qualitative research articles) related to your research topic from *MALL* journal articles. Work individually, and then share your work with your partners.

1) Describe the purposes, research questions, main methods, and conclusion of the articles briefly.
2) Describe how they relate to your study.

Appendix

The Chronological Table of *MALL*

* English: MALL article in English, Korean: MALL article in Korean

The Software Period (1998-2002)	
MALL Theory, Conceptualization, and Pedagogy	* English • Lee, C. H. (1998). On multimedia in foreign language teaching and learning. *Multimedia-Assisted Language Learning, 1*(1), 25-50. • Lee, C. H. (1999). Why use or not use computers? *Multimedia-Assisted Language Learning, 2*(2), 9-46. • Levy, M. (2002). Knowledge domains for the successful integration of CALL. *Multimedia-Assisted Language Learning, 5*(1), 243-257. • Myers, J., & Sung, K. (2002). Texts, technology, and pedagogy. *Multimedia-Assisted Language Learning. 5*(1), 151-166.
	* Korean • Cho, S. (1998). The applications of electronic mail to English education. *Multimedia-Assisted Language Learning, 1*(1), 213-227.
Listening and Speaking	English • Lee, C. H. (2000). Communicative activities applicable to CALL: Based on computer simulations. *Multimedia-Assisted Language Learning, 3*(2), 70-99.
	Korean • Keem, S. U. (2000). A field study : Multimedia-assisted English instruction to cultivate communicative competence. *Multimedia-Assisted Language Learning, 3*(1), 139-166.
Reading and Writing	Korean • Ihm, H. J. (2000). A case study of collaborative learning in a web-based writing program. *Multimedia-Assisted Language Learning, 3*(2), 175-197. • Kim, D. J. (2000). A study on the development of zone of proximal development for the optimization of English writing education through E-mail. *Multimedia-Assisted Language Learning, 3*(2), 100-118. • Kim, H. (2002) Web-integrated ESOL reading instruction: An idea for reading strategy practice. *Multimedia-Assisted Language Learning 5*(2), 83-102. • Yun, M. H., & Lee, C. H. (2001). A study of using CALL Software for the improvement of university students' reading speed in English. *Multimedia-Assisted Language Learning, 4*(1), 86-121.

Pronunciation, Vocabulary' and Grammar	English • Kim, I. S. (2002). Vocabulary acquisition research and development of a computer-assisted vocabulary learning program for EFL university students. *Multimedia-Assisted Language Learning, 5*(1), 59-82. • Lee, C. I., & Yoon, M. S. (2000). Use of a homepage for grammar practice based on error analysis of e-mail writings. *Multimedia-Assisted Language Learning, 3*(2), 53-69.
Computer-Mediated Communication (CMC)	English • Kim, S. Y. (2002). Korean college students' reflections of English language learning via CMC and FFC. *Multimedia-Assisted Language Learning, 5*(2), 9-28.
	Korean • Kim, D. (2002). A study on the pedagogical models for the optimum efficacy of the CMC instructions. *Multimedia-Assisted Language Learning, 5*(2), 47-64. • Min, D. G. & Choi, E. I. (2002). Using CMC to improve elementary school students' English proficiency: Focused on the analysis of discourse functions and syntactic complexity. *Multimedia-Assisted Language Learning, 5*(2), 103-129.
Collaborative Learning	English • Jung, Y. S. (2000). Effects of cooperative learning approach to MALL (Multimedia-Assisted Language Learning). *Multimedia-Assisted Language Learning, 3*(1), 9-46. • Son, J. B. & O'Neill, S. (1999). Collaborative e-mail exchange: A pilot study of peer editing. *Multimedia-Assisted Language Learning, 2*(2), 69-87.
Courseware Design and Evaluation	Korean • Choi, S. Y., Kim, K. S., Lee, C. K., & Sol, Y. H. (1999). Effective use of multimedia computer courseware in English language teaching and learning. *Multimedia-Assisted Language Learning, 2*(1), 179-256. • Kim, I. S. (2000). Development of web-based multimedia contents for foreign language education and their application: A case study of an OCU listening course. *Multimedia-Assisted Language Learning, 3*(2), 119-139. • Kim, J. R. (1999). A study of developing elementary English course design incorporating multimedia technology. *Multimedia-Assisted Language Learning, 2*(1), 74-99.

Assessment and Testing	English • Choi, I. C. (2002). Validation of computer-based/adaptive language tests focusing on response time. *Multimedia-Assisted Language Learning, 5*(1), 9-31. • Larson, J. W. (1998). An argument for computer adaptive language testing. *Multimedia-Assisted Language Learning, 1*(1), 9-24.
	Korean • Choi, I. C. (1999). Application of computational to linguistics language performance testing. *Multimedia- Assisted Language Learning, 2*(2), 245-278. • Choi, I. C., & Uhm, Y. H. (2001). Comparative analyses of computer-based ratings and human ratings based on performance testing of writing. *Multimedia-Assisted Language Learning, 4*(1), 165-184. • Kim, J. R., & Lim C. K. (1998). Developing computer-adaptive English testing for elementary school English. *Multimedia-Assisted Language Learning, 1*(1), 101-116.
Teacher Education	English • Davies, G. (2002). ICT and modern foreign languages: learning opportunities and training needs. *Multimedia-Assisted Language Learning, 5*(1), 200-221. • Lee, C. H. (2002). What is the most crucial factor in implementing computers into FLT/L? *Multimedia-Assisted Language Learning, 5*(1), 83-103.
	Korean • Han, J. I. (2001). A development of standards and a model of multimedia English education for pre-service teachers. *Multimedia-Assisted Language Learning, 4*(1), 185-213.
Other Foreign Language	Korean • Choi, J. C. (1999). Internet-based Spanish learning activities by using digital newspapers. *Multimedia-Assisted Language Learning, 2*(2), 279-313. • Choi, J. C., & Kim, K. (2001). The current state and perspective of web-based Spanish distance education. *Multimedia-Assisted Language Learning, 4*(2), 219-243. • Kim, K., & Choi, J. C. (2002). Construction and application of the web-based courseware "Spanish in multimedia." *Multimedia-Assisted Language Learning, 5*(2), 29-46.

Other Foreign Language	Korean • Kim, M. G. (2002). A study on the development of a web-based platform for French composition class. *Multimedia-Assisted Language Learning, 5*(2), 65-82. • Lee, H. Y. (2000). The application of the internet and the design for individualized teaching of Korean. *Multimedia-Assisted Language, 3*(1), 264-286.

The Internet Period (2003-2007)	
MALL Theory, Conceptualization, and Pedagogy	English • Han, K. (2004). L2 learners' self-efficacy beliefs: Interactive affects and effects of three different contexts. *Multimedia-Assisted Language Learning*, 8(1), 53-75. • Lee, S. (2005a). Translating constructivism into EFL classrooms through the use of technology. *Multimedia-Assisted Language Learning, 8*(1), 220-249. • Sung, K. (2004). Critical English language teaching using a multimedia and inquiry-based approach. *Multimedia-Assisted Language Learning, 7*(1), 169-198.
	Korean • Hwang, J. B. (2007). A study of the combining effects of the multimedia learning environment and the use of a focus-on-form technique. *Multimedia-Assisted Language Learning, 10*(3), 237-255. • Lee, J., & Lee, C. H. (2005). Teachers' perception of cyber homework for primary and secondary school students: A case study of d office of education. *Multimedia-Assisted Language Learning, 8*(2), 154-178. • Lee, S., & Kwon, C. J. (2007). The analysis of college students' English learning strategies in a CALL environment. *Multimedia-Assisted Language Learning, 10*(3), 155-186.

E-Learning, Online Learning and WBI	English • Kim, H. (2004). Analysis and application of web-based L2 tasks. *Multimedia-Assisted Language Learning*, 7(2), 81-101. • Lee, S. (2005b). ESL students' beliefs about the utility of synchronous online discussion (SOD) in language learning and their participation in the SOD. *Multimedia-Assisted Language Learning, 8*(2), 9-31.
	Korean • Cho, S. (2006). The use of podcasting for English learning. *Multimedia-Assisted Language Learning, 9*(3), 241-254. • Choi, S., & Lee, Y. (2003). The effectiveness of performing Internet-based English assignments in secondary English education. *Multimedia-Assisted Language Learning, 6*(2), 175-193. • Chung, S., & Choi, S. (2006). A study on the effects of teaching web-based English songs with Korean subtitles: For 3rd grade elementary school learners. *Multimedia-Assisted Language Learning, 9*(1), 146-166.
Blended Learning	English • Lee, C. H., & Pyo, K .H. (2003). A study on the effectiveness of online/offline English language learning at university level. *Multimedia-Assisted Language Learning, 6*(1), 90-110.
Listening and Speaking	English • Cha, K. W., & Rodriguez, F. (2004). Homework assignments for improving the English listening skills of Korean students: An investigative study. *Multimedia-Assisted Language Learning, 7*(2), 9-34. • Kim, I. S. (2005). Developing a web-based listening course. *Multimedia-Assisted Language Learning*, 8(1), 116-140. • Kim, K. W., & Kim, H. D. (2004). The effectiveness of Internet assisted instruction in English listening class. *Multimedia-Assisted Language Learning*, 7(2), 103-121.
	Korean • Choi, H., & Jung, B. (2006). The effects of the use of voice bulletin board on elementary school students' English speaking skills and affective domains: A case study. *Multimedia-Assisted Language Learning, 9*(3), 283-311. • Nam, J. Y., & Jeon, K. (2006). Study on the use of an English TV program for listening proficiency improvement of beginning young learners. *Multimedia-Assisted Language Learning, 9*(3), 127-149.

Reading and Writing	English • Chun, Y. V. (2004). EFL learners' use of print and online dictionaries in L1 and L2 writing processes. *Multimedia-Assisted Language Learning, 7*(1), 9-35. • Lee, S. (2004). Electronic spaces as a new writing and sharing arena. *Multimedia-Assisted Language Learning,* 7(2), 165-195.
	Korean • Kim, I. O., & Shim, K. A. (2003). A Study on the development of a primary English writing CD-ROM title and its effect on children's writing competence. *Multimedia-Assisted Language Learning, 6*(2), 71-95.
Pronunciation, Vocabulary' and Grammar	Korean • Kim, I. S., O, K. M., & Nation, P. (2005). The construction of an English word list for EFL university students and the development of its web-based levels test. *Multimedia-Assisted Language Learning, 8*(2), 58-88. • Lee, C. I. (2005). An authoring package for English vocabulary learning. *Multimedia-Assisted Language Learning, 8*(2), 179-197.
Computer-Mediated Communication (CMC)	English • Ahn, B., K. & Na, Y. H. (2005). Implementing an intercultural CMC project: A case study. *Multimedia-Assisted Language Learning, 8*(1), 9-33. • Cha, Y. (2007). A study of peer feedback patterns in CMC modes on Korean EFL students. *Multimedia-Assisted Language Learning, 10*(1), 9-35. • Chang, J. T. (2003). The use of CMC to improve communicative competence. *Multimedia-Assisted Language Learning, 6*(1), 18-41. • Choi, H. (2004). EFL students' perceptions on synchronous English text chatting: Implications for its implementation. *Multimedia-Assisted Language Learning, 7*(2), 35-63. • Ha, J. B., & Han, M. S. (2006). The role of meta-awareness and task type on the use of determiners during Internet chat. *Multimedia-Assisted Language Learning, 9*(2), 26-52. • Huh, K. (2007). CALL and creativity: Incorporating creativity task into CMC environments. *Multimedia-Assisted Language Learning, 10*(1), 36-61.

Computer-Mediated Communication (CMC)	English • Lee, S. W. (2004). Is synchronous computer mediated communication truly egalitarian?: A case study of computer-networked ESL classroom. *Multimedia- Assisted Language Learning, 7*(1), 109-141. • Park, E. Y. (2003). Strategies in negotiation of meaning and self- correction in CMC interaction. *Multimedia-Assisted Language Learning, 6*(2), 53-70.
	Korean • Cho, S. K. (2005). The development of an English learning program based on CMC activities. *Multimedia-Assisted Language Learning, 8*(2), 198-217. • Han, J. I. (2003). The effective use of CMC tools in teaching English as a foreign language. *Multimedia-Assisted Language Learning, 6*(2), 243-264. • Han, J. I. (2005). A case study on the accuracy of English and form-focused negotiation appearing in Korean college students' text-based chat scripts. *Multimedia-Assisted Language Learning, 8*(2), 262-287.
Courseware Design and Evaluation	English • Ohm, I. S. (2003). How to make CALL systems more intelligent. *Multimedia-Assisted Language Learning, 6*(2), 111-134.
	Korean • Kim, H. (2003). An idea of designing multifunctional English teacher homepage. *Multimedia-Assisted Language Learning, 6*(2), 97-118. • Kim, H. (2007). ICT-integrated English language curriculum for elementary school students: A case study of Apple Project. *Multimedia-Assisted Language Learning, 10*(1), 177-200. • Kim, H., & Chang, H. (2005). A case study of online college English: Effectiveness of language curriculum design in CALL. *Multimedia-Assisted Language Learning, 8*(2), 89-112. • Kim, J. R., & Hwang, S. Y. (2007). Connecting on-class elementary school English learning with selected on-line differentiated contents. *Multimedia-Assisted Language Learning, 10*(1), 130-154. • O, K. M. (2004). Developing web-based English achievement testing program. *Multimedia-Assisted Language Learning, 7*(2), 241-268.

Assessment and Testing	English	• Kim, J. (2006). A web-based speaking test development using Visual Basic 6.0. *Multimedia-Assisted Language Learning, 9*(2), 77-98. • Lee, H. (2004). Reliability of a repeated testing design: a handwritten and computerized ESL writing test. *Multimedia-Assisted Language Learning,* 7(2), 143-163.
	Korean	• Choi, I. C. (2005). Measurability of oral fluency through ASR-based COPI. *Multimedia-Assisted Language Learning, 8*(2), 240-261.
Other Foreign Language	Korean	• Cheon, S. (2006). Constructing an English loanwords contents (ELC) database. *Multimedia-Assisted Language Learning, 9*(1), 186-210. • Choi, H. (2007). The use of mind map software for Russian learning. *Multimedia-Assisted Language Learning, 10*(3), 221-235.

The Mobile Period (2008-2012)		
E-Learning, Online Learning, and WBI	English	• Jung, K., & Chang, K. (2009). A classroom-centered research on interaction through peer review in the online English class. *Multimedia-Assisted Language Learning, 12*(3), 67-92. • Lee, S. (2011a). A new convergence medium: IPTV in the English classrooms. *Multimedia-Assisted Language Learning, 14*(1), 95-120. • Lee, S. (2011b). Beyond the classroom: Videoconferencing English class in the study centers. *Multimedia-Assisted Language Learning, 14*(3), 109-132.
	Korean	• Kim, J. R., & Jang, Y. J. (2008). The effects of a massive multiplayer online role-playing game on English skills of elementary school students. *Multimedia-Assisted Language Learning, 11*(1), 103-125. • Park, S. H., & Lim, H. S. (2009). Elementary English teachers' perceptions and use of English learning websites of the public institutions. *Multimedia-Assisted Language Learning, 12*(3), 139-168.

Blended Learning	English • Cha, Y. (2012). Learners' perspectives and use of different learning methods on blended learning in English classes. *Multimedia-Assisted Language Learning, 15*(2), 11-40. • Cha, Y., & Kim, H. (2011). Implementation of instructional methods and learners' views in online/offline business English classes. *Multimedia-Assisted Language Learning, 14*(3), 11-35. • Lee, J., & Lee, C. H. (2012). Students' perspectives and the effectiveness of blended learning in L2 listening at university level. *Multimedia-Assisted Language Learning, 15*(1), 59-89. • Yoon, S. Y. (2011). Students' reflection on feedback in L2 writing in blended learning. *Multimedia-Assisted Language Learning, 14*(2), 235-261. • Yoon, S. Y., & Lee, C. H. (2010). The perspectives and effectiveness of blended learning in L2 writing of Korean university students. *Multimedia-Assisted Language Learning, 13*(2), 177-204. • Yoon, S. Y., & Lee, C. H. (2012). The impact of explicit listening instruction on teacher preparation practices in blended learning. *Multimedia-Assisted Language Learning, 15*(4), 175-200.
	Korean • Kim, J., & Kim, H. (2012). Developing a blended instructional learning model optimized for English teaching at off-line universities. *Multimedia-Assisted Language Learning, 15*(1), 135-155.
Social Network Services (SNS) and Smart Education	English • Kim, E. Y., Park, S. M., & Baek, S. H. (2011). Twitter and the implications for its use in EFL learning. *Multimedia-Assisted Language Learning, 14*(2), 113-137. • Kim, H. (2010). Three teachers' initial efforts to use Twitter for teaching English in public schools. *Multimedia-Assisted Language Learning, 13*(2), 129-154. • Kim, H., & Kwon, Y. (2012). Exploring smartphone applications for effective mobile-assisted language learning. *Multimedia-Assisted Language Learning, 15*(1), 31-57.

Social Network Services (SNS) and Smart Education	Korean • Cho, S. (2009). Smartphones used for foreign language learning. *Multimedia-Assisted Language Learning, 12*(3), 211-228. • Cho, S. (2011). Social networking sites and foreign language learning. *Multimedia-Assisted Language Learning, 14*(3), 315-334. • Park, H. J., & Kim, J. Y. (2011). The effects of the English writing activities using Twitter on learners' writing abilities at university level. *Multimedia-Assisted Language Learning, 14*(3), 245-264.
Reading and Writing	English • Kim, J. K. (2009). Effects of collaborative writing in weblogs. *Multimedia- Assisted Language Learning, 12*(2), 135-161. • Kim, S. Y., & Ryoo, Y. S. (2009). Korean college students' vocabulary profiles as predictors of English reading and writing proficiency. *Multimedia-Assisted Language Learning, 12*(3), 93-115. • Lee, S. (2008). Exploring the potential of a web-based writing instruction program and AES: An empirical study using My Access. *Multimedia-Assisted Language Learning, 11*(2), 103-125. • Lee, S. (2012b). Writing technologies and hypertext relay writing: Fostering collaborative writing. *Multimedia-Assisted Language Learning, 15*(2), 121-141. • Pae, J. K. (2011). Collaborative writing versus individual writing: Fluency, accuracy, complexity, and essay score. *Multimedia-Assisted Language Learning, 14*(1), 121-148. • Schenck, A., & Cho, Y. W. (2012). The efficacy of corpus-based pedagogical techniques for academic writing. *Multimedia-Assisted Language Learning, 15*(2), 167-186.
	Korean • Huh, K. (2012). A study of integrated reading and writing instruction through the use of multimedia. *Multimedia-Assisted Language Learning, 15*(1), 181-209. • Jang, N. R., & Lee, E. J. (2012). The effects of electronic teacher feedback and writing a self-evaluation form on writing ability and the affective domain of Korean EFL learners. *Multimedia-Assisted Language Learning, 15*(3), 113-143.

Reading and Writing	Korean • Kim, J. K. (2012). Effects of self-directed and guided self-directed e-portfolios on Korean college students' writing ability. *Multimedia-Assisted Language Learning, 15*(1), 115-134. • Oh, C. R., & Choi, S. Y. (2010). A study of developing speed reading skills in English using multimedia. *Multimedia-Assisted Language Learning, 13*(1), 147-171. • Park, S. H., & Choi, H. (2012). The effects of modified extensive reading activities using Internet English storybooks on elementary school students' English learning. *Multimedia-Assisted Language Learning, 15*(3), 57-82. • Ryu, J. A., & Lee, C. H. (2011). The impact of using a web-based speed reading program on the improvement of English reading speed at elementary school level. *Multimedia-Assisted Language Learning, 14*(3), 195-224.
Pronunciation, Vocabulary, and Grammar	English • Kim, A. Y. (2012). Investigating the effectiveness of computer-assisted language learning (CALL) in improving pronunciation: A case study. *Multimedia-Assisted Language Learning, 15*(3), 11-33. • Kim, Y. M. (2010). Spoken corpora of EFL learners: Collocations, vocabulary use, and their oral proficiency levels. *Multimedia-Assisted Language Learning, 13*(1), 9-28. • Lee, S. (2012a). Networked computer-supported intentional vocabulary learning: Make it active and interactive. *Multimedia-Assisted Language Learning, 15*(4), 81-102. • Lee, S. W. (2012). Receptive vocabulary size for reading English and American novels. *Multimedia-Assisted Language Learning, 15*(4), 103-125. • Yoon, S. Y., & Lee, C. H. (2009). A study on voice recordings and feedback through BBS in teaching and learning pronunciation. *Multimedia- Assisted Language Learning, 12*(2), 187-216.
	Korean • Min, D. G., Kim, S. R., & Kim, K. H. (2010). A study on the development of a corpus-based collocation book using children's English newspapers. *Multimedia-Assisted Language Learning, 13*(1), 173-200.

Pronunciation, Vocabulary, and Grammar	Korean • Shin, D., & Jeong, D. (2009). How can we make word family lists with graded affixes? *Multimedia-Assisted Language Learning, 12*(3), 169-193. • Shin, D., & Joo, H. (2008). Development of a vocabulary list for English textbook authorization: Reflection on vocabulary analysis programs and the basic vocabulary list. *Multimedia-Assisted Language Learning, 11*(3), 95-113. • Youk, S. Y., & Lee, C. H. (2008). The effective use of a web-based English grammar program for middle school students. *Multimedia-Assisted Language Learning, 11*(1), 155-177.
Focus on Form	English • Cho, Y. W. (2011). Triadic text-based SCMC and focus on form: Fluency, accuracy, and complexity. *Multimedia-Assisted Language Learning, 14*(2), 29-60. • Cho, Y. W., & Kim, I. H. (2010). The feasibility of using text-based online chat for communicative focus on form. *Multimedia-Assisted Language Learning, 13*(2), 37-58. • Cho, Y. W., Lee, Y. J., & Kim, S. (2012). Focus on form in text-based SCMC: Putting teachers' SLA knowledge into practice. *Multimedia-Assisted Language Learning, 15*(4), 11-37. • Hong, A. R., & Lee, C. H. (2008). The effects of focus on form in CMC: A case study of Korean adult learners. *Multimedia-Assisted Language Learning, 11*(2), 9-40.
Computer-Mediated Communication (CMC)	English • Cha, Y., & Park, L. E. (2010). An analysis of synchronous interaction and its influence on EFL writers' revisions. *Multimedia-Assisted Language Learning, 13*(2), 9-36. • Kwon, H., & Lee, C. H. (2011). Learner uptake of feedback in text-based synchronous computer mediated communication (SCMC). *Multimedia-Assisted Language Learning, 14*(2), 211-234. • Lim, K. (2012). Developing an English intensive course model based on CMC for Korean high school students. *Multimedia-Assisted Language Learning, 15*(4), 127-151. • Shim, Y. S. (2008). Stimulating negotiation of meaning in CMC interaction. *Multimedia-Assisted Language Learning, 11*(2), 142-168.

Computer-Mediated Communication (CMC)	Korean • Jung, Y. S. (2008). Exploring factors influencing the successful CMC based English learning. *Multimedia-Assisted Language Learning, 11*(3), 131-154. • Kim, S. Y., & Lee, H. J. (2012). A comparison of peer feedback in CMC and FFC contexts. *Multimedia-Assisted Language Learning, 15*(1), 91-114.
Collaborative Learning	English • Kim, B. G. (2010). Collaborative discussion and peer review activity in computer-mediated EFL writing. *Multimedia-Assisted Language Learning, 13*(2), 105-128. • Pae, J. K. (2012). How do Korean EFL students perform in computer-supported collaborative writing? *Multimedia-Assisted Language Learning, 15*(4), 153-174.
Courseware Design and Evaluation	English • Kim, T. E. (2010). Reflection on using the criterion online writing evaluation service. *Multimedia-Assisted Language Learning, 13*(3), 59-83. • Lee, S. (2009). Evaluation of English learning programs on EBSe. *Multimedia-Assisted Language Learning, 12*(3), 117-137. • Thorne, S. L. (2008). New media language use and "bridging activities": Implications for plurilingual life in a (partially) digital world. *Multimedia-Assisted Language Learning, 11*(1), 35-60.
	Korean • Cho, S., Lee, S., Kim, J, Ko, B., & Jeong, E. (2008). A development model of web-based English language learning programs. *Multimedia-Assisted Language Learning, 11*(1), 213-238. • Jun, H. C., & Choi, S. Y. (2008). A development of PDA vocabulary contents using cartoons for elementary school English language learning and teaching. *Multimedia-Assisted Language Learning, 11*(1), 179-212. • Kim, H., & Kim, E. (2010). The development of online-integrated college English curriculum for enhancing speaking performance. *Multimedia- Assisted Language Learning, 13*(3), 197-214.

Courseware Design and Evaluation	Korean • Moon, K., & Kim, J. (2012). Development and application of web-based Korean elementary English readability index software for measuring readability in extensive reading classrooms. *Multimedia-Assisted Language Learning, 15*(1), 157-179. • Ohm, I. S. (2008) A study of the design of curriculum-based progress monitoring systems. *Multimedia-Assisted Language Learning, 11*(1), 127-155.
Assessment and Testing	English • Choi, I. C. (2012). A validation of EFL essay assessment based on corpus indices and error analysis. *Multimedia-Assisted Language Learning, 15*(4), 39-60. • Craig, D. A., & Kim, J. (2010). Anxiety and performance in video- conferenced interviews. *Multimedia-Assisted Language Learning, 13*(3), 9-32. • Jin, K. A., & Park, T. (2012). Exploring automated scoring of Korean high school students' English composition. *Multimedia-Assisted Language Learning, 15*(1), 11-29. • Kim, H. J. (2011). Investigating effects of tasks on examinee performance in a computer-delivered speaking test. *Multimedia-Assisted Language Learning, 14*(1), 65-93. • Kim, J. (2011). The validation process in developing a web-based English speaking and writing test. *Multimedia-Assisted Language Learning, 14*(2), 181-209.
	Korean • Kim, J. (2009). The relationship between speaking test administration tools and item types. *Multimedia-Assisted Language Learning, 12*(1), 177-202.
Teacher Education	English • Ahn, K. (2009). Do innovative technologies bring about innovative instructional practices? A case study of a Korean EFL teacher's class under the curricular reform context. *Multimedia-Assisted Language Learning, 12*(2), 9-42.
	Korean • Gye, Y., Chang, J., & Jung, J. (2008). A case study of online in-service English teacher training program for language improvement. *Multimedia-Assisted Language Learning, 11*(3), 71-94.

Teacher Education	Korean • Jeon, Y. J., & Kang, H. Y. (2012). A study on the use of a web-based online in-service training program for the improvement of teaching skills for TaLK (Teach and Learn in Korea) scholars. *Multimedia-Assisted Language Learning, 15*(3), 145-164. • Kim, H. D. (2010). Study on teacher trainees' responses in blended TESOL intensive program. *Multimedia-Assisted Language Learning, 13*(3), 175-195. • Kim, H. O. (2011). The change in secondary school teachers' views and uses of multimedia-assisted language learning and the direction of teacher education. *Multimedia-Assisted Language Learning, 14*(1), 193-210. • Kim, S. (2012). Implementing digital portfolios in a pre-service English teachers' classroom. *Multimedia-Assisted Language Learning, 15*(3), 35-56. • Lee, J., & Lee, C. H. (2009). Elementary and secondary school teachers' perspectives and solutions for the improvement of online teacher training in foreign language education. *Multimedia-Assisted Language Learning, 12*(1), 203-229.

The Social Media and Artificial Intelligence (AI) period (2013-2020)	
E-Learning, Online Learning and WBI	English • Jung, H. J. (2016). Factors impacting learners satisfaction and continued use of e-learning in an EFL context. *Multimedia-Assisted Language Learning, 19*(2), 11-33. • Kim, H. S., & Cha, Y. (2017). A comparative study of pre-reading activities on university students' reading comprehension: learning vocabulary vs. watching YouTube. *Multimedia-Assisted Language Learning, 20*(1), 11-34. • Lee, S. E. (2018). "I'm So Excited About My Own Space for English": A Web-portfolio Project in a College English Writing Class. *Multimedia-Assisted Language Learning, 21*(1), 107-132. • Lee, Y. J., & Gerber, H. (2013). It's a WoW World: Second language acquisition and massively multiplayer online gaming. *Multimedia-Assisted Language Learning, 16*(2), 53-70. • Mo, S. K., & Lee, S. (2017). The relationships among the presences of community of inquiry and the perceptions of EFL college students in online learning. *Multimedia-Assisted Language Learning, 20*(2), 11-35.

E-Learning, Online Learning and WBI	English • Obari, H. (2013). The impact of employing mobile technologies and PC for learning Coursera on-line lectures and TOEIC practice kit. *Multimedia-Assisted Language Learning, 16*(4), 97-109.
	Korean • Ahn, J., & Shim, Y. (2015). A study on the perception and utilization of teachers' websites in Korean language teaching. *Multimedia-Assisted Language Learning, 18*(3), 198-230. • Han, J. I. (2017). The effects of creativity-based English teaching and learning using technology on Korean middle school students' English learning achievement and creativity. *Multimedia-Assisted Language Learning, 20*(4), 127-154. • Seo, Y. J., & Lee, E. J. (2014). The effects of storybook mind-mapping and summarizing activities on vocabulary acquisition, writing ability and the attitude of the elementary school students. *Multimedia-Assisted Language Learning, 17*(3), 121-153.
Blended Learning	English • Baek, J., & Lee, C. H. (2018). University students' perceptions and engagement in mobile assisted blended learning in English speaking classes. *Multimedia-Assisted Language Learning, 21*(4), 11-36. • Cha, Y. (2014). Effects of blended peer feedback modes on learners' writing performance and perspectives. *Multimedia-Assisted Language Learning, 17*(2), 11-42. • Jin, S. (2014). Implementation of smartphone-based blended learning in an EFL undergraduate grammar course. *Multimedia-Assisted Language Learning, 17*(4), 11-37. • Jung, R., & Lee, C. H. (2013). Using Internet video clips for university students' vocabulary development in blended learning. *Multimedia-Assisted Language Learning, 16*(4), 67-96. • Kim, H. S. (2014). Effects of using mobile devices in blended learning for English reading comprehension, *Multimedia-Assisted Language Learning, 17*(2), 64-85. • Kim, H., & Yoon, M. N. (2014). Adopting smartphone-based blended learning: An experimental study of the implementation of Kakao Talk and Mocafé. *Multimedia-Assisted Language Learning, 17*(2), 86-111.

Blended Learning	English • Kim, J. K., & Moon, E. J. (2013). The effect of online and coached online instructions on pronunciation and vocabulary in blended learning. *Multimedia-Assisted Language Learning, 16*(3), 39-67. • Kim, S. Y., & Lee, C. H. (2018). The impact of peer response on lexis and grammatical structure in L2 writing through blended learning. *Multimedia-Assisted Language Learning, 21*(4), 82-110. • Lee, J. (2015). The impact of metacognitive instruction in blended learning on L2 listeners' metacognitive awareness and comprehension. *Multimedia-Assisted Language Learning, 18*(4), 70-98. • Lee, Y. J., & Cho, Y. W. (2017). Coaching for Korean university students' English speaking and self-directed language learning: a blended learning approach. *Multimed Assist Lang Learn, 20*(1), 82-108. • Oh, E. (2017). The effect of peer teaching via flipped vocabulary learning on class engagement and learning achievements. *Multimedia-Assisted Language Learning, 20*(3), 105-127. • Park, S. M., & Cha, K. W. (2013). Pre-service teachers' perspectives on a blended listening course using TED Talks. *Multimedia-Assisted Language Learning, 16*(2), 93-116. • So, L. (2015). L2 writing instruction in blended learning for the development of fluency, complexity, and accuracy in higher education. *Multimedia-Assisted Language Learning, 18*(4), 121-147. • So, L., & Lee, C. H. (2016). Students' engagement in peer response and its influence on writing quality in blended learning at university level. *Multimedia-Assisted Language Learning, 19*(2), 61-90. • Yang, Z., & Lee, C. I. (2018). The effects of flipped vocabulary learning on Chinese college students' listening achievement. *Multimedia-Assisted Language Learning, 21*(1), 133-152. • Yee, W. H., & Lee, C. H. (2017). The impact of the problem-solution pattern instruction and collaborative revision on business writing in blended learning. *Multimedia-Assisted Language Learning, 20*(3), 128-156.

Blended Learning	English • Yoon, S. Y. (2014). The impact of language learning strategies in blended learning and students' perspectives. *Multimedia-Assisted Language Learning, 17*(4), 88-111. • Yoon, S. Y. (2015). The impact of voice journals on university students' speaking skills in blended learning. *Multimedia-Assisted Language Learning, 18*(4), 148-168.
Social Network Services (SNS) and Smart Education	English • Cho, H. (2018). An online survey tool as a learner response system: Use of Google Forms in university TOEIC courses. *Multimedia-Assisted Language Learning, 21*(2), 11-34. • Cho, Y. S. (2015). Exploration of a social networking site from L2 learners' perspectives: The case of Lang-8. *Multimedia-Assisted Language Learning, 18*(3), 11-40. • Jeong, M., Lee, J., & Kim, J. (2013). An analysis of learner interaction in Smart English education. *Multimedia-Assisted Language Learning, 16*(4), 39-65. • Ji, H. E., & Shin, H. W. (2019). Young foreign language learners' engagement and motivation in augmented reality-based vocabulary learning. *Multimedia-Assisted Language Learning, 22*(3), 9-31. • Jung, H. J. (2017). An empirical study of attributes influencing smart English learning. *Multimedia-Assisted Language Learning, 20*(3), 11-32. • Jung, H. J. (2019). Evaluating smart English classroom environments from the student satisfaction. *Multimedia-Assisted Language Learning, 22*(4), 34-56. • Kim, H. S. (2013). Emerging mobile apps to improve English listening skills. *Multimedia-Assisted Language Learning, 16*(2), 11-30. • Kim, S. Y. (2017). Smart learning: Approaches and materials for language learning. *Multimedia-Assisted Language Learning, 20*(3), 62-83. • Seo, W., & Choi, I. C. (2014). The effect of using a smart-phone speaking application on Korean middle school students' English expression learning and satisfaction. *Multimedia-Assisted Language Learning, 17*(1), 34-57. • Yoon, S. Y. (2017). Using learner response systems for EFL classrooms: Students' perspectives and experience. *Multimedia Assisted Language Learning, 20*(2), 36-58.

Social Network Services (SNS) and Smart Education	Korean • Choi, H., & Kim, J. (2013). Development of CAT smart app for elementary English reading evaluation. *Multimedia-Assisted Language Learning, 16*(1), 119-141. • Han, J. I. (2015). A study on the effective use of wiki software in the teaching of English writing. *Multimedia-Assisted Language Learning, 18*(3), 302-325. • Jin, S. (2013). The use of Facebook as a new pedagogical tool to promote EFL learners' writing. *Multimedia-Assisted Language Learning, 16*(3), 145-170. • Jin, S. (2018). The effects of using smartphone applications for vocabulary flashcards and SNS-based mobile collaborative learning on English vocabulary knowledge. *Multimedia-Assisted Language Learning, 21*(4), 298-322. • Jeong, N. S. (2017). The effects of mobile-mediated learning on university students' English writing achievement. *Multimedia-Assisted Language Learning, 20*(2), 84-113. • Kim, K. O., & Park, S. H. (2015). The Effects of process-based writing through the use of mobile SNS software on elementary English education. *Multimedia-Assisted Language Learning, 18*(1), 11-32. • Kim, G. (2019). An analysis of factor influencing Korean university students' use of mobile-assisted language learning environment. *Multimedia-Assisted Language Learning, 22*(2), 29-49. • Kwon, Y. (2013). A case study of college EFL learners' mobile-assisted language learning with smart applications. *Multimedia-Assisted Language Learning, 16*(1), 37-65. • Lee. C. H., & Cho, S. (2019). The application and effective use of MABL (Mobile-Assisted Language Learning) in university English classes. *Multimedia-Assisted Language Learning, 22*(4), 226-255. • Park, M. H., & Lee, S. W. (2017). The effect of using smart devices on the vocabulary learning for low English proficiency students. *Multimedia-Assisted Language Learning, 20*(1), 144-166. • Son, S. Y. (2018). Effects of using mobile-based vocabulary game activities on Korean middle school students' vocabulary learning and attitudes. *Multimedia-Assisted Language Learning, 21*(2), 104-133.

Listening and Speaking	English	• Kim, G. (2018). The effects of web-based dictation and group size on Korean university students' English listening performance. *Multimedia-Assisted Language Learning, 21*(2), 35-56. • Kim, J., Cho, Y. W., & Lee, Y. J. (2014). Exploring the effects of multimedia-based self-directed English speaking practice. *Multimedia-Assisted Language Learning, 17*(4), 61-87. • Kim, N. Y. (2016). Effects of voice chat on EFL learners' speaking ability according to proficiency levels. *Multimedia-Assisted Language Learning, 19*(4), 63-88. • Lee, E., & Park, S. D. (2014). Adult EFL learners' successful participation in Web-Talking for oral proficiency improvement. *Multimedia-Assisted Language Learning, 17*(2), 152-175.
	Korean	• Choe, Y. (2014). The effects of speaking task types and Korean EFL learners' English proficiency level on online speaking performance. *Multimedia-Assisted Language Learning, 17*(1), 106-131. • Jung, H. Y., & Cha, K. W. (2015). Effects of shadowing using TED on EFL learners' listening skills. *Multimedia-Assisted Language Learning, 18*(3), 257-276.
Reading and Writing	English	• Kim, H., & Cha, Y. (2015). Is self-directed learning effective in an online reading environment. *Multimedia-Assisteted Language Learning, 18*(3), 73-96. • Kim, K. S. (2017). Computer-aided analysis of L2 writers' source text borrowing. *Multimedia-Assisted Language Learning, 20*(1), 60-81. • Kim, M., & Cho, Y. W. (2016). The effects of metalinguistic and exemplar-based written corrective feedback on English verb complementation accuracy in multimedia-based EFL writing instruction. *Multimedia-Assisted Language Learning, 19*(2), 34-60. • Kim, N. Y. (2018). Effects of reading aloud tasks through a mobile phone on EFL vocabulary and reading comprehension skills. *Multimedia-Assisted Language Learning, 21*(1), 57-76. • Kim, P. (2018). Implementing digital storytelling and students' writing ability development in an EFL college classroom. *Multimedia-Assisted Language Learning, 21*(1), 77-106.

Reading and Writing	English • Kim, S. Y., & Pae, J. K. (2013). Computer-supported writing: A comparison of Wiki and Daedalus. *Multimedia-Assisted Language Learning, 16*(2), 31-52. • Lee, C., & Astle, R. (2014). Favorable types of medium in corrective feedback on writing: Harness the power of technologies or continue the traditional ways? *Multimedia-Assisted Language Learning, 17*(2), 112-129. • Lee, C. M., & Oh, E. (2014). Exploring the effects of a learner response system on EFL reading. *Multimedia-Assisted Language Learning, 17*(2), 130-151. • Wang, S. Y. (2018). Task complexity and media of L2 reading affecting Chinese intermediate EFL learners. *Multimedia-Assisted Language Learning, 21*(4), 211-230.
	Korean • Ahn, M. R. (2016). A study on the factors that influence the flipped class and learners' satisfaction level. *Multimedia-Assisted Language Learning, 19*(1), 114-136. • Lee, S. (2019). Korean college students' perception toward the effectiveness of machine translation on L2 revision. *Multimedia-Assisted Language Learning, 22*(4), 206-225.
Pronunciation, Vocabulary, and Grammar	English • Kang, N. (2015). The comparison between regular and flipped classrooms for EFL Korean adult learners. *Multimedia-Assisted Language Learning, 18*(3), 41-72. • Kim, H. S. (2019). The use of Socrative and Kahoot! in English Grammar. *Multimedia-Assisted Language Learning, 22*(4), 57-78. • Kim, H. S., & Choi, U. Y. (2019). Incidental development of tense-aspect in EFL through an interactive written discourse: Focusing on Aspectual Distinctions. *Multimedia-Assisted Language Learning, 22*(4), 79-102. • Kim, S. (2015). Calling on CALL to meet individual learner needs for grammar instruction in an EFL composition class. *Multimedia-Assisted Language Learning, 18*(3), 97-121. • Kim, S. M., & Lee, C. H. (2015). A case study on online peer feedback for learning English pronunciation at university level. *Multimedia-Assisted Language Learning, 18*(4), 42-69. • Ko, M. H. (2017). Output, feedback, technology, and L2 vocabulary learning. *Multimedia-Assisted Language Learning, 20*(3), 84-104.

Pronunciation, Vocabulary' and Grammar	• Ko, M. H., & Goranson, J. (2014). Technology-assisted vocabulary learning and student learning outcomes: A Case Study. *Multimedia-Assisted Language Learning, 17*(1), 11-33. • Oh, H., & Park, M. R. (2013). A case study of elementary school underachievers' SMART vocabulary learning experiences. *Multimedia-Assisted Language Learning, 16*(2), 71-92.
	Korean • Jeon, H. C. (2013). The effects of e-book contents using pseudo words on vocabulary learning. *Multimedia-Assisted Language Learning, 16*(1), 93-117. Yoon, S. Y. (2013). The effectiveness of online English pronunciation class and students' perspectives. *Multimedia-Assisted Language Learning, 16*(3), 97-123.
Courseware Design and Evaluation	English • Chun, S. (2016). High school teachers' needs for DDL materials: Appropriate amount of concordance input. *Multimedia-Assisted Language Learning, 19*(1), 32-57. • Han, J. I. (2014). The effects of learning models of English digital textbooks on Korean middle school students' English learning and attitudes toward English. *Multimedia-Assisted Language Learning, 17*(1), 132-158. • Ryu, J. (2017). The effects of digital textbooks on college EFL learners' self-regulated learning. *Multimedia-assisted language learning, 20*(4), 99-126. • Han, J. I. (2014). The effects of learning models of English digital textbooks on Korean middle school students' English learning and attitudes toward English. *Multimedia-Assisted Language Learning, 17*(1), 132-158.
	Korean • Jeon, Y. J., & Kang, M. K. (2013). A study of smart English teaching models using QR codes. *Multimedia-Assisted Language Learning, 16*(3), 125-143. • Kang, J. (2013). A study on elementary school students' acceptance of English digital textbooks using Technology Acceptance Model. *Multimedia-Assisted Language Learning, 16*(1), 11-36. • Kim, H., & Park, D. G. (2016). Mobile application design and evaluation for English speaking practice: Design-based research. *Multimedia-Assisted Language Learning, 19*(1), 58-85

Courseware Design and Evaluation	Korean • Kim, H., Lee, J. H., Kim, J. Y., & Lee, H. (2018). Design, implementation, and evaluation of open learning platform for teacher training. *Multimedia-Assisted Language Learning, 21*(3), 149-174. • Kim, S., & Kim, H. (2015). Designing scaffolding in a digital English textbook for high school low achievers: A case study. *Multimedia-Assisted Language Learning, 18*(1), 33-58. • Lee, D. K., & Kim, H. (2014). A study on online TEE teacher training programs in Korea. *Multimedia-Assisted Language Learning, 17*(1), 58-83. • Lee, M., & Joo, H. (2017). Development and field test of an online high school English speaking performance assessement support system. *Multimedia-Assisted Language Learning, 20*(1), 167-185. • Yun, J. H., Kwon, S. K., & Kim, S. Y. (2015). Development of a mobile English speaking app for middle school students: Speaking English Jr. *Multimedia-Assisted Language Learning, 18*(3), 231-256.
Assessment and Testing	English • Choi, I. C., & Jang, S. H. (2017). Task characteristics of a computerized TTS dictation test and diagnostic interpretability of qualitative error analysis. *Multimedia-Assisted Language Learning, 20*(4), 11-43. • Choi, I. C., & Park, S. Y. (2016). Efficacy of corpus-driven scoring methods for computer-based dictation tests. *Multimedia-Assisted Language Learning, 19*(4), 11-39. • Hong, W. (2016). The effect of presentation modes in computer-assisted language testing on cultural contents in Korean EFL classrooms. *Multimedia-Assisted Language Learning, 19*(3), 37-60. • Kim, J. E. (2014). The effectiveness of automated essay scoring in an EFL college classroom. *Multimedia-Assisted Language Learning, 17*(3), 11-36. • Moon, Y. S., & Choi, I. C. (2019). Salient linguistic features of EFL learner spoken corpus elicited by a computerized speaking test. *Multimedia-Assisted Language Learning, 22*(3), 54-83.
	Korean • Kim, J. (2017). A study on the correlation between the Korean college students' English reading speed and the scoring features of an English speaking test. *Multimedia-Assisted Language Leaning, 20*(3), 157-178.

Assessment and Testing	Korean • Kim, J., & Park, E. (2019). Development of task types and scoring constructs of computer-based English speaking test. *Multimedia-Assisted Language Learning, 22*(3), 150-178 • Lee, I., & Kim, J. (2018). The effect of task types and difficulty on Korean college students' CBT speaking test scores. *Multimedia-Assisted Language Learning, 21*(4), 247-266. • Lim, H., Park, D., & Si, K. (2014). Sophistication of an automated scoring system for large-scale essay writing tests. *Multimedia-Assisted Language Learning, 17*(1), 84-105. • Shin, D., Park, Y., Park, T., & Yim, S. Y. (2015). The present and future of an automated scoring program for speaking skills of English. *Multimedia-Assisted Language Learning, 18*(1), 93-114. • Shin, D., Chon, Y., Lee, S. W., & Park, M. (2017). Developing an English collocation proficiency text. *Multimedia-Assisted Language Learning, 20*(2), 59-83.
Teacher Education	English • Jung, H. J. (2018). An Exploration of English Teachers' Resistance to Technological Innovation. *Multimedia-Assisted Language Learning, 21*(1), 35-56. • Lim, S. H. (2017). Teachers empowering teachers in an online community of practice: A case study of Korean EFL teachers' learning to teach flipped classroom on NAVER BAND. *Multimedia-Assisted Language Learning, 20*(1), 109-143.
	Korean • Kim, H. S., & Kim, H. (2017). A study of Korean English teachers' future readiness for the fourth industrial revolution. *Multimedia-Assisted Language Learning, 20*(3), 179-205.
Artificial Intelligence (AI)	English • Kim, N. Y., Cha, Y., & Kim, H. S. (2019). Future English learning: chatbots and artificial intelligence. *Multimedia-Assisted Language Learning, 22*(3), 32-53. • Park, J. (2019). An AI-based English grammar checker vs. human raters in evaluating EFL learners' writing. *Multimedia-Assisted Language Learning, 22*(1), 112-131.

Artificial Intelligence (AI)	English • Yoon, S. Y. (2019). Student readiness for AI instruction: perspectives on AI in university EFL classrooms. *Multimedia-Assisted Language Learning, 22*(4), 134-160.
	Korean • Lee, J. H., Kim, H., Shin, D. K., & Yang, H. (2019). A study on the conversational interaction with chatbot for foreign language learning. *Multimedia-Assisted Language Learning, 22*(1), 132-153. • Yang, H., Kim, H., & Shin, D. (2019). A study on adopting AI-based chatbot in elementary English-speaking classes. *Multimedia-Assisted Language Learning, 22*(4), 184-205.
Corpus	English • Cho, H. (2016). An investigation of controlled corpus consultation of selected formulaic expressions in L2 Writing. *Multimedia-Assisted Language Learning, 19*(3), 11-36. • Chon, Y. V., & Shin, D. (2013). A corpus-driven analysis of spoken and written academic collocations. *Multimedia-Assisted Language Learning, 16*(3), 11-38. • Hong, J. Y. (2018). A corpus analysis of Korean EAP writers' acquisition of rhetorical structure and linguistic features. *Multimedia-Assisted Language Learning, 21*(3), 11-38. • Kang, H. Y., & Lee, C. H. (2014). Analysis of topic changes and moves in abstracts of Multimedia-Assisted Language Learning and Language Learning and Technology. *Multimedia-Assisted Language Learning, 17*(4), 38-60. • Kang, H. Y., & Lee, C. H. (2016). Move structures and lexico-grammatical patterns of abstracts of CALL research articles and MA theses: A Corpus-Based Comparative Analysis. *Multimedia-Assisted Language Learning, 19*(4), 40-62. • Nam, D. (2018). Lexical Bundle Uses in Prospective EFL Science and Engineering University Students' Writing. *Multimedia-Assisted Language Learning, 21*(4), 143-162. • Nam, D., & Park, K. (2015). Corpus-based analysis of thematic structure in L2 writing. *Multimedia-Assisted Language Learning, 18*(4), 99-120. • Le, T. H. T., & Kim, S. Y. (2018). A corpus analysis of collocational behaviors of near-synonyms adjective. *Multimedia-Assisted Language Learning, 21*(4), 181-210.

Corpus	Korean • Kim, J. E., & Choi, I. C. (2015). A corpus-based comparative analysis of linguistic difficulty among high school English textbooks, EBS-CSAT prep books, and College Scholastic Ability Test. *Multimedia-Assisted Language Learning, 18*(1), 59-92.

Appendices

Appendix 1 Web and App Resources

1.1 Websites and Apps for MALL and MABL

1. Listening

Esl-Lounge Student	https://www.esl-lounge.com/student/listening.php
Focus on English	https://www.focusenglish.com
LearnEnglish	https://learnenglish.britishcouncil.org/en/apps
Listen to English Podcasts	https://www.podcastsinenglish.com/
National Public Radio	https://www.npr.org
Naturalreader	https://www.naturalreaders.com/
PBS News hour	https://www.pbs.org/newshour
Randall's Cyber Listening Lab	https://www.esl-lab.com
TED	https://www.ted.com
VOA Learning English	https://learningenglish.voanews.com
Voki	https://www.voki.com
YouTube	https://www.youtube.com

Apps

English Listening Player
https://play.google.com/store/apps/details?id=com.talkenglish.player

English Listening
https://play.google.com/store/apps/details?id=com.talkenglish.listening

Learn English Listening
https://play.google.com/store/apps/details?id=com.ocoder.learn.english.free

2. Speaking

Animaker	https://www.animaker.com/
Focus on English	https://www.focusenglish.com
Kakao Talk	https://www.kakao.com

MS Teams	https://products.office.com/ko-kr/microsoft-teams/group-chat-software/
RhinoSpike	https://rhinospike.com
Voki	https://www.voki.com
Webex	https://www.webex.co.kr/
Xtranormal	https://www.xtranormal.com
Zoom	https://zoom.us/
WhaleOn	https://whale.naver.com/details/whaleon/

Apps

English Conversation Practice
https://play.google.com/store/apps/details?id=com.talkenglish.conversation

Learn to Speak English
https://play.google.com/store/apps/details?id=talkenglish.com.standard

Pronunciation

American English Pronunciation
https://pronuncian.com/

American English Pronunciation Practice
http://www.manythings.org/pp/

English Pronunciation
https://play.google.com/store/apps/details?id=com.study.english.pronunciation

Pronunciation and Conversation
https://www.thoughtco.com/esl-pronunciation-and-conversation-4133093

Sounds of English
https://www.soundsofenglish.org

Speakometer
https://play.google.com/store/apps/details?id=com.datawide.speakometer&hl=ko

3. Reading

English Newspaper: News for you	https://www.newreaderspress.com/news-for-you-online

Interactive Learning Resources	https://literacynet.org/cnnsf/week.html
PBS News hour	https://www.pbs.org/newshour
Rocket Reader	https://rocketreader.com
Storybird	https://storybird.com

Vocabulary

English Online	https://www.english-online.at
English Vocabulary Word Lists	https://www.manythings.org/vocabulary
Lextutor	https://www.lextutor.ca
The Corpus of Contemporary American	https://corpus.byu.edu/coca
English Cambridge Dictionaries Online	https://dictionary.cambridge.org

Collins COBUILD English Dictionary
https://www.collinsdictionary.com/dictionary/english

Dictionary.com	https://dictionary.reference.com
Merriam-Webster Learner's Dictionary	https://www.learnersdictionary.com
Oxford English Dictionary	https://www.oed.com

Apps

Aldiko Book Reader
https://play.google.com/store/apps/details?id=com.aldiko.android

AlReader -any textbook reader
https://play.google.com/store/apps/details?id=com.neverland.alreader

Cool Reader
https://play.google.com/store/apps/details?id=org.coolreader

FBReader: Favorite Book Reader
https://play.google.com/store/apps/details?id=org.geometerplus.zlibrary.ui.android

Kobo Books - Reading App
https://play.google.com/store/apps/details?id=com.kobobooks.android

4. Writing

Cambridge English Write & Improve
https://www.cambridgeenglish.org/learning-english/find-free-resources/write-and-improve

Online Writing Lab by D'Youville College
http://depts.dyc.edu/learningcenter/owl/grammar_topics.htm

Colorado State University's Writing Studio
https://writing.colostate.edu

LearnEnglish	https://learnenglish.britishcouncil.org/en/writing
LEO	https://leo.stcloudstate.edu/style/sentencev.html
Purdue's Online Writing lab	https://owl.english.purdue.edu
Small Seo Tools	https://smallseotools.com
Spellcheck	https://www.spellcheck.net
Word and Pictures	https://www.bbc.co.uk/schools/wordsandpictures

Grammar

English Learner	https://www.englishlearner.com
Grammarly	https://www.grammarly.com
Guide to Grammar & Writing	https://www.ccc.commnet.edu/grammar
LearnEnglish	https://learnenglish.britishcouncil.org/en/grammar
Purdue's Online Writing lab	https://owl.english.purdue.edu/owl/section/1/5/

Apps

JotterPad https://play.google.com/store/apps/details?id=com.jotterpad.x

English writing
https://play.google.com/store/apps/details?id=com.letters.templates

English Grammar Handbook
https://play.google.com/store/apps/details?id=com.ssstudio.grammarhandbook&hl=en

English Grammar Test
https://play.google.com/store/apps/details?id=english.grammar.test.app&hl=en

Writer
https://play.google.com/store/apps/details?id=com.jamesmc.writer

Writing Tips
https://play.google.com/store/apps/details?id=com.ictcontent.writingtips

Writer Plus (Write on the Go)
https://play.google.com/store/apps/details?id=co.easy4u.writer

1.2 Websites and Apps for Editing, Authoring, and Learning Tools

1. Learning tools

Words & Texts

Classcard https://www.classcard.net/
Tagxedo http://www.tagxedo.com/
Word Art https://wordart.com/

Images

PhotoScape http://www.photoscape.org/ps/main/index.php/
Snagit https://www.techsmith.com/screen-capture.html

Cartoons

Make Beliefs Comix https://www.makebeliefscomix.com/
Toonytool https://www.toonytool.com/

Sounds

Audacity https://www.audacityteam.org/
Goldwave https://www.goldwave.com/
1gram player http://www.1gram.net/
RhinoSpike https://rhinospike.com/

Videos

Camtasia	https://www.techsmith.com/video-editor.html
Gomcam	https://www.gomlab.com/gomcam-screen-recording/
Gommix	https://www.gomlab.com/gommix-video-editing/
Ocam	https://ohsoft.net/kor/ocam/download.php?cate=1002
1gram player	http://www.1gram.net/

Animations

Animaker https://www.animaker.com/

Draw Cartoon 2
https://play.google.com/store/apps/details?id=com.zalivka.animation2&hl

2. Authoring Tools

Kahoot	https://kahoot.com/
Quizlet	https://quizlet.com/
Socrative	https://www.socrative.com/

3. Other Learning Tools

Classting	https://www.classting.com/
Flipgrid	https://info.flipgrid.com/
Google Docs	https://docs.google.com/
Grammarly	https://app.grammarly.com/
Lextutor	https://www.lextutor.ca/
Mendeley	https://www.mendeley.com/
MS Teams	https://www.microsoft.com/ko-kr/microsoft-teams/free
OKMindmap	http://okmindmap.com/
Padlet	https://ko.padlet.com/

Appendix 2 Microteaching Evaluation Checklists for MALL

Microteaching Evaluation Checklists for MALL

Individual or Group Presentation: **Evaluator:**

*** Scale: 5 (Very good), 4 (Good), 3 (Average), 2 (Poor), 1 (Very poor)**

1. Content	5	4	3	2	1
Material					
Does the content meet the objectives of the syllabus/lesson plan?					
Is it suitable for the target group?					
Is it well organized?					
Is it interesting?					
Does it promote authentic use of language?					
Does it provide sufficient practice exercises?					
Is it adaptable and applicable in real classrooms?					
Instruction					
Is the instruction clear and level appropriate?					
Is it appropriate for the activities? (pre-, post-, while)					
Is it free of errors (content, grammar, etc.)?					
Does the teacher speak with clear and comprehensible pronunciation, stress, intonation, and rhythm?					
Is the instruction communicative (using real language)?					
Did the teacher use non-verbal properly?					
Is it well-matched with the materials used?					
Is the instruction given effectively and efficiently?					
Does it allow students to carry out individual/P/G work?					
Does the teacher build the students' knowledge throughout the lesson?					
Is there adequate and appropriate feedback?					
Is the teacher confident in delivering instruction?					

Activity					
Is the activity sufficient?					
Is it motivating and interesting?					
Is it level appropriate for the students?					
Does it include and practice the skills the students need?					
Does it promote adequate language production?					
Is it integrated into other language skills?					
Does it allow Learner (L)-Teacher and L-L interaction?					
Is there any feedback during the activity?					
Total					

2. Comments	
Which activity types were covered in the lesson?	
Which skills were supposed to be practiced? How was this achieved?	
Was the aim of the lesson attained?	
How can this lesson be applicable to your classes?	
Additional remarks	

Appendix 3 App Evaluation Checklists

3.1 Simple Evaluation Checklist for Apps

- Evaluator:
- E-mail:
- Date:
- Institution:
- Address/Phone number

Evaluation criteria	Elements	Quantitative evaluation	Qualitative evaluation
1. Aims & Objectives (5)	Learning and teaching goals	/5	
2. Administrative elements (5)	Author(s), Year Published, application capacity, battery consumption, E-mail/ Homepage, etc.	/5	
3. Pedagogical elements (50)	1) Learning objectives 2) Learning content 3) Feedback 4) Assessment	/8 /20 /12 /10	
4. Technical elements (30)	1) Screen display 2) Colors, sounds, graphics, and moving pictures 3) Ease of use and stability 4) Voice recognition 5) Link-up with the Web 6) Authorability	/5 /5 /6 /6 /4 /4	
5.Implementation and supportive elements (10)	1) Suitability of supportive materials 2) Management system and ease of implementation	/4 /6	
6. Ethical elements	1) Discrimination 2) Bias 3) Violence 4) Access to the harmful sites	-	
7. Final assessment	Total:	/100	

Ratings:

■ **Excellent: Over 90,** ■ **Good: 80-89,** ■ **Fair: 60-79,** ■ **Not Good: Under 59**

3.2 Comprehensive Evaluation Checklist for Apps

- Evaluator:
- E-mail:
- Date:
- Institution:
- Address/Phone number

1) Aims and objectives (5 points)				
Presentation of the objectives	**Presence**		**Absence**	
Aims and objectives				
Remarks				
Qualitative evaluation:				
Score				

2) Administrative elements (5)			
Content	Presence	Details	Absence
Title			
Author(s)			
Publisher			
Year published			
Update information			
Application capacity			
Battery consumption			
Address/Tel			
Email/ Homepage			
Hardware support needed			
Program type			
Price			
Remarks			
Qualitative evaluation:			
Score			

3) Pedagogical elements (50)			
Content (Details)		**Score**	**Comments**
Learning objectives (8)	Presentation of learning objectives (2)		
	Suitability of learning objectives for learners (2)		
	Suitability of learning content to learning objectives (2)		
	Appropriateness of learning materials for learning objectives (2)		
Learning content (22)	Suitability of learning content for learners (2)		
	Appropriateness of learning materials to learning content (2)		
	Validity in sequencing learning content (4)		
	Appropriateness in the quantity of learning content (4)		
	Accuracy in learning content (3)		
	Interaction between learners and learning content (3)		
	Up-to-date information* (4)		

Feedback (10)	Presentation of appropriate feedback (2)		
	Suitable form of feedback for learners (2)		
	Appropriateness in the content of feedback (2)		
	Accuracy in the content of feedback (2)		
	Appropriate control over feedback (2)		
Assessment (10)	Presence or absence of tests (2)		
	Appropriateness of test items (3)		
	Diversity and control over test items (2)		
	Accuracy and systematic test result (3)		
Qualitative evaluation:			
Score			

4) Technical elements (30)			
Content (Details)		**Score**	**Comments**
Screen displays (6)	Coordination of screen displays (1)		
	Suitability for learners (2)		
	Appropriate presentation of the content (2)		
	Recognition of learning pace (1)		
Color, sound, graphics, and moving pictures (5)	Suitability for learners (1)		
	Lucidity of color, sound and graphics (1)		
	Effectiveness of color, sound, and graphics (2)		
	Ease of control (1)		
Ease of use and stability (5)	Ease of access (2)*		
	Self-control of screen movement and close (1)		
	Ease of operation (1)		
	Functional stability (1)		

Voice recognition (6)	Accuracy of voice recognition technology (2)		
	Educational effectiveness of voice recognition technology (2)		
	Stability of voice recognition technology (2)		
Link-up with the Web (3)	Link-up between application and PC or other devices (2)		
	Educational effectiveness of web-connected materials (1)		
Authorability (4)	Modification or revision for program (2)		
	Addition for program (2)		
Qualitative evaluation:			
Score			

5) Implementation and supportive elements (10)			
Content (Details)		**Score**	**Comments**
Suitability of supportive materials (4)	Presence/absence of supportive materials (2)		
	Ease of implementation and usefulness (2)		
Management system and ease of implementation (6)	Record and management of accomplishment (3)		
	Ease of implementation of the program (3)		
Qualitative evaluation:			
Score			

6) Ethical Elements		
Contents (Details)	**Appropriateness or inappropriateness**	**Comments**
Discrimination for Gender, Age, Race, Region, and Culture		
Bias for Particular Notion and Theory		
Violence and Sexually Suggestive Content		
Access to the harmful sites		
Qualitative evaluation:		
Appropriateness		

7) Final assessment	
Final score	

Ratings:

■ Excellent: Over 90, ■ Good: 80-89, ■ Fair: 60-79, ■ Not Good: Under 59

Appendix 4 Homepages of CALL, MALL, and E-Learning Journals

■ Multimedia-Assisted Language Learning (Korea Association of Multimedia-Assisted Language Learning)
(http://journal.kamall.or.kr/)

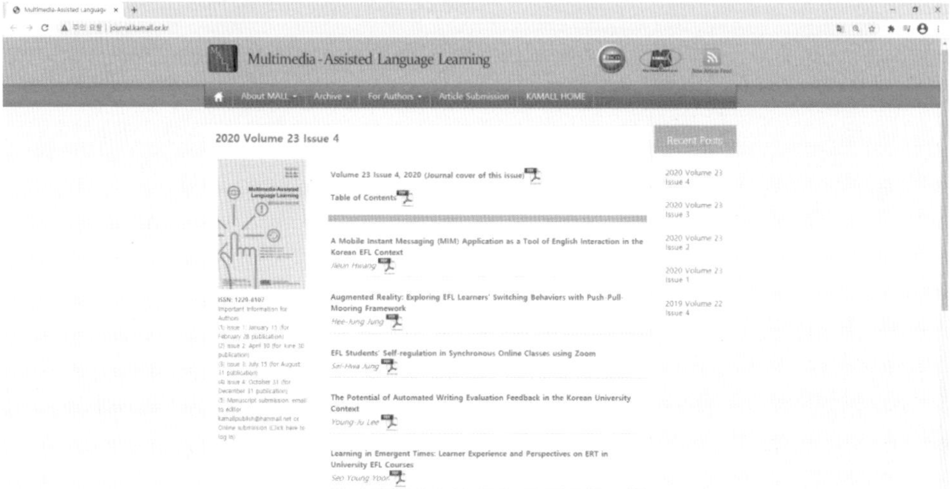

■ STEM Journal (The Society for Teaching English through Media)
(http://www.stemedia.co.kr/)

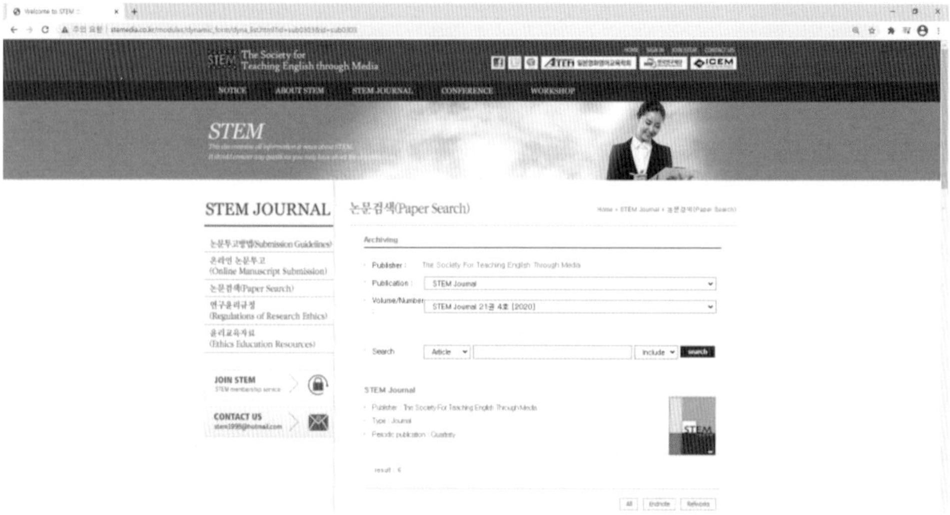

■ The Journal of Asia TEFL (Asia TEFL)
(http://journal.asiatefl.org/)

■ English Teaching (Korea Association of Teachers of English)
(http://journal.kate.or.kr/)

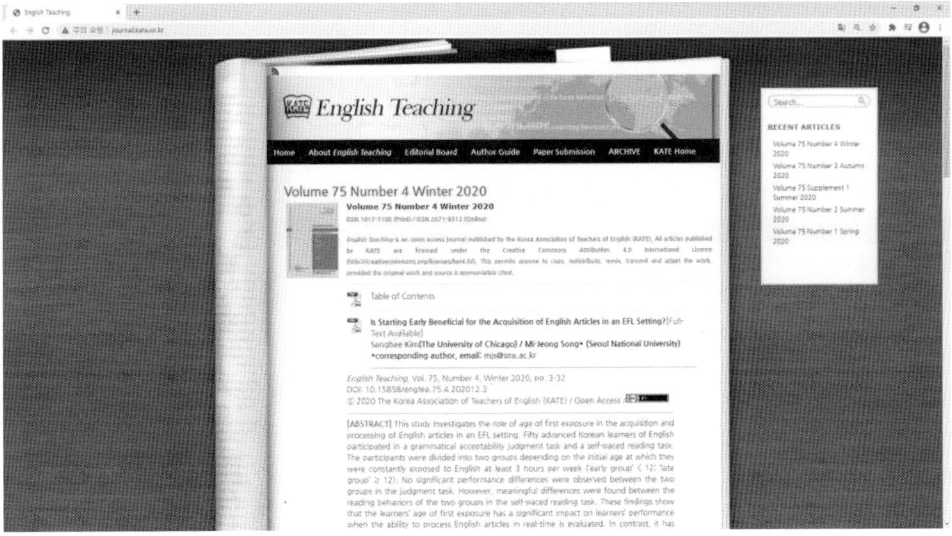

- **Korean Journal of English Language and Linguistics (The Korean Association for the Study of English Language and Linguistics)**
  (http://www.kasell.or.kr)

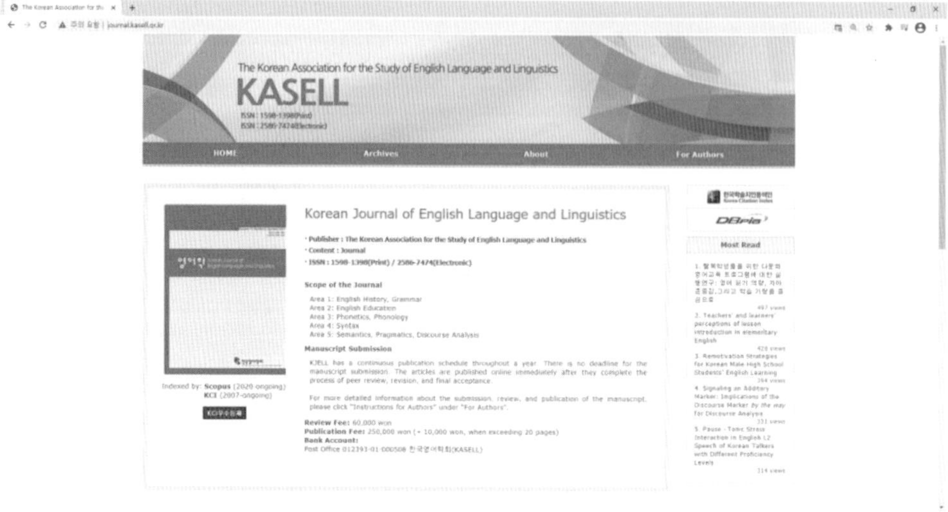

- **Foreign Languages Education (The Korea Association of Foreign Languages Education)**
  (http://www.kafle.or.kr/html/sub3_01.html)

■ Journal of Educational Technology (The Korean Society for Educational Technology)

(https://www.kset.or.kr:5003/sub.php?code=02_soci020601)

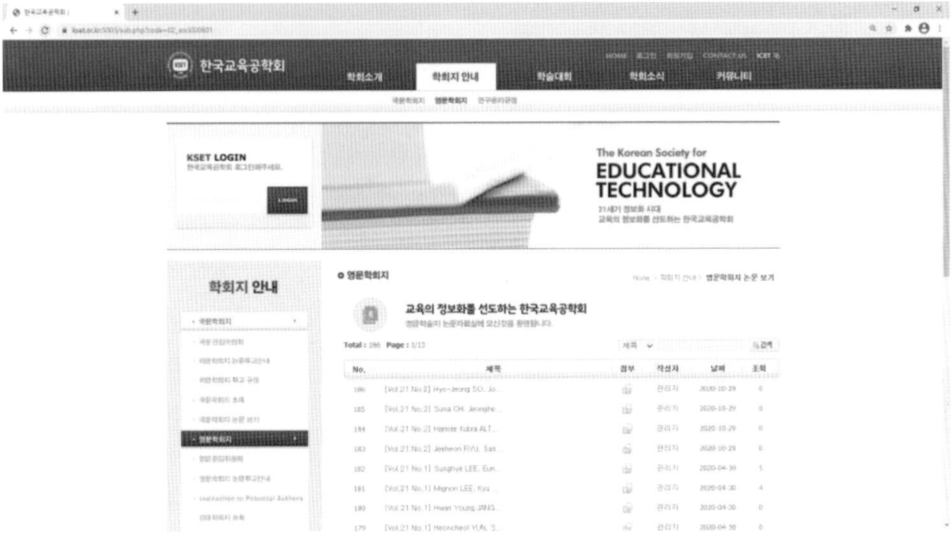

■ The Journal of Educational Information and Media (Korean Association for Educational Information and Media)

(https://kaeim.jams.or.kr/co/main/jmMain.kci/)

■ Language Learning & Technology (LLT)

(https://www.lltjournal.org/)

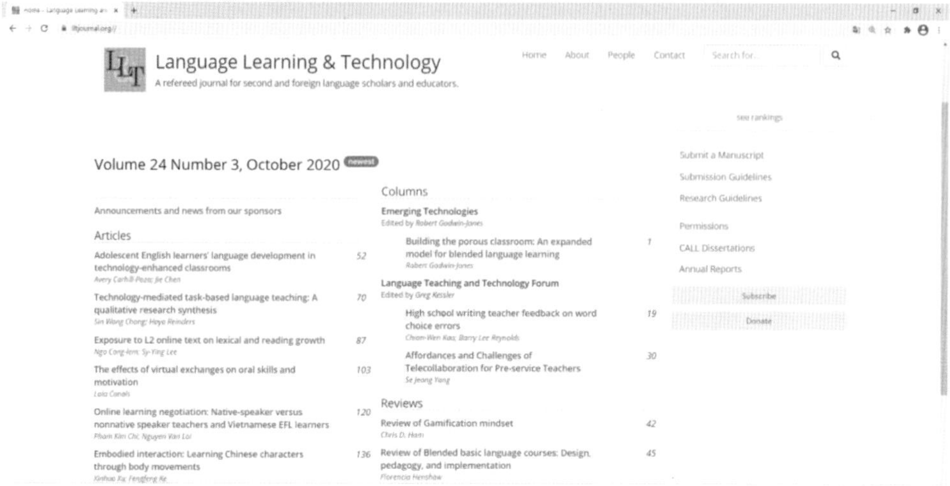

■ ReCALL (EUROCALL) (The journal of the European Association for Computer Assisted Language Learning)

(https://journals.cambridge.org/action/displayJournal?jid=REC)

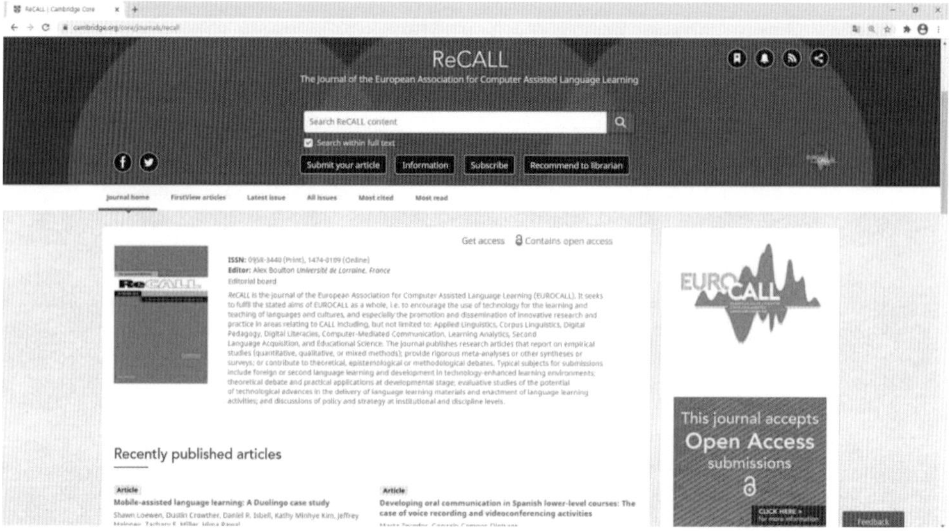

- **Computer Assisted Language Learning (CALL)**
  (https://www.tandfonline.com/loi/ncal20#.VcsWI_ntlBc)

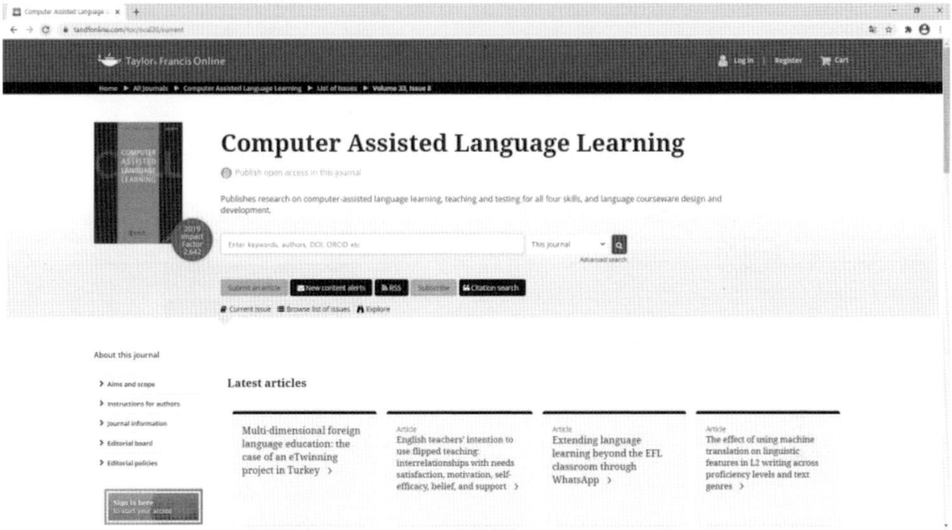

- **Computers and Education**
  (https://www.sciencedirect.com/journal/computers-and-education)

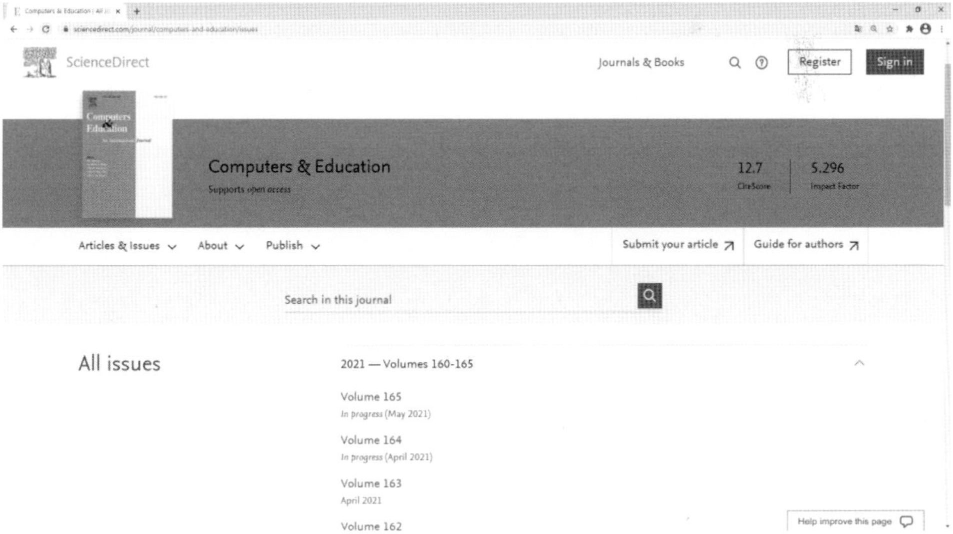

■ **British Journal of Educational Technology (BJET)**
(http://onlinelibrary.wiley.com/journal/10.1111/(ISSN)1467-8535)

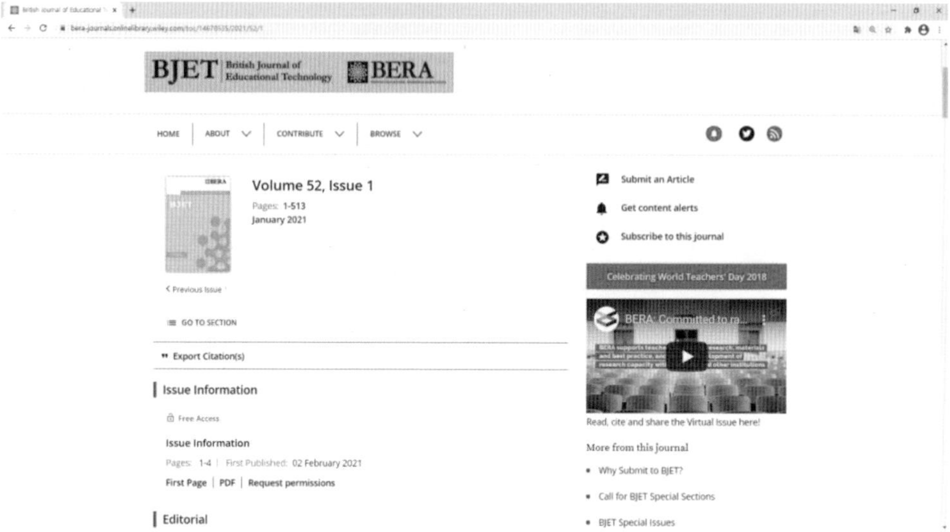

Bibliography

Abbott, M. L. (2006). ESL reading strategies: Differences in Arabic and Mandarin speaker test performance. *Language Learning, 56*(4), 633-670.

Abraham, L. B. (2008). Computer-mediated glosses in second language reading comprehension and vocabulary learning: A meta-analysis. *Computer Assisted Language Learning, 21*(3), 199-226.

AbuSeileek, A., & Abualsha'r, A. (2014). Using peer computer-mediated corrective feedback to support EFL learners' writing. *Language Learning & Technology, 18*(1), 76-95.

Adams, D. M. (1987). Communicating with electronic images: Transforming attitudes, knowledge and perception. *British Journal of Educational Technology, 18*(1), 15-20.

Ahmad, K., Corbett, G., Rogers, M., & Sussex, R. (1985). *Computers, language learning and language teaching.* Cambridge: Cambridge University Press.

Ahn, B. K., & Na, Y. H. (2005). Implementing an intercultural CMC project: A case study. *Multimedia-Assisted Language Learning, 8*(1), 9-33.

Ahn, K. (2009). Do innovative technologies bring about innovative instructional practices? A case study of a Korean EFL teacher's class under the curricular reform context. *Multimedia-Assisted Language Learning, 12*(2), 9-42.

Akyel, A., & Erçetin, G. (2009). Hypermedia reading strategies employed by advanced learners of English. *System, 37*(1), 136-152.

Alberta Education. (1987). *Vision 2000: A vision of educational technology in Alberta by the year 2000.* Edmonton: Alberta Education.

Alessi, S. M., & Trollip, S. R. (1985). *Computer-based instruction: Methods and development.* Englewood Cliffs, NJ: Prentice-Hall.

Alessi, S. M., & Trollip, S. R. (2001). *Multimedia for learning: Methods and development* (3rd ed.). Boston, MA: Allyn & Bacon, Inc.

Allan, M. (1985). *Teaching English with video.* Harlow, Essex: Longman.

Alptekin, C. (2006). Cultural familiarity in inferential and literal comprehension in L2 reading. *System, 34*(4), 494–508.

Al-Seghayer, K. (2001). The effect of multimedia annotation modes on L2 vocabulary acquisition: A comparative study. *Language Learning & Technology, 5*(1), 202-232.

Anderson, N. J. (2003). Scrolling, clicking, and reading English: Online reading strategies in a second/foreign language. *The Reading Matrix: An International*

Online Journal, 3(3), 1-33.

Ariew, R., & Frommer, J. G. (1987). Interaction in the computer age. In W. M. Rivers (Ed.), *Interactive language teaching* (pp. 177-194). Cambridge: Cambridge University Press.

Arnold, N., & Ducate, L. (2006). Future foreign language teachers' social and cognitive collaboration in an online environment. *Language Learning & Technology, 10*(1), 42-66.

Atkinson, T. (1992). *Hands off! - It's my go - IT in the Languages Classroom*. London: CILT.

Ausubel, D. A. (1964). Adults vs. children in second language learning: Psychological considerations. *Modern Language Learning, 48*(7), 420-424.

Aydin, Z., & Yildiz, S. (2014). Using wikis to promote collaborative EFL writing. *Language Learning & Technology, 18*(1), 160-180.

Ayoun, D. (2000). Web-based elicitation tasks in SLA research. *Language Learning & Technology, 3*(2), 77-98.

Bachman, L. F. (1990). *Fundamental considerations in language testing*. Oxford: Oxford University Press.

Bachman, L. F. (2000). Modern language testing at the turn of the century: Assuring that what we count counts. *Language Testing, 17*(1), 1-42.

Bachman, L. F., & Palmer, A. (1996). *Language testing in practice*. Oxford: Oxford University Press.

Baek, J. & Lee, C. H. (2018). University students' perceptions and engagement in mobile assisted blended learning in English speaking classes. *Multimedia-Assisted Language Learning, 21*(4), 11-36.

Bañados, E. (2013). A blended-learning pedagogical model for teaching and learning EFL successfully through an online interactive multimedia environment. *CALICO Journal, 23*(3), 533-550.

Barchan, J. (1986). New approaches to computer aided language learning. In K. C. Cameron, W. S. Dodd, & S. P. Q. Rahtz (Eds.), *Computers and modern language studies* (pp. 93-99). Chichester: Ellis Horwood Ltd.

Barr, D., Leakey, J., & Ranchoux, A. (2005). Told like it is! An evaluation of an integrated oral development project. *Language Learning & Technology, 9*(3), 55-78.

Barker, J., & Tucker, R. N. (1990). *The interactive learning revolution: Multimedia in education and training*. London: Kogan Page.

Baumbach, D. J. (1990). CD-ROM information sources for students: Anticipated outcomes and unexpected challenges. In A. McDougall & C. Dowling, (Eds.), *Computers in education* (pp. 19-24). Amsterdam: North-Holland.

Beattie, E. D., & Preston, N. R. (1989). *Selecting microcomputer courseware*. ERIC Digest. Retrieved from: http://files.eric.ed.gov/fulltext/ED315062.pdf

Beatty, K. (2003). *Teaching and researching computer-assisted language learning.* London: Longman.

Beebe, L. M. (1983). Risk-taking and the language learner. In H. W. Selinger & M. H. Long (Eds.), *Classroom oriented research in second language acquisition* (pp. 311-327). Rowley, MA: Newbury House.Behjat, F., Yamini, M., & Bagheri, M. S. (2011). Adjunct learning: Mixing the cyber world with face-to-face writing instruction. *International Review of Social Sciences and Humanities, 2*(1), 230-239.

Bell, F. (2011). Connectivism: Its place in theory-informed research and innovation in technology-enabled learning, *The International Review of Research in Open and Distance Learning, 12*(3), 4-13.

Belz, J. A. (2002). Social dimensions of telecollaborative foreign language study. *Language Learning & Technology, 6*(1), 60-81.

Belz, J. A. (2003). Linguistic perspectives on the development of intercultural competence in telecollaboration. *Language Learning & Technology, 7*(2), 68-117.

Berg, E. C. (1999). The effects of trained peer response on ESL students' revision types and writing quality. *Journal of Second Language Writing, 8*(3), 215-241.

Berne, J. E. (1995). How does varying pre-listening activities affect second language listening comprehension? *Hispania, 78*(2), 316-329.

Bersin, J. (2003). *The blended learning book: Best practices, proven methodologies, and lessons learned.* New York: John Wiley & Sons, Inc.

Biesenbach-Lucas, S. (2005). Communication topics and strategies in e-mail consultation: Comparison between American and international university students. *Language Learning & Technology, 9*(2), 24-46.

Biesenbach-Lucas, S. (2007). Students writing emails to faculty: An examination of e-politeness among native and non-native speakers of English. *Language Learning & Technology, 11*(2), 59-81.

Biesenbach-Lucas, S., & Weasenforth, D. (2001). E-mail and word processing in the ESL classroom: How the medium affects the message. *Language Learning & Technology, 5*(1), 135-165.

Blake, R. (2000). Computer mediated communication: A window on L2 Spanish interlanguage. *Language Learning & Technology, 4*(1), 120-136.

Blake, R., Wilson, N. L., Cetto, M., & Pardo-Ballester, C. (2008). Measuring oral proficiency in distance, face-to-face, and blended classrooms. *Language Learning & Technology, 12*(3), 114-127.

Bloch, J. (2007). Abdullah's blogging: A generation 1.5 student enters the blogosphere. *Language Learning & Technology, 11*(2), 128-141.

Bower, J., & Kawaguchi, S. (2011). Negotiation of meaning and corrective feedback in Japanese/English eTandem. *Language Learning & Technology, 15*(1), 41-71.

Briggs, N. (2018). Neural machine translation tools in the language learning classroom: Students' use, perceptions, and analyses. *The JALT CALL Journal, 14*(1), 3-24.

British Council. (1986). Fast Food [Computer software]. London: Author.

British Council. (1986). London Adventure [Computer software]. London: Author.

Brown, H. D. (2007a). *Principles of language learning and teaching* (5th ed.). White Plains, NY: Pearson Education.

Brown, H. D. (2007b). *Teaching by principles* (3rd ed.). White Plains, NY: Pearson Education.

Brown, J. D. (1997). Computers in language testing: Present research and some future directions. *Language Learning & Technology, 1*(1), 44-59.

Bunzel, M. J., & Morris, S. K. (1992). *Multimedia applications development.* New York: McGraw-Hill.

Byrne, D. (1986). *Teaching oral English.* Harlow, Essex: Longman.

Cakir, I. (2006). The use of video as an audio-visual material in foreign language teaching classroom. *The Turkish Online Journal of Educational Technology, 5*(4), 67-72.

Cameron, K. (1989). *Computer assisted language learning.* Oxford: Intellect.

Campbell-Howes, K. (2019, March 18). Why is AI a good thing for language teachers and learners? Retrieve from: https://www.oxfordtefl.com/blog/why-is-ai-a-good-thing-for-language-teachers-and-learners/

Carrell, P. L., Devine, J., & Eskey, D. E. (1988). *Interactive approaches to second language reading.* Cambridge: Cambridge University Press.

Celce-Murcia, M., Brinton, D., & Goodwin, J. (1996). *Teaching pronunciation: A reference for teachers of English to speakers of other languages.* Cambridge: Cambridge University Press.

Cha, K. W., & Rodriguez, F. (2004). Homework assignments for improving the English listening skills of Korean students: An investigative study. *Multimedia-Assisted Language Learning, 7*(2), 9-34.

Cha, Y. (2007). A study of peer feedback patterns in CMC modes on Korean EFL students. *Multimedia-Assisted Language Learning, 10*(1), 9-35.

Cha, Y. (2012). Learners' perspectives and use of different learning methods on blended learning in English classes. *Multimedia-Assisted Language Learning, 15*(2), 11-40.

Cha, Y. (2014). Effects of blended peer feedback modes on learners' writing performance and perspectives. *Multimedia-Assisted Language Learning, 17*(2), 11-42.

Cha, Y., & Kim, H. (2011). Implementation of instructional methods and learners' views in online/offline business English classes. *Multimedia-Assisted Language Learning, 14*(3), 11-35.

Cha, Y., & Park, L. E. (2010). An analysis of synchronous interaction and its influence on EFL writers' revisions. *Multimedia-Assisted Language Learning, 13*(2), 9-36.

Chalhoub–Deville, M., & Deville, C. (1999). Computer adaptive testing in second language contexts. *Annual Review of Applied Linguistics, 19*, 273-299.

Chang, J. T. (2003). The use of CMC to improve communicative competence. *Multimedia-Assisted Language Learning, 6*(1), 18-41.

Chao, C. C. (2015). Rethinking transfer: Learning from CALL teacher education as consequential transition. *Language Learning & Technology, 19*(1), 102-118.

Chapelle, C. A. (1997). CALL in the year 2000: Still in search of research paradigms? *Language Learning & Technology, 1*(1), 19-43.

Chapelle, C. A. (2001). *Computer applications in second language acquisition: Foundations for teaching, testing, and research*. Cambridge: Cambridge University Press.

Chapelle, C. A. (2009). The relationship between second language acquisition theory and computer-assisted language learning. *The Modern Language Journal, 93*(s1), *741*- 753.

Chapelle, C. A., & Jamieson, J. (1989). Research trends in computer-assisted language learning. In M. C. Pennington (Ed.), *Teaching languages with computers* (pp. 47-60). La Jolla: Athelstan.

Chapelle, C. A., & Jamieson, J. (2008). *Tips for teaching with CALL: Practical approaches to computer-assisted language learning*. White Plains, NY: Pearson Education.

Chapelle, C. A., Jamieson, J., & Heigelheimer, V. (2003). Validation of a web-based EFL test. *Language Testing, 20*(4), 409-439.

Chen, C. F. E. (2006). The development of e-mail literacy: From writing to peers to writing to authority figures. *Language Learning & Technology, 10*(2), 35-55.

Chen, C. F. E., & Cheng, W. Y. E. (2008). Beyond the design of automated writing evaluation: Pedagogical practices and perceived learning effectiveness in EFL writing classes. *Language Learning & Technology, 12*(2), 94-112.

Chen, H. I. (2013). Identity practices of multilingual writers in social networking spaces. *Language Learning & Technology, 17*(2), 143-170.

Chen, J., Belkada, S., & Okamoto, T. (2004). How a web-based course facilitates acquisition of English for academic purposes. *Language Learning & Technology, 8*(2), 33-49.

Chen, N. S., Hsieh, S. W., & Kinshuk, A. (2008). Effects of short-term memory and content representation type on mobile language learning. *Language Learning & Technology, 12*(3), 93-113.

Chen, N. S., & Wang, Y. (2008). Testing principles of language learning in a cyber face-to-face environment. *Educational Technology & Society, 11*(3), 97-113.

Chen, Y. H., & Baker, P. (2010). Lexical bundles in L1 and L2 academic writing. *Language Learning & Technology, 14*(2), 30-49.

Cheon, S. (2006). Constructing an English loanwords contents (ELC) database. *Multimedia-Assisted Language Learning, 9*(1), 186-210.

Cho, S. (1998). The applications of electronic mail to English education. *Multimedia-Assisted Language Learning, 1*(1), 213-227.

Cho, S. (2005). The development of an English learning program based on CMC activities. *Multimedia-Assisted Language Learning, 8*(2), 198-217.

Cho, S. (2006). The use of podcasting for English learning. *Multimedia-Assisted Language Learning, 9*(3), 241-254.

Cho, S. (2009). Smartphones used for foreign language learning. *Multimedia-Assisted Language Learning, 12*(3), 211-228.

Cho, S. (2011). Social networking sites and foreign language learning. *Multimedia-Assisted Language Learning, 14*(3), 315-334.

Cho, S., Lee, S., Kim, J., Ko, B., & Jeong, E. (2008). A development model of web-based English language learning programs. *Multimedia-Assisted Language Learning, 11*(1), 213-238.

Cho, Y. W. (2011). Triadic text-based SCMC and focus on form: Fluency, accuracy, and complexity. *Multimedia-Assisted Language Learning, 14*(2), 29-60.

Cho, Y. W., & Kim, I. H. (2010). The feasibility of using text-based online chat for communicative focus on form. *Multimedia-Assisted Language Learning, 13*(2), 37-58.

Cho, Y. W., Lee, Y. J., & Kim, S. (2012). Focus on form in text-based SCMC: Putting teachers' SLA knowledge into practice. *Multimedia-Assisted Language Learning, 15*(4), 11-37.

Choe, Y. (2014). The effects of speaking task types and Korean EFL learners' English proficiency level on online speaking performance. *Multimedia-Assisted Language Learning, 17*(1), 106-131.

Choi, H. (2004). EFL students' perceptions on synchronous English text chatting: Implications for its implementation. *Multimedia-Assisted Language Learning, 7*(2), 35-63.

Choi, H. (2007). The use of mind map software for Russian learning. *Multimedia-Assisted Language Learning, 10*(3), 221-235.

Choi, H., & Jung, B. (2006). The effects of the use of voice bulletin board on elementary school students' English speaking skills and affective domains: A case study. *Multimedia-Assisted Language Learning, 9*(3), 283-311.

Choi, H., & Kim, J. (2013). Development of CAT smart app for elementary English reading evaluation. *Multimedia-Assisted Language Learning, 16*(1), 119-141.

Choi, H., & Lee, C. H. (2020). Learner autonomy in EFL reading with digital technology at secondary school level. *The Journal of Asia TEFL, 17*(4), 1323-1345.

Choi, I. C. (1991). The current status and prospects of CALL. *English Teaching, 42,* 69-87.

Choi, I. C. (1999). Application of computational to linguistics language performance testing. *Multimedia Assisted Language Learning, 2*(2), 245-278.

Choi, I. C. (2002). Validation of computer-based/adaptive language tests focusing on response time. *Multimedia-Assisted Language Learning, 5*(1), 9-31.

Choi, I. C. (2005). Measurability of oral fluency through ASR-based COPI. *Multimedia-Assisted Language Learning, 8*(2), 240-261.

Choi, I. C. (2012). A validation of EFL essay assessment based on corpus indices and error analysis. *Multimedia-Assisted Language Learning, 15*(4), 39-60.

Choi, I. C., Kim, K. S., & Boo, J. (2003). Comparability of a paper-based language test and a computer-based language test. *Language Testing, 20*(3), 295-320.

Choi, I. C., & Uhm, Y. H. (2001). Comparative analyses of computer-based ratings and human ratings based on performance testing of writing. *Multimedia-Assisted Language Learning, 4*(1), 165-184.

Choi, J. C. (1999). Internet-based Spanish learning activities by using digital newspapers. *Multimedia-Assisted Language Learning, 2*(2), 279-313.

Choi, J. C., & Kim, K. (2001). The current state and perspective of web-based Spanish distance education. *Multimedia-Assisted Language Learning, 4*(2), 219-243.

Choi, S., & Lee, Y. (2003). The effectiveness of performing Internet-based English assignments in secondary English education. *Multimedia-Assisted Language Learning, 6*(2), 175-193.

Choi, S. Y. (1993). CALL for effective English language learning and teaching. *English Teaching, 46,* 31-65.

Choi, S. Y. (1994). CALL for improving English grammar, writing and speaking skills. *English Teaching, 49*, 31-65.

Choi, S. Y. (1996). The effectiveness of CD-ROM courseware in a high school setting in Korea. *English Teaching, 51*(4), 177-202.

Choi, S. Y., Kim, K. S., Lee, C. K., & Sol, Y. H. (1999). Effective use of multimedia computer courseware in English language teaching and learning. *Multimedia-Assisted Language Learning, 2*(1), 179-256.

Chon, Y. V., & Shin, D. (2013). A corpus-driven analysis of spoken and written academic collocations. *Multimedia-Assisted Language Learning, 16*(3), 11-38.

Chun, D. M. (1998). Signal analysis software for teaching discourse intonation. *Language Learning & Technology*, *2*(1), 61-77.

Chun, D. M. (2001). L2 reading on the Web: Strategies for accessing information in hypermedia. *Computer Assisted Language Learning, 14*(5), 367–403.

Chun, D. M., & Plass, J. L. (1996). Facilitating reading comprehension with multimedia. *System*, *24*(4), 503-519.

Chun, D. M., & Plass, J. L. (1997). Research on text comprehension in multimedia environments. *Language Learning & Technology, 1*(1), 60-81.

Chun, Y. V. (2004). EFL learners' use of print and online dictionaries in L1 and L2 writing processes. *Multimedia-Assisted Language Learning, 7*(1), 9-35.

Chung, S., & Choi, S. (2006). A study on the effects of teaching web-based English songs with Korean subtitles: For 3rd grade elementary school learners. *Multimedia-Assisted Language Learning, 9*(1), 146-166.

Chung, Y. G., Graves, B., Wesche, M., & Barfurth, M. (2005). Computer-mediated communication in Korean-English chat rooms: Tandem learning in an international languages program. *Canadian Modern Language Review, 62*(1), 49-86.

Clifford, R. (1987). The status of computer-assisted language instruction. *CALICO Journal, 4*(4), 9-16.

Coiro, J., & Dobler, E. (2007). Exploring the online reading comprehension strategies used by sixth-grade skilled readers to search for and locate information on the Internet. *Reading Research Quarterly, 42*(2), 214–257.

Collentine, J. (2000). Insights into the construction of grammatical knowledge provided by user-behavior tracking technologies. *Language Learning & Technology, 3*(2), 44-57.

Collentine, K. (2009). Learner use of holistic language units in multimodal, task-based synchronous computer-mediated communication. *Language Learning & Technology, 13*(2), 68-87.

Collentine, K. (2011). Learner autonomy in a task-based 3D world and production. *Language Learning & Technology, 15*(3), 50-67.

Conrad, S. M., & Goldstein, L. M. (1999). ESL student revision after teacher-written comments: Text, contexts, and individual. *Journal of Second Language Writing, 8*(2), 147-180.

Cook, V. J. (1988). Designing CALL programs for communicative teaching. *ELT Journal, 42*, 262-271.

Cope, B., & Kalantzis. M. (2016). Big data comes to school: Implications for learning, assessment, and research. *AERA Open*, *2*(2), 1–19.

Corbett, F., & Spinello, E. (2020). Connectivism and leadership: harnessing a learning theory for the digital age to redefine leadership in the twenty-first century. *Heliyon*, *6*(1), e03250.

Corston, N. (1993). *Video on windows multimedia.* New York: Interactive Developments Ltd.

Council of Ministers of Education. (1985). *Software evaluation: Criteria for computer software evaluation*. Toronto: Author.

Craig, D. A., & Kim, J. (2010). Anxiety and performance in video-conferenced interviews. *Multimedia-Assisted Language Learning, 13*(3), 9-32.

Cross, J. (2011). Comprehending news videotexts: The influence of the visual content. *Language Learning & Technology, 15*(2), 44-68.

Cummins, J., Brown, D., Edwards, P., Grady, M. O., Thrope, R., & Kingsbury, A. (1987). *Adult learning strategies and approaches: Resources for teachers of adults.* Leicester: NIACE.

Dalton, D. W. (1990). The effects of cooperative learning strategies on achievement and attitudes during interactive video. *Journal of Computer-Based Instruction, 17*(1), 8-16.

Davey, D., Jones, K. G., & Fox, J. (1995). Multimedia for language learning: Some course design issues. *Computer Assisted Language Learning, 8*(1), 31-44.

Davies, G. (2002). ICT and modern foreign languages: Learning opportunities and training needs. *Multimedia-Assisted Language Learning, 5*(1), 200-221.

Day, R. R., & Bamford, J. (2002). Top ten principles for teaching extensive reading. *Reading in a Foreign Language, 14*(2), 136-141.

deHaan, J., Reed, W. M., & Kuwada, K. (2010). The effect of interactivity with a music video game on second language vocabulary recall. *Language Learning & Technology, 14*(2), 74-94.

De Ridder, I. (2002). Visible or invisible links: Does the highlighting of hyperlinks affect incidental vocabulary learning, text comprehension, and the reading process. *Language Learning & Technology, 6*(1), 123-146.

Dever, S. Y., & Pennington, M. C. (1989). Computer capabilities underlying computer-learner interaction. In M. C. Pennington (Ed.), *Teaching languages with computers* (pp. 11-28). La Jolla: Athelstan.

Dewaele, J. (2012). Risk-taking and foreign language learning. In M. Byram & A. Hu (eds), *Routledge encyclopedia of language teaching and learning* (pp. 598-600). Oxford: Routledge.

Dias, J. (2002). Cellphones in the classroom: Boon or bane? *Calling Japan, 10*(3). 8-14.

DiGiovanni, E., & Nagaswami, G. (2001). Online peer review: An alternative to face-to-face? *ELT Journal, 55*(3), 263-272.

Dodigovic, M. (2007). Artificial intelligence and second language learning: An efficient approach to error remediation. *Language Awareness, 16*(2), 99-113.

Doering, A., & Beach, R. (2002). Preservice English teachers acquiring literacy practices through technology tools. *Language Learning & Technology, 6*(3), 127-146.

Dörnyei, Z. (2009) *The psychology of second language acquisition.* Oxford: Oxford University Press.

Doughty, C., & Long, M. (2003). Optimal psycholinguistic environments for distance foreign language learning. *Language Learning & Technology, 7*(3), 50-80.

Driscoll, M. (2002). *Blended learning: Let's get beyond the hype.* Retrieved March 19, 2015, from the World Wide Web: https://www-07.ibm.com/services/pdf/blended_learning.pdf

Ducate, L., & Lomicka, L. (2009). Podcasting: An effective tool for honing language students' pronunciation? *Language Learning & Technology, 13*(3), 66-86.

DuFon, M. A. (2002). Video recording in ethnographic SLA research: Some issues of validity in data collection. *Language Learning & Technology, 6*(1), 40-59.

Duke, B., Harper, G., & Johnston, M. (2013). Connectivism as a digital age learning theory. *The International HETL Review, Special Issue 2013*, 4-13.

Dunkel, P. (1999). Considerations in developing or using second/foreign language proficiency computer-adaptive tests. *Language Learning & Technology, 2*(2), 77-93.

Dupuy, B. C. (2000). Content-based instruction: Can it help ease the transition from beginning to advanced foreign language classes? *Foreign Language Annals, 33*(2), 205-223.

Durndell, A., Macleod H., & Siann, G. (1987). A survey of attitudes to knowledge about and experience of computers. *Computers & Education, 11*(3), 167-175.

Eastment, D. (1996). Survey review: CD-ROM materials for English language teaching. *ELT Journal, 50*(1), 69-79.

Edelhoff, C. (1978). Theme-oriented English teaching: Text-varieties, media, skills and project-work. In C. N. Candlin (Ed.), *The communicative teaching of English* (pp. 49-62). Harlow, Essex: Longman.

Egbert, J., Paulus, T. M., & Nakamichi, Y. (2002). The impact of CALL instruction on classroom computer use: A foundation for rethinking technology in teacher education. *Language Learning & Technology, 6*(3), 108-126.

Ehsani, F., & Knodt, E. (1998). Speech technology in computer-aided language learning: Strengths and limitations of a new CALL paradigm. *Language Learning & Technology, 2*(1), 45-60.

Elkhafaifi, H. (2005). The effect of pre-listening activities on listening comprehension in Arabic learners. *Foreign Language Annals, 38*(4), 505-513.

Ellis, R. (2006). Current issues in the teaching of grammar: An SLA perspective. *TESOL Quarterly, 40*(1), 83-107.

Elola, I., & Oskoz, A. (2010). Collaborative writing: Fostering foreign language and writing conventions development. *Language Learning & Technology, 14*(3), 51-71.

Eskenazi, M. (1999). Using automatic speech processing for foreign language pronunciation tutoring: Some issues and a prototype. *Language Learning & Technology, 2*(2), 62-76.

Fabos, B., & Young, M. D. (1999). Telecommunication in the classroom: Rhetoric versus reality. *Review of Educational Research, 69*(3), 217-259.

Fathman, A., & Whalley, E. (1990). Teacher response to student writing: Focus on form versus content. In B. Kroll (Ed.), *Second language writing: Research insights for the classroom* (pp. 178-190). Cambridge: Cambridge University Press.

Ferriman, N. (2013). The impact of blended e-learning on undergraduate academic essay writing in English (L2). *Computers & Education, 60*, 243-253.

Ferris, D. R. (1995). Student reactions to teacher response in multiple-draft composition classrooms. *TESOL Quarterly, 29*(1), 33-53.

Ferris, D. R. (1997). The influence of teacher commentary on student revision. *TESOL Quarterly, 31*(2), 315-339.

Ferris, D. R. (2001). Teaching writing for academic purposes. In J. Flowerdew & M. Peacock (Eds.), *Research perspectives on English for academic purposes* (pp. 298-314). Cambridge: Cambridge University Press.

Ferris, D. R. (2003). *Response to student writing: Implications for second language students.* Mahwah, NY: Lawrence Erlbaum Associate, Inc.

Feurzeig, W. (1988). Apprentice tools: Students as practitioners. In R. S. Nickerson & P. P. Zodhiates (Eds.), *Technology in education: Looking toward 2020* (pp. 97-120). Hillsdale, New Jersey: REA.

Fitze, M. (2006). Discourse and participation in ESL face-to-face and written electronic conferences. *Language Learning & Technology, 10*(1), 67-86.

Flowerdew, J., & Miller, L. (2005). *Second language listening: Theory and practice.* Cambridge University Press.

Flowers J. C. (2019). Strong and weak AI: Deweyan considerations. *AAAI Spring Symposium: Towards Conscious AI Systems.* Worcester State University, Worcester, Massachusetts.

Fox, J. (1986). Computer assisted reading - work in progress at the University of East Anglia. In K. C. Cameron, W. S. Dodd, & S. P. Q. Rahtz (Eds.), *Computers and modern language studies* (pp. 70-77). Chichester: Ellis Horwood Ltd.

Fox, J. (1990) A microcomputer-based approach to training in second language reading skills. *Computer-Assisted Language Learning, 1*(1), 29-40.

Fox, J., Labbett, B., Matthews, C., Romano-Hvid, C., & Schostak, J. (1992). *New perspectives in modern language learning.* Sheffield: Training Agency.

Fox, J., Matthews, A., Matthews, C., & Rope, A. (1990). *Educational technology in modern language learning.* Sheffield: Training Agency.

Fuchs, C., Hauck, M., & Müller-Hartmann, A. (2012). Promoting learner autonomy through multiliteracy skills development in cross-institutional exchanges. *Language Learning & Technology, 16*(3), 82-102.

Fuentes, A. C. (2001). Lexical behaviour in academic and technical corpora: Implications for ESP development. *Language Learning & Technology, 5*(3), 106-129.

Garcia E, Elbeltagi I, Brown M, Dungay K. (2015). The implications of a connectivist learning blog model and the changing role of teaching and learning. *British Journal of Educational Technology, 46*(4), 877–894.

Garcia, I., & Pena, M. I. (2011). Machine translation-assisted language learning: Writing for beginners. *Computer Assisted Language Learning, 24*(5), 471–487.

Gardner, J., & McNally, H. (1995). Supporting school-based initial teacher training with interactive video. *British Journal of Educational Technology, 26*(1), 30-41.

Garrett, N. (1991). Technology in the service of language learning: Trends and issues. *The Modern Language Journal, 75*(1), 74-101.

Garrison, D. R., & Kanuka, H. (2004). Blended learning: Uncovering its transformative potential in higher education. *Internet and Higher Education, 7*(2), 95-105.

Ghadirian, S. (2002). Providing controlled exposure to target vocabulary through the screening and arranging of texts. *Language Learning & Technology, 6*(1), 147-164.

Gilakjani, A. P., & Ahmadi, M. R. (2011). A study of factors affecting EFL learners' English listening comprehension and the strategies for improvement. *Journal of Language Teaching and Research, 2*(5), 977-988.

Goh, C., & Taib, Y. (2006). Metacognitive instruction in listening for young learners. *ELT Journal, 60*(3), 222-232.

Goldberg, A., Russell, M., & Cook, A. (2003). The effect of computers on student writing: A meta-analysis of studies from 1992 to 2002. *Journal of Technology, Learning, and Assessment, 2*(1), 1-52.

González-Bueno, M. (1998). The effects of electronic mail on Spanish L2 discourse. *Language Learning & Technology, 1*(2), 55-70.

González-Lloret, M. (2003). Designing task-based CALL to promote interaction: En busca de esmeraldas. *Language Learning & Technology, 7*(1), 86-104.

Goodwin, A., Hamrick, A., J., & Stewart, T. C. (1993). Instructional delivery via electronic mail. *TESOL Journal, 3*, 24-27.

Grabe, M., & Grabe, C. (2007). *Integrating technology for meaningful learning* (5th ed.). NY: Houghton Mifflin Company.

Grabe, W., & Stoller, F. (2002). *Teaching and research reading.* Harlow, UK: Longman.

Graham, C. R. (2006). Blended learning systems: Definition, current trends, and future directions. In C. J. Bonk & C. R. Graham (Eds.), *Handbook of blended learning: Global perspectives, local designs* (pp. 3-21). San Francisco: Pfeiffer.

Graham, S., & Macaro, E. (2008). Strategy instruction in listening for lower-intermediate learners of French. *Language Learning, 58*(4), 747-783.

Green, B. F. (1988). Construct validity of computer-based tests. In H. Wainer & H. I. Braun (Eds.), *Test validity* (pp. 77-86). Hillsdale, NJ: Lawrence Erlbaum.

Greenall, S., & Swan, M. (1986). *Effective reading.* Cambridge: Cambridge University

Press.

Grellet, F. (1981). *Developing reading skills: A practical guide to reading comprehension exercises.* Cambridge: Cambridge University Press.

Grgurović, M. (2011). Blended learning in an ESL class: A case study. *CALICO Journal, 29*(1), 100-117.

Grgurović, M., & Hegelheimer, V. (2007). Help options and multimedia listening: Students' use of subtitles and the transcript. *Language Learning & Technology, 11*(1), 45-66.

Groot, P. J. (2000). Computer assisted second language vocabulary acquisition. *Language Learning & Technology*, *4*(1), 60-81.

Gruba, P., & Corbel, C. (1997). Computer-based testing. In C. Clapham & D. Corson (Eds.), *Language testing and assessment. Volume 7: Language testing and assessment* (pp. 141-149). Dordrecht: Kluwer Academic.

Gye, Y., Chang, J., & Jung, J. (2008). A case study of online in-service English teacher training program for language improvement. *Multimedia-Assisted Language Learning, 11*(3), 71-94.

Ha, J. B., & Han, M. S. (2006). The role of meta-awareness and task type on the use of determiners during Internet chat. *Multimedia-Assisted Language Learning, 9*(2), 26-52.

Hafner, C. A., & Miller, L. (2011). Fostering learner autonomy in English for science: A collaborative digital video project in a technological learning environment. *Language Learning & Technology*, *15*(3), 68-86.

Haines, K. J. (2015). Learning to identify and actualize affordances in a new tool. *Language Learning & Technology*, *19*(1), 165-180.

Hainline, D. (1987). Computers in language instruction - trends and possibilities. In D. Hainline (Ed.), *New developments in computer-assisted language learning* (pp. 1-8). London: Croom Helm.

Hammadou, J. (2000). The impact of analogy and content knowledge on reading comprehension: What helps, what hurts. *The Modern Language Journal, 84*(1), 38-50.

Hamp-Lyons, L., & Heasley, B. (1987). *Study writing.* Cambridge: Cambridge University Press.

Han, J. I. (2001). A development of standards and a model of multimedia English education for pre-service teachers. *Multimedia-Assisted Language Learning, 4*(1), 185-213.

Han, J. I. (2003). The effective use of CMC tools in teaching English as a foreign language. *Multimedia-Assisted Language Learning, 6*(2), 243-264.

Han, J. I. (2005). A case study on the accuracy of English and form-focused negotiation appearing in Korean college students' text-based chat scripts.

Multimedia-Assisted Language Learning, 8(2), 262-287.

Han, J. I. (2014). The effects of learning models of English digital textbooks on Korean middle school students' English learning and attitudes toward English. *Multimedia-Assisted Language Learning, 17*(1), 132-158.

Han, K. (2004). L2 learners' self-efficacy beliefs: Interactive affects and effects of three different contexts. *Multimedia-Assisted Language Learning*, 8(1), 53-75.

Handley, Z., & Hamel, M. J. (2005). Establishing a methodology for benchmarking speech synthesis for computer-assisted language learning (CALL). *Language Learning & Technology*, *9*(3), 99-120.

Hanna, B. E., & De Nooy, J. (2003). A funny thing happened on the way to the forum: Electronic discussion and foreign language learning. *Language Learning & Technology, 7*(1), 71-85.

Hardison, D. M. (2004). Generalization of computer-assisted prosody training: Quantitative and qualitative findings. *Language Learning & Technology*, *8*(1), 34-52.

Hardisty, D. (1987). Towards a communications methodology: Natural and artificial language learning and teaching. In L. Legenhausen & D. Wolff (Eds.), *Computer assisted language learning and innovative EFL methodology* (pp. 13-26). Augsburg: Universitat Augsburg.

Hardisty, D., & Windeatt, S. (1989). *CALL*. Oxford: Oxford University Press.

Harmer, J. (2004). *How to teach writing*. Harlow, Essex: Pearson Education Limited.

Hawkridge, D. (1990). Software for school: British reviews in the late 1980s. In B. B. Oliver & S. Eileen (Eds.), *Computers and learning* (pp. 88-108). Wokingham, Berkshire: Addison-Wesley.

Hedgcock, J., & Lefkowitz, N. (1996). Some input on input: Two analyses of student response to expert feedback on L2 writing. *The Modern Language Journal, 80*(3), 287-308.

Hegelheimer, V., & Chapelle, C. A. (2000). Methodological issues in research on learner-computer interactions in CALL. *Language Learning & Technology*, *4*(1), 41-59.

Helm, F., Guth, S., & Farrah, M. (2012). Promoting dialogue or hegemonic practice: Power issues in telecollaboration. *Language Learning & Technology*, *16*(2), 103-127.

Hennessy, S., & O'Shea, T. (1993). Learner perceptions of realism and magic in computer simulations. *British Journal of Educational Technology*, *24*(2), 125-138.

Henning, G. (1987). *A guide to language testing: development, evaluation, research*. Rowley, Massachusetts: Newbury House.

Hewett, B. (2006). Synchronous online conference-based instruction: A study of whiteboard interactions and student writing. *Computers and Composition, 23*(1),

4-31.

Higgins, J. (1985). Should teachers learn to program? In C. Brumfit, M. Phillips, & P. Skehan (Eds.), *Computers in English language teaching. ELT documents 122* (pp. 69-78). Oxford: Pergamon.

Higgins, J. (1988). *Language, learners, and computers.* Harlow, Essex: Longman.

Higgins, J., & Johns, T. (1984). *Computers in language learning.* London: Collins ELT.

Hill, B. (1989). *Making the most of video.* London: CILT.

Hill, B. (1991). *Making the most of satellites and interactive video.* London: CILT.

Hincks, R., & Edlund, J. (2009). Promoting increased pitch variation in oral presentations with transient visual feedback. *Language Learning & Technology, 13*(3), 32-50.

Hinkel, E. (2006). Current perspectives on teaching the four skills. *TESOL Quarterly, 40*(1), 109-131.

Hinkelman, D., & Gruba, P. (2012). Power within blended language learning programs in Japan. *Language Learning & Technology, 16*(2), 46-64.

Hirvela, A. (1988). Marshall McLuhan and the case against CAI. *System, 16*(3), 299-311.

Hong, A. R., & Lee, C. H. (2008). The effects of focus on form in CMC: A case study of Korean adult learners. *Multimedia-Assisted Language Learning, 11*(2), 9-40.

Hope, G. R., Taylor, H. F., & Pusack, J. P. (1984). *Using computers in teaching foreign languages.* Englewood Cliffs, New Jersey: Prentice-Hall.

Horst, M., Cobb, T., & Nicolae, I. (2005). Expanding academic vocabulary with an interactive on-line database. *Language Learning & Technology, 9*(2), 90-110.

Hoven, D. (1999). A model for listening and viewing comprehension in multimedia environments. *Language Learning & Technology, 3*(1), 88-103.

Huang, H. T., & Liou, H. C. (2007). Vocabulary learning in an automated graded reading program. *Language Learning & Technology, 11*(3), 64-82.

Hubbard, P. (1987). Language teaching approaches, the evaluation of CALL software, and design implications. In W. F. Smith (Ed.), *Modern media in foreign language education: Theory and implementation* (pp. 228-254). Lincolnwood, IL: NTC.

Hubbard, P. (1988). An integrated framework for CALL courseware evaluation. *CALICO Journal, 6*(2), 51-72.

Hubbard, P. (2009). General introduction. In P. Hubbard (Ed.), *Computer assisted language learning: Vol 1* (pp. 1-20). London: Routledge.

Huffman, D. T., & Goldberg, J. R. (1987). Using wordprocessing to teach EFL composition. *System, 15*(2), 169-175.

Huh, K. (2007). CALL and creativity: Incorporating creativity task into CMC environments. *Multimedia-Assisted Language Learning, 10*(1), 36-61.

Huh, K. (2012). A study of integrated reading and writing instruction through the use of multimedia. *Multimedia-Assisted Language Learning, 15*(1), 181-209.

Hulstijn, J. H. (2000). The use of computer technology in experimental studies of second language acquisition: A survey of some techniques and some ongoing studies. *Language Learning & Technology, 3*(2), 32-43.

Hurley, R. (2019). *Big data: A guide to big data trends, artificial intelligence, machine learning, predictive analytics, internet of things, data science, data analytics, business intelligence, and data mining.* Independently published, USA.

Hwang, J. B. (2007). A study of the combining effects of the multimedia learning environment and the use of a focus-on-form technique. *Multimedia-Assisted Language Learning, 10*(3), 237-255.

Hyland, K. (2002). *Teaching and researching writing.* Essex: Pearson Education.

Ihm, H. J. (2000). A case study of collaborative learning in a web-based writing program. *Multimedia-Assisted Language Learning, 3*(2), 175-197.

Jacob, R. (1999). Treasure Hunt [Computer software]. London: Ron Jacob.

Jang, N. R., & Lee, E. J. (2012). The effects of electronic teacher feedback and writing a self-evaluation form on writing ability and the affective domain of Korean EFL learners. *Multimedia-Assisted Language Learning, 15*(3), 113-143.

Jeon, H. C. (2013). The effects of e-book contents using pseudo words on vocabulary learning. *Multimedia-Assisted Language Learning, 16*(1), 93-117.

Jeon, Y. J., & Kang, H. Y. (2012). A study on the use of a web-based online in-service training program for the improvement of teaching skills for TaLK (Teach and Learn in Korea) scholars. *Multimedia-Assisted Language Learning, 15*(3), 145-164.

Jeon, Y. J., & Kang, M. K. (2013). A study of smart English teaching models using QR codes. *Multimedia-Assisted Language Learning, 16*(3), 125-143.

Jeong, M., Lee, J., & Kim, J. (2013). An analysis of learner interaction in smart English education. *Multimedia-Assisted Language Learning, 16*(4), 39-65.

Jepson, K. (2005). Conversations and negotiated interaction in text and voice chat rooms. *Language Learning & Technology, 9*(3), 79-98.

Jiang, W., & Ramsay, G. (2005). Rapport-building through CALL in teaching Chinese as a foreign language: An exploratory study. *Language Learning & Technology, 9*(2), 47-63.

Jin, K. A., & Park, T. (2012). Exploring automated scoring of Korean high school students' English composition. *Multimedia-Assisted Language Learning, 15*(1), 11-29.

Jin, S. (2013). The use of Facebook as a new pedagogical tool to promote EFL learners' writing. *Multimedia-Assisted Language Learning, 16*(3), 145-170.

Jin, S. (2014). Implementation of smartphone-based blended learning in an EFL undergraduate grammar course. *Multimedia-Assisted Language Learning, 17*(4),

11-37.

Jones, C. (1998). *Wida's authoring suite: Guide for authors.* London: Wida Software Ltd.

Jones, C., & Fortescue, S. (1987). *Using Computers in the language classroom.* Harlow, Essex: Longman.

John, E. S. (2001). A case for using a parallel corpus and concordancer for beginners of a foreign language. *Language Learning & Technology, 5*(3), 185-203.

Jones, G. (1986). Computer simulations in language teaching–the Kingdom experiment. *System, 14*(2), 179-186.

Jones, K. (1982). *Simulations in language teaching.* London: Cambridge University Press.

Jones, L. (2004). Testing L2 vocabulary recognition and recall using pictorial and written test items. *Language Learning & Technology, 8*(3), 122-143.

Jones, R. H., Garralda, A., Li, D. C. S., & Lock, G. (2006). Interactional dynamics in on-line and face-to-face peer-tutoring sessions for second language writers. *Journal of Second Language Writing, 15*(1), 1-23.

Jones, R. J. D. (1991). Shaping educational technology: Ontario's educational computing initiative. *Educational & Training Technology International, 28*(2), 129-134.

Jones, S. (2003). *Encyclopedia of new media.* New York: SAGE.

Jun, H. C., & Choi, S. Y. (2008). A development of PDA vocabulary contents using cartoons for elementary school English language learning and teaching. *Multimedia-Assisted Language Learning, 11*(1), 179-212.

Jung, K., & Chang, K. (2009). A classroom-centered research on interaction through peer review in the online English class. *Multimedia-Assisted Language Learning, 12*(3), 67-92.

Jung, R., & Lee, C. H. (2013). Using Internet video clips for university students' vocabulary development in blended learning. *Multimedia-Assisted Language Learning, 16*(4), 67-96.

Jung, Y. S. (2000). Effects of cooperative learning approach to MALL (Multimedia-Assisted Language Learning). *Multimedia-Assisted Language Learning, 3*(1), 9-46.

Jung, Y. S. (2008). Exploring factors influencing the successful CMC based English learning. *Multimedia-Assisted Language Learning, 11*(3), 131-154.

Kabata, K., & Edasawa, Y. (2011). Tandem language learning through a cross-cultural keypal project. *Language Learning & Technology, 15*(1), 104-121.

Kang, H. Y., & Lee, C. H. (2014). Analysis of topic changes and moves in abstracts of multimedia-assisted language learning and language learning and technology. *Multimedia-Assisted Language Learning, 17*(4), 38-60.

Kang, H. Y., & Lee, C. H. (2020). Effects of focus on form instruction through listening in blended learning on the development of grammar and listening skills. *Korean Journal of English Language and Linguistics, 20*, 662-691.

Kang, J. (2013). A study on elementary school students' acceptance of English digital textbooks using technology acceptance model. *Multimedia-Assisted Language Learning, 16*(1), 11-36.

Kannan, J. & Munday, P., (2018). New trends in second language learning and teaching through the lens of ICT, networked learning, and artificial intelligence. *Círculo de Lingüística Aplicada a la Comunicación, 76*, 13-30.

Kasper, L. F. (2000). New technologies, new literacies: Focus discipline research and ESL learning communities. *Language Learning & Technology, 4*(2), 105-128.

Keem, S. U. (2000). A field study: Multimedia-assisted English instruction to cultivate communicative competence. *Multimedia-Assisted Language Learning, 3*(1), 139-166.

Kelm, O. (1996). The application of computer networking in foreign language learning education: Focus on principles of second language acquisition. In M. Warschauer (Ed.), *Telecollaboration in foreign language learning* (pp. 19-28). Honolulu, Hi: University of Hawaii Press.

Kennedy, C., & Miceli, T. (2001). An evaluation of intermediate students' approaches to corpus investigation. *Language Learning & Technology, 5*(3), 77-90.

Kennedy, C., & Miceli, T. (2010). Corpus-assisted creative writing: Introducing intermediate Italian learners to a corpus as a reference resource. *Language Learning & Technology, 14*(1), 28-44.

Kenning, M. J., & Kenning, M. M. (1983). *Introduction to computer assisted language teaching.* Oxford: Oxford University Press.

Kenworthy, J. (1987). *Teaching English pronunciation.* Harlow, Essex: Longman.

Kenyon, D. M., & Malabonga, V. (2001). Comparing examinee attitudes toward computer-assisted and other oral proficiency assessments. *Language Learning & Technology, 5*(2), 60-83.

Kern, R., Ware, P., & Warschauer, M. (2004). Crossing frontiers: New directions in online pedagogy and research. *Annual Review of Applied Linguistics, 24,* 243-260.

Kessler, G. (2009). Student-initiated attention to form in wiki-based collaborative writing. *Language Learning & Technology, 13*(1), 79-95.

Khan, B. H. (Ed.). (1997). *Web-based instruction.* Englewood Cliffs, NJ: Educational Technology Publications.

Kim, A. Y. (2012). Investigating the effectiveness of computer-assisted language learning (CALL) in improving pronunciation: A case study. *Multimedia-Assisted Language Learning, 15*(3), 11-33.

Kim, B. G. (2010). Collaborative discussion and peer review activity in computer-mediated EFL writing. *Multimedia-Assisted Language Learning, 13*(2), 105-128.

Kim, D. J. (2000). A study on the development of zone of proximal development for the optimization of English writing education through E-mail. *Multimedia-*

Assisted Language Learning, 3(2), 100-118.

Kim, D. J. (2002). A study on the pedagogical models for the optimum efficacy of the CMC instructions. *Multimedia-Assisted Language Learning, 5*(2), 47-64.

Kim, D., Rueckert, D., Kim, D. J., & Seo, D. (2013). Students' perceptions and experiences of mobile learning. *Language Learning & Technology, 17*(3), 52-73.

Kim, E. Y., Park, S. M., & Baek, S. H. (2011). Twitter and the implications for its use in EFL learning. *Multimedia-Assisted Language Learning, 14*(2), 113-137.

Kim, H. (2002) Web-integrated ESOL reading instruction: An idea for reading strategy practice. *Multimedia-Assisted Language Learning, 5*(2), 83-102.

Kim, H. (2003). An idea of designing multifunctional English teacher homepage. *Multimedia-Assisted Language Learning, 6*(2), 97-118.

Kim, H. (2004). Analysis and application of web-based L2 tasks. *Multimedia-Assisted Language Learning, 7*(2), 81-101.

Kim, H. (2007). ICT-integrated English language curriculum for elementary school students: A case study of Apple Project. *Multimedia-Assisted Language Learning, 10*(1), 177-200.

Kim, H. (2010). Three teachers' initial efforts to use Twitter for teaching English in public schools. *Multimedia-Assisted Language Learning, 13*(2). 129-154.

Kim, H., & Chang, H. (2005). A case study of online college English: Effectiveness of language curriculum design in CALL. *Multimedia-Assisted Language Learning, 8*(2), 89-112.

Kim, H., & Kim, E. (2010). The development of online-integrated college English curriculum for enhancing speaking performance. *Multimedia-Assisted Language Learning, 13*(3), 197-214.

Kim, H., & Kwon, Y. (2012). Exploring smartphone applications for effective mobile-assisted language learning. *Multimedia-Assisted Language Learning, 15*(1), 31-57.

Kim, H., & Yoon, M. N. (2014). Adopting smartphone-based blended learning: An experimental study of the implementation of Kakao Talk and Mocafé. *Multimedia-Assisted Language Learning, 17*(2), 86-111.

Kim, H. D. (2010). Study on teacher trainees' responses in blended TESOL intensive program. *Multimedia-Assisted Language Learning, 13*(3), 175-195.

Kim, H. J. (2011). Investigating effects of tasks on examinee performance in a computer-delivered speaking test. *Multimedia-Assisted Language Learning, 14*(1), 65-93.

Kim, H. O. (2011). The change in secondary school teachers' views and uses of multimedia-assisted language learning and the direction of teacher education. *Multimedia-Assisted Language Learning, 14*(1), 193-210.

Kim, H. S. (2013). Emerging mobile apps to improve English listening skills.

Multimedia-Assisted Language Learning, 16(2), 11-30.

Kim, H. S. (2014). Effects of using mobile devices in blended learning for English reading comprehension. *Multimedia-Assisted Language Learning, 17*(2), 64-85.

Kim, H. Y., & Kwon, Y. H. (2012). Exploring smartphone applications for effective mobile-assisted language learning. *Multimedia-Assisted Language Learning, 15*(1), 31-57.

Kim, I. O., & Shim, K. A. (2003). A Study on the development of a primary English writing CD-ROM title and its effect on children's writing competence. *Multimedia-Assisted Language Learning, 6*(2), 71-95.

Kim, I. S. (1996). CALL and its pedagogical implications for teaching foreign language at Korean university. *Journal of the Applied Linguistics Association of Korea*, 11, 3-23.

Kim, I. S. (1999). Theories and practices in evaluating foreign language software. *Multimedia-Assisted Language Learning, 2*(2), 104-135.

Kim, I. S. (2000). Development of web-based multimedia contents for foreign language education and their application: A case study of an OCU listening course. *Multimedia-Assisted Language Learning, 3*(2), 119-139.

Kim, I. S. (2002). Vocabulary acquisition research and development of a computer-assisted vocabulary learning program for EFL university students. *Multimedia-Assisted Language Learning, 5*(1), 59-82.

Kim, I. S. (2005). Developing a web-based listening course. *Multimedia-Assisted Language Learning, 8*(1), 116-140.

Kim, I. S., O, K. M., & Nation, P. (2005). The construction of an English word list for EFL university students and the development of its web-based levels test. *Multimedia-Assisted Language Learning, 8*(2), 58-88.

Kim, J. (2006). A web-based speaking test development using Visual Basic 6.0. *Multimedia-Assisted Language Learning, 9*(2), 77-98.

Kim, J. (2009). The relationship between speaking test administration tools and item types. *Multimedia-Assisted Language Learning, 12*(1), 177-202.

Kim, J. (2011). The validation process in developing a web-based English speaking and writing test. *Multimedia-Assisted Language Learning, 14*(2), 181-209.

Kim, J. (2014). Exploring the role of reflective journal by utilizing blog based on coaching in English education. *Multimedia-Assisted Language Learning, 17*(3), 95-120.

Kim, J., & Kim, H. (2012). Developing a blended instructional learning model optimized for English teaching at off-line universities. *Multimedia-Assisted Language Learning, 15*(1), 135-155.

Kim, J. E. (2014). The effectiveness of automated essay scoring in an EFL college classroom. *Multimedia-Assisted Language Learning, 17*(3), 11-36.

Kim, J. E., & Choi, I. C. (2015). A corpus-based comparative analysis of linguistic difficulty among high school English textbooks, EBS-CSAT prep books, and College Scholastic Ability Test. *Multimedia-Assisted Language Learning, 18*(1), 59-92.

Kim, J. K. (2009). Effects of collaborative writing in weblogs. *Multimedia-Assisted Language Learning, 12*(2), 135-161.

Kim, J. K. (2012). Effects of self-directed and guided self-directed e-portfolios on Korean college students' writing ability. *Multimedia-Assisted Language Learning, 15*(1), 115-134.

Kim, J. K., & Moon, E. J. (2013). The effect of online and coached online instructions on pronunciation and vocabulary in blended learning. *Multimedia-Assisted Language Learning, 16*(3), 39-67.

Kim, J. R. (1999). A study of developing elementary English course design incorporating multimedia technology. *Multimedia-Assisted Language Learning, 2*(1), 74-99.

Kim, J. R., & Jang, Y. J. (2008). The effects of a massive multiplayer online role playing game on English skills of elementary school students. *Multimedia-Assisted Language Learning, 11*(1), 103-125.

Kim, J. R., & Lim C. K. (1998). Developing computer-adaptive English testing for elementary school English. *Multimedia-Assisted Language Learning, 1*(1), 101-116.

Kim, J. R., & Hwang, S. Y. (2007). Connecting on-class elementary school English learning with selected on-line differentiated contents. *Multimedia-Assisted Language Learning, 10*(1), 130-154.

Kim, J., Cho, Y. W., & Lee, Y. J. (2014). Exploring the effects of multimedia-based self-directed English speaking practice. *Multimedia-Assisted Language Learning, 17*(4), 61-87.

Kim, K. O., & Park, S. H. (2015). The effects of process-based writing through the use of mobile SNS software on elementary English education. *Multimedia-Assisted Language Learning, 18*(1), 11-32.

Kim, K. W., & Kim, H. D. (2004). The effectiveness of Internet assisted instruction in English listening class. *Multimedia-Assisted Language Learning,* 7(2), 103-121.

Kim, K., & Choi, J. C. (2002). Construction and application of the web-based courseware "Spanish in Multimedia." *Multimedia-Assisted Language Learning, 5*(2), 29-46.

Kim, M. G. (2002). A study on the development of a web-based platform for French composition class. *Multimedia-Assisted Language Learning, 5*(2), 65-82.

Kim, N. Y., Cha, Y., & Kim, H. S. (2019). Future English learning: chatbots and artificial intelligence. *Multimedia-Assisted Language Learning, 22*(3), 32-53.

Kim, S. (2012). Implementing digital portfolios in a pre-service English teachers' classroom. *Multimedia-Assisted Language Learning, 15*(3), 35-56.

Kim, S., & Kim, H. (2015). Designing scaffolding in a digital English textbook for high school low achievers: A case study. *Multimedia-Assisted Language Learning, 18*(1), 33-58.

Kim, S. B. (1996). The effects of multimedia instruction on the L2 learners' achievement: An experiment. *English Teaching, 51*(4), 57-73.

Kim, S. Y. (2002). Korean college students' reflections of English language learning via CMC and FFC. *Multimedia-Assisted Language Learning, 5*(2), 9-28.

Kim, S. Y., & Lee, C. H. (2018). The impact of peer response on lexis and grammatical structure in L2 writing through blended learning. *Multimedia-Assisted Language Learning, 21*(4), 82-110.

Kim, S. Y., & Lee, H. J. (2012). A comparison of peer feedback in CMC and FFC contexts. *Multimedia-Assisted Language Learning, 15*(1), 91-114.

Kim, S. Y., & Pae, J. K. (2013). Computer-supported writing: A comparison of Wiki and Daedalus. *Multimedia-Assisted Language Learning, 16*(2), 31-52.

Kim, S. Y., & Ryoo, Y. S. (2009). Korean college students' vocabulary profiles as predictors of English reading and writing proficiency. *Multimedia-Assisted Language Learning, 12*(3), 93-115.

Kim, T. E. (2010). Reflection on using the criterion online writing evaluation service. *Multimedia-Assisted Language Learning, 13*(3), 59-83.

Kim, Y. M. (2010). Spoken corpora of EFL learners: Collocations, vocabulary use, and their oral proficiency levels. *Multimedia-Assisted Language Learning, 13*(1), 9-28.

Kitade, K. (2008). The role of offline metalanguage talk in asynchronous computer-mediated communication. *Language Learning & Technology, 12*(1), 64-84.

Klimanova, L., & Dembovskaya, S. (2013). L2 identity, discourse, and social networking in Russian. *Language Learning & Technology*, *17*(1), 69-88.

KMEC. (1998). *Criteria for quality of educational software.* Seoul: Author.

Knezek, G., Miyashita, K., & Sakamoto, T. (1993). Cross-cultural similarities in attitudes toward computers and the implications for teacher education. *Journal of Information Technology for Teacher Education, 2*, 193-204.

Ko, M. H., & Goranson, J. (2014). Technology-assisted vocabulary learning and student learning outcomes: A case study. *Multimedia-Assisted Language Learning, 17*(1), 11-33.

Kol, S., & Schcolnik, M. (2008). Asynchronous forums in EAP: Assessment issues. *Language Learning & Technology*, *12*(2), 49-70.

Kötter, M. (2003). Negotiation of meaning and codeswitching in online tandems. *Language Learning & Technology*, *7*(2), 145-172.

Kozlova, I., & Priven, D. (2015). ESL teacher training in 3D virtual worlds. *Language*

Learning & Technology, 19(1), 83-101.

Kramsch, C. (2000). Authenticity and authorship in the computer-mediated acquisition of L2 literacy. *Language Learning & Technology, 4*(2), 78-104.

Kukulska-Hulme, A. (2009). Will mobile learning change language learning? *ReCALL, 21*(2), 157-165.

Kukulska-Hulme, A., & Shield, L. (2008). An overview of mobile assisted language learning: From content delivery to supported collaboration and interaction. *ReCALL, 20*(3), 271–289.

Kwon, H., & Lee, C. H. (2011). Learner uptake of feedback in text-based synchronous computer mediated communication (SCMC). *Multimedia-Assisted Language Learning, 14*(2), 211-234.

Kwon, Y. (2013). A case study of college EFL learners' mobile-assisted language learning with smart applications. *Multimedia-Assisted Language Learning, 16*(1), 37-65.

Lafford, P. A., & Lafford, B. A. (2005). CMC technologies for teaching foreign languages: What's on the horizon? *CALICO Journal, 22*(3), 679-709.

Lai, C. (2013). A framework for developing self-directed technology use for language learning. *Language Learning & Technology, 17*(2), 100-122.

Lai, C., & Zhao, Y. (2006). Noticing and text-based chat. *Language Learning & Technology, 10*(3), 102-120.

Lam, F. S., & Pennington, M. C. (1995). The computer vs. the pen: A comparative study of word processing in a Hong Kong secondary classroom. *Computer Assisted Language Learning, 8*(1), 75-92.

Lamy, M. N., & Goodfellow, R. (1999). "Reflective Conversation" in the virtual language classroom. *Language Learning & Technology, 2*(2), 43-61.

Lan, Y. J., Sung, Y. T., & Chang, K. E. (2007). A mobile-device-supported peer-assisted learning system for collaborative early EFL reading. *Language Learning & Technology, 11*(3), 130-151.

Larreamendy-Joerns, J., & Leinhardt, G. (2006). Going the distance with online education. *Review of Educational Research, 76*(4), 567-605.

Larson, J. W. (1998). An argument for computer adaptive language testing. *Multimedia-Assisted Language Learning, 1*(1), 9-24.

Last, R. (1984). *Language teaching and the microcomputer.* Oxford: Basil Blackwell.

Latchem, C., Williamson, J., & Henderson-Lancett, L. (1993). IMM: An overview. In C. Latchem, J. Williamson, & L. Henderson-Lancett (Eds.), *Interactive multimedia* (pp. 19-38). London: Kogan Page.

Laufer, B., & Hill, M. (2000). What lexical information do L2 learners select in a call dictionary and how does it affect word retention? *Language Learning & Technology, 3*(2), 58-76.

Laurillard, D. (1987). The problems and possibilities of interactive video. In A. Jones, E. Scanlon, & T. O'Shea (Eds.), *The computer revolution in education: New technologies for distance* (pp. 129-142). Brighton, Sussex: Harvest Press.

Laurillard, D. (1995). Multimedia and the changing experience of the learner. *British Journal of Educational Technology, 26*(3), 179-189.

Lee, C., & Astle, R. (2014). Favorable types of medium in corrective feedback on writing: Harness the power of technologies or continue the traditional ways? *Multimedia-Assisted Language Learning, 17*(2), 112-129.

Lee, C. H. (1998a). The use of computers in foreign language teaching and learning effectively: Rethinking key issues. *Journal of the Applied Linguistics of Korea, 14*(1), 87-115.

Lee, C. H. (1998b). On multimedia in foreign language teaching and learning. *Multimedia-Assisted Language Learning, 1*(1), 25-50.

Lee, C. H. (1999). Why use or not use computers? *Multimedia-Assisted Language Learning, 2*(2), 9-46.

Lee, C. H. (2000a). Communicative activities applicable to CALL: Based on computer simulations. *Multimedia-Assisted Language Learning, 3*(2), 70-99.

Lee, C. H. (2000b). Multimedia courseware and content evaluation criteria. *Proceedings of 2000 KAMALL Conference, Korea,* 13-22.

Lee, C. H. (2000c). A Comparison between users' and non-users' attitudes towards the use of media technology in foreign language teaching at university level. *Journal of the Applied Linguistics Association of Korea, 16*(1), 17-50.

Lee, C. H. (2000d). Travelling around Korea [Computer software]. Seoul: Author.

Lee, C. H. (2002). What is the most crucial factor in implementing computers into FLT/L? *Multimedia-Assisted Language Learning, 5*(1), 83-103.

Lee, C. H. (2004). The effective use of live and recorded video on satellite TV and the Internet in FLT/L. *Multimedia-Assisted Language Learning, 7*(1), 83-108.

Lee, C. H. (2006). Computers and four language skills development. *Language and Linguistics, 38,* 59-87.

Lee, C. H. (2009). The effective contents and teaching methods for online multimedia English education course. *Studies in Foreign Language Education, 23*(1), 103-134.

Lee, C. H. (2012). Introduction. In KAMALL (Ed.), *The handbook of multimedia-assisted language learning* (pp. 11-16). Seongnam: Bookorea.

Lee, C. H. (2017). The impact and prospect of using digital technology in language education. *Proceedings of the Korean Education Conference*, Korea, *13*, 3-13.

Lee, C. H., & Cho, S. (2019). The application and effective use of MABL(Mobile-Assisted Blended Learning) in university English classes. *Multimedia-Assisted Language Learning, 22*(4), 226-255.

Lee, C. H., & Han, J. I. (2000). A study of a model of a teacher training program for effective multimedia English education. *Foreign Languages Education, 7*(1), 165-192.

Lee, C. H., Kwak, M. S., & Lynch, R. (2004). *ALL in ONE student book 1*. Seoul: Hanol Publishing Inc.

Lee, C. H., & Pyo, K. H. (2003). A study on the effectiveness of online/offline English language learning at university level. *Multimedia-Assisted Language Learning, 6*(1), 90-110.

Lee, C. H., & Yun, M. H. (2003). A study on the development of the evaluation criteria and model for multimedia courseware. *Foreign Languages Education, 10*(3), 187-217.

Lee, C. H., & Yun, M. H. (2005). Theories and practices of multimedia courseware evaluation. In B. Yoo et al. (Eds.), *The use of multimedia in ELT* (pp. 47-80). Seoul: Bookorea.

Lee, C. I. (2005). An authoring package for English vocabulary learning. *Multimedia-Assisted Language Learning, 8*(2), 179-197.

Lee, C. I., & Yoon, M. S. (2000). Use of a homepage for grammar practice based on error analysis of e-mail writings. *Multimedia-Assisted Language Learning, 3*(2), 53-69.

Lee, C. M., & Oh, E. (2014). Exploring the effects of a learner response system on EFL reading. *Multimedia-Assisted Language Learning, 17*(2), 130-151.

Lee, D. K., & Kim, H. (2014). A study on online TEE teacher training programs in Korea. *Multimedia-Assisted Language Learning, 17*(1), 58-83.

Lee, E., & Park, S. D. (2014). Adult EFL learners' successful participation in Web-Talking for oral proficiency improvement. *Multimedia-Assisted Language Learning, 17*(2), 152-175.

Lee, H. (2004). Reliability of a repeated testing design: A handwritten and computerized ESL writing test. *Multimedia-Assisted Language Learning, 7*(2), 143-163.

Lee, H. Y. (2000). The application of the Internet and the design for individualized teaching of Korean. *Multimedia-Assisted Language, 3*(1), 264-286.

Lee, J., & Lee, C. H. (2005). Teachers' perception of cyber homework for primary and secondary school students: A case study of D office of education. *Multimedia-Assisted Langage Learning, 8*(2), 154-178.

Lee, J., & Lee, C. H. (2009). Elementary and secondary school teachers' perspectives and solutions for the improvement of online teacher training in foreign language education. *Multimedia-Assisted Language Learning, 12*(1), 203-229.

Lee, J., & Lee, C. H. (2012). Students' perspectives and the effectiveness of blended learning in L2 listening at university level. *Multimedia-Assisted Language Learning, 15*(1), 59-89.

Lee, J., Yoon, S. Y., & Lee, C. H. (2013). Exploring online learning at primary schools: Students' perspectives on cyber home learning system through video conferencing (CHLS-VC). *The Turkish Online Journal of Educational Technology, 12*(1), 68-76.

Lee, L. (2008). Focus-on-form through collaborative scaffolding in expert-to-novice online interaction. *Language Learning & Technology, 12*(3), 53-72.

Lee, L. (2011). Blogging: Promoting learner autonomy and intercultural competence through study abroad. *Language Learning & Technology, 15*(3), 87-109.

Lee, S. (2004). Electronic spaces as a new writing and sharing arena. *Multimedia-Assisted Language Teaching, 7*(2), 165-195.

Lee, S. (2005a). Translating constructivism into EFL classrooms through the use of technology. *Multimedia-Assisted Language Learning, 8*(1), 220-249.

Lee, S. (2005b). ESL students' beliefs about the utility of synchronous online discussion (SOD) in language learning and their participation in the SOD. *Multimedia-Assisted Language Learning, 8*(2), 9-31.

Lee, S. (2008). Exploring the potential of a web-based writing instruction program and AES: An empirical study using My Access. *Multimedia-Assisted Language Learning, 11*(2), 103-125.

Lee, S. (2009). Evaluation of English learning programs on EBSe. *Multimedia-Assisted Language Learning, 12*(3), 117-137.

Lee, S. (2011a). A new convergence medium: IPTV in the English classrooms. *Multimedia-Assisted Language Learning, 14*(1), 95-120.

Lee, S. (2011b). Beyond the classroom: Videoconferencing English class in the study centers. *Multimedia-Assisted Language Learning, 14*(3), 109-132.

Lee, S. (2012a). Networked computer-supported intentional vocabulary learning: Make it active and interactive. *Multimedia-Assisted Language Learning, 15*(4), 81-102.

Lee, S. (2012b). Writing technologies and hypertext relay writing: Fostering collaborative writing. *Multimedia-Assisted Language Learning, 15*(2), 121-141.

Lee, S. (2019) The impact of using machine translation on EFL students' writing. *Computer Assisted Language Learning, 33*(3), 157-175.

Lee, S., & Kwon, C. J. (2007). The analysis of college students' English learning strategies in a CALL environment. *Multimedia-Assisted Language Learning, 10*(3), 155-186.

Lee, S. W. (2004). Is synchronous computer mediated communication truly egalitarian?: A case study of computer-networked ESL classroom. *Multimedia-Assisted Language Learning, 7*(1), 109-141.

Lee, S. W. (2012). Receptive vocabulary size for reading English and American novels. *Multimedia-Assisted Language Learning, 15*(4), 103-125.

Lee, Y. J., & Gerber, H. (2013). It's a WoW World: Second language acquisition and massively multiplayer online gaming. *Multimedia-Assisted Language Learning, 16*(2), 53-70.

Legenhausen, L., & Wolff, D. (1987). CALL at the crossroads? In L. Legenhausen & D. Wolff (Eds.), *Computer assisted language learning and innovative EFL methodology* (pp. 3-10). Augsburg: Thomas Finkenstaedt und Konrad Schroder.

Leonard, J. (1985). *Computers in language and literacy work*. London: ILEA.

Levy, M. (2002). Knowledge domains for the successful integration of CALL. *Multimedia-Assisted Language Learning, 5*(1), 243-257.

Levy, M., & Farrugia. D. (1988) *Computers in language teaching: Analysis, research and reviews*. Footscray: Footscray College of TAFE.

Levy, M., & Kennedy, C. (2004). A task-cycling pedagogy using stimulated reflection and audio-conferencing in foreign language learning. *Language Learning & Technology, 8*(2), 50-68.

Levy, M., & Kennedy, C. (2005). Learning Italian via mobile SMS. In A. Kukulska-Hulme & J. Traxler (Eds.), *Mobile learning: A handbook for educators and trainers*. (pp. 76-83). London, England: Routledge.

Levy, M., & Stockwell, G. (2006*). CALL dimensions: Options and issues in computer-assisted language learning*. Mahwah, NJ: Lawrence Erlbaum.

Li, Z., & Hegelheimer, V. (2013). Mobile-assisted grammar exercises: Effects on self-editing in L2 writing. *Language Learning & Technology*, *17*(3), 135-156.

Lian, A. (1992). Intelligence in computer-aided language learning. In M. C. Pennington & V. Stevens (Eds.), *Computers in applied linguistics* (pp. 110-126). Clevedon: Multilingual Matters.

Liang, M. Y. (2010). Using synchronous online peer response groups in EFL writing: Revision-related discourse. *Language Learning & Technology, 14*(1), 45-64.

Licklider, J. C. R. (1987). Information technology, education and the American future. In E. Scanlon & T. O'Shea (Eds.), *Educational computing* (pp. 253-270). Chichester: John Wiley and Sons.

Lim, H., Park, D., & Si, K. (2014). Sophistication of an automated scoring system for large-scale essay writing tests. *Multimedia-Assisted Language Learning, 17*(1), 84-105.

Lim, K. (2012). Developing an English intensive course model based on CMC for Korean high school students. *Multimedia-Assisted Language Learning, 15*(4), 127-151.

Lin, H., & Chen, T. (2007). Reading authentic EFL text using visualization and advance organizers in a multimedia learning environment. *Language Learning & Technology, 11*(3), 83-106.

Liou, H. C. (2013). Investigation of using text-critiquing programs in a process-oriented writing class. *CALICO Journal, 10*(4), 17-38.

Littlewood, W. (1981) *Communicative language teaching: An introduction.* Cambridge: Cambridge University Press.

Liu, J., & Hansen, J. (2002). *Peer response in second language writing classrooms.* Ann Arbor, MI: University of Michigan Press.

Liu, J., & Sadler, R. W. (2003). The effect and affect of peer review in electronic versus traditional modes on L2 writing. *Journal of English for Academic Purposes, 2*(3), 193-227.

Liu, M. H., & Kleinsasser, R. (2015). Exploring EFL teachers' knowledge and competencies: In-service program perspectives. *Language Learning & Technology, 19*(1), 119-138.

Lixun, W. (2001). Exploring parallel concordancing in English and Chinese. *Language Learning & Technology, 5*(3), 174-184.

Lomicka, L. (1998). "To gloss or not to gloss": An investigation of reading comprehension online. *Language Learning & Technology, 1*(2), 41-50.

Lonergan, J. (1984). *Video in language teaching.* Cambridge: Cambridge University Press.

Loranc-Paszylk, B. (2015). Videoconferencing as a tool for developing speaking skills. In M. Pawlak & E. Waniek-Klimczak (Eds.), *Issues in teaching, learning and testing speaking in a second language, second language learning and teaching* (pp. 189-203). Berlin: Springer Berlin Heidelberg.

Luckin, R., Holmes, W., Griffiths, M. & Forcier, L. B. (2016). *Intelligence unleashed. An argument for AI in Education.* London: Pearson.

Lys, F. (2013). The development of advanced learner oral proficiency using iPads. *Language Learning & Technology, 17*(3), 94-116.

Macaro, E. (2006). Strategies for language learning and for language use: Revising the theoretical framework. *The Modern Language Journal, 90*(3), 320-337.

Macaro, E., & Erler, L. (2008). Raising the achievement of young beginner readers of French through strategy instruction. *Applied Linguistics, 29*(1), 90-119.

Madsen, H. (1991). Computer-adaptive testing of listening and reading comprehension. In P. Dunkel (Ed.), *Computer-assisted language learning and testing* (pp. 237-257). New York: Newbury House.

Markee, N. (1994) Using electronic mail to manage the implementation of educational innovations. *System, 22*(3), 379-389.

Matthews. C. (1992). Going AI: Foundations of ICALL. *Computer Assisted Language Learning, 5*(1-2), 13-31.

Matthews, C. (1993). Grammar frameworks in intelligent CALL. *CALICO Journal, 11*(1), 5–27.

Mayer, R. E. (2002a). Cognitive theory and the design of multimedia instruction: An example of the two-way street between cognition and instruction. *New*

Directions for Teaching and Learning, 89, 55-71.

Mayer, R. E. (2002b). Multimedia learning. *Psychology of Learning and Motivation, 41,* 85-139.

Mayer-Schönberger, V., & Cukier, K. (2013). *Big data: A Revolution that will transform how we live, work, and think.* New York, NY: Houghton Mifflin Harcourt.

McCarthy, J., Minsky, M. L., Rochester, N., & Shannon, C. (2006). *A proposal for the Dartmouth summer research project on artificial intelligence,* august 31, 1955. *AI Magazine, 27*(4), 12-14.

McCarthy, M. (1990). *Vocabulary.* Oxford: Oxford University Press.

McCarthy, M., & O'Keeffe, A. (2004). Research in the teaching of speaking. *Annual Review of Applied Linguistics, 24,* 26-43.

McDonald, P., García-Carbonell, A., & Carot-Sierra, J. M. (2013). Computer learner corpora: Analysing interlanguage errors in synchronous and asynchronous communication. *Language Learning & Technology, 17*(2), 36-56.

McMinn, S. W. J. (2008). Podcasting possibilities: Increasing time and motivation in the language learning classroom. Retrieved March 24, 2015 from the World Wide Web: http://http://www.eife-l.org/publications/proceedings/ilf08/contributions/improving-quality-of-learning-with-technologies/McMinn.pdf

McNeil, L. (2014). Ecological affordance and anxiety in an oral asynchronous computer-mediated environment. *Language Learning & Technology, 18*(1), 142-159.

Megarry, J. (1989). Hypertext and compact discs: The challenge of multimedia learning. In C. Bell, J. Davies, & R. Winders (Eds.), *Promoting learning* (pp. 49-58). London: Kogan Page.

Merriam-Webster Dictionary. (2021). *Merriam-Webster's online dictionary.* Retrieved from: https://www.merriam-webster.com/dictionary/data/

Merrill, M. D. (1988). Applying component display theory to the design of courseware. In D. H. Jonassen (Ed.), *Instructional designs for microcomputer courseware* (pp. 61-102). Hillsdale, NJ: Lawrence Erlbaum Associates.

Meskill, C., Mossop, J., DiAngelo, S., & Pasquale, R. K. (2002). Expert and novice teachers talking technology: Precepts, concepts, and misconcepts. *Language Learning & Technology, 6*(3), 46-57.

Microsoft Research. (2013, February 13). The big bang: How the big data explosion is changing the world. Retrieved from: https://news.microsoft.com/2013/02/11/the-big-bang-how-the-big-data-explosion-is-changing-the-world/.

Min, D. G., & Choi, E. I. (2002). Using CMC to improve elementary school students' English proficiency: Focused on the analysis of discourse functions and syntactic complexity. *Multimedia-Assisted Language Learning, 5*(2), 103-129.

Min, D. G., Kim, S. R., & Kim, K. H. (2010). A study on the development of a corpus-based collocation book using children's English newspapers. *Multimedia-Assisted Language Learning, 13*(1), 173-200.

Min, H. T. (2006). The effects of trained peer review on EFL students' revision types and writing quality. *Journal of Second Language Writing, 15*(2), 118-141.

Miyazoe, T., & Anderson, T. (2010). Learning outcomes and students' perceptions of online writing: Simultaneous implementation of a forum, blog, and wiki in an EFL blended learning setting. *System, 38*(3), 185-199.

Mokhtari, K., & Reichard, C. (2004). Investigating the strategic reading processes of first and second language readers in two different cultural contexts. *System, 32*(3), 379-394.

Monteiro, K. (2014). An experimental study of corrective feedback during video-conferencing. *Language Learning & Technology, 18*(3), 56-79.

Moon, K., & Kim, J. (2012). Development and application of web-based Korean elementary English readability index software for measuring readability in extensive reading classrooms. *Multimedia-Assisted Language Learning, 15*(1), 157-179.

Morris, F. (2005). Child-to-child interaction and corrective feedback in a computer mediated L2 class. *Language Learning & Technology, 9*(1), 29-45.

Munby, J. (1968). *Read and think.* Essex: Longman.

Munby, J. (1979). Teaching intensive reading skills. In R. Mackay, B. Barknan, & R. R. Jordan (Eds.), *Reading in a second language* (pp. 142-159). Rowley, MA: Newbury House.

Murphy, J. M. (1991). Oral communication in TESOL: Integrating speaking, listening, and pronunciation. *TESOL Quarterly, 25*(1), 51-75.

Murphy, P. (2007). Reading comprehension exercises online: The effects of feedback, proficiency and interaction. *Language Learning & Technology, 11*(3), 107-129.

Murray, D. E. (2000). Changing technologies, changing literacy communities? *Language Learning & Technology, 4*(2), 43-58.

Myers, J., & Sung, K. (2002). Texts, technology, and pedagogy. *Multimedia-Assisted Language Learning, 5*(1), 151-166.

Nagata, N. (1998). Input vs. output practice in educational software for second language acquisition. *Language Learning & Technology, 1*(2), 23-40.

Nakano, M. (Ed). (2007). *World Englishes and miscommunications.* Tokyo: Waseda University International.

Nam, J. Y., & Jeon, K. (2006). Study on the use of an English TV program for listening proficiency improvement of beginning young learners. *Multimedia-Assisted Language Learning, 9*(3), 127-149.

Nassaji, H., & Fotos, S. S. (2010). *Teaching grammar in second language classrooms.* New

York: Routledge.

Nation, I. S. P. (2013). *Learning vocabulary in another language* (2nd ed.). Cambridge: Cambridge University.

Neri, A., Cucchiarini, C., Strik, H., & Boves, L. (2002). The pedagogy-technology interface in computer assisted pronunciation training. *Computer Assisted Language Learning, 15*(5), 441-447.

Neumeier, P. (2005). A closer look at blended learning: Parameters for designing a blended learning environment for language teaching and learning. *ReCALL, 17*(2), 163-178.

Nickerson, R. S. (1988). Technology in education in 2020: thinking about the not-distant future. In R. S. Nickerson & P. P. Zodhiates (Eds.), *Technology in education: Looking toward 2020* (pp. 1-10). Hillsdale, New Jersey: REA.

Nicolson, M., Murphy, L., & Southgate, M. (Eds). (2011). *Language teaching in blended contexts.* Edinburgh: Dunedin Academic Press.

Nielson, K. B. (2011). Self-study with language learning software in the workplace: What happens. *Language Learning & Technology, 15*(3), 110-129.

Nikolova, O. R. (2002). Effects of students' participation in authoring of multimedia materials on student acquisition of vocabulary. *Language Learning & Technology, 6*(1), 100-122.

Norris, N., Davies, R., & Beattie, C. (1990). Evaluating new technology: The case of the interactive video in schools programme. *British Journal of Educational Technology, 21*, 84-94.

Nuttall, C. (1996). *Teaching reading skills in a foreign language* (2nd ed.). Oxford: Heinemann.

Nuttall, C. (2005). *Teaching reading skills in a foreign language.* London: Macmillan.

O'Dowd, R. (2003). Understanding the "other side": Intercultural learning in a Spanish-English e-mail exchange. *Language Learning & Technology, 7*(2), 118-144.

O'Dowd, R. (2015). Supporting in-service language educators in learning to telecollaborate. *Language Learning & Technology, 19*(1), 63-82.

O, K. M. (2004). Developing web-based English achievement testing program. *Multimedia-Assisted Language Learning, 7*(2), 241-268.

O'Bryan, A., & Hegelheimer, V. (2009). Using a mixed methods approach to explore strategies, metacognitive awareness and the effects of task design on listening development. *Canadian Journal of Applied Linguistics, 12*(1), 9-38.

O'Shea, T., & Self, J. (1983). *Learning and teaching with computers.* Brighton, Sussex: Harvester Press.

Obari, H. (2013). The impact of employing mobile technologies and pc for learning Coursera on-line lectures and TOEIC practice kit. *Multimedia-Assisted Language Learning, 16*(4), 97-109.

Odell, A. (1986). Evaluating CALL software. In G. Leech & C. N. Candlin (Eds.), *Computers in English language teaching and research* (pp. 47-55). London: Longman.

OECD. (1987). *Information technologies and basic learning: Reading, writing, science and mathematics*. Paris: OECD.

Oh, C. R., & Choi, S. Y. (2010). A study of developing speed reading skills in English using multimedia. *Multimedia-Assisted Language Learning, 13*(1), 147-171.

Oh, H., & Park, M. R. (2013). A case study of elementary school underachievers' SMART vocabulary learning experiences. *Multimedia-Assisted Language Learning, 16*(2), 71-92.

Ohm, I. S. (2003). How to make call systems more intelligent. *Multimedia-Assisted Language Learning, 6*(2), 111-134.

Ohm, I. S. (2008). A study of the design of curriculum-based progress monitoring systems. *Multimedia-Assisted Language Learning, 11*(1), 127-155.

Olson, D. J. (2014). Benefits of visual feedback on segmental production in the L2 classroom. *Language Learning & Technology, 18*(3), 173-192.

O'Malley, J. M., & Chamot, A. U. (1990). *Learning strategies in second language acquisition*. Cambridge: Cambridge University Press.

O'Rourke, B. (2005). Form-focused interaction in online tandem learning. *CALICO Journal, 22*(3), 433-466.

Ortega, L. (1997). Processes and outcomes in networked classroom interaction: Defining the research agenda for L2 computer-assisted classroom discussion. *Language Learning & Technology, 1*(1), 82-93.

Osuna, M. M., & Meskill, C. (1998). Using the World Wide Web to integrate Spanish language and culture: A pilot study. *Language Learning & Technology, 1*(2), 71-92.

Oxford, R. (1990). *Language learning strategies: What every teacher should know*. New York: Newbury House.

Oxford, R. L., & Scarcella, R. C. (1994). Second language vocabulary learning among adults: State of the art in vocabulary instruction. *System, 22*(2), 231-243.

Pae, J. K. (2011). Collaborative writing versus individual writing: Fluency, accuracy, complexity, and essay score. *Multimedia-Assisted Language Learning, 14*(1), 121-148.

Pae, J. K. (2012). How do Korean EFL students perform in computer-supported collaborative writing? *Multimedia-Assisted Language Learning, 15*(4), 153-174.

Paine, N., & McAra, P. (1993). Interactive multimedia technology: A summary of current developments. In C. Latchem, J. Williamson., & L. Henderson-Lancett (Eds.), *Interactive multimedia* (pp. 39-56). London: Kogan Page.

Paivio, A. (1986). *Mental representations: A dual-coding approach*. New York: Oxford University Press.

Paris, S. G., Wasik, B. A., & Turner, J. C. (1991). The development of strategic readers.

In R. Barr, M. L. Kamil, P. B. Mosenthal, & P. D. Pearson (Eds.), *Handbook of reading research* (pp. 609-640). White Plains, NY: Longman.

Park, D. J. (1994). Toward the innovative EFL methodology for computer-assisted language learning. *English Teaching, 48,* 243-263.

Park, E. Y. (2003). Strategies in negotiation of meaning and self-correction in CMC interaction. *Multimedia-Assisted Language Learning, 6*(2), 53-70.

Park, H. J., & Kim, J. Y. (2011). The effects of the English writing activities using Twitter on learners' writing abilities at university level. *Multimedia-Assisted Language Learning, 14*(3), 245-264.

Park, J., Yang, J. S., & Hsieh, Y. C. (2014). University level second language readers' online reading and comprehension strategies. *Language Learning & Technology, 18*(3), 148-172.

Park, S. H., & Choi, H. (2012). The effects of modified extensive reading activities using Internet English storybooks on elementary school students' English learning. *Multimedia-Assisted Language Learning, 15*(3), 57-82.

Park, S. H., & Lim, H. S. (2009). Elementary English teachers' perceptions and use of English learning web sites of the public institutions. *Multimedia-Assisted Language Learning, 12*(3), 139-168.

Park, S. M., & Cha, K. W. (2013). Pre-service teachers' perspectives on a blended listening course using TED Talks. *Multimedia-Assisted Language Learning, 16*(2), 93-116.

Parks, S., Huot, D., Hamers, J., & Lemonnier, F. H. (2003). Crossing boundaries: Multimedia technology and pedagogical innovation in a high school class. *Language Learning & Technology*, *7*(1), 28-45.

Pawan, F., Paulus, T. M., Yalcin, S., & Chang, C. F. (2003). Online learning: Patterns of engagement and interaction among in-service teachers. *Language Learning & Technology*, *7*(3), 119-140.

Payne, J. S., & Ross, B. M. (2005). Synchronous CMC, working memory, and L2 oral proficiency development. *Language Learning & Technology*, *9*(3), 35-54.

Patterson, G. B. (1988). The benefits and implications of computer-assisted instruction in teaching English as a foreign language in Korea. *English Teaching, 35*, 191-208.

Pennington, M. C. (1989). Applications of computers in the development of speaking and listening proficiency. In M. C. Pennington (Ed.), *Teaching languages with computers* (pp. 99-122). La Jolla: Athelstan.

Pennington, M. C. (1991). The road ahead: A forward-looking view of computers in language learning. *Computer Assisted Language Learning, 4*(1), 3-19.

Pennington, M. C. (2004). Electronic media in second language writing: An overview of tools and research finding. In S. Fotos & C. M. Browne (Eds.), *New perspectives on CALL for second language classrooms* (pp. 69-92). Mahwah, NJ: Lawrence Erlbaum Associates.

Perez, M. M., Peters, E., Clarebout, G., & Desmet, P. (2014). Effects of captioning on video comprehension and incidental vocabulary learning. *Language Learning & Technology, 18*(1), 118-141.

Perzylo, L. (1993). The application of multimedia CD-ROMs in schools. *British Journal of Educational Technology, 24*, 191-197.

Peters, E. (2007). Manipulating L2 learners' online dictionary use and its effect on L2 word retention. *Language Learning & Technology, 11*(2), 36-58.

Phillips, M. (1985). Educational technology in the next decade: an ELT perspective. In C. Brumfit, M. Phillips, & P. Skehan (Eds.), *Computers in English Language Teaching. ELT documents 122* (pp. 99-120). Oxford: Pergamon.

Phinney, M. (1989). Computers, composition, and second language teaching. In M. C. Pennington (Ed.), *Teaching languages with computers* (pp. 81-96). La Jolla: Athelstan.

Piaget, J. (1972). *The principles of genetic epistemology*. New York: Basic Books.

Piper, A. (1987). Helping learners to write: A role for the word processor. *ELT Journal, 41*(2), 119-125.

Plass, J. L. (1998). Design and evaluation of the user interface of foreign language multimedia software: A cognitive approach, *Langauge Learning & Technology, 2*(1), 35-45.

Pokrivcakova, S. (2019). Preparing teachers for the application of AI-powered technologies in foreign language education. *Journal of Language and Cultural Education, 7*(3), 135-153.

Polat, N., Mancilla, R., & Mahalingappa, L. (2013). Anonymity and motivation in asynchronous discussions and L2 vocabulary learning. *Language Learning & Technology, 17*(2), 57-74.

Preece, J. (1993). Hypermedia, multimedia and human factors. In C, Latchem, J. Williamson, & L, Henderson-Lancett (Eds.), *Interactive multimedia* (pp. 135-150). London: Kogan Page.

Pusack, J. P., & Otto, S. (1990). Applying instructional technologies. *Foreign Language Annals, 23*(5), 409-417.

Pyo, J., & Lee, C. H. (2019). The effects of mitigation strategies instruction in peer response to L2 writing through computer-mediated communication at university level. *Multimedia-Assisted Language Learning, 22*(4), 103-133.

Pyo, J., & Lee, C. H. (2020). The incorporation of mitigation strategies in peer response to L2 writing via computer-mediated communication. *Studies in Foreign Language Education, 34*(4), 27-55.

Raimes, A. (1983). *Techniques in teaching writing.* New York: Oxford University Press.

Ranalli, J. (2013). Online strategy instruction for integrating dictionary skills and language awareness. *Language Learning & Technology, 17*(2), 75-99.

Reeder, K., Macfadyen, L. P., Roche, J., & Chase, M. (2004). Negotiating cultures in cyberspace: Participation patterns and problematics. *Language Learning & Technology, 8*(2), 88-105.

Reeves, T. C., & Reeves, P. M. (1997). Effective dimensions of interactive learning on the World Wide Web. In B. H. Khan (Ed.), *Web-based instruction* (pp. 59-66). Englewood Cliffs, NJ: Educational Technology Publications.

Rich, T. (1991). Computer technology and education: Past performance and future promise. *Innovations in Education & Training International, 28*(2), 147-153.

Richards, C. (2000). Hypermedia, Internet communication, and the challenge of redefining literacy in the electronic age. *Language Learning & Technology, 4*(2), 59-77.

Richards, C. (2005). The design of effective ICT-supported learning activities: Exemplary models, changing requirements, and new possibilities. *Language Learning & Technology, 9*(1), 60-79.

Richards, J. C., Platt, J., & Platt, H. (1992). *Longman dictionary of language teaching and applied linguistics* (2nd ed.). Essex: Longman.

Rivers, W. M. (1981). *Teaching foreign-language skills*. Chicago: The University of Chicago Press.

Robb, T. N., & Susser, B. (2000). The life and death of software: Examining the selection process. *CALICO Journal, 18*(1), 41-52.

Roever, C. (2001). Web-based language testing. *Language Learning & Technology, 5*(2), 84-94.

Romiszowski, A. J. (1988) *The selection and use of instructional media*. London: Kogan Page.

Romiszowski, A. J. (1993). Developing interactive multimedia courseware and networks: some current issues. In C. Latchem, J. Williamson, & L. Henderson-Lancett (Eds.), *Interactive multimedia* (pp. 57-78). London: Kogan Page.

Rooney, J. E. (2003). Blended learning opportunities to enhance educational programming and meetings. *Association Management, 55*(5), 26-32.

Rosell-Aguilar, F. (2013). Podcasting for language learning through iTunes U: The learner's view. *Language Learning & Technology, 17*(3), 74-93.

Ross, S. (1997). An introspective analysis of listener inferencing on a second language listening test. In G. Kasper & E. Kellerman (Eds.), *Communication strategies: Psycholinguistic and sociolinguistic perspectives* (pp. 216-237). New York: Routledge.

Rossett, A. (2002). *The ASTD e-learning handbook*. New York: McGraw-Hill.

Rott, S. (1999). The effect of exposure frequency on intermediate language learners' incidental vocabulary acquisition and retention through reading. *Studies in*

Second Language Acquisition, 21(4), 589–619.

Roussel, S., Rieussec, A., Nespoulous, J. L., & Tricot, A. (2008). Des baladeurs MP3 en classe d'allemand-L'effet de l'autorégulation matérielle de l'écoute sur la compréhension auditive en langue seconde. *Alsic. Apprentissage des Langues et Systèmes d'Information et de Communication*, *11*(2), 7-37.

Rülmann, F. (1995). Towards replacement of the teaching process: The emulation of the teaching process with CAL and its implications for the design of a multimedia CAL tutorial. *Computer Assisted Language Learning, 8*(1), 45-61.

Rumelhart, D. E. (1994). *Toward an interactive model of reading.* Newark, DE. International Reading Association.

Rüschoff, B. (1993). Language learning and information technology: State of art. *CALICO Journal, 10,* 5-17.

Russell, S. J., & Norvig, P. (2010). *Artificial Intelligence: A modern approach* (3rd ed.). Upper Saddle River, New Jersey: Prentice-Hall.

Russikoff, K., & Kogan, S. (1996, March). *Feedback on ESL writing.* Paper presented at the 31st Annual TESOL Convention, Chicago, IL.

Rutherford, W. E. (1987). *Second language grammar: Learning and teaching.* New York: Longman.

Ryu, J. A., & Lee, C. H. (2011). The impact of using web-based speed reading program on the improvement of English reading speed at elementary school level. *Multimedia-Assisted Language Learning, 14*(3), 195-224.

Sakar, A., & Ercetin, G. (2004). Effectiveness of hypermedia annotations for foreign language reading. *Journal of Computer Assisted Learning, 21,* 28-38.

Salaberry, M. R. (2001). The use of technology for second language learning and teaching: A retrospective. *The Modern Language Journal, 85*(1), 39-56.

Sampson, N. (2003). Meeting the needs of distance learners. *Language Learning & Technology, 7*(3), 103-118.

Sanne, S. M. (1993). Hypermedia in the teaching of Italian. *CALICO Journal 10*(4), 76-82.

Sauro, S. (2009). Computer-mediated corrective feedback and the development of L2 grammar. *Language Learning & Technology*, *13*(1), 96-120.

Sawaki, Y. (2001). Comparability of conventional and computerized tests of reading in a second language. *Language Learning & Technology*, *5*(2), 38-59.

Scarborough, D. (1988). Survey review of software for English language teaching. *ELT Journal, 24*(4), 68-76.

Schaffhauser, D. (2017). *Immersive Education: AR Comes of Age.* Retrieved from https://thejournal.com/articles/2017/03/06/immersive-education-ar-comes-of-age.aspx

Schank, R. C. (1984). *The cognitive computer: On language, learning, and artificial intelligence.*

Mass.: Addison-Wesley.
Schenck, A., & Cho, Y. W. (2012). The efficacy of corpus-based pedagogical techniques for academic writing. *Multimedia-Assisted Language Learning, 15*(2), 167-186.
Schmid, G. (1989). Teacher training in CALL: An Austrian view. *MUESLI News, Dec.*, 2-5.
Schmidt, R. (1990). The role of consciousness in second language learning. *Applied linguistics, 11*(2), 129-158.
Schmidt-Rinehart, B. C. (1994). The effects of topic familiarity on second language listening comprehension. *The Modern Language Journal, 78*(2), 179-189.
Schulze, M. (2008). AI in CALL—artificially inflated or almost imminent? *CALICO Journal, 25*(3), 510-527.
Schumann, J. H. (1997). *The neurobiology of affect in language.* Cambridge, MA: Blackwell.
Schwienhorst, K. (2003). Learner autonomy and tandem learning: Putting principles into practice in synchronous and asynchronous telecommunications environments. *Computer Assisted Language Learning, 16*(5), 427-443.
Scovel, T. (1969). Foreign accent, language acquisition, and cerebral dominance. *Language Learning, 19*(3-4), 245-253.
Scovel, T. (1988). *A time to speak: A psycholinguistic inquiry into the critical period for human speech.* New York: Newbury House.
Searle, J. R. (1980). Minds, brains, and programs. *Behavioral and Brain Sciences, 3*(3), 417-457.
Sengupta, S. (2001). Exchanging ideas with peers in network-based classrooms: An aid or a pain. *Language Learning & Technology, 5*(1), 103-134.
Seo, W., & Choi, I. C. (2014). The effect of using a smart-phone speaking application on Korean middle school students' English expression learning and satisfaction. *Multimedia-Assisted Language Learning, 17*(1), 34-57.
Seo, Y. J., & Lee, E. J. (2014). The effects of storybook mind-mapping and summarizing activities on vocabulary acquisition, writing ability and the attitude of the elementary school students. *Multimedia-Assisted Language Learning, 17*(3), 121-153.
Sherrington, R. (1973). *Television and language skills.* London: Oxford University Press.
Shim, Y. S. (2008). Stimulating negotiation of meaning in CMC interaction. *Multimedia-Assisted Language Learning, 11*(2), 142-168.
Shin, D., Park, Y., Park, T., & Yim, S. Y. (2015). The present and future of an automated scoring program for speaking skills of English. *Multimedia-Assisted Language Learning, 18*(1), 93-114.
Shin, D., & Jeong, D. (2009). How can we make word family lists with graded affixes? *Multimedia-Assisted Language Learning, 12*(3), 169-193.

Shin, D., & Joo, H. (2008). Development of a vocabulary list for English textbook authorization: Reflection on vocabulary analysis programs and the basic vocabulary list. *Multimedia-Assisted Language Learning, 11*(3), 95-113.

Shin, D. S. (2006). ESL students' computer-mediated communication practices: Context configuration. *Language Learning & Technology, 10*(3), 65-84.

Shin, S. K. (2015). Teaching critical, ethical, and safe use of ICT to teachers. *Language Learning & Technology, 19*(1), 181-197.

Shumin, K. (2002). Factors to consider: Developing adult EFL students' speaking abilities. In J. C. Richards & W. A. Renandya (Eds.), *Methodology in language teaching: An anthology of current practices* (pp. 204-211). Cambridge: Cambridge University Press.

Siemens, G. (2004). *Connectivism: A learning theory for the digital age.* Retrieved from http://www.elearnspace.org/Articles/connectivism.htm

Siemens, G. (2005). Connectivism: A learning theory for the digital age. *International Journal of Instructional Technology and Distance Learning, 2*(1). Retrieved from http://www.itdl.org/

Singh, H., & Reed, C. (2001). *A white paper: Achieving success with blended learning.* Centra Software. Retrieved May 20, 2015, from the World Wide Web: http://www.leerbeleving.nl/wbts/wbt2014/blend-ce.pdf

Skehan, P. (1985). A primer in CALL technology. In Brumfit, C., Phillips, M., & Skehan, P. (Eds.), *Computers in English Language Teaching. ELT documents 122* (pp. 121-136). Oxford: Pergamon.

Skinner, B. F. (1957). *Verbal behavior.* New York: Appleton-Century-Crofts.

Smith, B. (2012). Eye tracking as a measure of noticing: A study of explicit recasts in SCMC. *Language Learning & Technology, 16*(3), 53-81.

Smyth, R. (2005). Broadband videoconferencing as a tool for learner-centered distance learning in higher education. *British Journal of Educational Technology, 36*(5), 805-820.

Snow, M. A., Met, M., & Genesee, F. (1989). A conceptual framework for the integration of language and content in second/foreign language instruction. *TESOL Quarterly, 23*(2), 201-217.

Snyder, I. (1993). Writing with word processors: A research overview. *Educational Research, 35*(1), 49-68.

So, L., & Lee, C. H. (2013). A case study on the effects of an L2 writing instructional model for blended learning in higher education. *The Turkish Online Journal of Educational Technology, 12*(4), 1-10.

So, L., & Lee, C. H. (2014). The impact of peer response on L2 writing in blended learning in higher education. *Korean Journal of Applied Linguistics, 30*(4), 205-234.

Son, J. B. (2005). Exploring and evaluating language learning Web sites. In J. B. Son

& S. O'Neill (Eds.), *Enhancing learning and teaching: Pedagogy, technology, and language* (pp. 215-227). Flaxton, Australia: Post Pressed.

Son, J. B., & O'Neill, S. (1999). Collaborative e-mail exchange: A pilot study of peer editing. *Multimedia-Assisted Language Learning, 2*(2), 69-87.

Sotillo, S. M. (2000). Discourse functions and syntactic complexity in synchronous and asynchronous communication. *Language Learning & Technology, 4*(1), 82-119.

Spivey, N. N. (1997). *The constructivist metaphor: Reading, writing and the making of meaning.* San Diego: Academic Press.

Stepp-Greany, J. (2002). Student perceptions on language learning in a technological environment: Implications for the new millennium. *Language Learning & Technology, 6*(1), 165-180.

Stevens, V. (1989). A direction for CALL: From behavioristic to humanistic courseware. In M. C. Pennington (Ed.), *Teaching languages with computers* (pp. 31-44). La Jolla: Athelstan.

Stevens, V. (1992). Humanism and CALL: A coming of age. In M. C. Pennington & V. Stevens (Eds.), *Computers in applied linguistics* (pp. 11-38). Clevedon: Multilingual Matters.

Stockwell, G. (2007). A review of technology choice for teaching language skills in the CALL literature. *ReCALL, 19*(2), 105-120.

Stockwell, G. (2010). Using mobile phones for vocabulary activities: Examining the effect of the platform. *Language Learning & Technology, 14*(2), 95-110.

Strambi, A., & Bouvet, E. J. (2003). Flexibility and interaction at a distance: A mixed-model environment for language learning. *Language Learning & Technology, 7*(3), 81-101.

Suh, E. J., & Lee, C. H. (2014). A case study of elementary school students' English reading strategy use in blended learning. *Primary English Education, 20*(4), 297-320.

Sun, Y. C. (2009). Voice blog: An exploratory study of language learning. *Language Learning & Technology, 13*(2), 88-103.

Sun, Y. C., & Chang, Y. J. (2012). Blogging to learn: Becoming EFL academic writers through collaborative dialogues. *Language Learning & Technology, 16*(1), 43-61.

Sung, K. (2004). Critical English language teaching using a multimedia and inquiry-based approach. *Multimedia-Assisted Language Learning, 7*(1), 169-198.

Sydorenko, T. (2010). Modality of input and vocabulary acquisition. *Language Learning & Technology, 14*(2), 50-73.

Tai, S. J. D. (2015). From TPACK-in-action workshops to classrooms: CALL competency developed and integrated. *Language Learning & Technology, 19*(1), 139-164.

Tanner, M. W., & Landon, M. M. (2009). The effects of computer-assisted pronunciation readings on ESL learners' use of pausing, stress, intonation, and overall comprehensibility. *Language Learning & Technology, 13*(3), 51-65.

Tare, M., Golonka, E. M., Vatz, K., Bonilla, C. L., Crooks, C., & Strong, R. (2014). Effects of interactive chat versus independent writing on L2 learning. *Language Learning & Technology, 18*(3), 208-227.

Tarone, E. (2005). Speaking in a second language. In E. Hinkel (Ed.), *Handbook of research in second language teaching and learning* (pp. 485-502). Mahwah, NJ: Lawrence Erlbaum Associates.

Taylor, A., Stevens, J. R., & Asher, J. W. (2006). The effects of explicit reading strategy training on L2 reading comprehension. In J. Norris & L. Ortega (Eds.), *Synthesizing research on language learning and teaching* (pp. 213–244). Philadelphia: Benjamins.

Taylor, M. B. (1986). CALL-is correction. *System, 14*(3), 343-347.

TELL ME MORE [Computer software]. (1998, 2002). Viosins le Bretonneux: AURALOG.

Thompson, P., & Tribble, C. (2001). Looking at citations: Using corpora in English for academic purposes. *Language Learning & Technology, 5*(3), 91-105.

Thornbury, S. (1999). *How to teach grammar.* Harlow, Essex: Pearson Education Limited.

Thorne, S. L. (2003). Artifacts and cultures-of-use in intercultural communication. *Language Learning & Technology*, *7*(2), 38-67.

Thorne, S. L. (2008). New media language use and "bridging activities": Implications for plurilingual life in a (partially) digital world. *Multimedia-Assisted Language Learning, 11*(1), 35-60.

Thornton, P., & Houser, C. (2005). Using mobile phones in English education in Japan. *Journal of Computer Assisted Learning, 21*, 217-228.

Tomalin, B. (1986). *Video, TV & radio in the English class.* London: Macmillan.

Toyoda, E., & Harrison, R. (2002). Categorization of text chat communication between learners and native speakers of Japanese. *Language Learning & Technology*, *6*(1), 82-99.

Tribble, C. (1996). *Writing.* Oxford: Oxford University Press.

Tudini, V. (2003). Using native speakers in chat. *Language Learning & Technology*, *7*(3), 141-159.

UNESCO. (1988). *Informatics in education: trends and achievements by international organizations and prospects for further cooperation.* Paris: UNESCO.

Ur, P. (1984). *Teaching listening comprehension.* Cambridge: Cambridge University Press.

van Els, T., Bongaerts, T., Extra, G., van Os, C., & Janssen-van Dieten, A. (1984). *Applied linguistics and the learning and teaching of foreign languages.* London: Edward

Arnold.

Vandergriff, I. (2006). Negotiating common ground in computer-mediated versus face-to-face discussions. *Language Learning & Technology, 10*(1), 110-138.

Vandergrift, L. (1997). The comprehension strategies of second language (French) listeners: A descriptive study. *Foreign Language Annals, 30*(3), 387-409.

Vandergrift, L., & Goh, C. C. (2012). *Teaching and learning second language listening: Metacognition in action*. New York: Routledge.

Vandergrift, L., & Tafaghodtari, M. H. (2010). Teaching L2 learners how to listen does make a difference: An empirical study. *Language Learning, 60*(2), 470-497.

Vandergrift, L., Goh, C., Mareschal, C. J., & Tafaghodtari, M. H. (2006). The metacognitive awareness listening questionnaire: Development and validation. *Language Learning, 56*(3), 431-462.

Verdugo, D. R., & Belmonte, I. A. (2007). Using digital stories to improve listening comprehension with Spanish young learners of English. *Language Learning & Technology, 11*(1), 87-101.

Verhagen, P. (2006). *Connectivism: A new learning theory?* Retrieved from http://elearning.surf.nl/e-learning/english/3793

Vinagre, M., & Muñoz, B. (2011). Computer-mediated corrective feedback and language accuracy in telecollaborative exchanges. *Language Learning & Technology, 15*(1), 72-103.

Volle, L. M. (2005). Analyzing oral skills in voice e-mail and online interviews. *Language Learning & Technology, 9*(3), 146-163.

Vygotsky, L. S. (1978). *Mind in society: The development of higher psychological processes.* Cambridge: Harvard University Press.

Wagner, E. (2007). Are they watching? Test-taker viewing behavior during an L2 video listening test. *Language Learning & Technology, 11*(1), 67-86.

Walker, R. (2005). Using learner-produced recordings with monolingual groups to provide effective, individualized pronunciation practice. *TESOL Quarterly, 39*(3), 550-558.

Wang, S., & Smith, S. (2013). Reading and grammar learning through mobile phones. *Language Learning & Technology, 17*(3), 117-134.

Wang, Y. (2004). Supporting synchronous distance language learning with desktop videoconferencing. *Language Learning & Technology, 8*(3), 90-121.

Ward, J. S., & Barker, A. (2013). Undefined by data: A survey of big data definitions. arXiv: 1309.5821.

Ware, P. D., & O'Dowd, R. (2008). Peer feedback on language form in telecollaboration. *Language Learning & Technology, 12*(1), 43-63.

Warner, C. N. (2004). It's just a game, right? Types of play in foreign language CMC. *Language Learning & Technology, 8*(2), 69-87.

Warren, P., Elgort, I., & Crabbe, D. (2009). Comprehensibility and prosody ratings for pronunciation software development. *Language Learning & Technology, 13*(3), 87-102.

Warschauer, M. (Ed.) (1996). *Telecollaboration in foreign language learning.* Honolulu, HI: University of Hawaii. Second Language Teaching and Curriculum Center.

Warschauer, M., & Healey, D. (1998). Computers and language learning: An overview. *Language Teaching, 31*(2), 57-71.

Weasenforth, D., Biesenbach-Lucas, S., & Meloni, C. (2002). Realizing constructivist objectives through collaborative technologies: Threaded discussions. *Language Learning & Technology, 6*(3), 58-86.

Weinberg, A., Knoerr, H., & Vandergrift, L. (2011). Creating podcasts for academic listening in French: Student perceptions of enjoyment and usefulness. *CALICO Journal, 28*(3), 588-605.

White, K. D., & Heidrich, E. (2013). Our policies, their text: German language students' strategies with and beliefs about web-based machine translation. *Teaching German, 46*(2), 230–250.

Wilkins, D. A. (1972). *Linguistics in language teaching.* London: Arnold.

Williams, J. (2005a). *Teaching writing in second and foreign language classrooms.* Boston, MA: McGraw-Hill.

Williams, J. (2005b). Form-focused instruction. In E. Hinkel (Ed.), *Handbook of research in second language teaching and learning* (pp. 671-691). Mahwah, NJ: Lawrence Erlbaum Associates.

Williams, N. (1991). *The computer, the writer and the learner.* Berlin: Springer-Verlag.

Wilson, B. (1990). The preparedness of teacher trainees for computer utilisation: the Australian and British experiences. *Journal of Education for Teaching, 16*, 161-171.

Windeatt, S. (1987). The use of word-processors in language teaching. In L. Legenhausen & D. Wolff (Eds.), *Computer assisted language learning and innovative EFL methodology,* (pp. 145-166). Augusburg: Universitat Augusburg.

Windeatt, S. (1990). Teacher training for CALL. *MUESLI News,* Jan., 8-10.

Windeatt, S. (1995). Introduction to software evaluation. Unpublished manuscript, University of Newcastle.

Windeatt, S., Hardisty, D., & Eastment, D. (2000) *The Internet.* Oxford: Oxford University Press.

Winke, P., Gass, S., & Sydorenko, T. (2010). The effects of captioning videos used for foreign language listening activities. *Language Learning & Technology, 14*(1), 65-86.

Winston, P. H. (1987). An introduction to artificial intelligence. In E. Scanlon & T. O'Shea (Eds.), *Educational Computing* (pp. 181-192). Chichester: John Wiley and Sons.

Wood, J. (2001). Can software support children's vocabulary development? *Language Learning & Technology*, *5*(1), 166-201.

Woolf, B. P., Lane, H. C., Chaudhri, V. K., & Kolodner, J. L. (2013). AI grand challenges for education. *AI Magazine*, *34*(4), 66-84.

Wright, B., & Dillon, P. (1990). Some applications of interactive video in initial teacher training. *Educational & Training Technology International, 27*, 43-50.

Wu, H., & Zhang, W. (2014). Chinese EFL teachers' social interaction, socio-cognitive presence in synchronous computer-mediated communication. *Language Learning & Technology, 18*(3), 228-254.

Wyatt, D. H. (1984). *Computers and ESL*. Englewood Cliffs, New Jersey: Prentice-Hall.

Xu, C., & Ding, Y. (2014). An exploratory study of pauses in computer-assisted EFL writing. *Language Learning & Technology*, *18*(3), 80-96.

Yamashita, J. (2004). Reading attitudes in L1 and L2, and their influence on L2 extensive reading. *Reading in a Foreign Language*, *16*(1), 1-19.

Yang, Y. F. (2011). Learner interpretations of shared space in multilateral English blogging. *Language Learning & Technology*, *15*(1), 122-146.

Yang, S. C., & Chen, Y. (2007). Technology-enhanced language learning: A case study. *Computers in Human Behavior, 23,* 860-879.

Yang, Y. F., & Meng, W. T. (2013). The effects of online feedback training on students' text revision. *Language Learning & Technology*, *17*(2), 220-238.

Yanguas, Í. (2009). Multimedia glosses and their effect on L2 text comprehension and vocabulary learning. *Language Learning & Technology*, *13*(2), 48-67.

Yanguas, Í. (2010). Oral computer-mediated interaction between L2 learners: It's about time. *Language Learning & Technology*, *14*(3), 72-93.

Yoo, K. Y., & C. H. Lee (2002). An effective use of Korean middle school English textbook CD-ROM in teaching listening. *English Teaching*, *57*(2), 265-291.

Yoon, H. (2008). More than a linguistic reference: The influence of corpus technology on L2 academic writing. *Language Learning & Technology*, *12*(2), 31-48.

Yoon, H., & Jo, J. W. (2014). Direct and indirect access to corpora: An exploratory case study comparing students' error correction and learning strategy use in L2 writing. *Language Learning & Technology*, *18*(1), 96-117.

Yoon, S. Y. (2011). Students' reflection on feedback in L2 writing in blended learning. *Multimedia-Assisted Language Learning, 14*(2), 235-261.

Yoon, S. Y. (2013). The effectiveness of online English pronunciation class and students' perspectives. *Multimedia-Assisted Language Learning, 16*(3), 97-123.

Yoon, S. Y. (2014). The impact of language learning strategies in blended learning and students' perspectives. *Multimedia-Assisted Language Learning, 17*(4), 88-111.

Yoon, S. Y., & Lee, C. H. (2009). A study on voice recordings and feedback through

BBS in teaching and learning pronunciation. *Multimedia-Assisted Language Learning, 12*(2), 189-218.

Yoon, S. Y., & Lee, C. H. (2010). The perspectives and effectiveness of blended learning in L2 writing of Korean university students. *Multimedia-Assisted Language Learning, 13*(2), 177-204.

Yoon, S. Y., & Lee, C. H. (2011a). *Principles & practices in English pronunciation.* Seoul: Hankuk University of Foreign Studies Press Center.

Yoon, S. Y., & Lee, C. H. (2011b). Toward designing blended learning models for EFL classrooms: Blended learning models for spoken skills. *Proceedings of 2011 KAMALL International Conference*, 41-48.

Yoon, S. Y., & Lee, C. H. (2012). The impact of explicit listening instruction on teacher preparation practices in blended learning. *Multimedia-Assisted Language Learning, 15*(4), 175-200.

Yoon, S. Y., Lee, J., & Lee, C. H. (2013). Interacting with screenagers in classrooms. *Procedia-Social and Behavioral Sciences, 103*, 534-541.

Yoshii, M. (2006). L1 and L2 glosses: Their effects on incidental vocabulary learning. *Language Learning & Technology, 10*(3), 85-101.

Youk, S. Y., & Lee, C. H. (2008). The effective use of web-based English grammar program for middle school students. *Multimedia-Assisted Language Learning, 11*(1), 155-177.

Young, J. R. (2002). Hybrid teaching seeks to end the divide between traditional and online instruction. *The Chronicle of Higher Education, 48*(28), A33.

Yun, M. H., & Lee, C. H. (2001). A study of using CALL software for the improvement of university students' reading speed in English. *Multimedia-Assisted Language Learning, 4*(1), 86-121.

Zettersten, A. (1986). *New technologies in language learning.* Oxford: Pergamon.

Index

A

B

C

D

E

F

G

H

I

J

N

O

P

R

X

Y

Z